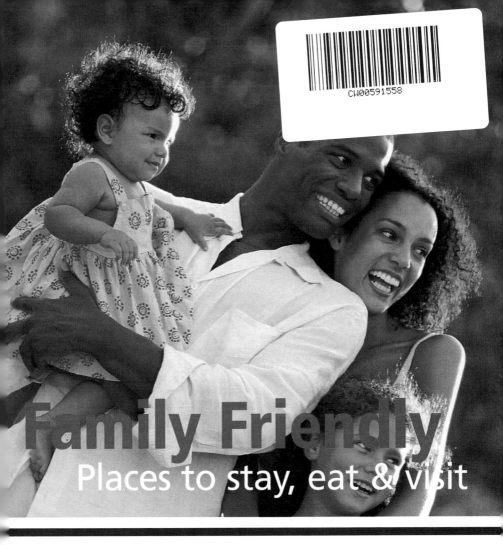

Family Friendly
Places to stay, eat & visit

attention wherever you go. Enjoy a warm welcome and memorable stay at a wide selection of hotels across the UK & Ireland.

Save 20% off a Marriott two night dinner, bed and breakfast Escape![sm] **Package – choose from 70 hotels across the UK and Ireland.***

Our superb range of hotels include something to satisfy every taste. Immerse yourself in the culture and energy of a city break. Get away from it all and relax in one of our Hotel & Country Clubs. Whatever your preference, you'll find the same Marriott care and

Call to action
Call 0845 600 2596 for reservations or to order a brochure - please quote "LYJI".

3rd edition published 2005

© Automobile Association Developments Limited 2005.
Automobile Association Developments Limited retains the
copyright in the current edition © 2005 and in all
subsequent editions, reprints and amendments to editions.

The information contained in this directory is partly sourced
from the AA's information resources.

⬛ Ordnance Survey® This product includes mapping data
licensed from Ordnance Survey ®
with the permission of the Controller of Her Majesty's
Stationery Office. © Crown copyright 2005. All rights
reserved. Licence number 399221

⬛ OS® This product includes mapping based upon
data licensed from Ordnance Survey of
Northern Ireland® reproduced by
permission of the Chief Executive, acting on behalf of the
Controller of Her Majesty's Stationery Office.
© Crown copyright 2005. Permit No 40073

Republic of Ireland mapping based on Ordnance Survey
Ireland Permit No. MP002104
© Ordnance Survey Ireland and Government of Ireland.

Maps prepared by the Cartography Department of The
Automobile Association. Maps © Automobile Association
Developments Limited 2005.

The Automobile Association would like to thank the
following agencies and libraries for their assistance in the
preparation of this book:
The Rising Sun tc; Digital Vision back cover and front tr;
Sheffield Marriott Hotel bl
The remaining pictures are held in the Association's
own library (AA WORLD TRAVEL LIBRARY)
with contributions from the following;
Chris Coe tl Max Jourdan br Paul Kenward bc

Typesetting and colour repro by Microset Graphics Ltd,
Basingstoke, Hampshire

Printed and bound in Spain by Graficas Estella, S.A., Navarra

Directory compiled by the AA Hotel Services Department
and generated from the AA establishment database.

The contents of this publication are believed correct at the
time of printing. Nevertheless, the publishers cannot be held
responsible for any errors or omissions or for any changes in
the details given in this guide or for the consequences of any
reliance on the information provided by the same. This does
not affect your statutory rights. Assessments of AA inspected
establishments are based on the experience of the Hotel and
Restaurant Inspectors on the occasion(s) of their visit(s) and
therefore descriptions given in this guide necessarily contain
an element of subjective opinion which may not reflect or
dictate a reader's own opinion on another occasion. The AA
strives to ensure accuracy of the information in this guide at
the time of printing. Due to the constantly evolving nature of
the subject matter the information is subject to change. The
AA will gratefully receive any advice from our readers of any
necessary updated information.

Please contact: Editorial department:
lifestyleguides@theAA.com
Advertisement department: advertisingsales@theAA.com
AA Hotel Scheme enquiries: 01256 844455

A CIP catalogue record for this book is available from the
British Library

ISBN-10 0 7495 42934
ISBN-13 978 0 7495 4291 7

Published by AA Publishing, a trading name of Automobile
Association Developments Limited whose registered office is
Southwood East, Apollo Rise, Farnborough, Hampshire
GU14 0JW

Registered number 1878835

A02157

Contents

AA Family Friendly
Places to stay, eat & visit
Where children can be seen and heard

This helpful guide from the AA features the hotels, bed and breakfasts, pubs and restaurants that go out of their way to cater for families with children of all ages. In these pages you can find family friendly places to stay in which children are not only welcomed, but in many cases have special facilities laid on to meet their needs, so you can relax and enjoy your holiday.

As well as providing practical accommodation with family rooms, hotels - particularly in larger towns - often provide baby-sitting services, play areas and entertainment as well as supervised activities for older children. Smaller hotels make children welcome by opening their gardens up and even providing their own children as playmates to visitors. Bed and breakfasts, particularly those in farmhouses, have farm animals as well as resident pets that always prove very popular!

Don't forget to let your hotel or bed and breakfast know any special requirements that you have such as cots and highchairs or special foods.

Of course there is always room for improvement, for places to provide baby-sitting services, laundry services and most importantly, in pubs and restaurants, baby-changing facilities. What we have tried to offer is a selection of places that are really making an effort to welcome families.

Whilst summer is an obvious time to book a holiday, you might like to consider taking an off-peak break when children are just as likely to enjoy cooler temperatures and crowd-free destinations.

Places to visit are recommended at the start of selected counties. These places are taken from the AA Days Out Guide which offers a more comprehensive choice, available from bookshops or www.theAA.com. Many hotels and B&Bs will recommend attractions in the area.

Whatever time of year you choose to go away, *AA Family Friendly Places to stay, eat & visit* is an essential guide to planning a break, offering a wide-ranging assortment of accommodation where every member of the family will be made welcome.

How to Use This Guide
Explanation of entries and notes on abbreviations

Sample Entry

➊ — **ANY TOWN,** Anyshire　　　　　　　　　**Map 00 NS00**

➋ ─ | Babies Welcome | Family Rooms | Children's Dishes | Minimum Age |

➌ ─ ◆◆◆ ❦ **Any Place** ─────────────────────────── **➍**
Any Walk XX37 6XX
☎ 09689 24444144 📠 09689 24444145
e-mail: address@test.co.uk

➎ ─ *Dir: on A422 900 yds NW of town centre*

➏ ─ **CHILD FACILITIES:** Food/bottle warming Ch menu Highchairs Family rooms from £65 **NEARBY:** Seafront location

This welcoming family home is conveniently situated for exploring Any Town and the surrounding area. Bedrooms are comfortable and well equipped, and public areas are cosy and inviting. Good value cuisine is served in the conservatory restaurant. Breakfast features home-made sausages and freshly made bread.

➐ ─ **ROOMS:** 19 en suite (3 fmly) s £35-38; d £68-76 ⊗ in bedrooms
➑ ─ **FACILITIES:** 🎣 Fishing Pool table
➒ ─ **NOTES:** RS Xmas **➓** ─ **PARKING:** 50

➊ The guide is divided into countries: England, Scotland, Wales, Northern Ireland and the Republic of Ireland. The Channel Islands and Isle of Man follow England. Each country is listed in county order, and then in alphabetical town/village order within each county.

Places on islands other than the Channel Islands and the Isle of Man are listed under their location name.

Within each location, hotels are listed first, in descending order of stars and Quality Assessment Score, followed by B&Bs in descending order of diamonds. If the establishment name is in italic type, the information that follows has not been confirmed by the management or proprietors for this year.
A company or consortium name or logo may appear.

Restaurants and pubs do not have ratings. Restaurants have Rosette awards and pubs are indicated by the tankard symbol. Some pubs may have Rosette awards. Please see pages 8 and 9 for further explanation.

The map reference gives the map page number, then the National Grid Reference. Read the first figure horizontally and the second figure vertically within the lettered square.

➋ **Children indicators**
Above the name of the establishment you will find at-a-glance indicators

| Babies Welcome | This indicates that the establishment has told us that they offer bottle/food warming and highchairs. Many places offer more than this. |

| Family Rooms | This indicates family rooms are available. |

| Children's Dishes | This indicates that children's portions or menu are available. |

| Minimum Age | This indicates that there is an age restriction, see Child Facilities box for details. |

🏖 This indicates the establishment is within walking distance or short drive of the seaside. Details of distance are given in the Child Facilities box.

5

❸The establishment name is preceded by the Star (hotels), Diamond (guest accommodation) or Rosette (restaurant) and followed by the address, phone/fax numbers and e-mail address where applicable. (Please note that e-mail addresses are believed correct at the time of printing but may change during the currency of the guide.) If the establishment name is in italic type the information that follows the Child Facilities box has not been confirmed by the proprietor or hotel management.

Hotels also show a Quality Assessment Score to offer a comparison of quality within their star rating.
Red diamonds are awarded to the top ten per cent of guest accommodation establishments within the three, four and five diamond ratings. Hotels and B&Bs may also have a Rosette award for food. B&Bs may also have egg cup and pie symbols, which indicate that, in the experience of our inspector, either breakfast or dinner exceeded their expectations at this diamond level.

Website Addresses
Web Site addresses are included where they have been supplied and specified by the respective establishment. Such Web Sites are not under the control of The Automobile Association Developments Limited and as such The Automobile Association Developments Limited has no control over them and will not accept any responsibility or liability in respect of any and all matters whatsoever relating to such Web Sites including access, content, material and functionality. By including the addresses of third party Web Sites the AA does not intend to solicit

business or offer any security to any person in any country, directly or indirectly.
❹➤ Farms are indicated by the cockerel symbol.
🍺 Pubs are indicated by the tankard symbol
❺**Dir:** Directions to the establishment as provided by the proprietor.
❻**Child facilities** are highlighted in a yellow box. Divided under the headings Child Facilities and Nearby, you will find specific details about family facilities including prices. The Nearby heading provides information about walks, farms, the seaside, parks etc that are near to the establishment. Please request any specific facilities and mention this guide when booking. A small number of establishments were unable to provide details at our press date, in this case we specify that you should telephone for information.

Room bed information is abbreviated.
S   single
D   double
B beds   bunk beds
T   twin

❼**Rooms** The first figure shows the number of en suite letting bedrooms, or total number of bedrooms, then the number with en suite facilities. Prices (per room per night) are provided by proprietors in good faith and are indications not firm quotations. Some establishments only accept cheques if notice is given and a cheque card produced. Not all establishments take travellers cheques.

❽**Facilities** Leisure facilities are as stated. Hotels only: Colour TV is provided in all bedrooms unless otherwise indicated.

❾**Notes RS** Some establishments have a restricted service during quieter months, when some of the listed facilities are not available: ask when booking.

❿**Parking** Shows numbers of spaces available for guests' use.

B&Bs only: Guests may have to order dinner (where this is available) in advance - please check when booking. *Licensed* indicates that the establishment is licensed to serve alcohol.

Further Information

Places to visit are taken from The AA Days Out Guide 2005. We have provided opening times as held on our database, but these may be subject to change. It is always advisable to telephone in advance for prices and to avoid disappointment.

Unclassified entries These are establishments which joined one of the AA schemes too close to guide deadlines for a full rating to be given.

Pubs with Stars and Diamonds Some pubs are shown with stars or diamonds but do not have accommodation details. This is because they belong to the AA accommodation schemes but it is their restaurants/bars which they have told us are family friendly, rather than their bedrooms. These places may have 'telephone for details' under the ROOMS but may not make provision for children. Small Stars and Diamonds under Rooms indicates inspections by other organisations only.

Symbols & Abbreviations

AWARDS & RATINGS

Hotels only

★ Star Classification
(see page 8)

% Quality Assessment score
(see page 8)

★ Red Stars indicate the AA's
highest quality award
(see page 8)

Country House Hotel

Town House Hotel

Restaurant with Rooms

Travel Accommodation
(see page 17-71)

B&Bs only

♦ Diamond Classification
(see page 9)

♦ Red Diamonds
*indicate the top 10% of 3, 4
and 5 diamond-rated
establishments*

Breakfast which exceeds
quality requirements at this
diamond level

Dinner which exceeds quality
requirements at this diamond
level

Farmhouse

Inn

Hotels and B&Bs
U Unclassified at time of
going to press

All Establishments
Rosette Award for
quality of food (see page 9)

ROOMS

s Single room

d Double room

*Bedroom restrictions are as stated,
e.g. ⊗ in 15 bedrooms*

∗ An asterisk indicates the prices
given are for 2004

FACILITIES

TV Television in bedrooms
(B&Bs only)

*Colour television is provided in all hotel
bedrooms unless otherwise stated*

STV Satellite television

ch fac Special facilities
for children

Xmas Special programme for
Christmas/ New Year

Leisure facilities are as stated
⬚ Indoor swimming pool
⬚ Heated indoor swimming pool
⌁ Outdoor swimming pool
⌁ Heated outdoor swimming pool
⚲ Tennis
⛳ Croquet
⛳ Golf Course

NOTES

RS Restricted opening,
e.g. RS Jan-Mar, Closed
Xmas/New Year

BB Bed and breakfast for up to
£20 per person per night

LB Short or Leisure Breaks
available

*Other restrictions are as stated,
e.g. ⊗ in restaurant*
🐕 No dogs

Stars, Diamonds and Rosette Awards

An important part of a holiday is knowing what amenities to expect of the hotel or bed and breakfast that you have booked. This is especially important when you are taking your children along too. From the definitions listed below, you can be very sure of what to expect and can make your choice accordingly.

All of the hotels and bed and breakfasts in this guide are inspected and rated according to the Star and Diamond Classification schemes. These ratings ensure that your accommodation meets the highest standards of cleanliness, with the emphasis on professionalism, proper booking procedures and a prompt and efficient service.

AA Star Classification

★ If you stay in a one-star hotel, you should expect a relatively informal yet competent style of service and an adequate range of facilities, including a television in the lounge or bedroom and a reasonable choice of hot and cold dishes. The majority of bedrooms are en suite, with a bath or shower room always available.

★★ A two-star hotel is run by smartly and professionally presented management and offers at least one restaurant or dining room for breakfast and dinner.

★★★ A three-star hotel includes direct dial telephones, a wide selection of drinks in the bar and last orders for dinner no earlier than 8pm.

★★★★ A four-star hotel is characterised by uniformed, well-trained staff, with additional services, a night porter and a serious approach to cuisine.

★★★★★ Finally, and most luxurious of all, is the five-star hotel, offering many extra facilities, attentive staff, top quality rooms and a full concierge service. A wide selection of drinks, including cocktails, is available in the bar, and the impressive menu reflects and complements the hotel's own style of cooking.

Quality percentage score In addition to the star classification, hotels receive a percentage score, based on an overall assessment of the 'guest experience'. The quality percentage score offers a comparison of quality within the star rating.

★ Top 200 Hotels
Red Stars indicate the AA's Top 200 Hotels in Britain and Ireland

AA Diamond Classification

 The AA's Diamond Awards cover bed and breakfast establishments only, reflecting guest accommodation at five grades of quality, with one Diamond indicating the simplest, and five Diamonds at the upper end of the scale.

The criteria for eligibility is guest care and quality rather than the choice of extra facilities. Establishments are vetted by a team of qualified inspectors to ensure that the accommodation, food and hospitality meets the AA's own exacting standards.

Guests should receive a prompt, professional check in and check out, comfortable accommodation equipped to modern standards, regularly changed bedding and towels, a sufficient hot water supply at all times, good, well-prepared meals, and a full English or continental breakfast.

 Red Diamonds recognise the very best 10% of guest accommodation within the three, four and five Diamond levels.

AA Rosettes

◉ Excellent local restaurants serving food prepared with care, understanding and skill, using good quality ingredients. These restaurants that stand out in their local area. The same expectations apply to hotel restaurants where guests should be able to eat in with confidence and a sense of anticipation. Around 50% of restaurants have one Rosette.

◉ ◉ The best local restaurants, which aim for and achieve higher standards, better consistency and where a greater precision is apparent in the cooking. There will be obvious attention to the selection of quality ingredients. Around 40% of restaurants have two Rosettes.

◉ ◉ ◉ Outstanding restaurants that demand recognition well beyond their local area. The cooking will be underpinned by the selection and sympathetic treatment of the highest quality ingredients. Timing, seasoning and the judgement of flavour combinations will be consistently excellent, supported by other elements such as intelligent service and a well-chosen wine list. Around 150 restaurants, less than 10%, have three Rosettes.

◉ ◉ ◉ ◉ Amongst the very best restaurants in the British Isles where the cooking demands national recognition. These restaurants will exhibit intense ambition, a passion for excellence, superb technical skills and remarkable consistency. They will combine appreciation of culinary traditions with a passionate desire for further exploration and improvement. About 15 restaurants have four Rosettes.

◉ ◉ ◉ ◉ ◉ The finest restaurants in the British Isles, where the cooking stands comparison with the best in the world. These restaurants will have highly individual voices, exhibit breathtaking culinary skills and set the standards to which others aspire. Around half a dozen restaurants have five Rosettes.

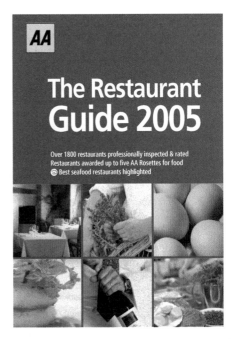

AA

The Restaurant Guide 2005

Over 1800 restaurants professionally inspected & rated
Restaurants awarded up to five AA Rosettes for food
◉ Best seafood restaurants highlighted

Useful Information

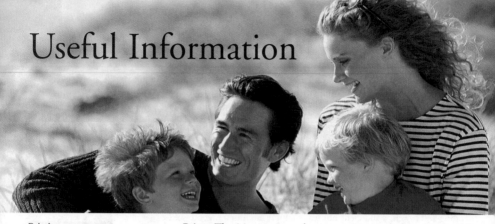

Britain

The Fire Precautions Act does not apply to the Channel Islands, Republic of Ireland, or the Isle of Man, which have their own rules. As far as we are aware, all establishments listed in Great Britain have applied for and not been refused a fire certificate.

Licensing laws differ in England, Wales, Scotland, the Republic of Ireland, the Isle of Man, the Isles of Scilly and the Channel Islands. Public houses are generally open from mid morning to early afternoon, and from about 6 or 7pm until 11pm, although closing times may be earlier or later and some pubs are open all afternoon. Unless otherwise stated, hotels listed in this guide are licensed. (For guest accommodation, please refer to the individual gazetteer entry. Note that licensed premises are not obliged to remain open throughout the permitted hours.) Hotel residents can obtain alcoholic drinks at all times, if the licensee is prepared to serve them. Non-residents eating at the hotel restaurant can have drinks with meals. Children under 14 (or 18 in Scotland) may be excluded from bars where no food is served. Those under 18 may not purchase or consume alcoholic drinks. Club licence means that drinks are served to club members only. 48 hours must elapse between joining and ordering.

Prices The AA encourages the use of the Hotel Industry Voluntary Code of Booking Practice, which aims to ensure that guests know how much they will have to pay and what services and facilities that includes, before entering a financially binding agreement. If the price has not previously been confirmed in writing, guests should be given a card stipulating the total obligatory charge when they register at reception.

The Tourism (Sleeping Accommodation Price Display) Order of 1977 compels hotels, travel accommodation, guest houses, farmhouses, inns and self-catering accommodation with four or more letting bedrooms, to display in entrance halls the minimum and maximum prices charged for each category of room. Tariffs shown are the minimum and maximum for one or two persons but they may vary without warning.

Northern Ireland & Republic of Ireland

The Euro Since 2002, Euro banknotes and coins have been in circulation throughout the Republic of Ireland.

The Fire Services (NI) Order 1984 covers establishments accommodating more than six people, which must have a certificate from the Northern Ireland Fire Authority. Places accommodating fewer than six

persons need adequate exits. AA officials inspect emergency notices, fire-fighting equipment and fire exits here. Republic of Ireland safety regulations are a matter for local authority regulations. For your own and others' safety, read the emergency notices and be sure you understand them.

In the Republic of Ireland there is a no smoking policy in restaurants and pubs.

Licensing Regulations
Northern Ireland: Public houses open Mon-Sat 11.30-23.00 and Sun 12.30-14.30 and 19.00-22.00. Hotels can serve residents without restriction. Non-residents can be served from 12.30-22.00 on Christmas Day. Children under 18 are not allowed in the bar area and may neither buy nor consume liquor in hotels.
Republic of Ireland: General licensing hours are Mon-Sat 10.30-23.00 (23.30 in summer). Sun and St Patrick's Day (17 March), 12.30-14.00 and 16.00-23.00. Hotels can serve residents without restriction. There is no service on Christmas Day (except for residents) or Good Friday.
Telephone numbers: Area codes for numbers in the Republic of Ireland apply only within the Republic. If dialling from outside, check the telephone directory. Area codes for numbers in Britain and Northern Ireland cannot be used directly from the Republic.

BEWLEY'S HOTELS

EACH HOTEL HAS ONE RATE, EVERY ROOM, EVERY NIGHT

Book Online:
www.BewleysHotels.com

Glasgow
(city centre)

£59

Newlands Cross
(off M50 Motorway)

€79

£59

Ballsbridge   DUBLIN
(served by Aircoach)

€99

Leeds
(now open)

€79

Manchester Airport
(5 mins walk from Terminals 1 & 3)

Leopardstown
(now served by Aircoach & Luas)

£59

Out and About with the Kids

When you're taking the kids away and planning to stay in a hotel or bed and breakfast establishment, choosing an establishment that can offer helpful staff and child-friendly facilities, means parents can feel their stay will be that much more relaxed.

First we'll look at staying in a hotel or bed and breakfast and some make-or-break differences that affect the quality of your stay.

Arriving with a young baby? First thing you might need to do is to mix a feed, or have a bottle warmed. Then you look for a cot nicely prepared, and later, somewhere to leave laundry to be washed (on a daily basis). Finally, you want to go and have dinner, but you can only relax if there is a baby listening service available.

Child a bit bigger? You will need a cot for this one too, plus a suitable eating area with highchair, nicely prepared little meals, small cutlery and maybe a family room where

you can put on your child's favourite video at the end of the day.

The fives upwards need toys and games, soft drinks available and, ideally, supervised activities during adult meal times. They should have an activities room suitably equipped with TV and video, and ideally, organised supervised activities laid on.

Some of the hotels and bed and breakfasts in this guide offer these specific extras. Some offer one or two of the facilities in the panel as shown on this page while others go the whole way to give all-round value to guests and in some cases go the extra mile by organising riding, tennis or similar activities, and putting on games shows, arranging competitions and running discos for the older children. Providing these are supervised, parents will then have time to relax on their own for a while.

Some family needs when staying away

- Baby listening service
- Babysitting service
- Warm baby bottles
- Highchairs
- Public area for families
- Indoor play area with some games
- Small cutlery
- Children's food from main menu
- Cots
- Laundry facilities
- Family bedrooms
- Soft drinks readily available

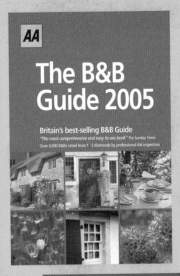
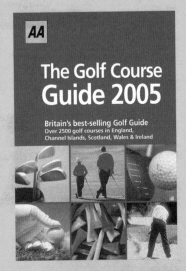
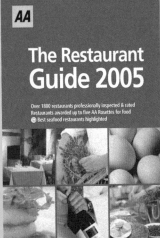
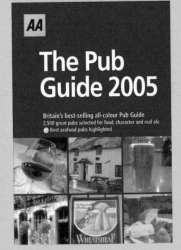

Beside the Seaside

Every year around 27 million seaside holidays are taken by the British in Britain, so there is no doubting the lure of the sea to natives of these islands, and there's plenty, too, to commend the coast to visitors from abroad. To help you plan a perfect seaside getaway in the UK and Ireland, in this year's Family Friendly guide we have included a seaside symbol to indicate those establishments within walking distance of the sea, or within a ten-minute drive of the coast. Details of distance to the sea are given in the Child Facilities box.

The British seaside holiday is the stuff of family memories, from the toe-squirming delights of the rock pool to the thrills of the end of the pier show. With over 11,000 miles of UK coastline and a further 7,500 miles in Ireland, some of it heart-stoppingly beautiful, there are plenty of beaches, resorts, villages and towns to choose from. Different families look for different seaside experiences, but why not combine an appreciation of the natural environment with a bit of kiss-me-quick razzmatazz?

Nice and natural

Privacy and a coastal environment rich in wildlife and spectacular scenery are more likely to be found in the more remote and rural areas, particularly in Wales, which is renowned for its glorious and very clean beaches. Typical of these are Pembrokeshire's beautiful Barafundle Bay, owned by the National Trust and accessible only by the coastal path, and the little cove at St Brides Haven, with its sandy beach and rock pools at low tide.

At these less developed sites, you may have to park at some distance and negotiate cliffs and steps with armfuls of beach equipment, and on-beach facilities may be more limited, but it's worth the trouble if you can manage it for the fabulous sands and luxurious amounts of personal space. Similar locations are dotted around the coastline, but more densely in the South West of England, the Channel Islands, Scotland and, of course, the Republic of Ireland.

These wild beaches are a natural playground where, equipped with a good book for identification purposes, a spade, net and bucket, you can discover the secrets of the underwater world; play hide-and-seek in the rough grass amid the sand dunes, fly your kite and chase your cricket ball into the sea. They are also subject to all the inherent dangers of the natural environment: sheer drops from high cliffs, slippery boulders, and unpredictable tidal movements, all of which parents should be alert to.

The first resort

Blackpool is the UK's top seaside resort, attracting over six million visitors a year. It is also the busiest resort in Europe. Attractions include the world-famous illuminations (stretching for six miles and incorporating 400,000 lights), three piers, the Golden Mile with its amusement arcades, the 518-foot Blackpool Tower, and the Pleasure Beach with one of the world's highest and fastest roller coasters, the Pepsi Max Big One. There is also a Sealife Centre, zoo, model village and Stanley Park with its attractive gardens and boating lake.

Brighton, another favourite resort, has a cool, arty atmosphere amid classic Regency architecture. Features include The Lanes, a network of narrow streets choc full of fascinating little shops, and the exotic oriental-style palace, the Royal Pavilion, built in 1787 for the Prince Regent, son of George III, later crowned George IV. Brighton has a renowned pier with a fun fair, sideshows, and amusement arcades, plus there's a Sealife Centre on the front.

Torquay, in the South West of England, has semi-tropical appeal with its palm trees and delectable beach. Torquay sand has actually been officially declared the best in Britain for making sandcastles, by a team of scientific researchers from Bournemouth University.

Southend is understandably popular with Londoners, being close to the capital. It has the longest pleasure pier in the world at 2,360 yards or 1.34 miles, boasting an upper deck, a pier railway and its own museum. Ayr, in Scotland, is popular with Glaswegians – again for its proximity – like Bangor in County Down, Northern Ireland's largest resort, on the south coast of Belfast Lough

and conveniently close to the city.

One of Southern Ireland's liveliest resorts is Bundoran in Donegal, on the Atlantic coast set against the Ben Bulben mountain range. Family-friendly facilities include a Blue-Flag beach, funfair, amusement arcades, the Donegal Adventure Centre with loads of outdoor activities aimed at families, Waterworld (an aqua adventure park), 10-pin bowling, and a six-screen Cineplex.

Seaside Awards

If you're keen to check out the cleanliness, range of facilities and general suitability of a beach for your family's needs, there are various inspection agencies that judge and make awards to beaches on a season by season basis. The Blue Flag scheme covers Europe and South Africa, and is owned and run by the Foundation for Environmental Education (FEE), but administered in the UK by Encams. The Blue Flag award (blue flag with a white circle) is based on water quality, environmental education and information, environmental management, safety and services. At the time of writing, the UK has 118 Blue Flag Beaches (England 70, Scotland 6, Wales 34, Northern Ireland 8), while the Republic of Ireland has 73.

Encams, the environmental campaigning group that runs the Keep Britain Tidy Campaign, also has its own UK Seaside Award (yellow flag with a blue flash and a black Encams logo). The Seaside Award acknowledges the difference between rural and resort beaches, rural beaches needing to meet only 13 criteria, while a resort beach must meet 29 to qualify. At the time of writing, the awards are distributed about the regions as follows:

East Midlands	3 (all resort)
East of England	26 (18 resort, 8 rural)
North East	15 (9 resort, 6 rural)
North West	16 (6 resort, 10 rural)
Northern Ireland	9 (8 resort and 1 rural)
Scotland	40 (8 resort, 32 rural)
South East of England	49 (25 resort, 24 rural)
South West of England	83 (37 resort, 46 rural)
The Channel Islands	8 (all rural)
Wales	108 (44 resort, 64 rural)
Yorkshire and the Humber	14 (9 resort, 5 rural)

The Keep Wales Tidy campaign also makes Green Coast Awards to Welsh beaches, to recognise 'those beaches which meet EC Guideline bathing water standards (the highest standard recognised under current EC legislation) but which are also prized for their natural, unspoiled environment'. Wales is particularly blessed with these.

Further information is available from:
www.blueflag.org
www.seasideawards.org.uk
www.keepwalestidy.org
(click on the tourism icon)

SeaBritain 2005, the Trafalgar Festival

During 2005 an even greater incentive to take a trip to the coast is the SeaBritain 2005 Trafalgar Festival, commemorating the 200th anniversary of the Battle of Trafalgar. Special events include a yacht race around the Isle of Wight on 13 June for the competitors of the Atlantic challenge. The Portsmouth Festivities, 18-25 June, will have a Trafalgar theme; and on 28 June there will be an International Fleet Review off Spithead (near Portsmouth) with ships from 35 nations taking part. During the evening there will also be a historic re-enactment of an early 19th-century sea battle in a Son et Lumière on the water off Southsea, culminating in one of the biggest fireworks displays ever to be held in Britain.

The International Festival of the Sea 2005, 30 June-3 July, will be held at the Royal Naval Base and Historic Dockyard at Portsmouth. Here actors will entertain the crowds with scenes that recapture life as it was in Nelson's day.

Between July and September a replica of the *HM Schooner Pickle* will be calling in at key British ports with a crew of re-enactors playing Nelson and his entourage, and between 21-23 October the nation will celebrate the 200th anniversary of the Battle of Trafalgar with church bells and beacons blazing across the land and national and local festivities.

Further information available from: www.trafalgar200.com & www.seabritain2005.com

Travel Accommodation Directory

This directory includes listings for Campanile, Days Inn, Hotel Ibis, Innkeeper's Lodge, Premier Lodge, Sleep Inn, Travel Inn, Travelodge and Welcome Break, with a section for each brand arranged in country, county, location order. Many of the establishments are conveniently situated on motorways and major roads, with a service station nearby and often feature adjacent popular family restaurants, ideal for breaking your journey as well as for overnight stays.

Campanile
020 7519 5045

Campanile offers modern accommodation for the budget market. Family rooms sleep up to 3 people, there are some communicating rooms in each hotel. Café-bistro offers children's menu. Room prices £29.95 - £46.95.

ENGLAND

BUCKINGHAMSHIRE
MILTON KEYNES
Campanile   80 rooms
40 Penn Road, Fenny Stratford, Bletchley MK2 2AU
☎ 01908 649819   📠 01908 649818
e: mk@envergure.co.uk
(M1 junct 14, follow A4146 to A5. Southbound on A5. 4th exit at 1st rdbt to Fenny Stratford. Hotel 500yds on left)

CHESHIRE
RUNCORN
Campanile   53 rooms
Lowlands Road WA7 5TP
☎ 01928 581771   📠 01928 581730
e: runcorn@envergure.co.uk
(M56 junct 12, take A557, then follow signs for Runcorn rail station)

ESSEX
BASILDON
Campanile   97 rooms
Pipps Hill, Southend Arterial Road SS14 3AE
☎ 01268 530810   📠 01268 286710
e: basildon@envergure.co.uk
(M25 junct 29 Basildon exit., back under A127, then left at rdbt)

GREATER MANCHESTER
MANCHESTER
Campanile   104 rooms
55 Ordsall Lane, Salford M5 4RS
☎ 0161 833 1845   📠 0161 833 1847
e: manchester@envergure.co.uk
(M602 to Manchester, then A57. After large rdbt with Sainsbury's on left, left at next traffic lights. Hotel on right)

KENT
DARTFORD
Campanile   125 rooms
1 Clipper Boulevard West, Crossways Business Park DA2 6QN
☎ 01322 278925   📠 01322 278948
e: dartford@envergure.co.uk
(Follow signs for Ferry Terminal from Dartford Bridge)

LEICESTERSHIRE
LEICESTER
Campanile Leicester   93 rooms
St Matthew's Way, 1 Bedford Street North LE1 3JE
☎ 0116 261 6600   📠 0116 2616601
e: leicester@envergure.co.uk
(From M69/M1 junct 21, follow city centre along Narborough Rd (A5460). Right at end of road, left at rdbt on A594. Follow Vaughn Way, Burleys Way then St. Matthews Way. Hotel on left)

MERSEYSIDE
LIVERPOOL
Campanile   100 rooms
Chaloner Street, Queens Dock L3 4AJ
☎ 0151 709 8104   📠 0151 709 8725
e: liverpool@envergure.co.uk
(Follow tourist signs marked Albert Dock. Hotel on waterfront)

TYNE & WEAR
WASHINGTON
Campanile   79 rooms
Emerson Road, District 5 NE37 1LE
☎ 0191 416 5010   📠 0191 416 5023
e: washington@envergure.co.uk
(A1 junct 64, A195 to Washington, 1st left at rdbt into Emerson Road, Hotel 800yds on left)

WEST MIDLANDS
BIRMINGHAM
Campanile   109 rooms
Aston Locks, Chester Street B6 4BE
☎ 0121 359 3330   📠 0121 359 1223
e: birmingham@envergure.co.uk
(Next to rdbt at junct of A4540/A38)

COVENTRY
Campanile   47 rooms
4 Wigston Road, Walsgrave CV2 2SD
☎ 024 7662 2311 📠 024 7660 2362
e: coventry@envergure.co.uk
(M6 exit 2, 2nd rdbt turn right)

WORCESTERSHIRE
REDDITCH
Campanile   46 rooms
Far Moor Lane, Winyates Green B98 0SD
☎ 01527 510710 📠 01527 517269
e: redditch@envergure.co.uk
(A435 towards Redditch, then A4023 to Redditch and Bromsgrove)

YORKSHIRE, EASt RIDING OF
KINGSTON UPON HULL
Campanile   47 rooms
Beverley Road, Freetown Way HU2 9AN
☎ 01482 325530 📠 01482 587538
e: hull@envergure.co.uk
(From M62 join A63 to Hull, pass Humber Bridge on right. Over flyover, follow railway station signs onto A1079. Hotel at bottom of Ferensway)

YORKSHIRE, SOUTH
DONCASTER
Campanile   50 rooms
Doncaster Leisure Park, Bawtry Road DN4 7PD
☎ 01302 370770 📠 01302 370813
e: doncaster@envergure.co.uk
(Follow signs to Doncaster Leisure Centre, left at rdbt before Dome complex)

ROTHERHAM
Campanile   50 rooms
Hellaby Industrial Estate, Lowton Way,
off Denby Way S66 8RY
☎ 01709 700255 📠 01709 545169
e: rotherham@envergure.co.uk
(M18 junct 1. Follow signs for Maltby off rdbt. Left at lights, 2nd on left)

YORKSHIRE, WEST
WAKEFIELD
Campanile   76 rooms
Monckton Road WF2 7AL
☎ 01924 201054 📠 01924 201055
e: wakefield@envergure.co.uk
(M1 junct 39, A636 1m towards Wakefield, left onto Monckton Rd, hotel on left)

WALES
CARDIFF
CARDIFF
Campanile   47 rooms
Caxton Place, Pentwyn CF23 8HA
☎ 029 2054 9044 📠 029 2054 9900
e: cardiff@envergure.co.uk
(Take Pentwyn exit from A48, follow signs for Pentwyn Industrial Estate)

Days Inn
0800 731 44 66

Family room sleep two adults and two children up to 12. Burger King, KFC and MacDonald's are available at most locations. Room prices £45-£69. For Welcome Break see page 71.

ENGLAND
BERKSHIRE
MEMBURY
Days Inn   38 rooms
Membury Service Area RG17 7TZ
☎ 01488 72336 📠 01488 72336
e: membury.hotel@welcomebreak.co.uk
(M4 between junct 14&15)

DERBYSHIRE
DERBY
Days Hotel Derby   100 rooms
Derbyshire C C Ground, Pentagon Roundabout
Nottingham Road DE21 6DA
☎ 01332 363600 📠 01332 200630
e: derby@kewgreen.co.uk
(M1 junct 25, take A52 towards Derby. At Pentagon rdbt take 4th exit and turn into cricket club)

SHARDLOW
Days Inn Donnington   47 rooms
Welcome Break Services DE72 2WW
☎ 01332 799666 📠 01332 794166
e: donnington.hotel@welcomebreak.co.uk
(M1junct 24/24a, onto A50 towards Stoke/Derby. Hotel between juncts 1 & 2)

ESSEX
STANSTED
Days Inn Stansted   60 rooms
Birchanger Green, Bishop Stortford CM23 5QZ
☎ 01279 656477 📠 01279 656590
e: birchanger.hotel@welcomebreak.co.uk
(M11 junct 8)

GLOUCESTERSHIRE
MICHAEL WOOD MOTORWAY SERVICE AREA
(M5)Days Inn 38 rooms
Michaelwood Service Area M5 Northbound,
Lower Wick GL11 6DD
☎ 01454 261513 📠 01454 269150
e: michaelwood.hotel@welcomebreak.co.uk
(M5 northbound between junct 13 and 14)

GREATER LONDON
SOUTH RUISLIP
Days Hotel 78 rooms
Long Drive, Station Approach HA4 0HN
☎ 020 8845 8400 📠 020 8845 5500
e: info@dayshotelheathrow.com
(turn off A40 at Polish War Memorial, follow signs to Ruislip and South Ruislip)

HAMPSHIRE
FLEET MOTORWAY SERVICE AREA
Days Inn 58 rooms
Fleet Services GU51 1AA
☎ 01252 15587 📠 01252 815587
e: fleethotel@welcomebreak.co.uk
(Welcome Break Fleet Motorway Service area between junct 4a & 5 southbound on the M3)

HERTFORDSHIRE
SOUTH MIMMS
Days Inn 74 rooms
Bignells Corner EN6 3QQ
☎ 01707 665440 📠 01707 660189
e: southmimmshotel@welcomebreak.co.uk
(M25 junct 23, at rdbt follow signs)

LEICESTERSHIRE
LEICESTER
Days Inn Leicester Central 71 rooms
14-17 Abbey Street LE1 3TE
☎ 0116 251 0666 📠 0870 033 9634
e: stephen.hughes@daysinn.co.uk

LEICESTER FOREST EAST MOTORWAY SERVICE AREA
Days Inn 92 rooms
Leicester Forest East, Junction 21 M1 LE3 3GB
☎ 0116 239 0534 📠 0116 239 0546
e: leicester.hotel@welcomebreak.co.uk
(on M1 northbound between junct 21 & 21A)

OXFORDSHIRE
OXFORD
Days Inn 59 rooms
M40 junction 8A, Waterstock OX33 1LJ
☎ 01865 877000 📠 01865 877016
e: oxford.hotel@welcomebreak.co.uk
(M40 junct 8a, Welcome Break service area)

SHROPSHIRE
TELFORD
Days Inn Telford 48 rooms
Telford Services, Priorslee Road TF11 8TG
☎ 01952 238400 📠 01952 238410
e: telford.hotel@welcomebreak.co.uk
(M54 junct 4)

SOMERSET
GORDANO SERVICE AREA (M5)
Days Inn 60 rooms
BS20 7XG
☎ 01275 373709 📠 01275 374104
e: gordano.hotel@welcomebreak.co.uk
(M5 junct 19, follow signs for Gordano services)

SEDGEMOOR MOTORWAY SERVICE AREA
Days Inn 40 rooms
M5 Northbound J22-21, Sedgemoor BS24 0JL
☎ 01934 750831 📠 01934 750808
e: sedgemoor.hotel@welcomebreak.co.uk
(M5 junct 21/22)

WARWICKSHIRE
WARWICK MOTORWAY SERVICE AREA
Days Inn Stratford-upon-Avon 54 rooms
Warwick Services, M40 Northbound junction 12-13,
Banbury Road CV35 0AA
☎ 01926 651681 📠 01926 651634
e: warwick.north.hotel@welcomebreak.co.uk
(M40 northbound between junct 12 & 13)

WARWICK MOTORWAY SERVICE AREA
Days Inn Stratford-upon-Avon 40 rooms
Warwick Services, M40 Southbound,
Banbury Road CV35 0AA
☎ 01926 650168 📠 01926 651601
(M40 southbound between junct 14 & 12)

YORKSHIRE, SOUTH
WOODALL
Days Inn Sheffield South 38 rooms
Woodall Service Area S26 7XR
☎ 0114 248 7992 📠 0114 248 5634
e: woodall.hotel@welcomebreak.co.uk
(M1 S'bound - Woodall Services - between juncts 30/31)

YORKSHIRE, WEST
HARTSHEAD MOOR SERVICE AREA
Days Inn 38 rooms
Hartshead Moor Service Area, Clifton HD6 4JX
☎ 01274 851706 📠 01274 855169
e: hartsheadmoor.hotel@welcomebreak.co.uk
(M62 between junct 25 and 26)

WAKEFIELD

Days Inn Hotel Wakefield   100 rooms
Fryers Way, Silkwood Park, Ossett WF5 9TJ
☎ 01924 274200 📠 01924 274246
e: wakefield@dayshotel.co.uk
(M1 junct 40 onto A638 to Wakefield. Take 1st left into Silkwood Park and hotel is on right)

SCOTLAND

DUMFRIES & GALLOWAY

GRETNA

Days Inn   64 rooms
Welcome Break Service Area DG16 5HQ
☎ 01461 337566 📠 01461 337823
e: gretna.hotel@welcomebreak.co.uk
(between junct 21/22 on M74 - accessible from both N'bound & S'bound carriageways)

DUNDEE CITY

DUNDEE

Days Inn   67 rooms
296a Strathmore Avenue DD3 6SH
☎ 01382 826000 📠 01382 825839
e: dundee@daysinn.co.uk
(leave A90 Kingsway at Ardler rdbt signed City Centre B960, Cledington Road. On Cledington Road 1st right into Johnston Avenue. Continue to end of avenue until reaching rdbt. Turn left into Strathmole Avenue and hotel on left)

SOUTH LANARKSHIRE

ABINGTON

Days Inn   52 rooms
ML12 6RG
☎ 01864 502782 📠 01864 502759
e: abington.hotel@welcomebreak.co.uk
(M74 junct 13, accessible from N'bound and S'bound carriageways)

Hotel Ibis
020 8283 4550

Ibis is a growing chain of modern travel accommodation with properties across the UK.

ENGLAND

BEDFORDSHIRE

LUTON

Hotel Ibis Luton   98 rooms
Spittlesea Road LU2 9NH
☎ 01582 424488 📠 01582 455511
e: H1040@accor-hotels.com
(from M1 junct 10 follow signs to Luton Airport. Hotel 600mtrs from airport)

CUMBRIA

CARLISLE

Hotel Ibis Carlisle   102 rooms
Portlands, Botchergate CA1 1RP
☎ 01228 518000 📠 01228 518010
e: H3443@accor-hotels.com
(M6 junct 42/43 follow signs for city centre.

DERBYSHIRE

BARLBOROUGH

Hotel Ibis Sheffield South   86 rooms
Tallys End, Chesterfield Road S43 4TX
☎ 01246 813222 📠 01246 813444
e: H3157@accor-hotels.com
(M1 junct 30. Towards A619, right at rdbt towards Chesterfield. Hotel immediately left)

CHESTERFIELD

Hotel Ibis Chesterfield
86 Lordsmill Street S41 7RW
☎ 01246 221333 📠 01246 221444
e: H3160@accor-hotels.com
(M1 junct 29, take A617 to Chesterfield. 2nd exit at 1st rdbt. Hotel situated on right at 2nd rdbt.)

DEVON

PLYMOUTH

Hotel Ibis Plymouth   52 rooms
Marsh Mills, Longbridge Road,
Forder Valley PL6 8LD
☎ 01752 601087 📠 01752 223213
e: H2093@accor-hotels.com
(A38 to Plymouth, 1st exit after flyover towards Estover, Leigham and Parkway Ind Est. At rdbt, hotel on 4th exit).

ESSEX

THURROCK

Hotel Ibis Thurrock   102 rooms
Weston Avenue RM20 3JQ
☎ 01708 686000 📠 01708 680525
e: H2176@accor-hotels.com
(M25 junct 31 to West Thurrock Services, right at 1st and 2nd rdbts then left at 3rd rdbt. Hotel on right after 500yds)

GREATER LONDON

BARKING

Hotel Ibis   86 rooms
Highbridge Road IG11 7BA
☎ 020 8477 4100 📠 020 8477 4101
e: H2042@accor-hotels.com
(exit Barking on A406)

HAYES

Hotel Ibis Heathrow   347 rooms
112/114 Bath Road UB3 5AL
☎ 020 8759 4888 📠 020 8564 7894
e: H0794@accor-hotels.com
(follow Heathrow terminals 1,2 & 3 signs, then onto the spur road, off at sign for A4 Central London. Hotel 0.5m on left)

WEMBLEY

Hotel Ibis Wembley   210 rooms
Southway HA9 6BA
☎ 0870 609 0963
e: H3141@accor-hotels.com
(From Hanger Lane on A40, follow A406 north, exit at Wembley. Follow A404 to traffic lights with Wembley Hill Road, turn right then 1st right into Southway. Hotel is 75mtrs on left.)

GREATER MANCHESTER
MANCHESTER

Hotel Ibis Manchester (Charles Street) 126 rooms
Charles Street, Princess Street M1 7DL
☎ 0161 272 5000   ▯ 0161 272 5010
e: H3143@accor-hotels.com
(M62, M602 towards Manchester Centre, follow signs to UMIST(A34))

Hotel Ibis Manchester City Centre   127 rooms
96 Portland Street M1 4GY
☎ 0161 234 0600   ▯ 0161 234 0610
e: H3142@accor-hotels.com
(In city centre, between Princess St & Oxford St. 10min walk from Piccadilly)

HAMPSHIRE
PORTSMOUTH

Hotel Ibis Portsmouth   144 rooms
Winston Churchill Avenue PO1 2LX
☎ 023 9264 0000   ▯ 023 9264 1000
e: H1461@accor-hotels.com
(M27 junct 2 onto M275. Follow signs for city centre then Sealife Centre and then Guildhall. Right at rdbt into Winston Churchill Ave)

SOUTHAMPTON

Hotel Ibis Southampton   93 rooms
West Quay Road, Western Esplanade SO15 1RA
☎ 023 8063 4463   ▯ 023 8022 3273
e: H1039@accor-hotels.com
(M27 junct 3/M271. Left to city centre (A35), follow Old Town Waterfront until 4th lights, left, then left again, hotel opposite station)

HERTFORDSHIRE
STEVENAGE

Hotel Ibis Stevenage   98 rooms
Danestrete SG1 1EJ
☎ 01438 779955   ▯ 01438 741880
e: H2497@accor-hotels.com
(in town centre adjacent to Tesco & Westgate Multi-Store)

LANCASHIRE
PRESTON

Hotel Ibis Preston North   82 rooms
Garstang Road, Broughton PR3 5JE
☎ 01772 861800   ▯ 01772 861900
e: H3162@accor-hotels.com
(M6 junct 32, then M55 J1. Left lane onto A6. Left at slip road and left again at mini rdbt. 2nd turn and hotel on right past pub)

LEICESTERSHIRE
LEICESTER

Hotel Ibis Leicester   94 rooms
St Georges Way, Constitution Hill LE1 1PL
☎ 0116 248 7200   ▯ 0116 262 0880
e: H3061@accor-hotels.com
(From M1/M69 J21, follow town centre signs, central ring rd (A594)/railway station, hotel opposite the Leicester Mercury.)

LINCOLNSHIRE
LINCOLN

Hotel Ibis Lincoln
86 Runcorn Rd (A46), off Whisby Road LN6 3QZ
☎ 01522 698333   ▯ 01522 698444
e: H3161@accor-hotels.com
(off A46 ring road onto Whisby Rd. 1st turning on left)

LONDON
E14

Hotel Ibis London Docklands   87 rooms
1 Baffin Way E14 9PE
☎ 020 7517 1100   ▯ 020 7987 5916
e: H2177@accor-hotels.com
(from Tower Bridge follow City Airport and Royal Docks signs, exit for 'Isle of Dogs'. Hotel on 1st left opposite McDonalds)

E15

Hotel Ibis London Stratford   108 rooms
1A Romford Road, Stratford E15 4LJ
☎ 020 8536 3700   ▯ 020 8519 5161
e: H3099@accor-hotels.com

E16

Hotel Ibis London ExCel   278 rooms
9 Western Gateway, Royal Victoria Docks E16 1AB
☎ 020 7055 2300   ▯ 020 7055 2310
e: H3655@accor-hotels.com
(M25 then A13 to London, City Airport, ExCel East)

NW1

Hotel Ibis London Euston   380 rooms
3 Cardington Street NW1 2LW
☎ 020 7388 7777   ▯ 020 7388 0001
e: H0921@accor-hotels.com
(from Euston Rd or station, right to Melton St leading to Cardington St)

Hotel Ibis

SE10

Hotel Ibis London Greenwich   82 rooms
30 Stockwell Street, Greenwich SE10 9JN
☎ 020 8305 1177   ≣ 020 8858 7139
e: H0975@accor-hotels.com
*(from Waterloo Bridge, Elephant & Castle, A2
to Greenwich.)*

MERSEYSIDE
LIVERPOOL
Hotel Ibis Liverpool   127 rooms
27 Wapping L1 8LY
☎ 0151 706 9800   ≣ 0151 706 9810
e: H3140@accor-hotels.com
*(from M62 follow signs for Albert Dock. Hotel opposite
entrance to Albert Dock)*

NORTHAMPTONSHIRE
CRICK
Hotel Ibis Rugby East   111 rooms
Parklands NN6 7EX
☎ 01788 824331   ≣ 01788 824332
e: H3588@accor-hotels.com
(M1 junct 18/A428)

NORTHAMPTON
Hotel Ibis Northampton   151 rooms
Sol Central, Marefair NN1 1SR
☎ 01604 608900   ≣ 01604 608910
e: H3657@accor-hotels.com
(M1 junct 15/15a & head for city centre railway station)

WELLINGBOROUGH
Hotel Ibis Wellingborough   78 rooms
Enstone Court NN8 2DR
☎ 01933 228333   ≣ 01933 228444
e: H3164@accor-hotels.com
*(located on junct of A45 & A509 towards Kettering on the
SW edge of Wellingborough)*

SUSSEX, WEST
CRAWLEY
Hotel Ibis London Gatwick   141 rooms
London Road, County Oak RH11 0PF
☎ 01293 590300   ≣ 01293 590310
e: H1889@accor-hotels.com
*(M23 junct 10, take A2011 to Crawley. At rdbt 3rd exit, at
next rdbt A23 London Rd towards Gatwick. Adjacent to
Manor Industrial Est)*

WEST MIDLANDS
BIRMINGHAM
Hotel Ibis Birmingham Holloway   51 rooms
55 Irving Street B1 1DH
☎ 0121 622 4925   ≣ 0121 622 4195
e: h2092@accor-hotels.com
(150yds from Dome Night Club, just off Bristol Street)

Hotel Ibis Birmingham Centre   159 rooms
Arcadian Centre, Ladywell Walk B5 4ST
☎ 0121 622 6010   ≣ 0121 622 6020
e: h1459@accor-hotels.com
*(Follow signs to city centre from all motorways. Then follow
'Markets Area' or 'Indoor Market' signs. Hotel next to
market.)*

Hotel Ibis Birmingham Bordesley   87 rooms
1 Bordesley Park Road, Bordesley B10 0PD
☎ 0121 506 2600   ≣ 0121 506 2610
e: H2178@accor-hotels.com

COVENTRY
Hotel Ibis Coventry South   51 rooms
Abbey Road Whitley CV3 4BJ
☎ 024 7663 9922   ≣ 024 7630 6898
e: H2094@accor-hotels.com
*(signed from A46/A423 rdbt. Take A423 towards A45.
Follow signs for Esporta Health Club and Jaguar Engineering
Plant)*

Hotel Ibis Coventry Centre   89 rooms
Mill Lane St John's Ringway CV1 2LN
☎ 024 7625 0500   ≣ 024 7655 3548
e: H2793@accor.hotels.com
*(from M45 junct 17 to Coventry. Follow City Centre/Ring
Road signs for Birmingham. A45 to Coventry, then A4114
signed to Jaguar Assembly Plant. At inner ring road towards
ring road S. Off exit 5 for Mill Lane)*

WILTSHIRE
SWINDON
Hotel Ibis Swindon   120 rooms
Delta Business Park, Great Western Way SN5 7XG
☎ 01793 514777   ≣ 01793 514570
e: H1041@accor-hotels.com
*(A3102 to Swindon, straight over rdbt, slip road onto Delta
Business Park and turn left)*

YORKSHIRE, EAST
KINGSTON UPON HULL
Hotel Ibis Hull   106 rooms
Osborne Street HU1 2NL
☎ 01482 387500   ≣ 01482 385510
e: h3479-gm@accor-hotels.com
*(M62/A63 straight across at rdbt, follow signs for Princes
Quay onto Myton St. Hotel on corner of Osborne St &
Ferensway)*

YORKSHIRE, SOUTH
ROTHERHAM
Hotel Ibis Rotherham   86 rooms
Moorhead Way, Bramley S66 1YY
☎ 01709 730333   ≣ 01709 730444
e: H3163@accor-hotels.com
*(M18 junct 1, left at rdbt & left at 1st lights. Hotel next to
supermarket)*

SHEFFIELD
Hotel Ibis Sheffield City   95 rooms
Shude Hill S1 2AR
☎ 0114 241 9600   🖷 0114 241 9610
e: H2891@accor-hotels.com
(M1 junct 33, follow signs to Sheffield City Centre(A630/A57), at rdbt take 5th exit, signed Ponds Forge, for hotel)

YORKSHIRE, WEST
SHIPLEY
Hotel Ibis Bradford   78 rooms
Quayside, Salts Mill Rd BD18 3ST
☎ 01274 589333   🖷 01274 589444
e: H3158@accor-hotels.com
(follow tourist signs for Salts Mill. Pick up A650 signs through & out of Bradford for approx 5m to Shipley. Hotel on Salts Mill Rd)

SCOTLAND
CITY OF EDINBURGH
EDINBURGH
Hotel Ibis Edinburgh   99 rooms
6 Hunter Square (off The Royal Mile) EH1 1QW
☎ 0131 240 7000   🖷 0131 240 7007
e: H2039@accor-hotels.com
(from Queen St (M8/M9) or Waterloo Pl (A1) over North Bridge (A7) & High St, take 1st right off South Bridge, into Hunter Sq)

CITY OF GLASGOW
GLASGOW
Hotel Ibis Glasgow City Centre   141 rooms
220 West Regent Street G2 4DQ
☎ 0141 225 6000   🖷 0141 225 6010
e: H3139@accor-hotels.com

WALES
CARDIFF
CARDIFF
Hotel Ibis Cardiff Gate   78 rooms
Malthouse Avenue, Cardiff Gate Business Park
Pontprennau CF23 8RA
☎ 029 2073 3222   🖷 029 2073 4222
e: H3159@accor-hotels.com
(M4 junct 30, take slip rd signed Cardiff Service Station. Hotel on left.)

Hotel Ibis Cardiff City Centre   102 rooms
Churchill Way CF10 2HA
☎ 029 2064 9250   🖷 029 2920 9260
e: H2936@accor-hotels.com
(M4, then A48 2nd exit A4232. Follow signs to City Centre on Newport Rd, left after railway bridge, left after Queen St station.)

Innkeeper's Lodge 0870 243 0500

A new concept in travel accommodation from Bass Leisure Retail, featuring comfortable rooms and complimentary breakfast. Family rooms have a double bed and a fold out double bed. From £39.95 - £79.95

ENGLAND
BEDFORDSHIRE
BEDFORD
Innkeeper's Lodge Bedford   47 rooms
403 Goldington Road MK41 0DS
☎ 0870 243 0500   🖷 01234 343926
(on A428)

BERKSHIRE
SLOUGH
Innkeeper's Lodge Slough/Windsor   57 rooms
399 London Road, Langley SL3 8PS
☎ 01753 591212   🖷 01753 211362
(M4 junct 5 onto London Rd, 100yds on right)

SUNNINGHILL
Innkeeper's Lodge Ascot   10 rooms
London Road, SL5 7SB
☎ 01344 870931   🖷 01344 870932
(M25 junct 13, at rdbt take A30 towards Sunningdale. Turn right onto A329 towards Ascot, continue for 1m and lodge on right)

WINDSOR
Innkeeper's Lodge Old Windsor   15 rooms
14 Straight Road, Old Windsor SL4 2RR
☎ 01753 860769   🖷 01753 851649

BUCKINGHAMSHIRE
ASTON CLINTON
Innkeeper's Lodge Aylesbury   11 rooms
London Road HP22 5HP
☎ 01296 632777   🖷 01296 632685
(on A41 in Aston Clinton, between Aylesbury & Tring)

AYLESBURY
Innkeeper's Lodge Aylesbury South   16 rooms
40 Main Street, Weston Turville HP22 5RW
☎ 01296 613131   🖷 01296 616902
(M25 junct 20/A41(Hemel Hempstead). Continue for 12m to Aston Clinton. Left onto B4544 to Weston Turville, lodge on left)

Innkeeper's Lodge

BEACONSFIELD
Innkeeper's Lodge   32 rooms
Aylesbury End HP9 1LW
☏ 01494 671211   🖷 01494 685042
(M40 junct 2 turn left at next two rdbts. Pub on rdbt)

CHESHIRE
ALDERLEY EDGE
Innkeeper's Lodge Alderley Edge   10 rooms
5-9 Wilmslow Road SK9 7NZ
☏ 01625 599959   🖷 01625 599432
(M56 junct 6, S on A538. Right at traffic lights towards Alderley Edge. Lodge on left, after 2nd rdbt)

CHESTER
Innkeeper's Lodge Chester   14 rooms
Whitchurch Road CH3 6AE
☏ 01244 332200   🖷 01244 336415
(on A41. 1m outside Chester towards Whitchurch)

Innkeeper's Lodge Chester Northeast 36 rooms
Warrington Road, Mickle Trafford CH2 4EX
☏ 01244 301391   🖷 01244 302002
(M53 junct 12, onto A56 signed Helsby, hotel 0.25m on right)

SANDBACH
Innkeeper's Lodge Sandbach   25 rooms
Bereton Green CW11 1RS
☏ 01477 544732
(M6, junction 17, at roundabout bear left towards Holmes Chapel, follow road until Breton, lodge on left at Breton Green)

WARRINGTON
Innkeeper's Lodge Warrington   58 rooms
322 Newton Road, Lowton Village WA3 1HD
☏ 0870 243 0500   🖷 01942 269692
(A580 via M56 junct 23 towards Manchester, follow signs for Toby Carvery)

CO DURHAM
CHESTER-LE-STREET
Innkeeper's Lodge Durham North   21 rooms
Church Mouse, Great North Road,
Chester Moor DH2 3RJ
☏ 0191 389 2628
(A1(M) junct 63, take A167 S Durham/Chester-Le-Street. Straight on at 3 rdbts, Inn on left)

DERBYSHIRE
CASTLETON
Innkeeper's Lodge Castleton   12 rooms
Castle Street S33 8WG
☏ 01433 620578   🖷 01433 622902
(on A6187, in the centre of the village)

DERBY
Innkeeper's Lodge Derby   29 rooms
Nottingham Road, Chaddesdon DE21 6LZ
☏ 0870 243 0500   🖷 01332 673306
(from M1 junct 25 take A52 towards Derby, take exit signed Spondon & Chaddesden, at rdbt take exit signed Chaddesden pass Asda store, 1m at lights right into car park)

DEVON
EXETER
Innkeeper's Lodge Exeter East   13 rooms
Clyst St George EX3 0QJ
☏ 01392 876121   🖷 01392 872022
(M5 junct 30, A376 towards Exmouth. Right at 1st rdbt, straight over 2nd rdbt, at 3rd rdbt turn into Bridge Hill, lodge on right)

DORSET
BOURNEMOUTH
Innkeeper's Lodge Bournemouth   28 rooms
Cooper Dean Roundabout, Castle Lane East BH7 7DP
☏ 01202 390837   🖷 01202 390378
(A338 Bournemouth spur road, follow until exit signed Bournemouth Hospital. Hotel on corner next to hospital)

GREATER LONDON
BECKENHAM
Innkeeper's Lodge   24 rooms
422 Upper Elmers End Road BR3 3HQ
☏ 020 8650 2233
(From M25 junct 6 Croydon, take A232 for Shirley. At West Wickham take A214 opposite Eden Park Station)

CROYDON
Innkeeper's Lodge Croydon South   30 rooms
415 Brighton Road CR2 6EJ
☏ 020 8680 4559   🖷 020 8649 9802
(M23 junct 7/ A23 or M25 junct 6/A22. At Purley take A235 Brighton Rd, N towards South Croydon, for 1m. Lodge on right.)

NORTHOLT
Innkeeper's Lodge   21 rooms
Mandeville Road UB5 4LU
☏ 020 8422 2050
(A40 at the Target roundabout)

GREATER MANCHESTER
STOCKPORT
Innkeeper's Lodge Stockport   22 rooms
271 Wellington Road, North Heaton Chapel SK4 5BP
☏ 0161 432 2753

HAMPSHIRE
FLEET
Innkeeper's Lodge   40 rooms
Cove Road GU51 2SH
01252 774600
(M3, junct 4A)

PORTSMOUTH

Innkeeper's Lodge Portsmouth 33 rooms
Copnor Road, Hilsea PO3 5HS
0870 243 0500
(From A27 take A2030. Right at lights, over 3 rdbts into Norway Road. Inn on A288)

ROWLAND'S CASTLE

Innkeeper's Lodge Portsmouth North 21 rooms
Whichers Gate Road PO9 6BB
☎ 0870 243 0500
(M3 junct 2, at rdbt, right onto the B2149 (Rowlands Castle). After 2m, left onto B2148 Whichers Gate Rd, lodge on left)

HERTFORDSHIRE
BOREHAMWOOD

Innkeeper's Lodge Borehamwood 55 rooms
Studio Way WD6 5JY
☎ 020 8905 1455 🖩 020 8236 9822
(M25 junct 23/A1(M) signed to London. Follow signs to Borehamwood after double rdbt turn into Studio Way)

ST ALBANS

Innkeeper's Lodge 13 rooms
1 Barnet Road AL2 1BL
☎ 01727 823698 🖩 01727 820902
(clockwise from Heathrow on M25 towards Harlow, exit at junct 22 staying in left lane, at rdbt take 1st left to London Colney. Straight over rdbt The Colney Fox is 450 yds on right)

KENT
CANTERBURY

Innkeeper's Lodge 9 rooms
162 New Dover Road CT1 3EL
☎ 01227 829951 🖩 01227 829952
(M2 junct 7, A2 left at junct for Rough Common onto A2050. At 2nd rdbt follow signs for Dover (A2), lodge on right)

MAIDSTONE

Innkeeper's Lodge Maidstone 12 rooms
Sandling Road ME14 2RF
☎ 01622 692212 🖩 01622 679265
(M20 junct 6, S onto A229 towards Maidstone. At 3rd rdbt, turn left and left again)

ROYAL TUNBRIDGE WELLS

Innkeeper's Lodge Tunbridge 15 rooms
21 London Road, Southborough TN4 0RL
☎ 01892 529292 🖩 01892 510620
(Off M25 onto A21, take A26 Tonbridge/Southborough turn off. Lodge located in Southborough on A26, opposite the cricket green on Church Road.)

LEICESTERSHIRE
LEICESTER

Innkeeper's Lodge Leicester 31 rooms
Hinckley Road LE3 3PG
☎ 0116 238 7878

LONDON
E11

Innkeeper's Lodge Snaresbrook 24 rooms
37 Hollybush Hill, Snaresbrook E11 1PE
☎ 020 8989 761

N14

Innkeeper's Lodge Southgate 19 rooms
22 The Green, Southgate N14 6EN
☎ 020 8447 8022 🖩 020 8447 8022
(take A111 from J24, 3m to rdbt for A1004, turn right into High Street , hotel at next rdbt)

MERSEYSIDE
LIVERPOOL

Innkeeper's Lodge Liverpool North 21 rooms
502 Queen's Drive, Stoneycroft L13 0AS
☎ 0151 254 2271 🖩 0151 254 2394
(from M62 take A5080 N towards Bootle Docks. Continue at lights at junct with A57. Hotel on left in Queen's Drive)

Innkeeper's Lodge 32 rooms
531 Aigburth Road L19 9DN
☎ 0151 494 1032 🖩 0151 494 3345
(on A56, opposite Liverpool cricket ground)

NORTHAMPTONSHIRE
NORTHAMPTON

Innkeeper's Lodge Northampton East 31 rooms
Talavera Way, Round Spinney NN3 8RN
☎ 01604 494241 🖩 01604 673701
(M1 junct 15a, N on A43. Right at rdbt, pass 2 further rdbts. At 3rd rdbt, A45 N until exit for A43, continue to Round Spinney rdbt and Talavera Way)

Innkeeper's Lodge Northampton South 51 rooms
London Road, Wootton NN4 0TG
☎ 01604 769676 🖩 01604 677981
(M1 junct 15 take A508, towards Northampton. Pass under flyover, exit left immediately & turn right at rdbt into London Rd. Lodge on right.)

NORTHUMBERLAND
CRAMLINGTON

Innkeeper's Lodge Cramlington 18 rooms
Blagdon Lane NE23 8AU
☎ 01670 736111 🖩 01670 715709
(from A1, exit for A19. At rdbt, left onto A1068, lodge at junct of Blagdon Lane and Fisher Lane)

NOTTINGHAMSHIRE
NOTTINGHAM
Innkeeper's Lodge Nottingham   34 rooms
Derby Road, Wollaton Vale NG8 2NR
☎ 0115 922 1691
(M1 junct 25, take A52 to Nottingham. At 3rd rdbt, left into Wollaton Vale, right across central reservation into car park)

STAFFORDSHIRE
LICHFIELD
Innkeeper's Lodge   10 rooms
Stafford Road WS13 8JB
☎ 01543 415789   🖷 01543 420752
(on A51, 0.75m outside city centre)

STOKE-ON-TRENT
Innkeeper's Lodge Stoke-on-Trent   30 rooms
Longton Road ST4 8BU
☎ 01782 644448   🖷 01782 644163
(M6 junct 15, follow A500 until the slip road for A34 towards Stone. At rdbt take left onto A5035, lodge is half a mile on right)

SURREY
FRIMLEY
Innkeeper's Lodge Frimley   43 rooms
114 Portsmouth Road GU15 1HS
☎ 01276 691939   🖷 01276 605900
(M3 junct 4/ A321 for Frimley take A325 (towards A30 Bagshot), over 1st rdbt past Frimley Park Hospital, straight over 2nd rdbt into Portsmouth Rd. Lodge 500mtrs on left.)

GODALMING
Innkeeper's Lodge   19 rooms
Ockford Road GU7 1RH
☎ 01483 419997   🖷 01483 410852
(Turn off A3/Milford at petrol station turn left onto A3100 through Milford under railway bridge. Lodge on rdbt on right)

REDHILL
Innkeeper's Lodge Redhill   37 rooms
2 Redstone Hill RH1 4BL
☎ 01737 768434   🖷 01737 770742
(M25 junct 8, follow signs for Redhill (A25). At railway station, left towards Godstone, located on right)

WALTON-ON-THAMES
Innkeeper's Lodge Walton-on-Thames 32 rooms
Ashley Park Road KT12 1JP
☎ 01932 220196   🖷 01932 220660
(M25 junct 11 east towards A317 towards Weybridge, at B365 roundabout for Ashley Park, turn left then right into Station Av, left opposite station)

WEYBRIDGE
Innkeeper's Lodge   18 rooms
25 Oatlands Chase KT13 9RW
☎ 01932 253277   🖷 01932 252412
badgers.rest@bass.com
(M25 junct 11, A317 towards Weybridge, at 3rd rdbt take A3050, left 1m. Turn into Oatlands Chase, lodge on right)

WOKING
Innkeeper's Lodge Woking   33 rooms
Chobham Road, Horsell GU21 4AL
☎ 01483 733047

SUSSEX, EAST
EASTBOURNE
Innkeeper's Lodge Eastbourne   42 rooms
Highfield Park Willingdon Drove, BN23 8AL
☎ 01323 507222

WICKFORD
Innkeeper's Lodge Basildon/Wickford 24 rooms
Runwell Road SS11 7QJ
☎ 01268 769671   🖷 01268 578012
(M25 junct 29/A127 Southend, leave at Basildon/Wickford, left at rdbt towards Wickford. Straight over next 2 rdbts 3rd rdbt 2nd exit)

TYNE & WEAR
NEWCASTLE UPON TYNE
Innkeeper's Lodge Newcastle   30 rooms
Kenton Bank NE3 3TY
☎ 0191 214 0877   🖷 0191 214 1922
(from A1(M), exit A696/B6918. At 1st rdbt, take B6918 (Kingston Park), 2nd rdbt turn right. Lodge located on left)

WARWICKSHIRE
RUGBY
Innkeeper's Lodge Rugby   16 rooms
The Green, Dunchurch CV22 6NJ
☎ 01788 810305   🖷 01788 810931
(M1 junct 17/M45/A45. Follow signs for Dunchurch B4429. Lodge located in the village centre on x-rds of the A426 and B4429)

WELLESBOURNE
Innkeeper's Lodge Stratford-upon-Avon East 9 rooms
Warwick Road CV35 9LX
☎ 01789 840206   🖷 01789 472902
(M40 junct 15 S onto A429 towards Wellesbourne. Turn left at rdbt onto B4086 & lodge is located 300yds on right.)

WEST MIDLANDS
BIRMINGHAM
Innkeeper's Lodge Birmingham West 24 rooms
563 Hagley Road, West Quinton B32 1HP
☎ 0870 243 0500
(M5 junct 3/A456 westbound. On opposite side of dual carriageway, accessed a short distance from rdbt)

Innkeeper's Lodge Birmingham South 85 rooms
2225 Coventry Road, Sheldon B26 3EH
☎ 0121 742 6201 📠 0121 722 2703
(M42 junct 6/A45 towards Birmingham for 2m. Lodge on left approaching overhanging traffic lights)

COVENTRY

Innkeeper's Lodge Meriden   13 rooms
Main Road, Meriden CV7 7NN
☎ 01676 523798 📠 01676 531922
(in village of Meriden, just off main A45 between Coventry & Birmingham on B4102. Lodge on left down the hill from Meriden Village Green)

KINGSWINFORD

Innkeeper's Lodge   22 rooms
Swindon Road DY6 9XA
☎ 01384 295254 📠 01384 287959
(A491 into Kingswinford, at x-rds lights, turn onto A4101 towards Kidderminster along 'Summerhill'. At 1st set of lights, hotel on right)

SOLIHULL

Innkeeper's Lodge Knowle   13 rooms
Warwick Road, Knowle B93 0EE
☎ 01564 771177 📠 01564 730862
(on A41)

SUTTON COLDFIELD

Innkeeper's Lodge Birmingham East 66 rooms
Chester Road, Streetley B73 6SP
☎ 0121 353 7785 📠 0121 352 1443
(M6 junct 7 to A34 heading S & turn left onto A4041. At 4th rdbt turn right onto A452-Chester Road, lodge located less 1m on right.)

WORCESTERSHIRE
BROMSGROVE

Innkeeper's Lodge Bromsgrove   29 rooms
462 Birmingham Road Marlbrook B61 0HR
☎ 01527 878060
(on the A38 0.5m between M5 & M42)

YORKSHIRE, EAST RIDING OF
WILLERBY

Innkeeper's Lodge Hull   32 rooms
Beverley Road HU10 6NT
☎ 01482 651518 📠 01482 658380
(M62/A63, Humber Bridge exit off A63, follow signs for A164. Lodge 3m on left opp Willerby shopping centre)

YORKSHIRE, NORTH
HARROGATE

Innkeeper's Lodge Harrogate West   11 rooms
Otley Road, Beckwith, Knowle HG3 1PR
☎ 01423 533091 📠 01423 533092
(from A1(M) junct 47, take A59 for Harrogate. Over 2 rdbts, at 3rd rdbt straight over onto B6162. Hotel on left.

KNARESBOROUGH

Innkeeper's Lodge Harrogate East   11 rooms
Wetherby Road, Plompton HG5 8LY
☎ 01423 797979 📠 01423 887276
(turn off A658 onto A661 towards Harrogate, lodge on left)

YORKSHIRE, SOUTH
SHEFFIELD

Innkeeper's Lodge Sheffield South   10 rooms
Hathersage Road, Longshaw S11 7TY
☎ 01433 630374 01433 637102
(8m from Sheffield city centre on A625 Sheffield Castleton Road at junction of A625 & B6051.)

YORKSHIRE, WEST
HUDDERSFIELD

Innkeeper's Lodge Huddersfield   23 rooms
36a Penistone Road HD8 0PQ
☎ 01484 602101 📠 01484 603938
(from A62 Huddersfield ring road onto A629 towards Wakefield)

ILKLEY

Innkeeper's Lodge   16 rooms
Hangingstone Road LS29 8BT
☎ 01943 607335 📠 01943 604712
(from A65 turn towards Ilkley town centre and then at the station turn right into Cowpasture Rd. The Cow & Calf is approx 0.75m on left)

KEIGHLEY

Innkeeper's Lodge   43 rooms
Bradford Road BD21 4BB
☎ 01535 610611
(From M606 rdbt take A6177, at next rdbt A641 & A650 towards Keighley. Lodge on 2nd rdbt)

LEEDS

Innkeeper's Lodge Leeds South   32 rooms
Bruntcliffe Road, Morley LS27 0LY
☎ 0113 253 3115 📠 0113 253 9365
(M62 junct 27 take A650 towards Morley. On junct of A650 and A643)

SCOTLAND
CITY OF EDINBURGH
EDINBURGH

Innkeeper's Lodge Edinburgh West   28 rooms
114-116 St John's Road, Corstophine EH12 8AX
☎ 0131 334 8235 📠 0131 316 5012
(M8 junct 1, N on A720. At Gogar rdbt, right onto A8, straight over next rdbt, hotel on left just past church at St John's Rd)

Innkeeper's Lodge - Premier Lodge

SOUTH QUEENSFERRY
Innkeeper's Lodge South Queensferry 16 rooms
7 Newhalls Road EH30 9TA
☎ 0131 331 1990 📠 0131 331 3168
(M8 follow signs for Forth Road Bridge exit at junct 2 onto M9/A8000. At rdbt take B907 follow until junction with B249. Turn right for lodge)

WEST DUNBARTONSHIRE
BALLOCH
Innkeeper's Lodge Loch Lomond   14 rooms
Balloch Road G83 8LQ
☎ 0870 243 0500
(M8 junct 30 onto M898. Left at Duntocher rdbt onto A82, right at rdbt (A811), left into Daluart Rd, lodge opposite)

WALES
CARDIFF
CARDIFF
Innkeeper's Lodge Cardiff   52 rooms
Tyn-y-Parc Road, Whitchurch CF14 6BG
☎ 029 2069 2554 📠 029 2052 7052
(M4 junct 32, southbound on A470. At 3rd set of T-lights, turn left).

Premier Lodge
08702 01 02 03

Modern travel accommodation across the UK. Every lodge features an adjacent licensed popular restaurant, such as Millers Restaurant, Outside Inn or Chef & Brewer. *Premier Lodge has now been acquired by Travel Inn and will be re-branded as Premier Travel Inn by Spring 2005.*

ENGLAND
BERKSHIRE
NEWBURY
Premier Lodge (Newbury)   49 rooms
Bath Road Midgham RG7 5UX
☎ 0870 9906556 📠 0870 9906557
(exit M4 at junct 12 for A4 towards Newbury. The hotel is 7m along on the right)

READING
Premier Lodge (Reading South)   32 rooms
Grazeley Green Road RG7 1LS
☎ 0870 9906454 📠 0870 9906455
(M4 junct 11 follow A33 towards Basingstoke, take Mortimer exit at 1st rdbt. 3rd right into Grazeley Rd, under railway bridge turn left, for the Lodge.

SLOUGH
Premier Lodge (Slough)   84 rooms
76 Uxbridge Road SL1 1SU
☎ 0870 9906500 📠 0870 9906501
(2m from M4 junct 5, just off A4)

BRISTOL
BRISTOL
Premier Lodge (Bristol North West) 106 rooms
Cribbs Causeway, Catbrain Lane BS10 7TQ
☎ 0870 9906570 📠 0870 9906571
(M5 junct 17, A4018. Take 1st left at rdbt into Lysander Rd. Right into Catbrain Hill leads into Catbrain Ln)

Premier Lodge (Bristol Filton) 60 rooms
Shield Retail Park, Gloucester Road North,
Filton BS34 7BR
☎ 0870 9906456 📠 0870 9906457
(exit M5 junct 16, towards A38 signed Filton & Patchway. Pass airport Royal Mail on right. At 2nd rdbt left, 1st left)

Premier Lodge (Bristol City Centre) 60 rooms
Llandoger Trow Kings Street BS1 4ER
☎ 0870 9906424 📠 0870 9906425
(follow A38 into city centre. Left onto B4053 right into Queen Charlotte St. On one-way system, right at river)

BUCKINGHAMSHIRE
MILTON KEYNES
Premier Lodge (Milton Keynes Central) 120 rooms
Shirwell Crescent, Furzton MK4 1GA
☎ 0870 9906396 📠 0870 9906397
(M1 junct 14, onto A509 to Milton Keynes. At 9th 'North Grafton' rdbt left onto V6. Right at Leadenhall rdbt onto H7. Over 'The Bowl' rdbt)

Premier Lodge (Milton Keynes South) 40 rooms
Bletcham Way, Caldecotte MK7 8HP
☎ 0870 9906558 📠 0870 9906559
(M1 junct 14, A509 to Milton Keynes. 1st rdbt take A4146, left at 2nd rdbt, over 3rd rdbt and right at 4th. Lodge over next rdbt on right)

CAMBRIDGESHIRE
ST NEOTS
Premier Lodge (Eaton Socon)   63 rooms
Great North Road, Eaton Socon PE19 8EN
☎ 0870 9906314 📠 0870 9906315
(just off A1 at rdbt with A428 and B1428 before St Neots, 1m from St Neots train station)

CHESHIRE
ALDERLEY EDGE
Premier Lodge (Alderley Edge)   37 rooms
Congleton Road, Alderley Edge SK9 7AA
☎ 0870 9906498 📠 0870 9906499
(From north, exit M56 junct 6 onto A538 towards Wilmslow then on A34 towards Alderley Edge.)

CHESTER
Premier Lodge (Chester)   31 rooms
76 Liverpool Road CH2 1AU
☎ 0870 9906470 📠 0870 9906471
(M53 junct 12 right for A56. At 2nd rdbt right signed A41 Chester Zoo. At 1st lights left into Heath Rd Mill Ln. Under rail bridge Lodge on right)

HANDFORTH

Premier Lodge (Manchester Airport North) 35 rooms
30 Wilmslow Road SK9 3EW
☎ 0870 9906602   ▤ 0870 9906603
(exit M56 junct 6 and follow the A538 towards town centre and bear to the left. Follow the road for approx 2m for hotel situated at the top of the hill on the right, just after Wilmslow Garden Centre)

KNUTSFORD

Premier Lodge (Knutsford North)   66 rooms
Bucklow Hill, WA16 6RD
☎ 0870 9906428   ▤ 0870 9906429
(M56 junct 7, take A556 towards Northwich and M6. Hotel 1m at lights on left)

Premier Lodge (Knutsford North West) 28 rooms
Warrington Road, Hoo Green, Mere WA16 0PZ
☎ 0870 9906482   ▤ 0870 9906483
(exit M6 junct 19 and follow the signs A556 Manchester. At the 1st set of lights turn left onto the A50 towards Warrington for hotel 1m on the right)

MACCLESFIELD

Premier Lodge (Macclesfield)   28 rooms
Congleton Road, Gawsworth SK11 7XD
☎ 0870 9906412   ▤ 0870 9906413
(2m from Macclesfield. Exit M6 junct 17 and follow the A534 to Congleton, then the A536 towards Macclesfield. Follow the road along to Gawsworth for hotel on left)

NANTWICH

Premier Lodge (Nantwich)   37 rooms
221 Crewe Road, CW5 6NE
☎ 0870 9906418   ▤ 0870 9906419
(exit M6 junct 16 for A500 signed Nantwich and Chester. At the 1st rdbt take 2nd exit and continue for approx 4m. At 3rd rdbt, take the 3rd exit signed A500 Chester, at the 4th turn left onto A534 towards Nantwich. The hotel is approx.100 yards on right)

NORTHWICH

Premier Lodge (Northwich South)   32 rooms
London Road, Leftwich CW9 8EG
☎ 0870 9906362   ▤ 0870 9906363
(off M6 junct 19, follow A556 to Chester. Turn right at the sign for Northwich and Davenham)

Premier Lodge (Northwich)   52 rooms
520 Chester Road Sandiway CW8 2DN
☎ 0870 9906494   ▤ 0870 9906495
(Situated 1m from M6 junct 19 on A556 towards Chester)

PUDDINGTON

Premier Lodge (Wirral South)   31 rooms
Parkgate Road, Two Mills CH66 9PD
☎ 0870 9906564   ▤ 0870 9906565
(5m from M56 junct 16 & M53 junct 5 on x-rds of A550 & A540)

WARRINGTON

Premier Lodge (Warrington Central) 105 rooms
Manchester Road, Woolston WA1 4GB
☎ 0870 9906524   ▤ 0870 9906525

Premier Lodge (Warrington North)   42 rooms
Golborne Road, Winwick WA2 8LF
☎ 0870 9906600   ▤ 0870 9906601
(M6 junct 22. Follow signs for A573 towards Newton-le-Willows. Follow dual carriageway to end & take 3rd exit at rdbt. Look out for church, opp lodge to right)

Premier Lodge (Warrington South)   29 rooms
Tarporley Road, Stretton WA4 4NB
☎ 0870 9906526   ▤ 0870 9906527
(Just off M56 junct 10. Follow A49 to Warrington & turn left at 1st set of traffic lights)

WILMSLOW

Premier Lodge (Manchester Airport South) 37 rooms
Racecourse Road SK9 5LR
☎ 0870 9906506   ▤ 0870 9906507

CUMBRIA
CARLISLE

Premier Lodge (Carlisle)   49 rooms
Kingstown Road CA3 0AT
☎ 0870 9906502   ▤ 0870 9906503
(1m from M6 junct 44 on the A7 towards Carlisle, on left)

DERBYSHIRE
DERBY

Premier Lodge (Derby North)   22 rooms
95 Ashbourne Road, Mackworth DE22 4LZ
☎ 0870 9906606   ▤ 0870 9906607
(M1 junct 25 on A52 towards Derby. At Pentagon Island straight towards city centre. Follow signs to A52 Ashbourne and into Mackworth)

Premier Lodge (Derby)   27 rooms
Foresters Leisure Park, Osmaston Park Road DE23 8AG
☎ 0870 9906306   ▤ 0870 9906307
(M1 junct 24 A6 to Derby. Left onto A5111 2m)

DEVON
PLYMOUTH

Premier Lodge (Plymouth City Centre) 107 rooms
Sutton Road, Shepherds Wharf PL4 0HT
☎ 0870 9906458   ▤ 0870 9906459
(from the Marsh Mills rdbt. follow signs City Centre (A374) Then Barbican Coxside signs. After Leisure Park right at lights hotel 50yds)

Premier Lodge

DORSET
POOLE
Premier Lodge (Poole)　　　126 rooms
Cabot Lane BH17 7DA
☎ 0870 9906332　🖷 0870 6606333
(from M27 onto the A31 towards Bournemouth. Follow signs for Poole/Channel Ferries and at Darby's Corner rdbt take 2nd exit. At the 2nd set of lights turn right)

ESSEX
BASILDON
Premier Lodge (Basildon)　　　64 rooms
Festival Leisure Park, Pipps Hill Road South,
off Cranes Farm Road SS14 3WB
☎ 0870 9906598　🖷 0870 9906599
(from M25 junct 29 follow A127 towards Basildon. Premier Lodge is 4 m outside Basildon off A1235)

CHELMSFORD
Premier Lodge (Chelmsford)　　　78 rooms
Main Road, Borham CM3 3HJ
☎ 0870 9906394　🖷 0870 9906395
(M25 junct 28, A12 to Colchester, then B1137 to Borham)

SOUTHEND-ON-SEA
Premier Lodge (Southend-on-Sea)　　42 rooms
213 Eastern Esplanade SS1 3AD
☎ 0870 9906370　🖷 0870 9906371
(on entering Southend follow the signs for the A1159 (A13) Shoeburyness onto a dual carriageway & at the rdbt forward signed Thorpe Bay seafront. At seafront turn right for hotel.)

THURROCK
Premier Lodge (Thurrock)　　　161 rooms
Stonehouse Lane RM19 1NS
☎ 0870 9906490　🖷 0870 9906491

WALTHAM ABBEY
Premier Lodge (Waltham Abbey)　　93 rooms
The Grange, Sewardstone Road EN9 3QF
☎ 0870 9906568　🖷 0870 9906569
(M25 junct 26 & follow A121 towards Waltham Abbey. Turn left onto A112, lodge 0.5m on left)

GLOUCESTERSHIRE
ALVESTON
Premier Lodge (Bristol North)　　74 rooms
Thornbury Road BS35 3LL
☎ 0870 9906496　🖷 0870 9906497
(from north exit the M5 at junct 14 onto the A38 towards Bristol. From the south exit the M5 at junct 16 and take the A38 towards Gloucester)

GLOUCESTER
Premier Lodge (Gloucester East)　　83 rooms
Barnwood GL4 3HR
0870 9906322　0870 9906323
(Exit M5 at junct 11. Follow the A40 towards Gloucester, at the 1st rbt take A417 towards Cirencester, at the next rdbt take the 4th exit)

Premier Lodge (Gloucester North)　　52 rooms
Tewkesbury Road, Twigworth GL2 9PG
☎ 0870 9906560　🖷 0870 9906561
(2m from Gloucester. Exit M5 at junct 11, take the A40 towards Gloucester and then A38 towards Tewkesbury)

STROUD
Premier Lodge (Stroud)　　　32 rooms
Stratford Lodge, Stratford Road GL5 4AF
☎ 0870 9906378　🖷 0870 9906379
(M5 junct 13, follow A419 to Stroud town centre, then follow signs for leisure centre, the lodge is opposite, next to Tesco)

GREATER LONDON
BARKING
Premier Lodge (Barking)　　　88 rooms
Highbridge Road IG11 7BA
☎ 0870 9906318　🖷 0870 9906319
(Situated 1.5m from Barking. Exit the M25 junct 30 onto the A13, signposted to London City and Docklands, onto the A406 North Circular)

BRENTFORD
Premier Lodge (London Brentford) 141 rooms
52 High Street TW8 0AW
☎ 0870 9906304　🖷 0870 9906305
(from Chiswick rdbt, take exit marked A205 towards Kew and Brentford. After approx 200 yds take the right fork onto A315 (High St) and follow road for 0.5m for hotel on left)

CROYDON
Premier Lodge (Croydon)　　　82 rooms
The Colonnades Leisure Park, 619 Purley Way CR0 4RQ
☎ 0870 9906554　🖷 0870 9906555
(from north, exit M1 onto the M25, then follow the A23 towards Croydon)

EDGWARE
Premier Lodge (London Edgware)　　111 rooms
435 Burnt Oak Broadway HA8 5AQ
☎ 0870 9906522　🖷 0870 9906523
(on A5, 11m from Central London and 3m from M1 junct 4. From M1 take A41 and then A5 towards Edgware. The hotel is situated on A5 opposite the Peugeot dealership)

HOUNSLOW
Premier Lodge (London Heathrow Airport 1) 133 rooms
Shepiston Lane, Heathrow Airport UB3 1RW
☎ 0870 9906612　🖷 0870 9906613
(from M4 junct 4 take 3rd exit off the rdbt and the hotel is situated on Shepiston Ln on right)

ROMFORD
Premier Lodge (Romford) 40 rooms
Whalebone Lane, North Chadwell Heath RM6 6QU
☎ 0870 9906450　🖷 0870 9906451
(6m from M25 junc 28 on the A12 at the junction with the A1112)

TWICKENHAM

Premier Lodge (Twickenham)   31 rooms
Chertsey Road, Whitton TW2 6LS
☏ 0870 9906416 🖹 0870 9906417
(M25 junct 12/M3 & follow signs for Central London. At end of M3, the road becomes the A316. In Richmond, 100 yards further go straight over the rdbt. Lodge 500 yards on left)

WEMBLEY

Premier Lodge (London Wembley)   154 rooms
151 Wembley Park Drive HA9 8HQ
☏ 0870 9906484 🖹 0870 9906485
(from A406 North Circular take A404 towards Wembley. After approx 2m right into Wembley Hill Rd, keep right into Empire Way (B4565) passing Wembley Arena on the right, and keep right round petrol station. Lodge is 200yds on left)

GREATER MANCHESTER
ALTRINCHAM

Premier Lodge (Altrincham South)   46 rooms
Manchester Road WA14 4PH
☏ 0870 9906580 🖹 0870 9906581
(From north M60 junct 7 and follow A56 towards Altrincham.)

Premier Lodge (Altrincham North)   48 rooms
Manchester Road, West Timperley WA14 5NH
☏ 0870 9906330 🖹 0870 9906631
(2 m from Altrincham off A56)

HYDE

Premier Lodge (Manchester East)   83 rooms
Stockport Road, Mottram SK14 3AU
☏ 0870 9906334 🖹 0870 9906335
(Situated at the end of M67, between A57 and A560)

MANCHESTER

Premier Lodge (Manchester City Centre) 170 rooms
North Tower Victoria Bridge Street Salford M3 5AS
☏ 0870 9906366 🖹 0870 9906367
(M602 to Manchester city centre, then A57(M) towards GMEX. 2nd exit following sign for A56 city centre. Turn left before the MEN arena onto A6 and 1st left)

Premier Lodge (City Centre GMEX 1) 147 rooms
Bishopsgate 7-11 Lower Mosley Street M2 3DW
☏ 0870 9906444 🖹 0870 9906445
(from M56 continue on A5103 towards Manchester city. Turn right at 2nd lights and at next set turn left onto Oxford Rd then left at the junction of St Peters Sq. The hotel is on the left hand side of Lower Mosley St)

Premier Lodge (City Centre GMEX 2) 200 rooms
Gaythorne, River Street M15 5FJ
☏ 0870 9906504 🖹 0870 9906505
(Adjacent to A57(M) (Mancunian Way) close to GMEX & Bridgewater Hall on A5103)

MIDDLETON

Premier Lodge (Manchester North) 42 rooms
818 Manchester Old Road, Rhodes M24 4RF
☏ 0870 9906406 🖹 0870 9906407
(M60/M62 junction 18 follow signs Manchester/Middleton. Leave M60 at junct 19, for A576 towards Middleton)

PENDLEBURY

Premier Lodge (Manchester North West) 31 rooms
219 Bolton Road M27 8TG
☏ 0870 9906528 🖹 0870 9906529
(from M60 junct 13 take A572 and rdbt 3rd exit towards Swinton. At next take A572 then after 2m right onto A580. After 2 sets of lights, take the A666 Kearsley, then 1st left at the rdbt. Pass fire station on right then 1st right)

STANDISH

Premier Lodge (Wigan North)   36 rooms
Almond Brook Road WN6 0SS
☏ 0870 9906474 🖹 0870 9906475
(M6 junct 27 follow signs for Standish. Turn left at T-junct, then take 1st right)

STOCKPORT

Premier Lodge (Stockport)   46 rooms
Churchgate SK1 1YG
☏ 0870 9906544 🖹 0870 9906545
(M60 junct 27 onto A626 St Marys Way, turn right at Behhams BMW garage into Spring Gdns then 2nd right into car park)

SWINTON

Premier Lodge (Manchester West)   27 rooms
East Lancs Road M27 0AA
☏ 0870 9906480 🖹 0870 9906481
(10 mins from Manchester city centre, off junct 13 of the M60 (Swinton/Leigh) on the A580)

URMSTON

Premier Lodge (Manchester Trafford Centre) 42 rooms
Trafford Boulevard M41 7JE
☏ 0870 9906310 🖹 0870 9906311
(from M6, join the M62 at junct 21a towards Manchester. Exit M62 at junct 1, taking the M60 south to junct 10, taking the B5214. The hotel is on the left just before Ellesmere Circle)

WIGAN

Premier Lodge (Wigan South)   28 rooms
53 Warrington Road, Ashton-in-Makerfield WN4 9PJ
☏ 0870 9906582 🖹 0870 9906583
(M6 junct 23, onto A49 towards Ashton. Hotel 0.5m on left)

HAMPSHIRE
NORTH WALTHAM
Premier Lodge (Basingstoke)   28 rooms
RG25 2BB
☎ 0870 9906476 📠 0870 9906477
(on A30 just off M3 junct 7. Follow signs North Waltham, Popham and Kings Worthy. Lodge located 2m on the right, before the A303)

ROMSEY
Premier Lodge (Southampton West) 67 rooms
Romsey Road, Ower SO51 6ZJ
☎ 0870 9906350 📠 0870 9906351
(M27 junct 2, follow A36 towards Salisbury, follow brown tourist sign 'The Vine Inn'. 200yds on Romsey Rd on right)

SOUTHAMPTON
Premier Lodge (Southampton Airport) 121 rooms
Mitchell Way SO18 2XU
☎ 0870 9906436 📠 0870 9906437
(off M27 junct 5 onto A335 towards Eastleigh. Turn right at the rdbt onto Wide Ln then 1st exit off next rdbt into Mitchell Way)

HERTFORDSHIRE
KING'S LANGLEY
Premier Lodge (King's Langley)   60 rooms
Hempstead Road WD4 8BR
☎ 0870 9906372 📠 0870 9906373
(1m from M25 junct 20, on the A4251 after Kings Langley)

WATFORD
Premier Lodge (Watford)   105 rooms
Timms Meadow Water Lane WD17 2NJ
☎ 0870 9906620 📠 0870 9906621
(M1 junct 5/A41 into town centre. At rdbt take 3rd exit & stay in left hand lane through traffic lights. Take 1st left into Water Ln lodge on left)

KENT
DOVER
Premier Lodge (Dover)   100 rooms
Marine Court, Marine Parade CT16 1LW
☎ 0870 9906516 📠 0870 9906517
(adjacent to ferry terminal)

GRAVESEND
Premier Lodge (Gravesend)   31 rooms
Hevercourt Road, Singlewell DA12 5UQ
☎ 0870 9906352 📠 0870 9906353
(off the A2 on the coastbound carriageway towards Rochester and the Channel Tunnel. Turn off at Singlewell Services Rd)

TONBRIDGE
Premier Lodge (Tonbridge)   38 rooms
Pembury Road TN11 0NA
☎ 0870 9906552 📠 0870 9906553
(M25 junct 5. Take A21 towards Hastings, pass junct for Tunbridge Wells (A26). Exit next junct then 1st exit at rdbt)

WATERINGBURY
Premier Lodge (Maidstone)   40 rooms
103 Tonbridge Road ME18 5NS
☎ 0870 9906346 📠 0870 9906347
(exit M25 junct 3 onto the M20. Exit at junct 4 onto the A228 towards West Malling. Follow the A26 towards Maidstone for approximately 3m)

LANCASHIRE
BILSBORROW
Premier Lodge (Preston North)   40 rooms
Garstang Road PR3 0RN
☎ 0870 9906410 📠 0870 9906411
(M6 junct 32 on A6 towards Garstang)

BLACKBURN
Premier Lodge (Blackburn)   20 rooms
Myerscough Road, Balderstone BB2 7LE
☎ 0870 9906388 📠 0870 9906389
(opp British Aerospace. M6 junct 31, A59 to Clitheroe)

BLACKPOOL
Premier Lodge (Blackpool)   81 rooms
Whitehills Park, Preston New Road FY4 5NZ
0870 9906608 📠 0870 9906609
(M55 junct 4 1st left off rdbt, lodge on right)

CHORLEY
Premier Lodge (Chorley South)   29 rooms
Bolton Road PR7 4AB
☎ 0870 9906604 📠 0870 9906605
(From south, exit M6 junct 27, follow signs for Standish. Turn left onto the A5106 to Chorley then the A6 towards Preston. The Lodge is 0.5m on the right)

Premier Lodge (Chorley)   81 rooms
Malthouse Farm, Moss Lane, Whittle le Woods PR6 8AB
☎ 0870 9906376 📠 0870 9906377
malthousefarm20@hotmail.com
(M6 junct 29 join M65. Exit at junct 2, taking the M61 (Manchester). Exit the M61 at junct 8, take the M674 (Wheelton), then 400 yds on the left turn into Moss Ln)

KIRKHAM
Premier Lodge (Blackpool East)   28 rooms
Fleetwood Road, Greenhalgh PR4 3HE
☎ 0870 9906636 📠 0870 9906637

LYTHAM ST ANNES
Premier Lodge (Lytham St Annes) 22 rooms
Church Road FY8 5LH
☎ 0870 9906548 📠 0870 9906549

PRESTON
Premier Lodge (Preston)   40 rooms
Lostock Lane, Bamber Bridge PR5 6BA
☎ 0870 9906462 📠 0870 9906463
(M65 junct 1, 0.5m from junct 29 of M6 close to rdbt of A582 and A6)

LEICESTERSHIRE
LEICESTER
Premier Lodge (Leicester West)   43 rooms
Leicester Road, Glenfield LE3 8HB
☎ 0870 9906520 🖹 0870 9906521
(exit M1 junction 21a onto A46 then onto the A50 for Glenfield and the County Hall. Turn off into County Hall, and hotel is on the left.)

Premier Lodge (Leicester South)   30 rooms
Glen Rise, Oadby LE2 4RG
☎ 0870 9906452 🖹 0870 9906453
(from M1 junct 21take A563 sign South. At Leicester racecourse rdbt turn right. Follow signs for Market Harborough and continue on dual carriageway and over the rdbt. As it becomes single lane the hotel is on right)

Premier Lodge (Leicester Central)   72 rooms
Heathley Park, Groby Road LE3 9QE
☎ 0870 9906398 🖹 0870 9906399

LONDON
N1
Premier Lodge (London King's Cross) 278 rooms
York Way, Kings Cross N1 9DZ
☎ 0870 9906414 🖹 0870 9906415
(Exit the M25 at junction 16 onto the M40 which becomes the A40. Follow the signs for the City and exit at Euston Rd, following the one-way system to York Way)

SE1
Premier Lodge (London Southwark) 56 rooms
Anchor Bankside, 34 Park Street SE1 9EF
☎ 0870 9906402 🖹 0870 9906403

MERSEYSIDE
BIRKENHEAD
Premier Lodge (Wirral)   30 rooms
Greasby Road CH49 2PP
☎ 0870 9906588 🖹 0870 9906589
(2m from M53 junct 2, just off B5139)

LIVERPOOL
Premier Lodge (Liverpool Albert Dock) 130 rooms
East Britannia Building, Albert Dock L3 4AD
☎ 0870 9906432 🖹 0870 9906433
(located just off the A5036. Once in city centre, follow the brown tourist signs for the Albert Dock. When inside the dock, the hotel is situated directly beside The Beatles Story)

Premier Lodge (Liverpool City Centre) 39 rooms
45 Victoria Street L1 6JB
☎ 0870 9906584 🖹 0870 9906585

Premier Lodge (Liverpool South East) 53 rooms
Roby Road, Huyton L36 4HD
☎ 0870 9906596 🖹 0870 9906597

Premier Lodge (Liverpool East)   34 rooms
804 Warrington Road, Rainhill L35 6PE
☎ 0870 9906446 🖹 0870 9906447
(off M62 junct 7, onto the A57 towards Rainhill)

ST HELENS
Premier Lodge (St Helens)   43 rooms
Garswood Old Road, East Lancs Road WA11 7LX
☎ 0870 9906374 🖹 0870 9906375
(3m from M6 junct 23, on A580 towards Liverpool)

NORTHAMPTONSHIRE
NORTHAMPTON
Premier Lodge (Northampton East) 60 rooms
Crow Lane, Great Billing NN3 9DA
☎ 0870 9906510 🖹 0870 9906511
(5m from the M1 junct 15. Take the A508 to A45 then follow signs for Billing Aquadrome)

Premier Lodge (Northampton South) 39 rooms
Newport Pagnell Road, West Wootton NN4 7JJ
☎ 0870 9906426 🖹 0870 9906427
(M1 junct 15 towards Northampton at A508/A45 junct. 5th exit off rdbt and lodge on right)

SILVERSTONE
Premier Lodge (Silverstone)   41 rooms
Brackley Hatch, Syresham NN13 5TX
☎ 0870 9906382 🖹 0870 9906383
(on A43 next to Green Man Chef & Brewer)

WEEDON
Premier Lodge (Daventry)   46 rooms
High Street NN7 4PX
☎ 0870 9906364 🖹 0870 9906365
(M1 junct 16; A45 towards Daventry. Through Upper Heyford and Flore Lodge on left)

NOTTINGHAMSHIRE
HUCKNALL
Premier Lodge (Nottingham North West) 35 rooms
Nottingham Road NG15 7PY
☎ 0870 9906518 🖹 0870 9906519
(From south, exit the M1 junct 26 onto A610 for approx 0.5m then follow signs for A611 North)

NOTTINGHAM
Premier Lodge (Nottingham City Centre) 87 rooms
Island Site, London Road NG2 4UU
☎ 0870 9906574 🖹 0870 9906575
(just off A6001, next to BBC building)

Premier Lodge (Nottingham North) 64 rooms
101 Mansfield Road, Daybrook NG5 6BH
☎ 0870 9906328 🖹 0870 9906329
(M1 junct 27 onto A60. M1 junct 26 onto A610 & A6514 towards A60. Turn off A60 for Mansfield)

Premier Lodge (Nottingham South) 42 rooms
Loughborough Road, Ruddington NG11 6LS
☎ 0870 9906422   📠 0870 9906423
*(exit M1 junct 24 and follow the signs for A453
Nottingham, then A52 Grantham. The hotel is situated at
1st rdbt on left)*

OXFORDSHIRE
BANBURY
Premier Lodge (Banbury)   39 rooms
Warwick Road, Warmington OX17 1JJ
☎ 0870 9906512   📠 0870 9906513
*(5 miles from Banbury. From north M40 junct 12 onto
B4100 towards Warmington. From south M40 junct 11
onto A423. Continue onto A442 and turn right onto
B4100.)*

SOMERSET
TAUNTON
Premier Lodge (Taunton)   38 rooms
Ilminster Road, Ruishton TA3 5LU
☎ 0870 9906534   📠 0870 9906535

WINSCOMBE
Premier Lodge (Bristol Airport)   31 rooms
Bridgwater Road BS25 1NN
☎ 0870 9906302   📠 0870 9906303
*(between M5 junct 21 and 22, 9 m from Bristol Airport.
Exit onto A371 to Banwell, Winscombe until you reach the
A38. At the lights turn right for Lodge 300yds on left)*

STAFFORDSHIRE
LICHFIELD
Premier Lodge (Lichfield)
30 Rykneld Street Fradley WS13 8RD
☎ 0870 9906438   📠 0870 9906439

STAFFORD
Premier Lodge (Stafford)   96 rooms
Hurricane Close ST16 1GZ
☎ 0870 9906478   📠 0870 9906479
(M6 junct 14. 2.5m NW of Stafford)

SURREY
COBHAM
Premier Lodge (Cobham)   48 rooms
Portsmouth Road Fairmile KT11 1BW
☎ 0870 9906358   📠 0870 9906359
*(M25 junct 10, follow the A3 towards London. Exit A3 to
join A245 towards Cobham and in town centre left onto
A307 Portsmouth Rd for Lodge on left)*

EPSOM
Premier Lodge (Epsom North)   29 rooms
272 Kingston Road, Ewell KT19 0SH
☎ 0870 9906466   📠 0870 9906467
*(exit M25 junct 8 and follow the A217 towards Sutton. At
junct with A240 follow the A240 towards Ewell. At the
Beggars Hill rdbt take the 2nd exit onto Kingston Rd)*

TADWORTH
Premier Lodge (Epsom South)   78 rooms
Brighton Road, Burgh Heath KT20 6BW
☎ 0870 9906442   📠 0870 9906443
(just off junct 8 of M25, on the A217 towards Sutton)

SUSSEX, EAST
BRIGHTON
Premier Lodge (Brighton City Centre) 160 rooms
144 North Street BN1 1RE
☎ 0870 9906340   📠 0870 9906341
*(from A23 follow city centre signs. At lights near Royal
Pavilion, turn right, take road ahead on left which runs
adjacent to Pavilion onto Church St, then 1st left onto New
Rd leading to North St)*

SUSSEX, WEST
BOGNOR REGIS
Premier Lodge (Bognor Regis)   24 rooms
Shripney Road PO22 9PA
☎ 0870 9906434   📠 0870 9906435
*(from the A27 take the Bognor Regis exit at the rdbt with the
junct of A29. A29 for approx 4m. Lodge on left)*

CHICHESTER
Premier Lodge (Chichester)   83 rooms
Chichester Gate Leisure Park,
Terminus Road PO19 8EL
☎ 0870 9906578   📠 0870 9906579

CRAWLEY
Premier Lodge (Gatwick South)   83 rooms
Crawley Avenue, Gossops Green RH10 8BA
☎ 0870 9906546   📠 0870 9906547
*(2m from M23 and just under 5m from Gatwick Airport.
Exit the M23 at junct 11 and follow the A23 towards
Crawley and Gatwick Airport)*

Premier Lodge (Gatwick Crawley)   57 rooms
Goffs Park Road RH11 8AX
☎ 0870 9906390   📠 0870 9906391
*(close to Gatwick Airport. Exit M23 at junct 11, follow the
A23 towards Crawley. At the 2nd rbt take 3rd exit for the
town centre, then 2nd right into Goffs Park Rd)*

GATWICK AIRPORT
Premier Lodge (Gatwick Airport)   102 rooms
London Road, Lowfield Heath RH10 9ST
☎ 0870 9906354   📠 0870 9906355
*(Near airport on A23, 2m from M23 junct 9a. Follow road
towards North Terminal rdbt then signs for A23 Crawley)*

TYNE & WEAR
GATESHEAD
Premier Lodge (Newcastle South)   40 rooms
Lobley Hill Road NE11 9NA
☎ 0870 9906590   📠 0870 9906591
*(off A1 on A692, 2m from Angel of the North and 3m from
the Metro Centre)*

NEWCASTLE UPON TYNE

Premier Lodge (Newcastle City Centre) 150 rooms
The Quayside NE1 3DW
☎ 0870 9906530 📠 0870 990653
(from north A1, A167, A186 Walker and Wallsend onto B1600 Quayside. From south A1, A184, A189 to the city centre. First exit onto the B1600 Quayside for the hotel next to Tyne Bridge)

NEWCASTLE UPON TYNE AIRPORT

Premier Lodge (Newcastle Airport) 52 rooms
Callerton Lane Ends, Woolsington NE13 8DF
☎ 0870 9906338 📠 0870 9906339
(A1 onto A696 Jedburgh Rd to Newcastle airport. 2nd slip road signed Throckley and Woolsington. Right at top of road, over 2 rdbts and level crossing. Hotel on left)

SUNDERLAND

Premier Lodge (Sunderland)   63 rooms
Timber Beach Road, Off Wessington Way,
Castletown SR5 3XG
☎ 0870 9906514 📠 0870 9906515
(A1 junct 64 onto A1231 towards Sunderland, lodge on last rdbt on right)

WEST MIDLANDS
BIRMINGHAM

Premier Lodge (Birmingham South) 62 rooms
Birmingham Great Park, Ashbrook Drive, Parkway,
Rubery B45 9PA
☎ 0870 9906538 📠 0870 9906539
(M5 junct 4 onto A38 towards Birmingham. Turn left into Birmingham Great Park, for Lodge behind superstore)

Premier Lodge (Birmingham City Centre) 60 rooms
80 Broad Street B15 1AU
☎ 0870 9906404 📠 0870 9906405
(M6 junct 6 onto A38 Aston Expressway and follow signs for the city centre, ICC and NIA then onto Broad St. Right at lights 2nd left at the rdbt for Lodge on left)

Premier Lodge (Birmingham NEC/Airport) 199 rooms
Bickenhill Parkway Northway N.E.C.   B40 3QE
☎ 0870 9906326 📠 0870 9906327
(M6 junct 4 follow A446 signed Warwick, exiting left after 0.5m signed NEC. At the rdbt take 2nd exit. At next rbt take 2nd exit onto Bickenhill Parkway and follow signs for Airport then at the next rdbt take 1st exit into Lodge)

COVENTRY

Premier Lodge (Coventry)   28 rooms
Combe Fields Road, Ansty CV7 9JP
☎ 0870 9906472 📠 0870 9906473
(10 mins from Coventry on the B4029. Exit M6 junct 2 onto the B4065 towards Ansty. After village turn right onto B4029 signed Brinklow and right into Coombe Fields Rd for Lodge on right)

SUTTON COLDFIELD

Premier Lodge (Birmingham North) 42 rooms
Whitehouse Common Road B75 6HD
☎ 0870 9906320 📠 0870 9906321
(M42 junct 9, follow A446 towards Lichfield, then A453 to Sutton Coldfield, and turn left into Whitehouse Common Rd for the Lodge on left)

WILTSHIRE
SWINDON

Premier Lodge (Swindon)   60 rooms
Ermin Street, Blunsdon SN26 8DJ
☎ 0870 9906356 📠 0870 9906357
(N of Swindon, 5m M4 junct 15 on M4 at junct of A419 & B4019)

WORCESTERSHIRE
BROMSGROVE

Premier Lodge (Bromsgrove)   27 rooms
Worcester Road, Upton Warren B61 7ET
☎ 0870 9906408 📠 0870 9906409
(1.5m from M5 junct 5 towards Bromsgrove on A38. From M42 junct 1 follow A38 south, cross over A448)

REDDITCH

Premier Lodge (Redditch)   33 rooms
Birchfield Road B97 6PX
☎ 0870 9906392 📠 0870 9906393
(A448 to Redditch & take 1st exit to Webheath, at rdbt take 3rd exit & 1st right)

YORKSHIRE, NORTH
GUISBOROUGH

Premier Lodge (Middlesbrough South) 20 rooms
Middlesbrough Road, Upsall TS14 6RW
☎ 0870 9906540 📠 0870 9906541

YORK

Premier Lodge (York City Centre)   86 rooms
20 Blossom Street YO24 1AJ
☎ 0870 9906594 📠 0870 9906595
(Just off A59)

YORKSHIRE, SOUTH
SHEFFIELD

Premier Lodge (Sheffield)   103 rooms
Sheffield Road, Meadowhall S9 2YL
☎0870 9906440 📠 0870 9906441
(1.5m from M1 junct 34 on A6178)

YORKSHIRE, WEST
BRIGHOUSE

Premier Lodge (Huddersfield North) 71 rooms
Wakefield Road HD6 4HA
☎ 0870 9906360 📠 0870 9906361
(exit M62 junct 25, at rdbt signed A644 Huddersfield/ Dewsbury/Wakefield. Lodge 500mtrs up hill on right)

Premier Lodge

CASTLEFORD
Premier Lodge (Castleford)   62 rooms
Pioneer Way WF10 5TG
☎ 0870 9906592 📠 0870 9906593
(M62 junct 31 onto A655 to Castleford. At traffic lights right onto Commerce Park. Lodge 2nd on left)

DARRINGTON
Premier Lodge (Pontefract)   28 rooms
Great North Road WF8 3BL
☎ 0870 9906386 📠 0870 9906387
(just off A1, 2m south of the A1/M62 interchange)

HALIFAX
Premier Lodge (Halifax)   31 rooms
Salterhebble Hill, Huddersfield Road HX3 0QT
☎ 0870 9906308 📠 0870 9906309
(off M62 junct 24, on the A629 towards Halifax)

HUDDERSFIELD
Lodge (Huddersfield)   40 rooms
New Hey Road, Ainley Top HD2 2EA
☎ 0870 9906488 📠 0870 9906489
(off M62 junct 24. After exiting, take the Brighouse exit from the rdbt (A643), take your 1st left into Grimescar Rd, turn right into New Hey Rd)

LEEDS
Premier Lodge (Leeds City West)   126 rooms
City West One Office Park, Gelderd Road LS12 6LX
☎ 0870 9906448 📠 0870 9906449
(exit M621 junct 1 and take ring road towards Leeds. At the 1st set of lights turn right onto Gelderd Rd then right at rdbt)

SCOTLAND
ABERDEEN CITY
ABERDEEN
Premier Lodge (Aberdeen West)   60 rooms
North Anderson Drive AB15 6DW
☎ 0870 9906430 📠 0870 9906431
(3m from the city centre and 5 m from Aberdeen airport. On approaching the city from the south, follow signs for the airport. The Premier Lodge is on North Anderson Dr, 1st left after fire station)

Premier Lodge (Aberdeen City Centre) 162 rooms
Inverlair House, West North Street AB24 5AR
☎ 0870 9906300 📠 0870 9906301
(From A90, follow A9013 into Aberdeen city centre. Turn onto A966 towards King St and take the 1st left)

Premier Lodge (Aberdeen South West) 61 rooms
Straik Road, Westhill AB32 6HF
☎ 0870 9906348 📠 0870 9906349
(Situated 6 miles from the city centre along the A944)

CITY OF EDINBURGH
EDINBURGH
Premier Lodge (Edinburgh City Centre) 112 rooms
Lauriston Place, Lady Lawson Street EH3 9HZ
☎ 0870 9906610 📠 0870 9906611
(from A8, right onto the A702 Lothian Rd and continue along until you reach Tollcross. Turn left into Lauriston Pl and Lodge is situated at the junction with Lauriston St, on left)

Premier Lodge (Edinburgh East)   42 rooms
91 Newcraighall Road, Newcraighall EH21 8RX
☎ 0870 9906336 📠 0870 9906337
(close to the city centre on the junction of the A1 and A6095 towards Musselburgh)

CITY OF GLASGOW
GLASGOW
Premier Lodge (Glasgow North East) 38 rooms
Cumbernauld Rd, Muirhead G69 9BS
☎ 0870 9906508 📠 0870 9906509
(off M8 junct 13, follow the M80 and A80 to the Stepps bypass. Turn left onto A80. The Lodge is 400 yards from the bypass on the left hand side)

Premier Lodge (Glasgow City Centre) 278 rooms
10 Elmbank Gardens G2 4PP
☎ 0870 9906312 📠 0870 9906313
e: glasgow@premierlodge.co.uk

DUNDEE CITY
BROUGHTY FERRY
Premier Lodge (Dundee East) 60 rooms
115-117 Lawers Drive, Panmurefield Village DD5 3UP
☎ 0870 9906324 📠 0870 9906325
(from north follow A92 Dundee to Arbroath. The Lodge is 1.5m past the group of 32 traffic lights, on right. From south, follow signs for A90 Perth to Dundee. At end of the dual carriageway follow signs for Dundee to Arbroath)

DUNDEE
Premier Lodge (Dundee North)   78 rooms
Dayton Drive, Camperdown Leisure Park, Kingsway DD2 3SQ
☎ 0870 9906420 📠 0870 9906421
(off A90 into Coupar Angus Rd, hotel visible from dual-carriageway, exit by slip road for Camperdown Leisure Park)

EAST DUNBARTONSHIRE
BEARSDEN
Premier Lodge (Glasgow North)   61 rooms
Milngavie Road G61 3TA
☎ 0870 9906532 📠 0870 9906533
(6m from the city centre. From east, exit the M8 at junct 16. From the west, exit at junct 17. Follow A81 signposted to Milngavie for Lodge on left)

FALKIRK

Premier Lodge (Falkirk)   60 rooms
Glenbervie Business Park, Bellsdyke Road,
Larbert FK5 4EG
☎ 0870 9906550 📠 0870 9906551
*(just off the A88, less than 1m from M876 junct 2 and 4m
from Falkirk town centre)*

SOUTH LANARKSHIRE

EAST KILBRIDE

Premier Lodge (East Kilbride)   40 rooms
Eaglesham Road G75 8LW
☎ 0870 9906542 📠 0870 9906543
(8m from M74 junct 5, on A726 at rdbt of B764)

WALES

CAERPHILLY
CAERPHILLY

Premier Lodge (Caerphilly)   40 rooms
Corbetts Lane CF83 3HX
☎ 0870 9906368 📠 0870 9906369
*(4m from M4 junct 32. Follow A470 and take the 2nd left
signposted Caerphilly. At rbt take the 4th exit and at next
rdbt take the 2nd exit. Over next rdbt and at Pwllypant
rdbt Lodge on left)*

Sleep Inn
0800 444 444

A new brand in the UK, Sleep Inn offers high
quality, air-conditioned accommodation with
power showers.

ENGLAND

CAMBRIDGESHIRE

BOXWORTH

Sleep Inn Cambridge
82 Cambridge Services, A14, CB3 8WU
☎ 01954 268400 📠 01954 268419
enquiries@hotels-cambridge.com
(A14 junct 28 6m N of Cambridge. 8m S of Huntington)

PETERBOROUGH

Sleep Inn Peterborough   82 rooms
Peterborough Services, Great North Road, Haddon
PE7 3UQ
☎ 01733 396850 📠 01733 396869
enquiries@hotels-peterborough.co.uk
*(At Junct 17 of A1(M) take the A605 towards Northampton.
Hotel is located 100mtrs on left)*

HERTFORDSHIRE

BALDOCK

Sleep Inn Baldock   62 rooms
Baldock Services (A1(M)/A507), Radwell SG7 5TR
☎ 01462 832900 📠 01462 832901
e: enquiries@hotels-baldock.com
(400yds E of A1(M) junct 10 & A507)

Travel Inn
0870 242 8000

Good quality, modern, budget accommodation in
over 300 locations throughout the UK. Every
Travel Inn has an adjacent licensed family
restaurant, often a Beefeater, Brewer's Fayre or TGI
Fridays.

ENGLAND

BEDFORDSHIRE

BEDFORD

Travel Inn   32 rooms
Priory Country Park, Barkers Lane MK41 9DJ
☎ 08701 977030 📠 01234 325697
*(M1 junct 13/A421/A6 towards Bedford then A428 signed
Cambridge. Cross River Ouse & right at next rdbt, follow
signs for Priory Country Park)*

DUNSTABLE

Travel Inn Dunstable/Luton   42 rooms
350 Luton Road LU5 4LL
☎ 08701 977083 📠 01582 664114
*(on A505. From M1 junct 11 follow signs to Dunstable. At
first rdbt turn right. The Travel Inn on left)*

Travel Inn Dunstable South   40 rooms
Watling Street, Kensworth LU6 3QP
☎ 08701 977082 📠 01582 842811
(M1 junct 9 towards Dunstable on A5, Inn on right)

LUTON

Travel Inn Luton Airport   129 rooms
Osbourne Road LU1 3HJ
☎ 08701 977166 📠 01582 421900
*(M1 junct 10 follow signs for Luton on A1081, at 3rd rdbt
turn left onto Gypsy Lane, turn left at next rdbt)*

BERKSHIRE

BRACKNELL

Travel Inn   60 rooms
Arlington Square, Wokingham Road RG42 1NA
☎ 08701 977036 📠 01344 319526
*(M4 (J10) A329(M) Bracknell to lights. 1st left, 3rd exit
rdbt by supermarket to town centre. Left at rdbt, left at next
rdbt. Travel Inn on left.)*

Travel Inn

BRISTOL

BRISTOL

Travel Inn Bristol South   40 rooms
Hengrove Leisure Park, Hengrove Way BS14 0HR
☎ 08701 977043 🖻 01275 834721
(From city centre take A37 to Wells & Shepton Mallet. Right onto A4174. Inn at 3rd traffic lights)

Travel Inn City Centre   224 rooms
Haymarket BS1 3LR
☎ 0870 238 3307 🖻 0117 9100619
(M4 junct 19/M32 towards city centre. Through 2 sets of lights, at 3rd set, turn right. To rdbt, take 2nd exit. Travel Inn on left.)

Travel Inn Bristol City East   40 rooms
200/202 Westerleigh Road,
Emersons Green BS16 7AN
☎ 08701 977042 🖻 0117 956 4644
(From M4 (J19) onto M32 (J1), turn left onto A4174 (Avon Ring Rd). Inn on 3rd rdbt)

BUCKINGHAMSHIRE

AYLESBURY

Travel Inn   64 rooms
Buckingham Road HP19 9QL
☎ 08701 977019 🖻 01206 330432
(N from Aylesbury centre on A413, Travel Inn 1m on left, adjacent to rdbt)

HIGH WYCOMBE

Travel Inn   81 rooms
Thanestead Farm, London Road, Loudwater HP10 9YL
☎ 08701 977135 🖻 01494 446855
(On A40 near M40(J3), 3 miles from High Wycombe. If approaching from M40 (West), take J2. Follow signs to High Wycombe via Beaconsfield)

MILTON KEYNES

Travel Inn Milton Keynes (Central) 38 rooms
Secklow Gate West MK9 3BZ
☎ 08701 977184 🖻 01908 607481
(from M1 junct 14 follow H6 route over 6 rdbts, at 7th (called Sth Secklow) turn right, Travel Inn on left)

Travel Inn Milton Keynes East   41 rooms
Willen Lake, Brickhill Street MK15 9HQ
☎ 08701 977185 🖻 01908 678561
(M1 junct 14 follow H6 Childsway. Turn right at 3rd rdbt into Brickhill St. Right at 1st mini rdbt, Travel Inn 1st left)

CAMBRIDGESHIRE

HUNTINGDON

Travel Inn   80 rooms
Brampton Hut PE28 4NQ
☎ 08701 977139 🖻 01480 811298
(junct of A1/A14. From north take next main exit for Huntingdon & Brampton not junct 14. Access via services)

PETERBOROUGH

Travel Inn Peterborough (Hampton) 80 rooms
4 Ashbourne Road, Off London Road, Hampton
PE7 8BT
☎ 08701 977206 🖻 01733 391055
(South: A1(M) J16, follow A15 through Yaxley. Travel Inn on the left at 1st rdbt.

Travel Inn Peterborough (Ferry Meadows) 40 rooms
Ham Lane, Orton Meadows, Nene Park PE2 5UU
☎ 08701 977205 🖻 01733 391055
(From south A1(M) (J16), then A15 through Yaxley. Left at rdbt.)

ST NEOTS

Travel Inn   41 rooms
Colmworth Business Park PE19 8YH
☎ 08701 977238 🖻 01480 408541
(from A1 at southern St Neots junct. Travel Inn at 1st rdbt (A428/B1428))

CHESHIRE

CHESTER

Travel Inn Chester (Central)   70 rooms
Caldy Valley Road CH3 5QJ
☎ 08701 977058 🖻 01244 403687
(Exit M53 (J12) and at rdbt 3rd exit onto A56 (signed Chester). At rdbt take 1st exit onto A41 (signed Whitchurch) then at 2nd rdbt take 3rd exit onto Caldy Valley Rd (signed Huntingdon) for The Travel Inn on right.)

CHESTER EAST SERVICE AREA (M56)

Travel Inn Chester (East)   40 rooms
Junction 14 M56 Chester East Service Area, Elton CH2 4QZ
☎ 08701 977059 🖻 01928 726721
(M56 junct 14/A5117 interchange)

CHILDER THORNTON

Travel Inn Wirral South   31 rooms
New Chester Road CH66 1QW
☎ 08701 977275 🖻 0151 347 1401
(Situated on the A41, near M53 (J5), heading towards Chester. Travel Inn is on the right, same entrance as Burleydam Garden Centre)

CREWE

Travel Inn   41 rooms
Coppenhall Lane, Woolstanwood CW2 8SD
☎ 08701 977068 🖻 01270 256316
(at junct of A530 & A532, 9m from M6 junct 16 N'bound)

MACCLESFIELD

Travel Inn   40 rooms
Tytherington Business Park, Springwood Way, Tytherington SK10 2XA
☎ 08701 977167 🖻 01625 422874
(on A523 Tytherington Business Park)

RUNCORN

Travel Inn   40 rooms
Chester Road, Preston Brook WA7 3BB
☎ 08701 977224 🖹 01928 719852
(1m from M56 junct 11, at Preston Brook)

WARRINGTON

Travel Inn Warrington North   40 rooms
Woburn Road WA2 8RN
☎ 08701 977260 🖹 01925 414544
(M62 junct 9 towards Warrington, 100yds from junct)

Travel Inn Warrington East   42 rooms
1430 Centre Park, Boulevard Park WA1 1QR
☎ 08701 977259 🖹 01925 244259
(at Bridgefoot junct of A49/A50/A56 in centre of Warrington)

CO DURHAM

DARLINGTON

Travel Inn   58 rooms
Morton Park Way, Morton Park DL1 4PJ
☎ 08701 977300 🖹 01325 373341

DURHAM

Travel Inn Durham (East)   40 rooms
Broomside Park, Belmont Industrial Estate DH1 1GG
☎ 08701 977084 🖹 0191 370 6501
(from A1(M) junct 62 take A690 west towards Durham. 1st exit, after 1m turn left. Travel Inn on left)

Travel Inn Durham South   38 rooms
Motorway Service Area, Tursdale Road, Bowburn DH6 5NP
☎ 08701 977087 🖹 0191 377 8722
(A1(M) junct 61& A177 Bowburn junction)

Travel Inn Durham (North)   60 rooms
Adj Arnison Retail Centre, Pity Me DH1 5GB
☎ 08701 977086 🖹 0191 383 1166
(A1(J63), then A167 to Durham. Over 5 rdbts and turn left at 6th rdbt. Travel Inn is on the right after 200 yds)

HARTLEPOOL

Travel Inn   40 rooms
Maritme Avenue, Hartlepool Marina TS24 0XZ
☎ 08701 977127 🖹 01429 233105
(approx 1m from A689/A179 link road on marina)

NEWTON AYCLIFFE

Travel Inn Durham (Newton Aycliffe) 44 rooms
Great North Road DL5 6JG
☎ 08701 977085 🖹 01325 324910
(Situated on the A167 east of Newton Aycliffe, 3 miles from the A1(M))

STOCKTON-ON-TEES

Travel Inn   62 rooms
Yarm Road TS18 3RT
☎ 08701 977243 🖹 01642 633339
(at junct A66/A135)

Travel Inn Stockton-on-Tees/Middlesbrough 40 rooms
Whitewater Way, Thornaby TS17 6QB
☎ 08701 977244 🖹 01642 671464
(A19 take A66 to Stockton/Darlington. Take 1st exit, Teeside Park/Teesdale. Right at lights over viaduct bridge rdbt & Tees Barrage)

CORNWALL

FRADDON

Travel Inn Newquay (Fraddon)   40 rooms
Penhale TR9 6NA
☎ 08701 977194 🖹 01726 860641
(on A30 2m S of Indian Queens)

HAYLE

Travel Inn   40 rooms
Carwin Rise TR27 4PN
☎ 08701 977133 🖹 01736 759514
(on A30 at Loggans Moor rdbt, take 1st exit on left, Carwin Rise, Travel Inn on right)

TRURO

Travel Inn   40 rooms
Old Carnon Hill, Carnon Downs TR3 6JT
☎ 08701 977255 🖹 01872 865620
(Situated on the A39 (Truro to Falmouth road), 3 miles south west of Truro)

CUMBRIA

CARLISLE

Travel Inn Carlisle (South)   40 rooms
Carleton CA4 0AD
☎ 08701 977054 🖹 01228 633313
(just off J42 on M6 south of Carlisle)

Travel Inn Carlisle (Central)   44 rooms
Warwick Road CA1 2WF
☎ 08701 977053 🖹 01228 534096
(M6 junct 43, on A69)

KILLINGTON LAKE MOTORWAY SERVICE AREA

Travel Inn   36 rooms
Killington Lake Motorway Service Area, Killington LA8 0NW
☎ 08701 977145 🖹 01539 621660
(From M6 Southbound, Travel Inn is 1 mile south of J37. From M6 northbound, exit J37 and rejoin southbound. Take the access road to the Travel Inn)

Travel Inn

WHITEHAVEN
Travel Inn 38 rooms
Howgate CA28 6PL
☎ 08701 977268 📠 01946 590106
(On outskirts of Whitehaven on A595 towards Workington)

DERBYSHIRE
CHESTERFIELD
Travel Inn 60 rooms
Tapton Lock Hill, Off Rotherway S41 7NJ
☎ 08701 977060 📠 01246 560707
(adjacent to Tesco, A61 and A619 rdbt, 1m N of city centre)

DERBY
Travel Inn Derby East 82 rooms
The Wyvern Business Park, Chaddesden
Sidings DE21 6BF
☎ 0870 238 3313 📠 01332 667827
(From M1 junct 25 follow A52 to Derby. After 6.5m take
exit for Wyvern/Pride Park. 1st exit at rdbt (A52
Nottingham), straight over next rdbt. Travel Inn on left)

Travel Inn Derby West 43 rooms
Uttoxeter New Road, Manor Park Way DE22 3HN
☎ 08701 977072 📠 01332 207506
(M1 (J25) take A38W towards Burton Upon Trent for
approx. 15 miles. Left at island (city hospital), right at lights,
3rd exit at city hospital island)

SOUTH NORMANTON
Travel Inn Mansfield 80 rooms
Carter Lane East DE55 2EH
☎ 08701 977180 📠 01773 861155
(just off M1 junct 28, on A38 signed Mansfield. Entrance
200yds on left)

TIBSHELF MOTORWAY SERVICE AREA
Travel Inn Mansfield (Tibshelf) 40 rooms
Tibshelf Motorway Service Area
DE55 5TZ
☎ 08701 977181 📠 01773 876609
(M1 northbound between junct 28/29, access available
southbound)

DEVON
BARNSTAPLE
Travel Inn 40 rooms
Eastern Avenue, Whiddon Drive EX32 8RY
☎ 08701 977025 📠 01271 377710
(adjacent to North Devon Link Rd at junct with A39)

EXETER
Travel Inn 44 rooms
398 Topsham Road EX2 6HE
☎ 08701 977097 📠 01392 876174
(2m from M5 junct 30/A30 junct 29. Follow signs for Exeter
& Dawlish (A379). On dual carriageway take 2nd slip road
on left at Countess Wear rdbt. Travel Inn next to Beefeater)

PLYMOUTH
Travel Inn 60 rooms
Lockyers Quay, Coxside PL4 0DX
☎ 08701 977207 📠 01752 663872
(A38 Marsh Mills rdbt then A374 into Plymouth. Follow
signs for Coxside & National Marine Aquarium)

Travel Inn Plymouth East 40 rooms
300 Plymouth Road, Crabtree Marsh Mills PL3 6RW
☎ 08701 977208 📠 01752 600112
(From E: Exit A38 Marsh Mill junction. Straight across
rbt, exit slip road 100mtrs on left. From W: Plympton junct
A38, at rdbt exit slip road next to A38 Liskeard)

DORSET
CHRISTCHURCH
Travel Inn (Christchurch East) 70 rooms
Somerford Road BH23 3QG
☎ 08701 977062 📠 01202 474939
(from M27 take A337 to Lyndhurst, then A35 to
Christchurch. On B3059 rdbt towards Somerford)

Travel Inn Christchurch West 42 rooms
Barrack Road BH23 2BN
☎ 08701 977063 📠 01202 483453
(from A338 take A3060 towards Christchurch. Turn left onto
A35 Travel Inn on right)

POOLE
Travel Inn 62 rooms
Holes Bay Road BH15 2BD
☎ 08701 977210 📠 01202 661497
(follow Poole Channel Ferry signs, hotel S of A35/A349 on
A350 dual carriageway)

WEYMOUTH
Travel Inn 40 rooms
Green Hill DT4 7SX
☎ 08701 977267 📠 01305 760589
(Follow signs to Weymouth, then brown signs to Lodmoor
Country Park)

ESSEX
BASILDON
Travel Inn Basildon (East Mayne) 32 rooms
Felmores, East Mayne SS13 1BW
☎ 08701 977026 📠 01268 530092
(M25 junct 29/A127 towards Southend, then A132 towards
Basildon)

Travel Inn Basildon South 60 rooms
High Road, Fobbing, Stanford le Hope SS17 9NR
☎ 08701 977027 📠 01268 581752
(From M25 (J30/31) take A13 towards Southend. Follow the
A13 for approx 10 miles then at the Five Bells rdbt turn right
onto Fobbing High Rd. Hotel on left)

BRAINTREE
Travel Inn   40 rooms
Cressing Road, Galley's Corner CM7 8GG
☎ 08701 977039 🖹 01376 555087
*(on A120 bypass at Braintree junction of Cressing Rd &
Galley's Corner)*

CHELMSFORD
Travel Inn   61 rooms
Chelmsford Service Area Colchester Road
Springfield CM2 5PY
☎ 0870 238 3310 🖹 01245 464010
*(on A12 (J19), Chelmsford by-pass, signed Chelmsford
Service Area. 2nd service area from A12 on M25)*

CLACTON-ON-SEA
Travel Inn   40 rooms
Crown Green Roundabout, Colchester Road,
Weeley CO16 9AA
☎ 08701 977064 🖹 01255 833106
*(take A120 off A12 towards Harwich. After 4m, A133 to
Clacton-on-Sea. Located on Weeley rdbt)*

COLCHESTER
Travel Inn   40 rooms
Ipswich Road CO4 9WP
☎ 08701 977065 🖹 01206 751327
*(take A120 (A1232) junct off A12, follow A1232 towards
Colchester, Travel Inn on right)*

GRAYS
Travel Inn Thurrock   62 rooms
Fleming Road, Unicorn Estate,
Chafford Hundred RM16 6YJ
☎ 08701 977253 🖹 01375 481876
*(from A13 follow signs for Lakeside Shopping Centre. Right
at 1st rdbt, over next rdbt then 1st slip rd. Left at rdbt)*

HARLOW
Travel Inn   61 rooms
Cambridge Road CM20 2EP
☎ 08701 977125 01279 452169
*(M11(J7) located off A414 on Sawbridgeworth to Bishop's
Stortford rd (A1184), by River Stort)*

PURFLEET
Travel Inn   30 rooms
High Street RM19 1QA
☎ 08701 977216 🖹 01708 860852
*(from Dartford Tunnel follow signs Dagenham (A13), at rdbt
take 1st exit to Purfleet (A1090))*

SOUTHEND-ON-SEA
Travel Inn   60 rooms
Thanet Grange SS2 6GB
☎ 08701 977235 🖹 01702 430838
(on A127 at intersection with B1013)

GLOUCESTERSHIRE
CHELTENHAM
Travel Inn Cheltenham (West)   40 rooms
Tewkesbury Road, Uckington GL51 9SL
☎ 08701 977055 🖹 01242 244887
*(opposite Sainsbury's & Homebase on A4019, 2m from J10
(southbound exit only) and 3m from J11 (both exits) of M5)*

Travel Inn Cheltenham Central   40 rooms
374 Gloucester Road GL51 7AY
☎ 08701 977056 🖹 01242 260042
*(M5 junct 11 onto A40 (Cheltenham). Follow dual carriage-
way to end, straight at 1st rdbt, turn right at 2nd)*

GLOUCESTER
Travel Inn Gloucester Longford   60 rooms
Tewkesbury Road, Longford GL2 9BE
☎ 08701 977115 🖹 01452 300924
*(Situated 10 minutes from M5 (J11), follow A40 to
Gloucester, A40 to Ross, then Travel Inn is on the A38 to
Gloucester on the Tewkesbury Rd)*

Travel Inn Gloucester Witcombe   39 rooms
Witcombe GL3 4SS
☎ 08701 977116   🖹 01452 864926
*(M5 junct 11A follow A417 (Cirencester) at 1st exit turn
right onto A46 towards Stroud/Witcombe. Left at next rdbt
by Crosshands PH)*

GREATER MANCHESTER
BOLTON
Travel Inn   40 rooms
991 Chorley New Road, Horwich BL6 4BA
☎ 08701 977282 🖹 01204 692585
*(M61 junct 6 follow dual carriageway to Bolton/Horwich
(Reebok Stadium on left,). continue & Inn on 2nd rdbt)*

CHADDERTON
Travel Inn Oldham (Chadderton)   40 rooms
The Broadway OL9 8DW
☎ 08701 977203 🖹 0161 682 7974
*(M60 ring road (anticlockwise) junct 21, signed Manchester
City Centre. A663, 400yds on left)*

CHEADLE
Travel Inn Manchester Cheadle   40 rooms
Royal Crescent SK8 3FE
☎ 08701 977172 🖹 0161 491 5886
(off Cheadle Royal rdbt off A34 behind TGI Friday's)

MANCHESTER
Travel Inn Manchester City South   226 rooms
Oxford Street M1 4WB
☎ 0870 238 3315 🖹 01823 322054
*(M6 junct 19 take 3rd exit onto A556. Join M56, exit junct
3 (A5103) to Medlock St, turn right into Whitworth St, then
left into Oxford St & right into Portland St.)*

Travel Inn Manchester Salford Quays 52 rooms
Basin 8 The Quays, Salford Quays M50 3SQ
☎ 08701 977176 📠 0161 876 0094
(From M602 (J3) take A5063 on Salford Quays, 1m from Manchester United's stadium.)

Travel Inn Manchester Denton   40 rooms
Alphington Drive, Manchester Road, South Denton
M34 3SH
☎ 08701 977173 📠 0161 337 9652
(M60 junct 24 onto A57 signed Denton. 1st right at lights, right at next lights, Travel Inn on left)

Travel Inn Manchester Trafford Centre 60 rooms
Wilderspool Wood, Trafford Centre,
Urmston M17 8WW
☎ 08701 977307 📠 0161 747 4763
(M60 junct 10 on W side of Manchester)

Travel Inn Manchester Heaton Park 45 rooms
Middleton Road, Crumpsall M8 6NB
☎ 08701 977174 📠 0161 740 9142
(off M60 junct 19, ring road east. Take A576 to Manchester through 2 sets of traffic lights. Travel Inn on left)

PRESTWICH

Travel Inn Manchester Prestwich   60 rooms
Bury New Road M25 3AJ
☎ 08701 977175 📠 0161 773 8099
(M60 junct 17, on A56)

ROCHDALE

Travel Inn   40 rooms
Newhey Road, Milnrow OL16 4JF
☎ 08701 977219 📠 01706 299074
(M62 junct 21 at rdbt, right towards Shaw, under motorway bridge & take 1st left)

SALE

Travel Inn Manchester South   40 rooms
Carrington Lane, Ashton-upon-Mersey M33 5BL
☎ 08701 977179 📠 0161 905 1742
(M60 junct 8 take A6144(M) towards Carrington. Left at 1st lights, Inn on left)

STOCKPORT

Travel Inn   40 rooms
Buxton Road SK2 6NB
☎ 08701 977242 📠 0161 477 8320
(on A6, 1.5m from town centre)

Travel Inn Manchester Airport   66 rooms
Finney Lane, Heald Green SK8 3QH
☎ 08701 977178 📠 0161 437 4910
(M56 junct 5 follow signs to Terminal 1, at rdbt take 2nd exit, at next rdbt follow signs for Cheadle. At traffic lights turn left, then right at next lights)

WIGAN

Travel Inn Wigan West   40 rooms
Orrell Road, Orrell WN5 8HQ
☎ 08701 977271 📠 01942 215002
(From M6 junct 26 follow signs for Upholland and Orrell. At first set of lights turn left. Travel Inn on right behind Priory Wood Beefeater)

Travel Inn Wigan South   40 rooms
Warrington Road, Marus Bridge WN3 6XB
☎ 08701 977270 📠 01942 498679
(M6 junct 25 (N'bound) slip road to rdbt turn left, to Inn)

HAMPSHIRE
ALDERSHOT

Travel Inn   60 rooms
7 Wellington Avenue GU11 1SQ
☎ 08701 977015 📠 01252 344073
(Exit M3 (J4), join A331 then A325 through Farnborough, past airfield, over rdbt. Travel Inn is ahead)

BASINGSTOKE

Travel Inn   71 rooms
Basingstoke Leisure Park, Worting Road RG22 6PG
☎ 08701 977028 📠 01256 819329
(M3 junct 6 follow signs for Leisure Park)

EASTLEIGH

Travel Inn   60 rooms
Leigh Road SO50 9YX
☎ 08701 977090 📠 023 8062 9048
(adjacent to M3 junct 13, near Eastleigh on A335)

FAREHAM

Travel Inn   41 rooms
Southampton Road, Park Gate SO31 6AF
☎ 08701 977100 📠 01489 577238
(on 2nd rdbt off M27 junct 9, signed A27 Fareham)

FARNBOROUGH

Travel Inn   62 rooms
Ively Road, Southwood GU14 0JP
☎ 08701 977101 📠 01252 546427
(From M3 (J4a), join A327 to Farnborough. Travel Inn on left hand side at 5th rbt (Monkey Puzzle rdbt))

HAVANT

Travel Inn Havant (Portsmouth)   36 rooms
65 Bedhampton Hill , Bedhampton PO9 3JN
☎ 08701 977130 📠 023 9245 3471
(on rdbt just off A3(M) to Bedhampton)

PORTSMOUTH

Travel Inn   64 rooms
Southampton Road, North Harbour, Cosham PO6 4SA
☎ 08701 977213 📠 023 9232 4895
(on A27, close to M27 junct 12)

Travel Inn Southsea   40 rooms
Long Curtain Road, Clarence Pier, Southsea PO5 3AA
☎ 08701 977236 📠 023 9273 3048
(Pier Rd leads to Clarence Pier. Travel Inn next to amusement park and Isle of Wight hovercraft)

ROWNHAMS MOTORWAY SERVICE AREA
Travel Inn Southampton West   39 rooms
Rownhams Service Area SO16 8AP
☎ 08701 977234 📠 023 8074 0204
(M27 Westbound - between junctions 3 & 4. No access from eastbound services)

SOUTHAMPTON
Travel Inn Southampton (City Centre) 172 rooms
New Road SO14 0AB
☎ 0870 238 3308 📠 023 8033 8395
(M27 junct 5/A335 towards city centre, at the Charlotte Place rdbt take 2nd left into East Park Terrace, then 1st left onto New Rd. Travel Inn on right)

Travel Inn Southampton North   32 rooms
Romsey Road, Nursling SO16 0XJ
☎ 08701 977233 📠 023 8074 0947
(M27 junct 3 take M271 towards Romsey. At next rdbt take 3rd exit towards Southampton (A3057) Travel Inn 1.5m on right)

WINCHESTER MOTORWAY SERVICE AREA
Travel Inn   40 rooms
SO21 1PP
☎ 08701 977272 📠 01962 791137
(M3 S'bound - between juncts 8 & 9. Note that distance to Travel Inn from Winchester is approx 26m due to location on motorway)

HEREFORDSHIRE
HEREFORD
Travel Inn   60 rooms
Holmer Road, Holmer HR4 9RS
☎ 08701 977134 📠 01432 343003
(from N M5 junct 7, follow A4103 to Worcester. M50 junct 4 take A49 Leominster road. Travel Inn 800yds on left)

ROSS-ON-WYE
Travel Inn   43 rooms
Ledbury Road HR9 7QL
☎ 08701 977221 📠 01989 566124
(1m from town centre on M50 rdbt)

STEVENAGE
Travel Inn   39 rooms
Corey's Mill Lane SG1 4AA
☎ 08701 977240 📠 01438 721609
(A1(M) junct 8, at intersection of A602 Hitchin Rd & Corey's Mill Lane)

TRING
Travel Inn   30 rooms
Tring Hill HP23 4LD
☎ 08701 977254 📠 01442 890787
(M25 junct 20 take A41 towards Aylesbury, at end of Hemel Hempstead/Tring bypass go straight over rdbt, Travel Inn on the right in approx 100yds)

WELWYN GARDEN CITY
Travel Inn   60 rooms
Gosling Park AL8 6DQ
☎ 08701 977263 📠 01707 393789
(on A6129 off junct 4 A1(M))

HERTFORDSHIRE
HATFIELD
Travel Inn   40 rooms
Comet Way, Lemsford Road AL10 0DA
☎ 08701 977129 📠 01707 256054
(From A1(M) junct 4, follow A1001 towards Hatfield. At next rbt take 2nd exit & 1st road on right)

HEMEL HEMPSTEAD
Travel Inn   61 rooms
Stoney Lane, Bourne End Services HP1 2SB
☎ 0870 238 3309 📠 01442 879149
(from M25 junct 20 (A41) exit at services. From M1 junct 8, follow A414, then A41, exit at services)

RADLETT
Travel Inn St Albans/Bricketwood   56 rooms
Smug Oak Lane AL2 3PN
☎ 08701 977040 📠 01727 873289
(From M10 take A5183 towards Radlett. After bridge over M25 turn right. From M25 or M1, follow signs to Bricketwood, turn into Smug Oak Lane at The Gate pub)

WATFORD
Travel Inn   45 rooms
859 St Albans Road, Garston WD25 0LH
☎ 08701 977261 📠 01923 682164
(On A412 St Albans Rd, 200yds past the North Orbital (A405), 0.5m S of M1 junct 6)

ISLE OF WIGHT
NEWPORT
Travel Inn Isle of Wight (Newport) 42 rooms
Seaclose, Fairlee Road PO30 2DN
☎ 08701 977144 📠 0870 241 9000
(From Newport town centre take A3054 signposted Ryde. After 0.75m at Seaclose lights, turn left. Travel Inn adjacent to council offices)

Travel Inn

KENT

ASHFORD

Travel Inn (Ashford Central)   60 rooms
Hall Avenue, Orbital Park, Sevington TN24 0GN
☎ 08701 977305 🖷 01233 500742
*(M20 junct 10. Southbound take 4th exit at rdbt.
Northbound take 1st exit/ A2070 for Brenzett. Inn at next
rdbt on right)*

Travel Inn Ashford (North)   60 rooms
Maidstone Road, Hothfield Common TN26 1AP
☎ 08701 977018 🖷 01233 713945
*(on A20, between Ashford & Charing, close to M20 junct
8/9)*

DOVER

Travel Inn Dover (West)   64 rooms
Folkestone Road CT15 7AB
☎ 08701 977076 🖷 01304 214504
*(M20 then A20 to Dover. Through tunnel, take 2nd exit
onto B2011. Take 1st left at rdbt. Travel Inn is on the left,
after 1 mile)*

Travel Inn Dover (East)   40 rooms
Jubilee Way, Guston Wood CT15 5FD
☎ 08701 977075 🖷 01304 240614
(on rdbt of A2 & A258)

FOLKESTONE

Travel Inn   79 rooms
Cherry Garden Lane CT19 4AP
☎ 08701 977103 🖷 01303 273641
*(M20 junct 13. At 1st rdbt turn right, at 2nd rdbt turn right
signed Folkestone A20. At traffic lights turn right, Travel Inn
is on the right.)*

GILLINGHAM

Travel Inn   45 rooms
Will Adams Way ME8 6BY
☎ 08701 977105 🖷 01634 261232
*(From M2 junct 4 turn left along A278 to A2. Turn left at
Tesco & Travel Inn is left at next rdbt, 5 minutes drive from
Priestfield Football Ground)*

GRAVESEND

Travel Inn   36 rooms
Wrotham Road DA11 7LF
☎ 08701 977118 🖷 01474 323776
(1 m from A2 on A227 towards Gravesend town centre)

MAIDSTONE

Travel Inn Maidstone (Allington) 40 rooms
London Road ME16 0HG
☎ 08701 977168 🖷 01622 672469
(M20 junct 5, 0.5m on London Rd towards Maidstone)

Travel Inn Maidstone (Hollingbourne) 58 rooms
ME17 1SS
☎ 08701 977169 🖷 01622 739535
(M20 junct 8)

Travel Inn Maidstone (Leybourne)   40 rooms
Castle Way ME19 5TR
☎ 08701 977170 🖷 01732 844474
(M20 junct 4, take A228, Travel Inn on left)

Travel Inn Maidstone (Sandling)   40 rooms
Allington Lock, Sandling ME14 3AS
☎ 08701 977308 🖷 01622 715159
(M20 junct 6 follow sign for Museum of Kent Life)

MARGATE

Travel Inn   44 rooms
Station Green, Marine Terrace CT9 5AF
☎ 08701 977182 🖷 01843 221101
(M2, A299, A28 to seafront. Inn station, facing sea)

SITTINGBOURNE

Travel Inn   40 rooms
Bobbing Corner, Sheppy Way, Bobbing ME9 8PD
☎ 08701 977229 🖷 01795 436748
*(M2 junct 5 take A249 towards Sheerness approx 2m, 1st
slip road after A2 underpass. Travel Inn on the left)*

WESTERHAM

Travel Inn Westerham (Clacket Lane) 58 rooms
TN16 2ER
☎ 08701 977265 🖷 01959 561311
(M25 between junct 5 & 6)

WHITSTABLE

Travel Inn   40 rooms
Thanet Way CT5 3DB
☎ 08701 977269 🖷 01227 263151
(2m W of town centre on B2205)

WROTHAM

Travel Inn Sevenoaks Maidstone   40 rooms
London Road, Wrotham Heath TN15 7RX
☎ 08701 977227 🖷 01732 870368
*(10 mins from M20 J2. 5mins from the M26 J2a. A20 to
Wrotham Heath/W.malling. Inn after lights on right)*

LANCASHIRE

BLACKPOOL

Travel Inn Blackpool Airport   39 rooms
Squires Gare Lane FY4 2QS
☎ 08701 977034 🖷 01253 362413
*(M55 junct 4/A5230 & turn left at 1st rdbt towards airport.
Travel Inn is just before Squires Gate railway station)*

Travel Inn Blackpool (South)   79 rooms
Yeadon Way, South Shore FY1 6BF
☎ 08701 977032 🖷 01253 343805
*(M55, follow signs for central car park/coach area. Located
next to Total garage)*

Travel Inn Blackpool Bispham   39 rooms
Devonshire Road, Bispham FY2 0AR
☎ 08701 977033   📠 01253 590498
(M55 junct 4 right onto A583. At 5th lights turn right (Whitegate Drive). 4-5m onto A587

BURNLEY
Travel Inn   40 rooms
Queen Victoria Road BB10 3EF
☎ 08701 977045   📠 01282 448431
(M65 junct 12 take 5th exit at rdbt, 1st exit at rdbt, keep in right lane at lights, next rdbt, 2nd exit then 3rd at next rdbt, under bridge turn left before football ground)

DARWEN
Travel Inn Blackburn   41 rooms
Oakenhurst Farm, Eccleslink Road BB3 0ST
☎ 08701 977 187   📠 08701 977701
(Situated directly off junction 4 of the M65, near Blackburn)

LANCASTER
Travel Inn   60 rooms
Lancaster Business Park, Caton Road LA1 3PE
☎ 0870 977 290   📠 01524 384801

PRESTON
Travel Inn Preston East   65 rooms
Bluebell Way, Preston East Link Road,
Fulwood PR2 5PZ
☎ 08701 977215   📠 01772 651619
(M6 junct 31A left at rdbt, follow ring road under motorway & Inn on left. No junct for southbound traffic so take junct 31 & join motorway northbound, take exit off junct 31A)

Travel Inn Preston (West)   38 rooms
Blackpool Road, Lea PR4 0XB
☎ 08701 977214   📠 01772 729971
(off A583, opposite Texaco garage.)

LEICESTERSHIRE
ASHBY-DE-LA-ZOUCH
Travel Inn   40 rooms
Flagstaff Island, Flagstaff Park LE65 1DS
☎ 08701 977281   📠 01530 561211
(Exit M1 (J23a), follow signs for A42 (M42) to Tamworth and Birmingham. Inn just off rdbt at J13 of A42)

LEICESTER
Travel Inn Leicester South   40 rooms
Hinckley Road, Leicester Forest East LE3 3GD
☎ 08701 977155   📠 0116 239 3429
(M1 junct 21 onto A5460. At major junct (Holiday Inn on right), left into Braunstone Lane. After 2m , left onto A47 towards Hinkley. 400yds on left)

Travel Inn Leicester (Thorpe Astley) 51 rooms
Meridian Business Park, Meridian Way,
Braunstone LE19 1LU
☎ 08701 977154   📠 0116 282 7486
(M1 junct 21 follow signs for A563 (outer ring road) W to Thorpe Astley. Slip road past Texaco garage, Travel Inn on left.)

LINCOLNSHIRE
BOSTON
Travel Inn   34 rooms
Wainfleet Road PE21 9RW
☎ 08701 977035   📠 01205 310908
(A52, 300yds E of junct with A16 Boston/Grimsby road. Nearest landmark is Pilgrim Hospital)

GRIMSBY
Travel Inn   40 rooms
Europa Park, Appian Way,
Off Gilbey Road DN31 2UT
☎ 08701 977121   📠 01472 241648
(From M180 (J5) take A180 towards Grimsby town centre. At 1st rdbt take 2nd exit. Take 1st left, then left at mini rdbt onto Appian Way)

LINCOLN
Travel Inn   40 rooms
Lincoln Road, Canwick Hill LN4 2RF
☎ 08701 977156   📠 01522 542521
(Approx 1 mile south of city centre at the junction of B1188 to Branston and B1131 to Brakebridge Heath)

SCUNTHORPE
Travel Inn   40 rooms
Lakeside Retail Park, Lakeside Parkway DN16 3UA
☎ 08701 977226   📠 01724 278651
(M180 junct 4, A18 towards Scunthorpe. At Morrisons rdbt left onto Lakeside Retail Park, Inn behind Morrisons petrol station)

LONDON, GREATER
CHESSINGTON
Travel Inn   42 rooms
Leatherhead Road KT9 2NE
☎ 08701 977057   📠 01372 720889
(From M25 (J9), head towards Kingston on A243, for approx. 2 miles. The Travel Inn is next to Chessington World of Adventures)

CROYDON
Travel Inn   39 rooms
104 Coombe Road CR0 5RB
☎ 08701 977069   📠 020 8686 6439
(M25 junct 7, A23 to Purley, then follow A235 to Croydon. Pass Tree House pub on left. Turn right at lights, onto A212)

Travel Inn

ENFIELD

Travel Inn   159 rooms
Innova Park, Mollison Avenue EN3 7XY
☎ 0870 238 3306   📠 01992 707070
(M25 (J25), A10 to London, left onto Bullsmoor Lane/Mollison Avenue. Over rdbt, right at lights into Innova Science Park.)

GREENFORD

Travel Inn   39 rooms
Western Avenue UB6 8TE
☎ 08701 977119   📠 020 8998 8823
(From the Western Avenue (A40), Eastbound, exit Perivale. Turn right, then at 2nd set of traffic lights turn left. Travel Inn is opposite the Hoover Building)

HAYES

Travel Inn Heathrow Hayes   62 rooms
362 Uxbridge Road UB4 0HF
☎ 08701 977132   📠 020 8569 1204
(M4 junct 3 follow A312 north, straight across next rdbt onto dual carriageway, at A4020 junct turn left, Travel Inn is 100yds on the right)

Travel Inn London Heathrow   590 rooms
362 Uxbridge Road UB4 0HF
☎ 08701 977 132   📠 020 8569 1204

HOUNSLOW

Travel Inn London Heathrow   590 rooms
Bath Road TW6 2AB
☎ 0870 6075 075   📠 0870 241 9000
(from M4 junct 4 follow signs for Heathrow Terminals 1, 2 & 3. Turn left onto Bath Rd signed A4/London. Travel Inn on right after 0.5 mile)

ILFORD

Travel Inn   44 rooms
Redbridge Lane East IG4 5BG
08701 977140   020 8550 6214
(M11 (signed London East/A12 Chelmsford) follow A12 Chelmsford signs, Travel Inn on left at bottom of slip road)

KENTON

Travel Inn Harrow   70 rooms
Kenton Road HA3 8AT
☎ 08701 977146   📠 020 8909 1604
(M1 junct 5 follow signs to Harrow & Kenton. Between Harrow & Wembley on A4006 opposite Kenton Railway Station)

RAINHAM

Travel Inn   60 rooms
New Road, Wennington RM13 9ED
☎ 08701 977217   📠 01708 634821
(M25 J30/31 - A13 for Dagenham/Rainham, then A1306 for Wennington, Aveley, Rainham. Inn 0.5m on right.)

ROMFORD

Travel Inn   40 rooms
Mercury Gardens RM1 3EN
☎ 08701 977220   📠 01708 760456
(off M25(J28), take A12 to Gallows Corner. Take A118 to next rdbt and turn left)

LONDON

E6

Travel Inn London Beckton   90 rooms
1 Woolwich Manor Way, Beckton E6 4NT
☎ 08701 977029   📠 020 7511 4214
(from A13 take A117, Woolwich Manor Way, towards City Airport, on left after 1st rdbt)

E16

Travel Inn London Docklands (ExCel) 202 rooms
Royal Victoria Dock E16 1SL
☎ 0870 238 3322   📠 020 7540 2250
(Situated on ExCel East. Follow A13 onto A1020. At the Connaught rdbt take 2nd exit into Connaught Road. The Travel Inn is on the right.)

SE1

Travel Inn London County Hall   313 rooms
Belvedere Road SE1 7PB
☎ 0870 238 3300   📠 020 7902 1619
(Situated in the historic County Hall building, next to the London Eye, opposite the Houses of Parliament, walking distance from West End and theatre land)

Travel Inn London Tower Bridge   195 rooms
Tower Bridge Road SE1 3LP
☎ 0870 238 3303   📠 020 7940 3719
(South of Tower Bridge)

SW5

Travel Inn London Kensington   183 rooms
11 Knaresborough Place, Kensington SW5 0TJ
☎ 0870 238 3304   📠 020 7370 9292
(Just off the A4 Cromwell Road, 2 minutes from Earls Court Tube Station)

SW6

Travel Inn London Putney Bridge   154 rooms
3 Putney Bridge Approach SW6 3JD
☎ 0870 238 3302   📠 020 7471 8315
(north bank of River Thames by Putney Bridge)

WC1

Travel Inn London Euston   220 rooms
1 Dukes Road WC1H 9PJ
☎ 0870 238 3301   📠 020 7554 3419
(On the corner of Euston Road (south side) and Duke's Road, between Kings Cross/St Pancras and Euston stations.)

MERSEYSIDE
BROMBOROUGH

Travel Inn Wirral Bromborough   32 rooms
High Street, Bromborough Cross CH62 7EZ
☎ 08701 977273 🖹 0151 344 0443
(on A41 New Chester Road, 2m from M53 junct 5)

HAYDOCK

Travel Inn   60 rooms
Yew Tree Way, Golborne WA3 3JD
☎ 08701 977131 🖹 01942 296100
(M6 junct 23, take A580 towards Manchester. Proceed for approx 2m passing over one major rdbt. Travel Inn on left)

HESWALL

Travel Inn Wirral North   37 rooms
Chester Road, Gayton CH60 3SD
☎ 08701 977274 🖹 0151 342 8983
(M53 junct 4 follow A5137 signed Heswall for 3m & turn left at next rdbt, Travel Inn on left)

LIVERPOOL

Travel Inn Liverpool Aintree   40 rooms
1 Ormskirk Road, Aintree L9 5AS
☎ 08701 977157 🖹 0151 525 8696
(M58/57 then follow A59 to Liverpool. Past Aintree Retail Park, left at lights into Aintree Racecourse. Travel Inn is on left)

Travel Inn Liverpool (City Centre)   165 rooms
Vernon Street L2 2AY
☎ 0870 238 3323 🖹 0870 241 9000
(from M62 follow Liverpool City Centre and then Birkenhead Tunnel signs. At rdbt take 3rd exit onto Dale St then right into Vernon St. The Travel Inn is on the left)

Travel Inn Liverpool West Derby   84 rooms
Queens Drive, West Derby L13 0DL
☎ 08701 977160 🖹 0151 220 7610
(At the end of M62 turn right under the flyover onto A5058 (following signs to the football stadium). Travel Inn is 1.5 m on the left, just past the Esso garage)

Travel Inn Liverpool Tarbock   40 rooms
Wilson Road, Tarbock L36 6AD
☎ 08701 977159 🖹 0151 480 9361
(at junct M62/M57. M62 junct 6 take A5080 Huyton then 1st right into Wilson Rd)

Travel Inn Liverpool North   63 rooms
Northern Perimeter Road, Bootle L30 7PT
☎ 08701 977158 🖹 0151 520 1842
(on A5207, off A5036, 0.25m from end of M58/M57)

ST HELENS

Travel Inn   40 rooms
Mickle Head Green, Eurolink, Lea Green WA9 4TT
☎ 08701 977237 🖹 01744 820531
(M62 junct 7, on A570 towards St Helens)

NORFOLK
KING'S LYNN

Travel Inn   40 rooms
Freebridge Farm PE34 3LJ
☎ 08701 977149 🖹 01553 775827
(junct of A47 & A17)

NORWICH

Travel Inn Norwich Airport   40 rooms
Holt Road, Norwich Airport NR6 6JA
☎ 08701 977 291 🖹 01603 428641

Travel Inn Norwich (East)   60 rooms
Broadland Business Park,
Old Chapel Way NR7 0WG
☎ 08701 977198 🖹 01603 307617
(A47 onto A1042, 3m E of city centre)

Travel Inn Norwich (Showground)   40 rooms
Longwater Interchange, Dereham Road,
New Costessey NR5 0TL
☎ 08701 977197 🖹 01603 741219
(Follow brown tourist signs for Royal Norfolk Showground on A47 and A1074. Travel Inn is situated opposite showground and junctions A47 and A1074)

NORTHAMPTONSHIRE
KETTERING

Travel Inn   39 rooms
Rothwell Road NN16 8XF
☎ 08701 977147 🖹 01536 415020
(on A14, off junct 7)

NORTHAMPTON

Travel Inn Northampton (East)   44 rooms
The Lakes, Bedford Road NN4 7YD
☎ 08701 977196 🖹 01604 621935
(M1 junct 15 follow A508 (A45) to Northampton. Take A428 exit then at rdbt take 4th exit (signed Bedford). Left at next rdbt for Travel Inn on right)

Travel Inn Northampton (West)   51 rooms
Harpole Turn, Weedon Road, Harpole NN7 4DD
☎ 08701 977195 🖹 01604 831807
(From M1 (J16), take A45 to Northampton. After 1 mile turn left into Harpole Turn. Travel Inn is on the left)

WATFORD GAP SERVICE AREA

Travel Inn Daventry   36 rooms
NN6 7UZ
☎ 08701 977301 🖷 01327 871333
(M1 southbound between J16/17. (Access from northbound via barrier access))

WELLINGBOROUGH

Travel Inn   40 rooms
London Road NN8 2DP
☎ 08701 977262 🖷 01933 275947
(0.5m from Wellingborough town centre on A5193 near Dennington Industrial Estate)

NORTHUMBERLAND

CRAMLINGTON

Travel Inn Newcastle-upon-Tyne Cramlington   40 rooms
Moor Farm Roundabout, off Front Street NE23 7QA
☎ 08701 977188   0191 250 2216
(at rdbt on junction of A19/A189 S of Cramlington)

PONTELAND

Travel Inn Newcastle Airport   86 rooms
Newcastle International Airport, Ponteland Road,
Prestwick NE20 9DB
☎ 08701 977190 🖷 01661 824940
(immediately adjacent to airport main entrance)

NOTTINGHAMSHIRE

NEWARK-ON-TRENT

Travel Inn   40 rooms
Lincoln Road NG24 2DB
☎ 08701 977186 🖷 01636 605135
(at intersection of A1/A46/A17, follow signs B6166)

NOTTINGHAM

Travel Inn Nottingham Riverside   86 rooms
The Phoenix Centre, Millennium Way West NG8 6AS
08701 977200   0115 977 0113
(M1 junct 26, 1m on A610 towards Nottingham)

Travel Inn Nottingham (City Centre) 161 rooms
Goldsmith Street NG1 5LT
☎ 0870 238 3314 🖷 0115 908 1388
(Follow A610 to City Centre. Follow signs for Nottingham Trent University into Talbot Street. Take 1st left into Clarendon Street and at lights turn right for Travel Inn on right.)

Travel Inn Nottingham South 38 rooms
Castle Marina Park, Castle Bridge Road NG7 1GX
☎ 08701 977199 🖷 0115 958 2362
(0.5m from Nottingham city centre, follow directions for Castle Marina)

OXFORDSHIRE

ABINGDON

Travel Inn   25 rooms
Marcham Road OX14 1AD
☎ 08701 977014 🖷 01235 554149
(On A415, 0.5 m from Abingdon town centre. Approx. 0.5m from the A34 at the Abingdon South junct)

DIDCOT

Travel Inn   60 rooms
Milton Interchange, Milton OX14 4DP
☎ 08701 977073 🖷 01235 820465
(on A4130 at junct with A34)

OXFORD

Travel Inn   120 rooms
Oxford Business Park, Garsington Road OX4 2JZ
☎ 08701 977204 🖷 01865 775887
(Situated on the Oxford Business Park, just off the A4142 on the junction with the B480, opposite the BMW Works, 3 miles from Oxford city centre)

SHROPSHIRE

TELFORD

Travel Inn   60 rooms
Euston Way TF3 4LY
☎ 08701 977251 🖷 01952 290742
(From M54 (J5) follow signs for Central Railway Station. Travel Inn is located on 2nd exit off rdbt)

SOMERSET

BRIDGWATER

Travel Inn   40 rooms
Express Park, Bristol Road TA6 4RR
☎ 0870 242 3344 🖷 0870 241 9000

PORTISHEAD

Travel Inn Bristol   40 rooms
Wyndham Way BS20 7GA
☎ 08701 977212 🖷 01275 846534
(From M5 (J19) follow A369 towards Portishead. Go across the first rdbt and the Travel Inn is situated on the next rdbt, 0.25 mile from the centre of Portishead.)

TAUNTON

Travel Inn Taunton (Central)   40 rooms
Massingham Park TA2 7RX
☎ 08701 977 293 🖷 01823 422350

Travel Inn Taunton (East)   40 rooms
81 Bridgwater Road TA1 2DU
☎ 08701 977249 🖷 01823 322054
(M5 junct 25 follow signs to Taunton over 1st rdbt & keep left at Creech Castle traffic lights, Travel Inn 200yds on right)

TAUNTON DEANE MOTORWAY SERVICE AREA

Travel Inn   39 rooms
Trull TA3 7PF
☎ 08701 977250   🖷 01823 338131
(M5 southbound between junct 25 & 26)

WESTON-SUPER-MARE

Travel Inn   60 rooms
Hutton Moor Road BS22 8LY
☎ 08701 977266   🖷 01934 627401
(From M25 (J21), follow A370 to Weston-Super-Mare. After 3rd rdbt turn right at traffic lights into Hutton Moor Leisure Centre. Turn left and follow road into car park)

STAFFORDSHIRE

CANNOCK

Travel Inn   60 rooms
Watling Street WS11 1SJ
☎ 08701 977048   🖷 01543 466130
(on at junct of A5/A460, 2m from M6 junct 11/12)

NEWCASTLE-UNDER-LYME

Travel Inn   58 rooms
Talke Road, Chesterton ST5 7AH
☎ 08701 977191   🖷 01782 578901
(Exit M6 (J16) - follow A500 for approx. 3.5 miles. Take A34 towards Newcastle-under-Lyme. Inn 0.5m on right)

NORTON CANES

Travel Inn Birmingham North (M6 Toll) 40 rooms
Norton Canes MSA M6 Toll Road,
North Canes WS11 9UX
☎ 08701 977070   🖷 08701 977 700
(Located on motorway service area between J6/7 of M6 toll road. Access from both sides via barrier and from A5)

STAFFORD MOTORWAY SERVICE AREA

Travel Inn Stafford (M6 Southbound) 40 rooms
Stafford Motorway Service Area ST15 0EY
☎ 08701 977239   🖷 01785 826303
(M6 southbound 8m S of junct 15)

TAMWORTH

Travel Inn   58 rooms
Bonehill Road, Bitterscote B78 3HQ
☎ 08701 977248   🖷 01827 310420
(M42 junct 10 follow A5 towards Tamworth. After 3m turn left onto A51. Straight over 1st rdbt, 3rd exit off next rdbt)

UTTOXETER

Travel Inn   41 rooms
Derby Road (A518/A50) ST14 5AA
☎ 08701 977256   🖷 01889 561801
(at junct of A50/A518, 1m of town centre)

SUFFOLK

IPSWICH

Travel Inn Ipswich North   59 rooms
Paper Mill Lane, Claydon IP6 0BE
☎ 0870 238 3311   🖷 01473 833127
e: ipswich.mti@whitbread.com
(on A14 NW of Ipswich at Great Blakenham/Claydon/RAF Wattisham junct, at rdbt take exit into Papermill Ln)

Travel Inn Ipswich (South)   40 rooms
Bourne Hill, Wherstead IP2 8ND
☎ 08701 977143   🖷 01473 692283
(From A14 follow signs for Ipswich Central A137 then Ipswich Central & Docks. At bottom of hill 2nd exit off rdbt)

LOWESTOFT

Travel Inn   40 rooms
249 Yarmouth Road NR32 4AA
☎ 08701 977165   🖷 01502 581223
(on A12, 2m N of Lowestoft)

SURREY

BAGSHOT

Travel Inn   40 rooms
1 London Road GU19 5HR
☎ 08701 977021   🖷 01276 451357
(on A30, 0.25m from Bagshot)

CAMBERLEY

Travel Inn   40 rooms
221 Yorktown Road, College Town GU47 0RT
☎ 08701 977047   🖷 01582 842811
(M3 junct 4 follow A331 to Camberley. At large rdbt, exit to A321 towards Bracknell. At 3rd set of traffic lights, Travel Inn on left)

EPSOM

Travel Inn   40 rooms
2-4 St Margarets Drive, Off Dorking Road KT18 7LB
☎ 08701 977096   🖷 01372 739761
(M25 junct 9, A24 towards Epsom, Travel Inn on left, just before town centre)

GUILDFORD

Travel Inn   87 rooms
Parkway GU1 1UP
☎ 08701 977122   🖷 01483 450678
(From M25 (J10) follow signs to Portsmouth (A3). Turn off signed Guildford centre/Leisure Centre (A322/A320/A25). Turn left and Travel Inn is on the left)

REDHILL

Travel Inn   48 rooms
Brighton Road, Salfords RH1 5BT
☎ 08701 977218   🖷 01737 778099
(on A23 , 2m S of Redhill, 3m N of Gatwick Airport)

WOKING

Travel Inn   34 rooms
Bridge Barn Lane GU21 6NL
☎ 08701 977276 📠 01483 771733
(M25 (J11) follow A320. Turn right at traffic lights by Toys R Us. Take 3rd mini rdbt 0.75m down Goldsworth Rd. Turn right into Bridge Barn Ln, Travel Inn on left)

SUSSEX, EAST
EASTBOURNE

Travel Inn   47 rooms
Willingdon Drive BN23 8AL
☎ 08701 977089 📠 01323 767379
(A22, towards Eastbourne. At next rdbt left. Inn on the left)

HASTINGS & ST LEONARDS

Travel Inn   44 rooms
1 John Macadam Way, St Leonards
TN37 7DB
☎ 08701 977128 📠 01424 756911
(travelling into Hastings on A21 London Rd, Travel Inn on right after junct with A2100 Battle road)

NEWHAVEN

Travel Inn   40 rooms
The Drove, Avis Road BN9 0AG
☎ 08701 977192 📠 01273 612359
(from A26 (New Rd) through Drove Industrial Estate, left turn after underpass. On same complex as Sainsburys, A259)

SUSSEX, WEST
ARUNDEL

Travel Inn   30 rooms
Crossbush Lane BN18 9PQ
☎ 08701 977016 📠 01903 884381
(1m E of Arundel at intersection of A27/A284)

CRAWLEY

Travel Inn Crawley   41 rooms
Balcombe Road RH10 3NL
☎ 08701 977067 📠 01293 873034
(On B2036 heading south towards Crawley from M23 junct 10)

Travel Inn Gatwick   219 rooms
North Terminal, Longbridge Way RH6 0NX
☎ 0870 238 3305 📠 01293 568278
(M23 junct 9/9A towards North Terminal, at rdbt take 3rd exit, hotel on right)

EAST GRINSTEAD

Travel Inn   41 rooms
London Road, Felbridge RH19 2QR
☎ 08701 977088 📠 01342 326187
(at junction of A22 & A264 south from M25 junct 6)

HORSHAM

Travel Inn   40 rooms
57 North Street RH12 1RD
☎ 08701 977136 📠 01403 270797
(opposite railway station, 5m from M23 junct 11)

TYNE & WEAR
GATESHEAD

Travel Inn   40 rooms
Derwent Haugh Road, Swalwell NE16 3BL
☎ 08701 977283 📠 0191 414 5032
(Off A1/A694 intersection. 1m N of Metro Centre)

NEWCASTLE UPON TYNE

Travel Inn Newcastle-upon-Tyne Holystone 40 rooms
Holystone Roundabout NE27 0DA
☎ 08701 977189 📠 0191 259 9509
(3m N of Tyne Tunnel, adjacent to A19. Take A191 signed Gosforth/Whitley Bay)

Travel Inn   81 rooms
City Road, Quayside NE1 2AN
☎ 0870 238 3318 📠 0191 232 6557
(at corner of City Rd (A186) & Crawhall Rd)

SUNDERLAND

Travel Inn   41 rooms
Wessington Way, Castletown SR5 3HR
☎ 08701 977245 📠 0191 548 4044
(A19, A1231 towards Sunderland, Inn 100yds)

WARWICKSHIRE
NUNEATON

Travel Inn Nuneaton/Coventry   48 rooms
Coventry Road CV10 7PJ
☎ 08701 977201 📠 024 7632 7156
(M6 junct 3, A444 towards Nuneaton. Inn on right)

RUGBY

Travel Inn Rugby   60 rooms
Central Park Drive, Central Park CV23 0WE
☎ 08701 977 223 📠 01788 565949

WEST MIDLANDS
BALSALL COMMON

Travel Inn   42 rooms
Kenilworth Road CV7 7EX
☎ 08701 977022 📠 01676 535929
(M42 junct 6, A45 towards Coventry for 0.5m, then A452 towards Leamington, Travel Inn 3m on right)

BIRMINGHAM

Travel Inn (City Centre)   53 rooms
20 Bridge Street B1 2JH
☎ 08701 977031 📠 0121 633 4779
(From M6/M5/M42 follow signs for city centre. Bridge St off A456 (Broad Street). Turn left in front of Hyatt Hotel Travel Inn on right)

Travel Inn Birmingham Central East 60 rooms
Richard Street, Aston Waterlinks B7 4AA
☎ 0870 238 3312 🖹 0121 333 6490
(On ring road A4540 at junct with A38M. From M6 junct 6 take 2nd exit off A38M, ring road, left at island, 1st left)

COVENTRY
Travel Inn   75 rooms
Rugby Road, Binley Woods CV3 2TA
☎ 08701 977066 🖹 024 7643 1178
(from M6 (J2) follow signs Warwick (A46 & M40). Follow "All traffic" signs, under bridge onto A46. Left at 1st rdbt to Binley. Travel Inn is on the right at next rdbt)

KINGSWINFORD
Travel Inn Dudley (Kingswinford)   43 rooms
Dudley Road DY6 8WT
☎ 08701 977303 🖹 01384 402736
(A4123 to Dudley, A461 following signs for Russell's Hall Hospital. On A4101 to Kingswinford, the Travel Inn is opposite Pensnett Trading Estate)

OLDBURY
Travel Inn   40 rooms
Wolverhampton Road B69 2BH
☎ 08701 977202 🖹 0121 552 1012
(M5 junct 2, take A4123 towards Wolverhampton, hotel 0.75m on left)

SOLIHULL
Travel Inn Solihull (North)   44 rooms
Stratford Road, Shirley B90 3AG
☎ 08701 977231 🖹 0121 733 2762
(M42 junct 4 follow signs for Birmingham. Travel Inn is situated in Shirley Town Centre, on A34)

Travel Inn Solihull Shirley   51 rooms
Stratford Road, Shirley B90 4EP
☎ 08701 977232 🖹 0121 733 7075
(Situated within a mile of J4 of the M42 on the A34, north)

Travel Inn Solihull (Hockley Heath) 55 rooms
Stratford Road, Hockley Heath B94 6NX
☎ 08701 977230 🖹 01564 783197
(on A3400, 2m S of M42 junct 4)

WALSALL
Travel Inn   40 rooms
Bentley Green, Bentley Road North WS2 0WB
☎ 08701 977258 🖹 01922 724098
(M6 junct 10, A454 signed Wolverhampton & then 2nd exit (Ansons junct). Left at rdbt, 1st left at next rdbt)

WEST BROMWICH
Travel Inn   40 rooms
New Gas Street B70 0NP
☎ 08701 977264 🖹 0121 500 5670
(From M5 junct 1 take A41 Expressway towards Wolverhampton. At 3rd rdt, Travel Inn on right)

WOLVERHAMPTON
Travel Inn   54 rooms
Wolverhampton Business Park
Stafford Road WV10 6TA
☎ 08701 977277 🖹 01902 785260
(The Travel Inn is located off the traffic lights approx. 100 yds off M54(J2))

WILTSHIRE
CHIPPENHAM
Travel Inn   79 rooms
Cepen Park, West Cepen Way SN14 6UZ
☎ 08701 977061 🖹 01249 461359
(M4 junct 17, take A350 towards Chippenham. Travel Inn is at 1st main rdbt at gateway to Chippenham)

SALISBURY
Travel Inn   60 rooms
Bishopdown Retail Park, Pearce Way SP1 3YU
☎ 08701 977225 🖹 01722 337889
(From Salisbury Centre, follow the A30 towards Marlborough for 1mile. Inn off Hampton Park at rdbt)

SWINDON
Travel Inn   63 rooms
Lydiard Way, Great Western Way SN5 8UY
☎ 08701 977247 🖹 01793 886890
(M4 junct 16, 3m SW of Swindon, take left lane towards Swindon, A3102)

WORCESTERSHIRE
BROMSGROVE
Travel Inn Bromsgrove   74 rooms
Birmingham Road B61 0BA
☎ 08701 977 044 🖹 01527 834719

EVESHAM
Travel Inn   40 rooms
Evesham Country Park A46 Trunk Road WR11 4TP
☎ 08701 977 288 🖹 01386 444301

HAGLEY
Travel Inn   40 rooms
Birmingham Road DY9 9JS
☎ 08701 977123 🖹 01562 884416
(5m off M5 junct 3 on opposite side of the A456 dual carriageway towards Kidderminster)

Travel Accommodation Directory

STRENSHAM MOTORWAY SERVICE AREA
Travel Inn Tewkesbury 49 rooms
WR8 0BZ
☎ 08701 977252 ▯ 01684 273606
(M5 Northbound J8 M5/M50 Interchange (access available to southbound))

WORCESTER
Travel Inn 60 rooms
Wainwright Way, Warndon WR4 9FA
☎ 08701 977278 ▯ 01905 756601
(M5 junct 6, at entrance of Warndon commercial development area)

YORKSHIRE, EAST RIDING OF
GOOLE
Travel Inn 41 rooms
Rawcliffe Road, Airmyn DN14 8JS
☎ 08701 977177 ▯ 01405 722661
(Leave M62 at junct 36, onto A614 signed Rawcliffe. Travel Inn immediately on left.)

KINGSTON UPON HULL
Travel Inn Hull West 40 rooms
Ferriby Road, Hessle HU13 0JA
☎ 08701 977138 ▯ 01482 645285
(From A63 take exit for A164/A15 to Humber Bridge, Beverley & Hessle Viewpoint. Travel Inn on 1st rdbt)

Travel Inn Hull North 42 rooms
Kingswood Park, Ennerdale HU7 4HS
☎ 08701 977137 ▯ 01482 820300
(N of Hull, Ennerdale link road in Kingswood Park. A63 to city centre, then A1079 north, right onto A1033, hotel on 2nd rdbt)

YORKSHIRE, NORTH
HARROGATE
Travel Inn Harrogate 50 rooms
Hornbeam Park Ave, Hornbeam Park HG2 8RA
☎ 08701 977 126 ▯ 01423 878581
(A1(M) junct 46 west then A661 to Harrogate. After 2m left at The Woodlands lights. Hornbeam Park Ave 1.5m on left)

YORK
Travel Inn York South West 59 rooms
Bilborough, Top Colton YO23 3PP
☎ 0870 238 3317 ▯ 01937 835934
(on A64 between Tadcaster & York)

Travel Inn York North West 44 rooms
White Rose Close, York Business Park,
Nether Poppleton YO26 6RL
☎ 08701 977280 ▯ 01904 787633
(on A1237 between A19 Thirsk road & A59 Harrogate road)

YORKSHIRE, SOUTH
BARNSLEY
Travel Inn 172 rooms
Meadow Gate, Dearne Valley, Wombwell S73 0UN
☎ 08701 977024 ▯ 01226 273810
(M1 junct 36, eastbound. Take A6195 (A635) to Doncaster for 5 miles. Travel Inn is adjacent to rdbt)

DONCASTER
Travel Inn 42 rooms
Wilmington Drive, Doncaster Carr DN4 5PJ
☎ 08701 977074 ▯ 01302 364811
(off A6182 near junct with access road to M18 junct 3)

ROTHERHAM
Travel Inn 37 rooms
Bawtry Road S65 3JB
☎ 08701 977222 ▯ 01709 531546
(on A631 towards Wickersley, between M18 junct 1 & M1 junct 33)

SHEFFIELD
Travel Inn Sheffield (Arena) 61 rooms
Attercliffe Common Road S9 2LU
☎ 0870 238 3316 ▯ 0114 242 3703
(M1 junct 34, follow signs to city centre. Travel Inn is opposite the Arena)

Travel Inn Sheffield (City Centre) 160 rooms
Angel St/Bank St Corner S3 8LN
☎ 0870 238 3324 ▯ 0870 241 9000
(from M1(J33), follow signs for Sheffield City Centre (A630 onto A57). At Park Square rdbt 4th exit (A61 Barnsley). Left at 4th set of lights into Snig Hill then right at lights)

TANKERSLEY
Travel Inn Sheffield Barnsley 42 rooms
Maple Road S75 3DL
☎ 08701 977228 ▯ 01226 741524
(M1 junct 35A (northbound exit only) follow A616 for 2m. From junct 36 take A61 towards Sheffield)

YORKSHIRE, WEST
BINGLEY
Travel Inn Bradford North 40 rooms
Off Bradford Road BD20 5NH
☎ 08701 977038 ▯ 01274 551692
(M62 junct 27 follow signs for A650, then to Bingley Main Street. At next rdbt straight on 50 mtrs on left)

CLECKHEATON
Travel Inn Bradford South 40 rooms
Whitehall Road BD19 6HG
☎ 08701 977037 ▯ 01274 855901
(on A58 at intersection with M62 & M606)

LEEDS

Travel Inn Leeds City Centre   139 rooms
Citygate, Wellington Street LS3 1LW
☎ 08701 977150   📠 0113 242 8105
(on junct of A65 & A58)

Travel Inn Leeds (East)   87 rooms
Selby Road, Whitkirk LS15 7AY
☎ 08701 977151   📠 0113 232 6195
(M1 junct 46 towards Leeds. At 2nd rdbt follow Temple Newsam signs. Inn 500mtrs on right.)

Travel Inn Leeds Airport   40 rooms
Victoria Avenue, Yeadon LS19 7AW
☎ 08701 977153   📠 0113 202 9383
(on A658, near Leeds/Bradford Airport)

Travel Inn Leeds Bradford South   42 rooms
Wakefield Road, Drighlington BD11 1EA
☎ 08701 977152   📠 0113 287 9115
(on Drighlington bypass, adjacent to M62 J27. A650 to Bradford then right to Drighlington, right and Inn on left)

PONTEFRACT

Travel Inn   40 rooms
Pontefract Road, Knottingley WF11 0BU
☎ 08701 977209   📠 01977 607954
(From M62 (J33) onto A1 North onto (A645) Pontefract. To T-junct, right towards Pontefract. Inn on right)

WAKEFIELD

Travel Inn   42 rooms
Thornes Park, Denby Dale Road WF2 8DY
☎ 08701 977257   📠 01924 373620
(From the M1 (J39) take the A636 towards Wakefield town centre. Travel Inn is on the left at the 3rd rdbt.)

SCOTLAND

ABERDEEN CITY

ABERDEEN

Travel Inn Aberdeen North   40 rooms
Ellon Road, Murcar, Bridge of Don AB23 8BP
☎ 08701 977012   📠 01224 706869
(From City Centre take A90 north. At rdbt, 1 mile past Exhibition Centre, turn left onto B999. Inn on right)

Travel Inn Aberdeen Dyce   40 rooms
Burnside Drive, off Riverside Drive,
Dyce AB21 0HW
☎ 08701 977304   📠 01224 772968
(from Aberdeen A96 towards Inverness, turn right at rdbt onto A947, at 2nd rdbt turn right then 2nd right)

Travel Inn Aberdeen South West   40 rooms
Mains of Balquharn, Portlethen AB12 4QS
☎ 08701 977013   📠 01224 783836
(on A90, exit signed Portlethen Shopping Centre)

CITY OF EDINBURGH

EDINBURGH

Travel Inn Edinburgh Inveresk   40 rooms
Carberry Road, Inveresk, Musselburgh EH21 8PT
☎ 08701 977092   📠 0131 653 2270
(from A1, take exit signed Dalkeith (A6094). Follow signs until rdbt, turn right, Travel Inn 300yds on right)

Travel Inn Edinburgh East   39 rooms
228 Willowbrae Road EH8 7NG
☎ 08701 977091   📠 0131 652 2789
(M8(J1) follow A720 (for 12m). Onto A1. At rdbt after ASDA turn left 2 miles. Inn on left)

Travel Inn Edinburgh City Centre   281 rooms
1 Morrison Link EH3 8DN
☎ 0870 238 3319   📠 0131 228 9836
(next to Edinburgh International Conference Centre)

Travel Inn Edinburgh Leith   60 rooms
Pier Place, Newhaven Dicks EH6 4TX
☎ 08701 977093   📠 0131 554 5994
(From A1 follow coast rd through Leith. Pass Ocean Terminal, over mini-rdbt, 2nd exit Harry Ramsden's car pk)

SOUTH QUEENSFERRY

Travel Inn Edinburgh Queensferry   46 rooms
Builyeon Road EH30 9YJ
☎ 08701 977094   📠 0131 319 1156
(M8 junct 2 follow signs M9 Stirling, leave at junct 1A take A8000 direction of Forth Road Bridge, at 3rd rdbt take 2nd exit into Builyeon Road, do not go onto Forth Road Bridge)

CITY OF GLASGOW

GLASGOW

Travel Inn Glasgow City Centre   254 rooms
Montrose House, 187 George Street G1 1YU
☎ 0870 238 3320   📠 0141 553 2719
(off M8(J15) 2 minutes walk of George Square)

Travel Inn Glasgow East   66 rooms
601 Hamilton Road G71 7SA
☎ 08701 977109   📠 0141 773 8554
(From J4 follow signs to Uddingston Mt. Vernon then Zoo Park. At entrance to Glasgow Zoo, by J4 of M73 & M74)

Travel Inn Glasgow Cambuslang   40 rooms
Cambuslang G32 8EY
☎ 08701 977306   📠 0141 778 1703
(on the rdbt at end of the M74, turn right at rdbt, at traffic lights turn right & Travel Inn on right)

DUMFRIES & GALLOWAY

ANNANDALE WATER SERVICE AREA

Travel Inn Lockerbie (Annandale Water) 42 rooms
Johnstonbridge DG11 1HD
☎ 08701 977163   📠 01576 470644
(A74(M) - adjacent to J16. Accessible north and southbound)

DUMFRIES
Travel Inn   40 rooms
Annan Road, Collin DG1 3JX
☎ 08701 977078   📠 01387 266475
(on main central rdbt junct of the Euroroute bypass (A75)

DUNDEE CITY
DUNDEE
Travel Inn Dundee (Centre)   40 rooms
Discovery Quay, Riverside Drive DD1 4XA
☎ 08701 977079   📠 01382 203237
(follow signs for Discovery Quay, situated on waterfront)

Travel Inn Dundee (West)   64 rooms
Kingsway West, Invergowrie DD2 5JU
☎ 08701 977081   📠 01382 568431
(approaching Swallow rdbt next to Technology Park rdbt take A90 towards Aberdeen, Travel Inn on left after 250yds)

Travel Inn Dundee East   40 rooms
Ethiebeaton Park, Arbroath Road,
Monifieth DD5 4HB
☎ 08701 977080   📠 01382 530468
(From A90 follow signs for A92)

EAST AYRSHIRE
KILMARNOCK
Travel Inn   40 rooms
Annadale KA1 2RS
☎ 08701 977148   📠 01563 570536
(from M74(J8) signed Kilmarnock (A71). From M77 join A71 to Irvine. At next rdbt turn right onto B7064 signed Crosshouse Hospital. Travel Inn is on the right)

EAST DUNBARTONSHIRE
MILNGAVIE
Travel Inn Glasgow North   60 rooms
103 Main Street G62 6BJ
☎ 08701 977112   📠 0141 956 7839
(On A81 6m N of Glasgow city centre. Close to Loch Mond. From M8 (J16) follow signs A879 to Milngavie)

FALKIRK POLMONT
Travel Inn Falkirk East
40 Beancross Road FK2 0YS
☎ 08701 977098   📠 01324 720777
(M9 junct 5 at rdbt take exit signed Polmont A9. Travel Inn is on the left hand side)

FIFE
GLENROTHES
Travel Inn   40 rooms
Beaufort Drive KY7 4UJ
☎ 08701 977114   📠 01592 773453
(From M90 (J2a), northbound, take A92 to Glenrothes. At 2nd rbt (Bankhead), take 3rd exit. Travel Inn is on the left (Beaufort Drive))

KINCARDINE
Travel Inn Falkirk North   40 rooms
Bowtrees Farm FK2 8PJ
☎ 08701 977099   📠 01324 831994
(From north M9 junct 7 towards Kincardine Bridge, from south M876 for Kincardine Bridge. On rdbt, end of slip rd)

HIGHLAND
FORT WILLIAM
Travel Inn   40 rooms
Loch Iall An Aird PH33 6AN
☎ 08701 977104   📠 01397 703618
(N end of Fort William Shopping Centre, just off A82)

INVERNESS
Travel Inn   39 rooms
Millburn Road IV2 3QX
☎ 08701 977141   📠 01463 717826
(on A9 junct with A96 (Raigmore Interchange, signed Airport/Aberdeen), follow B865 towards town centre, hotel 100yds past next rdbt)

Travel Inn Inverness East   60 rooms
Beechwood Business Park IV2 3BW
☎ 08701 977142   📠 01463 225233
(on A9, turn left sigposted Raigmore Hospital, Police HQ & Inshes Retail Park)

INVERCLYDE
GREENOCK
Travel Inn   40 rooms
1-3 James Watt Way PA15 2AJ
08701 977120   📠 01475 730890
(Follow M8 until it becomes A8 at Langbank, straight ahead through rdbt to Greenock, turn right off A8 at 3rd rdbt, next to McDonalds)

MORAY
ELGIN
Travel Inn   40 rooms
1 Linkwood Way IV30 1HY
☎ 08701 977095   📠 01343 540635
(on A96, 1.5m E of city centre)

NORTH LANARKSHIRE
BELLSHILL
Travel Inn Glasgow Bellshill   40 rooms
Belziehill Farm, New Edinburgh Road ML4 3HH
☎ 08701 977106   📠 01698 845969
(M74 junct 5 follow signs towards Coatbridge & Bellshill on A725. At 2nd exit off the A725. Travel Inn on left of rdbt)

CUMBERNAULD
Travel Inn Glasgow (Cumbernauld) 37 rooms
4 South Muirhead Road G67 1AX
☎ 08701 977108   📠 01236 736380
(From A80, A8011 following signs to Cumbernauld and town centre. Travel Inn opposite Asda/McDonalds. Turn at rdbt towards Esso garage. Turn right at mini-rdbt)

MOTHERWELL

Travel Inn Glasgow (near Motherwell) 40 rooms
Edinburgh Road, Newhouse ML3 6JW
☎ 08701 977164 🖹 01698 861353
*(From south M74 junct 5 onto A725 towards Coatbridge.
Take A8 towards Edinburgh & leave at junct 6, follow signs
for Lanark. Travel Inn 400yds on right)*

STEPPS

Travel Inn Glasgow (North East)   80 rooms
Crowood Roundabout, Cumbernauld Road G33 6LE
☎ 08701 977111 🖹 0141 779 8060
*(M8 junct 13 signposted M80. Exit M80 at Crowood rdbt,
take 3rd exit signposted A80 west. Travel Inn is 1st left)*

RENFREWSHIRE
PAISLEY

Travel Inn Glasgow Airport   104 rooms
Whitecart Road PA3 2TH
☎ 0870 238 3321 🖹 0141 842 1570
(close to airport terminal, follow signs)

Travel Inn Glasgow Paisley   40 rooms
Phoenix Retail Park PA1 2BH
☎ 08701 977113 🖹 0141 887 2799
*(M8 junct 28A St James Interchange follow A737 signed
Irvine, take 1st exit signed Linwood & turn left at 1st rdbt to
Phoenix Park)*

SOUTH AYRSHIRE
AYR

Travel Inn   40 rooms
Kilmarnock Road, Monkton KA9 2RJ
☎ 08701 977020 🖹 01292 678248
(on A77/A78 rdbt at Monkton, 2m from Prestwick Airport)

SOUTH LANARKSHIRE
EAST KILBRIDE

Travel Inn Glasgow East Kilbride   40 rooms
Brunel Way, The Murray G75 0JD
☎ 08701 977110 🖹 01355 230517
*(M74 junct 5, follow signs for East Kilbride A725, then signs
Paisley A726, left at Murray rdbt and left into Brunel Way)*

HAMILTON MOTORWAY SERVICE AREA

Travel Inn Glasgow (Hamilton)   36 rooms
Hamilton Motorway Service Area ML3 6JW
☎ 08701 977124 🖹 01698 891682
*(M74 n'bound, 1m N of junct 6. For s'bound access exit junct
6 onto A723, double back at rdbt & join M74 Glasgow exit)*

STIRLING
STIRLING

Travel Inn   60 rooms
Whins of Milton, Glasgow Road FK7 8EX
☎ 08701 977241 🖹 01786 816415
(on A872, 0.25m from M9/M80 junct 9 intersection)

WEST LOTHIAN
LIVINGSTON

Travel Inn   83 rooms
Deer Park Avenue, Knightsridge EH54 8AD
☎ 08701 977161 🖹 01506 438912
(on M8 (J3). Follow to rdbt Inn opposite rdbt)

WALES
BRIDGEND
BRIDGEND

Travel Inn   40 rooms
Pantruthyn Farm, Pencoed CF35 5HY
☎ 08701 977041 🖹 01656 864792
(M4 J35, behind the petrol station)

CAERPHILLY
CAERPHILLY

Travel Inn   40 rooms
Crossways Business Park, Pontypandy CF83 3NL
☎ 08701 977046 🖹 029 2086 5546
*(M4(J32) take A470 towards Merthyr Tydfil. J4 take A458
to Caerphilly. Stay on ring rd until Crossways Business Park
(5th rdbt). Travel Inn on the right of McDonald's rdbt.)*

CARDIFF
CARDIFF

Travel Inn Cardiff Bay   73 rooms
Keen Road CF24 5JT
☎ 08701 977050 🖹 029 2049 0403
*(Cardiff Docks & Bay signs from A48(M), over flyover &
next 4 rdbts. At 5th rdbt, take 3rd exit. Travel Inn 1st right
& 1st right again)*

Travel Inn Cardiff West   39 rooms
The Walston Castle, Port Road, Nantisaf,
Wenvoe CF5 6DD
☎ 08701 977052 🖹 029 2059 1436
*(From M4 (J33) south on A4232. Take 2nd exit (signed
Airport), then 3rd exit at Culverhouse Cross rdt. Travel Inn is
0.5m on Barry Rd (A4050))*

Travel Inn Cardiff (Roath)   70 rooms
David Lloyd Leisure Club, Ipswich
Road Roath CF23 9AQ
☎ 08701 977049 🖹 029 2046 2482
*(M4 (J30) take A4232 to A48. 2nd exit off A48 to Cardiff
East and Docks, (A4161). Follow signs for David Lloyd
Leisure Club.)*

CONWY
LLANDUDNO JUNCTION

Travel Inn   40 rooms
Afon Conway, Llandudno Junction LL28 5LB
☎ 08701 977162 🖹 01492 583614
*(Situated at J19 off the A55. Exit rdbt at A470 Betws-y-
Coed. The Travel Inn is immediately on the left, opposite the
petrol station)*

Travelodge
08700 850 950

Good quality, modern budget accommodation in over 240 locations acrooss the UK. Almost every lodge has an adjacent family restaurant, often a Little Chef, Harry Ramsden's or Burger King.

GWYNEDD

BANGOR

Travel Inn   40 rooms
Menai Business Park LL57 4FA
☎ 08701 977023   📠 01248 679214
(From A55 take 3rd Bangor turn off signed Caernarfon A487, Bangor & hospital. Take 3rd exit at 1st rdbt)

MERTHYR TYDFIL

MERTHYR TYDFIL

Travel Inn   40 rooms
Pentrebach CF48 4BD
☎ 08701 977183   📠 01443 699171
(M4 junct 32 follow A470 to Merthyr Tydfil. At 2nd rdbt turn right to Pentrebach, follow signs to Ind Estate)

NEATH PORT TALBOT

PORT TALBOT

Travel Inn   42 rooms
Baglan Road, Baglan SA12 8ES
☎ 08701 977211   📠 01639 823096
(Leave the M4 (J41 westbound). Follow road to rbt. Travel Inn just off 4th exit. J42 eastbound, left turn for Port Talbot. 2nd exit off 2nd rdbt.)

NEWPORT

CASTLETON

Travel Inn Cardiff East   49 rooms
Newport Road CF3 2UQ
☎ 08701 977051   📠 01633 681143
(M4 junct 8, at rdbt take 2nd exit A48 Castleton and follow for 3m, Travel Inn on right)

NEWPORT

Travel Inn Newport (South Wales)   63 rooms
Coldra Junction, Chepstow Road NP18 2NX
☎ 08701 977193   📠 01633 411376
(Just off J24 of M4. Take A48 to Langstone, at next rdbt return towards J24. The Travel Inn is 50 metres on the left.)

SWANSEA

SWANSEA

Travel Inn   40 rooms
Upper Fforest Way, Morriston SA6 8WB
☎ 08701 977246   📠 01792 311929
(M4 junct 45/A4067 towards Swansea. At 2nd exit, after 0.5m, turn left onto Clase Rd. Travel Inn 400yds on the left)

WREXHAM

WREXHAM

Travel Inn   36 rooms
Chester Road, Gresford LL12 8PW
☎ 08701 977279   📠 01978 856838
(on B5445 just off A483 dual carriageway near village of Gresford

ENGLAND

BEDFORDSHIRE

BEDFORD

Travelodge Bedford East   40 rooms
Black Cat Roundabout MK44 3OT
☎ 08700 850 950
(A1 North)

DUNSTABLE

Travelodge   28 rooms
Watling Street LU7 9LZ
☎ 08700 850 950   📠 01525 211177
(3m N, on A5)

LUTON

Travelodge   140 rooms
641 Dunstable Road LU4 8RQ
☎ 08700 850 950   📠 01582 490065
(M1 junct 11 towards Luton, hotel 100 yds on right)

MARSTON MORETAINE

Travelodge Bedford South West   54 rooms
Beancroft Road Junction MK43 0PZ
☎ 08700 850 950   📠 01234 766755
(on A421, northbound)

TODDINGTON MOTORWAY SERVICE AREA

Travelodge (Luton North)   66 rooms
LU5 6HR
☎ 08700 850 950   📠 01525 878452
(M1 between juncts 11 & 12)

BERKSHIRE

BINFIELD

Travelodge Bracknell   35 rooms
London Road RG12 4AA
☎ 08700 850 950   📠 01344 485940
(M4 junct 10 (Bracknell) take 1st exit towards Binfield)

NEWBURY

Travelodge (Newbury Chieveley)   127 rooms
Chieveley, Oxford Road RG18 9XX
☎ 08700 850 950   📠 01635 247886
(on A34 off junct 13 of M4)

READING

Travelodge   36 rooms
387 Basingstoke Road RG2 0JE
☎ 08700 850 950   📄 0118 975 1303
(On A33, southbound.)

Travelodge (Reading Central)   80 rooms
Oxford Road RG1 7LT
☎ 08700 850 950   📄 0118 950 3257

READING MOTORWAY
SERVICE AREA (EASTBOUND)
Travelodge Reading M4 (Eastbound) 86 rooms
Burghfield RG30 3UQ
☎ 08700 850 950   📄 0118 959 2045
(M4 between junct 11 and 12)

READING MOTORWAY
SERVICE AREA (WESTBOUND)
Travelodge Reading M4 (Westbound) 102 rooms
Burghfield RG30 3UQ
☎ 08700 850 950   📄 0118 958 2350
(M4 between junct 11 & 12)

SLOUGH
Travelodge   157 rooms
Landmark Place SL1 1BZ
☎ 08700 850 950   📄 01753 516897

TOT HILL SERVICES (A34 NEWBURY BYPASS)
Travelodge Newbury South   52 rooms
Tot Hill Services (A34), Newbury By-pass RG20 9ED
☎ 08700 850 950   📄 01635 278169
(Tot Hill Services on A34)

BRISTOL
BRISTOL
Travelodge (Bristol Cribbs Causeway) 56 rooms
Cribbs Causeway BS10 7TL
☎ 08700 850 950   📄 0117 950 1530
(A4018, off M5 junct 17)

Travelodge (Bristol Central)   119 rooms
Anchor Road, Harbourside BS1 5TT
☎ 08700 850 950   📄 0117 9255149

BUCKINGHAMSHIRE
MILTON KEYNES
Travelodge Milton Keynes North(Old Stratford) 33 rooms
Old Stratford Roundabout MK19 6AQ
☎ 08700 850 950   📄 01908 260802
(On A5 towards Towcester, Travelodge on A508/A422 rdbt)

Travelodge   80 rooms
109 Grafton Gate MK9 1AL
☎ 08700 850 950   📄 01908 241737

CAMBRIDGESHIRE
CAMBRIDGE
Travelodge (Cambridge)   120 rooms
Cambridge Leisure Park, Clifton Way CB1 7DY
☎ 0122 3241066

Travelodge (Cambridge South)   40 rooms
Fourwentways CB8 6AP
☎ 08700 850 950   📄 01223 839479
(adjacent to Little Chef at junct A11/A1307)

ELY
Travelodge   39 rooms
Witchford Road CB6 3NN
☎ 08700 850 950   📄 01353 668499
(at rdbt A10/A142)

FENSTANTON
Travelodge Huntingdon   40 rooms
PE18 9LP
☎ 08700 850 950   📄 01954 230919
(4m SE of Huntingdon, on A14 eastbound)

LOLWORTH
Travelodge   36 rooms
Huntingdon Road CB3 8DR
☎ 08700 850 950   📄 01954 781335
(on A14 northbound, 3m N of junct 14 on M11)

PETERBOROUGH
Travelodge Peterborough   42 rooms
Crowlands Road PE6 7SZ
☎ 08700 850 950   01733 223199
(at junct of A47 & A1073)

Travelodge Alwalton   32 rooms
Great North Road, Alwalton PE7 3UR
☎ 08700 850 950   📄 01733 231109
(on A1, southbound)

SWAVESEY
Travelodge Cambridge (West)   36 rooms
Cambridge Road CB4 5QR
☎ 08700 850 950   📄 01954 789113
(on eastbound carriageway of A14)

CHESHIRE
CREWE
Travelodge   42 rooms
Alsager Road, Barthomley CW2 5PT
☎ 08700 850 950   📄 01270 883157
(5m E, at junct 16 M6/A500)

Travelodge

KNUTSFORD
Travelodge   32 rooms
Chester Road, Tabley WA16 0PP
☎ 08700 850 950   📠 01565 652187
(on A556, northbound just E of junct 19 on M6)

KNUTSFORD MOTORWAY SERVICE AREA
Travelodge   54 rooms
Granada Services M6 junct 18/19 WA1 0TL
☎ 08700 850 950

LYMM
Travelodge   61 rooms
Granada Services A50 Cliffe Lane WA13 0SP
☎ 08700 850 950   📠 01925 759341

MACCLESFIELD
Travelodge Macclesfield   32 rooms
London Road South SK12 4NA
☎ 08700 850 950   📠 01625 875292
(on A523)

MIDDLEWICH
Travelodge   32 rooms
M6 Junction 18 A54 CW10 0JB
☎ 08700 850 950   📠 01606 738229

WARRINGTON
Travelodge   63 rooms
Kendrick/Leigh Street WA1 1UZ
☎ 08700 850 950   📠 01925 639432
(M6 junct 21, follow A57 towards Liverpool & Widnes to Warrington town centre, through Asda rdbt, lodge next left at lights)

WIDNES
Travelodge   32 rooms
Fiddlers Ferry Road WA8 2NR
☎ 08700 850 950   📠 0151 424 8930
(on A562)

CO DURHAM
DURHAM
Travelodge Durham   57 rooms
Station Road, Gilesgate DH1 1LJ
☎ 08700 850 950   📠 0191 386 5461

SEDGEFIELD
Travelodge   40 rooms
TS21 2JX
☎ 08700 850 950   📠 01740 623399
(on A689, 3m E of junct A1(M))

CORNWALL & ISLES OF SCILLY
SALTASH
Travelodge   53 rooms
Callington Road, Carkeel PL12 6LF
☎ 08700 850 950   📠 01752 841079
(on A38 Saltash by-pass - 1m from Tamar Bridge)

CUMBRIA
BURTON MOTORWAY SERVICE AREA
Travelodge   47 rooms
Burton in Kendal LA6 1JF
☎ 08700 850 950   📠 01524 784014
(between M6 junct 35/36 southbound)

CARLISLE
Travelodge (Carlisle North)   40 rooms
A74 Southbound, Todhills CA6 4HA
☎ 08700 850 950   📠 01228 674335

PENRITH
Travelodge   4 rooms
Redhills CA11 0DT
☎ 08700 850 950   📠 01768 866958
(on A66)

SOUTHWAITE MOTORWAY SERVICE AREA
Travelodge Carlisle (Southwaite) 38 rooms
Broadfield Site CA4 0NT
☎ 08700 850 950   📠 016974 75354
(M6 junct 41/42)

DERBYSHIRE
ALFRETON
Travelodge   60 rooms
Old Swanwick Colliery Rd DE55 1HJ
☎ 08700 850 950   📠 01773 520040
(3m from M1 junct 28 at A38/ A61 junct)

CHESTERFIELD
Travelodge   20 rooms
Brimmington Road, Inner Ring Road,
Wittington Moor S41 9BE
☎ 08700 850 950   📠 01246 455411
(on A61, N of town centre)

DERBY
Travelodge   40 rooms
Kingsway, Rowditch DE22 3NN
☎ 08700 850 950   📠 01332 367255

DEVON
EXETER
Travelodge   102 rooms
Moor Lane, Sandygate EX2 7HF
☎ 08700 850 950   📠 01392 410406
(M5 junct 30)

OKEHAMPTON
Travelodge (Okehampton East)   40 rooms
Whiddon Down EX20 2QT
☎ 08700 850 950   📠 01647 231626
(at Merrymeet rdbt on A30/A382)

PLYMOUTH
Travelodge   96 rooms
Derry's Cross PL1 2SW
☎ 08700 850 950

SAMPFORD PEVERELL
Travelodge Tiverton   40 rooms
Sampford Peverell Service Area EX16 7HD
08700 850 950   01884 821087
(M5 junct 27)

SOURTON CROSS
Travelodge Okehampton West   42 rooms
EX20 4LY
☎ 08700 850 950   🖶 0870 1911548
(4m W, at junct of A30/A386)

ESSEX
BASILDON
Travelodge Basildon   60 rooms
Festival Leisure Park, Festival Way SS14 3WB
☎ 08700 850 950   🖶 01268 186559
(M25 junct 29/A127, follow signs for Basildon centre to A176 and signs for Festival Park, lodge next to bowling alley)

EAST HORNDON
Travelodge Brentwood CM13 3LL   45 rooms
☎ 08700 850 950   🖶 01277 810819
(on A127, eastbound 4m off M25 junct 29)

FEERING
Travelodge (Colchester)   39 rooms
A12 London Road Northbound CO5 9EL
☎ 08700 850 950   🖶 01376 572848

HARLOW
Travelodge Harlow East (Stansted)   60 rooms
A414 Eastbound, Tylers Green, North Weald CM16 6BJ
☎ 08700 850 950   🖶 01992 523276

WEST THURROCK
Travelodge Thurrock   48 rooms
Arterial Road RM16 3BG
☎ 08700 850 950   🖶 01708 860971
(off A1306)

GLOUCESTERSHIRE
CIRENCESTER
Travelodge   43 rooms
Hare Bushes, Burford Road GL7 5DS
☎ 08700 850 950   🖶 01285 655290

SEVERN VIEW MOTORWAY SERVICE AREA
Travelodge   50 rooms
M48 Motorway, Severn Bridge BS35 4BH
☎ 08700 850 950   🖶 01454 632482
(M48 junct 21)

STONEHOUSE
Travelodge   40 rooms
A419 Easington GL10 3SQ
☎ 08700 850 950   🖶 01453 828590

GREATER LONDON
BRENTFORD
Travelodge (London Kew Bridge)   111 rooms
North Road, High Street TW8 0BO
☎ 08700 850 950   🖶 0208 758 1190
(M4 junct 2, Chiswick Roundabout turn right towards Kew, at traffic lights turn right in to Kew Bridge Road)

HESTON MOTORWAY SERVICE AREA
Travelodge (Eastbound)   66 rooms
Phoenix Way TW5 9NB
☎ 08700 850 950   🖶 020 8580 2028
(M4 junct 2 & 3 westbound)

Travelodge (Westbound)   145 rooms
Cranford Lane, TW5 9NB
☎ 08700 850 950   🖶 0208 580 20061

ILFORD
Travelodge London (Ilford Central)   91 rooms
Clements Road IG1 1BA
☎ 08700 850 950   🖶 020 8553 2920

Travelodge London (Ilford North)   32 rooms
Beehive Lane, Gants Hill IG4 5DR
08700 850 950   020 8551 1712

KINGSTON UPON THAMES
Travelodge London Kingston   72 rooms
21-23 London Road KT2 6ND
☎ 08700 850 950   🖶 0208 546 5904
(On Queen Elizabeth Road/London Road, opposite Rotunda complex)

MORDEN
Travelodge London Wimbledon   32 rooms
Epsom Road SM4 5PH
☎ 08700 850 950   🖶 020 8640 8227
(on A24)

GREATER MANCHESTER
BIRCH MOTORWAY SERVICE AREA
Travelodge Manchester North (Eastbound) 55 rooms
M62 Service Area East Bound OL10 2HQ
☎ 08700 850 950   🖶 0161 655 3716

Travelodge Manchester North (Westbound) 35 rooms
M62 Service Area West Bound OL10 2HQ
☎ 08700 850 950   🖶 0161 655 6422

BOLTON

Travelodge Bolton West   32 rooms
Bolton West Service Area, Horwich BL6 5UZ
☎ 08700 850 950   🖹 01204 668585

DIDSBURY

Travelodge Manchester South   62 rooms
Kingsway M20 5PG
☎ 08700 850 950   🖹 0161 448 0399

MANCHESTER

Travelodge (Manchester Central)   181 rooms
Townbury House, Blackfriars Street M3 5AB
☎ 08700 850 950   🖹 0161 839 5181

OLDHAM

Travelodge   50 rooms
432 Broadway, Chadderton OL9 8AU
☎ 08700 850 950   🖹 0161 681 9021

HAMPSHIRE
BARTON STACEY

Travelodge SO21 3NP   20 rooms
☎ 08700 850 950   🖹 01264 720260
(on A303)

BASINGSTOKE

Travelodge   44 rooms
Stag and Hounds, Winchester Road RG22 6H
☎ 08700 850 950   🖹 01256 843566
(off A30, S of town centre)

EASTLEIGH

Travelodge Southampton Eastleigh   32 rooms
Twyford Road SO50 4LF
☎ 08700 850 950   🖹 023 8061 6813
(M3 junct 12 on A335)

EMSWORTH

Travelodge Chichester (West)   36 rooms
PO10 7RB
☎ 08700 850 950   🖹 01243 370877
(A27)

FOUR MARKS

Travelodge Alton   31 rooms
156 Winchester Road GU34 5HZ
☎ 08700 850 950   🖹 01420 562659
(5m S of Alton on A31 northbound)

LIPHOOK

Travelodge   40 rooms
GU30 7TT
☎ 08700 850 950   🖹 01428 727619
(on northbound carriageway of A3, 1m from Griggs Green exit at Shell services)

LYNDHURST

Travelodge (New Forest)   32 rooms
A31 Westbound SO43 7GN
☎ 08700 850 950   🖹 02300 011544

PORTSMOUTH

Travelodge   78 rooms
Kingston Crescent, North End PO2 8AB
☎ 08700 850 950   🖹 02392 639121

RINGWOOD

Travelodge   31 rooms
St Leonards BH24 2NR
☎ 08700 850 950   🖹 01425 475941

SOUTHAMPTON

Travelodge   59 rooms
Lodge Road SO14 6QR
☎ 08700 850 950   🖹 023 8033 4569

SUTTON SCOTNEY

Travelodge Winchester (South)   40 rooms
SO21 3JY
☎ 08700 850 950   🖹 01962 761096
(on A34 southbound)

Travelodge Winchester (North)   31 rooms
SO21 3JY
☎ 08700 850 950   🖹 01962 761096
(on A34 northbound)

HERTFORDSHIRE
BALDOCK

Travelodge   40 rooms
Great North Road, Hinxworth SG7 5EX
☎ 08700 850 950   🖹 01462 835329
(on A1, southbound)

HEMEL HEMPSTEAD

Travelodge   53 rooms
Wolsey House, Wolsey Road HP2 4SS
☎ 08700 850 950   🖹 01442 266887

KENT
ASHFORD

Travelodge   67 rooms
Eureka Leisure Park TN25 4BN
☎ 08700 850 950   🖹 01233 622676
(M20 junct 9, take 1st exit on left)

CANTERBURY

Travelodge (Canterbury West)   40 rooms
A2 Gate Services, Dunkirk ME13 9LN
☎ 08700 850 950   🖹 01227 752781
(5m W on A2 northbound)

DARTFORD
Travelodge   65 rooms
Charles Street, Greenhithe DA9 9AP
☎ 08700 850 950 ▤ 01322 387854

FAVERSHAM
Travelodge Canterbury North   40 rooms
Thanet Way ME13 9EL
☎ 08700 850 950 ▤ 01227 281135
(from M2 junct 7, take A299)

GILLINGHAM
Travelodge Medway   58 rooms
Medway Motorway Service Area, Rainham ME8 8PQ
☎ 08700 850 950 ▤ 01634 263187
(between junct 4 & 5 of M2)

LANCASHIRE
BURNLEY
Travelodge   32 rooms
Cavalry Barracks, Barracks Road BB11 4AS
☎ 08700 850 950 ▤ 01282 416039
(junct A671/A679)

CHORLEY
Travelodge Preston Chorley   40 rooms
Preston Road, Clayton-le-Woods PR6 7JB
☎ 08700 850 950 ▤ 01772 311963
(from M6 junct 28 take B5256 for 2m, next to pub)

DARWEN
Travelodge Blackburn   48 rooms
Darwen Motorway Services BB3 0AT
☎ 08700 850 950 ▤ 01254 776058
(off M65 junct 4 towards Blackburn)

FORTON MOTORWAY SERVICE AREA
Travelodge Lancaster Forton   53 rooms
White Carr Lane, Bay Horse LA2 9DU
☎ 08700 850 950 ▤ 01524 791703
(between junct 32 & 33 of M6)

LEICESTERSHIRE
CASTLE DONINGTON
Travelodge Donington Park   80 rooms
Castle Donington DE74 2TN
☎ 08700 850 950 ▤ 01509 673494

LEICESTER
Travelodge (Leicester)   95 rooms
Vaughan Way LE1 4NN
☎ 0870 1911755 ▤ 0116 251 0560

MARKFIELD
Travelodge Leicester Markfield   60 rooms
Littleshaw Lane LE6 0PP
☎ 08700 850 950 ▤ 01530 244580
(on A50 from M1 junct 22)

THRUSSINGTON
Travelodge Leicester North   32 rooms
LE7 8TF
☎ 08700 850 950 ▤ 0870 1911584
(on A46, southbound)

LINCOLNSHIRE
COLSTERWORTH
Travelodge Grantham Colsterworth   31 rooms
NG35 5JR
☎ 08700 850 950 ▤ 01476 860680
(on A1/A151 southbound at junct with B151/B676)

GRANTHAM
Travelodge (Grantham North)   39 rooms
Grantham Service Area, Grantham North, Gonerby
Moor NG32 2AB
☎ 08700 850 950 ▤ 01476 577500
(4m N on A1)

LINCOLN
Travelodge   32 rooms
Thorpe on the Hill LN6 9AJ
☎ 08700 850 950 ▤ 01522 697213
(on A46)

LONG SUTTON
Travelodge Kings Lynn   40 rooms
Wisbech Road PE12 9AG
☎ 08700 850 950 ▤ 01406 362230
(on junct A17/A1101 rdbt)

SLEAFORD
Travelodge Holdingham NG34 8PN 40 rooms
☎ 08700 850 950 ▤ 01529 414752
(1m N, at rdbt A17/A15)

SOUTH WITHAM
Travelodge Grantham   32 rooms
New Fox NG33 5LN
☎ 08700 850 950 ▤ 0870 191 1576
(on A1, northbound)

LONDON
E1
Travelodge (London City)   142 rooms
1 Harrow Place E1 7DB
☎ 08700 850 950 ▤ 020 7626 1105

E14
Travelodge (London Dockland)   232 rooms
Coriander Avenue, East India Dock Road E14 2AA
☎ 08700 850 950 ▤ 020 7515 9178
(fronts A13 at East India Dock Rd)

SW11

Travelodge (London Battersea)   87 rooms
200 York Road, Battersea SW11 3SA
☎ 08700 850 950 🖻 0207 978 3898
*(from Wandsworth Bridge southern rdbt, take York Rd
A3205 towards Battersea. 0.5m on left)*

W3

Travelodge (London Park Royal)   64 rooms
A40 Western Ave, Acton W3 0TE
☎ 08700 850 950 🖻 020 8752 1134

WC1

Travelodge (London Kings Cross)   140 rooms
Willing House, Grays Inn Road,
Kings Cross WC1 8BH
☎ 08700 850 950 🖻 020 7278 7396

Travelodge (London Farringdon)   211 rooms
10-42 Kings Cross Road, WC1X 9QN
☎ 0870 1911774 🖻 020 7837 3776
*(M40 Marylebone Rd, Euston Rd, Kings Cross Rd; M1 West
End, St Johns Wood, Regents Park, Baker St, Marylebone Rd
Euston, Kings Cross Rd)*

Travelodge (London Islington)   351 rooms
100 Kings Cross Road WC1X 9DT
☎ 0870 1911773 🖻 020 7833 0798

WC2

Travelodge (London Covent Garden) 163 rooms
10 Drury Lane, High Holborn WC2B 5RE
☎ 020 7208 9988 🖻 020 7831 1548
*(Middle of Drury Lane, turn off at High Holborn. 5 mins
from High Holborn Tube & Covent Garden)*

MERSEYSIDE

BEBINGTON

Travelodge Wirral   31 rooms
New Chester Road CH62 9AQ
☎ 08700 850 950 🖻 0151 327 2489
(on A41, northbound off M53 junct 5)

HAYDOCK

Travelodge   62 rooms
Piele Road WA11 0JZ
☎ 08700 850 950 🖻 01942 272067
(2m W of junct 23 on M6, on A580 westbound)

LIVERPOOL

Travelodge (Liverpool Central)   105 rooms
25 Haymarket L1 6ER
☎ 08700 850 950 🖻 0151 227 5838
(Centre of Liverpool next to Birkenhead Tunnel.)

Travelodge (Liverpool South)   31 rooms
Brunswick Dock, Sefton Street L3 4BH
☎ 08700 850 950 🖻 0151 707 7769
*(Follow signs to City Centre & Docks, Travelodge 1 m after
Albert Docks,next to Royal Naval headquarters)*

NORFOLK

ACLE

Travelodge Great Yarmouth   40 rooms
NR13 3BE
☎ 08700 850 950 🖻 01493 751970
(junct of A47 & Acle by-pass)

NORWICH

Travelodge   62 rooms
Thickthorn Service Area, Norwich
Southern Bypass NR9 3AU
☎ 08700 850 950 🖻 0870 191 1704
(A11/A47 interchange)

NORTHAMPTONSHIRE

DESBOROUGH

Travelodge Market Harborough   32 rooms
Harborough Road NN14 2UG
☎ 08700 850 950 🖻 01536 762034
(on A6, southbound)

KETTERING

Travelodge   40 rooms
On the A14 (Westbound) NN14 1WR
☎ 08700 850 950

NORTHAMPTON

Travelodge   62 rooms
Upton Way NN5 6EG
☎ 08700 850 950 🖻 01604 758395
(A45, towards M1 junct 16)

RUSHDEN

Travelodge Wellingborough   40 rooms
Saunders Lodge NN10 9AP
☎ 08700 850 950 🖻 01933 57008
(on A45, eastbound)

THRAPSTON

Travelodge   40 rooms
Thrapston Bypass NN14 4UR
☎ 08700 850 950 🖻 01832 735199
(on A14 link road A1/M1)

TOWCESTER

Travelodge (Silverstone) 55 rooms
NN12 6TQ
☎ 08700 850 950 🖻 01327 359105
(A43 East Towcester by-pass)

NOTTINGHAMSHIRE

BLYTH

Travelodge   38 rooms
Hilltop Roundabout S81 8HG
☎ 08700 850 950 🖻 01909 591831
(at junct of A1M/A614)

MARKHAM MOOR
Travelodge Retford   40 rooms
DN22 0QU
☎ 08700 850 950 📠 01777 838091
(on A1 northbound)

NORTH MUSKHAM
Travelodge (Newark)   30 rooms
NG23 6HT
☎ 08700 850 950 📠 01636 703635
(3m N, on A1 southbound)

NOTTINGHAM
Travelodge (Nottingham Riverside) 61 rooms
Riverside Retail Park NG2 1RT
☎ 08700 850 950 📠 0115 986 0467
(on Riverside Retail Park)

TROWELL MOTORWAY SERVICE AREA
Travelodge Nottingham Trowell   35 rooms
NG9 3PL
☎ 08700 850 950 📠 0115 944 7815
(M1 junct 25/26 northbound)

WORKSOP
Travelodge   40 rooms
St Anne's Drive, Dukeries Drive S80 3QD
☎ 08700 850 950 📠 0870 191 1684
(on rdbt junct of A60/A57)

OXFORDSHIRE
BICESTER
Travelodge (Cherwell Valley)   98 rooms
Moto Service Area, Northampton Road, Ardley OX6 9RD
☎ 08700 850 950 📠 01869 346390
(M40 junct 10)

BURFORD
Travelodge (Cotswolds)   40 rooms
Bury Barn OX8 4JF
☎ 08700 850 950 📠 01993 822699
(A40)

OXFORD
Travelodge   150 rooms
Peartree Roundabout, Woodstock Road OX2 8JZ
☎ 08700 850 950 📠 01865 513474
(junct A34/A43)

Travelodge (Oxford East)   36 rooms
London Road, Wheatley OX33 1JH
☎ 08700 850 950 📠 01865 875905
(off A40 next to The Harvester on outskirts of Wheatley)

THAME
Travelodge   31 rooms
OX9 7XA
☎ 08700 850 950 📠 01844 218740
(A418/B4011)

RUTLAND
MORCOTT
Travelodge Uppingham   40 rooms
Uppingham LE15 8SA
☎ 08700 850 950 📠 01572 747719
(on A47, eastbound)

SHROPSHIRE
LUDLOW
Travelodge   32 rooms
Woofferton SY8 4AL
☎ 08700 850 950 📠 01584 711695
(on A49 at junct A456/B4362)

OSWESTRY
Travelodge   40 rooms
Mile End Service Area SY11 4JA
☎ 08700 850 950 📠 0870 191 1596
(junct A5/A483)

SHREWSBURY
Travelodge   40 rooms
Bayston Hill Services SY3 0DA
☎ 08700 850 950 📠 01743 874256
(A5/A49 junct)

TELFORD
Travelodge   40 rooms
Whitchurch Drive, Shawbirch TF1 3QA
☎ 08700 850 950 📠 01952 246534
(1m NW, on A5223)

SOMERSET
BATH
Travelodge Bath (Royal Oak)   66 rooms
York Buildings, George Street BA1 2EB
☎ 08700 850 950 📠 01225 442061

BECKINGTON
Travelodge   40 rooms
BA11 6SF
☎ 08700 850 950 📠 01373 830251
(on A36)

ILMINSTER
Travelodge   32 rooms
Southfields Roundabout, Horton Cross TA19 9PT
☎ 08700 850 950 📠 01460 53748
(on A303)

PODIMORE

Travelodge Yeovil   41 rooms
BA22 8JG
☎ 08700 850 950 🖹 01935 840074
(on A303, near junct with A37)

TAUNTON

Travelodge   48 rooms
Riverside Retail Park, Hankridge Farm TA1 2LR
☎ 08700 850 950 🖹 01823 444704
(M5 junct 25)

STAFFORDSHIRE

BARTON-UNDER-NEEDWOOD

Travelodge Burton-upon-Trent   20 rooms
DE13 8EG
☎ 08700 850 950 🖹 01283 716343
(on A38, northbound)

Travelodge Burton (South)   40 rooms
Rykneld Street DE13 8EH
08700 850 950 🖹 01283 716784
(on A38, southbound)

RUGELEY

Travelodge   32 rooms
Western Springs Road WS15 2AS
☎ 08700 850 950 🖹 01889 570096
(on A51/B5013)

STAFFORD MOTORWAY SERVICE AREA

Travelodge (Northbound only)   49 rooms
Moto Service Area, Eccleshall Road ST15 0EU
☎ 08700 850 950 🖹 01785 816107
(between M6 juncts 14 & 15 northbound only)

TALKE

Travelodge Stoke   62 rooms
Newcastle Road ST7 1UP
☎ 08700 850 950 🖹 01782 777000
(at junct of A34/A500)

TAMWORTH

Travelodge   62 rooms
Green Lane B77 5PS
☎ 08700 850 950 🖹 01827 260145
(A5/M42 junct 10)

UTTOXETER

Travelodge   32 rooms
Ashbourne Road ST14 5AA
☎ 08700 850 950 🖹 01889 562043
(on A50/A5030)

SUFFOLK

BARTON MILLS

Travelodge   40 rooms
Fiveways IP28 6AE
☎ 08700 850 950 🖹 01638 717675
(on A11)

IPSWICH

Travelodge (Ipswich Capel)   32 rooms
Capel St Mary IP9 2JP
☎ 08700 850 950 🖹 0870 1911542
(5m S on A12)

NEEDHAM MARKET

Travelodge Ipswich Beacon   40 rooms
Beacon Hill IP6 8LP
☎ 08700 850 950 🖹 01449 721640
(A14/A140)

STOWMARKET

Travelodge Ipswich Stowmarket   40 rooms
IP14 3PY
☎ 08700 850 950 🖹 01449 615347
(on A14 westbound)

SURREY

DORKING

Travelodge   55 rooms
Reigate Road RH4 1QB
☎ 08700 850 950 🖹 01306 741673
(0.5m E, on A25)

LEATHERHEAD

Travelodge (Leatherhead)   91 rooms
The Swan Centre, High Street KT22 8AA
☎ 0870 191 1748 🖹 01372 386577

STAINES

Travelodge   65 rooms
Hale Street, Two Rivers Retail Park TW18 4UW
☎ 08700 850 950 🖹 01784 491 026
(M25 junct 13, take B376 to Staines, Travelodge located in Two Rivers Retail Park.)

SUSSEX, EAST

BRIGHTON

Travelodge Brighton Central   94 rooms
Preston Road BN1 6AU
☎ 08700 850 950 🖹 01273 554917

HAILSHAM

Travelodge Hellingly Eastbourne   58 rooms
Boship Roundabout, Hellingly BN27 4DT
☎ 08700 850 950 🖹 01323 844556
(on A22 at Boship rdbt)

SUSSEX, WEST

CRAWLEY
Travelodge Gatwick Airport   186 rooms
Church Road, Lowfield Heath RH11 0PQ
☎ 08700 850 950   🖷 01293 535369
(M23 junct 10, 1m S off A23)

FIVE OAKS
Travelodge Billingshurst   26 rooms
Staines Street RH14 9AE
☎ 08700 850 950   🖷 01403 782711
(on A29, northbound, 1m N of Billingshurst)

FONTWELL
Travelodge Bognor Regis   62 rooms
BN18 0SB
☎ 08700 850 950   🖷 01243 543973
(on A27/A29 rdbt)

HICKSTEAD
Travelodge   55 rooms
Jobs Lane RH17 5NX
☎ 08700 850 950 🖷 01444 881377
(A23 southbound)

RUSTINGTON
Travelodge Littlehampton   36 rooms
Worthing Road BN17 6LZ
☎ 08700 850 950   🖷 01903 733150
(on A259, 1m E of Littlehampton)

TYNE & WEAR

NEWCASTLE UPON TYNE
Travelodge (Newcastle Central)   120 rooms
Forster Street NE1 2NH
☎ 08700 850 950   🖷 0191 261 7105

SEATON BURN
Travelodge (Newcastle North)   40 rooms
Front Street NE13 6ED
☎ 08700 850 950   🖷 0191 217 0107

SUNDERLAND
Travelodge Low Row SR1 3PT   60 rooms
☎ 08700 850 950   🖷 0191 514 3453

WARDLEY
Travelodge Newcastle East   71 rooms
Leam Lane, Whitemare Pool NE10 8YB
☎ 08700 850 950   🖷 0191 438 3333
(at junct of A194M/A184)

WASHINGTON SERVICE AREA
Travelodge (South)   36 rooms
Portobello DH3 2SJ
☎ 08700 850 950   🖷 0191 410 0057
(A1(M))

Travelodge (North)   31 rooms
Motorway Service Area Portobello DH3 2SJ
☎ 08700 850 950   🖷 0191 410 9258
(northbound carriageway of A1(M))

WARWICKSHIRE

ALCESTER
Travelodge Stratford Alcester   66 rooms
Oversley Mill Roundabout B49 6AA
☎ 08700 850 950   🖷 01789 766987
(at junct A46/A435)

DUNCHURCH
Travelodge Rugby   40 rooms
London Road, Thurlaston CV23 9LG
☎ 08700 850 950   🖷 01788 521538
(A45, westbound)

NUNEATON
Travelodge Bedworth   40 rooms
Bedworth CV10 7TF
☎ 08700 850 950   🖷 024 7638 2541
(2m S, on A444)

Travelodge   28 rooms
St Nicholas Park Drive CV11 6EN
☎ 08700 850 950   🖷 0870 1911594
(on A47)

WEST MIDLANDS

BIRMINGHAM
Travelodge (Birmingham Central)   136 rooms
230 Broad Street B15 1AY
☎ 08700 850 950   🖷 0121 644 5251

Travelodge (Birmingham East)   40 rooms
A45 Coventry Road, Acocks Green, Yardley B26 1DS
☎ 08700 850 950   🖷 0121 764 5882

DUDLEY
Travelodge Birmingham Dudley   32 rooms
Dudley Road, Brierley Hill DY5 1LQ
☎ 08700 850 950   🖷 0870 1911563
(3m W, on A461)

FRANKLEY MOTORWAY SERVICE AREA
Travelodge Birmingham South   62 rooms
Illey Lane, Frankley Motorway Service Area, Frankley
B32 4AR
☎ 08700 850 950   🖷 0121 501 2880
(between junct 3 and 4 on southbound carriageway of M5)

HILTON PARK MOTORWAY SERVICE AREA
Travelodge Birmingham North   63 rooms
Hilton Park Services (M6), Essington WV11 2AT
☎ 08700 850 950   🖷 01922 701967
(M6 between junct 10a & 11)

Travelodge

OLDBURY
Travelodge   33 rooms
Wolverhampton Road B69 2BH
☎ 08700 850 950 📠 0121 552 2967
(on A4123, northbound off junct 2 of M5)

SUTTON COLDFIELD
Travelodge Boldmere Road B73 5UP 32 rooms
☎ 08700 850 950 📠 0121 355 0017
(2m S, on B4142)

WILTSHIRE
AMESBURY
Travelodge   48 rooms
Countess Services SP4 7AS
☎ 08700 850 950 📠 01980 625273
(junct A345 & A303 eastbound)

LEIGH DELAMERE MOTORWAY SERVICE AREA
Travelodge Chippenham (Westbound) 31 rooms
Service Area SN14 6LB
☎ 08700 850 950 📠 01666 838529
(Between J17 & J18 on M4)

Travelodge Chippenham (Eastbound) 69 rooms
SN14 6LB
☎ 08700 850 950 📠 01666 837112
(Between junc 17 & 18 on the M4)

WARMINSTER
Travelodge   31 rooms
A36 Bath Road BA12 7RU
☎ 08700 850 950 📠 01985 214380
(junct A350/A36)

WORCESTERSHIRE
DROITWICH
Travelodge   32 rooms
Rashwood Hill WR9 8DA
☎ 08700 850 950 📠 01527 861807

HARTLEBURY
Travelodge   32 rooms
Shorthill Nurseries DY13 9SH
☎ 08700 850 950 📠 01299 251774
(A449 southbound)

YORKSHIRE, EAST RIDING OF
SOUTH CAVE
Travelodge Hull   40 rooms
Beacon Service Area HU15 1RZ
☎ 08700 850 950 📠 01430 424455
(at services on A63 eastbound)

YORKSHIRE, NORTH
BARNSDALE BAR SERVICE AREA
Travelodge Pontefract (Barnsdale Bar) 56 rooms
Wentbridge WF8 3QQ
☎ 08700 850 950 📠 01977 620711
(on A1, southbound)

BILBROUGH
Travelodge York   62 rooms
Tadcaster LS24 8EG
☎ 08700 850 950 📠 0870 1911685
(A64 eastbound)

HARROGATE
Travelodge (Harrogate)   46 rooms
The Gubbel HG1 2RF
☎ 0870 1911737 📠 01423562734

SCOTCH CORNER
Travelodge Skeeby (Scotch Corner) 40 rooms
Skeeby DL10 5EQ
☎ 08700 850 950 📠 0870 1911675
(0.5m S on A1)

Travelodge   50 rooms
Middleton Tyas Lane DL10 6PQ
☎ 08700 850 950 📠 01325 377616
(A1/A66)

SKIPTON
Travelodge Gargrave Road BD23 1UD 32 rooms
☎ 08700 850 950 📠 0870 1911676
(A65/A59 rdbt)

YORK
Travelodge (York Central)   90 rooms
90 Piccadilly YO1 9NX
☎ 08700 850 950 📠 01904 652171

YORKSHIRE, SOUTH
BARNSLEY
Travelodge School Street S70 3PE   32 rooms
☎ 08700 850 950 📠 01226 298799
(at Stairfoot rdbt A633/A635)

CARCROFT
Travelodge Doncaster   40 rooms
Great North Road DN6 9LF
☎ 08700 850 950 📠 0870 1911631
(on A1 northbound)

DONCASTER
Travelodge (Doncaster North)   39 rooms
DN8 5GS
☎ 08700 850 950 📠 01302 845469
(M18 junct 5)

SHEFFIELD
Travelodge   67 rooms
340 Prince of Wales Road S2 1FF
☏ 08700 850 950 🖹 0114 253 0935
(follow A630, take turn off for ring road & services)

YORKSHIRE, WEST
FERRYBRIDGE SERVICE AREA
Travelodge Pontefract Ferrybridge   36 rooms
WF11 0AF
☏ 08700 850 950 🖹 01977 622509
(M62 junct 33)

HALIFAX
Travelodge (Halifax Central)   52 rooms
Dean Clough Park HX3 5AY
☏ 08700 850 950 🖹 01422 362669

HUDDERSFIELD
Travelodge   27 rooms
Leeds Road, Mirfield WF14 0BY
☏ 08700 850 950 🖹 01924 489921
(M62 junct 25, follow A62 across 2 rdbts. Lodge on right)

LEEDS
Travelodge Leeds (Central)   100 rooms
Blaydes Court, Blaydes Yard,
off Swinegate LS1 4AD
☏ 08700 850 950 🖹 0113 246 0076

Travelodge Leeds (East)   60 rooms
Stile Hill Way, Colton LS15 9JA
☏ 08700 850 950 🖹 0113 264 8839

PUDSEY
Travelodge Bradford   48 rooms
1 Mid Point, Dick Lane BD3 8QD
☏ 08700 850 950 🖹 01274 665436

WOOLLEY EDGE MOTORWAY SERVICE AREA
Travelodge Wakefield (Southbound)   41 rooms
M1 Service Area Southbound, West Bretton WF4 4LQ
☏ 08700 850 950 🖹 01924 830174

Travelodge Wakefield (Northbound) 32 rooms
M1 Service Area, West Bretton WF4 4LQ
☏ 08700 850 950 🖹 01924 830609
(between junct 38/39, adj to service area)

NORTHERN IRELAND
BELFAST
BELFAST
Travelodge   90 rooms
15 Brunswick Street BT2 7GE
☏ 08700 850 950 🖹 028 9023 2999
*(from M2 follow city centre signs to Oxford St turn right to
May St, Brunswick St is 4th on left)*

CO LONDONDERRY
LONDONDERRY
Travelodge   39 rooms
22-24 Strand Road BT47 2AB
☏ 08700 850 950 🖹 01287 127 1277
*(approx 0.5m from Guildhall adjacent to shopping
centre/cinema)*

REPUBLIC OF IRELAND
CO CORK
CORK
Travelodge   60 rooms
Blackash
☏ 08700 850 950 🖹 021 4310723
(at rdbt junct of South Ring Road/Kinsale Rd R600)

CO DUBLIN
DUBLIN
Travelodge Dublin Airport   100 rooms
Swords By-Pass
☏ 08700 850 950 🖹 01 8409235
(on N1 Dublin/Belfast road)

Travelodge Dublin (Navan Road)   100 rooms
Auburn Avenue Roundabout, Navan Road
☏ 08700 850 950

CO GALWAY
GALWAY
Travelodge
Tuam Road
☏ 08700 850 950

CO WATERFORD
WATERFORD
Travelodge   32 rooms
Cork Road
☏ 08700 850 950 🖹 051 358890
(on N25, 1km from Waterford Glass Visitors Centre)

SCOTLAND
ABERDEEN CITY
ABERDEEN
Travelodge (Aberdeen West)   48 rooms
Inverurie Road, Bucksburn AB21 9BB
☏ 08700 850 950 🖹 01224 715609

Travelodge   97 rooms
9 Bridge St AB11 6JL
☏ 08700 850 950 🖹 01224 584587

Travelodge

CITY OF EDINBURGH

EDINBURGH

Travelodge (Edinburgh East)   45 rooms
Old Craighall EH21 8RE
☎ 08700 850 950 🖷 0131 653 6106
(off A1, 2m from E outskirts)

Travelodge (Edinburgh South)   72 rooms
46 Dreghorn Link EH13 9QR
☎ 08700 850 950 🖷 0131 441 4296
(6m S, A720 Ring Rd S)

Travelodge (Edinburgh Central)   193 rooms
33 Saint Marys Street EH1 1TA
☎ 08700 850 950 🖷 0131 557 3681

CITY OF GLASGOW

GLASGOW

Travelodge (Glasgow Airport)   98 rooms
Marchburn Drive, Glasgow Airport Business Park, Paisley
PA3 2AR
☎ 08700 850 950 🖷 0141 889 0583

Travelodge (Glasgow Paisley Road)   75 rooms
251 Paisley Road G5 8RA
☎ 08700 850 950 🖷 0141 420 3884
*(0.5m from city centre just off M8 junct 20 from S, M8
junct 21 M8 from N. Behind Harry Ramsden)*

Travelodge (Glasgow Central)   95 rooms
9 Hill Street G3 6PR
☎ 08700 850 950 🖷 0141 333 1221

DUMFRIES & GALLOWAY

DUMFRIES

Travelodge   40 rooms
Annan Road, Collin DG1 3SE
08700 850 950 🖷 01387 750658
(on A75)

DUNDEE CITY

DUNDEE

Travelodge   32 rooms
A90 Kingsway DD2 4TD
☎ 08700 850 950 🖷 01382 610488
(on A90)

EAST AYRSHIRE

KILMARNOCK

Travelodge   40 rooms
Kilmarnock By Pass KA1 5LQ
☎ 08700 850 950 🖷 01563 573810
(at Bellfield Interchange just off A77)

HIGHLAND

INVERNESS

Travelodge   50 rooms
Stoneyfield A96 Inverness Road IV2 7PA
☎ 08700 850 950 🖷 01463 718152
(Junct of A9 / A96)

PERTH & KINROSS

KINROSS

Travelodge   35 rooms
Kincardine Road KY13 7NQ
☎ 08700 850 950 🖷 01577 861641
(on A977, M90 junct 6 Turthills Tourist Centre)

PERTH

Travelodge PH2 0LP
☎ 08700 850 950 🖷 01738 444783

STIRLING

STIRLING

Travelodge   37 rooms
Pirnhall Roundabout Snabhead FK7 8EU
☎ 08700 850 950 🖷 01786 817646
(junct M9/M80)

WEST DUNBARTONSHIRE

DUMBARTON

Travelodge Milton G82 2TZ   32 rooms
☎ 08700 850 950 🖷 01389 765202
(1m E, on A82 westbound)

WALES

BRIDGEND

PENCOED

Travelodge   39 rooms
Old Mill, Felindre Road CF3 5HU
☎ 08700 850 950 🖷 01656 864404
(on A473)

CARDIFF

CARDIFF

Travelodge (Cardiff West)   50 rooms
Granada Service Area M4, Pontyclun CF72 8SA
☎ 08700 850 950 🖷 029 2089 9412
(M4, junct 33/A4232)

Travelodge (Cardiff East)   32 rooms
Circle Way East, Llanedeyrn CF23 9PD
☎ 08700 850 950 🖷 029 2054 9564
*(M4 junct 30, take A4232 to North Pentwyn Interchange.
A48 & signs for Cardiff East & Docks. 3rd exit at
Llanedeyrn Interchange, follow Circle Way East)*

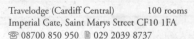

Travelodge (Cardiff Central)   100 rooms
Imperial Gate, Saint Marys Street CF10 1FA
☏ 08700 850 950   🖷 029 2039 8737

CROSS HANDS
Travelodge Llanelli   32 rooms
SA14 6NW
☏ 08700 850 950   🖷 0870 191 1729
(on A48, westbound)

ST CLEARS
Travelodge (Carmarthen)   32 rooms
Tenby Road SA33 4JN
☏ 08700 850 950   🖷 01994 231227

FLINTSHIRE
HALKYN
Travelodge CH8 8RF   31 rooms
☏ 08700 850 950   🖷 01352 781966
(on A55, westbound)

NORTHOP HALL
Travelodge   40 rooms
CH7 6HB
☏ 08700 850 950   01244 816473
(on A55, eastbound)

GWYNEDD
BANGOR
Travelodge   62 rooms
Llys-y-Gwynt LL57 4BG
☏ 08700 850 950   🖷 0870 1911561
(junct A5/A55)

MONMOUTHSHIRE
MAGOR
Travelodge   43 rooms
Magor Service Area NP26 3YL
☏ 08700 850 950   🖷 01633 881896
(M4 junct 23A)

RAGLAN
Travelodge Monmouth   43 rooms
Granada Services A40, Nr Monmouth NP5 4BG
☏ 08700 850 950   🖷 01600 740329
(on A40 near junct with A449)

SWANSEA
SWANSEA
Travelodge   50 rooms
Penllergaer SA4 1GT
☏ 08700 850 950   🖷 01792 898972
(M4 junct 47)

WREXHAM
WREXHAM
Travelodge   32 rooms
Wrexham By-Pass, Rhostyllen LL14 4EJ
☏ 08700 850 950   🖷 01978 365705
(2m S, A483/A5152 rdbt)

TULIP INN Tulip Inn

ENGLAND
GREATER MANCHESTER
MANCHESTER
Tulip Inn   121 rooms
Old Pack Lane, Manchester M17 8PG
☏ 0161 755 3355   🖷 0161 755 3344
e:info@tulipinnmanchester.co.uk
(from M60 J10 towards Trafford Centre)

SCOTLAND
CITY OF GLASGOW
GLASGOW
Tulip Inn   114 rooms
80, Balllater Street Glasgow G5 0TW
☏ 0141 429 4233   🖷 0141 429 4244
e:info@tulipinnglasgow.co.uk
*(From Glasgow Airport M8 J21 follow signs for East
Kilbride, turn R onto A8 along Kingston St, turn R onto
South Portland St, L to Norfolk St, straight through onto
Ballater St)*

Welcome Break
0800 731 446

Good quality, modern budget accommodation at motorway services.

ENGLAND

BUCKINGHAMSHIRE

MILTON KEYNES

Welcome Lodge   90 rooms
Newport Pagnell MK16 8DS
☎ 01908 610878 📄 01908 216539
e:newport.hotel@welcomebreak.co.uk
*(M1 junct 14-15. In service area - follow signs to Barrier
Lodge)*

CHESHIRE

BURTONWOOD MOTORWAY SERVICE AREA

Welcome Lodge   39 rooms
Burtonwood Services (M62), Great Sankey WA5 3AX
☎ 01925 710376 📄 01925 710378
e:burtonwood.hotel@welcomebreak.co.uk
(between M62 junct 7-9)

LANCASHIRE

CHORLEY

Welcome Lodge   100 rooms
Welcome Break Service Area PR7 5LR
☎ 01257 791746 📄 01257 793596
e:charnockhotel@welcomebreak.co.uk
*(between junct 27 & 28 of M6 northb'd. 500yds from
Camelot Theme Park via Mill Lane)*

WALES

BRIDGEND

BRIDGEND

Welcome Lodge   40 rooms
Sarn Park Services CF32 9RW
☎ 01656 659218 📄 01656 768665
e:sarnpark.hotel@welcomebreak.co.uk
(M4 junct 36)

England

BEDFORDSHIRE

England

Babies Welcome | **Children's Dishes**

◎ ◎ Paris House Restaurant
Woburn Park MK17 9QP
☎ 01525 290692 🖷 01525 290471
e-mail: gailbaker@parishouse.co.uk
web: www.parishouse.co.uk
Dir: M1 J13. From Woburn take A4012 Hockliffe, 1.75m out of Woburn village on L

CHILD FACILITIES: Outdoor play area Food/bottle warming Ch menu Ch portions Highchairs Ch cutlery **NEARBY:** Woburn Safari Park Cinema

🍴 The Chequers
Pertenhall Rd, Brook End MK44 2HR
☎ 01234 708678 🖷 01234 708678
e-mail: Chequers.keysoe@tesco.net
Dir: On B660 N of Bedford

CHILD FACILITIES: Please telephone for details

OPEN: 11.30-2.30 6.30-11 **BAR MEALS:** L served Wed-Mon 12-2 D served Wed-Mon 7-9.45 **FACILITIES:** Garden: Patio & grassed area fenced off from car park ✖ **PARKING:** 50

FOOD: Classic French **STYLE:** Country-house **SEATS:** 48
OPEN: 12-2/7-9.45, Closed Feb, Mon, D Sun **RESTAURANT:** Fixed L £20, Fixed D £55 **NOTES:** ⊗ in restaurant **PARKING:** 24

Children's Dishes

🍴 The Globe Inn
Globe Ln, Old Linslade LU7 2TA
☎ 01525 373338 🖷 01525 850551
Dir: A5 S to Dunstable, follow signs to Leighton Buzzard (A4146)

CHILD FACILITIES: Activities: colouring, bouncy castle (w/ends summer hols) Outdoor play area Ch menu Ch portions Highchairs **NEARBY:** Canal walks and feeding ducks

OPEN: 11-3 (Jan-Feb 12-3, 6-11, Summer 11-11) 6-11 (Sun 12-10.30) **BAR MEALS:** L served all week 12-9 D served all week 12-9 Av main course £7.50 **RESTAURANT:** L served all week 12-3 D served all week 6-9 Av 3 course à la carte £20 **FACILITIES:** Garden: Large, seats approx 200 **PARKING:** 150

Babies Welcome | **Children's Dishes**

🍴 The White Horse
High St SG18 9LD
☎ 01462 813364
e-mail: jack@ravenathexton.f9.co.uk

CHILD FACILITIES: Activities: Outdoor play area Food/bottle warming Ch menu Highchairs Ch cutlery Safe grounds Changing facilities

OPEN: 11-3 6-11 (Sun 12-10.30, all day BH's) **BAR MEALS:** L served all week 12-2 D served all week 6.10-10 Av main course £7.50 **FACILITIES:** Garden: Large grassed area with trees & seating **PARKING:** 40

How to use this guide & abbreviations are explained on pages 5-7

BERKSHIRE

Windsor Castle

BRACKNELL
The Look Out Discovery Centre RG12 7QW
thelookout@bracknell-forest.gov.uk ☎01344 354400
(3m S of town centre. From M3 junct 3, take A322
to Bracknell and from M4 junct 10, take A329(M)
to Bracknell. Follow brown tourist signs)
Open all year (Closed 24-26 Dec). £4.80 (ch &
concessions £3.20). Family (2 adults + 2 ch or 1
adult + 3 ch) £12.80.

HAMPSTEAD NORREYS
The Living Rainforest RG18 0TN
enquiries@livingrainforest.org ☎01635 202444
(follow brown tourist signs from M4/A34)
Open daily 10-5.15. (Closed from 1pm 24 Dec &
25-26 Dec)

READING
Museum of English Rural Life RG6 6AG
merl@reading.ac.uk ☎0118 378 8660
(2m SE on A327)
Open all year, Tue-Sat, 10-1 & 2-4.30. (Closed
BHs & Xmas-New Year).

RISELEY
Wellington Country Park RG7 1SP
info@wellington-county-park.co.uk ☎0118 932 6444
(signposted off A33, between Reading &
Basingstoke)
Open Mar-Oct, daily 10-5.30, £4.80 (ch £2.50)

WINDSOR
Legoland Windsor SL4 4AY
sales@legoland.co.uk ☎08705 040404
(on B3022 Windsor to Ascot road well signposted
from M3 junct 3 & M4 junct 6)
Open daily 20 Mar-Oct. Adult £21-£23 (ch under
3 free, ch 3-15 & pen £19-£20. Tickets can be
booked in advance by telephoning 08705 040404.
Windsor Castle SL4 1NJ
windsorcastle@royalcollection.org.uK ☎020 7766 7304
(M4 junct 6 & M3 junct 3)
Open all year, daily except Good Friday & 25-26
Dec. Nov-Feb, 9.45-4.15 (last admission 3), Mar-
Oct 9.45-5.15 (last admission 4). As Windsor
Castle is a royal residence the opening
arrangements may be subject to change at short
notice. £12 (ch 5-16 £6, under 5's free, pen &
stdents £10) Fam ticket £30 (2 adults & 2 ch).

BRACKNELL
Map 04 SU86

★★★★ 73% ⊛ ⊛ Coppid Beech
John Nike Way RG12 8TF
☎ 01344 303333 📠 01344 301200
e-mail: welcome@coppid-beech-hotel.co.uk
web: www.coppidbeech.com
*Dir: M4 junct 10 take Wokingham/Bracknell onto A329. In 2m take B3408
to Binfield at rdbt. Hotel 200yds on right*

CHILD FACILITIES: Please telephone for details

This chalet-style complex offers extensive facilities and includes a
ski-slope, ice rink, nightclub, health club and Bier Keller. Bedrooms
offer a range of suites and standard rooms, all of which are
impressively equipped. A choice of dining is offered and a full
bistro menu is available in the Keller. For more formal dining
Rowan's restaurant provides award-winning cuisine.
ROOMS: 205 en suite (6 fmly) ⊛ in 138 bedrooms s £110-£175;
d £120-£195 (incl. bkfst) **LB FACILITIES: Spa** STV ⊡ Sauna Solarium
Gym Jacuzzi Dry ski slope, Ice rink ♫ Xmas **PARKING:** 350

BRAY
Map 04 SU97

★★★★ 64% ⊛ Monkey Island
Old Mill Ln SL6 2EE
☎ 01628 623400 📠 01628 784732
e-mail: info@monkeyisland.co.uk
*Dir: M4 junct 8/9/A308 signed Windsor. 1st left into Bray, 1st right into Old
Mill Lane, opp Crown pub*

CHILD FACILITIES: Please telephone for details

This riverside hotel is charmingly set on an island in the Thames,
within easy reach of major routes. Access is by footbridge or boat,
but there is a large car park nearby. The hotel comprises two
buildings, one for accommodation and the other for dining and
drinking. Ample grounds are beautifully maintained and provide a
peaceful haven for wildlife.
ROOMS: 26 en suite (1 fmly) (12 GF) **FACILITIES:** STV Fishing ⏃
Boating ♫ Xmas **PARKING:** 100 **NOTES:** ✖ ⊛ in restaurant

COOKHAM
Map 04 SU88

Babies Welcome	Children's Dishes

⊛ ⊛ Malik's
High St SL6 9SF
☎ 01628 520085 📠 01628 529321
Dir: M4 J7, take A4 towards Maidenhead, 2 miles

CHILD FACILITIES: Food/bottle warming Ch menu Ch portions Highchairs Ch cutlery NEARBY: River walks Boulters Lock

FOOD: Indian **STYLE:** Classic **SEATS:** 70 **OPEN:** 12-2.30/6-11.00, Closed
25-26 Dec **RESTAURANT:** Fixed L £9.95, Fixed D £25, main £7.25-£15.95
NOTES: ⊛ area **PARKING:** 26

England

HUNGERFORD
Map 04 SU36

◆◆◆◆ 🍽 **Crown & Garter**
Great Common, Inkpen RG17 9QR
☎ 01488 668325
e-mail: gill.hern@btopenworld.com
web: www.crownandgarter.com
Dir: turn off A4 into Kintbury, turn opposite corner stores onto Inkpen Road, straight ahead for 2m, do not turn off this road

CHILD FACILITIES: Activities: toys, colouring Outdoor play area Food/bottle warming Ch menu Ch portions Highchairs Ch discounts Safe grounds Videos Family rms D rm with Z bed £85 Ch drinks Connecting rms **NEARBY:** Legoland Beale Park

Peacefully located in the attractive village of Inkpen, this charming 17th-century inn has a hop-draped bar where interesting well-prepared dishes are offered. The bedrooms, which are around a pretty garden, are more contemporary and are well equipped.
ROOMS: 8 annexe en suite (8 GF) s fr £50; d fr £70 * 🚭
FACILITIES: TVB tea/coffee No coaches Dinner Last d order 9.30pm
NOTES: 🚭 in restaurant Cen ht **LB PARKING:** 40

Children's Dishes

🍽 **The Swan Inn ◆◆◆◆**
Craven Rd, Lower Green, Inkpen RG17 9DX
☎ 01488 668326 📠 01488 668306
e-mail: enquiries@theswaninn-organics.co.uk
web: www.//theswaninn-organics.co.uk
Dir: S down Hungerford High St, L to common, R on common, pub 3m

CHILD FACILITIES: Outdoor play area Food/bottle warming Ch menu Ch portions Safe grounds Changing facilities **NEARBY:** Parks Walks

OPEN: 12-2.30 (Sat-Sun 12-3) 5-11 (Mon-Tue-7-11, Sun 7-10.30 All day weekends summer) Closed: 25-26 Dec **BAR MEALS:** L served all week 12-2 D served all week 7-9.30 **RESTAURANT:** L served Wed-Sun 12-2.30 12-2.30 D served Wed-Sat 7-9.30 7-9.30 Av 3 course à la carte £25
FACILITIES: Garden: Garden, terraces, both seating & tables 🐾
ROOMS: 10 bedrooms 10 en suite 2 family rooms s£40 d£75
PARKING: 50

READING
Map 04 SU77

🍽 **Fishermans Cottage**
224 Kennet Side RG1 3DW
☎ 0118 9571553 📠 0118 9571553
Dir: L from Kings Rd into Orts Rd then Canal Way

CHILD FACILITIES: Please telephone for details

OPEN: 12-11 (Sun 12-10.30, Jan-Feb closed Mon eve) **BAR MEALS:** L served all week 12-2.30 D served all week 6-9 Av main course £6
FACILITIES: Garden: **PARKING:** 10

STANFORD DINGLEY
Map 04 SU57

Babies Welcome **Children's Dishes**

🍽 **The Old Boot Inn**
RG7 6LT
☎ 01189 744292 📠 01189 744292
Dir: M4 J12, A4/A340 to Pangbourne. 1st L to Bradfield. Through Bradfield & follow signs for Stanford Dingley

CHILD FACILITIES: Outdoor play area Food/bottle warming Ch menu Ch portions Highchairs Ch cutlery Safe grounds **NEARBY:** Bucklebury Farm Park

continued

OPEN: 11-3 6-11 (Sun 12-3, 7-10.30) **BAR/RESTAURANT MEALS:** L served all week 12-2.15 D served all week 7-9.30
FACILITIES: Garden: 0.5 acre over-looking farmland **PARKING:** 40

WINDSOR
Map 04 SU97

Family Rooms

◆◆◆ Clarence Hotel
9 Clarence Rd SL4 5AE
☎ 01753 864436 📠 01753 857060
web: www.clarence-hotel.co.uk
Dir: M4 junct 6 follow dual-carriageway to Windsor, turn left at 1st rdbt

CHILD FACILITIES: Family area Food/bottle warming Safe grounds Family rms D rms with 1 or 2 S beds from £70 Connecting rms Laundry **NEARBY:** Legoland Chessington World of Adventure Thorpe Park

This Grade II listed Victorian town house is in the heart of Windsor. Space in some rooms is limited, but all are well maintained. Facilities include a lounge and a steam room. Breakfast is served in the dining room overlooking attractive gardens.
ROOMS: 20 en suite (6 fmly) (2 GF) s £40-£62; d £49-£72 *
FACILITIES: TVB tea/coffee TVL Sauna Steam room **NOTES:** 🚭 in restaurant Licensed Cen ht **PARKING:** 4

BRISTOL

BRISTOL
Map 03 ST57

Babies Welcome **Family Rooms** **Children's Dishes**

★★★★ 67%
Bristol Marriott City Centre
Lower Castle St BS1 3AD
☎ 0870 400 7210 📠 0870 400 7310
Dir: M32 follow signs to Broadmead, take slip road to rdbt, take 3rd exit

CHILD FACILITIES: Activities: Ch pack Food/bottle warming Ch menu Highchairs Ch discounts under 12s free Safe ground Family rms

Marriott
HOTELS · RESORTS · SUITES

Situated at the foot of the picturesque Castle Park, this hotel is well-placed for the city centre. Free parking is available for residents along with complimentary membership of the hotel's leisure club. In addition to a coffee bar and lounge menu, the Mediterrano restaurant offers an interesting selection of dishes.
ROOMS: 294 en suite (138 fmly) 🚭 in 221 bedrooms s fr £129; d fr £129 **LB FACILITIES:** Spa STV 🔲 Sauna Solarium Gym Jacuzzi Steam room **NOTES:** 🐾 🚭 in restaurant

BRISTOL, continued

England

Babies Welcome | **Children's Dishes**

◎ ◎ Bells Diner
1-3 York Rd, Montpellier BS6 5QB
☎ 0117 924 0357 ▤ 0117 924 4280
e-mail: info@bellsdiner.com
Dir: Telephone for further details

CHILD FACILITIES: **Activities:** crayons Food/bottle warming
Ch portions Highchairs Ch cutlery **NEARBY:** Park Paddling pool

FOOD: Mediterranean, European **STYLE:** Rustic **SEATS:** 60
OPEN: 12-2.30/7-10.30, Closed 24-30 Dec, SunL Mon & Sat
RESTAURANT: main £12.50-£19 **NOTES:** Smart Dress, ⊗ in restaurant,
⊗ area **PARKING:** On street

Babies Welcome | **Children's Dishes**

◎ riverstation
The Grove BS1 4RB
☎ 0117 914 4434 ▤ 0117 934 9990
e-mail: relax@riverstation.co.uk
Dir: Telephone for directions

CHILD FACILITIES: **Activities:** crayons Food/bottle warming
Ch menu (on request) Ch portions Highchairs Changing facilities
NEARBY: SS Great Britain Industrial museum @ Bristol

FOOD: Modern European **STYLE:** Modern Minimalist **SEATS:** 120
OPEN: 12-2.30/6-10.30, Closed Xmas, 1 Jan **RESTAURANT:** Fixed L
£11.50, main £12-£17.50 **NOTES:** ⊗ area **PARKING:** Pay & display, meter
parking opposite

All AA listed accommodation, restaurants
and pubs can be found on the AA's
website www.theAA.com

AA
The Pub Guide 2005

Over 2,500 pubs
hand-picked for their
great food and
authentic character.

www.theAA.com

Just AA sk.

AA
The Restaurant Guide 2005

The right choice
every time with this
invaluable guide for
food lovers.

www.theAA.com

Just AA sk.

BUCKINGHAMSHIRE

Bekonscot Model Village

BEACONSFIELD
Bekonscot Model Village HP9 2PL
bekonscot@dial.pipex.com ☎01494 672919
(2.7m M40 junct 2, 4m M25 junct 16)
Open mid Feb-Oct, 10-5. £5.30
(ch £3.20 concessions, students £4)

CHALFONT ST GILES
Chiltern Open Air Museum HP8 4AB
coamuseum@netscape.net ☎01494 871117
(M25 junct 17, M40 junct 2. Follow brown signs)
Open 31 Mar-Oct, daily 10-5.

CLIVEDEN
Cliveden SL6 0JA
cliveden@ntrust.org.uk ☎01628 605069
(2m N of Taplow, follow brown signs on A4)
Grounds 15 Mar-Oct daily 11-6, Nov-Dec daily
11-4 (Woodlands open all year). House Apr-Oct,
Thu & Sun 3-5.30 by timed ticket. Grounds: £7.50
House: £1 extra. Family ticket £17.20.

QUAINTON
Buckingham Railway Centre HP22 4BY
bucksrailcentre@btopenworld.com ☎01296 655720
(Off A41. 7m NW of Aylesbury)
Open with engines in steam Apr-Oct, Sun & BH
Mon; Jun-Aug, Wed; 10.30-5.30. Dec Sat & Sun
Santa's Magical Steamings-advanced booking
recommended. Also open for static viewing Wed-
Sun. Steaming Days; £6 (ch & pen £4). Family
ticket £18. BH wknds £7 (ch & pen £5). Family
ticket £20. Static viewing £3 (ch & pen £2).

STOWE
Stowe House MK18 5EH
sses@stowe.co.uk
(3m NW Buckingham) ☎01280 818282
Open 14-16 Mar, 25-31 May, 4 Sep-19 Oct, 14-16
Nov, daily (ex Mon & Tue, but open May BH Mon)
for guided tours only at 2pm; 3-27 Apr & 9 Jul-3
Sep, Wed-Sun 12-5 and daily tours at 2pm.

WEST WYCOMBE
The Hell-Fire Caves
HP14 3AJ ☎ 01494 524411
mary@west-wycombe-estate.co.uk
(On A40, West Wycombe)
Open all year, Mar-Oct, daily 11-6; Nov-Feb, Sat
& Sun 1-5. £4 (ch, pen & students £3). Family
ticket £12 (max 3 ch)

England

AMERSHAM
Map 04 SU99

Babies Welcome | **Children's Dishes**

◖ The Hit or Miss
Penn St Village HP7 0PX
☎ 01494 713109 ▤ 01494 718010
e-mail: enquiries@hitormiss.fsnet
Dir: Off the A404 Amersham-Wycombe Rd.

CHILD FACILITIES: Activities: colouring books, toddler toys Food/bottle warming Ch menu Ch portions Highchairs Safe grounds Changing facilities **NEARBY:** Odds Farm Animal Park Bekonscot Model Village

OPEN: 11-11 (Sun 12-10.30) **BAR MEALS:** L served all week 12-2.30 D served all week 6.45-9.30 Av main course £10 **RESTAURANT:** L served all week 12-2.30 D served all week 6.45-9.30 Av 3 course à la carte £19 **FACILITIES:** Garden: Lawn, patio area with picnic tables **PARKING:** 40

BUCKINGHAM
Map 04 SP63

Babies Welcome | **Children's Dishes**

◖ The Old Thatched Inn
Adstock MK18 2JN
☎ 01296 712584 ▤ 01296 715375

CHILD FACILITIES: Food/bottle warming Ch menu Ch portions Highchairs Safe grounds **NEARBY:** Stowe National Trust Gardens Cinemas

OPEN: 12-3 6-11 (open all day bank holidays & weekends) **BAR MEALS:** L served all week 12-2.35 D served all week 6-9.30 Av main course £10.95 **RESTAURANT:** L served all week 12-2.30 D served all week 6-9.30 Av 3 course à la carte £20 **FACILITIES:** Children's licence Garden: Floral terrace with tables, lawned area **PARKING:** 20

CHALFONT ST GILES
Map 04 SU99

Babies Welcome | **Children's Dishes**

◖ Ivy House
London Rd HP8 4RS
☎ 01494 872184 ▤ 01494 872870
web: www.theivyhouse-bucks.co.uk
Dir: On A413 2m S of Amersham & 1.5m N of Chalfont St Giles

CHILD FACILITIES: Activities: colouring, toddler toys Outdoor play area Food/bottle warming Ch menu Ch portions (where poss) Highchairs Ch cutlery Changing facilities **NEARBY:** Bekonscot Model Village Chiltern Open Air Museum

OPEN: 12-3.30 6-11 (Sat 12-11, Sun 12-10.30) **BAR MEALS:** L served all week 12-2.30 D served all week 6.30-9.30 **RESTAURANT:** L served all week 12-2.30 D served all week 6.30-9.30 Av 3 course à la carte £24 **FACILITIES:** Garden: Courtyard & garden with outstanding views **PARKING:** 45

CHESHAM
Map 04 SP90

Children's Dishes

◖ The Swan
Ley Hill HP5 1UT
☎ 01494 783075 ▤ 01494 783582
e-mail: swan@swanleyhill.com
Dir: E of Chesham by golf course

CHILD FACILITIES: Outdoor play area Food/bottle warming Ch menu Ch portions Ch cutlery Safe grounds **NEARBY:** Walks

OPEN: 12-3 5.30-11 (Sun 12-4, 7-10.30) **BAR MEALS:** L served all week 12-2.15 D served Tues-Sat **RESTAURANT:** L served all week 12-2 D served Tues-Sat 7-9 **FACILITIES:** Garden: Large garden, patio, benches ✶

FRIETH
Map 04 SU79

Babies Welcome | **Children's Dishes**

◖ The Yew Tree
RG9 6PJ
☎ 01494 882330
e-mail: yewtree2003@aol.com
Dir: From M40 towards Stokenchurch, thru Cadmore End, Lane End R to Frieth

CHILD FACILITIES: Activities: tree house Outdoor play area Family area Food/bottle warming Ch menu Highchairs Safe grounds **NEARBY:** Pet llamas Chiltern Valley walks

OPEN: 12-3 6-11 (Sun 12-5) **BAR MEALS:** L served all week 12-2.30 D served all week 6.30-10 **RESTAURANT:** L served all week 12-2.30 D served all week 6-10 **FACILITIES:** Garden: Well kept garden with seating **PARKING:** 60

HAMBLEDEN
Map 04 SP78

Children's Dishes

◖ The Stag & Huntsman Inn
RG9 6RP
☎ 01491 571227 ▤ 01491 413810
Dir: 5m from Henley-on-Thames on A4155 toward Marlow, L at Mill End towards Hambleden

CHILD FACILITIES: Food/bottle warming Ch menu Ch portions Ch cutlery **NEARBY:** River walks Boat hire Parks

OPEN: 11-2.30 6-11 (Sun 12-3, 7-10.30, Sat 11-3, 6-11) Closed: Dec 25, 26 Dec & 1 Jan (evening) **BAR MEALS:** L served all week 12-2 D served Mon-Sat 7-9.30 Av main course £8 **RESTAURANT:** 12-2 7-9.30 **FACILITIES:** Garden: large, landscaped, BBQ ✶ **PARKING:** 60

HIGH WYCOMBE
Map 04 SU89

★★★ 70% ◉ Ambassador Court
145 West Wycombe Rd HP12 3AB
☎ 01494 461818 ▤ 01494 461919
e-mail: ach@fardellhotels.com
web: www.fardellhotels.com/ambassadorcourt
Dir: M4 junct 4/A404 to A40 west towards Aylesbury. Hotel 0.5m on left next to petrol station

CHILD FACILITIES: Please telephone for details

A small privately owned hotel handily situated close to the M40 midway between London and Oxford. Bedrooms are pleasantly decorated and well equipped. Public rooms are contemporary in style and include a lounge with leather sofas, a cosy bar and Fusions restaurant.

ROOMS: 18 en suite (1 GF) ⊛ in all bedrooms s £50-£109; d £60-£119 (incl. bkfst) **FACILITIES:** STV Xmas **PARKING:** 18 **NOTES:** ✶ ⊛ in restaurant

England

MARLOW
Map 04 SU88

Babies Welcome | **Children's Dishes**

🍴 The Kings Head
Church Rd, Little Marlow SL7 3RZ
☎ 01628 484407 📠 01628 484407
Dir: M40 J4 take A4040 S 1st A4155

CHILD FACILITIES: Food/bottle warming Ch menu Ch portions Highchairs Changing facilities **NEARBY:** Parks River walks

OPEN: 11-3 5-11 (Sat-Sun 11-11) **BAR MEALS:** L served all week 12-2.15 D served all week 6.30-9.30 Av main course £8.25 **RESTAURANT:** L served all week 12-2.15 D served all week 6.30-9.30 Av 3 course à la carte £14 **FACILITIES:** Garden: Safely behind pub, lots of tables & chairs ✖
PARKING: 50

MILTON KEYNES
Map 04 SP83

Babies Welcome | **Family Rooms** | **Children's Dishes**

★★★ 70% Novotel Milton Keynes
Saxon St, Layburn Court, Heelands MK13 7RA
☎ 01908 322212 📠 01908 322235
e-mail: H3272@accor-hotels.com
Dir: M1 junct 14, follow Childsway signs towards city centre. Turn right into Saxon Way, continue straight across all rdbts hotel on left

CHILD FACILITIES: Activities: books, lego Dolfi corner Indoor play area Family area Food/bottle warming Ch menu Ch portions Highchairs Ch discounts under 16s free sharing with parents Safe grounds Games consoles Cots Family rms D rms with S beds from £65 Connecting rms **NEARBY:** Gulliver's Land amusement park Woburn safari park

Contemporary in style, this purpose-built hotel is situated on the outskirts of the town, just a few minutes' drive from the centre and mainline railway station. Bedrooms provide a good range of facilities, and public rooms include a children's play area and indoor leisure centre.
ROOMS: 124 en suite (40 fmly) (40 GF) ☺ in 105 bedrooms s £119; d £119 **LB FACILITIES:** STV 🏊 Sauna Gym Steam bath
PARKING: 130

OLNEY
Map 04 SP85

◆◆◆◆ Queen Hotel
40 Dartmouth Rd MK46 4BH
☎ 01234 711924 📠 01234 711924
e-mail: info@thequeenhotelolney.co.uk
Dir: on A509, in Olney town centre

CHILD FACILITIES: Please telephone for details

Located not far from the centre of the historic town, this 18th-century hotel has been lovingly renovated. Bedrooms are well appointed, featuring modern bathrooms. Breakfasts are
continued

served in the dining room, which is adjacent to a small, comfortable lounge.
ROOMS: 11 rms (9 en suite) (1 fmly) (3 GF) s £45-£49.50; d £65-£70 *
FACILITIES: TV9B tea/coffee **NOTES:** ✖ ☺ Licensed Cen ht **LB**
PARKING: 7

TAPLOW
Map 04 SU98

Babies Welcome | **Family Rooms** | **Children's Dishes**

★★★ 70% Taplow House Hotel
Berry Hill SL6 0DA
☎ 01628 670056 📠 01628 773625
e-mail: taplow@wrensgroup.com
web: www.taplowhouse.com
Dir: off A4 onto Berry Hill, hotel 0.5m on right

WREN'S HOTELS
The unique hotel collection

CHILD FACILITIES: Babysitting Activities: Sunday funday, colouring packs, outside games Outdoor play area Food/bottle warming Ch menu Ch portions Highchairs Ch discounts under 5s free Safe grounds Cots Family rms D rms with S beds
NEARBY: Riverside walks Cliveden

This elegant Georgian manor is set amid beautiful gardens and has been skilfully restored. Character public rooms are pleasing and include a number of air-conditioned conference rooms and an elegant restaurant. Comfortable bedrooms are individually decorated and furnished to a high standard.
ROOMS: 32 en suite (4 fmly) ☺ in all bedrooms **FACILITIES:** STV 🏊 ♿ Xmas **PARKING:** 100 **NOTES:** ✖ ☺ in restaurant

WEST WYCOMBE
Map 04 SU89

Babies Welcome | **Children's Dishes**

🍴 The George and Dragon Hotel
High St HP14 3AB
☎ 01494 464414 📠 01494 462432
e-mail: enq@george-and-dragon.co.uk
web: www.george-and-dragon.co.uk
Dir: On A40, close to M40

CHILD FACILITIES: Outdoor play area Food/bottle warming Ch menu Ch portions Highchairs Ch cutlery **NEARBY:** Walks West Wycombe Caves

OPEN: 11-2.30 5.30-11 (Sun 12-3, 7-10.30, Sat 12-3, 5.30-11) **BAR MEALS:** L served all week 12-2 D served all week 6-9.30 Av main course £8 **FACILITIES:** Garden: Large garden adjacent to car park
PARKING: 35

This symbol indicates establishments within walking distance or a short drive of the seaside.

CAMBRIDGESHIRE

ALCONBURY   Map 04 TL17

◆◆◆◆ 🛏 Manor House Hotel
20 Chapel St PE28 4DY
☎ 01480 890423 ▤ 01480 891663
e-mail: stayatmanorhouse@aol.com
Dir: signposted close to junct of A1/A14 N of Huntingdon

CHILD FACILITIES: Please telephone for details

This popular inn was originally a 16th-century manor farmhouse.
The accommodation has been refurbished to provide cheerfully
decorated, well-equipped bedrooms, some with four-poster beds.
The public rooms include a cosy, well-stocked bar with open fires,
as well as a more formal dining area.
ROOMS: 5 en suite 1 annexe en suite (6 fmly) s £39.95-£45;
d £49.95-£55 * ⊗ **FACILITIES:** TVB tea/coffee Direct dial from
bedrooms TVL Dinner Last d order 8.45pm **NOTES:** ✖ ⊗ in restaurant
⊗ in 1 lounge Cen ht **LB PARKING:** 25

CAMBRIDGE   Map 05 TL45

◆◆◆◆ *Acorn*
154 Chesterton Rd CB4 1DA
☎ 01223 353888 ▤ 01223 350527
e-mail: info@acornguesthouse.co.uk
web: www.acornguesthouse.co.uk
*Dir: From M1 J13. Right for city centre until mini rdbt. Turn left, straight for
about 1m, house on right*

CHILD FACILITIES: Please telephone for details

Close to the ring road and city centre, this attractive, yellow-brick
house has been extended and renovated by the owners to provide
homely accommodation. Tasty English breakfasts are served in the
cosy dining room, and service is friendly and attentive.
ROOMS: 10 en suite (1 fmly) **FACILITIES:** TVB tea/coffee Direct dial
from bedrooms TVL **NOTES:** ✖ ⊗ Cen ht **PARKING:** 7

⊚ ⊚ ⊚ Midsummer House
Midsummer Common CB4 1HA
☎ 01223 369299 ▤ 01223 302672
e-mail: reservations@midsummerhouse.co.uk
web: www.midsummerhouse.co.uk
Dir: Park in Pretoria Rd, then walk across footbridge. Restaurant on L

CHILD FACILITIES: Please telephone for details

FOOD: Modern French **STYLE:** Modern Traditional **SEATS:** 50
OPEN: 12-2/6-11, Closed 18 Dec-3 Jan, 20-29 Mar, 14-30 Aug, Sun-Mon
RESTAURANT: Fixed L £26, Fixed D £48.50 **NOTES:** ⊗ in restaurant, Air
con **PARKING:** On street

HUNTINGDON   Map 04 TL27

Babies Welcome   Children's Dishes

🛏 The Old Bridge Hotel ★★★ ⊚ ⊚
1 High St PE29 3TQ
☎ 01480 424300 ▤ 01480 411017
e-mail: oldbridge@huntsbridge.co.uk
web: www.huntsbridge.com
Dir: Signposted from A1 & A14

CHILD FACILITIES: Activities: toy box, colouring books Food/bottle
warming Ch menu Ch portions Highchairs Ch cutlery
NEARBY: Cinema Leisure centre Walks Cycling

OPEN: 11-11 (Sun 12-10.30) **BAR MEALS:** L served all week 12-2.30 D
served all week 6.30-10.30 Av main course £10 **RESTAURANT:** L served
all week 12-2.30 D served all week 6.30-10.30 Av 3 course à la carte £25 Av
2 course fixed price £12 **FACILITIES:** Garden: Drinks served only ✖
ROOMS: 24 bedrooms 24 en suite 1 family rooms s£85 d£125
PARKING: 60

KEYSTON   Map 04 TL07

Babies Welcome   Children's Dishes

⊚ Pheasant Inn
Village Loop Rd PE28 0RE
☎ 01832 710241 ▤ 01832 710340
e-mail: pheasant.keyston@btopenworld.com
web: www.huntsbridge.com
Dir: 0.5m off A14, clearly signposted.

CHILD FACILITIES: Food/bottle warming Ch menu Ch portions
Highchairs NEARBY: Walks

FOOD: British **STYLE:** Traditional, Rustic **SEATS:** 100
OPEN: 12-2.15/6.30-9.30 **RESTAURANT:** Fixed L £9.95, main
£9.75-£19.75 **NOTES:** ⊗ in restaurant **PARKING:** 40

All AA listed accommodation, restaurants
and pubs can be found on the AA's
website www.theAA.com

CHESHIRE

Macclesfield Canal

CHESTER
Chester Zoo CH2 1LH
marketing@chesterzoo.co.uk   ☎01244 380280
(2m N of city centre off A41& M53 Junct 10
southbound, Junct 12 all other directions)
Open all year, daily from 10. Last admission varies
with season from 5.30pm high summer to 3.30pm
winter. (Closed 25 Dec).
£12 Family ticket £39.50.

Deva Roman Experience
CH1 1NL   ☎01244 343407
(city centre)
Open daily Feb-Nov 9-5, Dec-Jan 10-4 . (Closed
25-26 Dec). £4.25 (ch £2.50, under 5's free, pen
£3.75, student £3.75). Family ticket £12. Party.

ELLESMERE PORT
Blue Planet Aquarium CH65 9LF
info@blueplanetaquarium.co.uk ☎0151 357 8804
(off M53 junct 10 at Cheshire Oaks. Follow signs
for aquarium).
Open all year, daily from 10. (Closed Xmas).
Seasonal variations in closing times, call to
confirm.

JODRELL BANK
Jodrell Bank Visitor Centre & Arboretum
SK11 9DL
visitorcentre@jb.man.ac.uk   ☎01477 571339
(M6 junct 18, A535 Holmes Chapel to Chelford rd)
Open Nov-Mid March 10.30-3, wknds 11-4. Mar-
Oct 10.30-5.30. £3 per car, £1 for 3D Show.

MOULDSWORTH
Mouldsworth Motor Museum
CH3 8AR   ☎01928 731781
(6m E of Chester, off B5393, close to Delamere
Forest & Oulton Park Racing Circuit, signposted.
Or M56 junct 12 into Frodsham then B5393 into
Mouldsworth, follow brown heritage signs.)
Open Feb-Nov (Sun only), Etr wknd, early May
BH Mon, Spring BH Sun-Mon & Aug BH wknd;
Sun, Feb-Nov; also Wed, Jul-Aug, noon-5.
£3 (ch £1.50)

WIDNES
Catalyst Science Discovery Centre WA8 0DF
info@catalyst.org.uk   ☎0151 420 1121
(signed from M62 junct 7 and M56 junct 12)
Open all year, Tue-Fri daily & BH Mon 10-5,
wknds 11-5.(Closed Mon ex BHs, 24-26 Dec & 1
Jan). £4.95

| Babies Welcome | Family Rooms | Children's Dishes |

★★ 69% **Curzon**
52/54 Hough Green CH4 8JQ
☎ 01244 678581 ▤ 01244 680866
e-mail: curzon.chester@virgin.net
web: www.curzonhotel.co.uk
Dir: on A5104

CHILD FACILITIES: Baby listening Activities: colouring books,
crayons, toys Food/bottle warming Ch portions Highchairs
Ch cutlery Ch discounts under 5s free Safe grounds Cots Family
rms D rm with 2 S beds, D rm with 1 S bed £90-£100 Ch drinks
NEARBY: Zoo Aquarium Sealife Centre Farm

This smart period property is located in a predominantly
residential suburb, close to the racecourse and a short walk from
the city centre. Spacious bedrooms are comfortable,
well-equipped and include family and four-poster rooms. The
atmosphere is friendly and the dinner menu offers a creative
choice of freshly prepared dishes.
ROOMS: 16 en suite (7 fmly) (1 GF) ❀ in 12 bedrooms s £55-£65;
d £75-£100 (incl. bkfst) **LB PARKING:** 20 **NOTES:** ✖ ❀ in restaurant
Closed 20 Dec-6 Jan

| Babies Welcome | Family Rooms | Children's Dishes |

◆◆◆◆ **Golborne Manor**
Platts Ln, Hatton Heath CH3 9AN
☎ 01829 770310 & 07774 695268 ▤ 01829 770370
e-mail: ann.ikin@golbornemanor.co.uk
web: www.golbornemanor.co.uk
*Dir: 5m S of A41 Whitchurch road. Turn right after van centre into Platts
Lane, then 400yds on left*

CHILD FACILITIES: Food/bottle warming Ch menu Ch portions
Highchairs Ch discounts Cots Family rms D rm with 2 S beds
Ch drinks **NEARBY:** Leisure centre

This elegant Edwardian house stands in beautiful gardens, with
spectacular views across open countryside. Accommodation is in
spacious bedrooms with either brass bedsteads or a richly carved
antique Arabian bed. Breakfast is served around a large table in
the dining room, and residents can relax in the comfortable
lounge.
ROOMS: 3 en suite (1 fmly) s £28-£40; d £58-£70 * **FACILITIES:** TVB
tea/coffee ♨ 3/4 snooker table, table tennis Dinner Last d order 1 day in
advance **NOTES:** Credit cards not taken ✖ ❀ Cen ht **LB PARKING:** 6

| Babies Welcome | Family Rooms | Children's Dishes |

◆◆◆ 🛏 🍴 **Cholmondeley Arms**
SY14 8HN
☎ 01829 720300 ▤ 01829 720123
e-mail: guy@cholmondeleyarms.co.uk
Dir: on A49, 6m N of Whitchurch

CHILD FACILITIES: Outdoor play area Food/bottle warming
Ch menu Ch portions Highchairs Ch discounts babies in cots free
Safe grounds Cots Family rms D rm with B beds Laundry

Complete with vaulted ceilings and open fires, this former village
school has been renovated to provide spacious public areas
furnished in rustic style - the setting for imaginative food and good
wines. Bedrooms are in a separate house, once the headmaster's
residence.
ROOMS: 6 en suite (1 fmly) (3 GF) s fr £50; d fr £65 * ❀
FACILITIES: TVB tea/coffee Direct dial from bedrooms No coaches
Dinner Last d order 10pm **NOTES:** Cen ht **LB PARKING:** 60

England

CHESHIRE

CONGLETON — Map 07 SJ86

Babies Welcome | **Children's Dishes**

🍺 Egerton Arms ♦♦♦♦
Astbury Village CW12 4RQ
☎ 01260 273946 📠 01260 277273
e-mail: egertonastbury@totalise.co.uk
Dir: Telephone for directions

CHILD FACILITIES: Outdoor play area Family area Food/bottle warming Ch menu Ch portions Highchairs Ch cutlery Safe grounds NEARBY: Little Moreton Hall Country Park Congleton Leisure Centre

OPEN: 11.15-11 (Sun 11-3, 7-10.30) BAR MEALS: L served all week 11.30-2 D served all week 6.30-9 Av main course £5.99 RESTAURANT: L served all week 11.30-1.45 D served all week 7-8.45 Av 3 course à la carte £14 Av 3 course fixed price £13.95 FACILITIES: Garden: Large grassed area with tables 🛏 ROOMS: 6 bedrooms 6 en suite s£45 d£60 PARKING: 100

KINGSLEY — Map 07 SJ57

♦♦♦♦ Charnwood
Hollow Ln WA6 8EF
☎ 01928 787097 📠 01928 788566
e-mail: susan.klin@talk21.com
Dir: from Frodsham take B5152 for approx 3m, then onto B5153 for Kingsley Hollow Lane. House just past church on right

CHILD FACILITIES: Please telephone for details

Set on the edge of a peaceful village, Charnwood offers two attractive, well-furnished bedrooms, one with a separate bathroom, and a comfortable lounge. Guests have their own entrance. Breakfast is served in a dining room that looks out on to the patio and pretty gardens.
ROOMS: 2 rms (1 en suite) (1 fmly) s £30-£40; d £40-£55 *
FACILITIES: TVB tea/coffee Direct dial from bedrooms TVL No coaches NOTES: Credit cards not taken 🛏 ⊗ Cen ht PARKING: 5

MALPAS — Map 07 SJ65

♦♦♦♦ 🌱 Millmoor Farm
Nomansheath SY14 8DY
☎ 01948 820304
e-mail: dave-sal@millmoor-farm.fsnet.co.uk
Dir: A41 S towards Whitchurch, right towards Nomansheath, 1m after Hampton Heath rdbt. Left at mini rdbt in village, Millmoor Farm signed after 0.5m

CHILD FACILITIES: Please telephone for details

Located in attractive gardens on a beef and dairy farm near Nomansheath, parts of this modernised farmhouse date back to the late 17th century. Bedrooms include one with a four-poster bed and some within a cottage, used also for self-catering. The attractive lounge-dining room features a welcoming log fire in the cooler months.
ROOMS: 3 rms (2 en suite) s £18-£24; d £36-£48 * FACILITIES: TVB tea/coffee Fishing 270 acres dairy & beef Dinner Last d order midday NOTES: Credit cards not taken ⊗ Cen ht LB BB PARKING: 11

NANTWICH — Map 07 SJ65

♦♦♦♦♦ Oakland House
252 Newcastle Rd, Blakelow, Shavington CW5 7ET
☎ 01270 567134
Dir: on A500 5m from M6 junct 16, and 2m from Nantwich, following the Nantwich and Chester signs, at 4th rdbt, take 1st exit

CHILD FACILITIES: Please telephone for details

Convenient for the motorway, Oakland House offers a friendly and
continued

---

relaxed atmosphere. Bedrooms, some of which are in a separate chalet, are attractively furnished and well equipped. There is a spacious sitting room and a modern conservatory overlooks the pretty garden and the Cheshire countryside. A substantial breakfast is served around one large table.
ROOMS: 3 en suite 6 annexe en suite (1 fmly) (6 GF) s £30-£35; d £44-£50 * FACILITIES: TVB tea/coffee TVL No coaches NOTES: ⊗ Cen ht PARKING: 14

PLUMLEY — Map 07 SJ77

Babies Welcome | **Children's Dishes**

🍺 The Smoker
WA16 0TY
☎ 01565 722338 📠 01565 722093
e-mail: smoker@plumley.fsword.co.uk
Dir: from M6 J19 take A556 W. Pub is 1.75m on L

CHILD FACILITIES: Outdoor play area Food/bottle warming Ch menu Ch portions Highchairs

OPEN: 11-3 6-11 (all day Sun) BAR MEALS: L served all week 11.30-2.30 D served all week 6.30-9.30 RESTAURANT: L served all week 11.30-2.30 D served all week 6.30-9.30 FACILITIES: Garden: Large lawned area, 15 large dining benches 🛏 PARKING: 100

SWETTENHAM — Map 07 SJ86

Babies Welcome | **Children's Dishes**

🍺 The Swettenham Arms
Swettenham Ln CW12 2LF
☎ 01477 571284 📠 01477 571284
e-mail: info@cheshireinns.co.uk
web: www.swettenhamarms.co.uk
Dir: M6 J18 to Holmes Chapel, then A535 towards Jodrell Bank. 3m take rd on R (Forty Acre Lane) to Swettenham

CHILD FACILITIES: Food/bottle warming Ch portions Highchairs Safe grounds Changing facilities NEARBY: Nature reserve Arboretum

OPEN: 12-3 6.30-11 (open all day Sun) BAR MEALS: L served all week 12-2.30 D served all week 7-9.30 RESTAURANT: 12-2.30 7-9.30 FACILITIES: Garden: Peaceful garden 🛏 PARKING: 150

TARPORLEY — Map 07 SJ56

♦♦♦♦ Hill House Farm
Rushton CW6 9AU
☎ 01829 732238 📠 01829 733929
e-mail: rayner@hillhousefarm.fsnet.co.uk
web: www.hillhousefarm.info
Dir: A51/A49 lights at Tilstone Fearnall take Eaton turning in 1m. Turn right at war memorial into Lower Lane, take 3rd road right into The Hall Lane. Farm in 0.5m

CHILD FACILITIES: Please telephone for details

This impressive brick farmhouse is set in very attractive gardens and nestles within 14 acres of rolling pastureland. The three stylish bedrooms have en suite or private facilities. There is a spacious and comfortable lounge and a traditionally furnished breakfast room. The proprietors are especially friendly.
ROOMS: 3 rms (2 en suite) (1 fmly) s £35-£40; d £60 *
FACILITIES: TVB tea/coffee No coaches NOTES: ⊗ Cen ht LB PARKING: 6

> Don't forget our travel accommodation section at the front of the guide

England

Babies Welcome | Children's Dishes

★★★★ 75%
De Vere Daresbury Park   DE VERE ● HOTELS
Chester Rd, Daresbury WA4 4BB
☎ 01925 267331 ▤ 01925 265615
e-mail: reservations.daresbury@devere-hotels.com
Dir: M56 junct 11, take 'Danesbury Park' exit at rdbt. Hotel is 100m along.

CHILD FACILITIES: Babysitting (chargeable) Food/bottle warming Ch menu Ch portions Highchairs Ch discounts under 4s free sharing with parents Safe grounds Games consoles Cots Connecting rms Laundry **NEARBY:** Chester Zoo Theme Park Aquarium Cinema

Close to the local motorway networks and tourist attractions, this modern hotel is a very popular venue for both business and leisure travellers. Public areas are themed around 'Alice in Wonderland' in tribute to local author Lewis Carroll. These include a range of eating and drinking options and leisure facilities.
ROOMS: 181 en suite (14 fmly) (62 GF) ⊛ in 128 bedrooms
s £70-£129; d £80-£139 **LB FACILITIES: Spa** STV ⊠ Squash Snooker Sauna Solarium Gym Jacuzzi Steam Room, Beauty salon Xmas
PARKING: 400

Babies Welcome | Family Rooms | Children's Dishes

♦♦♦ ❤ **Lea Farm**
Wrinehill Rd CW5 7NS
☎ 01270 841429 ▤ 01270 841429
e-mail: contactus@leafarm.co.uk
Dir: M6 junct 16, take A1550, at 1st rdbt Keele, 2nd rdbt Nantwich. Over railway bridge, 1st left to T-junct, turn left, 2nd farm on right

CHILD FACILITIES: Baby listening Activities: colouring books, toys, games Food/bottle warming Ch menu Ch portions Highchairs Ch cutlery Ch discounts Safe grounds Videos Cots Family rms D rm with S bed & child's bed Laundry **NEARBY:** Local gardens Craft centre

This working dairy farm is surrounded by delightful gardens and beautiful Cheshire countryside. Spacious bedrooms are equipped with modern facilities and the cosy lounge features a small snooker table. Hearty breakfasts are served in the attractive dining room, which looks out over the garden, with its resident peacocks.
ROOMS: 3 rms (2 en suite) (1 fmly) s £26-£29; d £44-£50 *
FACILITIES: TVB tea/coffee TVL Fishing Pool Table Bird watching 150 acres dairy & beer **NOTES:** Credit cards not taken ⊛ Cen ht
PARKING: 24

CORNWALL & ISLES OF SCILLY

St Ives beach

DOBWALLS
Dobwalls Family Adventure Park
PL14 6HD   ☎01579 320325
dobwallsadventurepark@hotmail.com
(Turn off A38 in centre of Dobwalls and follow the brown signs for approx 0.5m)
Open Etr. to Oct daily 10.30-5 10-5.30 in high season. *£8.95, ch under 2 free, pen & disabled £5.50. Family tickets available from £17.50-£52.95. Groups 20+ £5.50 each.

GOONHAVERN
World in Miniature TR4 9QE
info@worldinminiature.co.uk   ☎0870 458 4433
(Turn off A30 at Boxheater junct onto B3285)
Open Etr-Oct, daily from 10am.

GWEEK
National Seal Sanctuary
TR12 6UG   ☎01326 221361
slcgweek@merlin-entertainments.com
(pass RNAS Culdrose & take A3293 & then B3291 to Gweek. The sanctuary is signposted from village) Open all year, from 10am. Closed 25 Dec.

HELSTON
The Flambards Experience TR13 0QA
info@flambards.co.uk   ☎01326 573404

(0.5m SE of Helston on A3083, Lizard road)
Open daily 23 March - Oct, Nov - 22 March 11-4; Closed Thurs/Fri & 23 Dec - 10 Jan. *£9.95, ch 5-14 £8.95, pen £5.75. Family of 4 £36, family of 5 £44.00, family of 6 £51.50.

LOOE
Monkey Sanctuary PL13 1NZ
info@monkeysanctuary.org   ☎01503 262532
(Signposted on B3253 at No Man's Land between East Looe & Hessenford)
Open Sun-Thu 11-4.30 from the Sun before Etr-end Sep. Also open autumn half-term.
*£5, under 5s free, ch £3 & concession £4. Family ticket (2 ad + 2 ch) £15.

NEWQUAY
Blue Reef Aquarium TR7 1DU
info@bluereefaquarium.co.uk   ☎01637 878134
(From A30 follow signs to Newquay, follow Blue Reef Aquarium signs to car park in town centre)
Open all year, daily 10-5. Closed 25 Dec. Open until 6 during summer holidays.
*£5.95, ch 3-16 £3.95, pen & student £4.95. Family ticket £17.95.
Newquay Zoo TR7 2LZ
info@newquayzoo.co.uk   ☎01637 873342
(Off A3075 and follow signs to Zoo)
Open Apr-Oct, daily 9.30-6; Nov-Mar 10-dusk. Closed 25 Dec. *£6.95 ,ch 3+ £4.45, pen £5.45, ch under 3 free. Family ticket £19.95.

ST AUSTELL
Eden Project PL24 2SG
information@edenproject.com   ☎01726 811911
(Overlooking St Austell Bay signposted from A390/A30/A391) Open daily Mar-Oct 10-6 last admission 5pm, Nov-Feb 10-4.30 last admission 3pm. Closed 24-25 Dec.

BOSCASTLE Map 02 SX09

★★ 68% The Wellington Hotel

The Harbour PL35 0AQ
☎ 01840 250202 🖷 01840 250621
e-mail: info@wellingtonboscastle.co.uk
web: www.wellingtonboscastle.co.uk
Dir: A30/A395, right at Davidstow, signed to Boscastle

CHILD FACILITIES: Baby listening Nanny Activities: colouring, puzzles, games Food/bottle warming Ch menu Ch portions Highchairs Ch cutlery Ch discounts £15 extra bed 3-12s, under 2s free Videos Cots Family rms D rm with D sofa bed or D rm with Z bed £85-£140 **NEARBY:** Coast & countryside walks 8m to beach

Affectionately known as 'The Welly', this 16th-century coaching inn has an abundance of charm and character. The Long Bar is a popular watering hole for both visitors and locals alike. Bedrooms come in varying sizes, including the spacious Tower rooms; all are comfy and suitably equipped. There is a bar menu and, in the restaurant, a daily-changing carte.
ROOMS: 15 en suite (1 fmly) s £35-£45; d £70-£130 (incl. bkfst) LB
FACILITIES: ♫ Xmas **PARKING:** 20 **NOTES:** ✈ ⊗ in restaurant

◆◆◆◆ Old Coach House

Tintagel Rd PL35 0AS
☎ 01840 250398 🖷 01840 250346
e-mail: parsons@old-coach.demon.co.uk
Dir: at junct of B3266 and B3263

CHILD FACILITIES: Outdoor play area Food/bottle warming Ch portions Highchairs Ch discounts £18 sharing with family, under 8s £10, cots £5 Cots Family rms 1 king size rm with B beds, 2 D rms with S bed Laundry **NEARBY:** Coastal & woodland walks 5-min walk and 10-min drive to sea

Over 300 years old, the Old Coach House has lovely views over the village and the rolling countryside. The pleasant bedrooms are well equipped and include two rooms on the ground floor. A hearty breakfast is served in the conservatory, which overlooks the well-kept garden.
ROOMS: 8 en suite (3 fmly) (2 GF) s £38-£44; d £42-£44 *
FACILITIES: TVB tea/coffee TVL No coaches **NOTES:** ⊗ Cen ht LB
PARKING: 9

CALLINGTON Map 02 SX36

🍺 The Coachmakers Arms

6 Newport Square PL17 7AS
☎ 01579 382567 🖷 01579 384679
Dir: Telephone for directions

CHILD FACILITIES: Activities: toys, colouring Food/bottle warming Ch menu Ch portions Highchairs **NEARBY:** Donkey sanctuary Walks 15-min drive to sea

OPEN: 11-3 (Sun 12-3, 7-10.30) 6-11 **BAR MEALS:** L served all week 12-2 D served all week 7-9.30 Av main course £4.50 **RESTAURANT:** L served all week 12-2 D served all week 7-9.30 Av 3 course à la carte £15
PARKING: 10

All AA listed accommodation, restaurants and pubs can be found on the AA's website www.theAA.com

---

CRACKINGTON HAVEN Map 02 SX19

◆◆◆ 🍺 Coombe Barton

EX23 0JG
☎ 01840 230345 🖷 01840 230788
e-mail: info@coombebartoninn.co.uk
Dir: turn off A39 at Wainhouse corner, continue down lane to beach

CHILD FACILITIES: Please telephone for details

Overlooking the beach and surrounded by rugged cliffs, this long-established, family-run inn is popular with locals and visitors alike. A large selection of meals is available. The Sunday carvery is especially popular and booking is advised. Bedrooms are attractive and well equipped.
ROOMS: 6 rms (3 en suite) (1 fmly) s £30-£35; d £50-£96 *
FACILITIES: TV3B tea/coffee Pool Table Dinner Last d order 9.30pm
NOTES: ⊗ Cen ht LB **PARKING:** 25

CRANTOCK Map 02 SW76

★★★ 71% Crantock Bay

West Pentire TR8 5SE
☎ 01637 830229 🖷 01637 831111
e-mail: stay@crantockbayhotel.co.uk
Dir: at Newquay A3075 to Redruth. After 500yds rt towards Crantock, follow signs to West Pentire

CHILD FACILITIES: Baby listening Babysitting Activities: toys, colouring, books, puzzles, children's parties, treasure hunts, tennis court Indoor play area Outdoor play area Food/bottle warming Ch menu Ch portions Highchairs Ch cutlery Ch discounts free sharing with parents, under 12s discount in school hols Safe grounds Games consoles Videos Cots Family rms D rm with S bed or D rm with B bed from £64.50 Fridge Laundry Changing mats (if requested) **NEARBY:** Crealy Adventure Park Zoo Eden Project Museums Seafront location

This family-run hotel has spectacular sea views and a tradition of friendly and attentive service. With direct access to the beach from its four acres of grounds, and its extensive leisure facilities, the
continued on p84

England

CRANTOCK, continued

hotel is a great place for family guests. There are separate lounges, a spacious bar and enjoyable cuisine is served in the dining room.
ROOMS: 33 en suite (3 fmly) (10 GF) s £60-£90; d £120-£180 (incl. bkfst & dinner) LB **FACILITIES:** ⊠ ℺ Sauna Gym ♨ ♨ Jacuzzi Hotel leads on to sandy beach Xmas **PARKING:** 40 **NOTES:** ⊛ in restaurant Closed 2 wks Nov & Jan RS Dec & Feb

See advert on page 87

DULOE   Map 02 SX25

⊈ Ye Olde Plough House Inn
PL14 4PN
☎ 01503 262050 ▤ 01503 264089
e-mail: alison@ploughhouse.freeserve.co.uk
Dir: A38 to Dobwalls, take turning signed Looe

CHILD FACILITIES: Family area Food/bottle warming Ch menu Ch portions Highchairs **NEARBY:** Dobwalls Adventure Park 10-min drive to Looe

OPEN: 12-2.30 6.30-11 (Sun 7.00-10.30) Closed: Dec 25-26 **BAR MEALS:** L served all week 12-2 D served all week 6.30-9.30
RESTAURANT: L served all week 12-2 D served all week 6.30-9.30
FACILITIES: Garden: Fenced grassed area, four tables **PARKING:** 20

FALMOUTH   Map 02 SW83

★★★★ 72% ⊛ ⊛ Royal Duchy
Cliff Rd TR11 4NX
☎ 01326 313042 ▤ 01326 319420
e-mail: info@royalduchy.com
web: www.royalduchy.com
Dir: on Cliff Rd, along Falmouth seafront

CHILD FACILITIES: Baby listening Activities; board games, table tennis (during school hols) Food/bottle warming Ch menu Ch portions Highchairs Ch cutlery Ch discounts £15-51 Safe grounds Cots Family rms D rm with B beds Connecting rms Laundry **NEARBY:** Flambards theme park Seal sanctuary 2-min walk to sea

Looking out over the sea and towards Pendennis Castle, this hotel provides a friendly environment. The comfortable lounge and cocktail bar are well appointed, and leisure facilities are also available. The restaurant serves carefully prepared dishes and bedrooms vary in size and aspect, with many rooms having sea views.
ROOMS: 43 en suite (6 fmly) (1 GF) s £69-£93; d £130-£254 (incl. bkfst) LB **FACILITIES:** Spa STV ⊠ Sauna Table tennis ♫ Xmas **PARKING:** 50 **NOTES:** ✖ ⊛ in restaurant

See advert on opposite page

◆◆◆◆ Hawthorne Dene Hotel
12 Pennance Rd TR11 4EA
☎ 01326 311427 ▤ 01326 311994
e-mail: enquiries@hawthornedenehotel.co.uk
web: www.hawthornedenehotel.co.uk
Dir: A39 follow signs for town centre & beaches. Straight across at the lights and at the 1st mini rdbt. Next rdbt right into Pennance Rd. The hotel is on right.

CHILD FACILITIES: Activities: toys, games, cards Food/bottle warming Ch menu Ch portions Highchairs Ch discounts under 2s free, 2-12s 50% Safe grounds Videos Cots Family rms D rm with S beds £90 Ch drinks **NEARBY:** Leisure centre 10-min walk to sea

Picture windows in the lounge, dining room and many of the bedrooms look out over the sea at this comfortable house. Cuisine is a feature and dishes focus on the best of local and organic produce. A comfortable lounge is available, where a log fire burns in winter. Sign language is understood.
ROOMS: 10 en suite (1 fmly) (1 GF) s £35-£45; d £70-£90 * ⊛
FACILITIES: TVB tea/coffee No coaches Dinner Last d order 8.30pm
NOTES: ✖ ⊛ in restaurant Licensed Cen ht LB **PARKING:** 7

FEOCK   Map 02 SW83

⊈ The Punch Bowl & Ladle
Penelewey TR3 6QY
☎ 01872 862237 ▤ 01872 870401
Dir: Off A38 Falmouth Road

CHILD FACILITIES: Family area Ch menu Ch portions (some) Highchairs Safe grounds Changing facilities **NEARBY:** Walks Cycling Surfing Near sea

OPEN: 11.30 -11 (Sun 12-10.30) **BAR MEALS:** L served all week 12-2 D served all week 6-9 Av main course £7.95 **RESTAURANT:** L served all week 12-2.30 D served all week 6-9 Av 3 course à la carte £18
FACILITIES: Garden: lovely views **PARKING:** 60

FOWEY   Map 02 SX15

◆◆◆◆ Trevanion
70 Lostwithiel St PL23 1BQ
☎ 01726 832602 ▤ 01726 832602
e-mail: alisteve@trevanionguesthouse.co.uk
web: www.trevanionguesthouse.co.uk
Dir: A3082 into Fowey, down hill turn left (Lostwithiel Street), continue down hill. Trevanion next on left

CHILD FACILITIES: Activities: board games Food/bottle warming Ch portions Highchairs Ch cutlery Ch discounts Safe grounds Cots Family rms 2 D rms with S bed & sofa bed Ch drinks Laundry (on request) **NEARBY:** Tortoise Garden River trips Leisure centre 10-min walk

An ideal base for visiting The Eden Project and within easy walking distance of the historic town of Fowey, this 16th-century merchant's house provides comfortable accommodation. A hearty farmhouse-style cooked breakfast, using local produce, is served in the attractive dining room and other menu options are available.
ROOMS: 4 rms (3 en suite) (2 fmly) s £30-£35; d £50-£60 *
FACILITIES: TVB tea/coffee No coaches Garden Dinner Last d order morning **NOTES:** Credit cards not taken ⊛ Cen ht LB **PARKING:** 4

HELFORD PASSAGE
Map 02 SW72

⚓ Ferryboat Inn
TR11 5LB
☎ 01326 250625 ▯ 01326 250916
e-mail: ronald.brown7@btopenworld.co.uk
Dir: From A39 at Falmouth, towards River Helford

CHILD FACILITIES: Activities: activity packs, seasonal parties
Outdoor play area Family area Food/bottle warming Ch licence
Ch menu Highchairs Safe grounds Changing facilities
NEARBY: Eden Project Flambards Seafront location

OPEN: 11-11 Sun 12-10.30pm **BAR MEALS:** L served all week 12-2.30
D served all week 6.30-9 Av main course £6.25 **RESTAURANT:** L served
all week 12-2.30 D served all week 6.30-9 Av 3 course à la carte £10.95
FACILITIES: Garden: Patio, food served outdoors **PARKING:** 80

LAND'S END
Map 02 SW32

★★★ 64% *The Land's End Hotel*
TR19 7AA
☎ 01736 871844 ▯ 01736 871599
e-mail: landsendhotel@madasafish.co.uk
web: www.landsendhotel.co.uk
Dir: from Penzance take A30 and follow Land's End signs. After Sennen 1m to Land's End

CHILD FACILITIES: Please telephone for details

This famous location provides a most impressive setting for this attractive hotel. Bedrooms, many with stunning views of the Atlantic, are pleasantly decorated and comfortable. A relaxing lounge and attractive bar are provided and in the Longships restaurant, fresh local produce and fish dishes are a speciality.
ROOMS: 33 en suite (2 fmly) **FACILITIES:** Free entry Lands End visitor centre **PARKING:** 1000 **NOTES:** ⊛ in restaurant

LISKEARD
Map 02 SX26

♦♦♦♦ Trecarne House
Penhale Grange, St Cleer PL14 5EB
☎ 01579 343543 ▯ 01579 343543
e-mail: trish@trecarnehouse.co.uk
Dir: leave A38 at Liskeard onto A390 then B3254. Continue to St Cleer. Right at post office, 3rd left after church, 2nd right, house on the right

CHILD FACILITIES: Baby listening Babysitting Activities: games,
Lego, trampoline, table football, table tennis Indoor play area
Outdoor play area Family area Food/bottle warming Ch menu
Ch portions Highchairs Ch cutlery Ch discounts babies free,
children sharing with parents 50% Safe grounds Videos Family rms
D rms with sofa bed Ch drinks Laundry **NEARBY:** Dobwalls
Theme Park Walks Play Area 15-min drive to sea

continued

FALMOUTH'S FINEST

The Royal Duchy Hotel is the only 4 star hotel in Falmouth and has a reputation for luxurious accommodation, first class service and fine cuisine. It also sports excellent health and fitness facilities, which include an indoor pool and indoor games room. There is a full family entertainment programme during school holiday periods.

Enjoying panoramic views across Falmouth's famous bay, The Royal Duchy is the perfect base for exploring Cornwall. Discover the Eden Project, Flambards Theme Park, Gweek Seal Sanctuary, a beautiful cove or Falmouth's 300 years of maritime history.

Cliff Road, Falmouth, Cornwall, TR11 4NX
Tel: 01326 313042 Fax: 01326 319420
Web: www.royalduchy.co.uk

THE WESTCOUNTRY'S LEADING HOTEL GROUP

A warm and friendly welcome awaits at this large family home, peacefully located on the edge of the village. The stylish and spacious bedrooms, which enjoy magnificent country views, feature exposed pine floors and offer many thoughtful extras. A wide choice is available from the buffet-style breakfast, which can be enjoyed in the dining room and sun-filled conservatory overlooking rolling countryside.
ROOMS: 3 en suite (2 fmly) s £45-£55; d £66 * **FACILITIES:** TVB
tea/coffee TVL No coaches table tennis, trampoline, small snooker table
NOTES: Credit cards not taken ✖ ⊛ Cen ht **LB** **PARKING:** 6

LOOE
Map 02 SX25

★★★ 66% Hannafore Point
Marine Dr, West Looe PL13 2DG
☎ 01503 263273 ▯ 01503 263272
e-mail: stay@hannaforepointhotel.com
Dir: A38, left onto A385 to Looe. Over bridge left. Hotel 0.5m on left

CHILD FACILITIES: Baby listening Indoor play area Food/bottle
warming Ch menu Ch portions Highchairs Ch discounts under 5s
free, under 14s discount Safe grounds Games consoles Videos Cots
Family rms D rm with adj B bed rm £116-144 Connecting rms
Laundry **NEARBY:** Eden Project Monkey sanctuary Seafront
location

With panoramic coastal views embracing St George's Island around to Rame Head, this popular hotel provides a warm welcome. The wonderful view is also a feature of the spacious restaurant and bar, a scenic backdrop for dinners and breakfasts.
continued on p86

England

LOOE, continued

Additional facilities include a heated indoor pool, squash court and gymnasium.
ROOMS: 37 en suite (5 fmly) s fr £48; d fr £96 (incl. bkfst) **LB**
FACILITIES: Spa ⚲ Squash Sauna Solarium Gym Jacuzzi Tennis/bowls 200yds away ♫ Xmas **PARKING:** 32 **NOTES:** ⊗ in restaurant

MALPAS   Map 02 SW84

⌘ Heron Inn
Trenhaile Ter TR1 1SL
☎ 01872 272773 📠 01872 272773
CHILD FACILITIES: Family area Food/bottle warming Ch menu Ch portions (where possible) Highchairs Safe grounds **NEARBY:** Park River trips and walks Short drive to sea
OPEN: 11-3 6-11 **BAR MEALS:** L served all week 12-2 D served all week 6-9 Av main course £6.95 **RESTAURANT:** 12-2 7-9
FACILITIES: Children's licence **PARKING:** 13

MANACCAN   Map 02 SW72

⌘ The New Inn
TR12 6HA
☎ 01326 231323
e-mail: penny@macace.net
CHILD FACILITIES: Activities: crayons Outdoor play area Food/bottle warming Ch menu (early evening sitting) Ch portions Highchairs Ch cutlery Safe grounds **NEARBY:** 10-min walk to sea
OPEN: 12-3 (Sat-Sun all day in summer) 6-11 **BAR MEALS:** L served all week 12-2.30 D served all week 6-9.30 Av main course £9.50
FACILITIES: Garden: Large, natural, lots of flowers **PARKING:** 20

MARAZION   Map 02 SW53

★★ 77% ⊛ Mount Haven Hotel & St Michaels Restaurant
Turnpike Rd TR17 0DQ
☎ 01736 710249 📠 01736 711658
e-mail: reception@mounthaven.co.uk
web: www.mounthaven.co.uk
Dir: From A30 towards Penzance. At rdbt take exit for Helston onto A394. Next rdbt right into Marazion, hotel on left
CHILD FACILITIES: Baby listening Activities: board games Food/bottle warming Ch menu (on request) Ch portions Highchairs Ch discounts under 5s £10, under 13s 50%, under 16s 75% Cots Family rms £100-108 plus children Fridge Laundry (by arrangement) **NEARBY:** 0.5m to sea

Art and style abound at this delightfully located hotel where exceptional views can be enjoyed - sunsets and sunrises can be particularly splendid. Bedrooms, many with balconies, are comfortably appointed. Fresh seafood and local produce are simply treated to produce interesting menus and enjoyable dining. A range of holistic therapies is available. Service is attentive and friendly and a relaxing and enchanting environment has been created throughout.
ROOMS: 19 en suite (2 fmly) (6 GF) ⊗ in all bedrooms s £60-£80; d £84-£90 (incl. bkfst) **LB FACILITIES:** Spa Aromatherapy reflexology, massage & reiki **PARKING:** 30 **NOTES:** ⨯ ⊗ in restaurant Closed 20 Dec-5 Feb

MAWNAN SMITH   Map 02 SW72

★★★ 79% ⊛ ⬥ Meudon
TR11 5HT
☎ 01326 250541 📠 01326 250543
e-mail: wecare@meudon.co.uk
web: www.meudon.co.uk
Dir: from Truro A39 towards Falmouth at Hillhead rdbt, follow signs to Maenporth Beach. Hotel on left 1m after beach
CHILD FACILITIES: Please telephone for details

This charming late Victorian mansion, with its friendly hospitality, attentive service and impressive nine acres of gardens, which lead down to a private beach, provides a relaxing place to stay. Bedrooms are comfortable and spacious and cuisine features the best of local Cornish produce served in the conservatory restaurant.
ROOMS: 29 en suite (2 fmly) (15 GF) s £69-£125; d £138-£250 (incl. bkfst & dinner) **LB FACILITIES:** Fishing Riding Private beach, Hair salon, Yacht for skippered charter, sub-tropical gardens Xmas **PARKING:** 52 **NOTES:** ⊗ in restaurant Closed 3-31 Jan

MULLION   Map 02 SW61

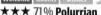

★★★ 71% Polurrian
TR12 7EN

THE INDEPENDENTS

☎ 01326 240421 📠 01326 240083
e-mail: polurotel@aol.com
Dir: A30 onto A3076 to Truro. Follow signs for Helston on A39 then A394 to The Lizard and Mullion
CHILD FACILITIES: Baby listening Activities: face painting, games Indoor play area Outdoor play area Family area Food/bottle warming Ch menu Ch portions Highchairs Ch cutlery Ch discounts under 5s free, 6-12s £25, 12-16s £35 Safe grounds Games consoles Videos Cots Family rms from £60 Laundry **NEARBY:** Flambards Village 2-min walk to own beach

This long-established hotel is set in 12 acres of landscaped gardens, 300 feet above the sea. The spectacular views over Polurrian Cove will remain long in the memory, along with the wonderful sunsets. Public areas are spacious and comfortable, and the bedrooms are individually styled. There is a well-equipped leisure centre.
ROOMS: 39 en suite (22 fmly) s £55-£120 (incl. bkfst & dinner) **LB FACILITIES:** STV ⬚ ⚲ ⚲ Squash Snooker Sauna Solarium Gym ⬚ ⬚ Jacuzzi Cricket net Whirlpool Mountain bikes Surfing Body boarding ♫ Xmas **PARKING:** 80 **NOTES:** ⊗ in restaurant

◆◆◆◆ Alma House
Churchtown TR12 7BZ
☎ 01326 240509
e-mail: almahousehotel@aol.co.uk
Dir: proceed into Mullion using the one way system and in centre of village turn left and Alma House is 200yds on right
CHILD FACILITIES: Food/bottle warming Ch menu Ch portions Highchairs Ch cutlery Ch discounts Safe grounds Videos Cots Family rms D rm with S bed Ch drinks **NEARBY:** Local park 10-min drive to sea

Alma House is a small Victorian hotel on the edge of the charming village of Mullion. Bedrooms are attractively decorated and have views across Mount's Bay. There is a relaxing lounge with a well-stocked bar. Dinner, featuring a choice of dishes, is available in the dining room.
ROOMS: 4 rms (3 en suite) **FACILITIES:** TVB tea/coffee TVL No coaches Dinner Last d order 9.30pm **NOTES:** ⨯ ⊗ Licensed Cen ht **PARKING:** 20

NEWQUAY Map 02 SW86

★★★★ 68% Headland

Fistral Beach TR7 1EW
☎ 01637 872211 ▤ 01637 872212
e-mail: office@headlandhotel.co.uk
web: www.headlandhotel.co.uk
Dir: off A30 onto A392 at Indian Queens, approaching Newquay follow signs for Fistral Beach, hotel adjacent

CHILD FACILITIES: Baby listening Babysitting (charge) **Activities:** supervised activities, surfing, entertainer during dinner, colouring, books, toys Indoor play area Outdoor play area Family area Food/bottle warming Ch menu Ch portions Highchairs Ch discounts under 4s £10, 5-10s £25, 11-15s £30 Safe grounds Videos Cots Family rms D rms with S beds £90-£270 Connecting rms Fridge Laundry **NEARBY:** Zoo Dairyland Seafront location

This Victorian hotel enjoys a stunning location overlooking the sea on three sides - views can be enjoyed from most of the windows. Bedrooms are comfortable and spacious, with a number having now been refurbished. Grand public areas, with impressive floral displays, include various lounges and dining options.
ROOMS: 104 en suite (40 fmly) s £70-£123; d £110-£197 (incl. bkfst)
LB FACILITIES: Spa STV ⌨ ⊀ Golf ⊕ Snooker Sauna Gym ⊿ ⊿ Jacuzzi Children's outdoor play area, Harry Potter playroom ♫ Xmas
PARKING: 400 **NOTES:** ⊗ in restaurant Closed 23-27 Dec

★★ 72% Whipsiderry

Trevelgue Rd, Porth TR7 3LY
☎ 01637 874777 ▤ 01637 874777
e-mail: info@whipsiderry.co.uk
Dir: right onto Padstow road (B3276) out of Newquay, in 0.5m right at Trevelgue Rd
CHILD FACILITIES: Please telephone for details
Quietly located, overlooking Porth Beach, this friendly hotel offers bedrooms in a variety of sizes and styles, many with superb views. A daily-changing menu offers interesting and well-cooked dishes with the emphasis on fresh, local produce. An outdoor pool is available, and at dusk guests can enjoy badger-watching in the attractive grounds.
ROOMS: 20 rms (19 en suite) (5 fmly) (3 GF) ⊗ in 8 bedrooms s £45-£54; d £90-£108 (incl. bkfst & dinner) **LB FACILITIES:** ⊀ Sauna American pool ♫ Xmas **PARKING:** 30 **NOTES:** ⊗ in restaurant Closed Nov-Etr (ex Xmas)

◆◆◆◆ Priory Lodge Hotel

30 Mount Wise TR7 2BN
☎ 01637 874111 ▤ 01637 851803
e-mail: fiona@priorylodgehotel.fsnet.co.uk
Dir: left at traffic lights in town centre onto Berry Rd, right onto Mount Wise B3282. Hotel approx 0.5m on right

continued

CHILD FACILITIES: Baby listening **Activities:** magician, disco twice weekly, colouring, puzzles, toys Indoor play area Outdoor play area Food/bottle warming Ch menu Ch portions Highchairs Ch discounts 2 under 14s free sharing parents' room in certain seasons Safe grounds Games consoles Cots Family rms Connecting rms Laundry **NEARBY:** Zoo Sealife centre 5-min walk to sea

A short stroll from the town centre and beaches, this pleasant hotel provides an impressive range of facilities. The bedrooms are spacious, and some have a balcony and a sea view. Dinner is a pleasant range of choices, including vegetarian. In summer, entertainment is provided in the bar most evenings.
ROOMS: 22 rms (20 en suite) 6 annexe en suite (13 fmly) (1 GF) s £30-£38; d £60-£76 * ⊗ in 2 bedrooms **FACILITIES:** TVB tea/coffee Direct dial from bedrooms TVL ⊀ Sauna Solarium Pool Table Video machines Outdoor jacuzzi Dinner Last d order 7.30pm **NOTES:** ⊀ ⊗ in restaurant ⊗ in 1 lounge Licensed Cen ht **LB PARKING:** 30

◆◆◆ Rolling Waves

Alexandra Rd, Porth TR7 3NB
☎ 01637 873236 ▤ 01637 873236
e-mail: enquiries@rollingwaves.co.uk
Dir: off A30 & join A3059 then onto B3276 into Porth, past beach, opposite pitch and putt on right
CHILD FACILITIES: Please telephone for details
This peaceful hotel occupies an elevated position away from the bustle of Newquay, overlooking Porth Beach and the coastline. The friendly proprietors are most attentive and many guests return to this comfortable establishment. Dinner is served in an airy dining room and there are panoramic views from the bar.
ROOMS: 9 rms (8 en suite) (2 fmly) (5 GF) s £20-£25; d £42-£54 *
FACILITIES: TVB tea/coffee TVL No coaches Dinner Last d order 3pm **NOTES:** ⊀ ⊗ Licensed Cen ht **LB PARKING:** 9

NEWQUAY, continued

◆◆◆ Tir Chonaill Lodge
106 Mount Wise TR7 1QP
☎ 01637 876492
e-mail: tirchonaillhotel@talk21.com
web: www.tirchonaill.co.uk
Dir: Mount Wise signposted from both boating lake rdbts on entering Newquay. Hotel is on Mount Wise above town centre

CHILD FACILITIES: Please telephone for details

Family-owned and long established, Tir Chonaill Lodge is close to the beaches and the town centre. Bedrooms are neatly presented and some have wonderful views across town to the sea. A warm welcome is extended to all guests, and wholesome dinners and ample breakfasts are sure to satisfy.

ROOMS: 9 en suite (9 fmly) (1 GF) s £30-£40; d £55-£60 * ⊗
FACILITIES: TVB tea/coffee TVL Dinner Last d order 5pm **NOTES:** ⊗ in restaurant Licensed Cen ht **LB PARKING:** 10

PADSTOW
Map 02 SW97

Babies Welcome	Family Rooms	Children's Dishes	

◆◆◆◆ Roselyn
20 Grenville Rd PL28 8EX
☎ 01841 532756 ▤ 01841 532756
e-mail: padstowbbroselyn@bushinternet.com
web: www.padstowbbroselyn.co.uk
Dir: after passing 'Welcome to Padstow' sign, Grenville Road is 1st on left with school on corner

CHILD FACILITIES: Baby listening Activities: puzzles and games Food/bottle warming Ch portions Highchairs Ch cutlery Ch discounts Cots Family rms D rm with S bed & folding bed Fridge Laundry NEARBY: Adventure park Animal centre Short walk to sea

This charming small guest house is in a quiet residential area just a 10-minute walk from the centre of the delightful fishing village. The owners provide warm hospitality, and smartly furnished and well-equipped bedrooms. A good choice of breakfast options is available.

ROOMS: 3 en suite (1 fmly) s fr £35; d fr £55 * **FACILITIES:** TVB tea/coffee No coaches **NOTES:** Credit cards not taken ✖ ⊗ Cen ht LB **PARKING:** 5

PENZANCE
Map 02 SW43

◆◆◆ Carlton Private Hotel
The Promenade TR18 4NW
☎ 01736 362081 ▤ 01736 362081
e-mail: carltonhotelpenzance@talk21.com
Dir: from railway/bus/coach station, follow signs for harbour and Newlyn. Hotel approx 0.75m on right

CHILD FACILITIES: Please telephone for details

Situated on the pleasant promenade and having sea views from many of its rooms, the Carlton is an easy stroll from the town centre and amenities. Rooms are practically furnished and traditionally styled, and a pleasant lounge and spacious dining room are provided.
ROOMS: 12 rms (9 en suite) (6 fmly) s £18-£25; d £44-£50 * ⊗
FACILITIES: TVB tea/coffee TVL No coaches **NOTES:** ✖ ⊗ in restaurant LB BB

Babies Welcome	Family Rooms	Children's Dishes	

◆◆◆ Penmorvah Hotel
61 Alexandra Rd TR18 4LZ
☎ 01736 363711
Dir: from A30 follow Penzance town centre signs past rail station. Follow coast road to mini-rdbt. Right into Alexandra Rd. Penmorvah is on right with blue sign

CHILD FACILITIES: Activities: puzzles, games, books Family area Food/bottle warming Ch menu Ch portions Highchairs Ch cutlery Ch discounts under 5s free, under 15s half price Safe grounds Cots Family rms D rm with 1 S bed, D with 2 S beds £20-£25 Ch drinks Changing mats NEARBY: Land's End Flambards Seal sanctuary Swimming pool 5-min walk to sea

Situated in a quiet, tree-lined road just a short walk from the seafront and town centre, and convenient for the ferry port, the Penmorvah has a friendly and relaxing atmosphere. Bedrooms are well appointed and equipped with many thoughtful extras. Well-cooked breakfasts are served in the attractive dining room.
ROOMS: 8 en suite (2 fmly) (1 GF) s £20-£25; d £40-£50 *
FACILITIES: TVB tea/coffee TVL **NOTES:** ⊗ Cen ht

POLKERRIS
Map 02 SX05

▦ The Rashleigh Inn
PL24 2TL
☎ 01726 813991 ▤ 01726 815619
e-mail: jonspode@aol.com
Dir: Off A3082 outside Fowey

CHILD FACILITIES: Please telephone for details

OPEN: 11-11 **BAR MEALS:** L served all week 12-2 D served all week 6-9 Av main course £6.75 **RESTAURANT:** L served all week 12-2 D served all week 6-9 Av 3 course à la carte £20 **FACILITIES:** Garden: Multi-level terrace, overlooks Polkerris etc ✖ **PARKING:** 22

PORT ISAAC
Map 02 SW98

◆◆◆◆ The Corn Mill
Port Isaac Rd, Trelill PL30 3HZ
☎ 01208 851079
Dir: between villages of Pendoggett and Trelill

CHILD FACILITIES: Please telephone for details

Dating from the 18th century, this former mill has been restored to provide a charming home, packed full of character. The bedrooms

continued

continued

are individually styled and personal touches contribute to a relaxed and homely atmosphere. The farmhouse kitchen is the venue for a delicious breakfast.
ROOMS: 3 rms (2 en suite) (1 fmly) d £60 * ⊗ **FACILITIES:** TV1B tea/coffee No coaches **NOTES:** Credit cards not taken ⊗ in restaurant Cen ht **PARKING:** 3

PORTREATH
Map 02 SW64

Babies Welcome | Children's Dishes

ⓖ Tabb's Restaurant
Railway Ter TR16 4LD
☎ 01209 842488 🖷 01209 842488
Dir: In village centre, near seafront

CHILD FACILITIES: Food/bottle warming Ch portions Highchairs NEARBY: 400yds to sea

FOOD: British, Mediterranean **STYLE:** Rustic **SEATS:** 35
OPEN: 12.15-2.15/7-9.30, Closed 2 wks Jan & Nov, TueL Mon-Sat
RESTAURANT: Fixed L £15, Fixed D £19.50, main £11.50-£19.75
NOTES: ⊗ in restaurant **PARKING:** 4

PORTSCATHO
Map 02 SW83

Babies Welcome | Family Rooms | Children's Dishes

★★★ ⓖ ⓖ Rosevine
TR2 5EW
☎ 01872 580206 🖷 01872 580230
e-mail: info@rosevinehotels.co.uk
web: www.rosevine.co.uk
Dir: from St Austell take A390 for Truro. Left onto B3287 to Tregony. Take A3078 through Ruan High Lanes. Hotel 3rd left

CHILD FACILITIES: Baby listening Activities: puzzles, games, toys, colouring, tree house Indoor play area Outdoor play area Food/bottle warming Ch menu Ch portions Highchairs Ch cutlery Ch discounts discounts vary with age Games consoles Videos Cots Family rms 2 rms or D bed with S or T bed from £184 Connecting rms Laundry Changing mats NEARBY: Coastal walks Cinema Sailing Horseriding 3-min walk to sea

Set in secluded splendour, with views over beautifully tended gardens towards the sea, this Georgian country house has its own beach at the head of the Roseland peninsula. The proprietors and staff are attentive and friendly and create a relaxed atmosphere. Bedrooms are impressively equipped, with fresh fruit, flowers and up-to-date reading material - most enjoy the views and some have balconies. Cuisine features the local harvest of fresh fish and shellfish and the best of Cornish produce.
ROOMS: 11 en suite 6 annexe en suite (7 fmly) (3 GF) s £126-£178; d £168-£224 (incl. bkfst) **LB FACILITIES:** 🏓 Table tennis Children's playroom 🎵 **PARKING:** 20 **NOTES:** ⊗ in restaurant Closed Dec-8 Feb

PRAA SANDS
Map 02 SW52

Babies Welcome | Family Rooms | Children's Dishes

◆◆◆◆ 🏛 Gwynoon
Chy-an-Dour Rd TR20 9SY
☎ 01736 763508
e-mail: enquiries@gwynoon.co.uk
web: www.gwynoon.co.uk
Dir: M5 junct 31 at Exeter, A30 to Penzance. A394 towards Helston, 7m Germoe X-rds, right by golf club to Praa Sands, down hill past holiday village, 2nd left after post office to Chy-an-Dour Road, Guest house immediately left

continued

CHILD FACILITIES: Food/bottle warming Ch menu Ch portions Highchairs Ch cutlery Ch discounts under 2s £10 per stay, 2-12s £22.50 pn, 12+s £27.50 pn Safe grounds Cots £5 Family rms suites with D rm & D/T rm Ch drinks Connecting rms Laundry (charge) NEARBY: Flambards 100 yds to sea

Gwynoon is located in Praa Sands, one of Cornwall's dazzling beaches. There are excellent views from the front bedrooms, balcony and the well-tended gardens. Bedrooms are well furnished and have many extras. The hosts are very attentive and provide a peaceful atmosphere. The enjoyable breakfasts feature fresh local produce.
ROOMS: 3 en suite (2 fmly) (1 GF) s £27.50; d £55 * **FACILITIES:** TVB tea/coffee No coaches **NOTES:** Credit cards not taken 🐾 ⊗ Cen ht **PARKING:** 6

ST AGNES
Map 02 SW75

Babies Welcome | Family Rooms | Children's Dishes

◆◆◆◆ 🍴 Driftwood Spars Hotel
Trevaunance Cove TR5 0RT
☎ 01872 552428 & 553323 🖷 01872 553701
e-mail: driftwoodspars@hotmail.com
web: www.driftwoodspars.com
Dir: off A30 at rdbt signed St Agnes, through village bear right past church, left at bottom of hill, hotel on right

CHILD FACILITIES: Food/bottle warming Ch menu Ch portions Highchairs Ch discounts babies free, £2 per year old Videos Cots Family rms D rms with B beds £40pppn, plus child rate Connecting rms Fridge NEARBY: Rock pools 100 yds to sea

This historic inn was built from shipwreck timbers - hence the name. Bedrooms are attractively decorated in a bright seaside style, with comfortable furnishings and many interesting features. A good range of local produce is offered, especially delicious smoked fish.
ROOMS: 9 en suite 6 annexe en suite (5 fmly) (5 GF) s £37-£55; d £74-£84 * **FACILITIES:** TVB tea/coffee Direct dial from bedrooms TVL Snooker Pool Table Sea fishing, surfing Dinner Last d order 9.30pm **NOTES:** ⊗ in restaurant ⊗ in 1 lounge Cen ht **PARKING:** 81

England

ST AUSTELL Map 02 SX05

★★★★ 75% 🌐 **Carlyon Bay**

Sea Rd, Carlyon Bay PL25 3RD

☎ 01726 812304 📠 01726 814938

e-mail: reservations@carlyonbay.com

web: www.carlyonbay.com

Dir: from St Austell, follow signs for Charlestown. Carlyon Bay signed on left, hotel at end of Sea Road

CHILD FACILITIES: Baby listening Babysitting Activities: games, putting green, tennis courts, 2 swimming pools, archery Indoor play area Outdoor play area Food/bottle warming Ch menu Ch portions Highchairs Ch cutlery Ch discounts 0-3s £5 per day, 3-8s 75% discount, 9-13s 45% discount, own room 25% discount Safe grounds Games consoles Videos Cots Family rms D rms with B beds £200 Connecting rms Laundry **NEARBY:** Eden Project Seal sanctuary Flambards 5-min walk to sea

Originally built in the 1920s, this long-established hotel lies on the clifftop in 250 acres of grounds, which include indoor and outdoor pools and a golf course. Bedrooms are well-maintained, many with marvellous views across St Austell Bay. A good choice of comfortable lounges is available, whilst facilities for families include kids clubs and entertainment.

ROOMS: 87 en suite (14 fmly) ⊗ in 14 bedrooms s £90 £106; d £170-£280 (incl. bkfst) **LB FACILITIES: Spa** STV ⊡ ⚑ Golf 18 ⚒ Snooker Sauna Solarium ⌁ Table tennis 9-hole approach course, Health and beauty salon ♫ Xmas **PARKING:** 100 **NOTES:** ✻ ⊗ in restaurant

See advert on opposite page

ST IVES Map 02 SW54

★★★ 68% **Chy-an-Albany**

Albany Ter TR26 2BS

☎ 01736 796759 📠 01736 795584

e-mail: info@chyanalbanyhotel.com

Dir: from A30 onto A3074 signed St Ives, hotel on left just before junct

CHILD FACILITIES: Baby listening Activities: puzzles, colouring Food/bottle warming Ch menu Ch portions Highchairs Ch discounts under 2s free, 2-7s 75% discount, 8-12s half price Safe grounds Cots Family rms D rms with S bed, D rms with 2 S beds Laundry **NEARBY:** Dairyland Flambards Short walk to sea

Conveniently located, this pleasant hotel enjoys splendid sea views. Comfortable bedrooms, some with balconies and sea views, come in a variety of sizes. Friendly staff and the relaxing environment mean that guests return on a regular basis. Freshly prepared and appetising cuisine is served in the dining room.

ROOMS: 40 en suite (11 fmly) ⊗ in all bedrooms **FACILITIES:** STV ♫ Xmas **PARKING:** 37 **NOTES:** ✻ ⊗ in restaurant

★★★ 65% **Tregenna Castle Hotel**

TR26 2DE

☎ 01736 795254 📠 01736 796066

e-mail: hotel@tregenna-castle.co.uk

Dir: A30 from Exeter to Penzance, at Lelant W of Hayle take A3074 to St Ives, through Carbis Bay, signed main entrance on left

CHILD FACILITIES: Babysitting Outdoor play area Food/bottle warming Ch menu Ch portions Highchairs Ch discounts under 3s free, 3-12s up to 50% Safe grounds Cots Family rms Connecting rms Laundry

Sitting at the top of town in beautiful landscaped gardens, this popular hotel boasts spectacular views of St Ives. Many leisure facilities are available, including indoor and outdoor pools, gymnasium and sauna. Families are particularly welcome. Bedrooms are generally spacious. A carte menu or carvery buffet are offered in the restaurant.

ROOMS: 83 en suite (12 fmly) (16 GF) ⊗ in 49 bedrooms s £50-£95; d £80-£170 (incl. bkfst & dinner) **FACILITIES:** STV ⊡ ⚑ Golf 18 ⚒ Squash Sauna Solarium Gym ⌁ Jacuzzi Health spa Steam room Xmas **PARKING:** 200 **NOTES:** ✻ ⊗ in restaurant

◆◆◆◆◆ 🏛 **Lumiere**

Consols TR26 2HD

☎ 01736 799902 & 07971 809883 📠 01736 799902

Dir: leave A30 southbound at St Ives exit, over 1st rdbt, left at 2nd rdbt, T-junct after 3m, turn right, entrance 150yds on right

CHILD FACILITIES: Activities: toys Outdoor play area Food/bottle warming Ch menu Ch portions Highchairs Ch cutlery Ch discounts under 2s free Safe grounds Videos Cots Family rms D with connecting child's rm Ch drinks Laundry Changing mats **NEARBY:** Horse riding Coastal walks Cinema Park Swimming pool 15-min walk to sea

Lumiere is a friendly, modern house, located above the busy town but set in quiet grounds. The stylish building has spacious rooms, well equipped with many thoughtful extras. Guests can relax in the garden in summer. Cornish breakfasts add to a memorable stay.

ROOMS: 2 en suite (1 fmly) (1 GF) s £30; d £60 * **FACILITIES:** TVB tea/coffee No coaches **NOTES:** Credit cards not taken ✻ ⊗ Cen ht **LB PARKING:** 3

◆◆◆◆ 🏛 **Primrose Valley Hotel**

Primrose Valley, Porthminster Beach TR26 2ED

☎ 01736 794939 📠 01736 794939

e-mail: info@primroseonline.co.uk

web: www.primroseonline.co.uk

Dir: from A30 follow St Ives signs, right into Primrose Valley 25mtrs after the 'St Ives - Porthia' sign, bear left under bridge, along beach front, turning left back under bridge, hotel on left

CHILD FACILITIES: Baby listening Activities: toys, books, colouring, games Indoor play area Food/bottle warming Ch menu Ch portions Highchairs Ch cutlery Ch discounts under 3s free (charge for cot), 3-9s 1/3 cost, 10-16s 50% when sharing Safe grounds Videos Cots Family rms D rms with S beds/B beds from £73 Connecting rms Laundry Changing mats **NEARBY:** Beach adjacent

St Ives is just a short walk from this friendly, family-run hotel. Porthminster beach is nearby. The hotel has a light and airy atmosphere and a good level of comfort. Some bedrooms have a balcony. There is a lounge and bar area, and dinner is available. Breakfast features local produce and home-made items.

ROOMS: 10 en suite (4 fmly) s £37.50-£53.50; d £55-£99 * ⊗ **FACILITIES:** TVB tea/coffee TVL No coaches Dinner Last d order 6.30pm **NOTES:** ✻ ⊗ in restaurant ⊗ in lounges Licensed **LB PARKING:** 10

Babies Welcome | Family Rooms | Children's Dishes

◆◆◆ Thurlestone Hotel

St Ives Rd, Carbis Bay TR26 2RT
☎ 01736 796369
e-mail: anna.monkman@virgin.net
Dir: off A30 follow A3074 St Ives signs. Through Lelant onto Carbis Bay, pass convenience store on left. Hotel is 0.25m on left next to newsagents

CHILD FACILITIES: Baby listening **Activities:** games, puzzles **Food/bottle warming Ch portions Highchairs Ch discounts under 2s free, 2-12s half price, 13-16s 3/4 price Games consoles Cots Family rms 2 D rms with S beds, D rm with B beds £52.50-£81 Laundry **NEARBY:** 5-min walk to sea

Built in 1843 as a chapel, this granite house now provides pleasant, modern accommodation. The proprietors offer a friendly and comfortable environment, and many guests return regularly. There is a cosy lounge bar. Some of the bedrooms have sea views and all are well equipped.

ROOMS: 8 en suite (3 fmly) d £42-£60 * **FACILITIES:** TVB tea/coffee TVL **NOTES:** ✠ ⊘ Licensed Cen ht **LB PARKING:** 5

ST JUST (NEAR LAND'S END)   Map 02 SW33

Babies Welcome | Family Rooms | Children's Dishes

◆◆◆ 🍷 Wellington Hotel

Market Square TR19 7HD
☎ 01736 787319 📠 01736 787906
e-mail: wellingtonhotel@msn.com
Dir: take A30 to W of Penzance then take A3071. St Just is 6m W of Penzance. Hotel overlooks Main Square

CHILD FACILITIES: Indoor play area Outdoor play area Family area Food/bottle warming Ch menu Highchairs Ch discounts children from £5 Safe grounds Cots Family rms D rm with B beds or T rm with B beds Connecting rms Laundry **NEARBY:** Country club Flambards Paradise park

This friendly inn, situated in busy Market Square, offers comfortable accommodation and is popular with locals and visitors alike. Bedrooms are spacious and well equipped. Home-cooked food makes for a pleasant stay.

ROOMS: 5 en suite 6 annexe en suite (4 fmly) (3 GF) s £30-£35; d £50-£65 * ⊘ in 1 bedrooms **FACILITIES:** TVB tea/coffee TVL Pool Table Dinner Last d order 9pm **NOTES:** ⊘ in restaurant Cen ht **LB**

ST MELLION   Map 02 SX36

★★★ 68% St Mellion International

PL12 6SD
☎ 01579 351351 📠 01579 350537
e-mail: stmellion@americangolf.uk.com
web: www.st-mellion.co.uk
Dir: from M5/A38 towards Plymouth & Saltash. St Mellion off A38 on A388 towards Callington & Launceston

CHILD FACILITIES: Please telephone for details

This purpose-built hotel, golfing and leisure complex is surrounded by 450 acres of land with two highly regarded 18-hole golf courses. The bedrooms generally have views over the courses and public areas include a choice of eating options. Function suites are also available.

ROOMS: 39 annexe en suite (15 fmly) (8 GF) s £75-£105; d £100-£160 (incl. bkfst) **LB FACILITIES:** Spa 🏊 Golf 18 ⚼ Squash Snooker Sauna Solarium Gym ⚓ Jacuzzi Steam room Skincare Xmas **PARKING:** 400 **NOTES:** ✠ ⊘ in restaurant

---

THE CARLYON BAY HOTEL AA★★★★

FIRST FOR FAMILIES

The Carlyon Bay Hotel is set in 250 acres of landscaped grounds with beautiful views of St. Austell Bay and the Carlyon Bay Championship Golf Course, a spectacular 18 hole course – free to guests. The hotel also sports excellent health and fitness facilities, including superb outdoor and indoor swimming pool, tennis courts, health and beauty salon, sauna, solarium and spa bath. During School Holiday periods there is a full family entertainment programme.

It's perfect for exploring Cornwall; the Lost Gardens of Heligan, Eden Project or pretty fishing villages.

Carlyon Bay, St. Austell, Cornwall PL25 3RD
Tel: 01726 812304 Fax: 01726 814938
Web: www.carlyonbay.co.uk

THE WESTCOUNTRY'S LEADING HOTEL GROUP

SALTASH   Map 02 SX45

Babies Welcome | Family Rooms | Children's Dishes

★★★ 67% China Fleet Country Club

PL12 6LJ
☎ 01752 848668 📠 01752 848456
e-mail: sales@china-fleet.co.uk
Dir: A38 towards Plymouth/Saltash. Cross Tamar Bridge taking slip road before tunnel. Right at lights, 1st left follow signs 0.5m.

CHILD FACILITIES: Baby listening **Activities:** sport in school hols, afternoon club, Lego tables, books, soft play area Indoor play area Outdoor play area Food/bottle warming Ch menu Ch portions Highchairs Ch discounts children free Safe grounds Cots Family rms Apartments- 2 rm or T beds with S beds £72-88 Fridge Laundry **NEARBY:** Ski slope Cinema Aquarium Plymouth Dome

In a convenient, quiet location, ideal for access to Plymouth and the countryside, the China Fleet Country Club offers an extensive range of sporting and leisure facilities including an impressive golf course. Bedrooms are all located in annexe buildings; each is equipped with its own kitchen. There is a range of dining options, and the newly refurbished restaurant offers some interesting and imaginative choices.

ROOMS: 40 en suite (21 GF) ⊘ in 30 bedrooms s £42-£72; d £42-£88 **FACILITIES:** Spa STV 🏊 Golf 18 ⚼ Squash Sauna Solarium Gym ⚓ Jacuzzi 28 bay Floodlit driving range Health & beauty suite Hairdressers Xmas **PARKING:** 400 **NOTES:** ✠ ⊘ in restaurant

England

SCILLY, ISLES OF

BRYHER — Map 02

★★★ 81% 🏵 🏵 Hell Bay Hotel
TR23 0PR
☎ 01720 422947 📠 01720 423004
e-mail: contactus@hellbay.co.uk
Dir: Island location means it is only accessible by helicopter from Penzance, ship from Penzance or plane from Southampton, Bristol, Exeter, Plymouth or Land's End

CHILD FACILITIES: Please telephone for details

Located on the smallest of the inhabited Scilly islands, this hotel provides a really special destination. Much of the hotel has been completely refurbished and bedrooms, many with garden access and stunning sea views, are stylish and very well equipped. Cuisine features fresh local produce and is a delight.
ROOMS: 12 en suite 11 annexe en suite (4 fmly) (18 GF) 🚭 in all bedrooms d £180-£400 (incl. bkfst & dinner) **LB FACILITIES:** STV ⚐ Golf 9 Sauna Gym 🎵 Jacuzzi Boules Par 3 golf **NOTES:** 🚭 in restaurant Closed Jan-Feb

ST MARTIN'S — Map 02

★★★ 🏵 🏵 🏵
St Martin's on the Isle
Lower Town TR25 0QW
☎ 01720 422090 📠 01720 422298
e-mail: stay@stmartinshotel.co.uk web: www.stmartinshotel.co.uk
Dir: 20-minute helicopter flight to St Mary's, then 20-minute launch to St Martin's

CHILD FACILITIES: Baby listening Babysitting Indoor play area Outdoor play area Food/bottle warming Ch menu Ch portions Highchairs Ch cutlery Ch discounts under 12s free Safe grounds Videos Cots Family rms rms with B beds Ch drinks Connecting rms Fridge Laundry Changing mats **NEARBY:** Seafront location

This attractive hotel, complete with its own sandy beach, enjoys an idyllic position on the waterfront overlooking Tresco and Tean. Bedrooms are brightly appointed, comfortably furnished and overlook the sea or the well-tended gardens. There is an elegant, award-winning restaurant and a split-level lounge bar where guests can relax and enjoy the memorable view. Locally caught fish features significantly on the daily-changing menus.
ROOMS: 30 en suite (10 fmly) (14 GF) s £125-£175; d £250-£350 (incl. bkfst & dinner) **LB FACILITIES:** 🏊 ⚐ Snooker Clay pigeon shooting Boating Bikes Diving Snorkelling **NOTES:** 🚭 in restaurant Closed Nov-Feb

TRESCO — Map 02

★★★ 🏵 🏵 The Island
TR24 0PU
☎ 01720 422883 📠 01720 423008
e-mail: islandhotel@tresco.co.uk
web: www.tresco.co.uk/holidays/island_hotel.asp
Dir: helicopter service Penzance to Tresco, hotel on NE of island

CHILD FACILITIES: Baby listening Nanny Babysitting Activities: board games, sailing school, table football, table tennis, badminton, cricket, shrimping Indoor play area Outdoor play area Family area Food/bottle warming Ch menu Ch portions Highchairs Ch cutlery Ch discounts Safe grounds Games consoles Videos Cots Family rms D rm with B beds £30 sharing with adults, 30% in own room Connecting rms Fridge Laundry Changing mats **NEARBY:** Gardens Playpark Cliff Cutter Private beach

continued

This delightful colonial-style hotel enjoys a waterside location in its own attractive gardens. The spacious, comfortable lounges, airy restaurant and many of the bedrooms enjoy stunning sea views. All of the rooms are brightly furnished and many benefit from lounge areas, balconies or terraces. Carefully prepared, imaginative cuisine makes good use of locally caught fish.
ROOMS: 48 en suite (27 fmly) s £117-£283; d £117-£283 (incl. bkfst & dinner) **LB FACILITIES:** ⚐ ⚒ Fishing 🎵 Boating Table tennis Bowls, boutique, internet access **NOTES:** 🐾 🚭 in restaurant Closed Nov-Feb

SEATON — Map 02 SX35

◆◆◆◆ ☐ Smugglers Inn
Treunnick Ln PL11 3JD
☎ 01503 250646
web: www.the-smugglers-inn.co.uk
Dir: A387 towards Hessonford, onto Downderry Road (B3247) for 2m

CHILD FACILITIES: Family area Food/bottle warming Ch menu Ch portions Highchairs Ch cutlery Safe grounds Cots Family rms Connecting rms **NEARBY:** Country park Seafront location

Close to the fishing port of Looe, this friendly inn has an enviable location close to the waters edge. Bedrooms are pleasantly appointed and attractively decorated. Entertainment features in the bar on certain nights of the week. The menu has a wide range of choices and there is also a children's menu.
ROOMS: 5 en suite (2 fmly) s £17.50-£50; d £35-£60 * 🚭 **FACILITIES:** TVB tea/coffee Pool Table Dinner Last d order 9pm **NOTES:** 🐾 🚭 in restaurant Cen ht **BB**

TINTAGEL — Map 02 SX08

☐ The Port William ◆◆◆◆
Trebarwith Strand PL34 0HB
☎ 01840 770230 📠 01840 770936
e-mail: theportwilliam@btinternet.com
Dir: Off B3263 between Camelford & Tintagel

CHILD FACILITIES: Please telephone for details

OPEN: 11-11 (Sun 12-10.30) 12 opening in winter **BAR/RESTAURANT MEALS:** L all week 12-2.30 D all week 6.30-9.30 **FACILITIES:** Garden: Patio **ROOMS:** 8 bedrooms 8 en suite s£55 d£75 **PARKING:** 75

CUMBRIA

Wooden boats on the shore near Cragwood

ALSTON
Nent Valley
Nenthead Mines Heritage Centre CA9 3PD
administration.office@virgin.net ☎01434 382726
(5m E, on A689)
Open Etr-Oct, daily 10.30-5. Mine tours at 12, 1.30
& 3 daily. £4-£6.50, pen £3.25-5.50, ch site free,
mine £2. Family ticket £15.30

BASSENTHWAITE
Trotters World of Animals CA12 4RD
info@trottersworld.com ☎017687 76239
Open all year, except 25 Dec & Jan. Summer
10 - 5.30, Winter 11 - 4.30. *£5.50, ch £4.25,
under 3yrs free.

CARLISLE
Carlisle Castle
CA3 8UR ☎01228 591992
(North side of city centre, close to station)
Open all year, Apr-Sep, daily 9.30-6 Oct-Mar, daily
10-4. Closed 24-26 Dec & 1 Jan. £3.80, ch £1.90,
concessions £2.90.

CARLISLE
Tullie House Museum & Art Gallery CA38TP
barbaral@carlisle-city.gov.uk ☎01228 534781
(M6, junct 42, 43 or 44 follow signs to city centre.
Car park located in Devonshire Walk)
Open Nov-Mar, Mon-Sat 10-4, Sun 12-4; Apr-Jun
& Sep-Oct, Mon-Sat 10-5, Sun 12-5. Jul-Aug,
Mon-Sat 10-5, Sun 11-5. Closed 25-26 Dec & 1
Jan. Ground floor including Art Gallery & Old Tullie
House - Free.Upper floors & New Millennium
Gallery *£5.20, concessions £3.60 Family ticket 2
adults 3 ch £14.50

DALTON-IN-FURNESS
South Lakes Wild Animal Park LA15 8JR
office@wildanimalpark.co.uk ☎01229 466086
(M6 junct 36, A590 to Dalton-in-Furness, follow
tourist signs)
Open all year, daily 10-5, last admission 4.15;
Nov-Feb 10-4.30, last admission 3.45. Closed 25
Dec. *£9.50, ch, pen, wheelchair users &
registered blind £6. Reduced prices Nov-Mar.

HARDKNOT CASTLE ROMAN FORT
Hardknot Castle Roman Fort
(9m NE of Ravenglass, at end of Hardknott Pass)
Open any reasonable time. Access may be
hazardous in winter.

HAWKSHEAD
Beatrix Potter Gallery LA22 ONS
Main St ☎01229 466086
(on the main street in village centre)
beatrixpotterygallery@nationaltrust.org.uk
Open 3 Apr-Oct & Good Fri Sat-Wed 10.30-4.30
(last admission 4). Admission is by timed ticket
including NT menbers. £3 ch £1.50, Family ticket
£7.50 (2ad+3ch).

KENDAL
Museum of Lakeland Life LA9 5AL
info@lakelandmuseum.org.uk ☎01539 722464
(M6 junct 36, follow signs to Kendal. Located at
south end of Kendal beside Abbot Hall Art Gallery)
Open 20 Jan-23 Dec, Mon-Sat 10.30-5 (closing at
4pm Jan, Feb, Mar, Nov, Dec) £3.50, ch &
students £2. Family ticket £9.50 Combined ticket
with Abbot Hall & Lakeland Life same day, £6.50.

LAKESIDE
Aquarium of the Lakes
LA12 8AS ☎015395 30153
aquariumofthelakes@reallive.co.uk
(M6, junct 36, take A590 to Newby Bridge. Turn
right over bridge, follow Hawkshead road to
Lakeside. Well signposted)
Open all year, daily from 9am. Closed 25 Dec.
*£5.95, ch £3.75, pen £4.95. Family ticket 2 adult
& 2 ch £16.95, 2 adult & 3 ch £19.95, 2 adult & 4
ch £22.95.

PENRITH
Rheged - The Village in the Hill CA11 0DQ
enquiries@rheged.com ☎01768 868000
(M6 junct 40, on A66 towards Keswick)
Open daily 10-5.30. Closed 25 Dec
*Each attraction £5.50, ch £3.90 & pen £4.70.
Family ticket £16

RAVENGLASS
Ravenglass & Eskdale Railway
CA18 1SW ☎01229 717171
steam@ravenglass-railway.co.uk
(Close to A595, Barrow to Carlisle road)
Open: trains operate daily Mid Mar-early Nov. Most
winter wknds, plus daily in Feb Half-term.
*Return fare £8.20, ch 5-15 £4.10. 1 adult half
price with 2+ fare paying children.

WINDERMERE
Lake District Visitor Centre at Brockhole
LA23 1LJ
infodesk@lake-district.gov.uk ☎015394 46601
(On A591, between Windermere and Ambleside,
follow brown tourist signs)
Open Etr-Oct, 10-5 daily. Grounds & gardens open
all year.
Windermere Steamboat Centre LA23 1BN
steamboat@ecosse.net ☎015394 45565
(0.5m N of Bowness-on-Windermere on A592)
Open 17 Mar-7 Nov daily, 10-5. Steamboat trips
subject to availability & weather.
£4.25, ch £2.25 Family ticket £8.50, season ticket
£15.

AMBLESIDE
Map 07 NY30

Babies Welcome | Family Rooms | Children's Dishes

★★★ 78% 🌸 Rothay Manor
Rothay Bridge LA22 0EH
☎ 015394 33605 📠 015394 33607
e-mail: hotel@rothaymanor.co.uk
web: www.rothaymanor.co.uk
Dir: In Ambleside follow signs for Coniston (A593). Hotel 0.25 mile SW of Ambleside opposite rugby pitch

CHILD FACILITIES: Baby listening Activities: croquet, boules, games Outdoor play area Food/bottle warming Ch menu Ch portions Highchairs Ch discounts under 3s free Safe grounds Videos Cots Family rms D rm with 2 S beds £140-£200 Ch drinks Fridge Laundry **NEARBY:** Children's playground Lake Leisure club

The former home of a Liverpool merchant, this attractive listed building, built in Regency style, is a short walk from both the town centre and Lake Windermere. Spacious bedrooms, including suites, family rooms and rooms with balconies, have been refurbished to a high standard. Public areas include a choice of lounges and a spacious restaurant.
ROOMS: 17 en suite 2 annexe en suite (7 fmly) (3 GF) 🚭 in all bedrooms s £70-£95; d £120-£180 (incl. bkfst) **LB FACILITIES:** Nearby leisure centre free to guests Xmas **PARKING:** 15 **NOTES:** ✸ 🚭 in restaurant Closed 3-28 Jan

◆◆◆◆ 🍴 Wateredge Inn
Waterhead Bay LA22 0EP
☎ 015394 32332 📠 015394 31878
e-mail: rec@wateredgeinn.co.uk
web: www.wateredgeinn.co.uk
Dir: On A591, at Waterhead, 1m S of Ambleside. Wateredge situated at end of promenade by lake

CHILD FACILITIES: Please telephone for details

This modern inn has an idyllic location on the shore of Windermere at Waterhead Bay. The pretty bedrooms are particularly smart and generally spacious, and all offer a high standard of quality and comfort. The airy, open-plan

continued

bar-restaurant opens onto attractive gardens, which have magnificent lake views. There is also a comfortable lounge.
ROOMS: 15 en suite 6 annexe en suite (3 fmly) (3 GF) s £35-£50; d £70-£140 * 🚭 in 1 bedrooms **FACILITIES:** TVB tea/coffee Complimentary membership to nearby leisure club Dinner Last d order 8.30pm **NOTES:** 🚭 in area of dining room 🚭 in lounges Cen ht **LB PARKING:** 40

◆◆◆◆ 🍴 Glen Rothay Hotel
Rydal LA22 9LR
☎ 015394 34500 📠 34505
e-mail: jhpckrng9@aol.com
Dir: on A591, 1.5m NW of Ambleside on right opposite Rydal water
CHILD FACILITIES: Please telephone for details

Dating in part back to 1624, this Grade II listed building offers spacious bedrooms furnished to a high standard, including four-poster and family rooms. A wide choice of meals using local produce is available in the Badger Bar or in the restaurant, and there is an atmospheric oak-panelled lounge to relax in after dinner.
ROOMS: 8 en suite (1 fmly) 🚭 **FACILITIES:** TVB tea/coffee Direct dial from bedrooms Dinner Last d order 8.45pm **NOTES:** 🚭 in restaurant 🚭 in 1 lounge Cen ht **PARKING:** 30

APPLEBY-IN-WESTMORLAND
Map 12 NY62

Babies Welcome | Family Rooms | Children's Dishes

★★★ 78% 🌸 🌸
Appleby Manor Country House
Roman Rd CA16 6JB
☎ 017683 51571 📠 017683 52888
e-mail: reception@applebymanor.co.uk
web: www.applebymanor.co.uk
Dir: M6 junct 40/A66 towards Brough. Take Appleby turn, then immediately right. Continue 0.5m

Best Western

CHILD FACILITIES: Baby listening Activities: puzzles, board games, table tennis, pool table Outdoor play area Food/bottle warming Ch menu Ch portions Highchairs Ch cutlery Ch discounts under 16s free sharing with 2 adults, 50% discount for own room Safe grounds Videos Cots Family rms 8 family rms Connecting rms Laundry **NEARBY:** Ostrich sanctuary Discovery centre Cinema

This imposing country mansion is set in extensive grounds amid fabulous Cumbrian scenery. The Dunbobbin family and their experienced staff ensure a warm welcome and attentive service. Bedrooms, including a number with patios, vary in style, with the garden rooms now refurbished. The restaurant serves carefully prepared meals.
ROOMS: 23 en suite 7 annexe en suite (9 fmly) 🚭 in 23 bedrooms s £84-£94; d £128-£148 (incl. bkfst) **LB FACILITIES:** STV 🔄 Sauna Solarium ♨ Jacuzzi Steam room, Table tennis, Pool table **PARKING:** 53 **NOTES:** 🚭 in restaurant Closed 24-26 Dec

BASSENTHWAITE
Map 11 NY23

Babies Welcome | Family Rooms | Children's Dishes

★★★★ 72% 🏵 Armathwaite Hall
CA12 4RE
☎ 017687 76551 📠 017687 76220
e-mail: reservations@armathwaite-hall.com
web: www.armathwaite-hall.com
Dir: M6 junct 40/A66 to Keswick rdbt then A591 signed Carlisle. 8m to Castle Inn junct, turn left. Hotel 300yds

CHILD FACILITIES: Baby listening Babysitting Activities: colouring, puzzles, Freebee Club Outdoor play area Food/bottle warming Ch menu Ch portions Highchairs Ch discounts under 12s free when sharing with 2 adults Safe grounds Games consoles Videos Cots Family rms D & T rms with Z bed or adj B bed rm Connecting rms Laundry **NEARBY:** Animal park on estate

Enjoying fine views over Bassenthwaite Lake, this impressive mansion, dating from the 17th century, is peacefully situated amid 400 acres of deer park. Comfortably furnished bedrooms are complemented by a choice of public rooms featuring splendid wood panelling and roaring log fires in the cooler months. The indoor and outdoor leisure facilities are also an added attraction.
ROOMS: 43 en suite (4 fmly) (8 GF) s £119-£155; d £150-£290 (incl. bkfst) **LB FACILITIES: Spa** STV 🏊 ◈ Fishing Snooker Sauna Solarium Gym ♨ ♿ Jacuzzi Archery, Beauty salon, Clayshooting, Quad bikes, Falconry, Mountain Bikes Xmas **PARKING:** 100 **NOTES:** ⊗ in restaurant

BOOT
Map 07 NY10

🍴 The Boot Inn (formerly The Burnmoor Inn)
CA19 1TG
☎ 019467 23224 📠 019467 23337
e-mail: stay@burnmoor.co.uk
web: www.burnmoor.co.uk
CHILD FACILITIES: Please telephone for details

OPEN: 11-11 **BAR MEALS:** L served all week 11-5 D served all week 6-9 Av main course £7.50 **RESTAURANT:** L served all week 11-5 D served all week 6-9 Av 3 course à la carte £17.50 **FACILITIES:** Children's licence Garden: Part paved part grassed, seating 40 people **ROOMS:** 9 bedrooms 8 en suite 2 family rooms s£30 d£60 (♦♦♦) **PARKING:** 30

Babies Welcome | Children's Dishes

🍴 Brook House Inn
CA19 1TG
☎ 019467 23288 📠 019467 23160
e-mail: stay@brookhouseinn.co.uk
CHILD FACILITIES: Food/bottle warming Ch licence Ch menu Ch portions (some main courses) Highchairs Ch cutlery Changing facilities **NEARBY:** Ravenglass & Eskdale Railway

continued

OPEN: 11-11 Closed: 25 Dec **BAR MEALS:** L served all week 12-5.30 D served all week 5.30-8.30 Av main course £8 **RESTAURANT:** L served all week 12-4.30 D served all week 6-8.30 **FACILITIES:** Children's licence Garden: Terrace with seating; views across valley **ROOMS:** 7 bedrooms 7 en suite s£40 d£60 (♦♦♦♦) **PARKING:** 25

BRAITHWAITE
Map 11 NY22

♦♦♦♦ 🍺 🍴 The Royal Oak
Braithwaite CA12 5SY
☎ 017687 78533 📠 017687 78533
e-mail: tpfranks@hotmail.com
web: www.royaloak-braithwaite.co.uk
Dir: turn off A66 and follow Whinlatter Pass. Hotel in middle of Braithwaite.
CHILD FACILITIES: Please telephone for details

The Royal Oak, in the pretty village of Braithwaite, has delightful views of Skiddaw and Barrow, and is an ideal base for tourists and walkers. Some of the well-equipped bedrooms are furnished with four-poster beds. Hearty meals and traditional Cumbrian breakfasts are served in the restaurant.
ROOMS: 10 en suite (1 fmly) s £30-£37; d £60-£74 * ⊗
FACILITIES: STV TVB tea/coffee ◈ local golf available, bowling green Dinner Last d order 9pm **NOTES:** ⊗ in restaurant Cen ht **LB**
PARKING: 20

CALDBECK
Map 11 NY34

♦♦♦♦ 🌱 Swaledale Watch Farm
Whelpo CA7 8HQ
☎ 016974 78409 📠 016974 78409
e-mail: nan.savage@talk21.com
Dir: 1m SW of Caldbeck village on B5299
CHILD FACILITIES: Please telephone for details

This attractive farmhouse, within its own nature reserve, is in a peaceful location with a backdrop of picturesque fells. The en suite bedrooms are spacious and well equipped. Two rooms are in an adjacent converted farm building and share a comfortable sitting room. Traditional hearty breakfasts are served in the attractive dining room overlooking the garden, with views to the fells.
ROOMS: 2 en suite 2 annexe en suite (2 fmly) (4 GF) s £22-£7; d £40-£48 * **FACILITIES:** TVB tea/coffee TVL 100 acre Nature Reserve 150 acres Sheep **NOTES:** Credit cards not taken 🐾 ⊗ Cen ht **BB**
PARKING: 8

Many proprietors are happy to provide extra facilities for children, but let them know in advance what you need so they can be prepared

COCKERMOUTH · Map 11 NY13

| Babies Welcome | Family Rooms | Children's Dishes |

★★★ 76% 🏵 The Trout
Crown St CA13 0EJ
☎ 01900 823591 📠 01900 827514
e-mail: enquiries@trouthotel.co.uk web: www.trouthotel.co.uk
Dir: next to Wordsworth House

CHILD FACILITIES: Baby listening Activities: colouring Food/bottle warming Ch licence Ch menu Ch portions Highchairs Ch cutlery Ch discounts under 5s free in adults room Cots Family rms D rm with B beds from £80 Connecting rms Fridge Laundry **NEARBY:** Muncastle Castle Aquarium

Dating back to 1670, this privately owned hotel has an enviable setting on the banks of the River Derwent. The well-equipped bedrooms, some contained in a new wing overlooking the river, are mostly spacious and comfortable. The new Terrace bar and bistro, serving food all day, has a sheltered patio area. There is a choice of lounge areas and an attractive, traditional style dining room offering fixed price à la carte dishes.
ROOMS: 43 en suite (4 fmly) (15 GF) ⊗ in 12 bedrooms
s £59.95-£129; d £109-£149 (incl. bkfst) **LB FACILITIES:** STV Fishing Xmas **PARKING:** 40 **NOTES:** ⊗ in restaurant

CONISTON · Map 07 SD39

| Babies Welcome | Children's Dishes |

🍴 Black Bull Inn & Hotel
1 Yewdale Rd LA21 8DU
☎ 015394 41335 📠 015394 41168
e-mail: i.s.bradley@btinternet.com

CHILD FACILITIES: Family area Food/bottle warming Ch licence Ch menu Ch portions Highchairs Ch cutlery Safe grounds Changing facilities **NEARBY:** Walks Lake activities

OPEN: 11-11 (Sun 12-10.30) Closed: 25 Dec **BAR MEALS:** L served all week 12-9.30 D served all week **RESTAURANT:** L served by appointment only D served all week 6-9 **FACILITIES:** Children's licence Garden: Riverside patio outside **PARKING:** 12

CROOK · Map 07 SD49

| Babies Welcome | Children's Dishes |

🍴 The Sun Inn
LA8 8LA
☎ 01539 821351 📠 01539 821351
Dir: off the B5284

CHILD FACILITIES: Food/bottle warming Ch menu Ch portions Highchairs Ch cutlery

OPEN: 12-2.30 6-11 (Sat 12-11, Sun 12-10.30) **BAR MEALS:** L served all week 12-2.15 D served all week 6-8.45 Av main course £7 **RESTAURANT:** L served all week 12-2.30 D served all week 6-9 Av 3 course à la carte £18 **FACILITIES:** Garden: Terrace **PARKING:** 20

ELTERWATER · Map 07 NY30

| Babies Welcome | Children's Dishes |

🍴 The Britannia Inn
LA22 9HP
☎ 015394 37210 📠 015394 37311
e-mail: info@britinn.co.uk
Dir: A593 from Ambleside, then B5343 to Elterwater

continued

CHILD FACILITIES: Activities: colouring books, books, games Food/bottle warming Ch licence Ch menu Ch portions Highchairs Ch cutlery Safe grounds Changing facilities **NEARBY:** River & wildlife walks

OPEN: 11-11 (Sun 12-10.30) Closed: 25-26 Dec **BAR MEALS:** L served all week 12-2 D served all week 6.30-9.30 Av main course £8.95 **RESTAURANT:** L served all week 12-2 D served all week 6.30-9.30 **FACILITIES:** Children's licence Patio **ROOMS:** 9 bedrooms 8 en suite s£66 d£76 no children overnight **PARKING:** 10

HAWKSHEAD · Map 07 SD39

| Babies Welcome | Family Rooms | Children's Dishes |

◆◆◆ 🍴 Kings Arms Hotel
LA22 0NZ
☎ 015394 36372 📠 36006
e-mail: info@kingsarmshawkshead.co.uk
web: www.kingsarmshawkshead.co.uk
Dir: from Windermere take A591 to Ambleside then B5286 to Hawkshead, in main square

CHILD FACILITIES: Activities: colouring, jigsaws, toys Food/bottle warming Ch menu Ch portions Highchairs Ch discounts babies free, under 14s £12 Safe grounds Cots Family rms with S bed, 1 D rm with T beds £38 per adult Ch drinks Connecting rms Laundry **NEARBY:** Animal parks Beatrix Potter exhibitions Adventure playgrounds

A traditional Lakeland inn in the heart of a conservation area. The cosy, thoughtfully equipped bedrooms retain much character and are traditionally furnished. A good choice of freshly prepared food is available in both the lounge bar and the neatly presented dining room.
ROOMS: 9 rms (8 en suite) (3 fmly) s £34-£43; d £58-£76 *
FACILITIES: TVB tea/coffee Direct dial from bedrooms Fishing Dinner Last d order 9.30pm **NOTES:** ⊗ in restaurant ⊗ in lounges Cen ht **LB**

KENDAL · Map 07 SD59

| Babies Welcome | Children's Dishes |

🍴 Gateway Inn
Crook Rd LA8 8LX
☎ 01539 720605 & 724187 📠 01539 720581
Dir: From M6 J36 take A590/A591, follow signs for Windermere, pub on L after 9m

CHILD FACILITIES: Activities: colouring Outdoor play area Food/bottle warming Ch menu Ch portions Highchairs Ch cutlery Safe grounds Changing facilities **NEARBY:** Lake Windermere Walks

OPEN: 11-11 (all day wknds) **BAR MEALS:** L served all week 12-2 D served all week 6-9 Av main course £8.50 **RESTAURANT:** L served all week 12-2 D served all week 6-9 Av 3 course à la carte £15 **FACILITIES:** Garden: Terrace, food served outside **PARKING:** 50

Babies Welcome | **Children's Dishes**

🍴 The Gilpin Bridge Inn ◆◆◆
Bridge End, Levens LA8 8EP
☎ 015395 52206 🖹 015395 52444
Dir: Telephone for directions

CHILD FACILITIES: Activities: toys, colouring Outdoor play area Family area Food/bottle warming Ch licence Ch menu Ch portions Highchairs Ch cutlery Safe grounds Changing facilities NEARBY: Lake Windermere Leisure centre

OPEN: 11.30-2.30 5.30-11 (Open all day Summer, BH's) BAR MEALS: L served all week 11.30-2 D served all week 5.30-9 Av main course £5.50
RESTAURANT: L served all week 11.30-2 D served all week 6-9 Av 3 course à la carte £13.50 Av 2 course fixed price £4.95
FACILITIES: Children's licence Garden ROOMS: 10 bedrooms 10 en suite 2 family rooms s£40 d£55 PARKING: 60

KESWICK
Map 11 NY22

Babies Welcome | **Family Rooms** | **Children's Dishes**

★★★ 69% Keswick Country House
Station Rd CA12 4NQ
☎ 0845 458 4333 🖹 01253 754222
e-mail: reservations@choice-hotels.co.uk
web: www.thekeswickhotel.co.uk
Dir: M6 junct 40/A66 , 1st slip road into Keswick, then follow signs for leisure pool.

CHILD FACILITIES: Baby listening Activities: colouring Food/bottle warming Ch menu Ch portions Highchairs Ch discounts under 3s free, 4-11s £15, 12-14s £20 Safe grounds Cots Family rms Laundry NEARBY: Tennis court Play area Leisure centre with slides

This impressive Victorian hotel is set amid landscaped gardens. Eight superior bedrooms have been created in the Station Wing, which is accessed through the Victorian conservatory. Main house rooms, undergoing refurbished, are comfortably modern in style and offer a good range of amenities. Public areas include a spacious and relaxing lounge, and an attractive restaurant.
ROOMS: 74 en suite (6 fmly) s£42-£108; d£84-£216 (incl. bkfst & dinner) FACILITIES: STV Snooker ♨ ♒ Leisure facilities close by. Xmas PARKING: 70 NOTES: ✈ ⊛ in restaurant

◆◆◆◆ Hazeldene Hotel
The Heads CA12 5ER
☎ 017687 72106 🖹 017687 75435
e-mail: info@hazeldene-hotel.co.uk
Dir: from A66 follow signs for Borrowdale and lake. Turn right into The Heads opposite central car park

CHILD FACILITIES: Please telephone for details

Overlooking Hope Park, and having views of Catbells, Causey Pike and Walla Crag, this friendly family-run hotel is within walking distance of the town centre. Bedrooms are comfortably proportioned, brightly decorated and well equipped. There are two lounges, a games room, and a spacious dining room where hearty breakfasts are served.
ROOMS: 17 en suite (4 fmly) s£25-£35; d£50-£100 * ⊛
FACILITIES: TVB tea/coffee Direct dial from bedrooms TVL No coaches Pool Table NOTES: ⊛ in restaurant Licensed Cen ht LB PARKING: 12

Babies Welcome | This symbol indicates the establishment provides food & bottle warming and highchairs

Babies Welcome | **Family Rooms** | **Children's Dishes**

◆◆◆◆ Skiddaw Grove Country House
Vicarage Hill CA12 5QB
☎ 017687 73324 🖹 017687 73324
e-mail: skiddawgrove@hotmail.com
Dir: exit M6 junct 40 then A66 W, turn off left at Crosthwaite rdbt, into Keswick, immediately right into Vicarage Hill. House 50yds on left

CHILD FACILITIES: Baby listening Outdoor play area Food/bottle warming Ch menu Ch portions Highchairs Ch cutlery Ch discounts under 2s free, up to 5s £5, 5-15s £15 Safe grounds Cots Family rms D rm with 2 S beds (on request) Changing mats (on request) NEARBY: Cinema Theatre Leisure centre Playground

Skiddaw Grove Country House stands in lovely gardens just off the bypass. It has an outdoor pool and magnificent views of Bassenthwaite Lake and Skiddaw. Bedrooms are thoughtfully equipped, and there is a cosy lounge.
ROOMS: 5 en suite (1 fmly) s £26-£30; d £52-£60 * FACILITIES: TVB tea/coffee No coaches ⊁ Table tennis NOTES: Credit cards not taken ✈ ⊛ Licensed Cen ht LB PARKING: 6

KIRKBY STEPHEN
Map 12 NY70

Family Rooms | **Children's Dishes**

◆◆◆ 🍴 Southview Farm
Winton CA17 4HS
☎ 01768 371120 🖹 01768 371120
e-mail: southviewwinton@hotmail.com
Dir: M6 junct 38, take A685 to Brough for approx 10m. Signposted Winton

CHILD FACILITIES: Activities: colouring, toys Food/bottle warming Ch portions Ch cutlery Ch discounts under 5s free, then £1 per yr of age Safe grounds Family rms D rm with S bed, D rm with Z bed Laundry NEARBY: Swings Walks

A friendly family home, South View lies in the centre of the village of Winston, in a terraced row with the working farm to the rear. Two well-proportioned bedrooms are available and there is a cosy combined lounge/dining room where traditional breakfasts are served around one table.
ROOMS: 2 rms (2 fmly) s £18; d £34-£36 * FACILITIES: tea/coffee TVL 280 acres beef, dairy Dinner Last d order 8am NOTES: Credit cards not taken ⊛ BB PARKING: 2

LAZONBY
Map 12 NY53

Babies Welcome | **Family Rooms** | **Children's Dishes**

◆◆◆◆ Bracken Bank Lodge
CA10 1AX
☎ 01768 898241 🖹 01768 898221
e-mail: info@brackenbank.co.uk
web: www.brackenbank.co.uk
Dir: from M6 junct 41 follow signs for A6 Carlisle at 1st rdbt. At the 2nd rdbt take A6 towards Carlisle. Continue for approx. 2m, at Plumpton take a right to Lazonby (B6413). After 3m turn left at x-rds. Bracken Bank 1st building on right.

CHILD FACILITIES: Nanny Babysitting Activities: art classes, treasure hunts, face painting, stories, board games, outdoor games, jigsaws, toys Food/bottle warming Ch menu Ch portions Highchairs Ch discounts under 5s free sharing with parents Safe grounds Videos Cots Family rms T rm with adjoining T rm Ch drinks Connecting rms Laundry NEARBY: Falconry Cinema Go Karting Quad Bikes Animal Centre

This 17th-century shooting lodge stands within a 700-acre estate, which offers fishing on the River Eden, riding stables and boarding kennels. Original features include polished wooden floors, and all
continued on p98

England

LAZONBY, continued

bedrooms are individually designed. The house is furnished with antiques, oil paintings, hunting trophies and sporting prints, and has a full-size billiard table.

ROOMS: 4 en suite s £35; d £70 * **FACILITIES:** TV2B tea/coffee TVL Fishing Riding Snooker ♘ Clay pigeon shooting Golf nearby Dinner Last d order 24hrs notice **NOTES:** Credit cards not taken ✖ ⊘ Licensed Cen ht **LB PARKING:** 10

LITTLE LANGDALE   Map 07 NY30

🍴 Three Shires Inn ★★

LA22 9NZ
☎ 015394 37215 📠 015394 37127
e-mail: enquiries@threeshiresinn.co.uk
web: www.threeshiresinn.co.uk
Dir: Turn off A593, 2.3m from Ambleside at 2nd junct signposted for The Langdales. 1st L 0.5m, Hotel 1m up lane

CHILD FACILITIES: Please telephone for details

OPEN: 11-11 (Sun 12-10.30) (Dec-Jan 12-3, 8-10.30) Closed: Dec 25 **BAR MEALS:** L served all week 12-2 D served all week 6-8.45 Av main course £9.95 **RESTAURANT:** L served none D served all week 6.30-8 Av 3 course à la carte £18.95 **FACILITIES:** Children's licence Garden: Terrace and gardens next to stream **ROOMS:** 10 bedrooms 10 en suite 1 family rooms s£36 d£72 **PARKING:** 20

LORTON   Map 11 NY12

Babies Welcome	Family Rooms	Children's Dishes

♦♦♦♦♦ 🍴 Winder Hall Country House

CA13 9UP
☎ 01900 85107 📠 01900 85479
e-mail: nick@winderhall.co.uk
web: www.winderhall.co.uk
Dir: from Keswick take A66 W, at Braithwaite then B5292 Whinlatter Pass to Lorton. Continue to T junct signed Buttermere, turn left. Winderhall approx. 0.5m on right hand side.

CHILD FACILITIES: Baby listening Activities: games, toys Outdoor play area Food/bottle warming Ch menu Ch portions Highchairs Ch cutlery Ch discounts under 5s free, 5-12 sharing with 2 adults, over 12s sharing with 2 adults Safe grounds Videos Cots Family rms D rms with S beds Ch drinks Laundry Changing mats **NEARBY:** Adventure playground Walks

Impressive Winder Hall dates back to the 14th century. The lounge is luxuriously furnished and the elegant, spacious dining room is the venue for skilfully prepared meals. The smart, individually styled bedrooms are thoughtfully equipped, and all are furnished with fine antiques or pine. Two rooms have beautiful four-poster beds.

ROOMS: 7 en suite (2 fmly) s £90-£100; d £110-£160 *
FACILITIES: TVB tea/coffee Direct dial from bedrooms No coaches Fishing Complimentary leisure facilities at nearby hotel Dinner Last d order 7pm **NOTES:** ✖ ⊘ Licensed Cen ht **LB PARKING:** 10

NEWBY BRIDGE   Map 07 SD38

★★★ 67% Whitewater

The Lakeland Village LA12 8PX
☎ 015395 31133 📠 015395 31881
e-mail: enquiries@whitewater-hotel.co.uk
web: www.whitewater-hotel.co.uk
Dir: M6 junct 36 follow signs for A590 Barrow, 1m through Newby Bridge. Right at sign for Lakeland Village, hotel on left

CHILD FACILITIES: Please telephone for details

continued

This tasteful conversion of an old mill on the River Leven is close to the southern end of Lake Windermere. Bedrooms, many with lovely river views, are spacious and comfortable. Public areas include a luxurious, well-equipped spa, squash courts, and a choice of dining options. Mountain bikes are available. The Fisherman's bar hosts regular jazz nights that are popular with locals.

ROOMS: 35 en suite (10 fmly) (2 GF) ⊛ in 10 bedrooms s £92-£97; d £128-£195 (incl. bkfst) **LB FACILITIES: Spa** STV ⊠ ⚲ Squash Sauna Solarium Gym ⚒ Beauty treatment Table tennis Steam room Golf driving range ♫ Xmas **PARKING:** 50 **NOTES:** ✖ ⊘ in restaurant

♦♦♦♦ Hill Crest

Brow Edge LA12 8QP
☎ 015395 31766 📠 015395 31986
e-mail: enquiries@hillcrest.gbr.cc
Dir: 1m after Newby Bridge on A590 turn left into Brow Edge Rd, guest house 0.75m on right

CHILD FACILITIES: Please telephone for details

A warm welcome is offered at this well-kept family home, which has stunning views. The stone house is ideal for a quiet getaway, providing thoughtfully equipped and attractive bedrooms. The pleasant lounge doubles as a breakfast room, where the menu makes good use of local produce.

ROOMS: 3 en suite (2 fmly) (1 GF) s £35.50-£40; d £50-£60 *
FACILITIES: TVB tea/coffee TVL No coaches Free use of health & fitness club **NOTES:** ✖ ⊘ Cen ht **LB PARKING:** 4

PENRITH   Map 12 NY53

Babies Welcome	Family Rooms	Children's Dishes

★★★★ 72%

North Lakes Hotel & Spa

Ullswater Rd CA11 8QT
☎ 01768 868111 📠 01768 868291
e-mail: nlakes@shirehotels.co.uk
Dir: M6 junct 40 at junct with A66

SHIRE HOTELS

CHILD FACILITIES: Babysitting Activities: Trekkers Club, movies, Megasplash, games, toys, air hockey, pool table Indoor play area Family area Food/bottle warming Ch menu Ch portions Highchairs Ch cutlery Ch discounts under 16s free sharing with parents (not Xmas/New Yr) Games consoles Videos Cots Family rms D rm with B bed and S bed from £57 Ch drinks Connecting rms Fridge Laundry Changing mats **NEARBY:** Rheged Ostrich sanctuary Beatrix Potter exhibition

With its great location, it is no wonder that this hotel enjoys a busy trade. Amenities include excellent health and leisure facilities including full spa. Themed public areas have a contemporary Scandinavian country style and offer plenty of space and comfort. **ROOMS:** 84 en suite (6 fmly) (2 GF) ⊛ in 57 bedrooms s £108-£123; d £114-£134 (incl. bkfst) **LB FACILITIES: Spa** STV ⊠ Squash Sauna Solarium Gym Childrens pool, 5 Health & Beauty rooms, Steam room Xmas **PARKING:** 150 **NOTES:** ✖ ⊘ in restaurant

RAVENSTONEDALE
Map 07 NY70

Babies Welcome | **Family Rooms** | **Children's Dishes**

★★ 66% The Fat Lamb
Crossbank CA17 4LL
☎ 01539 623242 📠 623285
e-mail: fatlamb@cumbria.com
Dir: on A683, between Kirkby Stephen and Sedbergh

CHILD FACILITIES: Outdoor play area Food/bottle warming Ch menu Ch portions Highchairs Ch discounts under 6s free, 6-12s £10, 12s+ 1/2 price if sharing with parents Safe grounds Cots Family rms D rm with S beds Laundry

Open fires and solid stone walls are a feature of this 17th-century inn, set in its own nature reserve. There is a choice of dining options with an extensive menu available in the traditional bar or a more formal dining experience in the restaurant. Bedrooms are bright and cheerful and include family rooms and easily accessible rooms for guests with limited mobility.
ROOMS: 12 en suite (4 fmly) ⊛ in all bedrooms s £48-£50; d £76-£80 (incl. bkfst) **LB FACILITIES:** Fishing Private 5 acre nature reserve Xmas **PARKING:** 60 **NOTES:** ⊛ in restaurant

◆◆◆ 🍴 The Kings Head Hotel
CA17 4NH
☎ 015396 23284
e-mail: enquiries@kings-head.net web: www.kings-head.net
Dir: off M6 at junct 38, 6m down A685 to village of Ravenstonedale, 2mins off A65 in heart of village

CHILD FACILITIES: Please telephone for details

This delightful village inn offers comfortably furnished bedrooms and characterful public areas. The bar, warmed by log fires in cooler months, attracts locals and visitors, while an extensive menu, featuring local produce whenever possible, is served here or in the candlelit restaurant.
ROOMS: 4 rms (2 en suite) (1 fmly) **FACILITIES:** TVB tea/coffee Pool Table Dinner Last d order 9pm **NOTES:** ⊛ in restaurant ⊛ in lounges Cen ht **PARKING:** 10

SEATHWAITE
Map 07 SD29

Babies Welcome | **Children's Dishes**

🍴 The Newfield Inn
LA20 6ED
☎ 01229 716208
e-mail: paul@seathwaite.freeserve.co.uk
Dir: A590 toward Barrow, then R onto A5092, becomes A595, follow for 1m, R at Duddon Bri, 6m to Seathwaite

CHILD FACILITIES: Activities: games, drawing Outdoor play area Food/bottle warming Ch menu Ch portions Highchairs Ch cutlery Safe grounds Changing facilities **NEARBY:** River walk

OPEN: 11-11 Rest: variations over Christmas & New Year **BAR MEALS:** L served all week 12-9 D served all week 12-9 Av main course £6 **RESTAURANT:** L served all week 12-9 D served all week 12-9 Av 3 course à la carte £14 **FACILITIES:** Garden: Sheltered, seating for 40, stunning views **PARKING:** 30

SILLOTH
Map 11 NY15

Babies Welcome | **Family Rooms** | **Children's Dishes**

★★★ 59% The Skinburness
CA7 4QY
☎ 016973 32332 📠 32549
Dir: from Wigton take B5302 to Silloth & follow brown tourist signs to hotel
continued

CHILD FACILITIES: Baby listening Food/bottle warming Ch menu Ch portions Highchairs Ch cutlery Ch discounts under 5s free sharing with parents Safe grounds Games consoles Videos Cots Family rms Ch drinks (on request) Connecting rms Laundry (on request) Changing mats (on request) **NEARBY:** Seafront location

Located on the peaceful Solway Estuary, close to sandy beaches and coastal walks, this popular hotel provides traditionally furnished bedrooms with a host of modern facilities. There is also a small leisure complex with a pool, sauna and spa. Good meals are available in the popular bar and the pleasant hotel restaurant.
ROOMS: 26 en suite (8 fmly) (1 GF) ⊛ in 4 bedrooms s £60; d £120 (incl. bkfst) **LB FACILITIES:** ⊠ Sauna Solarium Gym Jacuzzi ♫ Xmas **PARKING:** 50

TEMPLE SOWERBY
Map 12 NY62

Babies Welcome | **Family Rooms** | **Children's Dishes**

◆◆◆ 🌱 Skygarth Farm
CA10 1SS
☎ 01768 361300 📠 01768 361300
e-mail: enquire@skygarth.co.uk
Dir: Turn off A66 at Temple Sowerby for Morland, Skygarth is 500yds on the right

CHILD FACILITIES: Activities: working farm, toys, puzzles, books Food/bottle warming Ch menu Ch portions Highchairs Ch cutlery Ch discounts under 4s free, under 13s reduced Videos Cots Family rms 2 D rms with 2 S beds Laundry **NEARBY:** River walks Swimming pools

Skygarth is just south of the village, 0.5 mile from the busy main road. The house stands in a cobbled courtyard surrounded by cowsheds and with gardens to the rear, where red squirrels feed. There are two well-proportioned bedrooms and an attractive lounge where tasty breakfasts are served.
ROOMS: 2 rms (2 fmly) s fr £25; d fr £40 * ⊛ **FACILITIES:** TVB tea/coffee 200 acres Mixed **NOTES:** Credit cards not taken ✈ Cen ht **PARKING:** 4

TROUTBECK (NEAR WINDERMERE)
Map 12 SD49

◆◆◆◆ 🍴 Queens Head Hotel
Town Head LA23 1PW
☎ 015394 32174 📠 015394 31938
e-mail: enquiries@queensheadhotel.com
web: www.queensheadhotel.com
Dir: M6 junct 36, take A590/591 W towards Windermere. Right at mini-rdbt onto A592 signed Penrith/Ullswater. Queens Head 2m on right

CHILD FACILITIES: Please telephone for details

This 17th-century coaching inn has stunning views of the Troutbeck Valley. The delightful bedrooms, several with four-poster beds, are traditionally furnished and equipped with modern facilities. Beams, flagstone floors, and a bar that was once an Elizabethan
continued on p100

TROUTBECK (NEAR WINDERMERE), continued

four-poster, provide a wonderful setting in which to enjoy imaginative food.

ROOMS: 11 en suite 3 annexe en suite s £60-£70; d £75-£105 * ⊛
FACILITIES: TVB tea/coffee No coaches Dinner Last d order 9pm
NOTES: ✖ Cen ht **LB PARKING:** 75

ULVERSTON   Map 07 SD27

Babies Welcome | Children's Dishes

🍴 Royal Oak
Spark Bridge LA12 8BS
☎ 01229 861006
Dir: From Ulverston take A590 N. Village off A5092

CHILD FACILITIES: Activities: games, books, toys **Indoor play area Outdoor play area Food/bottle warming Ch menu Ch portions Highchairs Ch cutlery Safe grounds NEARBY:** Parks Walks Steam train Lake cruises 5-min drive to sea

OPEN: 12-3 6-11 **BAR MEALS:** L served all week 12-2 D served all week 6-9 Av main course £7 **FACILITIES:** Garden: Food served outside
PARKING: 30

WATERMILLOCK   Map 12 NY42

Babies Welcome | Family Rooms | Children's Dishes

♦♦♦♦ 🍴 Brackenrigg
CA11 0LP
☎ 017684 86206 📠 017684 86945
e-mail: enquiries@brackenrigginn.co.uk
web: www.brackenrigginn.co.uk
Dir: 6m from M6. Take A66 towards Keswick and A592 to Ullswater. Turn right at lake & continue about 3m

CHILD FACILITIES: Food/bottle warming **Ch menu Ch portions Highchairs Ch discounts under 3s free, 3-16s £10 sharing with parents Cots Family rms D rm with S bed from £69 Connecting rms NEARBY:** Rheged Ostrich sanctuary Alpaca centre

An 18th-century coaching inn with superb views of Ullswater and the surrounding countryside. Freshly prepared dishes and daily specials are served by friendly staff in the traditional bar and restaurant. The bedrooms include six attractive rooms in the stable cottages.

ROOMS: 11 en suite 6 annexe en suite (8 fmly) (3 GF) s £32-£37; d £54-£69 * ⊛ **FACILITIES:** TVB tea/coffee small field out the back Dinner Last d order 9pm **NOTES:** ⊛ in restaurant ⊛ in lounges Cen ht **LB PARKING:** 40

WINDERMERE   Map 07 SD49

★★★★ 66% Low Wood
LA23 1LP
☎ 015394 33338 📠 015394 34072
e-mail: lowwood@elhmail.co.uk
Dir: M6 junct 36, follow A590 then A591 to Windermere, then 3m towards Ambleside, hotel on right

CHILD FACILITIES: Please telephone for details

Benefiting from a lakeside location, this hotel offers an excellent range of leisure facilities. Bedrooms, many with panoramic lake views, are attractively furnished, and include a number of larger executive rooms and suites. There is a choice of bars, a spacious restaurant and the more informal Café del Lago. The Poolside bar offers internet and e-mail access.

ROOMS: 110 en suite (13 fmly) ⊛ in 55 bedrooms s £103-£120; d £150-£190 (incl. bkfst) **LB FACILITIES:** Spa STV 🎣 Fishing Squash Snooker Sauna Solarium Gym Jacuzzi Water skiing Canoeing, Beauty salon, Spa 🎵 Xmas **PARKING:** 200 **NOTES:** ⊛ in restaurant

---

Babies Welcome | Family Rooms | Children's Dishes

★★★ 72% ⊛ Langdale Chase
Langdale Chase LA23 1LW
☎ 015394 32201 📠 015394 32604
e-mail: sales@langdalechase.co.uk
web: www.langdalechase.co.uk
Dir: 2m S of Ambleside and 3m N of Windermere, on A591

CHILD FACILITIES: Baby listening Babysitting (by prior arrangement) Activities: board games, puzzles, books, mini golf Outdoor play area Food/bottle warming Ch menu Ch portions Highchairs Ch discounts babies in cot half price Safe grounds Family rms from £85 Connecting rms Laundry NEARBY: Lakeside location with private pebble beach Adventure park Gardens

Enjoying unrivalled views of Lake Windermere, this imposing country manor has been trading as a hotel for over 70 years. Public areas feature carved fireplaces, oak panelling and a galleried staircase. Bedrooms, many now refurbished, have stylish, spacious bathrooms and outstanding views.

ROOMS: 20 en suite 7 annexe en suite (2 fmly) (1 GF) s £65-£99 (incl. bkfst) **LB FACILITIES:** Fishing 🎵 ♿ Sailing boats Xmas **PARKING:** 50 **NOTES:** ⊛ in restaurant

Babies Welcome | Family Rooms | Children's Dishes

★★★ 71% ⊛ ⊛ Beech Hill
Newby Bridge Rd LA23 3LR
☎ 015394 42137 📠 015394 43745
e-mail: reservations@beechhillhotel.co.uk
web: www.beechhillhotel.co.uk
Dir: A592 towards Bowness, hotel on left, 4m S from Bowness

Best Western

CHILD FACILITIES: Baby listening Nanny (charge) Babysitting Food/bottle warming Ch menu Ch portions Highchairs Ch discounts under 3s free, 4-8s £15, 8-14s £25 Safe grounds Videos Cots Family rms, Double rms with B beds Connecting rms Laundry NEARBY: Lakeside location Beatrix Potter exhibition Aquarium Lake cruises

This stylish, terraced hotel is set on high ground leading to the shore of Lake Windermere and has a spacious, open-plan lounge which, like the restaurant, affords splendid views across the lake. Bedrooms offer a range of styles; some have four-poster beds, and all are well-equipped. Leisure facilities available.

ROOMS: 58 en suite (4 fmly) (4 GF) ⊛ in 10 bedrooms s £50-£85; d £100-£170 (incl. bkfst) **LB FACILITIES:** 🎣 Fishing Sauna Solarium 🎵 Xmas **PARKING:** 70 **NOTES:** ⊛ in restaurant

♦♦♦♦ Blenheim Lodge
Brantfell Rd, Bowness on Windermere LA23 3AE
☎ 015394 43440 📠 015394 43440
e-mail: blenheimlodge@supanet.com
Dir: A591 Bowness village, left at mini-rdbt, turn first left and left again, house is at the top

CHILD FACILITIES: Please telephone for details

From a peaceful position above the town of Bowness, Blenheim
continued

England

Lodge has stunning views over the lake. Bedrooms are traditionally furnished and some have four-poster or half-tester beds. There is a comfortable lounge and a pleasing dining room where hearty breakfasts are served at individual tables.
ROOMS: 11 en suite (2 fmly) (2 GF) s £37-£45; d £62-£100 *
FACILITIES: TVB tea/coffee TVL No coaches Membership of Country Club with sports facilities **NOTES:** ✖ ⊗ Licensed Cen ht **LB**
PARKING: 11

♦♦♦♦ The Fairfield Garden Guest House
Brantfell Rd, Bowness-on-Windermere LA23 3AE
☎ 015394 46565 ⊠ 015394 46565
e-mail: tonyandliz@the-fairfield.co.uk
Dir: follow signs to Bowness town centre, turn opposite St Martins Church and immediately left by Spinnery restaurant, house is 200yds on right
CHILD FACILITIES: Please telephone for details

This welcoming house is in a quiet lane above the town and within walking distance of the lake and Bowness. Bedrooms are comfortably furnished and thoughtfully equipped. Public rooms include an inviting lounge with adjacent bar, and an attractive dining room overlooking the landscaped gardens.
ROOMS: 10 rms (9 en suite) (2 fmly) (3 GF) **FACILITIES:** TVB tea/coffee TVL ₤ Dinner Last d order 24hrs **NOTES:** ⊗ Licensed Cen ht **PARKING:** 9

Babies Welcome | Family Rooms | Children's Dishes

♦♦♦♦ White Lodge Hotel
Lake Rd LA23 2JJ
☎ 015394 43624 ⊠ 015394 44749
e-mail: enquiries@whitelodgehotel.com
web: www.whitelodgehotel.com
Dir: on main lake road, on right
CHILD FACILITIES: Food/bottle warming Ch menu Ch portions Highchairs Ch cutlery Ch discounts under 5s free, 5-10s 60% off, over 10s 50% Cots Family rms with D & T beds Connecting rms **NEARBY:** Lake boat trips Tennis World of Peter Rabbit
This stylish Victorian house stands in gardens at the north end of Bowness. The comfortable lounge and main dining room are furnished with antiques, and the modern bedrooms offer high levels of comfort and have quality pine furniture. There is an attractive bar, which doubles as the breakfast room.
ROOMS: 12 en suite (3 fmly) s £33-£37; d £64-£72 * ⊗ in 4 bedrooms **FACILITIES:** TVB tea/coffee TVL No coaches Dinner Last d order 6.30pm **NOTES:** ✖ ⊗ in restaurant ⊗ in lounges Licensed Cen ht **LB** **PARKING:** 14

♦♦♦ Rosemount
Lake Rd LA23 2EQ
☎ 015394 43739 ⊠ 015394 48978
e-mail: rosemt3739@aol.com
web: www.lakedistrictguesthouse.com
Dir: turn off A591, through village & Rosemount is on left just beyond modern Catholic church

continued

CHILD FACILITIES: Please telephone for details
This large Victorian property stands midway between Windermere and Bowness and is convenient for the lake. Hearty Cumbrian breakfasts, freshly prepared using good-quality local produce, are served in the Rennie Mackintosh inspired dining room. Bedrooms are cheerfully decorated and there is an airy modern lounge with a piano.
ROOMS: 16 rms (15 en suite) (4 fmly) (3 GF) s £25-£35; d £45-£85 *
FACILITIES: TVB tea/coffee Golf can be arranged.Free entry local leisure club **NOTES:** ✖ ⊗ Licensed Cen ht **LB** **PARKING:** 11

WORKINGTON   Map 11 NY02

Babies Welcome | Children's Dishes |

★★★ 82% ⊚ Washington Central
Washington St CA14 3AY
☎ 01900 65772 ⊠ 01900 68770
e-mail: kawildwchotel@aol.com
web: www.washingtoncentralhotelworkington.com
Dir: M6 junct 40 towards Keswick, follow to Workington. At lights at bottom of Ramsey Brow, turn right and follow signs for hotel
CHILD FACILITIES: Babysitting Activities: books, colouring, games, swimming pool Family area Food/bottle warming Ch licence Ch menu Ch portions Highchairs Ch cutlery Ch discounts under 5s free, 5-11s £15, 11-16s £20 Safe grounds Cots Ch drinks (by request) Connecting rms Laundry Changing mats **NEARBY:** Lake District National Park Cinema Aquarium 2m to sea

Enjoying a prominent town centre location, this modern hotel boasts memorably hospitable staff. The well-maintained and comfortable bedrooms are equipped with a range of thoughtful extras. Public areas include numerous lounges, a spacious bar, Ceasars leisure club, a smart restaurant and a popular coffee shop.
ROOMS: 46 en suite (4 fmly) ⊗ in 37 bedrooms s £77-£89.95; d £109.95-£159.95 (incl. bkfst) **LB** **FACILITIES:** STV ⊠ Sauna Solarium Gym Jacuzzi Free bike hire, Nightclub ♬ **PARKING:** 16 **NOTES:** ✖ ⊗ in restaurant RS 25 Dec

Babies Welcome | Children's Dishes

⊠ The Old Ginn House
Great Clifton CA14 1TS
☎ 01900 64616 ⊠ 01900 873384
e-mail: enquiries@oldginnhouse.co.uk
Dir: 3 miles from Workington, 4 miles from Cockermouth, just off the A66
CHILD FACILITIES: Food/bottle warming Ch menu Ch portions Highchairs Safe grounds **NEARBY:** Maryport Aquarium
OPEN: 12-2 6-11 Closed: 24-26 Dec, 1 Jan **BAR MEALS:** L served all week 12-1.45 D served all week 6-9.30 Av main course £7.95
RESTAURANT: L served all week 12-1.45 D served all week 6-9.30
FACILITIES: Garden: Courtyard ✖ **ROOMS:** 20 bedrooms 20 en suite s £45 d£60 (♦♦♦♦) **PARKING:** 40

YANWATH   Map 12 NY52

⊠ The Yanwath Gate Inn
CA10 2LF
☎ 01768 862386 ⊠ 01768 864006
e-mail: deanchef@hotmail.com
CHILD FACILITIES: Please telephone for details
OPEN: 12-2.30 6.30-11 Closed: Jan **BAR MEALS:** L served all week 12-2 D served all week 6-9 Av main course £10.50 **RESTAURANT:** L served all week 12-2 D served all week 6-9.15 Av 3 course à la carte £20 Av 2 course fixed price £7.50 **FACILITIES:** Children's licence Garden: Secluded terrace, lawns, landscaped garden ✖ **PARKING:** 20

England

DERBYSHIRE

Chatsworth House

BOLSOVER
Bolsover Castle
S446 PR ☎01246 822844
(On A632)
Open all year, Apr & Sep-Oct Thu-Mon 10-5; May-July daily 10-6; Aug daily 10-7, Nov-Mar Thurs-Mon 10-4. Closed 24-26 Dec & 1 Jan. £6.50, ch £3.30, concessions £4.90.

BUXTON
Poole's Cavern - Buxton Country Park
SK17 9DH ☎01298 26978
info@poolescavern.co.uk
(1m from Buxton town centre, off A6 and A515)
Open Mar-Oct, daily 10-5. Open in winter for groups only.

CASTLETON
Blue-John Cavern & Mine
S33 8WP ☎01433 620638
lesley@bluejohn.gemsoft.co.uk
(Follow Blue-John Cavern signs from Castleton)
Open all year daily 9.30-5 or dusk. 1hr guided tours every 10 mins.

Peak Cavern
S33 8WS ☎01433 620285
info@peakcavern.co.uk
(On A6187, in centre of Castleton)
Open Etr-Oct, 10-5. Nov-Etr wknds only 10-5.

Speedwell Cavern S33 8WA
info@speedwellcavern.co.uk ☎01433 620512
(A625 becomes A6187 at Hathersage. 0.5m W of Castleton)
Open all year, Etr-Oct daily 9.30-5.30, Nov-Etr 10-5. Closed 25 Dec. Phone to check winter opening times due to weather. *£6, ch £4.

Treak Cliff Cavern
S33 8WP ☎01433 620571
treakcliff@bluejohnstone.com
(0.75m W of Castleton on A6187)
Open all year, Mar-Oct, daily 10-last tour 4.20, Aug only, last tour 4.45; Nov-Feb daily 10-last tour at 3.20. Closed 24-26 & 31 Dec-1 Jan. All tours are guided & last about 40 mins.
*Adults £5.80, ch 5-15 £3.20 Fam. 2 ad & 2 ch £16.

CHATSWORTH
Chatsworth DE45 1PP
visit@chatsworth.org ☎01246 582204
(8m N of Matlock off B6012. 16m from M1 junct 29, signposted via Chesterfield, follow brown signs)
Open 17 Mar-19 Dec, House & garden 11-5.30, Farmyard 10.30-5.30.
*House & Garden £9.00, ch £3.50, students & pen £7.00. Family ticket £21.50. Pre-booked group discounts available. Garden only £5.50, ch £2.50, students & pen £4. Family ticket £13.50.
Farmyard & Adventure Playground £4 pen £3.
Groups 5+ £3.50. Family pass to all attractions £35.

CRESWELL
Creswell Crags Museum and Education Centre
S80 3LH
info@creswell-crags.org.uk ☎01909 720378
(On the B6042, Crags Road, between A616 and A60, 1m E of Creswell village)
Open all year, Feb-Oct, daily, 10.30-4.30; Nov-Jan Sun only 10.30-4.30. * Free. Cave & site tour £2.75 (ch £2, no under 5's). £1 parking donation requested.

CRICH
Crich Tramway Village DE4 5DP
enquiry@tramway.co.uk ☎0870 758 7267
(Off B5035, 8m from M1 junct 28)
Open Apr-Oct, daily 10-5.30 6.30pm wknds Jun-Aug & BH wknds. Nov-Dec open wknds 10.30-4
*£8, ch 3-15 £4, pen £7. Family ticket 2 adults & 3 ch £21.

ILKESTON
American Adventure Theme Park
DE7 5SX ☎0845 330 2929
sales@americanadventure.co.uk
(Off M1 junct 26, signposted, take A610 to A608 then A6007)
Open 23 Mar-3 Nov, daily from 10.

MATLOCK BATH
Peak District Mining Museum DE4 3NR
mail@peakmines.co.uk ☎01629 583834
(On A6 by River Derwent.)
Open all year, daily 11-4 later in summer season. Closed 25 Dec.

The Heights of Abraham Cable Cars, Caverns & Hilltop Park DE4 3PD
enquiries@h-of-a.co.uk ☎01629 582365
(On A6, signposted from M1 junct 28 & A6. Base station next to Matlock Bath railway station)
Open daily 14-22 Feb & Etr-Oct 10-5 28 Feb-26 Mar wknds only. *£8.50, ch £5.50, pen £6.50.

ROWSLEY
The Wind in the Willows
DE4 2NP ☎01629 733433
enquiries@windinthewillows.info
(At junct of A6 & B6012)
Open Apr-Sep, daily 10-5.30; Oct-Mar, daily 10-4.30. Closed 25 Dec & 28-30 Jan.

ALFRETON   Map 08 SK45

🔲 White Horse Inn
Badger Ln, Woolley Moor DE55 6FG
☎ 01246 590319 🖷 01246 590319
e-mail: info@the-whitehorse-inn.co.uk
Dir: From A632 (Matlock/Chesterfield rd) take B6036. Pub 1m after Ashover. From A61 take B6036 to Woolley Moor
CHILD FACILITIES: Please telephone for details
OPEN: 12-3 6-11 (Sun 12-10.30, all day summer wknds) **BAR MEALS:** L served all week 12-2 D served Tues-Sat 6-9 Av main course £7.50
RESTAURANT: L served all week 12-2 D served Tues-Sat 6-9 Av 3 course à la carte £16 Av 3 course fixed price £14.95 **FACILITIES:** Children's licence Garden: Large patio with picnic benches **PARKING:** 50

ALKMONTON   Map 07 SK13

◆◆◆◆ The Courtyard
Dairy House Farm DE6 3DG
☎ 01335 330187 🖷 01335 330187
e-mail: andy@dairyhousefarm.org.uk
Dir: off A50 at Foston, approx 3.5m up Woodyard Lane
CHILD FACILITIES: Please telephone for details
Surrounded by open countryside, this is a delightful conversion of Victorian farm buildings in the Derbyshire Dales. The bedrooms are well furnished and thoughtfully equipped. A hearty breakfast is provided in the bright dining room and dinner is available by prior arrangement. Two rooms are approved as providing suitable facilities for the less able.
ROOMS: 7 en suite (1 fmly) (7 GF) **FACILITIES:** TVB tea/coffee No coaches Fishing Dinner Last d order 4pm **NOTES:** ✖ ⊗ Cen ht **PARKING:** 12

ASHBOURNE   Map 07 SK14

| Babies Welcome | Family Rooms | Children's Dishes |

★★ 64%
The Dog & Partridge Country Inn   THE INDEPENDENTS
Swinscoe DE6 2HS
☎ 01335 343183 🖷 01335 342742
e-mail: info@dogandpartridge.co.uk
web: www.dogandpartridge.co.uk
Dir: A52 towards Leek, hotel 4m on left
CHILD FACILITIES: Baby listening Activities: play area, board games, pets corner Indoor play area Outdoor play area Family area Food/bottle warming Ch menu Ch portions Highchairs Ch cutlery Ch discounts under 4s free Safe grounds Videos Cots Family rms Connecting rms Fridge **NEARBY:** Alton Towers Zoo Trail cycle tracks American adventure theme park

This 17th-century inn is situated in the hamlet of Swinscoe, within easy reach of Alton Towers. Bedroom have direct access and are sited within the hotel's grounds. Well-presented self-catering family suites are also available. Meals are served every evening until late and can be enjoyed either in the bar, the conservatory or an outdoor terrace weather permitting.
ROOMS: 25 en suite (15 fmly) s £45-£90; d £75-£100 (incl. bkfst) **LB** **FACILITIES:** Fishing Xmas **PARKING:** 115 **NOTES:** ⊗ in restaurant

◆◆◆◆ 🍴 🚬 Bramhall's
6 Buxton Rd DE6 1EX
☎ 01335 346158
e-mail: info@bramhalls.co.uk
web: www.bramhalls.co.uk
Dir: from market square take Buxton road N up hill, Bramhall's 30yds on left
CHILD FACILITIES: Please telephone for details

continued

Located within the heart of the historic market town, this restaurant with rooms occupies a conversion of two cottages and an Edwardian house. It is increasingly popular for its imaginative food and attentive service. Quality bedrooms are filled with thoughtful extras and a warm welcome is assured.
ROOMS: 10 rms (8 en suite) (1 fmly) (1 GF) s £25-£27.50; d £49.50-£60 * ⊗ **FACILITIES:** TVB tea/coffee No coaches Dinner Last d order 9.30pm **NOTES:** ✖ ⊗ in area of dining room ⊗ in 1 lounge Licensed Cen ht **PARKING:** 6

| Babies Welcome | Children's Dishes |

🔲 The Green Man Royal Hotel ◆◆◆
St Johns St DE6 1GH
☎ 01335 345783 🖷 01335 346613
Dir: In town centre off A52
CHILD FACILITIES: Food/bottle warming Ch menu Ch portions Highchairs Safe grounds **NEARBY:** Parks Walks Skate park
OPEN: 11-11 (Sun 12-10.30) Closed: Dec 25 & Jan 1 **BAR MEALS:** L served all week 12-3.00 D served all week 6-9 Av main course £12
FACILITIES: Garden: courtyard ✖ **ROOMS:** 18 bedrooms 18 en suite 1 family room s£40 d£60 **PARKING:** 12

BAKEWELL   Map 08 SK26

| Babies Welcome | Family Rooms | Children's Dishes |

◆◆◆◆ Wyedale
Wyedale House, 25 Holywell DE45 1BA
☎ 01629 812845
Dir: approaching Bakewell on A6 from Matlock turn left into Holywell immediately before pelican crossing, B & B directly ahead – 30mtrs
CHILD FACILITIES: Family area Food/bottle warming Ch menu Ch portions Highchairs Safe grounds Cots Family rms D rm with 2 S beds & cot £60-£80 Laundry **NEARBY:** Park Swimming pool Cycle hire Playground

Wyedale is located close to the town centre and is an ideal base for relaxing or touring the surrounding area. Bedrooms, one of which is situated on the ground floor, are spacious and each is freshly decorated. Breakfast can be taken in the attractive dining room, which overlooks the rear patio.
ROOMS: 3 en suite (1 fmly) (1 GF) **FACILITIES:** TVB tea/coffee No coaches **NOTES:** Credit cards not taken ✖ ⊗ Cen ht **PARKING:** 3

BASLOW   Map 08 SK27

| Babies Welcome | Family Rooms | Children's Dishes |

★★★ 77% 🍴 Cavendish
DE45 1SP
☎ 01246 582311 🖷 01246 582312
e-mail: info@cavendish-hotel.net
web: www.cavendish-hotel.net
Dir: M1 junct 29/A617 W to Chesterfield & A619 to Baslow. Hotel in village centre, off main road
CHILD FACILITIES: Baby listening Food/bottle warming Ch portions Highchairs Safe grounds Cots Family rms T rm with B beds, D rm with 2 beds Connecting rms Ch drinks Fridge Laundry **NEARBY:** Chatsworth House

This stylish property, dating back to the 18th century, is delightfully situated on the edge of the Chatsworth Estate. Elegantly appointed bedrooms offer a host of thoughtful amenities, while comfortable public areas are furnished with period pieces and paintings. Guests have a choice of dining in the informal conservatory Garden Room or Gallery Restaurant.
ROOMS: 24 en suite (3 fmly) (2 GF) ⊗ in 2 bedrooms s £103-£115; d £135-£148 **LB** **FACILITIES:** STV Fishing ⚓ Xmas **PARKING:** 50 **NOTES:** ✖ ⊗ in restaurant

BUXTON — Map 07 SK07

◆◆◆ Hawthorn Farm

Fairfield Rd SK17 7ED
☎ 01298 23230 ▨ 01298 71322
e-mail: alan.pimblett@virgin.net
Dir: on A6 Manchester/Stockport rd opposite St Peter's church

CHILD FACILITIES: Please telephone for details

A delightful Tudor farmhouse, set back from the Manchester road, in attractive gardens. The lounge boasts a feature stone fireplace and many rooms display original beams. Some of the bedrooms are in converted farm buildings.

ROOMS: 3 en suite 6 annexe rms (4 en suite) (1 fmly) (4 GF)
s £30-£50; d £55-£65 * **FACILITIES:** TVB tea/coffee TVL No coaches
NOTES: ⊗ Cen ht **PARKING:** 12

CASTLETON

Babies Welcome Children's Dishes

◆◆◆◆ ◖ The Peaks Inn

How Ln S33 8WJ
☎ 01433 620247 ▨ 01433 623590
e-mail: info@peaks-inn.co.uk
web: www.peaks-inn.co.uk
Dir: on main A425 in centre of Castleton

CHILD FACILITIES: Activities: colouring, games Food/bottle warming Ch menu Ch portions Highchairs Ch cutlery Safe grounds
NEARBY: Peveril Castle Castleton Caverns Museums Theatres

Located in the heart of this historic village, the Peaks Inn has been sympathetically renovated to provide spacious tastefully furnished bedrooms with smart modern en suite bathrooms. Open plan public areas offer both character and comfort and an attractive beer garden is also available for use.

ROOMS: 4 en suite d £80-£90 * ⊗ **FACILITIES:** TVB tea/coffee Direct dial from bedrooms TVL Dinner Last d order 9pm **NOTES:** ✻ ⊗ in area of dining room ⊗ in 1 lounge Cen ht **LB** **PARKING:** 40

CHESTERFIELD — Map 08 SK37

◆◆◆◆ ⊜ Hornbeam House

Mile Hill, Mansfield Rd, Hasland S41 0JN
☎ 01246 556851 ▨ 0870 0521647
e-mail: enquiries@hornbeam4t.demon.co.uk
Dir: from M1 junct 29 take A617 towards Chesterfield, approx 1.5m 1st exit turn left at top of slip road, 200yds turn right towards Hasland. Hornbeam House is 0.75m on right

CHILD FACILITIES: Please telephone for details

Conveniently located for both the M1 and touring around the area, yet on an easy approach to Chesterfield, this large suburban detached house stands in substantial grounds. Attentive and

continued

helpful service is the hallmark, and fresh and healthy cooking is enjoyed both at breakfast and dinner.

ROOMS: 2 en suite (1 fmly) s £30-£34; d £52-£60 *
FACILITIES: tea/coffee TVL No coaches Dinner Last d order 10am
NOTES: ✻ ⊗ Cen ht **PARKING:** 3

DOE LEA — Map 08 SK46

Babies Welcome Children's Dishes

◖ Hardwick Inn

Hardwick Park S44 5QJ
☎ 01246 850245 ▨ 01246 856365
e-mail: Batty@hardwickinn.co.uk
web: www.hardwickinn.co.uk
Dir: M1 J29 take A6175. 0.5m L (signed Stainsby/Hardwick Hall). After Stainsby, 2m L at staggered junction. Follow brown Tourist Board signs.

CHILD FACILITIES: Outdoor play area Family area Food/bottle warming Ch menu Ch portions Highchairs Ch cutlery Safe grounds
NEARBY: Hardwick Hall Hardwick Park & Lakes

OPEN: 11.30-11 **BAR MEALS:** L served all week 11.30-9.30 D served all week Av main course £6.50 **RESTAURANT:** L served Tues- Sun 12-2 D served Tues-Sat 7-9 Av 3 course à la carte £16.50 Av 3 course fixed price £13.20 **FACILITIES:** Garden: Lrg garden, pond & picnic table, extensive lawns ✻

EYAM — Map 08 SK27

◆◆◆◆ ◖ Miners Arms

Water Ln S32 5RG
☎ 01433 630853 ▨ 01433 639050
e-mail: minersarms@plaguevillage.fsnet.co.uk
Dir: M1 junct 29, take A619 to Chesterfield then A623 to Baslow and follow signs to Calver. Through Stoney Middleton turn right for Eyam.

CHILD FACILITIES: Please telephone for details

Located within the historic centre, this 17th century inn is very much the focal point of local life and has a strong following for both its imaginative food and well-stocked bars. Bedrooms are brightly decorated and comfortable and public areas include an attractive restaurant, a cosy separate breakfast room and bars with polished brasses and ornaments.

ROOMS: 7 en suite (1 fmly) (1 GF) s £25-£40; d £50-£80 * ⊗
FACILITIES: TVB tea/coffee Dinner Last d order 9pm **NOTES:** ⊗ in restaurant ⊗ in 1 lounge Cen ht **LB** **PARKING:** 75

FOOLOW — Map 08 SK17

◆◆◆◆ ◖ Bulls Head

S32 5QR
☎ 01433 630873 ▨ 01433 631738
Dir: M1 junct 29 follow signs to Bakewell. At Baslow take A623 Foolow, is 3m after Stoney-Middleton

CHILD FACILITIES: Please telephone for details

continued

Located centrally in the village this popular inn retains many original features and offers comfortable, well-equipped bedrooms. Extensive and imaginative bar meals are served in both the traditionally furnished dining room or in the cosy bar areas. The inn welcomes well behaved dogs in the bar, and doesn't even mind muddy boots on the stone flagged areas.
ROOMS: 3 en suite (1 fmly) s fr £50; d fr £70 * ⊛ **FACILITIES:** TVB tea/coffee Dinner Last d order 8.45pm **NOTES:** ⊛ in restaurant Cen ht **PARKING:** 20

GREAT HUCKLOW   Map 08 SK17

Babies Welcome | Children's Dishes

♦♦♦ 🍴 The Queen Anne
SK17 8RF
☎ 01298 871246
e-mail: mal@thequeenanne.net
Dir: on A623, turn off at Anchor pub junct towards Bradwell, 2nd right to Great Hucklow

CHILD FACILITIES: Family area Food/bottle warming Ch portions Highchairs Ch cutlery **NEARBY:** Walks

Located in the heart of this pretty hamlet, the Queen Anne has been a licensed inn for over three hundred years and public areas retain many original features. The cosy bedrooms are situated in a separate building and benefit from modern en suite shower rooms.
ROOMS: 2 en suite (2 GF) d £55-£65 * ⊛ **FACILITIES:** TVB tea/coffee Darts, Shove Ha'penny, cards & other pub games Dinner Last d order 8.30pm **NOTES:** ⊛ in area of dining room ⊛ in 1 lounge Cen ht **PARKING:** 30

HATHERSAGE   Map 08 SK28

♦♦♦♦ Sladen Cottage
Castleton Rd S32 1EH
☎ 01433 650104
e-mail: colley@sladencottage.co.uk
web: www.sladencottage.co.uk
Dir: on A6187 towards Hope/Castleton, 200yds past George Hotel on right immediately before railway bridge
CHILD FACILITIES: Please telephone for details

This delightful, newly refurbished stone property enjoys an elevated position overlooking the rolling countryside of Hope Valley; minutes' walk from the village centre. Modern contemporary bedrooms are smartly appointed and guests have use of two smart lounges and a small kitchen. A hearty breakfast is served in the spacious, attractive pine dining room.
ROOMS: 5 en suite (1 fmly) d £48-£59 * **FACILITIES:** TVB tea/coffee No coaches **NOTES:** Credit cards not taken 🐾 ⊛ Cen ht **PARKING:** 8

LONG EATON   Map 08 SK43

Babies Welcome | Family Rooms | Children's Dishes

★★★ 66%
Novotel Nottingham/Derby
Bostock Ln NG10 4EP
☎ 0115 946 5111 📠 0115 946 5900
e-mail: H0507@accor-hotels.com
Dir: M1 junct 25 onto B6002 to Long Eaton. Hotel 400yds on left
CHILD FACILITIES: Activities: toys, themed gifts Indoor play area Outdoor play area Family area Food/bottle warming Ch menu Ch portions Highchairs Ch cutlery Ch discounts under 16s free sharing with parents Safe grounds Games consoles Cots Family rms D rms with S beds from £70 Connecting rms Laundry **NEARBY:** Sherwood Forest Castle Alton Towers Theme parks Cinema

continued

In close proximity to M1 junction 25, this purpose-built hotel has much to offer. Bedrooms are spacious; all have sofa beds. Public rooms include a bright brasserie, which is open all day and provides extended dining.
ROOMS: 108 en suite (40 fmly) ⊛ in 66 bedrooms s £49-£75; d £49-£75 **LB FACILITIES:** STV 🪝 **PARKING:** 220

LONGFORD   Map 07 SK23

♦♦♦♦ Russets
Off Main St DE6 3DR
☎ 01335 330874 📠 01335 330874
e-mail: geoffrey.nolan@virgin.net
web: www.russets.com
Dir: from A516 turn into Sutton Lane in Hatton. Follow this until T-junction, R onto Long Lane. Next R into Longford & R before telephone box on Main St
CHILD FACILITIES: Please telephone for details

An indoor swimming pool is available at this beautifully maintained bungalow, which is peacefully located near Alton Towers. Bedrooms are well equipped and have smart modern bathrooms. Comprehensive breakfasts are taken at one family table in a homely dining room, and a comfortable guest lounge is also available.
ROOMS: 2 en suite (1 fmly) (2 GF) s £30; d £50 * **FACILITIES:** STV TVB tea/coffee TVL No coaches 🐾 Gymnasium **NOTES:** Credit cards not taken ⊛ Cen ht **PARKING:** 4

MATLOCK   Map 08 SK36

Babies Welcome | Family Rooms | Children's Dishes

♦♦♦♦ 🏫 Old Sunday School
New St DE4 3FH
☎ 01629 583347 📠 01629 583347
e-mail: davhpatrick@hotmail.com
Dir: turn off A6 at Crown Square up Bank Rd (steep hill) to Derby County Council Office car park, New St is directly opposite
CHILD FACILITIES: Activities: colouring, toys, Lego Family area Food/bottle warming Ch menu Ch portions Highchairs Ch cutlery Ch discounts Videos Family rms Adjoining room with S/T beds £15 per rm for children Ch drinks Connecting rms Laundry **NEARBY:** Heights of Abraham Park Theme park

A warm welcome is assured at this early Victorian former chapel, built of mellow sandstone and sympathetically restored, and just a few minutes' walk from central attractions. The comfortable, homely bedroom is complemented by a modern shower room, and the spacious open-plan living area includes a period dining table, the setting for comprehensive breakfasts and (by arrangement) imaginative dinners.
ROOMS: 1 en suite (1 fmly) s £22.50-£25; d £45-£50 * **FACILITIES:** TVB tea/coffee TVL No coaches Dinner Last d order 5pm **NOTES:** Credit cards not taken 🐾 ⊛ Cen ht **LB**

England

MATLOCK, continued

Family Rooms | Children's Dishes

♦♦♦ ❦ Farley

Farley DE4 5LR
☎ 01629 582533 & 07801 756409 🖅 01629 584856
e-mail: eric.b@ukgateway.net
Dir: A6 Buxton/Bakewell 1st R after rdbt in Matlock. Turn R at top of hill, then L up Farley Hill, 2nd farm on L

CHILD FACILITIES: Indoor play area Outdoor play area Food/bottle warming Ch menu Ch portions Ch cutlery Ch discounts under 2s free, children sharing with parents 50% Safe grounds Family rms D rm with 2 S beds Ch drinks Laundry **NEARBY:** Farm animals Matlock Park Cinema Bowling Theme parks

Guests can expect a warm welcome at this traditional stone-built farmhouse dating back to the 12th century. In addition to farming, the proprietors also breed dogs and horses. The bedrooms are pleasantly decorated and equipped with many useful extras. Breakfast is served communally around one large table and dinner is available by prior arrangement.
ROOMS: 2 en suite (2 fmly) s fr £25; d £40-£45 * ⊗
FACILITIES: TVB tea/coffee TVL Riding 165 acres arable beef dairy Dinner Last d order 5pm **NOTES:** Credit cards not taken ⊗ in area of dining room Cen ht **LB PARKING:** 8

MELBOURNE
Map 08 SK32

Babies Welcome | Family Rooms | Children's Dishes

♦♦♦ 🍴 The Melbourne Arms

92 Ashby Rd DE73 1ES
☎ 01332 864949 🖅 01332 865525
e-mail: info@melbournearms.com
Dir: Aprox 3m from Nottingham East Midlands Airport

CHILD FACILITIES: Activities: bouncy castle, playground Outdoor play area Family area Food/bottle warming Highchairs Ch cutlery Safe grounds Family rms 2 D beds £65 Connecting rms Fridge **NEARBY:** Alton Towers Race circuit Alvaston Castle

Ideally located for both the airport and Donnington Park, this Grade II listed inn provides modern, thoughtfully equipped bedrooms, one of which is housed in a sympathetic conversion of a former outbuilding. Ground floor areas include two bars, a coffee shop and an elegant Indian restaurant.
ROOMS: 5 en suite (1 fmly) s £35-£40; d £50-£55 * ⊗
FACILITIES: TVB tea/coffee TVL Dinner Last d order 11pm **NOTES:** ✖ ⊗ in area of dining room ⊗ in 1 lounge Cen ht **PARKING:** 52

How to use this guide & abbreviations are explained on pages 5-7

SOUTH NORMANTON
Map 08 SK45

Babies Welcome | Family Rooms | Children's Dishes

★★★★ 70% Renaissance Derby/Nottingham Hotel

RENAISSANCE HOTELS

Carter Ln East DE55 2EH
☎ 01773 812000 🖅 01773 580032
e-mail: derby@renaissancehotels.co.uk
Dir: M1 junct 28, E on A38 to Mansfield

CHILD FACILITIES: Babysitting Activities: colouring Food/bottle warming Ch menu Ch portions Highchairs Ch discounts Cots Family rms Ch drinks Connecting rms Fridge Laundry **NEARBY:** Alton Towers American Adventure Park Chatsworth House

This hotel provides comfortable bedrooms, stylishly furnished and decorated with a range of extras provided. Public rooms include a smart leisure centre and Chatterley's Restaurant.
ROOMS: 158 en suite (7 fmly) (61 GF) ⊗ in 100 bedrooms s £120-£132; d £140-£152 (incl. bkfst) **LB FACILITIES:** STV ☒ Sauna Solarium Gym Jacuzzi Steam room, Whirlpool Xmas **PARKING:** 220 **NOTES:** ⊗ in restaurant

♦♦♦♦ The Boundary Lodge

Lea Vale, Broadmeadows DE55 3NA
☎ 01773 819066 🖅 01773 819006
e-mail: manager@boundarylodge.fsnet.co.uk
web: www.theboundary.co.uk
Dir: M1 junct 28, join B6019 to South Normanton, continue for 0.5 mile and over mini-rdbt, at 2nd mini-rdbt turn left into Birchwood Lane, Lea Vale is next left, Lodge 3rd on left

CHILD FACILITIES: Please telephone for details

Ideally located for the M1, this modern public house, now under new ownership, provides a range of food and drink suitable for all tastes, and families are especially welcome. The spacious bedrooms are situated in separate purpose-built accommodation and contain many practical and homely extras to ensure guest comfort.
ROOMS: 14 en suite (2 fmly) d £44.95; (room only) * ⊗ in 6 bedrooms **FACILITIES:** STV TVB tea/coffee Direct dial from bedrooms TVL Pool Table Indoor & outdoor play areas for children Dinner Last d order 8.45pm **NOTES:** ✖ ⊗ in area of dining room ⊗ in 1 lounge Licensed Cen ht **LB PARKING:** 96

SWADLINCOTE
Map 08 SK21

Family Rooms | Children's Dishes

♦♦♦♦ Overseale House

Acresford Rd, Overseal DE12 6HX
☎ 01283 763741 🖅 01283 760015
e-mail: oversealehouse@hotmail.com
web: www.overseale.co.uk
Dir: in the village of Overseal on the A444 between Burton-on-Trent & M42 junct 11

CHILD FACILITIES: Outdoor play area Food/bottle warming Ch portions Ch cutlery Ch discounts under 2s free Family rms D rm with 2nd T rm Ch drinks Connecting rms Fridge **NEARBY:** NEC Conkers discovery centre Zoo Drayton Manor Park

Located in the village of Overseal, this well-proportioned Georgian mansion, built for a renowned industrialist, retains many original features including a magnificent ornately decorated dining room. The period-furnished ground floor areas include a cosy sitting room, and bedrooms contain many thoughtful extras.
ROOMS: 4 en suite 1 annexe rms (3 fmly) (2 GF) s £25-£30; d £50-£60 * **FACILITIES:** TVB tea/coffee No coaches 3 acre garden **NOTES:** Credit cards not taken ⊗ Cen ht **PARKING:** 6

TIDESWELL
Map 07 SK17

Babies Welcome	Family Rooms	Children's Dishes

◆◆◆ Jaret House
Queen St SK17 8JZ
☎ 01298 872470
e-mail: jarethouse@tesco.net
Dir: A6/A623-B6049, Jaret House in centre of village opposite Hills and Dales Tearooms

CHILD FACILITIES: Activities: books Food/bottle warming Ch menu Ch portions Highchairs Ch discounts under 12s free Videos Cots Family rms D rm with S bed £45-£60 Ch drinks
NEARBY: Chatsworth Farmyard

This typical Derbyshire cottage offers traditionally furnished bedrooms, all with en suite shower rooms. Friendly and attentive service is provided. A comfortable sitting room is warmed by a log fire during the colder months and substantial freshly-prepared breakfasts are served in a cosy dining room.
ROOMS: 3 en suite (1 fmly) s £25; d £45-£50 * **FACILITIES:** TVB tea/coffee No coaches **NOTES:** Credit cards not taken ✖ ⊗ Cen ht LB

TISSINGTON
Map 07 SK15

Babies Welcome	Family Rooms	Children's Dishes

◆◆◆ ❤ Bent Farm
DE6 1RD
☎ 01335 390214 ▤ 01335 390214
e-mail: mike.hil@bentfarm.fsnet.co.uk
Dir: A515 Ashbourne to Buxton rd, turn off at Tissington, through avenue of trees to village, past pond, Bent Farm 0.5m on left

CHILD FACILITIES: Outdoor play area Food/bottle warming Ch menu Ch portions Highchairs Ch cutlery Ch discounts free in cots, under 16s £15 when sharing with parents Videos Cots Family rms D rm with 1 or 2 S beds £80 Laundry (by arrangement)
NEARBY: Carsington Water Alton Towers Heights of Abraham

Set amid rolling hills and open pastures, this 17th-century Grade II listed farmhouse is part of a dairy farm and also a furniture makers. The spacious bedrooms match the character of the house. Breakfast includes fresh milk and eggs from the farm and is served in the traditional dining room. There is also a large, comfortable lounge.
ROOMS: 2 en suite (1 fmly) d £24.50-£49 * **FACILITIES:** tea/coffee TVL Farming activities 280 acres dairy **NOTES:** Credit cards not taken ✖ ⊗ Cen ht LB BB **PARKING:** 6

DEVON

Beach huts in Torquay

CLYST ST MARY
Crealy Adventure Park EX5 1DR
fun@crealy.co.uk
☎01395 233200
(Leave M5 junct 30 onto A3052) Open all year, Jan-Mid Jul & 6 Sep-Dec daily 10-5 Mid Jul-5 Sep, daily 10-6. Closed winter term time Mon-Tue. *£7.95-£8.95, ch under 90cm free, pen £5.20-£6.20 Party 4+ £7.70-£8.70.

COMBE MARTIN
Combe Martin Wildlife & Dinosaur Park
EX34 ONG
☎01271 882486
info@dinosaur-park.com
(M5 junct 27 then A361 towards Barnstaple and turn right on to A399) Open 20 Mar-Oct daily, 10-4 last admission 3pm *£10, ch 3-15 £6, ch under 3 free, pen £7. Family 2 adults & 2 ch £29.

CULLOMPTON
Diggerland
EX15 2PE
☎08700 344437
mail@diggerland
(M25 junct 27. E on A38 & at rdbt turn right onto A3181. Diggerland is 3m on left.) Open 12 Feb-27 Nov, 12-5, wkends, BHs & school holidays. £2.50 (pen £1.25, under 2s free). Additonal charge to drive/ride machinery.

DARTMOUTH
Woodlands Leisure Park TQ9 7DQ
fun@woodlandspark.com
☎01803 712598

(W, off A3122) Open 26 Mar-5 Nov daily, also wknds & school holidays.
*£8.25. Family ticket £31.20 2 ad & 2 ch.

ILFRACOMBE
Watermouth Castle & Family Theme Park
EX34 9SL
☎01271 863879
enquiries@watermouthcastle.com
(3m NE off A399, midway between Ilfracombe & Combe Martin)
Open Apr-Oct, closed Sat. Also closed some Mon & Fri off season. Ring for further details. *£9.00, ch 3-13 £7.50 & pen £6.50

NEWTON ABBOT
Hedgehog Hospital at Prickly Ball Farm
TQ12 6BZ
☎01626 362319
hedgehog@hedgehog.org.uk
(1.5m from Newton Abbot on A381 towards Totnes, follow brown heritage signs)
Open wk before Etr-end Oct, 10.30-5. Last admission 1hr before closing.

PAIGNTON
Paignton Zoo Environmental Park TQ4 7EU
info@paigntonzoo.org.uk
☎01803 697500
(1m from Paignton town centre on A3022 Totnes) road. Open all year, daily 10-6 5pm in winter. Last admission 5pm, 4pm in winter. Closed 25 Dec. £8.50, ch 3-15 £6.20, students £7. Family ticket £26.70

TORQUAY
Babbacombe Model Village
TQ1 3LA
☎01803 328669
ss@babbacombemodelvillage.co.uk
(follow brown tourist signs from outskirts of town) Apr-May, 10-5.30; Jun-Aug, 10am-10.30pm; Sep; 10-9.30; Oct, 10-5; Nov-Feb 10-4.30. Closed 25 Dec. *£6.40, ch £3.95, pen £5.40. Family ticket £18.50.

ASHBURTON
Map 03 SX76

★★★ 74% ◎ ◎ Holne Chase
Two Bridges Rd TQ13 7NS
☎ 01364 631471 🖷 01364 631453
e-mail: info@holne-chase.co.uk
web: www.holne-chase.co.uk
Dir: 3m N on unclass Two Bridges/Tavistock road

CHILD FACILITIES: Please telephone for details

This former hunting lodge is peacefully situated in a secluded position, with sweeping lawns leading to the river and panoramic views of the moor. Bedrooms are attractively and individually furnished, and there are a number of split-level suites available. Good quality local produce features on the daily-changing menu.
ROOMS: 10 en suite 7 annexe en suite (9 fmly) (1 GF) s £95-£125; d £140-£230 (incl. bkfst) **LB FACILITIES:** Fishing Riding 🐎 ⛵ Fly fishing, Riding, Beauty treatments for people and dogs Xmas
PARKING: 40 **NOTES:** ⊛ in restaurant

♦♦♦♦ Greencott
Landscove TQ13 7LZ
☎ 01803 762649
Dir: take A38 to Plymouth, then 2nd exit signed Landscove. At top of slip rd turn left, follow for 2m, keep village green on right, opposite village hall

CHILD FACILITIES: Please telephone for details

Greencott enjoys a peaceful village location and superb country views. Your hosts extend a warm and genuinely friendly welcome and a relaxed home-from-home atmosphere prevails. Service is attentive and caring and many guests return time and again. Bedrooms are attractive, comfortable and very well equipped. Delicious country cooking is served around the oak dining table.
ROOMS: 2 en suite s £19-£21; d £38-£42 ⊛ **FACILITIES:** tea/coffee No coaches Dinner Last d order by arrangement **NOTES:** Credit cards not taken 🐾 ⊛ in restaurant Cen ht **LB BB PARKING:** 3

♦♦♦♦ 🏆 🍴 The Rising Sun
Woodland TQ13 7JT
☎ 01364 652544 🖷 01364 654202
e-mail: mail@risingsunwoodland.co.uk
web: www.risingsunwoodland.co.uk
Dir: turn off A38 Exeter/Plymouth at sign for Woodland and Denbury (which is shortly after sign Plymouth 26m) continue down lane 1.5m Rising Sun is on left

CHILD FACILITIES: Activities: toys, books, colouring Indoor play area Outdoor play area Family area Food/bottle warming Ch menu Ch portions Highchairs Safe grounds Family rms D rm with B bed or adjoining room £75 Connecting rms NEARBY: Dartmoor Farm Museum

Peacefully situated in the scenic South Devon countryside and an excellent base for touring the area, this inn is just a short drive from the A38. A friendly welcome is extended to all guests: business, leisure and families alike. Bedrooms are comfortable and well equipped. Dinner and breakfast feature much local and organic produce. A good selection of homemade puddings and West Country cheeses is available.
ROOMS: 6 en suite (2 fmly) (2 GF) s £38-£45; d £60-£70 * ⊛ **FACILITIES:** TVB tea/coffee Dinner Last d order 9.15pm **NOTES:** ⊛ in restaurant Cen ht **PARKING:** 30

All information was correct at the time of going to press; we recommend you confirm details on booking

---

Babies Welcome | Children's Dishes

◎ ◎ Agaric
30 North St TQ13 7QD
☎ 01364 654478
e-mail: eat@agaricrestaurant.co.uk
Dir: opposite town hall. Ashburton off A38 between Exeter & Plymouth

**CHILD FACILITIES: Activities: Food/bottle warming Ch portions Highchairs Ch cutlery Safe grounds Changing facilities
NEARBY: Otter and butterfly farm Steam railway Children's farm Walks**

FOOD: British, Mediterranean **STYLE:** Chic Rustic **SEATS:** 30
OPEN: 12-2.30/7-9.30, Closed 2 wks Oct, Xmas, 1wk Jan, 2 wks Feb, Mon-TueL Sat, D Sun **RESTAURANT:** main £12.95-£16.95 **NOTES:** ⊛ in restaurant **PARKING:** Car park opposite

BARNSTAPLE
Map 02 SS53

Babies Welcome | Family Rooms | Children's Dishes 🏐

★★★ 74% Barnstaple Hotel
Braunton Rd EX31 1LE
☎ 01271 376221 🖷 01271 324101
e-mail: info@barnstaplehotel.co.uk
web: www.barnstaplehotel.co.uk
Dir: outskirts of Barnstaple on A361

CHILD FACILITIES: Baby listening Food/bottle warming Ch menu Ch portions Highchairs Ch cutlery Ch discounts free sharing with parents, own rm £35 Safe grounds Cots Family rms D rm with S bed from £70 Connecting rms Laundry NEARBY: Cinema Karting Tenpin bowling 10-min drive to sea

This well-established hotel enjoys a convenient location on the edge of town. Bedrooms are spacious and well equipped, many with access to a balcony overlooking the outdoor pool and garden. A wide choice is offered from various menus based on local produce, and there is an extensive range of leisure facilities making this an ideal destination for family breaks.
ROOMS: 60 en suite (3 fmly) (17 GF) s £57-£80; d £65-£90 **LB**
FACILITIES: Spa STV 🎱 🏹 Snooker Sauna Solarium Gym Xmas
PARKING: 250 **NOTES:** 🐾

BIDEFORD
Map 02 SS42

Babies Welcome | Family Rooms | Children's Dishes 🏐

♦♦♦♦ Pines at Eastleigh
The Pines, Eastleigh EX39 4PA
☎ 01271 860561
e-mail: pirrie@thepinesateastleigh.co.uk
Dir: turn off A39 Barnstaple/Bideford rd onto A386 signed Torrington. Take first left signed Eastleigh, 500yds, 1st left also signed Eastleigh, 1.5m to village, house on right

CHILD FACILITIES: Baby listening Activities: table tennis, table football, snooker, games, archery on request Indoor play area Outdoor play area Family area Food/bottle warming Ch menu Ch portions Highchairs Ch cutlery Ch discounts under 1s free, under 18s up to 25% Safe grounds Videos Cots Family rms D rm with separate T rm from £75 Ch drinks Connecting rms Laundry Changing mats NEARBY: Cycle trail Adventure park Outdoor adventure schools 5-min drive to sea

Friendly hospitality is assured at this Georgian farmhouse, set in seven acres of gardens. Two of the comfortable bedrooms are located in the main house, the remainder in converted barns around a charming courtyard, with a pretty pond and well.
continued

A delicious breakfast featuring local and home-made produce is served in the dining room and a guest lounge is also available.
ROOMS: 6 en suite (3 fmly) (4 GF) s £25-£45; d £60-£100 *
FACILITIES: TVB tea/coffee Direct dial from bedrooms No coaches ♨ Badminton, Link with outdoor activity centre **NOTES:** ⊛ Licensed Cen ht **LB PARKING:** 20

BRENDON   Map 03 SS74

♦♦♦♦ Leeford Cottage
EX35 6PS
☎ 01598 741279 ◨ 01598 741392
e-mail: g.linley@virgin.net
web: www.leefordcottage.com
Dir: approx. 4.5m E of Lynton. Off A39 at Brendon sign, cross packhorse bridges and village green, straight over x-rds Leeford Cottage is on left

CHILD FACILITIES: Baby listening Activities: books, puzzles, games, balls Indoor play area Outdoor play area Food/bottle warming Ch menu Ch portions Highchairs Ch cutlery Ch discounts under 2s free, reductions sharing with parents Safe grounds Videos Cots Ch drinks Connecting rms Laundry **NEARBY:** Butlins Walks Sheep centre Zoo Adventure park 8 min to sea

Situated in the quiet hamlet of Brendon, this 400-year-old cottage is steeped in character. The welcoming proprietors grow their own vegetables and rear hens, which provide the eggs for breakfasts. Bedrooms are cosy and comfortable and dinner features good home cooking.
ROOMS: 3 rms (1 en suite) s £27-£28; d £45-£47 *
FACILITIES: tea/coffee TVL No coaches Dinner Last d order 5pm
NOTES: Credit cards not taken ⊛ Cen ht **LB PARKING:** 10

CHAWLEIGH   Map 03 SS71

Family Rooms | Children's Dishes

♦♦♦♦ ≣ The Barn-Rodgemonts
Rodgemonts EX18 7ET
☎ 01769 580200
e-mail: pyerodgemonts@btinternet.com
Dir: from Exeter take A377 at Eggesford Stn (level crossing on left) right B3042 to Chawleigh, 1.5m at T- junct left onto B3096 towards Chulmleigh, 0.5m signed Chawleigh Week, fork left after 250mtrs Rodgemonts drive on right

CHILD FACILITIES: Food/bottle warming Ch menu Ch portions Ch cutlery Ch discounts Family rms D & T connecting rms Connecting rms

Set amid peaceful countryside, this attractive house offers friendly hospitality. Bedrooms are located in the thatched, converted former hay barn, each with views of the orchard from which the proprietors produce their own apple juice which features in the delightful breakfasts. By prior arrangement, Aga cooked dinners are served in the farmhouse kitchen, overlooking the gardens.
ROOMS: 2 en suite (1 fmly) d £42-£52 * **FACILITIES:** TVB tea/coffee No coaches Dinner **NOTES:** Credit cards not taken ⊛ Cen ht **LB PARKING:** 3

COLYTON   Map 03 SY29

♦♦♦♦ Colyton Holiday Cottages
The White Cottage, Dolphin St EX24 6NA
☎ 01297 552401 ◨ 01297 553207
e-mail: hello@colytoncottages.com
web: www.colytoncottages.com
Dir: turn off A3052 towards Colyton, through town centre towards Shute, cottage right after Kingfisher pub

continued

CHILD FACILITIES: Please telephone for details
Centrally located in this picturesque village, these charming comfortable cottages have been converted from an old barn, retaining the character and beams of the original building. Each cottage includes lounge/dining room and fully equipped kitchen; two units are situated on the ground floor. A hearty cooked breakfast will be delivered to your cottage.
ROOMS: 4 en suite (2 GF) s fr £25; d fr £50 * **FACILITIES:** TVB tea/coffee Direct dial from bedrooms TVL No coaches **NOTES:** Credit cards not taken ✖ ⊛ Cen ht **LB PARKING:** 8

CREDITON   Map 03 SS80

♦♦♦♦ Fircroft
George Hill EX17 2DS
☎ 01363 774224
e-mail: fircroftbb@talk21.com
Dir: on A377 to Barnstaple at the green turn right. At x-roads straight over 1st on right

CHILD FACILITIES: Please telephone for details
This delightful double-fronted Victorian family home is quietly located with views over the market town below. It provides guests with spacious bedrooms, which are thoughtfully equipped with numerous useful facilities. In warmer weather guests can relax in the south-facing gardens.
ROOMS: 2 en suite (2 fmly) d £48 * **FACILITIES:** TVB tea/coffee No coaches **NOTES:** Credit cards not taken ✖ ⊛ Cen ht **PARKING:** 6

CULMSTOCK   Map 03 ST11

Babies Welcome | Children's Dishes

⌂ Culm Valley Inn
EX15 3JJ
☎ 01884 840354 ◨ 01884 841659

CHILD FACILITIES: Food/bottle warming Ch portions Highchairs **NEARBY:** Diggerland

OPEN: 12-3 6-11 (Open All Day Sun) Closed: 25 Dec **BAR MEALS:** L served all week 12-2 D served Mon-Sat 7-9 Av main course £10
RESTAURANT: L served all week 12-2 D served Mon-Sat 7-9 Av 3 course à la carte £21.50 **FACILITIES:** Garden: Old Railway embankment overlooking River Culm **NOTES:** Credit cards not taken **PARKING:** 40

DARTMOUTH   Map 03 SX85

♦♦♦♦ ⌂ Seale Arms
10 Victoria Rd TQ6 9SA
☎ 01803 832719 ◨ 01803 839366
e-mail: sealearms@hotmail.com
Dir: turn off A38 at Buckfastleigh then A384 to Totnes. At Totnes take A381 to Halwell, then A3122 to Dartmouth

CHILD FACILITIES: Activities: toys, games, books Indoor play area Family area Food/bottle warming Ch menu Ch portions Highchairs Ch cutlery Ch discounts Safe grounds Games consoles Cots Family rms D rm with S bed & cot Ch drinks **NEARBY:** Adventure park Farm Zoo 10-min drive to sea

A friendly inn, the Seale Arms is conveniently located only a short walk from the quayside. Bedrooms are attractively decorated, spacious and stylish and are provided with a range of extras. The well-stocked bar is popular with locals and visitors alike and offers a good selection of freshly cooked dishes. Breakfast is served in the dining room.
ROOMS: 4 en suite (2 fmly) s £30-£35; d £50-£65 * ⊛
FACILITIES: TVB tea/coffee Pool Table **NOTES:** ✖ ⊛ in restaurant ⊛ in 1 lounge Cen ht

England

DAWLISH
Map 03 SX97

Babies Welcome | **Family Rooms** | **Children's Dishes**

★★★ 71% Langstone Cliff
THE INDEPENDENTS
Dawlish Warren EX7 0NA
☎ 01626 868000 ▤ 01626 868006
e-mail: reception@langstone-hotel.co.uk
web: www.langstone-hotel.co.uk
Dir: 1.5m NE off A379 Exeter road to Dawlish Warren

CHILD FACILITIES: Baby listening Babysitting (by prior request) **Activities:** paddling pools, discos, face painting, toys, books, board games Indoor play area Outdoor play area Family area Food/bottle warming Ch menu Ch portions Highchairs Ch cutlery Ch discounts under 10s sharing free, 10-16s sharing 50% Safe grounds Cots Family rms suites - 2 rms Ch drinks (not complementary) Connecting rms Laundry Changing mats (by request) **NEARBY:** 500yds to sea

A family owned and run hotel, the Langstone Cliff offers a range of leisure and function facilities. Bedrooms, many with sea views and balconies, are spacious, comfortable and well equipped. There are a number of attractive lounges. Dinner is served, often carvery style, in the restaurant.
ROOMS: 62 en suite 4 annexe en suite (52 fmly) (10 GF) s £62-£71; d £106-£154 (incl. bkfst) LB **FACILITIES:** STV ▣ ↘ ✎ Snooker Gym Table tennis, Golf practice area, Hair and beauty salon ♫ Xmas **PARKING:** 200

See advert on opposite page

EXETER
Map 03 SX99

◆◆◆◆ The Edwardian
30/32 Heavitree Rd EX1 2LQ
☎ 01392 276102 & 254699 ▤ 01392 253393
e-mail: michael@edwardianexeter.co.uk
web: www.edwardianexeter.co.uk
Dir: M5 junct 29. R at lights signed city centre. On Heavitree Rd after Exeter University, School of Education on L

CHILD FACILITIES: Please telephone for details

Tastefully decorated in period style, this attractive Edwardian terraced property is situated within walking distance of the city centre. All of the bedrooms feature personal touches and a number have four-poster beds. Books and local tourist information are provided in the comfortable lounge, and the resident proprietors are on hand to help guests plan their stay.
ROOMS: 12 en suite (4 fmly) (3 GF) ❀ **FACILITIES:** TVB tea/coffee Direct dial from bedrooms TVL No coaches **NOTES:** ❀ in restaurant Cen ht **PARKING:** 3

How to use this guide & abbreviations are explained on pages 5-7

Babies Welcome | **Family Rooms** | **Children's Dishes**

◆◆◆◆ 🍴 Gissons Arms
Kennford EX6 7UD
☎ 01392 832444
Dir: along A38 towards Torquay, before fork in road, go up slip road on left

CHILD FACILITIES: Family area Food/bottle warming Ch menu Highchairs Ch cutlery Ch discounts Safe grounds Family rms £60 + £10 extra bed **NEARBY:** Woodland walks

With parts dating back to the 15th century, this delightful inn offers comfortable, well-equipped bedrooms, some boasting four-poster beds. The bars retain the original character and charm of the building and have a relaxed atmosphere. In addition to the extensive choice of dishes from the carvery, a range of daily special dishes and a tempting selection of desserts are available.
ROOMS: 14 en suite s £40; d £60 * **FACILITIES:** TVB tea/coffee Direct dial from bedrooms Dinner Last d order 10pm **NOTES:** ❀ in area of dining room Cen ht **PARKING:** 100

Family Rooms | **Children's Dishes** | **Minimum Age**

◆◆◆ Sunnymede
24 New North Rd EX4 4HF
☎ 01392 273844
Dir: from M5, junct 30, follow City Centre signs into one-way system. Pass Central Station in Queen St. At clocktower rdbt turn right. Sunnymede on left

CHILD FACILITIES: Food/bottle warming Ch menu Ch portions Ch cutlery Ch discounts Family rms triple rm £55-£60 **NEARBY:** Cathedral Museum Quayside

The Sunnymede enjoys a central location in this historic city and is convenient for the college, shopping centre and tourist attractions. A compact guest house, it offers well-presented, comfortable bedrooms. A good choice is available at breakfast. This is a no-smoking establishment.
ROOMS: 9 en suite (1 fmly) s £25-£28; d £42-£45 * **FACILITIES:** TV6B tea/coffee TVL No coaches **NOTES:** ✖ ❀ Cen ht

Babies Welcome | **Children's Dishes**

🏅 Brazz
10-12 Palace Gate EX1 1JA
☎ 01392 252525 ▤ 01392 253045
e-mail: exeter@brazz.co.uk
Dir: exit M5 J30, follow Topsham Rd then first right off South Street.

CHILD FACILITIES: Activities: colouring, games Food/bottle warming Ch licence Ch portions Highchairs Safe grounds Changing facilities **NEARBY:** Crealy Adventure Park Underground passages

FOOD: British, French **STYLE:** Modern **SEATS:** 150 **OPEN:** 12-3/6-10.30, Closed 25 Dec **RESTAURANT:** Fixed L £13.50, Fixed D £16.50, main £7.50-£15.95 **NOTES:** ❀ in restaurant, Air con **PARKING:** On street

Babies Welcome | **Children's Dishes**

🏅🏅 The Puffing Billy
Station Rd, Exton EX3 0PR
☎ 01392 877888 ▤ 01392 876212
e-mail: the_billy@hotmail.com
Dir: Three miles from J30 M5 take A376 signposted Exmouth, pass through Ebford and follow signs for The Puffing Billy

CHILD FACILITIES: Food/bottle warming Ch licence Ch menu Ch portions Highchairs Ch cutlery **NEARBY:** Playground Estuary

FOOD: Modern European **STYLE:** Chic, Modern **SEATS:** 75 **OPEN:** 12-3/6-10, Closed 25 Dec, 1 Jan **RESTAURANT:** Fixed L £10.50, Fixed D £14, main £10.95-£21 **NOTES:** ❀ area, Air con **PARKING:** 25

HARTLAND Map 02 SS22

Babies Welcome	Family Rooms	Children's Dishes

◆◆◆ Fosfelle

EX39 6EF
☎ 01237 441273 🖷 01237 441273
Dir: off A39 onto B3248 for 2m entrance on right

CHILD FACILITIES: Indoor play area Outdoor play area Family area Food/bottle warming Ch menu Ch portions Highchairs Ch cutlery Ch discounts under 12s 50% Safe grounds Cots Family rms D rm with B beds/S beds from £70 Ch drinks Connecting rms Laundry **NEARBY:** Adventure park Coastal paths

Dating back to the 17th century, this delightful manor house offers comfortable accommodation close to the village of Hartland. It is set in six acres of gardens with two fishing lakes. The restaurant offers a range of freshly prepared dishes.
ROOMS: 7 rms (4 en suite) (2 fmly) s £26-£32; d £52-£60 * 🛇
FACILITIES: TV6B tea/coffee TVL Fishing Pool Table Dinner Last d order 9pm **NOTES:** ✖ Licensed Cen ht **LB PARKING:** 20

HOLBETON Map 02 SX65

🛱 The Mildmay Colours Inn

PL8 1NA
☎ 01752 830248 🖷 01752 830432
e-mail: louise@mildmaycolours.fsnet.co.uk
Dir: S from Exeter on A38, Yealmpton/Ermington, S past Ugborough & Ermington R onto A379. After 1.5m, turn R, signposted Mildmay Colours/Holbeton

CHILD FACILITIES: Please telephone for details

OPEN: 11-3 6-11 (Sun 12-3, 7-10.30) **BAR MEALS:** L served all week 12-2 D served all week 6-9 **RESTAURANT:** L served Sun 12-2 Av 3 course à la carte £12 **FACILITIES:** Garden: Nice flower arrangements, 10 picnic benches **PARKING:** 20

HONITON Map 03 ST10

Babies Welcome	Family Rooms	Children's Dishes

★★★

Combe House Hotel & Restaurant

Gittisham EX14 3AD
☎ 01404 540400 🖷 01404 46004
e-mail: stay@thishotel.com web: www.thishotel.com
Dir: off A30 1m S of Honiton, follow Gittisham Heathpark signs

CHILD FACILITIES: Baby listening Babysitting Activities: toys, colouring, jigsaws, table tennis, games Food/bottle warming Ch menu Ch portions Highchairs Ch cutlery Ch discounts under 3s free, 3-12s £15 sharing with parents Safe grounds Games consoles Videos Cots Family rms D rms with sofa beds from £275 Ch drinks Connecting rms Laundry Changing mats **NEARBY:** Crealy Adventure Park Cinema Leisure centre

Standing proud in an elevated position, this Elizabethan mansion enjoys uninterrupted views over acres of its own woodland, meadow and pasture. Bedrooms are a blend of comfort and quality with relaxation being the ultimate objective. A range of atmospheric public rooms retain all the charm and history of the old house. Dining is equally impressive, a skilled kitchen brigade maximises the best of local and home-grown produce, augmented by excellent wines. Private dining is available in the magnificently restored old kitchen.
ROOMS: 15 en suite s £125-£165; d £140-£148 (incl. bkfst) **LB**
FACILITIES: Fishing 🗇 Jacuzzi Xmas **PARKING:** 51 **NOTES:** 🛇 in restaurant

---

Nestling in 20 acre grounds overlooking the sea at Dawlish is the family owned Langstone Cliff Hotel.

AA ★★★

66 en-suite rooms and a host of public rooms give the hotel great versatility. Situated just 10 miles from both Exeter and Torbay, only a 30 minute drive from Dartmoor yet just 500 yards from 2 miles of sand, an 18 hole golf course and an internationally renowned bird sanctuary makes the hotel a perfect family holiday venue.

The hotel offers extensive business and banqueting facilities. Star cabaret weekends are also featured regularly throughout the year.

Langstone Cliff Hotel, Dawlish, South Devon, EX7 0NA
Tel: 01626 868000 Fax: 01626 868006
website: www.langstone-hotel.co.uk
email: aa@langstone-hotel.co.uk

◆◆◆◆ Atwell's at Wellington Farm

Wilmington EX14 9JR
☎ 01404 831885
e-mail: wilmington@btinternet.com
Dir: 3m from Honiton, take A35 towards Dorchester, approx 500yds through village of Wilmington on left

CHILD FACILITIES: Please telephone for details

Convenient for Honiton and the coast, this delightful Grade II listed 16th-century farmhouse is set in five acres, which also accommodates a rescue centre for animals including hens, a goat, sheep and horses of varying sizes - from Shire to Shetland. This friendly house offers comfortable accommodation, hearty breakfasts using fresh local produce and cream teas.
ROOMS: 3 rms (2 en suite) (1 GF) s fr £20; d £44-£50 *
FACILITIES: TVB TVL No coaches **NOTES:** Credit cards not taken 🛇 Cen ht **PARKING:** 10

Babies Welcome	Family Rooms	Children's Dishes

◆◆◆◆ 🐾 Courtmoor Farm

Upottery EX14 9QA
☎ 01404 861565
e-mail: courtmoor.farm@btinternet.com
web: www.courtmoor.farm.btinternet.co.uk
Dir: off A30, 0.5m W of A30 & A303 junct, approx 4m from Honiton

CHILD FACILITIES: Activities: toys, games Outdoor play area Family area Food/bottle warming Ch menu Ch portions Highchairs Ch cutlery Ch discounts under 2s free, 2-7s £8, 8-16s £12 Safe grounds Cots Family rms D rms with S beds, cot or Z bed £56-£72 Laundry (on request) Changing mats (on request) **NEARBY:** Donkey sanctuary

This guest house, set in attractive grounds, overlooks the attractive
continued on p112

HONITON, continued

Otter Valley. Bedrooms all have views, and are spacious, comfortable and well equipped. Dinner, by prior arrangement, provides freshly cooked local produce. Guests have access to the leisure room, gym and sauna. Self-catering cottages are also available.

ROOMS: 3 en suite (1 fmly) s £32; d £48 * **FACILITIES:** STV TVB tea/coffee Fishing Sauna Gymnasium childrens play area & equipment 17 acres non-working Dinner Last d order 10am **NOTES:** ✱ ⊗ Licensed Cen ht **PARKING:** 20

HOPE COVE   Map 03 SX64

★★ 70% **Cottage**
TQ7 3HJ
☎ 01548 561555 ▤ 01548 561455
e-mail: info@hopecove.com
web: www.hopecove.com
Dir: from Kingsbridge on A381 to Salcombe. 2nd right at Marlborough, left for Inner Hope

CHILD FACILITIES: Baby listening Indoor play area Food/bottle warming Ch menu Ch portions Highchairs Ch cutlery Ch discounts under 1s £2, 1-3s £7, 4-8s £11.50, 9-12s £16 Games consoles Videos Cots Family rms (seasonal) Laundry NEARBY: Woodlands Leisure Park Seafront location

Glorious sunsets can be seen over the attractive bay from this popular hotel. Friendly and attentive service from the staff and management mean many guests return here. Bedrooms, many with sea views and some with balconies, are well equipped. There are three lounges and particularly interesting is the cabin, built from shipwrecked timbers. The restaurant offers an enjoyable dining experience.

ROOMS: 35 rms (26 en suite) (5 fmly) (7 GF) s £52.75-£77.50; d £85.50-£135 (incl. bkfst & dinner) **LB FACILITIES:** Table Tennis Xmas **PARKING:** 50 **NOTES:** ⊗ in restaurant Closed Early Jan - Early Feb

ILFRACOMBE   Map 02 SS54

◆◆◆◆ **Strathmore Hotel**
57 St Brannock's Rd EX34 8EQ
☎ 01271 862248
e-mail: peter@small6374.fsnet.co.uk
web: www.strathmore.ukhotels.com
Dir: take A361 from Barnstaple to Ilfracombe, Strathmore is approx 1.5m from Mullacot Cross entering Ilfracombe

CHILD FACILITIES: Food/bottle warming Ch menu Ch portions Highchairs Ch discounts under 4s free in cot or £7.50 in bed, 5-9s £10, 10-15s £15 Safe grounds Videos Cots Family rms D rms with S beds NEARBY: Dinosaur Park Castle Zoo 10-min walk to sea

Situated within walking distance of the town centre and beach, this charming Victorian hotel offers guests a very warm welcome. Bedrooms are attractively decorated and comfortably furnished. Public areas include an attractive terraced garden and an elegant breakfast room.

ROOMS: 8 en suite (3 fmly) s £30-£40; d £48-£70 * **FACILITIES:** TVB tea/coffee No coaches **NOTES:** ⊗ Licensed Cen ht **LB PARKING:** 5

◆◆◆◆ **Norbury House Hotel**
Torrs Park EX34 8AZ
☎ 01271 863888
e-mail: info@norburyhousehotel.co.uk
web: www.norburyhousehotel.co.uk
Dir: A361 from Barnstaple, 1st set of traffic lights turn left. At 2nd set, turn left & left again into Torrs Park, Norbury House on right

CHILD FACILITIES: Baby listening Activities: toys, puzzles Food/bottle warming Ch menu Ch portions Highchairs Ch cutlery Ch discounts under 3s free Safe grounds Videos Cots Family rms D with 1 or 2 S beds £65 per rm Fridge Laundry (by request) NEARBY: Wildlife and dinosaur park Zoo 10-min walk to sea

This establishment is quietly located in an elevated position, with views over the town and the sea in the distance. Norbury House was built as a gentleman's residence in 1870. The well-equipped bedrooms are comfortable and there is an inviting lounge. Breakfast is served in the pleasant dining room.

ROOMS: 8 rms (6 en suite) (3 fmly) s £25-£27; d £50-£54 * **FACILITIES:** TVB tea/coffee TVL No coaches Dinner Last d order 10am **NOTES:** ⊗ Licensed Cen ht **LB PARKING:** 6

INSTOW   Map 02 SS43

◉ **Decks Restaurant**
Hatton Croft House, Marine Pde EX39 4JJ
☎ 01271 860671 ▤ 01271 860820
e-mail: decks@instow.net
web: www.decksrestaurant.co.uk
Dir: Telephone for directions

CHILD FACILITIES: Outdoor play area Food/bottle warming Ch portions Highchairs Ch cutlery Safe grounds NEARBY: Cinema Leisure centre Walks Seafront location

FOOD: Modern British **STYLE:** Chic Formal **SEATS:** 50 **OPEN:** 12-2.30/7-9.30, Closed 25-26 Dec, 1 Jan, Sun-Mon **RESTAURANT:** Fixed L £17, Fixed D £22.50, main £12.50-£21 **NOTES:** ⊗ area, Air con **PARKING:** On street; beach car park

KINGSBRIDGE   Map 03 SX74

⬛ **The Crabshell Inn**
Embankment Rd TQ7 1JZ
☎ 01548 852345 ▤ 01548 852262

CHILD FACILITIES: Activities: games room, pool table Indoor play area Outdoor play area Food/bottle warming Ch menu Ch portions Highchairs Ch cutlery Safe grounds NEARBY: Quayside location Sorley tunnel & farm Woodlands Park fun park Near sea

continued

OPEN: 11-11 (Sun 12-10.30) **BAR MEALS:** L served all week 12-2.30 D served all week 6-9.30 Av main course £5.50 **RESTAURANT:** L served all week 12-2.30 D served all week 6-9.30 Av 3 course à la carte £11.75 **FACILITIES:** Garden: Patio area with tables & seats **PARKING:** 40

LUSTLEIGH   Map 03 SX78

 Babies Welcome | Children's Dishes

🕮 The Cleave
TQ13 9TJ
☎ 01647 277223 📠 01647 277223
e-mail: alisonperring@supanet.com
Dir: Off A382 between Bovey Tracy and Moretonhampstead

CHILD FACILITIES: Activities: books, colouring, games Family area Food/bottle warming Ch portions Highchairs Safe grounds Changing facilities

OPEN: 11-3 6.30-11 (summer 11-11) Closed: Mon Nov-Feb **BAR MEALS:** L served all week 12-2.30 D served all week 6.30-9 Av main course £6.95 **RESTAURANT:** L served all week 12-2 D served all week 6.30 Av 3 course à la carte £18 **FACILITIES:** Garden: Traditional cottage style garden **PARKING:** 10

LYNMOUTH   Map 03 SS74

 Babies Welcome | Family Rooms | Children's Dishes

★★★ 65% Tors
EX35 6NA
☎ 01598 753236 📠 01598 752544
e-mail: torshotel@torslynmouth.co.uk
web: www.torslynmouth.co.uk
Dir: adjacent to A39 on Countisbury Hill just before entering Lynmouth from Minehead

CHILD FACILITIES: Baby listening Activities: board games, swimming, table tennis Indoor play area Outdoor play area Food/bottle warming Ch menu Ch portions Highchairs Ch cutlery Ch discounts Safe grounds Videos Cots Family rms D rm with B bed £63 per adult, £5 per child Ch drinks Connecting rms Laundry NEARBY: Zoo Cinema Farm 2-min walk to sea

In an elevated position overlooking Lynmouth Bay, this friendly hotel is set in five acres of woodland. The majority of the bedrooms benefit from the superb views, as do the public areas; which are generous and well-presented. Both fixed-price and short arte menus are offered in the restaurant.
ROOMS: 31 en suite (6 fmly) s £68-£170; d £96-£200 (incl. bkfst) **LB FACILITIES:** Table tennis Pool table Xmas **PARKING:** 40 **NOTES:** ⊗ in restaurant Closed 4-31 Jan RS Feb (wknds only)

 Babies Welcome | Family Rooms | Children's Dishes

★★ 68% Bath
Sea Front EX35 6EL
☎ 01598 752238 📠 01598 753894
e-mail: bathhotel@torslynmouth.co.uk
Dir: M5 junct 25, follow A39 to Minehead then Porlock and Lynmouth

CHILD FACILITIES: Baby listening Food/bottle warming Ch menu Ch portions Highchairs Ch discounts under 14s free Cots Family rms 3 bed rm, D rm with T beds, D rm with S bed £66-90 Laundry NEARBY: Park Country walks Cinema Seafront location

This well-established, friendly hotel is situated near the harbour and offers lovely views from the attractive, sea-facing bedrooms and an excellent starting point for scenic walks. There are two

continued

lounges and a sun lounge and the restaurant menu makes good use of fresh produce and local fish.
ROOMS: 22 en suite (9 fmly) ⊗ in 1 bedroom s £40-£53; d £66-£116 (incl. bkfst) **LB FACILITIES: PARKING:** 12 **NOTES:** ⊗ in restaurant Closed Jan & Dec RS Feb-Mar and Nov

MOLLAND   Map 03 SS82

 Babies Welcome | Children's Dishes

🕮 The London Inn
EX36 3NG
☎ 01769 550269

CHILD FACILITIES: Activities: toys, puzzles, colouring Food/bottle warming Ch menu Ch portions Highchairs Safe grounds NEARBY: Exmoor Wildlife Walks

OPEN: 11.30 -11 (Sun 12-3, 7-10.30) **BAR MEALS:** L served all week 12-2 D served all week 7-9 Av main course £6.50 **RESTAURANT:** L served all week D served all week Av 3 course à la carte £12 **FACILITIES:** Garden **NOTES:** Credit cards not taken **PARKING:** 12

MORETONHAMPSTEAD   Map 03 SX78

Family Rooms | Children's Dishes

Ⓤ Bovey Castle
TQ13 8RE
☎ 01647 445000 📠 01647 440961
e-mail: reception@boveycastle.com
web: www.boveycastle.com
Dir: 2m from Moretonhampstead towards Princetown on B3212

CHILD FACILITIES: Baby listening Babysitting Activities: children's playbarn Indoor play area Outdoor play area Food/bottle warming Ch menu Ch discounts under 2s free, over 2s sharing with parents £65 Safe grounds Games consoles Videos Cots Family rms D rms with cot Connecting rms Laundry NEARBY: Miniature pony centre Children's camp site

At the time of going to press, the star classification for this hotel was not confirmed. Please refer to the AA internet site www.theAA.com for current information.
ROOMS: 60 en suite 5 annexe en suite (5 fmly) (2 GF) ⊗ in all bedrooms s £145-£550; d £145-£550 **FACILITIES:** Spa STV 🎾 Golf 18 ⚲ Fishing Snooker Sauna Solarium Gym ♨ Jacuzzi clay pigeon shooting, archery, fly-fishing ♫ Xmas **PARKING:** 100 **NOTES:** ✖ ⊗ in restaurant

PAIGNTON   Map 03 SX86

★★★ 71% Redcliffe   THE INDEPENDENTS
Marine Dr TQ3 2NL
☎ 01803 526397 📠 01803 528030
e-mail: redclfe@aol.com
Dir: Hotel on seafront at Torquay end of Paignton Green

CHILD FACILITIES: Please telephone for details

Set on the edge of the sea in three acres of well-tended grounds, this popular hotel enjoys uninterrupted views across Tor Bay. Offering a diverse range of facilities, including leisure and beauty treatments, the Redcliffe is suitable for all guests. Bedrooms are pleasantly appointed and comfortably furnished, whilst public areas offer ample space for rest and relaxation.
ROOMS: 67 en suite (8 fmly) (2 GF) s £52-£57; d £104-£114 (incl. bkfst) **FACILITIES:** Spa STV 🎾 Fishing Sauna Solarium Gym ♨ Jacuzzi Table tennis, Carpet Bowls Xmas **PARKING:** 80 **NOTES:** ✖ ⊗ in restaurant

England

PAIGNTON, continued

Babies Welcome | **Family Rooms** | **Children's Dishes**

◆◆◆◆ Aquamarine Hotel

8 St Andrews Rd TQ4 6HA
☎ 01803 551193
e-mail: aquahotel@aol.com
Dir: from seafront along Esplanade with sea on left, right at mini rdbt into Sands Rd, St Andrews Rd 2nd on left

CHILD FACILITIES: Baby listening Outdoor play area Food/bottle warming Ch menu Ch portions Highchairs Ch cutlery Ch discounts under 5s £5, 5-10s half price, 10-14s 25% off Safe grounds Videos Cots Family rms 2 rms with B beds & S bed, 1 with S beds & 2 with D beds Ch drinks

The friendly proprietors at this small hotel extend a warm welcome to their guests. Just a short distance from the town centre and the seafront, the hotel is well placed for visiting the many local attractions. A comfortable lounge, small bar and a pleasant garden with decking are available, and tasty home-cooked evening meals are available by prior arrangement.
ROOMS: 8 en suite (3 fmly) s £20-£24; d £40-£48 * ⊗
FACILITIES: TVB tea/coffee TVL Dinner Last d order 4.30pm
NOTES: ✠ ⊗ in restaurant ⊗ in lounges Licensed Cen ht **LB**
PARKING: 4

Babies Welcome | **Family Rooms** | **Children's Dishes**

◆◆◆ Bay Cottage Hotel

4 Beach Rd TQ4 6AY
☎ 01803 525729
e-mail: info@baycottagehotel.co.uk
Dir: travel along B3201(Esplanade Rd) having past Paignton Pier, Beach Rd is 2nd on the right. Bay Cottage is the 4th Hotel

CHILD FACILITIES: Baby listening Activities: books, games, colouring Food/bottle warming Ch menu Ch portions Highchairs Ch cutlery Ch discounts under 2s free, 2-5s £8, 6-15s half price Safe grounds Cots Family rms 1D rm with B beds, 2 D rms with S bed Ch drinks Connecting rms **NEARBY:** Paignton Zoo Adventure park 100 metres to sea

With easy level access to the beach, theatre and the shops, Bay Cottage offers friendly accommodation. In the bedrooms, the best possible use has been made of available space. Dinner, by prior arrangement, offers home-cooked food served in the pleasant surroundings of the pine-furnished dining room, and a comfortable lounge is provided for guests' use.
ROOMS: 8 en suite (3 fmly) ⊗ **FACILITIES:** TVB tea/coffee TVL No coaches Dinner Last d order 9.30am **NOTES:** Credit cards not taken ⊗ in restaurant Cen ht **LB**

Babies Welcome | **Family Rooms** | **Children's Dishes**

◆◆◆ The Sealawn Hotel

Sea Front, 20 Esplanade Rd TQ3 3RT
☎ 01803 559031 ▤ 01803 666285
e-mail: westernbc@barbox.net
Dir: M5 towards Torquay turn right at large rdbt. Towards seafront situated between pier & cinema on left

CHILD FACILITIES: Baby listening Activities: colouring, puzzles, books, toys Outdoor play area Food/bottle warming Ch menu Ch portions Highchairs Ch cutlery Ch discounts under 2s free, 2-16s 50% Safe grounds Videos Cots Family rms D rms with S or T beds £60-70 Laundry **NEARBY:** Zoo Cinema Leisure centre Swimming pool Water park 2 min to sea

Ideally located on the seafront, The Sealawn, which is under new ownership, is a convenient and pleasant place to stay. Bedrooms
continued

are comfortable and well equipped, and some are located on the ground floor. Many have excellent views over the bay. Dinner is provided in the lower ground-floor dining room where hearty portions are served at breakfast.

ROOMS: 12 en suite (3 fmly) (3 GF) s £30-£32; d £50-£54 *
FACILITIES: TVB tea/coffee Direct dial from bedrooms TVL Dinner Las' d order 9.30pm **NOTES:** ✠ ⊗ in restaurant Licensed Cen ht **LB**
PARKING: 12

◆◆◆ Wentworth Hotel

18 Youngs Park Rd, Goodrington TQ4 6BU
☎ 01803 557843
e-mail: thewentworthhotel@blueyonder.co.uk
Dir: through Paignton on A378, after 1m turn left at rdbt. Immediately righ' onto Roundham Rd, turn right and right again onto Youngs Park Rd

CHILD FACILITIES: Please telephone for details

Within 200 metres of the beach, this Victorian house overlooks Goodrington Park and is conveniently placed for many attractions and the town centre. The bedrooms are attractively decorated an' well-equipped and feature many thoughtful extras. A traditional English breakfast provides an enjoyable and tasty start to the day, with evening meals also available by prior arrangement. Additional facilities include a bar and relaxing guest lounge.
ROOMS: 9 en suite (2 fmly) ⊗ in 7 bedrooms **FACILITIES:** TVB tea/coffee TVL No coaches Dinner Last d order by booking
NOTES: Credit cards not taken ⊗ in restaurant ⊗ in lounges Licensed Cen ht **BB PARKING:** 4

PLYMOUTH   Map 02 SX4

Babies Welcome | **Children's Dishes**

★★★★ 62%
Copthorne Hotel Plymouth

Armada Way PL1 1AR
☎ 01752 224161 ▤ 01752 670688
e-mail: sales.plymouth@mill-cop.com
web: www.copthorne.com/plymouth
Dir: from M5 follow A38 to Plymouth city centre. Follow ferryport signs ov 3 rdbts. Hotel on 1st exit left before 4th rdbt

CHILD FACILITIES: Babysitting Food/bottle warming Ch menu Ch portions Highchairs Ch discounts Cots Connecting rms Fridge Laundry **NEARBY:** Cinema Tenpin bowling Laser Quest Near sea

Located right in the city centre, this hotel possesses plentiful facilities and parking. Suites, Connoisseur and Classic rooms are available; all are spacious and well-equipped. Public areas are spread over two floors and include Bentley's brasserie and bar and a small leisure centre with a pool and gym.
ROOMS: 135 en suite (29 fmly) ⊗ in 93 bedrooms s £72-£135; d £72-£145 **LB FACILITIES:** STV ▣ Gym Steam room Xmas
PARKING: 50 **NOTES:** ✠ ⊗ in restaurant

★★★ 69% Duke of Cornwall
Millbay Rd PL1 3LG
☎ 01752 275850 📠 01752 275854
e-mail: info@thedukeofcornwallhotel.com
web: www.thedukeofcornwallhotel.com
Dir: follow city centre, then Plymouth Pavilions Conference & Leisure Centre signs past hotel

CHILD FACILITIES: Baby listening Babysitting Activities: toys, colouring Family area Food/bottle warming Ch menu Ch portions Highchairs Ch cutlery Ch discounts Safe grounds Videos Cots Family rms several options Ch drinks (by request) Connecting rms Laundry Changing mats (specific area) **NEARBY:** Aquarium Park Swimming pools 5 mins to sea

An historic landmark, this city centre hotel is conveniently located. The spacious public areas include a popular bar, comfortable lounge and multi functional ballroom. Bedrooms, many with far reaching views, are individually styled and comfortably appointed. A range of dining options include bar meals, or the more formal atmosphere in the elegant dining room.
ROOMS: 71 en suite (6 fmly) ⊛ in 20 bedrooms s £94-£160; d £104-£135160 (incl. bkfst) LB **FACILITIES:** STV Xmas **PARKING:** 50 **NOTES:** ⊛ in restaurant Closed 24 Dec-1st Mon in Jan

★★★ 65% Novotel Plymouth
Marsh Mills PL6 8NH
☎ 01752 221422 📠 01752 223922
e-mail: H0508@accor-hotels.com
Dir: Exit A38 at Marsh Mills, follow Plympton signs, hotel on left

CHILD FACILITIES: Babysitting (arranged in advance) Activities: gift bag Indoor play area Family area Food/bottle warming Ch menu Ch portions Highchairs Ch cutlery Ch discounts under 16s free sharing with parents Safe grounds Games consoles Videos Cots Family rms D rms with S beds £85 Connecting rms Laundry Changing mats **NEARBY:** Woodlands adventure park

Conveniently located on the outskirts of the city, close to Marsh Mills roundabout, this modern hotel offers good value accommodation. All rooms are spacious and designed with flexibility for family use. Public areas are open-plan with meals available throughout the day in either the Garden Brasserie, the bar, or from room service.
ROOMS: 100 en suite (17 fmly) (18 GF) ⊛ in 80 bedrooms s £50-£70; d £50-£85 LB **FACILITIES:** STV ⚲ Xmas **PARKING:** 140

◆◆◆◆ Cranbourne Hotel
278-282 Citadel Rd, The Hoe PL1 2PZ
☎ 01752 263858 & 224646 📠 01752 263858
-mail: cran.hotel@virgin.net

CHILD FACILITIES: Food/bottle warming Ch menu Ch portions Highchairs Ch discounts under 2s free, 2-5s £6, 5-12s £8, over 12s £10 Cots Family rms D rm with 2 S beds **NEARBY:** Near sea

This attractive Georgian terrace house has been extensively renovated, and is located just a short walk from The Hoe, The Barbican and the city centre. Bedrooms are practically furnished and well equipped. Hearty breakfasts are served in the elegant dining room.
ROOMS: 40 rms (28 en suite) (5 fmly) s £20-£35; d £40-£50 * **FACILITIES:** TVB tea/coffee TVL **NOTES:** ⊛ in restaurant Licensed Cen t **PARKING:** 14

◆◆◆ Caraneal
12/14 Pier St, West Hoe PL1 3BS
☎ 01752 663589 📠 01752 663589
e-mail: caranealhotel@hotmail.com
Dir: from A38 follow signs for city centre, then signs for The Hoe & seafront. On seafront pass Plymouth Dome, turn right after Dome

CHILD FACILITIES: Activities: board games Food/bottle warming Ch portions Highchairs Ch discounts £5 per child sharing rm with adults Cots Family rms D rm with S beds from £50 Ch drinks **NEARBY:** Play park Leisure pool Ice rink 100 metres to sea

Within walking distance of the Hoe, city centre and numerous other attractions, this small hotel offers stylish, well-equipped accommodation. Some rooms are situated on the ground floor, suitable for the less mobile. A comfortable lounge and residents' bar are available to guests, while full English breakfasts are served in the dining room.
ROOMS: 9 en suite (1 fmly) (2 GF) s £25-£35; d £40-£50 * ⊛ in 3 bedrooms **FACILITIES:** TVB tea/coffee TVL No coaches **NOTES:** ✱ ⊛ in restaurant Licensed Cen ht **PARKING:** 2

ROCKBEARE   Map 03 SY09

◆◆◆ ❤ Lower Allercombe Farm
EX5 2HD
☎ 01404 822519 📠 01404 822519
e-mail: susie@allercombe.fsnet.co.uk
web: www.lowerallercombefarm.co.uk
Dir: exit A30 at Daisy Mount onto B3180. After 200yds turn right to Allercombe. In 1m at Allercombe x-rds turn right , farm is 50yds on right

CHILD FACILITIES: Ch portions Ch cutlery Ch discounts under 3s free Safe grounds Family rms D rm with put-up bed £60-65 **NEARBY:** Theme park

Rurally situated, Lower Allercombe dates back to the 17th century and offers comfortable accommodation. It is located close to the A30 and Exeter Airport, and makes an ideal base for visiting the many local attractions. A self-catering cottage is also available.
ROOMS: 3 rms (1 en suite) (1 fmly) s fr £30; d fr £50 * ⊛ **FACILITIES:** TVB tea/coffee 180 acres competition horses & Stud **NOTES:** Credit cards not taken ⊛ in restaurant Cen ht

⊛ ⊛ The Jack In The Green
EX5 2EE
☎ 01404 822240 📠 01404 823445
e-mail: info@jackinthegreen.uk.com
web: www.jackinthegreen.uk.com
Dir: 5m E of Exeter. From M5 J29 take A30 towards Honiton, turn off for Clyst, Honiton and Rockbeare.

CHILD FACILITIES: Family area Food/bottle warming Ch menu Ch portions Safe grounds Changing facilities **NEARBY:** Crealy Adventure Park

FOOD: Eclectic **STYLE:** Traditional, Rustic **SEATS:** 60
OPEN: 11-2/5.30-9.30, Closed 25 Dec-2 Jan **RESTAURANT:** Fixed L £18.95, Fixed D £24.95 **NOTES:** Smart Dress, ⊛ in restaurant, Air con **PARKING:** 120

Please mention AA Family Friendly Places to Stay, Eat and Visit when booking

SALCOMBE
Map 03 SX73

Babies Welcome | Family Rooms | Children's Dishes

★★★★ 73% ◉ ◉ Soar Mill Cove
Soar Mill Cove, Malborough TQ7 3DS
☎ 01548 561566 🖷 01548 561223
e-mail: info@soarmillcove.co.uk
web: www.soarmillcove.co.uk
Dir: 3m W of town off A381 at Malborough. Follow 'Soar' signs

CHILD FACILITIES: Baby listening Babysitting Activities: weekly rain forest fun, colouring, games Indoor play area Outdoor play area Food/bottle warming Ch menu Ch portions Highchairs Ch cutlery Ch discounts babies free, 1-5s 75%, 6-15s 66% Safe grounds Videos Cots Family rms D rm with 2 S beds from £250 Ch drinks Connecting rms Fridge Laundry Changing mats NEARBY: Walks Leisure park Aquarium Sailing Fishing Near sea

Situated amid spectacular scenery with dramatic sea views, this hotel provides a relaxing stay. Family-run, with a committed team, keen standards of hospitality and service are apparent. Bedrooms are well equipped and many rooms have private terraces. There are different seating areas where impressive cream teas are served, or, for the more active, a choice of swimming pools. Local produce is used to good effect in the restaurant.
ROOMS: 22 en suite (5 fmly) (21 GF) ⊗ in all bedrooms s £150-£180; d £180-£220 (incl. bkfst) LB **FACILITIES:** ▣ ⸯ ⸞ Sauna ⸜ Table tennis, Games room, 9 hole Pitch n putt, Spa treatment suite ♫ Xmas
PARKING: 30 **NOTES:** ⊗ in restaurant Closed 1 Nov-11 Feb

★★★★ 72% ◉ Thurlestone Hotel
TQ7 3NN
☎ 01548 560382 🖷 01548 561069
e-mail: enquiries@thurlestone.co.uk
web: www.thurlestone.co.uk
CHILD FACILITIES: Please telephone for details
(For full entry see Thurlestone)

> All information was correct at the time of going to press; we recommend you confirm details on booking

SAUNTON
Map 02 SS43

Babies Welcome | Family Rooms | Children's Dishes

★★★★ 70% Saunton Sands
EX33 1LQ
☎ 01271 890212 🖷 01271 890145
e-mail: info@sauntonsands.com
web: www.sauntonsands.com
Dir: off A361 at Braunton, signposted Croyde B3231, hotel 2m on left

CHILD FACILITIES: Baby listening Nanny Babysitting Activities: entertainment in school hols, toys, putting green, adventure area Indoor play area Outdoor play area Food/bottle warming Ch menu Ch portions Highchairs Ch discounts vary according to age Safe grounds Games consoles Videos Cots Family rms D rm with S beds from £202 Connecting rms Fridge Laundry NEARBY: Zoo Wildlife and dinosaur park Adventure park Theme park Seafront location

Stunning sea views and direct access to five miles of sandy beach are just two of the features of this popular hotel. The majority of sea-facing rooms benefit from balconies, and splendid views can be enjoyed from all of the public areas, which include comfortable
continued

lounges. The Sands café/bar is a successful innovation and provides an informal eating option.

ROOMS: 92 en suite (39 fmly) s £73-£110; d £146-£320 (incl. bkfst) LB
FACILITIES: STV ▣ ⸯ ⸞ Squash Snooker Sauna Solarium Gym ⸜ Table tennis, Sun Shower, Health and beauty salon ♫ Xmas
PARKING: 142 **NOTES:** ✱ ⊗ in restaurant

See advert on opposite page

SIDMOUTH
Map 03 SY18

Babies Welcome | Family Rooms | Children's Dishes

★★★★ 75% ◉ Victoria
Brend Hotels
The Esplanade EX10 8RY
☎ 01395 512651 🖷 01395 579154
e-mail: info@victoriahotel.co.uk
web: www.victoriahotel.co.uk
Dir: on Sidmouth seafront

CHILD FACILITIES: Baby listening Activities: entertainment in school hols, swimming pool, tennis court, table tennis Food/bottle warming Ch menu Ch portions Highchairs Ch cutlery Ch discounts under 3s free, varying other rates Safe grounds Games consoles Cots Family rms D rm with B beds from £200 Connecting rms Laundry NEARBY: Donkey sanctuary Karting Aquatic centre Theme park 2-min walk to sea

This imposing building, with manicured gardens, is situated overlooking the town. Wonderful sea views can be enjoyed from many of the comfortable bedrooms and elegant lounges. With indoor and outdoor leisure, the hotel caters to a year-round clientele. Carefully prepared meals are served in the refined atmosphere of the restaurant, with staff providing a professional and friendly service.
ROOMS: 61 en suite (18 fmly) s £100-£200; d £140-£250 LB
FACILITIES: Spa STV ▣ ⸯ ⸞ Snooker Sauna Solarium Gym ⸜ ♫ Xmas **PARKING:** 104 **NOTES:** ✱ ⊗ in restaurant

★★★ 73% Sid Valley Country House
Sidbury EX10 0QJ
☎ 01395 597274 & 597587
e-mail: sidvalleyhotel@totalise.co.uk
web: www.sidvalleyhotel.co.uk
Dir: off A375, 2.5m from Sidmouth in village of Sidbury, hotel is clearly signposted
CHILD FACILITIES: Please telephone for details
Situated in an Area of Outstanding Natural Beauty, this family-run hotel has glorious views down the valley. Friendly, unobtrusive service is the key here. Bedrooms vary in size and are equipped with numerous thoughtful extras. Every evening an imaginative menu is served using the best of fresh, local produce. A selection of well-equipped, self-catering cottages is also available.
ROOMS: 10 en suite (2 fmly) (1 GF) ⊗ in all bedrooms s £49.50-£65; d £99-£130 (incl. bkfst) LB **FACILITIES:** STV ⸯ Riding Xmas
PARKING: 32 **NOTES:** ⊗ in restaurant

★★★ 66% Fortfield
EX10 8NU
☎ 01395 512403 📠 01395 579366
e-mail: reservations@fortfield-hotel.co.uk

CHILD FACILITIES: Baby listening Activities: colouring, jigsaws Outdoor play area Food/bottle warming Ch menu Ch portions Highchairs Ch discounts under 4s free sharing with parents, 5-10s 40%, 11-14s 20% Safe grounds Videos Cots Family rms Ch drinks (on request) Connecting rms Laundry (on request) **NEARBY:** Cinema Adventure Park Countryside Park Walks Near sea

Offering good standards of hospitality and service, this long-established hotel overlooks the sea and cricket ground. A choice of comfortable lounges is available. Bedrooms are undergoing a programme of extensive upgrading; a number of rooms have the benefit of sea views. A new leisure complex is due for completion in 2004.
ROOMS: 52 en suite 3 annexe en suite (7 fmly) (4 GF) ⊛ in all bedrooms s £56.50-£79.50; d £102-£148 (incl. bkfst & dinner) **LB FACILITIES:** Sauna Health & beauty salon ♫ Xmas **PARKING:** 60 **NOTES:** 🐾 ⊛ in restaurant

---

SLAPTON   Map 03 SX84

The Tower Inn
Church Rd TQ7 2PN
☎ 01548 580216 📠 01548 580140
e-mail: towerinn@slapton.org
Dir: Off A379 south of Dartmouth, turn L at Slapton Sands

CHILD FACILITIES: Activities: colouring Family area Food/bottle warming Ch menu Ch portions Highchairs Safe grounds **NEARBY:** Woodlands Park fun park Steam railway 10-min walk to sea

OPEN: 12-3 6-11 (Sun 7-10.30) Closed: 25 Dec **BAR MEALS:** L served all week 12-2.30 D served all week 6-9.30 **RESTAURANT:** L served all week 12-2.30 D served all week 7-9.30 Av 3 course à la carte £25 **FACILITIES:** Garden: Beautiful walled garden **PARKING:** 6

STOCKLAND   Map 03 ST20

The Kings Arms Inn ◆◆◆◆
EX14 9BS
☎ 01404 881361 📠 01404 881732
e-mail: info@kingsarms.net
web: www.kingsarms.net

CHILD FACILITIES: Food/bottle warming Ch menu Ch portions Highchairs Safe grounds **NEARBY:** Crealy Adventure Park Donkey sanctuary

OPEN: 12-3 6.30-11.30 Closed: Dec 25 **BAR MEALS:** L served Mon-Sat 12-2 Av main course £10.50 **RESTAURANT:** L served all week 12-2 D served all week 6.30-9 **FACILITIES:** Garden: Part lawn part patio, Seating for 30 **ROOMS:** 3 bedrooms 3 en suite 1 family rooms s£40 d£60 **PARKING:** 45

TAVISTOCK   Map 02 SX47

◆◆ ♥ Sowtontown Farm
Peter Tavy PL19 9JR
☎ 01822 810058
e-mail: sowtownfarm@msn.net
Dir: turn off A386 to Peter Tavy. Over bridge, turn right, then 2nd left, house on left

CHILD FACILITIES: Baby listening Activities: toys, Lego, books, lamb feeding, egg collecting Food/bottle warming Ch menu Ch portions Highchairs Ch cutlery Ch discounts under 2s free, 2-5s £10 Safe grounds Cots Family rms D rm with put-up bed or cot £45-£65 Ch drinks Laundry **NEARBY:** Animal farm Model village Theme park

Relax at this informal, comfortable and welcoming family home. The family pets wander free and you can see the Dartmoor ponies in their field, or the hens (which provide the eggs for breakfast). The home cooking is tasty and plentiful. Pets can be accommodated by arrangement.
ROOMS: 3 en suite s £25; d £40-£45 * ⊛ in 1 bedrooms **FACILITIES:** TV1B tea/coffee 5 acres small holding Dinner Last d order 24hrs notice **NOTES:** Credit cards not taken **PARKING:** 6

THURLESTONE
Map 03 SX64

★★★★ 72% @ Thurlestone
TQ7 3NN
☎ 01548 560382 📠 01548 561069
e-mail: enquiries@thurlestone.co.uk
web: www.thurlestone.co.uk
Dir: *A38 take A384 into Totnes, A381 towards Kingsbridge, onto A379 towards Churchstow, onto B3197 turn into lane signed to Thurlestone*

CHILD FACILITIES: Please telephone for details

This perennially popular hotel has been in the same family-ownership since 1896. A range of indoor and outdoor leisure facilities provide something for everyone and wonderful views of the south Devon coast can be enjoyed from several vantage points, including many of the bedrooms, some of which also have balconies. Elegant public rooms are styled to ensure rest and relaxation.
ROOMS: 64 en suite (23 fmly) s £60-£125; d £120-£250 (incl. bkfst & dinner) **LB FACILITIES:** Spa STV ☒ ⅋ Golf 9 ⅋ Squash Snooker Sauna Solarium Gym ♒ ♨ Jacuzzi ♫ Xmas **PARKING:** 121 **NOTES:** ⊛ in restaurant Closed Jan

TIVERTON
Map 03 SS91

★★★ 68% Tiverton
Blundells Rd EX16 4DB
☎ 01884 256120 📠 01884 258101
e-mail: sales@tivertonhotel.co.uk
web: www.tivertonhotel.co.uk
Dir: *M5 junct 27, onto dual carriageway A361 Devon link road, Tiverton exit 7m W. Hotel on Blundells Rd next to business park*

CHILD FACILITIES: Baby listening Babysitting (subject to availability) Activities: toys, colouring Food/bottle warming Ch menu Ch portions Highchairs Ch cutlery Ch discounts under 16s sharing free Safe grounds Videos Cots Family rms D rm with S beds from £90 Connecting rms Laundry NEARBY: Leisure centre Cinema Museum

Conveniently situated on the outskirts of the town, with easy access to the M5, this comfortable hotel has a relaxed atmosphere. The spacious bedrooms are well-equipped and decorated in a contemporary style. A formal dining option is offered by the Gallery Restaurant, while lighter snacks are served in the bar area. Room service is extensive.
ROOMS: 69 en suite (10 fmly) ⊛ in 53 bedrooms s fr £65; d fr £92 (incl. bkfst) **LB FACILITIES:** STV Xmas **PARKING:** 130 **NOTES:** ⊛ in restaurant

◆◆◆ Angel
13 St Peter St EX16 6NU
☎ 01884 253392 📠 01884 251154
e-mail: cerimar@eurobell.co.uk
Dir: *A361to Gornhay Cross, follow signs to Bickleigh, at 5th rdbt right then right again at next junct follow road round to left at triangle, 200mtrs on right*

CHILD FACILITIES: Please telephone for details

Guests are assured of a warm welcome at this personally run establishment, conveniently located in a quiet area close to the town centre. In addition to the neatly furnished and well-presented bedrooms, a comfortable lounge is available. A variety of local eateries are within easy walking distance.
ROOMS: 7 rms (3 en suite) (2 fmly) s £19-£20; d £38-£46 *
FACILITIES: TVB tea/coffee TVL No coaches **NOTES:** Credit cards not taken ➤ Cen ht **BB PARKING:** 2

TORQUAY
Map 03 SX96

Babies Welcome | Family Rooms | Children's Dishes

★★★★★ 68% The Imperial
Park Hill Rd TQ1 2DG
☎ 01803 294301 📠 01803 298293
e-mail: imperialtorquay@paramount-hotels.co.uk
Dir: *A380 towards the seafront. Turn left and follow road to harbour, at clocktower turn right. Hotel 300yds on right*

PARAMOUNT GROUP OF HOTELS

CHILD FACILITIES: Babysitting Activities: entertainment in school hols, quiz, crayons Indoor play area Outdoor play area Food/bottle warming Ch menu Ch portions Highchairs Ch cutlery Ch portions under 5s free Games consoles Videos Cots Family rms £40-60 Connecting rms Fridge Laundry NEARBY: Zoo Leisure park Model village Water park Near sea

This hotel has an enviable location with extensive views of the coastline. Traditional in style, public areas are elegant with choice of dining including the informal TQ1 brasserie or the more formal Regatta Restaurant. Bedrooms are spacious, most with private balconies, and the hotel has an extensive range of indoor and outdoor leisure facilities.
ROOMS: 152 en suite (7 fmly) ⊛ in 26 bedrooms s £120-£130; d £210-£220 (incl. bkfst) **LB FACILITIES:** STV ☒ ⅋ ⅋ Squash Snooker Sauna Solarium Gym Jacuzzi Beauty salon Hairdresser ♫ Xmas **PARKING:** 140

Family Rooms | Children's Dishes

★★★ 58% Rainbow International
Belgrave Rd TQ2 5HJ
☎ 01803 213232 📠 01803 212925
e-mail: enquiries@rainbow-hotel.co.uk
web: www.rainbow-hotel.co.uk
Dir: *Close to harbour and marina*

CHILD FACILITIES: Baby listening Babysitting (by arrangement & cost) Activities: Rainbow Kids Club Outdoor play area Ch menu Ch portions Highchairs Ch cutlery (by prior request) Ch discounts one child under 12 free Safe grounds Games consoles Videos Cots Family rms Laundry NEARBY: Parks Gardens 4-min walk to sea

This large hotel is located within easy walking distance of the seafront. Bedrooms vary in size and shape; many family rooms are available. Entertainment is provided every evening in the nightclub and the residents' ballroom. A leisure club and gymnasium are also on offer.
ROOMS: 134 en suite (70 fmly) **FACILITIES:** ☒ ⅋ Solarium Gym Table tennis Steam room ♫ **PARKING:** 100 **NOTES:** ⊛ in restaurant

Babies Welcome | Family Rooms | Children's Dishes

★★ 70% Red House
Rousdown Rd, Chelston TQ2 6PB
☎ 01803 607811 📠 01803 200592
e-mail: stay@redhouse-hotel.co.uk
web: www.redhouse-hotel.co.uk
Dir: *towards seafront/Chelston, turn into Avenue Rd, 1st lights turn right. Follow road past shops and church, take next left. Hotel on right*

CHILD FACILITIES: Activities: swimming pools, table tennis, pool table Indoor play area Food/bottle warming Ch menu Ch portions Highchairs Ch discounts under 6s free, 6-12s 50% off, 13-16s 25% off Safe grounds Cots Family rms D rm with connecting twin/ D rm with S beds £22-£35 Connecting rms Laundry NEARBY: Zoo Model village Leisure park Water park 10-min walk to sea

With views over Torbay, this pleasant and relaxing hotel enjoys a quiet location close to Cockington village. The comfortable bedrooms are well equipped and a good choice of bar meals are
continue

available in addition to the fixed price menu for residents. Many guests return here on a regular basis for the excellent range of leisure facilities.

Red House, Torquay

ROOMS: 10 en suite (5 fmly) s £25-£35; d £50-£70 (incl. bkfst) **FACILITIES:** Spa ⌨ ⤳ Sauna Solarium Gym Games room Table tennis Beauty salon pool table Xmas **PARKING:** 10 **NOTES:** ⊗ in restaurant

★★ 70% Torcroft
28-30 Croft Rd TQ2 5UE
☎ 01803 298292 📠 01803 291799
e-mail: enquiries@torcroft.co.uk
web: www.torcroft.co.uk
Dir: from A390 take A3022 to Avenue Rd. Follow signs to seafront then turn left, cross lights and up Shedden Hill, 1st left into Croft Rd

CHILD FACILITIES: Baby listening Outdoor play area Food/bottle warming Ch menu Ch portions Highchairs Ch cutlery Ch discounts under 3s free, 3-13s sharing 50% Safe grounds Cots Family rms D rm with B beds, D rm with S bed Ch drinks Connecting rms Laundry Changing mats NEARBY: 300yds to sea

This elegant, Grade II listed Victorian property is pleasantly located in a quiet area, just a short stroll from the seafront. The delightful garden and patio are very popular with guests, ideal for a spot of sunbathing or relaxing with a good book! The comfortable bedrooms are individually furnished, two of which have balconies. Pleasant, home-cooked meals are enthusiastically offered and provide enjoyable dining.
ROOMS: 15 en suite (2 fmly) ⊗ in all bedrooms s £25-£40; d £50-£80 (incl. bkfst) **LB FACILITIES:** Xmas **PARKING:** 11 **NOTES:** ✈ ⊗ in restaurant

◆◆◆ The Cranmore
89 Avenue Rd TQ2 5LH
☎ 01803 298488
e-mail: thecranmore@tesco.net
Dir: A380 onto A3022, from Newton Abbot at Torre station right at lights, premises 200yds on left

CHILD FACILITIES: Activities: games, cards, books Food/bottle warming Ch menu Ch portions Highchairs Ch cutlery Ch discounts under 2s free, 2-6s 25%, 7-11s 50%, 12-15s 75% Safe grounds Videos Cots Family rms Ch drinks Laundry NEARBY: Leisure Centre Cinema Water Park 10-min walk to sea

A family run hotel, The Cranmore offers comfortable accommodation in a relaxed and friendly atmosphere and is conveniently located for the town centre and the seafront. Bedrooms are attractive and well furnished, and family rooms are available. Breakfast is taken in the pleasant dining room and

continued

special dietary requirements can be catered for. Dinner is also available by prior arrangement.
ROOMS: 6 en suite (1 fmly) s £25-£28; d £40-£52 * **FACILITIES:** TVB tea/coffee TVL No coaches Dinner Last d order 12.00 **NOTES:** ✈ ⊗ Licensed Cen ht **LB PARKING:** 4

◆◆◆◆ Glenorleigh Hotel
26 Cleveland Rd TQ2 5BE
☎ 01803 292135 📠 01803 213717
e-mail: glenorleighhotel@btinternet.com
web: www.glenorleigh.co.uk
Dir: follow A3022 Newton Abbot/Torquay road to lights at Torre Station, bear right into Avenue Rd & Cleveland Rd is 1st left

CHILD FACILITIES: Baby listening Activities: games, jigsaws, toys Food/bottle warming Ch portions Highchairs Ch cutlery Ch discounts under 2s free, 2-6s 25%, 7-16s 50% Safe grounds Cots Family rms Connecting rms Changing mats NEARBY: Paignton Zoo Crealy Adventure Park Walks 10-min walk to sea

Conveniently located in a residential area, The Glenorleigh provides a smart range of attractively decorated bedrooms, a number of which are on the ground floor. A host of other facilities such as a solarium, an outdoor pool and terrace make this small, family-run hotel ideal for leisure use.
ROOMS: 16 rms (13 en suite) (6 fmly) (6 GF) s £28-£38; d £56-£76 * ⊗ **FACILITIES:** TVB tea/coffee TVL No coaches ⤳ Solarium Pool Table, Darts, Board Games. Dinner Last d order 2pm **NOTES:** ✈ ⊗ in restaurant ⊗ in 1 lounge Licensed Cen ht **LB PARKING:** 10

◆◆◆◆ Norwood Hotel
60 Belgrave Rd TQ2 5HY
☎ 01803 294236 📠 01803 294224
e-mail: enquiries@norwoodhoteltorquay.co.uk.
web: www.norwoodhoteltorquay.co.uk
Dir: from Princess Theatre head towards Paignton, at 1st lights turn right into Belgrave Rd. At x-rds straight over, hotel 3rd building on left

CHILD FACILITIES: Please telephone for details

Guests are assured of a warm welcome at this privately owned and personally run hotel. Fronted by attractive floral displays, it is conveniently located for the town centre and most attractions. The well-equipped accommodation includes a family room. Public areas include a comfortable lounge and both dinner and breakfast are served at separate tables in the pleasant dining room.
ROOMS: 11 en suite (5 fmly) (2 GF) d £40-£60 * ⊗ in 4 bedrooms **FACILITIES:** TVB tea/coffee TVL No coaches Dinner Last d order noon **NOTES:** ✈ ⊗ in restaurant Licensed Cen ht **LB PARKING:** 3

◆◆◆ Devon Court Hotel
24 Croft Rd TQ2 5UE
☎ 01803 293603 📠 01803 213660
e-mail: info@devoncourt.co.uk
Dir: from A380 take A3022 to Avenue Rd, left at seafront. Cross lights & up Sheddon Hill. 1st left at church into Croft Rd, hotel 100yds on right

CHILD FACILITIES: Baby listening Activities: toys, jigsaws Food/bottle warming Ch menu Ch portions Highchairs Ch cutlery Ch discounts under 2s free, 2-6s 50%, 7-14s 80% Safe grounds Cots Family rms D rm with Z or B beds Ch drinks Connecting rms NEARBY: Model Village Fun House Cinema Near sea

Located in a quiet residential area close to the town centre and the seafront, this attractive family-run Victorian house offers comfortable, pleasantly decorated bedrooms. The atmosphere is relaxed and welcoming and facilities include a heated outdoor

continued on p120

TORQUAY Map 03 SX96

pool, a no-smoking lounge, a spacious lounge/bar and a dining room where dinner and full English breakfasts are served.
ROOMS: 15 rms (13 en suite) (1 fmly) (3 GF) s £30-£50; d £48-£80 * ⊛ **FACILITIES:** TVB tea/coffee TVL No coaches ⚓ Dinner Last d order 10am **NOTES:** ⊛ in restaurant ⊛ in 1 lounge Licensed Cen ht **LB PARKING:** 12

◆◆◆ *Fircroft*
69 Avenue Rd TQ2 5LG
☎ 01803 211634
e-mail: havanakid546@aol.com
CHILD FACILITIES: Please telephone for details
Handily placed within strolling distance of the beach and town centre, this comfortable establishment offers a friendly welcome to all. Bedrooms, including one on the ground floor, are attractively decorated and neatly furnished. Additional facilities include the relaxing conservatory and smart dining room, the latter being the venue for tasty breakfasts and evening meals.
ROOMS: 8 rms (7 en suite) (1 GF) ⊛ **FACILITIES:** TVB tea/coffee TVL No coaches Dinner Last d order 3pm **NOTES:** Credit cards not taken ⊛ in restaurant Cen ht **PARKING:** 5

◆◆◆ The Palms Hotel
537 Babbacombe Rd TQ1 1HQ
☎ 01803 293970 🖷 01803 298573
e-mail: grahamaward@yahoo.co.uk
web: www.palmshoteltorquay.com
Dir: follow signs to Torquay Harbour on B3199 Babbacombe Rd 300yds from harbour opposite Torwood gardens
CHILD FACILITIES: Activities: colouring, puzzles, toys, games Food/bottle warming Ch menu Ch portions Highchairs Ch discounts Safe grounds Games consoles Videos Cots Family rms 2 D rms with B beds Ch drinks Laundry **NEARBY:** Play area 10-min walk to sea

The owners here at Palms Hotel extend a very warm welcome to their guests. Family friendly, the hotel offers comfortable accommodation, with many books, games and videos available for the children. The Cyber café, a well stocked bar and light bar meals are welcome facilities. Breakfast is taken in the dining room, which overlooks Torwood Gardens.
ROOMS: 9 en suite (4 fmly) s £20-£25; d £40-£50 * ⊛ **FACILITIES:** STV TVB tea/coffee No coaches Internet facilities in dry bar Dinner Last d order 8pm **NOTES:** ⊛ in area of dining room ⊛ in 1 lounge Licensed Cen ht **LB PARKING:** 4

TOTNES Map 03 SX86

◆◆◆◆ The Old Forge at Totnes
Seymour Place TQ9 5AY
☎ 01803 862174 🖷 01803 865385
e-mail: eng@oldforgetotnes.com
web: www.oldforgetotnes.com
Dir: turn off A38 towards Totnes. From town centre cross river bridge and take 2nd right
CHILD FACILITIES: Activities: books, games, colouring Food/bottle warming Ch portions Highchairs Ch cutlery Ch discounts babies in cots free, under 7s £12.50, 7-12s £15 Safe grounds Cots Family rms D rm with 2 S beds, cottage with D & T rm £76 for 2 nights Ch drinks Fridge Laundry **NEARBY:** Zoo Farm River and steam train trips 5m to sea

continued

Over 600-years-old, this delightful property is close to the town centre and Steamer Quay. Bedrooms vary from spacious suites to cosy cottage-style, all of which have been equipped with numerous thoughtful extras. Public areas include a conservatory overlooking the gardens and a comfortable lounge. Breakfast is a leisurely and enjoyable affair, served in the pleasantly appointed dining room.
ROOMS: 10 rms (9 en suite) (2 fmly) (3 GF) s fr £46; d £56-£76 * **FACILITIES:** TVB tea/coffee Direct dial from bedrooms TVL No coaches Whirlpool spa **NOTES:** ✖ ⊛ Licensed Cen ht **LB PARKING:** 9

TYTHERLEIGH Map 03 ST30

◗ Tytherleigh Arms Hotel
EX13 7BE
☎ 01460 220400 & 220214 🖷 01460 220406
e-mail: TytherleighArms@aol.com
CHILD FACILITIES: Please telephone for details
OPEN: 11-2.30 6.30-11 **BAR MEALS:** L served all week 12-2.30 D served all week 6.30-9 Av main course £8.95 **RESTAURANT:** L served all week 12-2.30 D served all week 6.30-9 Av 3 course à la carte £16.95
FACILITIES: Children's licence Garden: Courtyard, very pretty ✖
PARKING: 60

UMBERLEIGH Map 02 SS62

◗ The Rising Sun Inn ★★
EX37 9DU
☎ 01769 560447 🖷 01769 564764
e-mail: risingsuninn@btinternet.com
web: www.risinguninn.com
Dir: on A377, Exeter/Barnstaple road, at junct with B3227
CHILD FACILITIES: Please telephone for details
OPEN: 11-3 6-11 (open all day Sat-Sun) **BAR MEALS:** L served all week 12-2 D served all week 7-9 **RESTAURANT:** L served all week 12-2 D served all week 7-9 Av 3 course à la carte £19 **FACILITIES:** Children's licence Garden: Patio garden overlooking the river **ROOMS:** 9 bedrooms 9 en suite s£46 d£80 **PARKING:** 30

WOOLACOMBE Map 02 SS44

★★★ 74% Woolacombe Bay
South St EX34 7BN
☎ 01271 870388 🖷 01271 870613
e-mail: woolacombe.bayhotel@btinternet.com
web: www.woolacombe-bay-hotel.co.uk
Dir: from A361 take B3343 to Woolacombe. Hotel in centre on left
CHILD FACILITIES: Baby listening Nanny (only at creche times) Babysitting Activities: children's club in hols, jigsaws, games Indoor play area Outdoor play area Family area Food/bottle warming Ch menu Highchairs Ch cutlery Ch discounts Safe grounds Games consoles Videos Cots Family rms Connecting rms Laundry **NEARBY:** Sheep centre Gardens Walks 1 min to sea

This family-friendly hotel is adjacent to the beach and the village centre, and has a welcoming and friendly environment. The public areas are spacious and comfortable, and many of the well-equipped bedrooms have balconies with splendid views over the bay. In addition to the fixed price menu served in the stylish restaurant, Maxwell's bistro offers an informal alternative.
ROOMS: 64 en suite (27 fmly) (2 GF) ⊛ in all bedrooms s £53-£147; d £106-£294 (incl. bkfst & dinner) **LB FACILITIES:** Spa STV ⛱ ⚓ Golf 9 ⛳ Squash Snooker Sauna Solarium Gym Jacuzzi Beauty salon, Creche, Childrens club, Table Tennis, Hairdresser ♫ Xmas **PARKING:** 150
NOTES: ✖ ⊛ in restaurant Closed 3 Jan-mid Feb

DORSET

Weymouth Beach

ABBOTSBURY
Abbotsbury Swannery
DT3 4JG ☎01305 871858
info@abbotsbury-tourism.co.uk
(Turn off A35 at Winterborne Steepleton near
Dorchester. Abbotsbury on B3157 coastal road
between Weymouth and Bridport)
Open 24 Mar-2 Nov, daily 10-6, last admission 5.

BOURNEMOUTH
Oceanarium
BH2 5AA ☎01202 311993
oceanarium@reallive.co.uk
(From A338 Wessex Way, follow the Oceanarium
tourist signs)
Open all year, daily from 10am. Closed 25 Dec.

BOVINGTON CAMP
Clouds Hill
BH20 7NQ ☎01929 405616
(1m N of Bovington Camp & Tank Museum)
Open Apr-Oct, Thu-Sun, 12-5.
*£3.10.
The Tank Museum BH20 6JG
info@tankmuseum.co.uk ☎01929 405096
(Off A352 or A35, follow brown tank signs from
Bere Regis & Wool)
Open all year, daily 10-5 Closed 23-28 Dec.
*£8, ch £6, pen £7.50. Family saver £23 2 adult &
2 ch, £22 1 adult & 3 ch. Group rates available.

BROWNSEA ISLAND
Brownsea Island
BH15 7EE ☎01202 707744 ▤01202 701635
(located in Poole Harbour)
Open: 12 Mar-22 Jul, 10-5 all week; 23 Jul-2 Sep
10-6 all week; 3-30 Sep 10-5 all week; 1-30 Oct,
10-4 all week.
*£4.20 (ch £2). Family ticket £10.40. Party

DORCHESTER
Dinosaur Museum DT1 1EW
info@thedinosaurmuseum.com ☎01305 269880
(Off A35 into Dorchester; museum in town centre
just off High East Street)
Open all year, daily 9.30-5.30 10-4.30 Nov-Mar.
Closed 24-26 Dec.
*£6, ch £4.50, pen & student £5.25, under 4s free.
Family ticket £18.50.

Dorset Teddy Bear Museum
DT1 1BE ☎01305 263200
info@teddybearmuseum.co.uk
(Turn off A35 and museum in town centre near
Tourist Information Centre)
Open daily, Mon-Sat 9.30-5, Sun 10-4.30. Closed
25-26 Dec.
*£3.50, ch £2.50, under 4s free. Family £10.50.
Tutankhamun Exhibition
DT1 1UW ☎01305 269571
info@tutankhamun-exhibition.co.uk
(off A35 into Dorchester town centre)
Open all year daily, Apr-Oct, 9.30-5.30; Nov-Mar
wkdays 9.30-5, wknds 10-4.30. Closed 24-26 Dec.
*£6, ch £4.50, pen & student £5.25, under 5s free.
Family ticket £18.50

PORTLAND
Portland Castle
DT5 1AZ ☎01305 820539
(Overlooking Portland harbour) Open, Apr-June &
Sep, daily 10-5; Jul-Aug, daily 10-6, Oct, daily 10-
4. Closed Nov-Mar. £3.50 (ch £1.80, concessions
£2.60).

SWANAGE
Swanage Railway
BH19 1HB ☎01929 425800 ▤01929 426680
general@swanrail.freeserve.co.uk
(signed from A351)
Open every weekend throughout the year, daily
Apr-Oct.

WEST LULWORTH
Lulworth Castle
BH20 5QS ☎01929 400352 ▤01929 400563
estate.office@lulworth.com
(from Wareham, W on A352 for 1m, left onto
B3070 to E Lulworth, follow tourist signs)
Open Castle: Summer 10.30-6; Winter 10.30-4.
Lulworth Castle House open Wed 28 May-30 Jul,
2-5.

WEYMOUTH
Deep Sea Adventure & Sharky's Play & Party
DT4 8BG ☎0871 222 5760
enquiries@deepsea-adventure.co.uk
(Follow signs on A35 to Weymouth. Follow signs
to the Deep Sea Adventure, which is located on
the Old Harbour between pavillion and town
bridge) Open all year, daily 9.30-7 high season
9.30-8. Closed 25 Dec & 1 Jan.
*Sharky's Play Zone: Adults free, ch £3.30. Deep
Sea Adventure: £3.75, ch 5-15 £2.75, pen &
student £3.25. Combined ticket for both
attractions, ch £4.75.

WOOL
Monkey World
BH20 6HH ☎01929 462537
apes@monkeyworld.org
(1m N of Wool on Bere Regis Rd)
Open daily 10-5 Jul-Aug 10-6. Last admission
1 hour before closing.

BOURNEMOUTH
Map 04 SZ09

| Babies Welcome | Family Rooms | Children's Dishes |

★★★ 77% ⚙ Chine

Best Western

Boscombe Spa Rd BH5 1AX
☎ 01202 396234 📠 01202 391737
e-mail: reservations@chinehotel.co.uk
web: www.chinehotel.co.uk

Dir: Follow BIC signs, A338/Wessex Way to St Pauls rdbt. 1st exit - St Pauls Rd to next rdbt, 2nd exit signed Eastcliff/Boscombe/Southbourne. Next rdbt, 1st exit into Christchurch Rd. After 2nd lights, right into Boscombe Spa Rd

CHILD FACILITIES: Baby listening Babysitting Activities: entertainment during hols, children's welcome pack, colouring, games Indoor play area Outdoor play area Family area Food/bottle warming Ch menu Ch portions Highchairs Ch discounts £25 per child, under 2s free Safe grounds Games consoles Videos Cots Family rms D & T rm with B beds £180 Ch drinks (on request) Connecting rms Fridge Laundry NEARBY: Swimming pools Cinema Aquarium Gardens 2-min walk to sea

Benefiting from superb views, this popular hotel is set in delightful gardens with private access to the seafront and beach. The excellent range of facilities includes an indoor and outdoor pool, a small leisure centre and a selection of meeting rooms. The spacious bedrooms, some of which have balconies, are well appointed and thoughtfully equipped.
ROOMS: 65 en suite 22 annexe en suite (13 fmly) ⊗ in 14 bedrooms s £70-£90; d £140-£180 (incl. bkfst) LB **FACILITIES: Spa** STV 🎬 ⚡ Sauna Solarium Gym 🏋 ⚓ Jacuzzi Games room, Outdoor & indoor childrens play area Xmas **PARKING:** 50 **NOTES:** 🐾 ⊗ in restaurant

See advert on opposite page

All AA listed accommodation, restaurants and pubs can be found on the AA's website www.theAA.com

| Babies Welcome | Family Rooms | Children's Dishes |

★★★ 68% *Royal Exeter*

Exeter Rd BH2 5AG
☎ 01202 438000 📠 01202 297963
e-mail: royalexeterhotel@aol.com
web: www.royalexeterhotel.com

Dir: opposite Bournemouth International Centre

CHILD FACILITIES: Food/bottle warming Ch menu Highchairs Ch discounts under 5s free sharing with parent Cots Family rms Laundry Changing mats NEARBY: Cinemas 5-min walk to sea

Ideally located opposite the Bournemouth International Centre, and convenient for the beach and town centre. New and extensive refurbishment of the public areas has resulted in a smart, modern

continued

and open-plan lounge bar and restaurant together with an exciting adjoining bar complex.

ROOMS: 54 en suite (13 fmly) **FACILITIES:** STV **PARKING:** 50 **NOTES:** 🐾

| Babies Welcome | Family Rooms | Children's Dishes |

★★★ 65% Cumberland

East Overcliff Dr BH1 3AF
☎ 01202 290722 📠 01202 311394
e-mail: cumberland@bluemermaidhotels.com

CHILD FACILITIES: Babysitting Indoor play area Outdoor play area Food/bottle warming Ch menu Ch portions Highchairs Ch cutlery Ch discounts under 5s free, 5-10s £5, 11-15s £10 Safe grounds Games consoles Videos Cots Family rms 3 or 4 bed rms (seasonal) Ch drinks Connecting rms Laundry NEARBY: Imax cinema Oceanarium Ice skating Vistarama balloon Seafront location

Many of the well-equipped and attractively decorated bedrooms at this hotel benefit from sea views and balconies. The lounges and restaurant are spacious and comfortable. The restaurant offers a daily changing fixed price menu. Guests may use the leisure club at the sister hotel, The Queens.
ROOMS: 102 en suite (12 fmly) s £52.50-£70; d £52.50-£70 (incl. bkfst) **LB FACILITIES:** ⚡ Free membership of nearby Leisure Club in sister hotel Xmas **PARKING:** 51 **NOTES:** ⊗ in restaurant

| Babies Welcome | Family Rooms | Children's Dishes |

★★★ 63% Ocean View Hotel

East Overcliff Dr BH1 3AR
☎ 01202 558057 📠 01202 556285
e-mail: enquiry@oceanview.uk.com

CHILD FACILITIES: Baby listening Babysitting Food/bottle warming Ch menu Ch portions Highchairs Ch discounts 4s and under sharing £10, 5-15s 50% Safe grounds Videos Cots Family rms D rm with 1-3 S beds Ch drinks Laundry NEARBY: Gardens Parks Seafront location

Splendid sea views can be enjoyed from all of the public rooms at this popular East Cliff hotel. Bedrooms vary in size, and all are light, airy and well equipped. A comfortable bar/lounge offers an informal alternative to the drawing room, whilst the spacious restaurant offers a fixed-price menu every evening.
ROOMS: 52 rms (51 en suite) (13 fmly) s £56-£64; d £112-£128 (incl. bkfst & dinner) **LB FACILITIES:** ⚡ Indoor leisure suite at Bayview Court Hotel (sister hotel) 🎵 Xmas **PARKING:** 39 **NOTES:** ⊗ in restaurant

◆◆◆◆ The Boltons Hotel

9 Durley Chine Rd South, West Cliff BH2 5JT
☎ 01202 751517
e-mail: info@boltonshotel.co.uk

Dir: turn off A338 onto B3066 (Durley Chine Rd) at 2nd rdbt turn right onto West Cliff Rd, Durly Chine Rd South is 2nd on right

CHILD FACILITIES: Please telephone for details

continued

Located in a quiet position close to the town centre, this fine Victorian property offers appealing public rooms, including a lounge, dining room and cosy residents' bar. The secluded gardens contain a swimming pool. The comfortable bedrooms vary in size and are well equipped and furnished.
ROOMS: 13 en suite (2 fmly) (1 GF) d £50-£80 * ⊗ **FACILITIES:** TVB tea/coffee Direct dial from bedrooms ⚲ **NOTES:** ✈ ⊗ in restaurant ⊗ in 1 lounge Licensed Cen ht **PARKING:** 12

♦♦♦ Fenn Lodge
11 Rosemount Rd, Alum Chine BH4 8HB
☎ 01202 761273 📠 01202 761273
e-mail: fennlodge@btconnect.com
web: www.fennlodge.co.uk
Dir: Take A338 into Poole until it ends at rdbt, exit down 'The Avenue' signposted Alum Chine & Sandbanks. Turn left at traffic lights & then right at rdbt into Alumhurst, take 3rd left into Rosemount Rd
CHILD FACILITIES: Please telephone for details
A warm welcome is assured at this family run hotel located within walking distance of Alum Chine and the beach. Westbourne, Sandbanks, Bournemouth and Poole just a short drive away. Bedrooms are comfortably furnished with many useful extra facilities provided. There is a bar and newly refurbished lounge available to guests.
ROOMS: 11 en suite (2 fmly) (1 GF) s £20-£27.50; d £40-£55 * **FACILITIES:** TVB tea/coffee No coaches **NOTES:** ✈ ⊗ Licensed Cen ht **LB PARKING:** 6

Please mention AA Family Friendly Places to Stay, Eat and Visit when booking

♦♦♦ East Cliff Cottage Hotel
57 Grove Rd BH1 3AT
☎ 01202 552788 📠 01202 552788
e-mail: info@otel57.freeserve.co.uk
web: www.otel57.freeserve.co.uk
Dir: Wessex Way into Bournemouth, left at East Cliff Rd sign, right at next rdbt, left (Meyrick Rd), left (Grove Rd).
CHILD FACILITIES: Please telephone for details
Situated just 300 yards from the seafront and conveniently close to the town centre and the East Cliff Lift, this charming small hotel offers comfortable accommodation. Home-cooked meals are served in the spacious dining room. Guests can relax in the cosy lounge or in the delightful garden in fine weather.
ROOMS: 10 rms (7 en suite) (4 fmly) s £20-£65; d £50-£80 * **FACILITIES:** STV TVB tea/coffee Direct dial from bedrooms TVL No coaches Dinner Last d order 4pm **NOTES:** ⊗ in restaurant Licensed Cen ht **LB PARKING:** 10

⊛ Bistro on the Beach
Solent Promenade, Southbourne Coast Rd, Southbourne BH6 4BE
☎ 01202 431473 📠 01202 434606
e-mail: info@bistroonthebeach.co.uk
web: www.bistroonthebeach.co.uk
Dir: From Bournemouth take coast road to East Cliff, at lights R, then R again. Join overcliff. 1m to mini rdbt, take 2nd turn. 400yds to car park.
CHILD FACILITIES: Food/bottle warming Ch menu Ch portions Highchairs Safe grounds Changing facilities **NEARBY:** Seafront location

continued on p124

The Chine Hotel
★★★

On the cliff tops overlooking Poole Bay, with easy access to the beaches and town centre, this attractive Victorian hotel boasts three acres of secluded gardens and family friendly amenities including children's entertainment, dedicated play areas, a leisure club and an award winning restaurant.

The Chine Hotel
Boscombe Spa Road, Bournemouth, Dorset BH5 1AX
Tel: +44 (0)1202 396234 Fax: +44 (0)1202 391737
e-mail: reservations@chinehotel.co.uk
www.fjbhotels.co.uk

BOURNEMOUTH, continued

FOOD: Modern British **STYLE:** Traditional Bistro **SEATS:** 67
OPEN: 6.30-12, Closed L Mon-Sun, D Sun-Mon **RESTAURANT:** Fixed D
£18.95, main £9.95-£19.95 **NOTES:** ⊗ in restaurant, Air con
PARKING: Public car park nearby

BRIDPORT   Map 03 SY49

◆◆◆◆ Britmead House
West Bay Rd DT6 4EG
☎ 01308 422941
e-mail: britmead@talk21.com
web: www.britmeadhouse.co.uk
Dir: approaching Bridport on A35 follow signs for West Bay, Britmead House is 800yds S of A35

CHILD FACILITIES: Food/bottle warming Ch menu Ch portions
Highchairs Ch discounts babies free sharing with parents, other
reductions for under 15s Safe grounds Cots Family rms D rm with
1 or 2 S beds £76-£90 Connecting rms **NEARBY:** Leisure centre
Monkey sanctuary Aquarium Walks Fossil hunts Short walk to sea

Britmead House is located south of Bridport, within easy reach of
the town centre and West Bay harbour. Family-run, the
atmosphere is friendly and the accommodation well-appointed
and comfortable. Many guests return on a regular basis. A choice
of breakfast is served in the light and airy dining room.
ROOMS: 8 en suite (2 fmly) (2 GF) s £34-£48; d £50-£66 *
FACILITIES: TVB tea/coffee No coaches **NOTES:** ⊗ Cen ht **LB**
PARKING: 12

⊛ Riverside Restaurant
West Bay DT6 4EZ
☎ 01308 422011 ▤ 01308 458808
e-mail: artwatfish@hotmail.com
Dir: In the centre of West Bay by the river.

CHILD FACILITIES: Activities: colouring Outdoor play area
Food/bottle warming Ch menu Ch portions Highchairs Ch cutlery
Changing facilities **NEARBY:** River bank location Coastal path
Leisure centre Swannery 200 metres to beach

FOOD: Seafood **SEATS:** 80 **OPEN:** 11.30-2.20/6.30-8.30, Closed 1
Dec-mid Feb, Mon (ex BHs), D Sun **RESTAURANT:** Fixed D £12.95, main
£9.50-£20 **NOTES:** ⊗ in restaurant **PARKING:** Public car park

⟁ Shave Cross Inn
Shave Cross, Marshwood Vale DT6 6HW
☎ 01308 868358 ▤ 01308 867064
e-mail: roy.warburton@virgin.net
Dir: From Bridport take B3162 2m turn L signed 'Broadoak/Shave Cross' then Marshwood

CHILD FACILITIES: Activities: colouring books and pens Outdoor
play area Family area Food/bottle warming Ch menu Ch portions
Highchairs Ch cutlery Safe grounds **NEARBY:** Walks Jurassic
coast Fossil hunting 3.5m to sea

OPEN: 10.30-3 5-11 (all day Sat-Sun in Summer, BHs) Rest: 25 Dec Closed
eve **BAR MEALS:** L served Tue-Sun 12-3 D served Tue-Sun 5-9.30
RESTAURANT: L served Tue-Sun 12-3 D served Tue-Sat 7-9.30 Av 3 course
à la carte £25 **FACILITIES:** Children's licence Garden: Cottage garden
PARKING: 30

BUCKLAND NEWTON   Map 03 ST60

⟁ Gaggle of Geese
DT2 7BS
☎ 01300 345249
e-mail: gaggle@bucklandnewton.freeserve.co.uk
Dir: On B3143 N of Dorchester

CHILD FACILITIES: Outdoor play area Food/bottle warming
Ch menu Ch portions Highchairs Ch cutlery Safe grounds Changing
facilities **NEARBY:** Henley Hillbillies Badger & Wildlife Night
Watch

OPEN: 12-2.30 6.30-11 **BAR MEALS:** L served all week 12-2 D served all
week 7-10 Av main course £6.95 **RESTAURANT:** L served all week 12-2 D
served all week 7-10 **FACILITIES:** Garden: Pub on 5 acres. Pond & stream
PARKING: 30

CASHMOOR   Map 03 ST91

◆◆◆◆ ⌂ Cashmoor House
DT11 8DN
☎ 01725 552339 ▤ 01725 552291
e-mail: spencer.jones@ukonline.co.uk
Dir: on A354 Salisbury-Blandford, 3m S of Sixpenny Handley rdbt just passed Inn on the Chase

CHILD FACILITIES: Baby listening Activities: books, toys, jigsaws
Food/bottle warming Ch portions Highchairs Ch cutlery
Ch discounts under 3s free, £10 per child sharing Safe grounds
Family rms rms with B Beds & extra S beds D rm £45, £10 additional
bed Ch drinks Laundry **NEARBY:** Cinema Leisure centre

Situated virtually midway between Blandford and Salisbury, parts
of Cashmoor House date back to the 17th century. Retaining its
original character and charm, the whole property is attractively
furnished and decorated, with a warm and homely farmhouse
ambience. Traditional Aga cooked breakfasts, featuring
home-made bread and preserves, plus eggs laid by their own
hens, are served in the beamed dining room; suppers available by
prior arrangement.
ROOMS: 4 en suite (2 fmly) (2 GF) s £25-£30; d fr £45 *
FACILITIES: TVB tea/coffee TVL No coaches Dinner Last d order
breakfast **NOTES:** Credit cards not taken ⊗ Cen ht **PARKING:** 8

CORFE CASTLE   Map 03 SY9

⟁ The Greyhound Inn
The Square BH20 5EZ
☎ 01929 480205 ▤ 01929 481483
e-mail: mjml@greyhound-inn.fsnet.co.uk
Dir: W from Bournemouth, take A35, after 5m L onto A351, 10m to Corfe Castle

CHILD FACILITIES: Activities: books, games, puzzles Outdoor play
area Family area Food/bottle warming Ch menu Ch portions
Highchairs Safe grounds **NEARBY:** Corfe Castle Walks
Steam train

OPEN: 11-3 Summer open all day 6-11.30 **BAR MEALS:** L served all week
12-2.30 D served all week 6-9 Av main course £12.95 **RESTAURANT:** L
served all week 12-2.30 D served all week 6-9 Av 3 course à la carte £17.95
FACILITIES: Garden: BBQ & hog roast in summer; castle views

MOTCOMBE — Map 03 ST82

◐ The Coppleridge Inn ♦♦♦♦
SP7 9HW
☎ 01747 851980 📠 01747 851858
e-mail: thecoppleridgeinn@btinternet.com
web: www.coppleridge.com

CHILD FACILITIES: Please telephone for details

Overlooking the Blackmore Vale, this 18th-century converted farmhouse offers a quiet village location combined with the traditional hospitality of a popular inn. A wide range of meals is available in the bar, the restaurant or the comfortable lounge which has flagstone floors and a log fire. Typical specials range from turkey and bacon pie, beef lasagne to pork, bacon and cider casserole, and home-made crêpe stuffed with spinach and Stilton. There is also an extensive choice of snacks.
OPEN: 11-3 5-11 All day Sat & Sun **BAR MEALS:** L served all week 12-2.30 D served all week 6-9.30 Av main course £7.50 **RESTAURANT:** L served all week 12-2.30 D served all week 6-9.30 Av 3 course à la carte £17.50 **FACILITIES:** Garden: 15 acres including lawns, wood, pond area **ROOMS:** 10 bedrooms 10 en suite 3 family rooms s£42.50 d£75 **PARKING:** 60

NETTLECOMBE — Map 03 SY59

Babies Welcome | Children's Dishes | Minimum Age

◐ Marquis of Lorne ♦♦♦♦
DT6 3SY
☎ 01308 485236 📠 01308 485666
e-mail: julie.woodroffe@btinternet.com
web: www.marquisoflorne.com
Dir: 3m E of A3066 Bridport-Beaminster rd. From Bridport North to Beaminster after 1.5m turn right signed Powerstock, West Milton & Mill after 3m at a T Jct, pub up hill on left

CHILD FACILITIES: Activities: games, books, drawing Outdoor play area Family area Food/bottle warming Ch menu Ch portions Highchairs Ch cutlery Safe grounds Changing facilities **NEARBY:** Swannery 10-min drive to sea

OPEN: 11.30-2.30 6.30-11 (Sun all day) **BAR MEALS:** L served all week 12-2 D served all week 6.30-9 Av main course £8 **RESTAURANT:** L served all week 12-2 D served all week 6.30-9 Av 3 course à la carte £15 **FACILITIES:** Garden: Well kept garden with good views & play area **ROOMS:** 7 bedrooms 7 en suite s£45 d£70 **PARKING:** 50

> Many proprietors are happy to provide extra facilities for children, but let them know in advance what you need so they can be prepared

NORTH WOOTTON — Map 03 ST61

Babies Welcome | Children's Dishes

◐ The Three Elms
DT9 5JW
☎ 01935 812881 📠 01935 812881
Dir: From Sherborne take A352 towards Dorchester then A3030. Pub 1m on R

CHILD FACILITIES: Outdoor play area Food/bottle warming Ch menu Ch portions Highchairs Safe grounds

OPEN: 11-2.30 6.30-11 (Sun 12-3, 7-10.30) Closed: 25-26 Dec **BAR MEALS:** L served all week 12-2 D served all week 6.30-10 Av main course £8 **RESTAURANT:** L served all week 12-2 D served all week 6.30-10 **FACILITIES:** Garden: **PARKING:** 50

PIDDLETRENTHIDE — Map 03 SY79

Babies Welcome | Family Rooms | Children's Dishes

♦♦♦♦ ◐ The Poachers
DT2 7QX
☎ 01300 348358 📠 01300 348153
e-mail: thepoachersinn@piddletrenthide.fsbusiness.co.uk
web: www.thepoachersinn.co.uk
Dir: 8m from Dorchester on B3143, 2m into Piddletrenthide, inn on left

CHILD FACILITIES: Activities: colouring, wooden garden games Food/bottle warming Ch menu Ch portions Highchairs Ch cutlery Ch discounts under 10s £10, 10-15s £15 Safe grounds Cots Family rms D rm with S bed & B beds in adj rm Laundry **NEARBY:** Monkey World Dinosaur Museum

A warm welcome is assured at this friendly inn. The bar and dining areas retain much of their original 16th-century character and charm with home-cooked meals a key feature. Extensions have allowed for good-sized bedrooms, the majority of which are situated around the swimming pool, garden and adjacent stream.
ROOMS: 5 en suite 15 annexe en suite (1 fmly) (13 GF) s £35-£45; d £65-£85 * **FACILITIES:** TVB tea/coffee Direct dial from bedrooms 🎣 Skittle alley Dinner Last d order 9pm **NOTES:** ⊗ in area of dining room Cen ht **LB** **PARKING:** 40

POOLE — Map 04 SZ09

Babies Welcome | Family Rooms | Children's Dishes

★★★★ 70% Harbour Heights
73 Haven Rd, Sandbanks BH13 7PS
☎ 01202 707272 📠 01202 708594
e-mail: enquiries@harbourheights.net
web: www.fjbhotels.co.uk
Dir: Follow signs for Sandbanks, hotel on left after Canford Cliffs

Best Western

CHILD FACILITIES: Baby listening Babysitting Food/bottle warming Ch menu Ch portions Highchairs Ch cutlery Ch discounts 0-3s £5, 4-14s £25 Cots Family rms from £235 Ch drinks Fridge Laundry **NEARBY:** Museums Farms Sea Life Sanctuary Near sea

The unassuming appearance of this hotel belies a wealth of innovation, quality and style. Following a four million pound refit, contemporary bedrooms now combine state-of-the-art facilities with traditional comforts. Throughout the smart public areas, which include a choice of dining options, popular bars and sitting areas, picture windows accentuate panoramic views of Poole Harbour. The sun deck, elevated above terraced gardens, is the perfect setting for watching the cross channel ferries come and go.
ROOMS: 38 en suite (2 fmly) ⊗ in all bedrooms s £105-£175; d fr £210 (incl. bkfst) **FACILITIES:** STV Spa bath in all rooms Xmas **PARKING:** 50 **NOTES:** ✖ ⊗ in restaurant

England

POOLE, continued

Babies Welcome | Family Rooms | Children's Dishes

★★★ 75% ⊛ Sandbanks
15 Banks Rd, Sandbanks BH13 7PS
☎ 01202 707377 ▯ 01202 708885
e-mail: reservations@sandbankshotel.co.uk
web: www.sandbankshotel.co.uk
Dir: A338 from Bournemouth onto Wessex Way, to Liverpool Victoria rdbt. Left and take 2nd exit onto B3965. Hotel on left

CHILD FACILITIES: Baby listening Babysitting Activities: entertainment in hols, table tennis, pool table, soft playroom Indoor play area Outdoor play area Family area Food/bottle warming Ch menu Ch portions Highchairs Ch cutlery Ch discounts (depending on age) Safe grounds Games consoles Videos Cots Family rms D rms with adj S or T rms, D or T rms with adj B bed rms Connecting rms Fridge Laundry Changing mats
NEARBY: Bowling Cinema Harbour Seafront location

Set on the delightful Sandbanks Peninsula, this large and popular hotel has direct access to a blue flag beach and stunning views across Poole Harbour. Most of the spacious bedrooms have sea views, and there is an extensive range of leisure facilities, which now include a state-of-the-art creche.
ROOMS: 110 en suite (31 fmly) (4 GF) ⊛ in 40 bedrooms s £70-£128; d £140-£256 (incl. bkfst & dinner) **LB FACILITIES:** STV ⊠ Sauna Solarium Gym Jacuzzi Sailing, Mntn bikes, kids play area, massage room ♫ Xmas **PARKING:** 120 **NOTES:** ✖ ⊛ in restaurant

POWERSTOCK
Map 03 SY59

Babies Welcome | Family Rooms | Children's Dishes

◆◆◆◆ ◀ Three Horseshoes Inn
DT6 3TF
☎ 01308 485328
e-mail: info@threehorseshoesinn.com
web: www.threehorseshoesinn.com
Dir: Powerstock signposted off Bridport to Beaminster Rd A3066. 3m from Bridport

CHILD FACILITIES: Activities: colouring, board games Outdoor play area Food/bottle warming Ch menu Ch portions Highchairs Safe grounds Videos Family rms D rm with S beds up to £90 Laundry NEARBY: Monkey World Museums 5m to sea

From its elevated position in the village of Powerstock, The Three Horseshoes overlooks rolling hills. The unpretentious bar and cosy dining room appeal to both locals and visitors alike. A wide range of meals is available, with the emphasis on local, and organic where possible, produce, cooked with care. The spacious bedrooms offer comfort and all the expected facilities.
ROOMS: 1 en suite 2 annexe en suite (1 fmly) (2 GF) s £40-£60; d £60-£80 * **FACILITIES:** TVB tea/coffee Dinner Last d order 9pm **NOTES:** ⊛ in restaurant ⊛ in lounges Cen ht **LB PARKING:** 25

SHERBORNE
Map 03 ST61

◆◆◆◆◆ ▣ Munden House
Munden Ln, Alweston DT9 5HU
☎ 01963 23150 ▯ 01963 23153
e-mail: admin@mundenhouse.demon.co.uk
web: www.mundenhouse.demon.co.uk
Dir: from Sherborne A352, left onto A3030 to Alweston. Pass village shop on right and after 250yds on left at Oxfords Bakery sign, left

CHILD FACILITIES: Please telephone for details

Dating back to mid-Victorian times, Munden House enjoys a peaceful location in the picturesque Blackmore Vale, within three miles of Sherborne. Beautifully restored throughout - bedrooms and bathrooms are elegantly decorated and furnished. Guests are invited to use the luxurious sitting room to view the glorious surrounding countryside and the well-tended gardens. Memorable breakfasts are served in the impressive dining room.
ROOMS: 6 en suite 1 annexe en suite (2 GF) s £42-£55; d £65-£90 *
FACILITIES: TVB tea/coffee Direct dial from bedrooms No coaches Table tennis **NOTES:** ✖ ⊛ Cen ht **PARKING:** 20

Babies Welcome | Children's Dishes

◀ White Hart
Bishops Caundle DT9 5ND
☎ 01963 23301 ▯ 01963 23301 (by arrangement)
Dir: On A3030 between Sherborne & Sturminster Newton

CHILD FACILITIES: Activities: trampoline, play adventure trail Outdoor play area Food/bottle warming Ch menu Ch portions (if possible) Highchairs

OPEN: 11.30-3 6.30-11 (Sun 12-3, 7-10.30) **BAR MEALS:** L served all week 12-2 D served all week 6.45-9.30 Av main course £6.10
RESTAURANT: L served all week 12-2 D served all week 6.30-9.30
FACILITIES: Garden: Patio area, 6 benches **PARKING:** 32

STURMINSTER NEWTON
Map 03 ST71

Babies Welcome | Family Rooms | Children's Dishes

◆◆◆◆ ⬭ ❤ Honeysuckle House
1995 Fifehead St Quintin DT10 2AP
☎ 01258 817896
Dir: turn off A357 up Glue Hill (signed Hazelbury Bryan). Take next left, after sharp bend. Follow road for approx 2.5m

CHILD FACILITIES: Baby listening Nanny Babysitting Activities: farm tours, animal feeding, toys, colouring, puzzles, games, pony rides, trampoline Indoor play area Outdoor play area Family area Food/bottle warming Ch menu Ch portions Highchairs Ch cutlery Ch discounts under 4s 50% Safe grounds Games consoles Videos Cots Family rms D rm with S bed £62.50-£75 Ch drinks Laundry
NEARBY: Monkey sanctuary Longleat safari park Water park Theme park Cinema

Peace and tranquillity can be found at this 400-acre working dairy farm. The young proprietors offer a particularly friendly welcome and ensure all guests are very well looked after. Bedrooms are comfortable and include some welcome extras. Breakfasts are enormous, and be sure to book for dinner which is a real highlight of any stay.
ROOMS: 3 en suite (1 fmly) s £25-£35; d £45-£65 * ⊛
FACILITIES: TVB tea/coffee TVL ⚲ Fishing Riding ♫ Pony rides, farm tours, children's tractor rides 400 acres Dairy Dinner Last d order Previous day **NOTES:** Credit cards not taken Cen ht **LB PARKING:** 6

How to use this guide & abbreviations
are explained on pages 5-7

SWANAGE   Map 04 SZ07

| Babies Welcome | Family Rooms | Children's Dishes |

★★★ 69% **The Pines**

Burlington Rd BH19 1LT

☎ 01929 425211 📠 01929 422075

e-mail: reservations@pineshotel.co.uk

web: www.pineshotel.co.uk

Dir: A351 to seafront, left then 2nd right. Hotel at end of road

CHILD FACILITIES: Baby listening Nanny (by prior arrangement) Food/bottle warming Ch menu Ch portions Highchairs Ch discounts under 2s free, under 16s £19.50 Safe grounds Cots Family rms adjoining rms, rms with B beds Connecting rms Laundry **NEARBY:** Ask at reception for guide Seafront location

Enjoying a peaceful location with spectacular views over the cliffs and sea, The Pines is a pleasant place to stay. Bedrooms, many with sea views, are comfortable and some have now been refurbished. Guests can take tea in the lounge, enjoy appetising bar snacks in the attractive bar and interesting and accomplished cuisine in the restaurant.

ROOMS: 49 en suite (26 fmly) (6 GF) s £54.50-£72.50; d £109-£157 incl. bkfst) **LB FACILITIES:** Xmas **PARKING:** 60 **NOTES:** 🚭 in restaurant

---

TARRANT MONKTON   Map 03 ST90

| Babies Welcome | Family Rooms | Children's Dishes |

◆◆◆◆ 🚻 🍴 **The Langton Arms**

DT11 8RX

☎ 01258 830225 📠 01258 830053

e-mail: info@thelangtonarms.co.uk

Dir: Turn off A354 in Tarrant Hinton for Tarrant Monkton, follow country road to Tarrant Monkton, through ford. Langton Arms opposite

CHILD FACILITIES: Baby listening Activities: play table Indoor play area Outdoor play area Family area Food/bottle warming Ch menu Ch portions Highchairs Ch discounts Cots free Safe grounds Family rms **NEARBY:** Walks Farm

Tucked away in the sleepy Dorset village of Tarrant Monkton, the Langton Arms offers the delights and charm of an old English inn and is an ideal base for touring this attractive area. Bedrooms, all situated in the modern annexe, are very well equipped and comfortable. The bar, and restaurant (open Wednesday til Sunday lunch), are popular, and both offer appetising dishes.

ROOMS: 6 annexe en suite (6 fmly) (6 GF) s £55-£60; d £75-£85 * 🚭 **FACILITIES:** TVB tea/coffee Direct dial from bedrooms Pool Table Skittle Alley, Beer Garden Dinner Last d order 9.30pm **NOTES:** 🚭 in restaurant **LB PARKING:** 100

England

WEYMOUTH
Map 03 SY67

♦♦♦ Westwey Hotel
62 Abbotsbury Rd DT4 0BJ
☎ 01305 784564 ▤ 01305 770920
e-mail: sales@westweyhotel.co.uk
Dir: follow Espanade towards Jubilee clock, right into King St, 2nd exit from
rdbt, onto next rdbt, 2nd exit into Abbotsbury Rd, pass lights, hotel on right

CHILD FACILITIES: Please telephone for details

Well located for the town centre and beach, this friendly hotel
provides comfortable accommodation. It offers well-equipped
bedrooms, a small lounge and a bar. Dinner and breakfast, both
with a choice of menu, are served in the bright and pleasant
dining room.

ROOMS: 9 rms (7 en suite) (2 fmly) s £22-£38; d £44-£80 *
FACILITIES: TVB tea/coffee TVL Dinner Last d order 3pm **NOTES:** ✖
⊗ Licensed Cen ht **PARKING:** 9

WIMBORNE MINSTER
Map 04 SZ09

♦♦♦♦ Ashton Lodge
10 Oakley Hill BH21 1QH
☎ 01202 883423 ▤ 01202 886180
e-mail: ashtonlodge@ukgateway.net
web: www.ashtonlodge.ukgateway.net
Dir: from A31 S of Wimborne take A349 towards Poole, exit left at next rdbt
signed Wimborne/Canford Magna. House on right after 200yds

CHILD FACILITIES: Please telephone for details

A warm welcome is assured at this delightful modern home, which
provides comfortable bedrooms, stylishly furnished with
attractively co-ordinated decor and fabrics. All are well equipped,
with many extra facilities provided. Hearty breakfasts are served in
the spacious dining room, which overlooks the well-maintained
garden.

ROOMS: 5 rms (2 en suite) (2 fmly) s fr £30; d £55-£60 *
FACILITIES: TVB tea/coffee TVL No coaches **NOTES:** Credit cards not
taken ✖ ⊗ Cen ht **LB PARKING:** 4

♦♦ Peacehaven
282 Sopwith Crescent, Merley BH21 1XL
☎ 01202 880281
Dir: turn off A31 at Merley rdbt onto A349in 200yds at rdbt turn left onto
Oakley Hill, 1st right onto Oakley Lane, 1st right onto Oakley Straight, 1st
left Sopwith Crescent

CHILD FACILITIES: Please telephone for details

A warm welcome is assured at this cosy, family-run bungalow
located in a quiet residential area on the edge of town. Bedrooms
are comfortable and the lounge is available for relaxation. Guests
share one large table for breakfast and evening meals are
available by prior arrangement.

ROOMS: 2 rms (2 GF) s £25-£30; d £40-£50 * **FACILITIES:** TVB
tea/coffee No coaches Dinner Last d order 24hrs **NOTES:** Credit cards
not taken ✖ ⊗ Cen ht **LB PARKING:** 3

Babies Welcome | Children's Dishes

⊚ ⊚ Les Bouviers
Oakley Hill, Merley BH21 1RJ
☎ 01202 889555 ▤ 01202 889555
e-mail: info@lesbouviers.co.uk
Dir: 1m S of Wimborne on A349

CHILD FACILITIES: Food/bottle warming Ch menu (by special
request) Ch portions Highchairs Ch cutlery **NEARBY:** Wimborne
model village Alice in Wonderland

FOOD: French **STYLE:** Formal **SEATS:** 50 **OPEN:** 12-2.45/7-10.30,
Closed 26 Dec, 1st wk Jan **RESTAURANT:** Fixed L £12.95, Fixed D £21.95
NOTES: Smart Dress, ⊗ area, Air con **PARKING:** 15

Co DURHAM

BARNARD CASTLE
Map 12 NZ01

Babies Welcome | Family Rooms | Children's Dishes

★★★ 73% ⊚ The Morritt Arms Hotel & Restaurant
Greta Bridge DL12 9SE
☎ 01833 627232 ▤ 01833 627392
e-mail: relax@themorritt.co.uk
web: www.themorritt.co.uk
Dir: turn off A1 at Scotch Corner onto A66 towards Penrith. Greta Bridge
9m on left

CHILD FACILITIES: Baby listening Babysitting Activities: toy
cupboard (prior arrangement) Outdoor play area Food/bottle
warming Ch menu Ch portions Highchairs Ch cutlery Safe grounds
Cots Family rms D rm with 2 T beds £140 Ch drinks Laundry
Changing mats (some) **NEARBY:** Farms Walks Leisure centre
Horse riding

Set off the main road at Greta Bridge, this 17th-century coaching
house provides comfortable public rooms full of character. The bar
is focused on food and has an interesting Dickensian mural. A fine
dining experience is offered in the oak-panelled restaurant.
Bedrooms come in individual styles and varying sizes. The
attentive service will leave a lasting impression.

ROOMS: 23 en suite (3 fmly) ⊗ in 17 bedrooms s £59.50-£75;
d £87.50-£126.50 (incl. bkfst) **LB FACILITIES:** Xmas **PARKING:** 40
NOTES: ⊗ in restaurant

BEAMISH
Map 12 NZ2

Babies Welcome | Family Rooms | Children's Dishes

★★★ 69% ⊚ ⊚ Beamish Park
Beamish Burn Rd NE16 5EG
☎ 01207 230666 ▤ 01207 281260
e-mail: reception@beamish-park-hotel.co.uk
web: www.beamish-park-hotel.co.uk
Dir: A1(M)/A692 towards Consett, then A6076 towards Stanley. Hotel on
left behind Causey Arch Inn

CHILD FACILITIES: Baby listening Babysitting (by arrangement)
Food/bottle warming Ch menu Ch portions Highchairs Ch discounts
under 12s sharing with 2 adults Safe grounds Cots Family rms D rm
with 5 beds £60 Connecting rms Laundry **NEARBY:** Beamish
Museum Tanfield Railway Metroland

continue

The Metro Centre, Beamish Museum and south Tyneside are all within striking distance of this modern hotel, set in open countryside alongside its own golf course and floodlit range. Bedrooms, some with their own patios, provide a diverse mix of styles and sizes. The conservatory bistro offers a modern menu.
ROOMS: 47 en suite (7 fmly) ⊗ in 20 bedrooms s £40-£59; d £50-£71
LB FACILITIES: STV Golf 9 ⅃ 20 bay floodlit golf driving range. Golf tuition by PGA professional **PARKING:** 100

COWSHILL   Map 12 NY84

♦♦♦♦ ❤ **Low Cornriggs Farm**
Cowshill-in-Weardale DL13 1AQ
☎ 01388 537600 ▤ 01388 537777
e-mail: enquiries@lowcornriggsfarm.fsnet.co.uk
web: www.alstonandkillhoperidingcentre.co.uk
Dir: on the A689 10m W of Stanhope, on the right hand side of the road between villages of Cowshill & Lanehead.

CHILD FACILITIES: Please telephone for details

Situated in the heart of Weardale yet also close to Cumbria, this delightful farmhouse enjoys stunning views. Original stone and stripped pine are combined to provide a house with real character. Excellent home-cooked dinners are offered along with charming hospitality. Bedrooms are attractive and thoughtfully equipped with many practical and homely extras. There is a riding stable available on the farm.
ROOMS: 3 en suite (1 fmly) s £28-£30; d £45-£48 * **FACILITIES:** TVB tea/coffee TVL ⅂ Golf 9 Fishing Riding Riding school & Trekking centre, Pool supervised 42 acres Hereford cows, ponies Dinner Last d order noon **NOTES:** Credit cards not taken ⊗ Licensed Cen ht **LB**
PARKING: 10

SEDGEFIELD   Map 08 NZ32

Babies Welcome | Children's Dishes

🍴 **Dun Cow Inn** ♦♦♦
43 Front St TS21 3AT
☎ 01740 620894 ▤ 01740 622163
e-mail: duncowinn@grayner.fsnet.co.uk
Dir: At junct of A177 & A689. Inn in centre of village

CHILD FACILITIES: Food/bottle warming Ch portions Highchairs
NEARBY: Local park Country park

Parts of this well-known English inn date from the 17th century. The spacious bedrooms are well appointed and come with a range of thoughtful extras. This is also the pub that can claim to be Prime Minister Tony Blair's local, as he is the constituency MP. Here he hosted the 'million pound lunch' for American President George W Bush. A good range of dishes can be enjoyed in the bar areas as well as the dining room, all of which are adorned with a range of local photographs and bric-a-brac.
OPEN: 11-3 6.30-11 **BAR MEALS:** L served all week 12-2 D served all week 7-10 Av main course £8.95 **RESTAURANT:** L served all week 12-2 D served all week 7-10 Av 3 course à la carte £19 **FACILITIES:** 🛠
ROOMS: 6 bedrooms 6 en suite s£49.50 d£65 **PARKING:** 30

> Don't forget to let proprietors know when you book that you're bringing the kids

---

ESSEX

Walton on the Naze

COLCHESTER
Colchester Castle Museum
CO1 1TJ   ☎01206 282939
(at E end of High St)
Open all year, Mon-Sat 10-5, Sun 11-5. Closed Xmas/New Year £4.50 (ch under 5's free, ch & concessions £2.90).
Colchester Zoo CO3 0SL
enquiries@colchester-zoo.co.uk ☎01206 331292
(turn off A12 onto A1124 and follow elephant signs) Open all year, daily from 9.30. Last admission 5.30 (1hr before dusk out of season). Closed 25 Dec. £11.99 (ch 3-14 £6.99, disabled £4.99).

NEWPORT
Mole Hall Wildlife Park CB11 3SS
enquiries@molehall.co.uk   ☎01799 540400
(M11 junct 8.Situated between Stansted & Saffron Walden, off B1383) Open all year, daily 10.30-6 (or dusk). (Closed 25 Dec). Butterfly House open mid Mar-Oct.

SOUTHEND-ON-SEA
Southend Museum, Planetarium & Discovery Centre
SS2 6ES   ☎01702 434449
southendmuseum@hotmail.com
(Take A217 or A13 towards town centre. Museum is adjacent to Southend Victoria Railway Station). Open Central Museum: Tues-Sat 10-5 (Closed Sun-Mon & BH); Planetarium; Wed-Sat, shows at 11, 2 & 4. Central Museum free. Planetarium £2.40 (ch & pen £1.70). Family tickets £7.50 Party rates on request.

STANSTED
House on the Hill Museum Adventure
CM24 8SP   ☎01279 813567
mountfitchetcastle1066@btinternet.com
(off B1383 in the centre of Stansted Mountfitchet) Open daily, 10-5; (closed for a few days over the Xmas period) £3.80 (ch under 14's £3, pen £3.50). Party 15+.
Mountfitchet Castle & Norman Village
CM24 8SP   ☎01279 813237
mountfitchetcastle1066@btinternet.com
(off B1383, in centre of village. 5 min from M11 junct 8) Open daily, 13 Mar-13 Nov, 10-5. £6 (ch under 2 free, ch 2-14 £5, pen £5.50).

England

Babies Welcome | **Children's Dishes**

🍺 The Bell Inn
St James St CO9 3EJ
☎ 01787 460350
e-mail: bell-inn@ic24.net
Dir: On A1124 N of Halstead, R to Castle Hedingham

CHILD FACILITIES: Activities: colouring books, rocking horse, blocks Outdoor play area Food/bottle warming Ch menu Ch portions Highchairs Safe grounds Changing facilities **NEARBY:** Castle Steam train Walks

OPEN: 11.30-3 Open all day Friday 6-11 (Sun 12-3, 7-10.30) Closed: 25 Dec (eve) **BAR MEALS:** L served all week 12-2 D served all week 7-9.30 Av main course £7.50 **FACILITIES:** Garden: Large walled orchard garden **PARKING:** 15

Babies Welcome | **Family Rooms** | **Children's Dishes**

◆◆◆◆ Boswell House Hotel
118/120 Springfield Rd CM2 6LF
☎ 01245 287587 📠 01245 287587
e-mail: boswell118@aol.com
Dir: follow directions to Riverside Ice and Leisure Centre, over river premises at Victoria/Springfield Rd junct

CHILD FACILITIES: Baby listening Babysitting Activities: books, puzzles, games, toys Food/bottle warming Ch menu Ch portions Highchairs Ch cutlery Videos Cots Family rms D rm with 2 S beds £75-£80 Ch drinks Laundry **NEARBY:** Ice rink Swimming pool Cinema Tenpin bowling Parks

A warm welcome and attentive service can be expected from the caring hosts at this well maintained, privately owned hotel. The pleasantly decorated, thoughtfully equipped bedrooms have well chosen pine furnishings and co-ordinated soft fabrics. Breakfast and dinner are served in the attractive dining room and pre-dinner drinks can be taken in the comfortable lounge bar.
ROOMS: 13 en suite (2 fmly) (4 GF) s £50-£52; d £65-£70 * ❀
FACILITIES: TVB tea/coffee Direct dial from bedrooms TVL No coaches Dinner Last d order 8.30pm **NOTES:** ✖ ❀ in restaurant ❀ in 1 lounge Licensed Cen ht **PARKING:** 15

Babies Welcome | **Children's Dishes**

⊛ Russells
Bell St, Great Baddow CM2 7JF
☎ 01245 478484 📠 01245 478484
e-mail: russells@russells.sagehost.co.uk
web: www.russellsrest.co.uk
Dir: Telephone for directions

CHILD FACILITIES: Activities: books, drawing Food/bottle warming Ch licence Ch menu Ch portions Highchairs Safe grounds **NEARBY:** Parks Cinema Walks

FOOD: British, French **STYLE:** Modern, Formal **SEATS:** 70
OPEN: 12-2.30/7-11.30, Closed 2 wks from 2 Jan, MonL Sat, D Sun
RESTAURANT: Fixed L £9.95, Fixed D £21.95, main £12.95-£19.95
NOTES: Smart Dress, ❀ in restaurant, Air con **PARKING:** 40

Babies Welcome | **Family Rooms** | **Children's Dishes**

◆◆◆ Sandrock Hotel
1 Penfold Rd, Marine Pde West CO15 1JN
☎ 01255 428215 📠 01255 428215
Dir: A12 to A120, to town/seafront, R at pier, signed Sandrock, 2nd rd on R

CHILD FACILITIES: Baby listening Food/bottle warming Ch menu Ch portions Highchairs Ch cutlery Ch discounts under 3s free Cots Family rms **NEARBY:** Pier Leisure centre 100yds to sea

A warm welcome is offered at this Victorian property which is situated just off the seafront and within easy walking distance of the town centre. Bedrooms vary in size and style, and each is attractively decorated and thoughtfully equipped, some with sea views. Breakfast is served in the smart restaurant/bar and guests also have the use of a cosy residents' lounge. Dinner is available by prior arrangement.
ROOMS: 9 en suite (3 fmly) (1 GF) d £54-£56 * ❀ in 2 bedrooms
FACILITIES: TVB tea/coffee TVL No coaches **NOTES:** ❀ in restaurant Licensed Cen ht **LB** **PARKING:** 6

FRINTON-ON-SEA Map 05 TM22

Babies Welcome | Family Rooms | Children's Dishes

♦♦♦ Uplands

41 Hadleigh Rd CO13 9HQ
☎ 01255 674889 & 679232 📠 01255 678870
e-mail: info@uplandsguesthouse.com
web: www.uplandsguesthouse.com
Dir: A12 to A120, signed Harwich, A133 signed Clacton, through Weeley onto B1033, Thorpe-le-Soken & Kirby Cross. R into Frinton over level crossing, Hadleigh Rd 3rd L, Uplands 250yds on L

CHILD FACILITIES: Activities: colouring, board games Food/bottle warming Ch portions Highchairs Ch cutlery Ch discounts under 3s free, 4-5s £5, 5-14s £10 Videos Cots Family rms 2 S beds & B beds £60-£75 Ch drinks Laundry NEARBY: Tenpin bowling Seal watching boat trip Crazy golf Cinema Piers 3-min walk to sea

Large Edwardian house situated in a peaceful side road just a short walk from the shops and seafront. Bedrooms are pleasantly decorated and thoughtfully equipped with a good range of useful extras. Public rooms include a large lounge/dining room where breakfast is served at individual tables.

ROOMS: 4 rms (2 en suite) s £23-£28; d £46-£56 *
FACILITIES: tea/coffee No coaches **NOTES:** Credit cards not taken 🐕 ⊗ Cen ht LB **PARKING:** 4

GREAT YELDHAM Map 05 TL73

Babies Welcome | Children's Dishes

White Hart

CO9 4HJ
☎ 01787 237250 📠 01787 238044
e-mail: reservations@whitehartyeldham.co.uk
web: www.whitehartyeldham.co.uk
Dir: On A1017, between Halstead and Haverhill.

CHILD FACILITIES: Food/bottle warming Ch licence Ch menu Ch portions Highchairs Safe grounds NEARBY: Colne Vally Steam Railway Hedingham Castle

FOOD: Modern British **STYLE:** Traditional **SEATS:** 60
OPEN: 12-2/6.30-9.30, Closed D 25-26 Dec **RESTAURANT:** Fixed L £10.50, main £10-£18 **NOTES:** ⊗ in restaurant, ⊗ area **PARKING:** 40

Many proprietors are happy to provide extra facilities for children, but let them know in advance what you need so they can be prepared

LITTLE CANFIELD Map 05 TL52

Babies Welcome | Children's Dishes

The Lion & Lamb

CM6 1SR
☎ 01279 870257 📠 01279 870423
e-mail: info@lionandlamb.co.uk
web: www.lionandlamb.co.uk
Dir: M11 J8 B1256 towards Takeley

CHILD FACILITIES: Activities: colouring Outdoor play area Food/bottle warming Ch menu Ch portions Highchairs Ch cutlery Safe grounds Changing facilities NEARBY: Forest Cinema Walk

OPEN: 11-11 (Sun 12-10.30) **BAR MEALS:** L served all week 11-10 D served all week 11-10 Av main course £12.50 **RESTAURANT:** L served all week 11-10 D served all week 11-10 Av 3 course à la carte £22.50 Av 3 course fixed price £16 **FACILITIES:** Garden: Lrg enclosed garden overlooking farmland 🐕 **PARKING:** 50

SOUTHEND-ON-SEA Map 05 TQ88

♦♦♦ Terrace Hotel

8 Royal Ter SS1 1DY
☎ 01702 348143 📠 01702 348143
e-mail: info@theterracehotel.co.uk
Dir: Royal Terrace can only be approached from Southend seafront, via Pier Hill, opposite the pier

CHILD FACILITIES: Please telephone for details

On a raised terrace above the main seafront promenade, this guest house has a comfortable, informal atmosphere. There is a cosy bar, elegant sitting room and breakfast room, and the spacious and well-planned bedrooms consist of three en suite rear-facing rooms and six front-facing rooms which share two bathrooms.

ROOMS: 9 rms (3 en suite) (2 fmly) s £28.20-£39.95; d £42.30-£54.05 * ⊗ in 3 bedrooms **FACILITIES:** TVB tea/coffee TVL No coaches
NOTES: ⊗ in restaurant ⊗ in lounges Cen ht LB

GLOUCESTERSHIRE

Cotswold Farm Park

BOURTON-ON-THE-WATER

Birdland GL54 2BN
sb.birdland@virgin.net ☎01451 820480
(On A429)
Open all year, Apr-Oct daily 10-6; Nov-Mar daily
10-4. Last admission 1hr before closing. Closed
25 Dec.
*£4.85, ch 4-14 £2.85, pen £3.85. Family ticket
2 ad & 2 ch £14.00. Party 10+.
Model Village GL54 2AF
reception@theoldnewinn.co.uk ☎01451 820467
Open all year 9-5.45 summer, 10-dusk winter.
Closed 25 Dec.

CHEDWORTH

Chedworth Roman Villa
GL54 3LJ ☎01242 890256
chedworth@smtp.ntrust.org.uk
(3m NW of Fossebridge on A429)
Open 8 Feb-26 Mar, daily ex Mon 11-4; 27 Mar-24
Oct, daily ex Mon 10-5; 26 Oct-14 Nov, daily ex
Mon 11-4. Closed Mon ex BH Mons.
*£4.10, ch £2. Family ticket £10.20.

CIRENCESTER

Corinium Museum GL7 2BX
museums@cotswold.gov.uk ☎01285 655611
(In town centre)
Open Mon-Sat 10-5, Sun 2-5 (closed 1 Jan, 25-26
Dec) *£3.50, ch £2, students £2, pen £2.50.
Family ticket £8.

CLEARWELL

Clearwell Caves Ancient Iron Mines
GL16 8JR ☎01594 832535
jw@clearwellcaves.com
(1.5m S of Coleford town centre, off B4228. Follow
brown tourist signs)
Open Mar-Oct daily 10-5. Jan-Feb Sat-Sun 10-5.
Christmas Fantasy 1-24 Dec, daily 10-5.
*£4, ch £2.50, concessions £3.50 Family ticket
£11.

GLOUCESTER

Gloucester City Museum & Art Gallery
GL1 1HP ☎01452 396131
city.museum@gloucester.gov.uk
(City centre)
Open all year, Tue-Sat 10-5.

GUITING POWER

Cotswold Farm Park GL54 SUG
info@cotswoldfarmpark.co.uk ☎01451 850307
(Signposted off B4077 from M5 Junct 9)
Open 20 Mar-12 Sep, daily 10.30-5 then open
wknds only until end Oct & Autumn half term
10.30-4. *£4.95, ch £3.50, pen £4.65. Family ticket
£15.50.

MORETON-IN-MARSH

Cotswold Falconry Centre
GL56 9QB
geoffdalton@yahoo.co.uk ☎01386 701043
(1m W of Moreton-in-Marsh on A44).
Open mid Feb-mid Nov, 10.30-5.30. (Last
admission 5pm). £5 (ch 4-15 £2.50, concession
£4). Joint ticket with Batsford Arboretum £8.50 (ch
4-15 £3, concession £8).

NEWENT

The National Birds of Prey Centre GL18 1JJ
katherine@nbpc.co.uk ☎0870 9901992
(Follow A40, right on to B4219 towards Newent.
Follow brown tourist signs from Newent town)
Open Feb-Oct, daily 10.30-5.30 *£6.75, ch £4, pen
£5.75. Family ticket £18.50 (2+2). Party 12+.

NEWENT

The Shambles
GL18 1PP ☎01531 822144
(close to town centre near church)
Open mid Mar-end Oct, Tue-Sun & BH's 10-5 or
dusk; Nov-Dec wknds only.
*£4.25, ch £2.65, pen £3.65.

SLIMBRIDGE

WWT Slimbridge GL2 7BT
slimbridge@wwt.org.uk ☎01453 891900
(Off A38, signed from M5 junct 13 & 14)
Open all year, daily from 9.30-5, winter 4pm.
Closed 25 Dec.
*£6.75, ch £4, pen £5.50. Family ticket £17.50.

WESTONBIRT

Westonbirt Arboretum
GL8 8QS ☎01666 880220
(3m S Tetbury on A433)
Open all year, daily 10-8 or sunset. Visitor centre
& shop all year.
Closed Xmas & New Year
Jun-nov £7.50, pen £6.50 Family ticket £15. Nov-
Mar £5 (pen £4) Family ticket £11. Apr-Jun £6
(pen £5) Family ticket £12.

WINCHCOMBE

Sudeley Castle & Gardens GL54 5JD
marketing@sudeley.org.uk ☎01242 602308
(B4632 to Winchcombe. Castle is signed from
town)
Open daily Mar-Oct, Grounds, Gardens, exhibition,
shop & plant centre 10.30-5.30. 29 Mar-2 Nov,
Castle apartments & Church & restaurant 11-5.
*Castle & Gardens £6.85-£7.85, ch 5-15 £3.85-
£4.85 & concessions £5.85-£6.85. Gardens only
£5.50-£6.50, ch £2.75-£3.75 & concessions £4.50-
£5.50. Family ticket 2 ad & 2 ch £18.50-£22. Party
20+ £5.85, ch £3.85, concessions £4.85.

England

BERKELEY   Map 03 ST69

Babies Welcome | **Children's Dishes**

🍴 The Malt House ★★
Marybrook St GL13 9BA
☎ 01453 511177 📠 01453 810257
e-mail: the-malthouse@btconnect.com
web: www.themalthouse.uk.com
*Dir: From A38 towards Bristol from exit 13 or 14 of M5, after approx 8m
Berkeley is signposted, the Malthouse is situated on the main road
heading towards Sharpness*

CHILD FACILITIES: Food/bottle warming Ch menu Ch portions
Highchairs Safe grounds **NEARBY:** Castle Wildfowl trust

OPEN: 12-11 (Sun 12-4, Mon 4-11) **BAR MEALS:** L served Tues-Sat 11-2
D served Mon-Sat 6-9.00 **RESTAURANT:** L served Tues-Sat 12-2.00 D
served Mon-Sat 6-9 Av 3 course à la carte £15 **FACILITIES:** Garden: Small
garden; Food served outside in summer 🎯 **ROOMS:** 9 bedrooms 9 en
suite 1 family room s£49 d£69 **PARKING:** 40

BOURTON-ON-THE-WATER   Map 04 SP12

Babies Welcome | **Children's Dishes**

🍴 The Duke of Wellington
Sherborne St GL54 2BY
☎ 01451 820539 📠 01451 810919

CHILD FACILITIES: Family area Food/bottle warming Ch menu
Ch portions Highchairs Ch cutlery Safe grounds Changing facilities
NEARBY: Motor museum Bird zoo Model village

OPEN: 12-3 6-11 (Summer all day) **BAR MEALS:** L served all week
12-2.30 D served all week 6-9.30 **RESTAURANT:** L served all week
12-2.30 D served Mon-Sat 7-9 Av 3 course à la carte £20
FACILITIES: Garden: Overlooking local river with seating 🎯

CHELTENHAM   Map 03 SO92

Babies Welcome | **Family Rooms** | **Children's Dishes**

◆◆◆◆ Beechworth Lawn Hotel
133 Hales Rd GL52 6ST
☎ 01242 522583 📠 01242 574800
e-mail: info@beechworthlawnhotel.co.uk
web: www.beechworthlawnhotel.co.uk
Dir: from A40 London Rd, turn into Hales Rd. Hotel approx 0.5m on right

CHILD FACILITIES: Baby listening Food/bottle warming Ch menu
(breakfast only) Ch portions (breakfast only) Highchairs Ch cutlery
Cots Family rms D rm with S bed, D rm with 2 S beds or cot £65-95
Ch drinks (on request) Laundry **NEARBY:** Outdoor swimming
pool Play area Mini zoo Sudeley Castle Roman villa

Located in the residential area of Battledown, close to the
racecourse, town centre and GCHQ, this elegant Victorian house
offers thoughtfully furnished bedrooms, a light and airy breakfast
room and a spacious guest lounge, complete with piano. Cooked
breakfasts, with an emphasis on local produce, are a strong point,
ensuring a satisfying start to the day.
ROOMS: 7 en suite (2 fmly) (2 GF) d £60-£95 * **FACILITIES:** TVB
tea/coffee TVL No coaches **NOTES:** ⊗ Cen ht **LB PARKING:** 10

◆◆◆◆ Moorend Park Hotel
Moorend Park Rd GL53 0LA
☎ 01242 224441 📠 01242 572413
e-mail: moorendpark@freeuk.com
*Dir: M5 J11A, A417 (Cirencester), A46 (Cheltenham). After 3m L at lights to
enter hotel car park.*

CHILD FACILITIES: Please telephone for details

continued

A warm welcome is extended at this elegant early Victorian house,
located a short distance from the town centre. All bedrooms are
neatly presented, bright and spacious, and suitably equipped for
all guests. Delicious breakfasts are served in the spacious dining
room and there is also a cosy bar in addition to a peaceful reading
lounge.
ROOMS: 9 en suite (2 fmly) s £52-£56; d £62-£86 * **FACILITIES:** TVB
tea/coffee Direct dial from bedrooms No coaches **NOTES:** 🎯 ⊗
Licensed Cen ht **LB PARKING:** 20

◆◆◆ Montpellier Hotel
33 Montpellier Ter GL50 1UX
☎ 01242 526009 📠 01242 261953
e-mail: montpellierhotel@btopenworld.com
*Dir: M5 J11, follow A40 to rdbt at Montpellier, continue on A40, hotel
100mtrs on R beyond rdbt, overlooking tennis courts*

CHILD FACILITIES: Please telephone for details

Forming part of an elegant Georgian terrace overlooking the
municipal gardens in a fashionable area of town, this friendly and
welcoming hotel is convenient for the shops, restaurants and local
amenities. Bedrooms are soundly appointed and comfortably
furnished with a range of practical extras and thoughtful touches.
ROOMS: 7 en suite (5 fmly) s £28-£40; d £48-£60 * ⊗ in 3 bedrooms
FACILITIES: TVB tea/coffee No coaches Dinner Last d order 5pm
NOTES: Credit cards not taken 🎯 ⊗ in restaurant Licensed Cen ht **LB**
PARKING:

CHIPPING CAMPDEN   Map 04 SP13

Family Rooms | **Children's Dishes**

◆◆◆◆ Holly House
Ebrington GL55 6NL
☎ 01386 593213 📠 01386 593181
e-mail: hutsby@talk21.com
web: www.hollyhousebandb.co.uk
*Dir: from Chipping Campden take B4035 towards Shipston on Stour. After
0.5m turn left to Ebrington & follow signs*

CHILD FACILITIES: Food/bottle warming Ch menu Ch portions
Ch cutlery Ch discounts children £10-15 Safe grounds Family rms
D rms with 2/3 S beds or cot Laundry **NEARBY:** Farm Zoo Bird
sanctuary Model village Butterfly farm

Set in the heart of the pretty Cotswold village of Ebrington, this
late Victorian house offers thoughtfully equipped accommodation.
Bedrooms are housed in buildings that were formerly used by the
local wheelwright, and offer level access, seclusion and privacy.
Quality English breakfasts are served in the light and airy dining
room. For other meals, the village pub is just a few minutes'
walk away.
ROOMS: 2 en suite 1 annexe en suite (1 fmly) (3 GF) s £40-£65;
d £55-£65 * **FACILITIES:** TVB tea/coffee No coaches **NOTES:** Credit
cards not taken 🎯 ⊗ Cen ht **PARKING:** 5

🍴 Eight Bells
Church St GL55 6JG
☎ 01386 840371 📠 01386 841669
e-mail: neilhargreaves@bellinn.fsnet.co.uk
web: www.eightbellsinn.co.uk

CHILD FACILITIES: Please telephone for details

OPEN: 11-3 5.30-11 (all day Jul-Aug) Closed: 25 Dec **BAR MEALS:** L
served all week 12-2.30 D served all week 6.30-9.30 Av main course £9.50
RESTAURANT: L served all week 12-2.30 D served all week 6.30-9.30 Av 3
course à la carte £20 **FACILITIES:** Garden: Terrace, courtyard, great views
ROOMS: 4 bedrooms 4 en suite 1 family room s£50 d£85 (◆◆◆)

Babies Welcome	Children's Dishes

🍴 The Noel Arms Hotel ★★★ ⊚

High St GL55 6AT
☎ 01386 840317 🖷 01386 841136
e-mail: reception@noelarms.com
web: www.noelarmshotel.com
Dir: Telephone for directions

CHILD FACILITIES: **Activities:** Food/bottle warming Ch menu Ch portions Highchairs

This historic 14th-century establishment has a wealth of character and charm, and is renowned for accommodating Charles II in 1651 after his defeat by Cromwell at Worcester. Bedrooms are very individual in style, but all have high levels of comfort and interesting interior design. There is the popular Dover's bar where light meals may be taken and also the award-winning Gainsborough restaurant where booking is essential.
OPEN: 11-11 (Sun 12-10.30) **BAR MEALS:** L served all week 12-2 D served all week 7-9 Av main course £8 **RESTAURANT:** L served Sun 12-2 D served all week 7-9 **ROOMS:** 26 bedrooms 26 en suite 1 family room s£90 d£120 **PARKING:** 25

EWEN   Map 04 SU09

★★ 67% ⊚ Wild Duck Inn

Drakes Island GL7 6BY
☎ 01285 770310 🖷 01285 770924
e-mail: wduckinn@aol.com
web: www.thewildduckinn.co.uk
Dir: from Cirencester take A429. At Kemble left to Ewen. Pub in village centre

CHILD FACILITIES: **Please telephone for details**

This bustling, ever-popular inn dates back to the early 16th century and is full of character. Bedrooms vary in style and are well equipped and tastefully furnished. Open fires, old beams and rustic pine tables add to the charm in the bar and restaurant, where imaginative, robust cooking has earned a loyal following and well-deserved reputation.
ROOMS: 11 en suite s £60-£80; d £80-£130 (incl. cont bkfst)
FACILITIES: Discounted leisure facilities within 3m Garden: Enclosed courtyard, giant chess board **PARKING:** 50 **NOTES:** RS 25 Dec
See advert on opposite page

GREET   Map 03 SP03

Babies Welcome	Children's Dishes

🍴 The Harvest Home

Evesham Rd GL54 5BH
☎ 01242 602430
e-mail: sworchardbarn@aol.com
Dir: M5 J9 take A435 towards Evesham, then B4077 & B4078 towards Winchcombe. 200yds from station.

CHILD FACILITIES: Food/bottle warming Ch licence Ch menu Ch portions Highchairs Ch cutlery Safe grounds **NEARBY:** Steam railway Sudeley Castle

OPEN: 12-3 6-11 (Sun 6-10.30) Rest: 25 & 31 Dec closed eve **BAR MEALS:** L served all week 12-2 D served all week 6-9 Av main course £8 **RESTAURANT:** L served all week 12-2 D served all week 6-9 Av 3 course à la carte £16 Av 2 course fixed price £5.95 **FACILITIES:** Children's licence Garden: Grass area, picnic tables, countryside views **PARKING:** 30

MARSHFIELD   Map 03 ST77

Babies Welcome	Children's Dishes

🍴 The Lord Nelson Inn

1 & 2 High St SN14 8LP
☎ 01225 891820 & 891981
e-mail: clair.vezey@btopenworld.com

CHILD FACILITIES: **Activities:** colouring books, baby slides Food/bottle warming Ch menu Ch portions Highchairs Ch cutlery Safe grounds Changing facilities **NEARBY:** Walks Bath city centre Local park

OPEN: 12-2.30 Summer: Sun 12-10.30 5.30-11 Winter: Sun 12-3, 6.30-10.30 **BAR MEALS:** L served all week 12-2 D served all week 6-9 Av main course £9.75 **RESTAURANT:** L served all week 12-2 D served all week 6-9 Av 3 course à la carte £22.50 **FACILITIES:** Garden: small patio area with seating

---

NAILSWORTH   Map 03 ST89

Babies Welcome	Children's Dishes

🍴 The Britannia

Cossack Square GL6 0DG
☎ 01453 832501 🖷 01453 872228
e-mail: pheasantpluckers2003@yahoo.co.uk

CHILD FACILITIES: Food/bottle warming Ch menu Ch portions Highchairs Safe grounds **NEARBY:** Walks in Cotswolds

OPEN: 11-11 Closed: 25 Dec **BAR MEALS:** L served all week 11-2.45 D served all week 5.30-10 **RESTAURANT:** L served all week 11-2.45 D served all week 5.30-10 **FACILITIES:** Garden: Heated terrace & lawns **PARKING:** 100

How to use this guide & abbreviations are explained on pages 5-7

NEWNHAM Map 03 SO61

Babies Welcome | **Family Rooms** | **Children's Dishes**

♦♦♦♦ Swan House Country Guest House
Swan House, High St GL14 1BY
☎ 01594 516504 ▤ 01594 516177
e-mail: enquiries@swanhousenewnham.co.uk
web: www.swanhousenewnham.co.uk
Dir: on service road set back from A48 between clock tower & Ship PH.

CHILD FACILITIES: Baby listening Activities: toys, games Food/bottle warming Ch menu Ch portions Highchairs Ch cutlery Ch discounts under 3s free, 3-13 £15 Cots Family rms D rms with S beds £62.50-£75 Laundry Changing mats **NEARBY:** History centre Model village

This Grade II listed house, parts of which date back to 1640, is centrally placed in this picturesque village. No two bedrooms are alike, but all share similarly high standards of comfort and quality. Breakfast, and dinner by prior arrangement, are served in the cosy dining room with local produce used whenever possible. A guest lounge is also available, complete with honesty bar.
ROOMS: 6 en suite (1 GF) s £28-£38; d £56-£76 * **FACILITIES:** TVB tea/coffee No coaches Secure storage for bicycles, surf boards & canoes Dinner Last d order 6pm **NOTES:** ⊗ in restaurant ⊗ in lounges Licensed Cen ht **PARKING:** 5

STOW-ON-THE-WOLD Map 04 SP12

Babies Welcome | **Family Rooms** | **Children's Dishes**

★★ 68% Old Stocks
 THE INDEPENDENTS
The Square GL54 1AF
☎ 01451 830666 ▤ 01451 870014
e-mail: aa@theoldstockshotel.co.uk
web: www.oldstockshotel.co.uk
Dir: turn off A429 to town centre. Hotel is facing Village Green

CHILD FACILITIES: Baby listening Activities: games Food/bottle warming Ch menu Ch portions Highchairs Ch cutlery Ch discounts under 5s £5, 5-10s £10, 10-15s £15 Safe grounds Cots Family rms D rms with S bed & rm for cot £40 per adult plus child Ch drinks (on request) Changing mats (on request) **NEARBY:** Farm Park Falconry Centre Maize Wildlife Park Birdland

Overlooking the old market square, this Grade II listed, mellow Cotswold stone building is a comfortable and friendly base from which to explore this picturesque area. There is a lot of character and atmosphere with bedrooms all offering individuality and charm. Facilities include guest lounge, restaurant and bar, whilst outside, the patio is a popular summer venue for refreshing drinks and good food.
ROOMS: 15 en suite 3 annexe en suite (5 fmly) (4 GF) ⊗ in 10 bedrooms s £45-£60; d £90-£120 (incl. bkfst) **LB FACILITIES:** Xmas **PARKING:** 12 **NOTES:** ⊗ in restaurant

The Wild Duck Inn

Drakes Island, Ewen Cirencester, Gloucester GL7 6BY Tel: 01285 770310 Fax: 01285 770924 Email: wildduck@btconnect.com
AA ★★ **www.thewildduckinn.co.uk** ◉

An attractive 16th century inn of great character, built of Cotswold stone. A typical local English inn with a warm and welcoming ambience. The hotel is an ideal venue for a long or short stay. The secluded garden is perfect for 'alfresco' dining in the summer. In winter a large open log fire burns in the bar. The Country style dining room offers fresh seasonal food with fresh fish delivered overnight from Devon. Eleven bedrooms, two of which have four poster beds overlook the garden and have full facilities.

 The Wild Duck Inn is the centre for many sporting venues and places of interest.

Babies Welcome | **Family Rooms** | **Children's Dishes**

♦♦♦♦ 🏠 The Mews
Fox Ln, Digbeth St GL54 1BN
☎ 01451 831633 ▤ 01451 831633
e-mail: enquiries@themewsfoxlane.co.uk
web: www.themewsfoxlane.co.uk
Dir: exit SE corner Stow Square to the right of Barclays Bank into Digbeth St. Left after 2nd speed bump. The Mews is half way down on left

CHILD FACILITIES: Food/bottle warming Ch portions Highchairs Ch cutlery Ch discounts babies free Cots Family rms T rms with cot/roll away bed from £60 Ch drinks (on request) Laundry

Peacefully located down a quiet lane in this popular market town, The Mews offers an impressive standard of accommodation and guests are assured of a genuinely warm welcome. The one bedroom is spacious and brimming with generous extras. A delicious breakfast, which features quality local produce and home-made preserves, can be enjoyed in the smart dining room.
ROOMS: 1 en suite (1 fmly) s £40-£50; d £55-£65 * **FACILITIES:** TVB tea/coffee TVL No coaches **NOTES:** Credit cards not taken ✖ ⊗ Cen ht **PARKING:** 1

Many proprietors are happy to provide extra facilities for children, but let them know in advance what you need so they can be prepared

STOW-ON-THE-WOLD, continued

Babies Welcome	Family Rooms	Children's Dishes

◆◆◆ Limes

Evesham Rd GL54 1EJ
☎ 01451 830034 📠 01451 830034
e-mail: thelimes@zoom.co.uk
Dir: turn off A429 towards Evesham on A424. The Limes 800yds on left

CHILD FACILITIES: Food/bottle warming Ch portions Highchairs Safe grounds Cots Family rms D rm with 2 S beds and put-up if needed **NEARBY:** Bird sanctuary Zoo

Just a few minutes' walk from the village centre, this Victorian house provides a comfortable base from which to explore this beautiful area. Bedroom styles vary, with both four-poster and ground-floor rooms offered. A warm and genuine welcome is extended to all guests, many of whom return on a regular basis. A spacious lounge is available and breakfast is served in the light and airy dining room.

ROOMS: 4 en suite 1 annexe en suite (1 fmly) (1 GF) s £30-£46; d £46-£50 * ⊗ **FACILITIES:** STV TVB tea/coffee TVL No coaches **NOTES:** Credit cards not taken ⊗ in restaurant Cen ht **PARKING:** 4

Babies Welcome	Children's Dishes

⊚ Hamilton's Brasserie

Park St GL54 1AQ
☎ 01451 831700 📠 01451 831388
e-mail: goodfood@hamiltons.br.com
Dir: Telephone for directions

CHILD FACILITIES: Activities: colouring books, quiz sheets Food/bottle warming Ch portions Highchairs

FOOD: Modern International **STYLE:** Modern, Chic **SEATS:** 55 **OPEN:** 12-2.30/6-9.30, Closed 25-26 Dec, D Sun **RESTAURANT:** main £12-£16.50 **NOTES:** ⊗ in restaurant, Air con **PARKING:** On street; car park nearby

STROUD   Map 03 SO80

◆◆◆ ⬛ George

Frocester GL10 3TQ
☎ 01453 822302 📠 01453 791612
e-mail: enquiries@georgeinn.fsnet.co.uk
Dir: M5 junct 13, onto A419 towards Stroud, at rndbt take Easington exit. Through Eastington, turn left in front of Kings Head to Frocester. Pub is 400yds past railway bridge on right

CHILD FACILITIES: Please telephone for details

Located in the village of Frocester, this popular Georgian posting house retains many original features. Public areas include a superb function suite, whilst bedrooms offer ample space and comfort. The inn enjoys a good reputation for food and good old traditional hospitality!

ROOMS: 9 rms (6 en suite) (4 fmly) s £29-£39; d £55-£59 * ⊗ in 3 bedrooms **FACILITIES:** TVB tea/coffee Boules Pitch Dinner Last d order 9.30pm **NOTES:** ✖ ⊗ in restaurant Cen ht **PARKING:** 30

Don't forget our travel accommodation section at the front of the guide

TETBURY   Map 03 ST89

Babies Welcome	Family Rooms	Children's Dishes

★★★ ⊚ Calcot Manor

Calcot GL8 8YJ
☎ 01666 890391 📠 01666 890394
e-mail: reception@calcotmanor.co.uk
web: www.calcotmanor.co.uk
Dir: 3m West of Tetbury at junct A4135/A46

CHILD FACILITIES: Baby listening Nanny Babysitting Activities: Playzone, small cinema, toys Indoor play area Outdoor play area Food/bottle warming Ch menu Ch portions Highchairs Ch cutlery Ch discounts under 12s £20, 13s+ £25 Safe grounds Games consoles Videos Cots Family rms from £215 Ch drinks Connecting rms Fridge Laundry **NEARBY:** Bowood House Wildlife Park Arboretum

Cistercian monks built the ancient barns and stables around which this lovely English farmhouse is set. No two rooms are identical, and each is beautifully decorated in country-house style and equipped with the comforts of home. Sumptuous sitting rooms, with crackling log fires in the winter, look out over well-kept gardens. There are two dining options: the elegant conservatory restaurant and the informal Gumstool Inn. A superb health and leisure spa includes an indoor pool, high-tech gym, massage tables, complementary therapies and much more. For children, a crèche and 'playzone' have been provided.

ROOMS: 9 en suite 21 annexe en suite (10 fmly) s £120-£150; d fr £190 (incl. bkfst) LB **FACILITIES:** Spa ☒ ⸙ ⸙ Sauna Solarium Gym ⬚ Jacuzzi Clay pigeon shooting Xmas **PARKING:** 120 **NOTES:** ✖ ⊗ in restaurant

WOODCHESTER   Map 03 SO80

Babies Welcome	Children's Dishes

⬛ The Old Fleece

Bath Rd, Rooksmoor GL5 5NB
☎ 01453 872582 📠 01453 872228
e-mail: pheasantpluckers2003@yahoo.co.uk
Dir: 2m S of Stroud on the A46

CHILD FACILITIES: Food/bottle warming Ch menu Ch portions Highchairs Safe grounds **NEARBY:** Walks in Cotswolds

OPEN: 11-11 Closed: 25 Dec **BAR MEALS:** L served all week 11-2.45 D served all week 5.30-10 Av main course £9.95 **RESTAURANT:** L served all week 11-2.45 D served all week 5.30-10 **FACILITIES:** Garden: Heated terrace **PARKING:** 40

GREATER LONDON

Chessington World of Adventures

HAMPTON
Hampton Court Palace
KT8 9AU ☎0870 752 7777 & 8781 9501
(On A308, close to A3, M3 & M25 exits. Train from
Waterloo - Hampton Court, 2 mins walk from
station). Open mid Mar-mid Oct. daily 9.30-6
(10.15-6 on Mon); mid Oct-mid Mar, daily, 9.30-
4.30 (10.15-4.30 on Mon).

CHERTSEY
Thorpe Park
KT16 8PN ☎0870 444 4466
(M25 junct 11 or 13 and follow signs via A320 to
Thorpe Park) Open from 5 Apr-2 Nov ex some off-
peak days 9/10-5/6 times vary, 7.30pm from 25
Jul-7 Sep, until 8pm on fireworks night & from
noon-11 on Fri nights.

CHESSINGTON
Chessington World of Adventures
KT9 2NE ☎0870 444 7777
(M25 junct 9/10, on A243) Open 10 Apr-2 Nov
(excluding some off peak days) either 10-5, 10-6 or
10-7 (telephone for details)

KEW
Kew Gardens (Royal Botanics Gardens)
TW9 3AB ☎020 8332 5655
info@kew.org
(Underground - Kew Gardens)
Open all year, Gardens daily 9.30-between 4 &
7.30pm (seasonal, visit website or phone to
verify) (Closed 25 Dec & 1 Jan). £8.50
(concessions £6.50, ch under 17 free).

TWICKENHAM
Museum of Rugby & Twickenham Stadium Tours
TW1 1DZ ☎020 8892 8877
(take M3 into London, then onto A316 following
signs to museum.) Open, Tue-Sat 10-5 (last
admission 4.30pm), Sun 11-5 (last admission
4.30pm). (Closed post Twickenham match days,
Etr Sun, 24-26 Dec & 1 Jan). Museum Tour; £8
(concessions £5).

| Babies Welcome | Family Rooms | Children's Dishes |

★★★ 69%
Novotel London Heathrow
Junction 4 M4, Cherry Ln UB7 9HB
☎ 01895 431431 ▪ 01895 431221
e-mail: H1551@accor-hotels.com
*Dir: M4 junct 4, follow Uxbridge signs on A408. Keep left and take 2nd exit
off traffic island into Cherry Ln signed West Drayton. Hotel on left*

CHILD FACILITIES: Activities: Lego Indoor play area Family area
Food/bottle warming Ch menu Ch portions Highchairs Ch discounts
under 16s free sharing with parents Safe grounds Games consoles
Cots Family rms D rms with S beds Connecting rms Fridge Laundry
NEARBY: Legoland Chessington Thorpe Park

Conveniently located for Heathrow and the motorway network,
this modern hotel provides comfortable accommodation. The
large, airy indoor atrium creates a good sense of space in public
areas, which include a bar, fitness centre and swimming pool.
Hotel boasts a safer car park award for its security measures.
ROOMS: 178 en suite (34 fmly) (10 GF) ❄ in 112 bedrooms
s £115-£125; d £115-£125 **LB FACILITIES:** STV ☞ Gym **PARKING:** 100

♦♦♦♦ Harmondsworth Hall
Summerhouse Ln, Harmondsworth Village UB7 0BG
☎ 020 8759 1824 & 07713 104229 ▪ 020 8897 6385
e-mail: Elaine@harmondsworthhall.com
web: www.harmondsworthhall.com
*Dir: M4 junct 4 left onto A3044 Holloway Lane towards Harmondsworth.
After 3rd rdbt into Harmondsworth village after Crown Pub on left next left
into Summerhouse Lane*

CHILD FACILITIES: Please telephone for details

Hidden away in the old part of the village, this guest house is
ideally located for the airport and motorways. Breakfast is served
in an attractive wood-panelled dining room, which looks out on to
the gardens, and guests have the use of a spacious comfortably
appointed lounge. Each bedroom is well-equipped and
individually furnished and decorated.
ROOMS: 10 en suite (4 fmly) (2 GF) s £55-£65; d £70-£75 *
FACILITIES: TVB tea/coffee Direct dial from bedrooms TVL No coaches
Dinner Last d order by arrangement **NOTES:** ❄ Licensed Cen ht **LB**
PARKING: 8

| Babies Welcome | Family Rooms | Children's Dishes |

♦♦♦ Shepiston Lodge
31 Shepiston Ln UB3 1LJ
☎ 020 8573 0266 ▪ 020 8569 2536
e-mail: shepistonlodge@aol.com
*Dir: leave M4 junct 4, follow Hayes sign, from slip road onto Shepiston
Lane. 50yds from fire station, almost opposite Great Western pub*

continued on p138

England

HEATHROW AIRPORT, continued

CHILD FACILITIES: Activities: books, games Outdoor play area Food/bottle warming Ch menu Ch portions Highchairs Ch discounts Safe grounds Cots Family rms D rms with S beds £75 Ch drinks **NEARBY:** Model village Model railway Tenpin bowling Swimming pool

Located close to Heathrow Airport, this small private hotel offers smartly presented and well-equipped bedrooms. Public rooms include an informal bar and spacious dining room, in which freshly cooked breakfasts and, by request, dinners are served. Ample, secure car parking is available.

ROOMS: 22 en suite (2 fmly) (9 GF) s fr £45; d fr £60 *
FACILITIES: TVB tea/coffee TVL Dinner Last d order 6pm **NOTES:** ✖ ⊛ in restaurant ⊛ in 1 lounge Licensed Cen ht **PARKING:** 20

KEW
Map 04 TQ17

Babies Welcome | Children's Dishes

⊛ ⊛ The Glasshouse
14 Station Rd TW9 3PZ
☎ 020 8940 6777 🖷 020 8940 3833
Dir: Telephone for directions

CHILD FACILITIES: Food/bottle warming Ch menu Ch portions Highchairs **NEARBY:** Kew Gardens

FOOD: Modern British **STYLE:** Modern **SEATS:** 60
OPEN: 12-2.30/7-10.30, Closed Xmas, New Year **RESTAURANT:** Fixed L £20, Fixed D £32.50 **NOTES:** ⊛ in restaurant, Air con **PARKING:** On street; metered

KINGSTON UPON THAMES
Map 04 TQ16

Babies Welcome | Children's Dishes

⊛ Frère Jacques
10-12 Riverside Walk, Off Bishops Hall KT1 1QN
☎ 020 8546 1332 🖷 020 8546 1956
e-mail: john@frerejacques.co.uk
web: www.frerejacques.co.uk
Dir: 50mtrs S of Kingston side of Kingston Bridge, by the river

CHILD FACILITIES: Activities: colouring Food/bottle warming Ch menu Highchairs **NEARBY:** Riverside walks Cinema

FOOD: French **STYLE:** Rustic, French **SEATS:** 130 **OPEN:** 12, Closed 25-26 Dec, 1 Jan, D 24 Dec **RESTAURANT:** Fixed L £8.90, main £11.25-£15.50 **NOTES:** ⊛ area, Air con **PARKING:** Euro car park - Thames St.

NORTHWOOD
Map 04 TQ09

♦♦♦ Frithwood House
31 Frithwood Av HA6 3LY
☎ 01923 827864 🖷 01923 824720
e-mail: frithwood_31@hotmail.com
Dir: A404 to Northwood. Off Watford Rd past RAF & NATO Headquarters

CHILD FACILITIES: Please telephone for details

This Edwardian property is located in quiet residential surroundings close to the town centre and the style is very relaxed and informal. Bedrooms are both practical and homely. Guests have the use of a TV lounge and breakfast is served communally in the kitchen/dining room.

ROOMS: 12 en suite (4 fmly) (3 GF) s £37-£44; d £54-£66 * ⊛
FACILITIES: STV TVB Direct dial from bedrooms TVL **NOTES:** ✖ ⊛ in restaurant Cen ht **PARKING:** 10

PINNER
Map 04 TQ18

Babies Welcome | Children's Dishes

⊛ Friends Restaurant
11 High St HA5 5PJ
☎ 020 8866 0286 🖷 020 8866 0286
e-mail: info@friendsrestaurant.co.uk
web: www.friendsrestaurant.co.uk
Dir: In centre of Pinner. 2 mins' walk from underground station

CHILD FACILITIES: Food/bottle warming Ch licence Ch portions Highchairs

FOOD: Modern British **STYLE:** Traditional **SEATS:** 50
OPEN: 12-3/6.30-10.30, Closed 25 Dec, BHs, D Sun **RESTAURANT:** Fixed D £28.50 **NOTES:** ⊛ in restaurant, ⊛ area, Air con **PARKING:** nearby car parks x3

RICHMOND (UPON THAMES)   Map 04 TQ17

★★★ 63% *Bingham Hotel*
61-63 Petersham Rd TW10 6UT
☎ 020 8940 0902 📠 020 8948 8737
e-mail: reservations@binghamhotel.co.uk
Dir: on A307

CHILD FACILITIES: Please telephone for details

This Georgian building overlooks the Thames and is within walking distance of the town centre. Bedrooms vary in size and style and comfortable public rooms enjoy views of the pretty garden and river. Diners can choose from a selection of meals from light snacks to three-course dinners.
ROOMS: 23 en suite (2 fmly) **FACILITIES:** Gym **PARKING:** 12

SURBITON   Map 04 TQ16

Babies Welcome | Children's Dishes

🏵 The French Table
85 Maple Rd KT6 4AW
☎ 0208 3992 365 📠 0208 390 5353
Dir: 5 minute walk from Surbiton Station, 1 mile from Kingston.

CHILD FACILITIES: Activities: colouring Food/bottle warming Ch portions Highchairs **NEARBY:** River Thames Parks

FOOD: French, Mediterranean **STYLE:** Modern Chic **SEATS:** 48
OPEN: 12-2.30/7-10.30, Closed 25-26 Dec, 10 days Jan, last 2 wks Aug, MonL Tue & Sat, D Sun **RESTAURANT:** Fixed L £12.50, main £10.50-£14.80 **NOTES:** Smart Dress, ⊘ area, Air con **PARKING:** On street

 This symbol indicates establishments within walking distance or a short drive of the seaside.

GREATER MANCHESTER

Aerospace Hall at the Museum of Science and Industry

MANCHESTER
Manchester Museum M13 9PL
anna.j.davey@man.ac.uk   ☎0161 275 2634
(S of city centre on B5117)
Open all year, Mon-Sat 10-5, Sun & BHs 11-4.
Manchester United Museum & Tour Centre
M16 0RA
tours@manutd.co.uk   ☎0870 442 1994
(2m from city centre, off A56)
Open daily 9.30-5 (open until 30 mins before kick off on Match Days). (Closed some days over Xmas & New Year)
* Stadium tour & Museum: £9 (ch & pen £6) Family ticket £25. Museum only: £5.50 (ch & pen £3.75) Family ticket £15.50.
Museum of Science and Industry in Manchester
M3 4FP
marketing@msim.org.uk   ☎0161 832 2244
(follow brown tourist signs from city centre)
Open all year, daily 10-5. Last admission 4.30.
(Closed 24-26 Dec).
Urbis M4 3BG
info@urbis.org.uk   ☎0161 907 9099
Open all year daily 10-6
SALFORD
The Lowry M50 3AZ
info@thelowry.com   ☎0870 787 5774
(from M60 take junct 12 for M602. Salford Quays is 0.25m from junct 3 of the M602, follow Lowry signs) Open daily from 10am Galleries, Sun-Fri from 11, Sat from 10. (Closed 25 Dec).
WIGAN
*Wigan Pie*r WN3 4EF
wiganpier@wlct.org   ☎01942 323666
(follow brown tourist signs from M6 junct 25-27 / M61 junct 6-8)
Open all year, Mon-Thu 10-5; Sat & Sun 11-5.(Closed every Fri ex Good Fri, 25-26 Dec, 1 Jan). *£8.50 (concessions £6.25). Site ticket £23.50 (2 ad & 2 concessions).

England

Babies Welcome | **Family Rooms** | **Children's Dishes**

★★★ 68% Cresta Court

Church St WA14 4DP
☎ 0161 927 7272 📠 0161 929 6548
e-mail: stewart5738@btconnect.com
web: www.cresta-court.co.uk

CHILD FACILITIES: Baby listening Activities: activity pack (on request) Family area Food/bottle warming Ch menu Ch portions Highchairs Ch discounts under 16s sharing free Safe grounds Cots Family rms Laundry **NEARBY:** Park Gardens Old Trafford Safari park Boat trips

This modern hotel enjoys a prime location on the A56, close to the station and town centre shops and amenities. Bedrooms vary in style from spacious four-posters to smaller, traditionally furnished rooms. Public areas include a choice of bars, a small gym, beauty salon and extensive function facilities.

ROOMS: 136 en suite (8 fmly) ⊗ in 80 bedrooms s £49-£69; d £49-£69 **LB FACILITIES:** STV ℞ Solarium Gym ⚓ Beauty salon/fitness & cardiovascular training room ♫ Xmas **PARKING:** 200 **NOTES:** ⊗ in restaurant

◆◆◆ Broomfield Hotel

33-35 Wigan Rd, Deane BL3 5PX
☎ 01204 61570 📠 01204 650932
e-mail: chris@broomfield.force9.net
Dir: M61 J5, take A58 to 1st set lights, straight on A676, hotel on R

CHILD FACILITIES: Please telephone for details

A friendly relaxed atmosphere prevails at this hotel conveniently located close to the motorway and west of the town centre. The bedrooms, some suitable for families, are equipped with modern facilities. Public areas include a bar, a lounge and a dining room, which offers good-value dinners and hearty breakfasts.

ROOMS: 20 en suite (2 fmly) (2 GF) s £36-£40; d £50 * ⊗ in 4 bedrooms **FACILITIES:** TVB tea/coffee TVL Pool Table 3/4 Snooker table & darts Dinner Last d order 8.30pm **NOTES:** ⊗ in restaurant Licensed Cen ht **PARKING:** 12

Babies Welcome | **Family Rooms** | **Children's Dishes**

◆◆◆ 🐄 Needhams

Uplands Rd, Werneth Low, Gee Cross SK14 3AG
☎ 0161 368 4610 📠 0161 367 9106
e-mail: charlotte@needhamsfarm.co.uk
Dir: A560 at Gee Cross turn into Joel Lane, left at top of hill (Werneth Low Rd), 0.5m. Uplands Rd on right

CHILD FACILITIES: Food/bottle warming Ch menu Ch portions Highchairs Ch cutlery Ch discounts Safe grounds Cots Family rms D rm with 1/2 S bed or cot Ch drinks **NEARBY:** Country park Cinema Science museum

This old stone-built farmhouse has been extensively restored to provide modern accommodation. The bedrooms are well-equipped and include many personal touches. There is an open fire in the spacious lounge/dining room. Home cooking is served by arrangement.

ROOMS: 7 rms (6 en suite) (1 fmly) ⊗ **FACILITIES:** TVB tea/coffee Direct dial from bedrooms TVL Golf 12 Riding 30 acres Non working Dinner Last d order 8pm **NOTES:** ⊗ in restaurant Licensed Cen ht **PARKING:** 14

Babies Welcome | **Children's Dishes**

★★★★★ 72% ⊛ ⊛

The Lowry Hotel

50 Dearmans Place, Chapel Wharf, Salford
M3 5LH
☎ 0161 827 4000 📠 0161 827 4001
e-mail: enquiries@thelowryhotel.com
web: www.roccofortehotels.com
Dir: M6 junct 19, A556 & M56 follow signs for Manchester. A5103 for 4.5m. At rdbt take A57(M) to lights & turn right onto Water St . Left to New Quay St/Trinity Way. At 1st lights turn right onto Chapel St to Hotel

CHILD FACILITIES: Baby listening Nanny (by prior arrangement) Babysitting (by prior arrangement) Activities: colouring Food/bottle warming Ch menu Ch portions Highchairs Ch discounts £25 extra bed, cots free Videos Cots Connecting rms Fridge Laundry Changing mats

This modern hotel, set beside the River Irwell in the centre of the city, offers well-equipped spacious bedrooms. Many of the rooms look out over the river, as do the sumptuous suites. The River Room restaurant produces good brasserie cooking. Extensive function facilities are available, together with a spa to provide extra pampering.

ROOMS: 165 en suite (7 fmly) ⊗ in 90 bedrooms s fr £189; d fr £214 **LB FACILITIES:** STV Sauna Gym Spa facilities & swimming available offsite ♫ Xmas **PARKING:** 100 **NOTES:** ✹

★★★★ 68% *The Palace*

Oxford St M60 7HA
☎ 0161 288 1111 📠 0161 288 2222
web: www.principal-hotels.com
Dir: opposite Oxford Rd Railway Station

CHILD FACILITIES: Please telephone for details

Formerly the offices of the Refuge Life Assurance Company, this impressive neo-Gothic building occupies a central location. There is a vast lobby, spacious open-plan bar-lounge and restaurant and extensive function facilities. Bedrooms vary in size and style and are all spacious and well equipped.

ROOMS: 252 en suite (59 fmly) ⊗ in 30 bedrooms **FACILITIES:** STV ♫ **NOTES:** ✹ ⊗ in restaurant

Babies Welcome | **Family Rooms** | **Children's Dishes**

★★★ 68%

Novotel Manchester Centre

21 Dickinson St M1 4LX
☎ 0161 235 2200 📠 0161 235 2210
e-mail: H3145@accor-hotels.com
Dir: from Oxford St, into Portland St, left into Dickinson St. Hotel located on right

CHILD FACILITIES: Activities: Indoor play area Food/bottle warming Ch menu Ch portions Highchairs Ch discounts under 16s free sharing with parents Games consoles Cots Family rms D rms with S beds Connecting rms Laundry **NEARBY:** Cinema Museum Laser Quest Urbis

This smart, modern property enjoys a central location convenient for theatres, shops and Manchester's business district. Spacious bedrooms are thoughtfully equipped and brightly decorated. Open plan, contemporary public areas include an all day restaurant and a stylish bar.

ROOMS: 164 en suite (60 fmly) ⊗ in 123 bedrooms s fr £103; d fr £103 **LB FACILITIES:** STV Sauna Gym Steam room

◆◆◆ *Victoria Park Hotel*

4 Park Crescent, Victoria Park M14 5RE
☎ 0161 224 1399 0161 224 2219 📠 0161 225 4949
e-mail: vph.manchester@claranet.co.uk
Dir: A6010 to B5117 Park Cres directly off Wilmslow Rd

CHILD FACILITIES: Please telephone for details

A large Victorian house situated in a quiet crescent close to the city centre, university buildings and hospitals. Bedrooms are simply furnished and there is a comfortable guest lounge. A vegetarian continental breakfast is served in the attractive dining room. No alcohol is allowed on the premises.

ROOMS: 20 rms (19 en suite) (5 fmly) (4 GF) ⊗ in 14 bedrooms
FACILITIES: tea/coffee Direct dial from bedrooms **NOTES:** ✟ ⊗ in restaurant ⊗ in lounges Cen ht **PARKING:** 40

MANCHESTER AIRPORT　　　　　Map 07 SJ88

★★★★ 69%
Manchester Airport Marriott

Hale Rd, Hale Barns WA15 8XW
☎ 0161 904 0301 📠 0161 980 1787
e-mail: manchesterairportmarriott@whitbread.com

CHILD FACILITIES: Please telephone for details

With good airport links and convenient access to the thriving city, this sprawling modern hotel is a popular destination. The hotel offers leisure facilities, a choice of eating and drinking options and ample car parking. Bedrooms are situated around a courtyard.

ROOMS: 215 en suite (22 fmly) ⊗ in 160 bedrooms s £80-£129;
d £84-£129 **LB FACILITIES:** Spa STV ⊠ Sauna Solarium Gym Jacuzzi
PARKING: 400 **NOTES:** ✟ ⊗ in restaurant

★★★ 67% Bewley's Hotel Manchester Airport

Outwood Ln M90 4HL
☎ 0161 498 0333 📠 0161 498 0222
e-mail: man@bewleyshotels.com
web: www.bewleyshotels.com/man_index.asp
Dir: at Manchester Airport. Follow signs to Manchester Airport Terminal 3. Hotel on left on Terminal 3 rdbt.

CHILD FACILITIES: Please telephone for details

Located adjacent to the airport this modern, stylish hotel is ideal for air travellers and families alike. All bedrooms are spacious and well equipped and include a wing of newly-built superior rooms. Open-plan day rooms continue the contemporary theme.

ROOMS: 226 en suite ⊗ in 158 bedrooms s £59; d £59
FACILITIES: STV **PARKING:** 120 **NOTES:** ✟

◆◆◆ Rylands Farm

Altrincham Rd SK9 4LT
☎ 01625 535646 & 548041 📠 01625 255256
e-mail: info@rylandsfarm.com
web: www.rylandsfarm.com
Dir: M56 junct 6 take A538 towards Wilmslow. Guest house 1.5m on left.

continued

CHILD FACILITIES: Please telephone for details

Situated in pretty gardens and convenient for Manchester Airport, this property provides a range of bedrooms, some of which are well furnished and located in a separate building. Breakfast is taken in an attractive conservatory dining room, which also contains a comfortable lounge area.

ROOMS: 3 en suite 6 annexe en suite (3 fmly) (3 GF) s £42.50-£45;
d £49.50-£54.50 * **FACILITIES:** TV6B tea/coffee TVL No coaches
NOTES: ✟ ⊗ Licensed Cen ht **PARKING:** 15

OLDHAM　　　　　Map 07 SD90

Babies Welcome	Family Rooms	Children's Dishes

◆◆◆◆ 🍴 Mallons Restaurant with Guest Rooms

792-794 Huddersfield Rd, Austerlands OL4 3QB
☎ 0161 622 1234 📠 0161 622 1234
Dir: A62 Oldham to Huddersfield road, 2m from Oldham on Sadleworth border

CHILD FACILITIES: Please telephone for details

Situated a couple of miles from the town centre with good views of the surrounding hills, this restaurant with rooms offers a wide choice of modern style dishes and good honest hospitality. Stylish bedrooms are modern, well equipped and comfortably furnished. There is also a garden with decking at the rear.

ROOMS: 5 rms (4 en suite) (1 fmly) s £40-£47; d £65 * ⊗
FACILITIES: TVB tea/coffee No coaches Solarium Dinner Last d order 10pm **NOTES:** ✟ ⊗ in restaurant ⊗ in 1 lounge Licensed Cen ht
PARKING: 22

WORSLEY　　　　　Map 07 SD70

Babies Welcome	Family Rooms	Children's Dishes

★★★ 63%
Novotel Manchester West

Worsley Brow M28 2YA
☎ 0161 799 3535 📠 0161 703 8207
e-mail: H0907@accor-hotels.com
Dir: adjacent to M60 junct 13

CHILD FACILITIES: Activities: welcome bag Indoor play area
Outdoor play area Food/bottle warming Ch menu Ch portions
Highchairs Ch discounts under 16s free when sharing with parents
Safe grounds Games consoles Cots Family rms D rms with S beds
Connecting rms Laundry **NEARBY:** MUFC Camelot theme park
Shire horse centre Aquarium

Well-placed for access to the Peak and Lake Districts, as well as the thriving city of Manchester, this modern hotel successfully caters for both families and business guests. Spacious bedrooms all have sofa beds and a large work area, and the hotel also boasts an outdoor swimming pool and children's play area.

ROOMS: 119 en suite (4 fmly) **FACILITIES:** STV ⚲ **PARKING:** 140

HAMPSHIRE

Southsea Castle

ANDOVER

Finkley Down Farm Park SP11 6NF
admin@finkleydownfarm.co.uk ☎01264 352195
(Signposted from A303 & A343, 1.5m N of A303
and 2m E of Andover)
Open mid Mar-Oct, daily 10-6. Last admission
5pm. *£4.75, ch £3.75, pen £4.25. Family ticket
£16, 2 ad & 2ch.

BASINGSTOKE

Milestones - Hampshire's Living History Museum
RG21 6YR ☎01256 477766
jane.holmes@hants.gov.uk
(M3 junct 6, take ringway road West and follow
signs for Leisure Park)
Open Tue-Fri & BHs 10-5, Sat-Sun 11-5 Closed
24-26 Dec & 1 Jan. *£6.50, ch £3.50, concessions
£5.75. Family ticket 2 adults & 2 ch £16.50.
Group discounts 15+.

BEAULIEU

Beaulieu: National Motor Museum
SO42 7ZN ☎01590 612345
info@beaulieu.co.uk
(M27 junct 2, A326, B3054, then follow tourist
signs)
Open all year - Palace House & Gardens,
National Motor Museum, Beaulieu Abbey &
Exhibition of Monastic Life. Open May-Sep 10-6;
Oct-Apr 10-5. Closed 25 Dec.
*£15, ch 5-12 £7.50, 12-17 £8.50, pen £13.50.
Family ticket £42.

GOSPORT

Explosion! Museum of Naval Firepower
PO12 4LE ☎023 9250 5600
info@explosion.org.uk
(A32 and follow signs)
Open all year, Apr-Oct & all school hols, daily 10-
5.30; Nov-Mar, Thurs Sat/Sun 10-4.30. Closed
24-26 Dec.
*£5, ch £3.50, pen £4.50 Family ticket £15

LYNDHURST

New Forest Museum & Visitor Centre
SO43 7NY ☎023 8028 3444
office@newforestmuseum.org.uk
(Leave M27 at Cadnam & follow A337 to
Lyndhurst. Museum signposted)
Open daily, from 10am. Closed 25 & 26 Dec.

MARWELL

Marwell Zoological Park
SO21 1JH ☎01962 777407
marwell@marwell.org.uk
(M3 junct 11 or M27 junct 5. Zoo on B2177, follow
brown tourist signs)
Open all year, daily ex 25 Dec, 10-6 in summer,
10-4 in winter. Last admission 90 mins before
closing.
*£11.50 ch £8, pen £9.50 Family ticket 2 ad & 2
ch £37.50.

OWER

Paultons Park SO51 6AL
info@paultons.co.uk ☎023 8081 4442
(Exit M27 junct 2, near junct A31 & A36)
Open mid Mar-Oct, daily 10-6; Nov & Dec, wknds
only until Xmas.
*£13.50, ch under 14. Children under 1m tall enter
for free. Range of Family Supersavers.

PORTSMOUTH

Blue Reef Aquarium
PO5 3PB ☎023 9287 5222
portsmouth@bluereefaquarium.co.uk
(Follow brown tourist signs)
Open daily from 10am. Closing times vary with
season, please telephone for details.
*£5.95, pen £4.95, ch 3-16 £3.95

Portsmouth Historic Dockyard
PO1 3LJ ☎023 9287 0999
mail@historicdockyard.co.uk
(Follow brown historic ships sign from M27/M275)
Open all year, Apr-Oct, daily 10-5; Nov-Mar,
daily 10-5. Closed 25 Dec. All inclusive ticket:
£15.50 (ch & pen £12.50, under 5's free) Family
£45.

RINGWOOD

Moors Valley Country Park
BH242ET ☎01425 470721
mvalley@eastdorsetdc.gov.uk
(1.5m from Ashley Heath rdbt on A31 near Three
Legged Cross)
Open all year ex 25 Dec, 8-dusk. Visitor centre
open 9.30-4.30, later in summer. *No admission
charge but parking up to £5 per day.

WEYHILL

The Hawk Conservancy and Country Park
SP11 8DY ☎01264 772252
info@hawk-conservancy.org
(3m W of Andover, signposted from A303)
Open Feb half-term-Oct half-term, daily from
10.30 last admission 4pm.
*£7.25, ch £4.65, pen & student £6.70. Family
ticket £23.

WINCHESTER

INTECH - Hampshire Technology Centre
SO21 1HX ☎01962 863791
htct@intech-uk.com
(On B3404; Alresford road)
Open daily 10-4. Closed Xmas & 1 Jan
*£5.95, pen £3.75, ch £4.30

🍺 The Globe on the Lake
The Soke, Broad St SO24 9DB
☎ 01962 732294 📠 01962 736211
e-mail: duveen-conway@supanet.com
Dir: Telephone for directions

CHILD FACILITIES: Please telephone for details

OPEN: 11-3 Summer Sat-Sun all day 6-11 Winter Sun 12-8 Closed: 25-26 Dec **BAR MEALS:** L served all week 12-2 D served all week 6.30-9.30 Av main course £8.25 **RESTAURANT:** L served all week 12-2 D served all week 6.30-9 **FACILITIES:** Garden: Large lakeside garden ✈

Children's Dishes

🍺 Wyke Down Country Pub & Restaurant
Wyke Down, Picket Piece SP11 6LX

CHILD FACILITIES: Outdoor play area Ch menu Ch portions Highchairs (booster seats) Safe grounds NEARBY: Farm Park

OPEN: 12-3 6-11 Closed: Christmas Day, Boxing Day **BAR MEALS:** L served all week 12-2 D served all week 6-9 Av main course £7 **RESTAURANT:** L served all week 12-2 D served all week 6-9 Av 3 course à la carte £21 **FACILITIES:** Garden: Enclosed area with bench seating **PARKING:** 90

♦♦♦ Crossings Cottage
Lyndhurst Rd SO42 7RL
☎ 01590 622478
e-mail: lisa@crossings-brockenhurst.co.uk
Dir: in centre of village just before rail crossing and opposite cycle hire shop

CHILD FACILITIES: Please telephone for details

Crossings is centrally situated for the town, and is aptly named due to its close proximity to the station and level crossing. Guests can be sure of a warm welcome from the friendly proprietor. Rooms are comfortably furnished and equipped. Full English breakfasts are served at individual tables.

ROOMS: 3 rms s £35-£40; d £44-£50 * **FACILITIES:** TVB tea/coffee No coaches **NOTES:** Credit cards not taken ✈ ⊗ Cen ht **LB PARKING:** 2

♦♦♦♦ 🍺 The Compasses
Damerham SP6 3HQ
☎ 01725 518231 📠 01725 518880
e-mail: info@compassesinn.net
Dir: centre of Fordingbridge at mini rdbt take rd marked Sandleheath/Damerham, 3m to Damerham. On left after garage

CHILD FACILITIES: Please telephone for details

This friendly, 400-year-old traditional inn enjoys a peaceful village location just three miles from Fordingbridge and is an ideal base for exploring this delightful area. The comfortable bedrooms are pleasantly furnished and well-equipped. Tasty meals are available at both lunch and dinner. Two self-catering units will be available in 2004.

ROOMS: 6 en suite (1 fmly) s £39.50-£45; d £69-£80 * **FACILITIES:** TVB tea/coffee Direct dial from bedrooms Pool Table Large garden & bar games Dinner Last d order 9.30pm **NOTES:** ⊗ in restaurant ⊗ in 1 lounge Cen ht **LB PARKING:** 30

Babies Welcome | Children's Dishes

🍺 The Royal Oak
SO41 0LA
☎ 01590 642297 📠 01590 641798
e-mail: enquiries@oakdownton.freeuk.com
Dir: Situated on A337 between Lymington & Christchurch.

CHILD FACILITIES: Food/bottle warming Ch menu Ch portions Highchairs NEARBY: Beaulieu Motor Museum New Forest Near sea

OPEN: 11.30-2.30 6-11 **BAR MEALS:** L served all week 12-2 D served all week 6-9.00 Av main course £9.50 **RESTAURANT:** 12-2 D served all week 6-9 Av 3 course à la carte £20 Av 3 course fixed price £14.50 **FACILITIES:** Garden: Large grassed area, picnic tables & umbrellas **PARKING:** 40

Babies Welcome | Children's Dishes

🍺 The Queen Inn
Down St RG25 2AD
☎ 01256 397367 📠 01256 397601
Dir: from M3 J7, follow signs to Dummer

CHILD FACILITIES: Outdoor play area Food/bottle warming Ch menu Ch portions Highchairs Safe grounds

OPEN: 11.30-2.30 6-11 (Sun 12-3 7-10.30) **BAR MEALS:** L served all week 12-2.30 D served all week 6-9.30 **RESTAURANT:** L served all week 12-1.30 D served all week 6-9.30 **FACILITIES:** Garden: Benches, tables, chairs ✈ **PARKING:** 20

Family Rooms | Children's Dishes

🏨 ⊛⊛⊛ 36 on the Quay
47 South St PO10 7EG
☎ 01243 375592 372257

CHILD FACILITIES: Baby listening Food/bottle warming Ch menu (on request) Ch portions Ch discounts under 5s free Safe grounds Family rms D rms with 2 S beds Ch drinks (on request) NEARBY: Animal park Walks

Occupying a prime position on the Quay with far reaching views over the estuary, this 16th-century house is the scene for the proprietor's accomplished and exciting cuisine. As would be expected the elegant restaurant occupies centre stage with peaceful pastel shades and crisp napery together with glimpses of the bustling harbour outside. The smart bedrooms offer style, comfort and thoughtful extras.

ROOMS: 4 en suite s £60-£85; d £85-£120 (incl. bkfst) **PARKING:** 6 **NOTES:** ⊗ in restaurant Closed 3wks Jan, 1wk Oct

♦♦♦ Travelrest-Avenue House Hotel
22 The Avenue PO14 1NS
☎ 01329 232175 📠 01329 232196
Dir: on A27, 0.5m from town centre, 500mtrs from railway station

CHILD FACILITIES: Please telephone for details

Conveniently situated just west of the town centre, this well-presented hotel is ideally located for the continental ferry terminals and naval heritage sites. The comfortable bedrooms are

continued on p144

FAREHAM, continued

spacious, attractive and well-equipped and one has a four-poster bed. Breakfast is served in the cosy conservatory dining room.
ROOMS: 19 en suite (3 fmly) (6 GF) s £45-£53; d £50-£62.50 * ⊗ in 10 bedrooms **FACILITIES:** TVB tea/coffee Direct dial from bedrooms Landscaped garden **NOTES:** ⊗ in restaurant ⊗ in lounges Cen ht **PARKING:** 27

FORDINGBRIDGE
Map 04 SU11

Babies Welcome	Family Rooms	Children's Dishes

◆◆◆◆◆ ◉ ◉ ◉ 🏆 🍴 The Three Lions
Stuckton SP6 2HF
☎ 01425 652489 📠 01425 656144
e-mail: the3lions@btinternet.com
Dir: 0.5m E of Fordingbridge from A338 or B3078. At Q8 garage follow Three Lions tourist signs

> **CHILD FACILITIES:** Baby listening Outdoor play area Food/bottle warming Ch menu Ch portions Highchairs Ch cutlery Ch discounts Safe grounds Videos Cots Family rms Ch drinks
> **NEARBY:** Paultons Park Moors Valley Country Park Walks

Set in a quiet hamlet near to Fordingbridge, this charming and friendly inn offers high levels of comfort and quality. Well-equipped bedrooms and a locally popular and award-winning restaurant combine to make this a delightful place to stay. There is an attractive garden complete with hot tub in which to relax.
ROOMS: 3 en suite (1 fmly) ⊗ **FACILITIES:** TV4B tea/coffee No coaches Sauna Whirlpool spa in garden Dinner Last d order 9.45pm **NOTES:** ⊗ in restaurant Cen ht **PARKING:** 50

◆◆◆ 🍴 The Fighting Cocks
Godshill SP6 2LL
☎ 01425 652462 📠 01425 652462
Dir: From M27 junct 1 follow signs to Fordingbridge for approx 6m, pub just before cattlegrid on right

> **CHILD FACILITIES:** Please telephone for details

Ideally located for walkers and cyclists on a day out in the New Forest, this friendly inn is situated in the village of Godshill with views across adjoining heathland. Bedrooms and comfortably furnished and equipped. Light snacks and meals are available from noon till late in the various bar areas.
ROOMS: 3 en suite (2 fmly) s £40-£75; d £70-£75 * ⊗
FACILITIES: TVB tea/coffee Pool Table Dinner Last d order 10pm **NOTES:** ✈ ⊗ in area of dining room Cen ht **PARKING:** 50

LYMINGTON
Map 04 SZ39

Babies Welcome	Family Rooms	Children's Dishes

★★★ 72% Elmers Court
South Baddesley Rd SO41 5ZB
☎ 01590 676011 📠 01590 679780
e-mail: elmerscourt@macdonald-hotels.co.uk
Dir: M27 junct 1, through Lyndhurst, Brockenhurst & Lymington, hotel 200yds right after Lymington ferry terminal

MACDONALD HOTELS

> **CHILD FACILITIES:** Babysitting Activities: children's club, games, colouring Outdoor play area Food/bottle warming Ch menu Ch portions Highchairs Ch discounts under 4s free, over 4s £20 Safe grounds Videos Cots Family rms D rm plus rm with B beds, D rm with D sofa bed from £150 Connecting rms Fridge Laundry
> **NEARBY:** Paultons Park Marwell Zoo Moors Valley Country Park Leisure World

Originally known as The Elms, this Tudor-gabled manor house dates back to the 1820s. Ideally located at the edge of the New
continued

Forest and overlooking The Solent with views towards the Isle of Wight, the hotel offers suites and self-catering accommodation, along with well-appointed leisure facilities.

ROOMS: 42 annexe en suite (8 fmly) (22 GF) ⊗ in 16 bedrooms s £82-£105; d £144-£170 (incl. bkfst) **LB FACILITIES: Spa** 🏊 🕴 ❊ Squash Sauna Solarium Gym 🏋 ⛵ Jacuzzi Beauty treatment rooms,, Steam room, Aerobics classes 🎵 Xmas **PARKING:** 100 **NOTES:** ✈ ⊗ in restaurant

---

LYNDHURST
Map 04 SU30

◆◆◆◆ Heather House Hotel
Southampton Rd SO43 7BQ
☎ 023 8028 4409 📠 023 8028 4431
e-mail: enquiries@heatherhouse.co.uk
web: www.heatherhouse.co.uk
Dir: from A31/junct1 M27 take A337 to Lyndhurst. At lights in centre of village turn left, establishment approx 800yds on left

> **CHILD FACILITIES:** Please telephone for details

Located on the edge of town with views over the New Forest, this impressive double-fronted Edwardian house is set in its own attractive gardens. Bedrooms are comfortably appointed and include rooms suitable for families. Breakfast is served in the pleasant, tastefully furnished dining room.
ROOMS: 11 en suite (1 GF) ⊗ **FACILITIES:** TVB tea/coffee Direct dial from bedrooms TVL Dinner **NOTES:** ✈ ⊗ in restaurant Licensed Cen ht **PARKING:** 15

Babies Welcome	Family Rooms	Children's Dishes

◆◆◆◆ Penny Farthing Hotel
Romsey Rd SO43 7AA
☎ 023 80284422 📠 023 80284488
e-mail: stay@pennyfarthinghotel.co.uk
web: www.pennyfarthinghotel.co.uk
Dir: from M27 junct 1 follow A337, hotel on left as coming into village

> **CHILD FACILITIES:** Food/bottle warming Ch portions Highchairs Cots Family rms D rm with adjoining B bed rm £125 Connecting rms **NEARBY:** New Forest Theme park Dairy farm

This well-appointed, friendly hotel on the edge of town is ideally situated for guests wishing exploring the New Forest and local
continued

attractions. Bedrooms are well-equipped and attractively decorated with some located in an adjacent cottage. There is a spacious breakfast room, a comfortable lounge bar and a bicycle store.
ROOMS: 16 en suite 4 annexe en suite (2 fmly) (3 GF) s £59-£78; d £78-£98 * ⊗ **FACILITIES:** TVB tea/coffee Direct dial from bedrooms TVL No coaches **NOTES:** ✈ ⊗ in restaurant ⊗ in 1 lounge Licensed Cen ht **PARKING:** 23

Babies Welcome | Family Rooms | Children's Dishes

♦♦♦♦ Whitemoor House Hotel

Southampton Rd SO43 7BU
☎ 023 8028 2186
e-mail: whitemoor@aol.com
web: www.whitemoorhotel.co.uk
Dir: entering town from E on A35, hotel on right just past golf course and 40mph signs.

CHILD FACILITIES: Activities: games, puzzles Food/bottle warming Ch menu Ch portions Highchairs Ch discounts under 2s free, then £1 per year of age Cots Family rms D rm with S and Z bed Ch drinks NEARBY: Theme park Activity farm Otter and owl sanctuary

A warm welcome is assured at this non-smoking hotel, which has the New Forest on its doorstep and provides an excellent base from which to explore the area. Bedrooms are comfortable and brightly decorated. There is a cosy lounge where drinks can be enjoyed and tasty dinners are served by prior arrangement (except Sundays).
ROOMS: 8 en suite (1 fmly) s £38-£45; d £62-£80 * **FACILITIES:** TVB tea/coffee Direct dial from bedrooms No coaches Dinner Last d order 5pm **NOTES:** ✈ ⊗ Licensed Cen ht LB **PARKING:** 8

♦♦♦ *Clarendon Villa*

Gosport Ln SO43 7BL
☎ 023 80282803 🖷 023 80284303
e-mail: clarendonvilla@i12.com
web: www.clarendonvilla.i12.com
Dir: behind New Forest Visitor Information Centre, next to Gosport Lane entrance to car park

CHILD FACILITIES: Please telephone for details

This centrally located guesthouse provides guests with a warm and friendly environment from which to explore the New Forest. The bedroom available is bright, airy and neatly appointed, and has a fridge, video and a library of films. A cooked breakfast is served in your room at a time of your choice.
ROOMS: 3 en suite (1 fmly) **FACILITIES:** TVB tea/coffee No coaches **NOTES:** ✈ ⊗ Cen ht **PARKING:** 3

MAPLEDURWELL — Map 04 SU65

Babies Welcome | Children's Dishes

The Gamekeepers

Tunworth Rd RG25 2LU
☎ 01256 322038 🖷 01256 322038
e-mail: phil_costello64@hotmail.com
Dir: 3m from J6 M3. Turn R at the Hatch pub on A30 towards Hook. Gamekeepers is signposted

CHILD FACILITIES: Food/bottle warming Ch menu Ch portions Highchairs Ch cutlery Safe grounds NEARBY: Walks Parks Cinema

OPEN: 12-3 6-11 **BAR MEALS:** L served all week 12-2.30 D served all week 6.30-9.30 Av main course £10.75 **RESTAURANT:** L served all week 12-2.30 D served all week 6.30-9.30 Av 3 course à la carte £21.50 **FACILITIES:** Garden: Large, secluded garden area **PARKING:** 50

OVINGTON — Map 04 SU53

Children's Dishes

The Bush

SO24 0RE
☎ 01962 732764 🖷 01962 735130
e-mail: thebushinn@wadworth.co.uk
Dir: A31 from Winchester, E to Alton & Farnham, approx 6m turn L off dual carriageway to Ovington. 0.5m to pub

CHILD FACILITIES: Food/bottle warming Ch menu Ch portions (limited) NEARBY: Walks

OPEN: 11-3 6-11 (Sun 12-3, 7-10.30) Closed: Dec 25 **BAR MEALS:** L served all week 12-2 D served Mon-Sat 6.30-9.30 Av main course £13.50 **FACILITIES:** Garden: Pretty, alongside river **PARKING:** 40

OWSLEBURY — Map 04 SU52

Children's Dishes

The Ship Inn

Whites Hill SO21 1LT
☎ 01962 777358 🖷 01962 777458
e-mail: theshipinn@freeuk.com
Dir: M3 J11 take B3335 follow signs for Owslebury

CHILD FACILITIES: Activities: bouncy castle Outdoor play area Food/bottle warming Ch menu Ch portions Safe grounds Changing facilities NEARBY: Marwell Zoological Park

OPEN: 11-3 (Sun 12-10.30, Sat Apr-Sep 11-11) 6-11 (Jul-Aug 11-11 all week) **BAR MEALS:** L served all week 12-2 D served all week 6.30-9.30 Av main course £9 **RESTAURANT:** L served all week 12-2 D served all week 6.30-9.30 Av 3 course à la carte £18 **FACILITIES:** Garden: Garden with pond, horse park **PARKING:** 50

PORTSMOUTH — Map 04 SU60

Babies Welcome | Family Rooms | Children's Dishes

★★★★ 65%

Portsmouth Marriott Hotel

Marriott HOTELS · RESORTS · SUITES

Southampton Rd PO6 4SH
☎ 0870 400 7285 🖷 0870 400 7385
e-mail: reservations.portsmouth@marriotthotels.com
Dir: M27 junct 12 keep left and hotel on left

CHILD FACILITIES: Activities: entertainment in school hols Food/bottle warming Ch menu Ch portions Highchairs Ch discounts children free when sharing Safe grounds Games consoles Cots Family rms D rms with S beds Ch drinks Connecting rms Fridge Laundry NEARBY: Cinema Historic dockyard Fun fair 10 min to sea

Close to the motorway and ferry port, this hotel is well suited to all kinds of guests. The comfortable and well laid-out bedrooms provide a comprehensive range of facilities including up-to-date

continued on p146

PORTSMOUTH, continued

workstations. The leisure club offers a pool, a gym, and a health and beauty salon.
ROOMS: 174 en suite (77 fmly) ⊛ in 130 bedrooms s £67-£155; d £84-£185 **FACILITIES:** STV ⊡ Sauna Solarium Gym Jacuzzi Exercise studio, Beauty salon Xmas **PARKING:** 250

Babies Welcome	Family Rooms	Children's Dishes

♦♦♦♦ Hamilton House
95 Victoria Rd North, Southsea PO5 1PS
☎ 023 9282 3502 ▤ 023 9282 3502
e-mail: sandra@hamiltonhouse.co.uk
web: www.hamiltonhouse.co.uk
Dir: M275 junct 12 into Portsmouth, past ferry port, at rdbt take 1st exit & follow road to right, then to left, cross 3 rdbts. 0.5m into Victoria Rd N

CHILD FACILITIES: Food/bottle warming Ch portions Highchairs Ch cutlery Ch discounts when sharing with 2 adults Cots Family rms 4 rms with D & S bed, 1 D rm with up to 3 S beds & Z bed £63-£100 **NEARBY:** Historic dockyard Aquarium Fun fair Swimming pool Short walk to sea

This spacious Victorian property, carefully renovated by Graham and Sandra Tubb, provides bright, comfortable accommodation with many thoughtful extra facilities. The property is well located for exploring historic Portsmouth and is close to the University. A full cooked breakfast is available from 6.15am for those catching the cross channel ferry. Easy street parking is available.
ROOMS: 9 rms (5 en suite) (3 fmly) s £40-£50; d £48-£60
FACILITIES: TVB tea/coffee TVL **NOTES:** ✖ ⊛ Cen ht

ROCKBOURNE   Map 04 SU11

Children's Dishes

🍴 The Rose & Thistle
SP6 3NL
☎ 01725 518236
e-mail: enquiries@roseandthistle.co.uk
Dir: Rockbourne is signposted from B3078 and from A354

CHILD FACILITIES: Food/bottle warming Ch licence Ch portions **NEARBY:** Walks New Forest

OPEN: 11-3 6-11 Oct-Apr closed Sun from 8 **BAR MEALS:** L served all week 12-2.30 D served all week 6.30-9.30 Av main course £12
RESTAURANT: L served all week 12-2.30 D served all week 6.30-9.30 Av 3 course à la carte £18 **FACILITIES:** Children's licence Garden: An English country garden ✖ **PARKING:** 28

Babies Welcome	This symbol indicates the establishment provides food & bottle warming and highchairs

ROMSEY   Map 04 SU32

⊛ Bertie's
80 The Hundred SO51 8BX
☎ 01794 830708 ▤ 01794 507507
e-mail: sales@berties.co.uk
web: www.berties.co.uk
Dir: 200yds from Broadlands' gate in town centre

CHILD FACILITIES: Please telephone for details

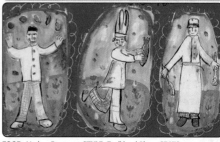

FOOD: Modern European **STYLE:** Traditional Bistro **SEATS:** 34
OPEN: 12-2.30/7-10, Closed 26-30 Dec, Sun **RESTAURANT:** Fixed L £11.95, Fixed D £14.95, main £9.95-£18.95 **NOTES:** ⊛ area **PARKING:** 10

ROTHERWICK   Map 04 SU75

Babies Welcome	Family Rooms	Children's Dishes

★★★★ ⊛ ⊛ ⚜ Tylney Hall
RG27 9AZ
☎ 01256 764881 ▤ 01256 768141
e-mail: sales@tylneyhall.com
web: www.tylneyhall.com
Dir: M3 junct 5, A287 to Basingstoke, over junct with A30, over railway bridge, towards Newnham. Right at Newnham Green. Hotel 1m on left

CHILD FACILITIES: Baby listening Babysitting Activities: swimming pools Food/bottle warming Ch menu Ch portions Highchairs Ch cutlery Ch discounts cots free, extra bed £30 Safe grounds Cots Family rms £325-430 Connecting rms Laundry **NEARBY:** Bird sanctuary Zoo

A superb Grade II listed Victorian country house, set in 66 acres of beautiful parkland. The hotel offers very high standards of comfort in relaxed yet elegant surroundings, featuring magnificently restored water gardens, which were originally laid out by famous 19th-century gardener, Gertrude Jekyll. The spacious public rooms include the Wedgwood drawing room and panelled Oak Room, which are filled with fresh flowers and warmed by log fires in winter. The spacious bedrooms are traditionally furnished and offer a high degree of comfort.
ROOMS: 35 en suite 77 annexe en suite (1 fmly) s £135-£400; d £165-£430 (incl. bkfst) **LB FACILITIES:** Spa STV ⊡ ⚲ ⚲ Snooker Sauna Solarium Gym ♫ Clay pigeon shooting, Archery, Falconry, Balloon rides, Laser shooting ♫ Xmas **PARKING:** 120 **NOTES:** ✖ ⊛ in restaurant

ROWLAND'S CASTLE   Map 04 SU71

Babies Welcome | **Family Rooms** | **Children's Dishes**

◆◆◆◆ The Fountain Inn

34 The Green PO9 6AB
☎ 023 9241 2291 ▤ 023 9241 2291
e-mail: Fountaininn@amserve.com
Dir: A3(M) junct 2, follow B2149 for 2m, turn left at rdbt down Redlands Lane. Inn overlooks village green

CHILD FACILITIES: Nanny Babysitting Outdoor play area Food/bottle warming Ch portions Highchairs Ch discounts under 5s free, under 12s sharing £5 Safe grounds Cots Family rms king size with put up bed/cot £65 plus child's cost Ch drinks (on request) **NEARBY:** Children's zoo Fun fair 5m to sea

A charming coaching inn set back from the road and overlooking the village green. The well-equipped bedrooms have been tastefully refurbished and have many thoughtful touches; one room has a lovely four-poster bed. Public areas consist of a popular local bar and a cosy Thai restaurant.
ROOMS: 4 en suite (1 fmly) **FACILITIES:** TVB tea/coffee Dinner Last d order 9.30pm **NOTES:** ⊗ Cen ht **LB**

SOUTHAMPTON   Map 04 SU41

Babies Welcome | **Family Rooms** | **Children's Dishes**

★★★ 65% Novotel Southampton

1 West Quay Rd SO15 1RA
☎ 023 8033 0550 ▤ 023 8022 2158
e-mail: H1073@accor-hotels.com
Dir: M27 junct 3 & signs for City Centre (A33). After 1m take right hand lane for West Quay & Dock Gates 4-10. Hotel entrance on left. Turn at lights by McDonalds, left at rdbt, hotel straight ahead

CHILD FACILITIES: Activities: colouring, puzzles Indoor play area Family area Food/bottle warming Ch menu Ch portions Highchairs Ch cutlery Ch discounts under 16s free sharing with parents Safe grounds Games consoles Cots Family rms from £75 Connecting rms Laundry **NEARBY:** Play park 10-min walk to sea

Modern purpose-built hotel situated close to the city centre, railway station, ferry terminal and major road networks. The brightly decorated bedrooms are ideal for families; four rooms have facilities for the less mobile. The open-plan public areas include the Garden brasserie, a bar and a leisure complex.
ROOMS: 121 en suite (50 fmly) ⊗ in 98 bedrooms s fr £89; d fr £89 **LB FACILITIES:** STV ⊠ Sauna Gym **PARKING:** 300

◆◆◆◆ Alcantara

20 Howard Rd, Shirley SO15 5BN
☎ 023 8033 2966 ▤ 023 8049 6163
e-mail: alcantara@btconnect.com
Dir: M3/A33, follow city centre signs, turn 1st right after Cowherds pub into Northlands Rd, right at T-junct, straight at traffic lights

CHILD FACILITIES: Please telephone for details

A warm welcome is assured at this Victorian property, named after the ocean liner to reflect the establishment's shipping connections and close location to the city centre. The comfortable bedrooms are well decorated and have many thoughtful extras.
ROOMS: 9 rms (6 en suite) (3 fmly) (2 GF) s £26-£34; d £52 *
FACILITIES: TVB tea/coffee No coaches Limited access to nearby leisure facilities **NOTES:** ✖ ⊗ Cen ht **PARKING:** 7

SWAY   Map 04 SZ29

Babies Welcome | **Family Rooms** | **Children's Dishes**

◆◆◆◆ Acorn Shetland Pony Stud

Meadows Cottage, Arnewood Bridge Rd SO41 6DA
☎ 01590 682000 ▤ 01590 682000
e-mail: meadows.cottage@virgin.net
Dir: M27 through Lyndhurst towards Brockenhurst, take B3055 signed Sway, pass Birchy Hill Nursing Home, over x-rds, take 2nd entrance left

CHILD FACILITIES: Baby listening Activities: Food/bottle warming Ch menu Ch portions Highchairs Ch cutlery Ch discounts for under 13s Safe grounds Videos Cots Family rms suite - D rm with T rm Ch drinks Connecting rms Fridge Laundry **NEARBY:** New Forest Theme park Museums 10-min drive to sea

Peacefully located on the outskirts of Sway this comfortable establishment is set in over six acres of pony paddocks and a landscaped water garden. The ground-floor bedrooms are well furnished and have direct access onto patios. The enjoyable breakfasts use a good range of freshly-cooked produce including delicious home-made bread.
ROOMS: 2 en suite (1 fmly) (2 GF) d fr £48 * **FACILITIES:** TVB tea/coffee No coaches Carriage driving **NOTES:** Credit cards not taken ⊗ Cen ht **LB PARKING:** 3

WARSASH   Map 04 SU40

Babies Welcome | **Children's Dishes**

▥ The Jolly Farmer Country Inn

29 Fleet End Rd SO31 9JH
☎ 01489 572500 ▤ 01489 885847
e-mail: mail@thejollyfarmeruk.com
Dir: Exit M27 Jct 9, head towards A27 Fareham, turn R onto Warsash Rd Follow for 2m then L onto Fleet End Rd

CHILD FACILITIES: Activities: colouring books Outdoor play area Family area Food/bottle warming Ch licence Ch menu Ch portions Highchairs Ch cutlery Safe grounds Changing facilities **NEARBY:** Paultons Park Marwell Zoological Park

OPEN: 11-11 **BAR MEALS:** L served all week 12-2.30 D served all week 6-10 Av main course £6.95 **RESTAURANT:** L served all week 12-2.30 D served all week 6-10 Av 3 course à la carte £15 **FACILITIES:** Garden: Large play area **PARKING:** 50

England

WHITCHURCH
Map 04 SU44

🍺 Watership Down Inn
Freefolk Priors RG28 7NJ
☎ 01256 892254
Dir: On B3400 between Basingstoke & Andover

CHILD FACILITIES: Please telephone for details

OPEN: 11.30-3.30 6-11 Rest: 25/26/31 Dec Evening **BAR MEALS:** L served all week 12-2.30 D served all week 6-9.30 Av main course £6.95 **FACILITIES:** Garden: Beer garden, patio, heaters ✖ **PARKING:** 18

WICKHAM
Map 04 SU51

Babies Welcome	Family Rooms	Children's

★★ 70% ◉ ◉ Old House Hotel & Restaurant
The Square PO17 5JG
☎ 01329 833049 📠 01329 833672
e-mail: oldhousehotel@aol.com
web: www.oldhousehotel.co.uk
Dir: M27 junct 10, N on A32 for 2m towards Alton. See website for directions.

CHILD FACILITIES: Baby listening Food/bottle warming Ch menu Ch portions Highchairs Ch discounts Safe grounds Games consoles Videos Cots Family rms 2 D rms or rm with 2 D beds Connecting rms Laundry **NEARBY:** Historic dockyard Cinema Tenpin bowling Zoo New Forest

This creeper-clad former Georgian residence occupies a prime position in a charming square in the centre of town. Ongoing refurbishment is resulting in smart and comfortable public areas that include a choice of eating areas and an inviting bar and lounge. Bedrooms are well equipped although some are larger than others.
ROOMS: 8 en suite 4 annexe en suite ◉ in all bedrooms s fr £70; d £85-£120 (incl. cont bkfst) **LB FACILITIES: PARKING:** 8 **NOTES:** ✖ ◉ in restaurant

WINCHESTER
Map 04 SU52

Babies Welcome	Family Rooms	Children's Dishes

★★★★ 63% The Wessex
Paternoster Row SO23 9LQ
☎ 0870 400 8126 📠 01962 841503
e-mail: wessex@macdonald-hotels.co.uk
Dir: M3, follow signs for town centre, at rdbt by King Alfred's statue past Guildhall, next left, hotel on right

MACDONALD HOTELS

CHILD FACILITIES: Baby listening Babysitting Activities: activity packs, fun bags Food/bottle warming Ch menu Ch portions Highchairs Ch cutlery Ch discounts children sharing free, in own room 50% Videos Cots Family rms D rm with 1/2 S beds Ch drinks Connecting rms Fridge Laundry Changing mats **NEARBY:** Zoo Theme park

A modern hotel occupying an enviable location in the centre of this historic city and adjacent to the spectacular cathedral, yet quietly situated on a side street. Inside, the ambience is modern, restful and welcoming, with many public areas and bedrooms enjoying unrivalled views of the hotel's centuries-old neighbour.
ROOMS: 94 en suite (6 fmly) ◉ in 61 bedrooms s £65-£160; d £110-£250 (incl. bkfst) **LB FACILITIES:** STV Solarium Gym Free use of local leisure centre, beauty therapy Xmas **PARKING:** 60 **NOTES:** ◉ in restaurant

How to use this guide & abbreviations are explained on pages 5-7

HEREFORDSHIRE

Goodrich Castle

BROCKHAMPTON
Brockhampton Estate
WR6 5TB ☎01885 482077
brockhampton@nationaltrust.org.uk
(2m E of Bromyard on A44)
Open Mar-Oct daily (ex Mon/Tue) but open BH Mon's Apr-Oct 12-5 (12-4 in Oct). Woodland walks open to dusk throughout the year.
*Lower Brockhampton £3.50 (ch £1.75) Family £8.50.

GOODRICH
Goodrich Castle
HR9 6YH ☎01600 890538
(5m S of Ross-on-Wye, off A40)
Open all year, Mar, daily, 10-5; Apr-May, daily 10-5; Jun-Aug, daily 10-6; Sep-oct, daily 10-5; Nov-Feb Thu-Mon 10-4. (Closed 24-26 Dec & 1 Jan).
*£4 (ch £2, concessions £3 family £10).

HEREFORD
Hereford Cathedral HR1 2NG
office@herefordcathedral.co.uk ☎01432 374200
(A49 signed from city inner ring roads)
Cathedral open daily for visitors 9.30-5; Mappa Mundi & Chained Library Exhibition Summer: Mon-Sat 10-4.15, Sun 11-3.15. Winter: Mon-Sat 11-3.15 (closed Sun).
Old House
HR1 2AA ☎01432 260694
(located in the centre of the High Town)
Open all year, 10-5. Apr-Sep, Tue-Sat 10-5, Sun & BH Mon 10-4.

LEDBURY
Eastnor Castle HR8 1RL
eastnorcastle@eastnorcastle.co ☎01531 633160
(the castle is 2.5m E of Ledbury on the A438 Tewkesbury road)
Open 11 Apr-3 Oct, Sun & BH Mon; Jul & Aug, Sun-Fri 11-5.

SWAINSHILL
The Weir Gardens
HR4 7QF ☎01981 590509
(5m W of Hereford, on A438)
Open mid-Jan Feb wknds only, 11-4. Mar daily 11-6, Apr-Sep, Wed-Sun & BH's, 11-6 Oct, Wed-Sun 11-4 (closed Nov-mid Jan) £3.50 (ch £1.75) Family £8.

BROMYARD
Map 03 SO65

◆◆◆◆ 😋 Linton Brook Farm
Malvern Rd, Bringsty WR6 5TR
☎ 01885 488875 & 01885 488875 📠 01885 488875
Dir: from A44 onto B4220 signed to Malvern. Farm 0.5m

CHILD FACILITIES: Please telephone for details

Dating back some 400 years, this large house has a wealth of character and has been sympathetically renovated to provide modern comforts. Accommodation is spacious. There is a comfortable sitting room with a wood-burning stove and a breakfast room with exposed beams and an inglenook fireplace.
ROOMS: 3 en suite **FACILITIES:** TV2B tea/coffee TVL 68 acres grassland **NOTES:** Credit cards not taken 🐾 ⊗ Cen ht **PARKING:** 12

CANON PYON
Map 03 SO44

Babies Welcome | **Children's Dishes**

🍺 The Nags Head Inn ◆◆◆
HR4 8NY
☎ 01432 830252

CHILD FACILITIES: Outdoor play area Food/bottle warming Ch menu Ch portions Highchairs Ch cutlery Safe grounds Changing facilities **NEARBY:** Walks

Situated a few miles north of Hereford this 400-year-old inn offers a warm welcome. Bedrooms are located in a separate, self-contained building, and all are equipped with modern comforts. The bar is the hub of proceedings, and here an extensive menu is available, including vegetarian options. The large garden has a children's adventure playground.
OPEN: 11-2.30 6-11 **BAR MEALS:** L served Tue-Sun 12-2.30 D served all week 6.30-9.30 **RESTAURANT:** L served Tue-Sun 12-2.30 D served all week 6.30-9.30 **FACILITIES:** Beer garden, patio, seating for 60 🐾 **ROOMS:** 6 en suite 1 family rooms s£35 d£45 **PARKING:** 50

DORMINGTON
Map 03 SO54

Babies Welcome | **Children's Dishes**

🍺 Yew Tree Inn
Len Gee's Restaurant, Priors Frome HR1 4EH
☎ 01432 850467 📠 01432 850467
e-mail: len@lengees.info
web: www.lengees.info
Dir: On A438 at Dormington turn towards Mordiford, 0.5m on L.

CHILD FACILITIES: Activities: children's quiz, colouring Outdoor play area Food/bottle warming Ch menu Ch portions Highchairs Ch cutlery Safe grounds **NEARBY:** Newbridge animal farm Walks

OPEN: 12-2 7-11 (Closed Tue Jan-Mar) **BAR MEALS:** L served all week 12-2 D served all week 7-9 Av main course £8.95 **RESTAURANT:** L served all week 12-2 D served all week 7-9 Av 3 course à la carte £18 Av 3 course fixed price £14.95 **FACILITIES:** Garden: Terraced with views of Black Mountains **PARKING:** 40

LEDBURY
Map 03 SO73

Babies Welcome | **Family Rooms** | **Children's Dishes**

★★ 72% 🏵 Verzon Bar, Brasserie & Hotel
Hereford Rd, Trumpet HR8 2PZ
☎ 01531 670381 📠 01531 670830
e-mail: info@theverzon.co.uk
web: www.theverzon.co.uk
Dir: 2m W of Ledbury on A438

CHILD FACILITIES: Activities: colouring, jigsaws, games Outdoor play area Food/bottle warming Ch menu Ch portions Highchairs Ch cutlery Ch discounts under 5s free sharing with parents Safe grounds Cots Family rms D rm with S beds Laundry **NEARBY:** Eastnor Castle

Dating back to 1790 this elegant establishment stands in extensive gardens, from which far-reaching views over the Malvern Hills can be enjoyed. Bedrooms are well-appointed and spacious; one of them has a four-poster bed. Stylish public areas include the popular bar and the brasserie restaurant which serves a range of well executed and flavour packed dishes.
ROOMS: 8 en suite (1 fmly) 🏵 in all bedrooms s £55-£70; d £78-£98 (incl. bkfst) **LB** **FACILITIES:** STV **PARKING:** 60 **NOTES:** 🐾 ⊗ in restaurant

PEMBRIDGE
Map 03 SO35

Children's Dishes

🍺 The Cider House Restaurant
Dunkerton's Cider Mill, Luntley HR6 9ED
☎ 01544 388161 📠 01544 388654
Dir: W on A44 from Leominster, L in Pembridge centre by New Inn, 1m on L

CHILD FACILITIES: Food/bottle warming Ch portions Safe grounds **NEARBY:** River walks Small breeds farm

OPEN: 10-5 Please telephone 1st Closed: 1 Oct - Easter **BAR MEALS:** L served Wed-Sat 12-2.30 D served none Av main course £10 **RESTAURANT:** L served Mon-Sat 12-2.30 D served None Av 3 course à la carte £18.50 **FACILITIES:** Terrace overlooking fields 🐾 **PARKING:** 30

ROSS-ON-WYE
Map 03 SO52

Babies Welcome | **Family Rooms** | **Children's Dishes**

◆◆◆◆ Brynheulog
Howle Hill HR9 5SP
☎ 01989 562051 📠 01989 562051
Dir: from Ross-on-Wye take B4234, after 1 mile turn left, (signed Howle Hill). After 250yds 1st right (signed Howle Hill). At x-roads turn left, first house on right, past church

CHILD FACILITIES: Baby listening Activities: colouring, jigsaws, toys Indoor play area Outdoor play area Family area Food/bottle warming Ch menu Ch portions Highchairs Ch cutlery Ch discounts under 5s free, under 12s 50% Safe grounds Games consoles Videos Cots Family rms Ch drinks Connecting rms Fridge Laundry Changing mats

This highly individual guest house has been lovingly designed by the owner to provide a high level of comfort and it benefits from superb views. The bedrooms are full of character and well equipped, with furniture built by a local craftsman. Two are in a self-contained wing with its own private lounge. Public areas consist of a tastefully decorated dining room and a relaxing lounge.
ROOMS: 4 en suite (1 fmly) (2 GF) s £20-£30; d £40-£60 * **FACILITIES:** TV3B tea/coffee TVL No coaches Dinner **NOTES:** Credit cards not taken ⊗ Cen ht **LB** **PARKING:** 7

England

SELLACK — Map 03 SO52

◐▊ The Lough Pool Inn
HR9 6LX
☎ 01989 730236 ▤ 01989 730462
Dir: A49 from Ross-on-Wye toward Hereford, side rd signed Sellack/Hoarwithy, pub 3m from R-on-W

CHILD FACILITIES: Outdoor play area Food/bottle warming Ch menu Ch portions Highchairs Safe grounds **NEARBY:** Wye Valley walk

OPEN: 11.30-2.30 6.30-11 (Sun 12-2 7-10.30) Closed: 25 Dec, 26 Dec (eve) **BAR MEALS:** L served all week 12-2 D served all week 7-9.15 Av main course £12.50 **RESTAURANT:** L served all week 12-2 D served all week 7-9.15 Av 3 course à la carte £23 **FACILITIES:** Garden: Lawn outside pub **PARKING:** 40

SYMONDS YAT (EAST) — Map 03 SO51

◐▊ The Saracens Head Inn ◆◆◆◆
HR9 6JL
☎ 01600 890435 ▤ 01600 890034
e-mail: email@saracensheadinn.co.uk
web: www.saracensheadinn.co.uk

CHILD FACILITIES: Food/bottle warming Ch menu Ch portions Highchairs Ch cutlery Changing facilities **NEARBY:** Puzzle Wood Cycling trails Maze Walks

Dating from the 16th century, this popular and friendly family-run hotel faces the River Wye and enjoys wonderful views. Bedrooms are well equipped and sympathetically decorated in a cottage style. There is also a separate cosy residents' lounge, an attractive dining room and an atmospheric public bar with riverside patio seating.
OPEN: 11-11 **BAR MEALS:** L served all week 12-2.30 D served all week 7-9.15 Av main course £8 **RESTAURANT:** D served all week 7-9.15 **FACILITIES:** Garden: 2 riverside terraces **ROOMS:** 11 bedrooms 11 en suite 1 family rooms s£48 d£69 **PARKING:** 38

HERTFORDSHIRE

ALDBURY — Map 04 SP91

◐▊ The Valiant Trooper
Trooper Rd HP23 5RW
☎ 01442 851203 ▤ 01442 851071
Dir: A41 at Tring junct, follow railway station signs, 0.5m and at village green turn R then 200yds on L

CHILD FACILITIES: Outdoor play area Family area Food/bottle warming Ch menu Ch portions Highchairs Safe grounds **NEARBY:** Walks National Trust forest

OPEN: 11-11 (Sun 12-10.30) **BAR MEALS:** L served all week 12-2.30 D served Tue-Sat 6.30-9.15 **RESTAURANT:** L served Tue-Sun 12-2 D served Tue-Sun 6.30-9.15 **FACILITIES:** Garden: **PARKING:** 36

BUNTINGFORD — Map 05 TL32

◐▊ The Sword in Hand
Westmill SG9 9LQ
☎ 01763 271356
e-mail: heather@swordinhand.ndo.co.uk
Dir: Off A10 1.5m S of Buntingford

CHILD FACILITIES: Activities: trampoline Outdoor play area Family area Food/bottle warming Ch licence Ch menu Ch portions Highchairs Safe grounds **NEARBY:** Walks Zoo Wildlife park

OPEN: 12-3 Open Mon L in Summer) 5.30-11 **BAR MEALS:** L served Tue-Sun 12-2.30 D served Tue-Sun 6.30-9.30 Av main course £10 **RESTAURANT:** L served Tue-Sun 12-2.30 D served Tue-Sun 6.30-9.30 Av 3 course à la carte £20 **FACILITIES:** Garden: Large, beautiful view, patio area, pergola **PARKING:** 25

FLAUNDEN — Map 04 TL00

◐▊ The Bricklayers Arms
Hogpits Bottom HP3 0PH
☎ 01442 833322 ▤ 834841
e-mail: goodfood@bricklayersarms.co.uk
web: www.bricklayersarms.co.uk
Dir: M1 J8 through H Hempstead to Bovington then follow Flaunden sign. M25 J18 through Chorleywood to Chenies/Latimer then Flaunden

CHILD FACILITIES: Food/bottle warming Ch menu Ch portions Highchairs Ch cutlery Safe grounds **NEARBY:** Walks Parks

OPEN: 11.30 -11.30 **BAR MEALS:** L served all week 12-2 D served all week 6-9.30 Av main course £13 **RESTAURANT:** L served all week 12-3 D served all week 6-9.30 Av 3 course à la carte £23 **FACILITIES:** Garden: Sunny & secluded **PARKING:** 40

England

RICKMANSWORTH
Map 04 TQ09

| Babies Welcome | Family Rooms | Children's Dishes |

 ★★★★★ 72% The Grove

Chandler's Cross WD3 4TG
☎ 01923 807807 🖷 01923 221008
e-mail: info@thegrove.co.uk
web: www.thegrove.co.uk
Dir: From M25 follow signs for the A411 towards Watford, entrance to The Grove is on the right. From M1 follow brown signs to The Grove.

CHILD FACILITIES: Babysitting Activities: Anouska's Kids Club, seasonal entertainment, colouring, books, toys, games Indoor play area Outdoor play area Food/bottle warming Ch menu Ch portions Highchairs Ch cutlery Ch discounts 50% child rm, free when sharing Safe grounds Games consoles Cots Family rms D or T rms connecting £260 Ch drinks Connecting rms Fridge Laundry Changing mats (on request) **NEARBY:** Animal park Dry ski slope

Set in 300 acres of grounds, this splendid new hotel combines historic character with marvellous modern design. The spacious bedrooms feature the latest in temperature control, flat-screen TV and lighting technology. Many have balconies and separate showers. Suites in the original mansion are particularly stunning. There is an impressive range of facilities including championship golf, a luxurious spa and three dining rooms.
ROOMS: 227 en suite (31 fmly) (35 GF) ⊗ in 144 bedrooms s fr £282
FACILITIES: Spa STV 🖭 Golf 18 ⚲ Fishing Sauna Solarium Gym ♨ ♨ Jacuzzi 12 Treatment rooms, cycling, kids club ♫ Xmas
PARKING: 400 **NOTES:** ✱

ST ALBANS
Map 04 TL10

| Babies Welcome | Family Rooms | Children's Dishes |

♦♦♦♦ Ardmore House
54 Lemsford Rd AL1 3PR
☎ 01727 859313 🖷 01727 859313
e-mail: info@ardmorehousehotel.co.uk
Dir: off Hatfield Rd, near St Albans Railway Station

CHILD FACILITIES: Outdoor play area Food/bottle warming Ch menu Ch portions Highchairs Safe grounds Cots Family rms D rm with 2 S beds, D rm with 3 S beds £105

Located in immaculate surroundings close to the town centre and cathedral, this extended Edwardian house has been carefully renovated. The practically furnished bedrooms offer a good range of facilities and the extensive public areas include a spacious conservatory dining room.
ROOMS: 40 en suite (5 fmly) (7 GF) s £45-£63; d £60-£95 * ⊗ in 20 bedrooms **FACILITIES:** STV TVB tea/coffee Direct dial from bedrooms TVL Dinner Last d order 8.30pm **NOTES:** ⊗ in restaurant ⊗ in 1 lounge Licensed Cen ht **PARKING:** 40

STANDON
Map 05 TL32

| Babies Welcome | Children's Dishes |

◀ Nag's Head ♦♦♦♦
SG11 1NL
☎ 01920 821424
Dir: Telephone for directions

CHILD FACILITIES: Outdoor play area Food/bottle warming Ch portions Highchairs Ch cutlery Safe grounds Changing facilities **NEARBY:** Park Walks

A warm welcome and friendly service is just part of the appeal of this popular, family-run inn, situated in the sleepy hamlet of Wellpond Green. Modern bedrooms are well appointed and have good, en suite showers. The spacious restaurant and the bar offer a good range of dishes.
OPEN: 12-2.30 6-11 **BAR MEALS:** L served Tue-Sun 12-2 D served Mon-Sat 6.30-9.30 Av main course £6.95 **RESTAURANT:** L served Tue-Sun 12-2 D served Mon-Sat 6.30-9.30 Av 3 course à la carte £18
FACILITIES: Garden: Lawn, full size boules pitch, Patio ✱ **ROOMS:** 5 bedrooms 5 en suite 1 family rooms s£50 d£70 **PARKING:** 28

STEVENAGE
Map 04 TL22

| Babies Welcome | Family Rooms | Children's Dishes |

★★★ 66% Novotel Stevenage
Knebworth Park SG1 2AX
☎ 01438 346100 🖷 01438 723872
e-mail: H0992@accor-hotels.com
Dir: A1(M) junct 7, at entrance to Knebworth Park

CHILD FACILITIES: Baby listening Babysitting Activities: welcome pack, toys Indoor play area Outdoor play area Food/bottle warming Ch menu Ch portions Highchairs Ch discounts 2 under 16s sharing free Safe grounds Games consoles Videos Cots Family rms D rm with S beds £55-99 Connecting rms Laundry **NEARBY:** Knebworth Park Dinosaur park

With an accessible location just off the A1(M), this hotel is a popular and convenient choice. There's plenty for guests to do: Knebworth Park is a noteworthy neighbour and the hotel's outdoor pool and children's play area add to the appeal for families.
ROOMS: 100 en suite (20 fmly) (30 GF) ⊗ in 85 bedrooms s £55-£95; d £55-£95 **LB FACILITIES:** STV ⚲ Special rates at local health club ♫ Xmas **PARKING:** 100

Please mention AA Family Friendly Places to Stay, Eat and Visit when booking

KENT

Carousel in Folkestone

BEKESBOURNE

Howletts Wild Animal Park CT4 5EL
info@howletts.net ☎01303 264647
(Off A2, 3m S of Canterbury, follow brown tourist
signs) Open all year, daily 10-6 during summer
last admission 4.30, 10-dusk during winter last
admission 3. Closed 25 Dec.

BELTRING

Hop Farm & Country Park TN12 6PY
enquiry@thehopfarm.co.uk ☎01622 872068
(On A228 at Paddock Wood)
Open from 10am. Closed 24-26 Dec, 23 May & 20
Jun. *£7.50, ch under 4 free, ch 4-15 & pen £6.50.
Family ticket 2 ad & 2 ch £27.

CANTERBURY

Canterbury Roman Museum CT1 2RA
museums@canterbury.gov.uk ☎01227 785575
(In the centre close to the cathedral and city
centre car parks)
Open all year, Mon-Sat 10-5 & Sun Jun-Oct 1.30-
5. Last admission 4pm. Closed Good Fri & Xmas
period. *£2.80, ch 5-18, disabled, pen & students
£1.75. Family ticket £7.20.

The Canterbury Tales CT1 2TG
info@canterburytales.org.uk ☎01227 479227
(In heart of city centre, follow finger sign-posting)
Open all year, Mar-Jun 10-5, Jul-Aug 9.30-5, Sep-
Oct 10-4 & Nov-Feb 10-4.30.*£6.95, ch £5.25, pen
& student £5.95 Family ticket 2 ad & 2 ch £22.50.

CHATHAM

The Historic Dockyard Chatham ME4 4TZ
info@chdt.org.uk ☎01634 823800
(From M20 & M2 junct 3, follow signs for Chatham
on A229.Then take A230 and A231, following
brown tourist signs. Brown anchor signs lead to
visitors' entrance) Open mid Feb-early Nov, daily
10-6. Last entry 4pm. *£10, ch 5-15 £6.50,
concession £7.50 Family ticket 2 ad & 2 ch
£26.50, additional child £3.25.

DOVER

Dover Castle & Secret Wartime Tunnels
CT16 1HU ☎01304 211067
Open all year, Apr-Jun & Sep, daily 10-6; Jul-Aug
daily 9.30-6.30; Oct daily 10-5; Nov-Jan, Thu-Mon
10-4; Feb-Mar daily 10-4. Closed 24-26 Dec & 1
Jan. £8.50, ch £4.30, concessions £6.40.

GROOMBRIDGE PLACE

**Groombridge Place Gardens & Enchanted
Forest**
TN3 9QG office ☎01892 861444
office@groombridge.co.uk
(Turn off A264 onto B2110 0.5m from Langton
Green. Follow signs to Groombridge. Entrance at
bottom of Groombridge Hill in Groombridge
village.) Open 21 Mar-5 Nov, daily 9.30-6 or dusk.
£8.50, ch 3-12 £7, pen £7.20. Family ticket 2 ad &
2 ch £29.50. Groups 20+ available on request.

HEVER

Hever Castle & Gardens TN8 7NG
mail@hevercastle.co.uk ☎01732 865224
(M25 junct 5 or 6, 3m SE of Edenbridge, off
B2026)
Open Mar-Nov, daily. Castle 12-6, Gardens 11-6.
Last admission 5pm. Closes 4pm Mar & Nov.
*Castle & Gardens £8.80, ch 5-14 £4.80, pen
£7.40.Family ticket £22.40. Gardens only £7 ch 5-
14 £4.60, pen £6. Family ticket £18.60. Party 15+.

LYMPNE

**Port Lympne Wild Animal Park,
Mansion & Garden**
CT21 4PD ☎01303 264647
info@howletts.net
(Off M20 junct 11, follow brown tourist signs. Also
follow brown tourist signs from A20 between
Ashford and Folkeston) Open all year, daily 10-6
closes at dusk in summer, last admission 4.30pm
summer, 3pm winter. Closed 25 Dec.

MAIDSTONE

Leeds Castle ME17 1PL
enquiries@leeds-castle.co.uk ☎01622 765400
(7m E of Maidstone at junct 8 of M20/A20, clearly
signposted) Open daily, Mar-Oct 10-5 (Castle 11-
5.30). Nov-Mar 10-3 (Castle 10-3) Closed 26 Jun;
3 Jul; 5 Nov; 25 Dec. Mar-Oct, Castle, Park &
Gardens, £12.50 (ch 4-15 £9, students & pen
£11); Family ticket (2ad & 2ch) £39. Nov-Feb,
Castle Park & gardens £10.50 (ch £7, students &
pen £9). Family ticket £33.

MAIDSTONE

Museum of Kent Life
ME14 3AU ☎01622 763936
enquiries@museum-kentlife.co.uk
(From M20 junct 6 onto A229 Maidstone road,
follow signs for Aylesford) Open Feb-1 Nov, daily
10-5.30, in winter open every wknd 10-3.

STROOD

Diggerland ME2 2NU
mail@diggerland.com ☎08700 344437
(M2 junct 2, follow A228 towards Rochester. At
rdbt turn right. Diggerland on right). Open 10-5
wknds, BHs & school hols. £2.50 for all over 2yrs
(pen £1.25) Additional charges to ride/drive
machinery.

SWINGFIELD MINNIS

The Butterfly Centre
CT15 7HX ☎01303 844244
(On A260 by junction with Elham-Lydden road)
Open Apr-1 Oct, daily 10-5. Closed Easter
Sunday.

ASHFORD
Map 05 TR04

Babies Welcome | **Family Rooms** | **Children's Dishes**

◆◆◆◆ Croft
Canterbury Rd, Kennington TN25 4DU
☎ 01233 622140 🖷 01233 635271
e-mail: info@crofthotel.com
Dir: M20 junct 10 onto A28 signed Canterbury

CHILD FACILITIES: Baby listening Outdoor play area Family area
Food/bottle warming Ch menu (by request) Ch portions Highchairs
Ch cutlery Safe grounds Cots Family rms £73 Ch drinks
Connecting rms Laundry

An attractive redbrick house situated in two acres of smart,
landscaped grounds just a short drive from Ashford railway
station. The generously proportioned bedrooms are located in the
main house and in pretty cottages; all are pleasantly decorated
and thoughtfully equipped. Public rooms include a smart new
restaurant, a bar and a cosy residents' lounge.
ROOMS: 27 en suite (6 fmly) (8 GF) ⊗ in 13 bedrooms
FACILITIES: TVB tea/coffee Direct dial from bedrooms TVL Dinner Last
d order 9.30pm **NOTES:** ⊗ in restaurant Licensed Cen ht **PARKING:** 30

BEARSTED
Map 05 TQ85

Babies Welcome | **Children's Dishes**

◉ ◉ Soufflé Restaurant
31 The Green ME14 4DN
☎ 01622 737065 🖷 01622 737065
Dir: Telephone for directions

CHILD FACILITIES: Food/bottle warming Ch portions Highchairs
Ch cutlery Safe grounds Changing facilities NEARBY: Play area

FOOD: Mediterranean, European **STYLE:** Classic Chic **SEATS:** 40
OPEN: 12-2.30/7-10, Closed MonL Sat, D Sun **RESTAURANT:** Fixed L
£13.50, Fixed D £22.50, main £16.50-£18.50 **PARKING:** 15

CANTERBURY
Map 05 TR15

Babies Welcome | **Family Rooms** | **Children's Dishes**

◆◆◆◆◆ Thanington Hotel
140 Wincheap CT1 3RY
☎ 01227 453227 🖷 01227 453225
e-mail: thanington@lineone.net
web: www.thanington-hotel.co.uk
Dir: on A28, just outside city walls

CHILD FACILITIES: Activities: games Food/bottle warming
Ch portions Highchairs Safe grounds Cots Family rms D rm with
2-3 beds £100-£135 NEARBY: Cinema Animal park Roman
museum Cathedral

This fine Georgian property is situated close to the town centre
and cathedral. The spacious bedrooms are located in the main
house or in the smart modern extension; all have excellent
facilities. Two bedrooms in the main house have four-posters.
There is a spacious lounge, magnificent dining room and a
swimming pool overlooking the elegant courtyard. Secure parking
is a bonus.
ROOMS: 15 en suite (2 fmly) (4 GF) ⊗ **FACILITIES:** TVB tea/coffee
Direct dial from bedrooms TVL ▣ Pool Table Threequarter size snooker
table, games room **NOTES:** ⊗ in restaurant Licensed Cen ht
PARKING: 13

◆◆◆◆ Yorke Lodge Hotel
50 London Rd CT2 8LF
☎ 01227 451243 🖷 01227 462006
e-mail: enquiries@yorkelodge.com
web: www.yorkelodge.com
Dir: turn off A2 onto A2050, left at 1st rdbt into London Rd, hotel on left

CHILD FACILITIES: Please telephone for details

This charming 18th-century property is situated in a tree-lined
road about 10 minutes' walk from the town centre and railway
station. The spacious bedrooms are thoughtfully equipped and
tastefully decorated; some rooms have four-poster beds. Public
rooms include a stylish dining room and a small reception area
with a library.
ROOMS: 8 en suite (1 fmly) s £38-£45; d £65-£88 * ⊗
FACILITIES: TVB tea/coffee TVL No coaches **NOTES:** ⊗ in restaurant
Cen ht **LB** **PARKING:** 5

🍴 The Chapter Arms
New Town St, Chartham Hatch CT4 7LT
☎ 01227 738340
e-mail: chapterarms@clara.co.uk
Dir: 3m from Canterbury. Off A28 in Chartham Hatch

CHILD FACILITIES: Please telephone for details

OPEN: 11-3 6.30-11 Closed: 25 Dec (eve) **BAR MEALS:** L served all week
12-2 D served Mon-Sat 7-9 Av main course £10 **RESTAURANT:** L served
all week 12-2 D served Mon-Sat 7-9 Av 3 course à la carte £25
FACILITIES: Garden: 1 acre of lawn, fish ponds & flower beds ✈
PARKING: 40

CHIDDINGSTONE
Map 05 TQ54

Babies Welcome | **Children's Dishes**

🍴 Castle Inn
TN8 7AH
☎ 01892 870247 🖷 01892 870808
e-mail: info@castleinn.co.uk
web: www.castleinn.co.uk
Dir: S of B2027 between Tonbridge & Edenbridge

CHILD FACILITIES: Food/bottle warming Ch licence Ch menu
Ch portions Highchairs Ch cutlery Changing facilities
NEARBY: Hever Castle Penhurst Place Walks

OPEN: 11-11 **BAR MEALS:** L served all week 11-9.30 D served all week
Av main course £6.40 **RESTAURANT:** L served Wed-Mon 12-2 D served
Wed-Mon 7.30-9.30 Av 3 course à la carte £22 Av 3 course fixed price £22
FACILITIES: Children's licence Garden: Patio, lawn, sheltered, bar

DOVER
Map 05 TR34

◆◆◆◆ 🍴 The Park Inn
1-2 Park Place, Ladywell CT16 1DQ
☎ 01304 203300 🖷 01304 203324
e-mail: theparkinn@aol.com
Dir: M20-A20, follow signs for town centre, opposite police station

CHILD FACILITIES: Please telephone for details

A charming 18th-century inn situated in the heart of the town
centre. The open plan public rooms offer a good level of comfort
throughout and include a popular bar and a smart restaurant with
an open fireplace. Bedrooms are generally quite spacious; each is
tastefully decorated with quality soft furnishings and many
thoughtful touches.
ROOMS: 5 en suite (1 fmly) ⊗ **FACILITIES:** STV TVB tea/coffee
Direct dial from bedrooms Dinner Last d order 9.30pm **NOTES:** ✈ ⊗ in
area of dining room ⊗ in lounges Cen ht

DOVER, continued

◆◆◆ *Longfield*
203 Folkestone Rd CT17 9SL
☎ 01304 204716 📠 01304 204716
e-mail: res@longfieldguesthouse.co.uk
Dir: M20 to Dover, continue past junct 13, exit at Court Wood junction B2011. At rdbt turn left into Folkestone Rd. House 3m on right

CHILD FACILITIES: Please telephone for details

This friendly, family-run guest house is gradually being upgraded and is ideally situated close to the station, town centre, ports and Channel Tunnel. Bedrooms are pleasantly appointed and equipped with a good range of useful extras. Continental and English breakfasts are offered in the separate dining room, and secure parking is a real bonus.
ROOMS: 8 rms (3 en suite) (2 fmly) (1 GF) **FACILITIES:** TVB tea/coffee No coaches Dinner Last d order 2pm **NOTES:** ✖ ⊗ in restaurant ⊗ in lounges Cen ht **PARKING:** 11

◆◆◆ Peverall House
28 Park Av CT16 1HD
☎ 01304 202573 📠 01304 240034
e-mail: info@peverellhouse.co.uk
Dir: from A2 turn right at rdbt signed Dover Castle, take 2nd right (opp Castle entrance), then 1st left

CHILD FACILITIES: Please telephone for details

Close to Connaught Park, this impressive Victorian house has a large, attractive garden. The pine-furnished accommodation includes an airy sun lounge and a breakfast room. Most bedrooms have a sunny aspect, and those on the top floor have views of the castle and town. The atmosphere is very informal and friendly.
ROOMS: 7 rms (3 en suite) (4 fmly) d £40-£50 * **FACILITIES:** TVB tea/coffee No coaches **NOTES:** ✖ ⊗ in restaurant ⊗ in lounges Cen ht
LB PARKING: 8

◆◆◆ 🍴 Swingate Inn & Hotel
Deal Rd CT15 5DP
☎ 01304 204043 📠 01304 204043
e-mail: terry@swingate.com
web: www.swingate.com
Dir: turn off A2 onto 258 Deal road, hotel 0.25m on the right

CHILD FACILITIES: Activities: bouncy castle, toys, colouring, pets corner, climbing frame Outdoor play area Family area Food/bottle warming Ch menu Ch portions Highchairs Ch cutlery Ch discounts Safe grounds Games consoles Videos Cots Family rms D rm with 2 S beds Ch drinks Laundry **NEARBY:** Walks Parks Castles Pony riding 10-min drive to sea

Pleasantly located on the edge of Dover and most convenient for the ferry port, this friendly inn offers modern and spacious accommodation. The bar offers informal dining and in the restaurant an à la carte menu provides greater choice. Jazz

continued

evenings on Thursdays prove particularly popular and family entertainment is provided on Sunday evenings.
ROOMS: 11 en suite (2 fmly) s £42; d £50 * ⊗ in 1 bedrooms
FACILITIES: TVB tea/coffee Pets' corner Bird aviary Bouncy castle Gazebo Dinner Last d order 9.45pm **NOTES:** ✖ ⊗ in area of dining room ⊗ in 1 lounge Cen ht **PARKING:** 60

FAVERSHAM   Map 05 TR06

🍴 The Albion Tavern
Front Brents, Faversham Creek ME13 7DH
☎ 01795 591411 📠 01795 591587
e-mail: jenniferkent@msn.com
Dir: From Faversham take A2 W. In Ospringe turn R just before Ship Inn, at Shepherd Neame Brewery 1m turn L over creek bridge

CHILD FACILITIES: Activities: toys, books Food/bottle warming Ch portions Highchairs Safe grounds Changing facilities
NEARBY: Creekside walk

OPEN: 11-3 6-11 (Sun 12-10.30) **BAR MEALS:** L served all week 12-2.30 D served all week 6.30-9.30 Av main course £5 **RESTAURANT:** L served all week 12-2 D served all week 7-9 Av 3 course à la carte £16
FACILITIES: Garden: **PARKING:** 20

FOLKESTONE   Map 05 TR23

🍴 The Lighthouse
Old Dover Rd, Capel le Ferne CT18 7HT
☎ 01303 223300 📠 01303 256501

CHILD FACILITIES: Activities: colouring books, toys Indoor play area Outdoor play area Family area Food/bottle warming Ch menu Ch portions Highchairs Ch cutlery Safe grounds Changing facilities
NEARBY: 10-min drive to sea

BAR MEALS: L served all week 12-2.15 D served all week 5.30-9 Av main course £7 **RESTAURANT:** L served all week 12-2.15 D served all week 5.30-9 Av 3 course à la carte £17 **FACILITIES:** Garden: lawn, large patio ✖ **ROOMS:** 8 bedrooms 8 en suite 2 family rooms s£40 d£50 (◆◆◆◆)
PARKING: 80

FORDCOMBE   Map 05 TQ54

🍴 Chafford Arms
TN3 0SA
☎ 01892 740267 📠 01892 740703
e-mail: bazzer@chafford-arms.fsnet.co.uk
Dir: On B2188 (off A264) between Tunbridge Wells & E Grinstead

CHILD FACILITIES: Outdoor play area Food/bottle warming Ch portions Ch cutlery Safe grounds Changing facilities
NEARBY: Groombridge Place Penshurst Place Hever Castle The Pantiles Tunbridge Wells

OPEN: 11.45-3 6.30-11 (All day Sat) **BAR MEALS:** L served all week 12.30-2 D served Tue-Sat 7.30-9 Av main course £7.95 **RESTAURANT:** L served all week 12.30-2 D served Tue-Sat 7.30-9 Av 3 course à la carte £17.50 **FACILITIES:** Garden: Enclosed garden, patio **PARKING:** 16

This symbol indicates establishments within walking distance or a short drive of the seaside.

HERNHILL Map 05 TR06

🍺 Red Lion
The Green ME13 9JR
☎ 01227 751207 📠 01227 752990
e-mail: theredlion@lineone.net
Dir: S of A299 between Faversham & Whitstable

> CHILD FACILITIES: Please telephone for details

OPEN: 11.30-3 6-11 (Sun 12-3.30, 7-10.30) Closed: 25 Dec & 26 Dec, 1 Jan eves **BAR MEALS:** L served all week 12-2.30 D served all week 6-9.30 Av main course £8 **RESTAURANT:** L served (Sat & Sun only) 12-2.30 D served all week 6-9.30 Av 3 course à la carte £16.50 **FACILITIES:** Garden: Food served outside, attractive garden 🐾 **PARKING:** 40

MAIDSTONE Map 05 TQ75

> Babies Welcome | Family Rooms | Children's Dishes

♦♦♦♦ Langley Oast
Langley Park, Langley ME17 3NQ
☎ 01622 863523 📠 01622 863523
e-mail: margaret@langleyoast.freeserve.co.uk
Dir: From junct 6 follow signs to Maidstone town centre then Hastings. At Wheatsheaf traffic lights take A274 to Tenterden. Past Parkwood Business state turn right into lane signed Maidstone Golf Centre

> CHILD FACILITIES: Food/bottle warming Ch portions Highchairs Ch cutlery Ch discounts Safe grounds Cots Family rms D rm with S bed, sofa bed or travel cot Fridge NEARBY: Rare breeds centre Walks

This traditional Kentish oast house is a short drive from the town centre and enjoys views of the surrounding countryside. Bedrooms are spacious and well appointed; two of the rooms occupy the 24 feet diameter roundel towers and one has a Jacuzzi bath. Breakfast is taken in the airy dining room around one large table.
ROOMS: 3 rms (2 en suite) (1 fmly) **FACILITIES:** TVB tea/coffee No coaches Jacuzzi in 1 bedroom **NOTES:** Credit cards not taken 🐾 ⊗ Cen ht **PARKING:** 5

> Babies Welcome | Children's Dishes

🍺 The Ringlestone Inn ♦♦♦♦♦
Ringlestone Hamlet, Nr Harrietsham ME17 1NX
☎ 01622 859900 📠 01622 859966
e-mail: bookings@ringlestone.com
web: www.ringlestone.com
Dir: Take A20 E from Maidstone/at rndbt opp Great Danes Hotel turn to Hollingbourne. Through village, R at crossroads at top of hill

> CHILD FACILITIES: Activities: colouring, crayons Food/bottle warming Ch licence Ch menu Ch portions Highchairs Ch cutlery Safe grounds NEARBY: Leeds Castle Mote Park Museum of Kent Life

continued

OPEN: 12-3 6-11 (Sat-Sun 12-11) Closed: 25 Dec **BAR MEALS:** L served all week 12-2 D served all week 7-9.30 **RESTAURANT:** L served all week 12-2 D served all week 7-9.30 Av 3 course à la carte £24.50 **FACILITIES:** Children's licence Garden: Five acres of landscaped gardens, seating 🐾 **ROOMS:** 3 bedrooms 3 en suite s£89 d£99 **PARKING:** 50

SEVENOAKS Map 05 TQ55

♦♦♦ Barn Cottage
Seven Mile Ln, Borough Green TN15 8QY
☎ 01732 883384
e-mail: suzifilleul@aol.com
Dir: from A20 take B2016 (Seven Mile Lane) for 1m. Over x-roads, Barn Cottage on left opp sign for Viking Oak Kennels

> CHILD FACILITIES: Please telephone for details

This pretty white-boarded cottage is set in a pleasant courtyard amidst attractive gardens. The bedrooms are neat and comfortably furnished. Breakfast is served in the flower-filled conservatory, which overlooks the garden. Guests also have use of a comfortably furnished lounge.
ROOMS: 3 rms s £27.50; d £55 * **FACILITIES:** tea/coffee No coaches Cycling **NOTES:** Credit cards not taken 🐾 ⊗ Cen ht **PARKING:** 5

SHEPHERDSWELL Map 05 TR24

> Family Rooms | Children's Dishes

♦♦♦ Bishops Lodge
The Green, 2 Mill Ln CT15 7NB
☎ 01304 832010 & 832292
Dir: Leave A2 approx 5m from Dover, right at lights into Coxhill, Shepherdswell. Into village then right Church Hill onto the green, opposite school house

> CHILD FACILITIES: Baby listening Babysitting (not registered) Activities: toys, puzzles, books, dolls house, board games Outdoor play area Family area Food/bottle warming Ch menu Ch portions Ch cutlery Ch discounts under 5s free Safe grounds Games consoles Videos Cots Family rms D rm with 1/2 S beds £48-£52 Ch drinks Laundry NEARBY: Park Walks Leisure centre Cinema Swimming pool Zoo Animal park 5m to sea

Expect a warm welcome at this delightful detached property ideally situated in a peaceful rural location just a short drive from the A2 and Dover. Bedrooms are cheerfully decorated with co-ordinated fabrics and have many thoughtful touches. Breakfast, which includes locally sourced produce, is served in the smart dining room.
ROOMS: 3 rms (1 fmly) s £20-£25; d £45-£50 * **FACILITIES:** TVB tea/coffee No coaches Dinner Last d order 8pm **NOTES:** Credit cards not taken 🐾 ⊗ Cen ht LB **PARKING:** 5

SITTINGBOURNE Map 05 TQ96

> Babies Welcome | Family Rooms | Children's Dishes

★★★ 71% ⊛ Hempstead House Country Hotel
London Rd, Bapchild ME9 9PP
☎ 01795 428020 📠 01795 436362
e-mail: info@hempsteadhouse.co.uk
web: www.hempsteadhouse.co.uk
Dir: 1.5m from Sittingbourne town centre on A2 towards Canterbury

> CHILD FACILITIES: Baby listening Activities: swimming pool, trampoline Food/bottle warming Ch menu Ch portions Highchairs Ch cutlery Ch discounts children £10 when sharing room Safe grounds Games consoles Videos Cots Family rms D rm with 1-3 S beds Ch drinks Laundry NEARBY: Castles Leisure centre Farms Walks Cinema

continued on p156

SITTINGBOURNE, continued

Expect a warm welcome at this charming detached Victorian property, which is situated amidst three acres of mature landscaped gardens. Bedrooms are attractively decorated with lovely co-ordinated fabrics, tastefully furnished and equipped with many thoughtful touches. Public rooms feature a choice of beautifully furnished lounges as well as a superb conservatory dining room.
ROOMS: 27 en suite (7 fmly) (1 GF) ⊗ in all bedrooms s £75-£95; d £85-£105 (incl. bkfst) **LB** **FACILITIES:** STV ᴿ Xmas **PARKING:** 100 **NOTES:** ⊗ in restaurant

SMARTS HILL   Map 05 TQ54

🍺 The Bottle House Inn
Coldharbour Rd TN11 8ET
☎ 01892 870306 🖷 01892 871094
e-mail: info@thebottlehouseinnpenshurst.co.uk
Dir: From Tunbridge Wells take A264 W then B2188 N

CHILD FACILITIES: Activities: colouring Food/bottle warming Ch licence Ch menu Ch portions Highchairs Safe grounds **NEARBY:** Hever Castle Penshurst Place Groombridge Place The Pantiles

OPEN: 11-11 (Sun 12-10.30pm) Closed: Dec 25 **BAR MEALS:** L served all week 12-10 D served all week 12-10 Av main course £10 **RESTAURANT:** L served all week 12-10 D served all week 12-10 Av 3 course à la carte £20 **FACILITIES:** Children's licence Garden: Front raised terrace garden and side patio **PARKING:** 36

TUNBRIDGE WELLS (ROYAL)   Map 05 TQ53

Babies Welcome | Family Rooms | Children's Dishes

★★★★ 71% ⊛ *The Spa*
Mount Ephraim TN4 8XJ
☎ 01892 520331 🖷 01892 510575
e-mail: info@spahotel.co.uk
web: www.spahotel.co.uk
Dir: off A21 to A26, follow signs to A264 East Grinstead, hotel on right

CHILD FACILITIES: Baby listening Activities: pony riding for under 10s, board games, jigsaws Food/bottle warming Ch menu Ch portions Highchairs Ch discounts under 14s free when sharing with parents Safe grounds Cots Family rms D/T rm with interconnecting room £130 Connecting rms Laundry **NEARBY:** Castle Walks

This imposing 18th-century country house is set in 14 acres of
continued

attractive landscaped grounds, overlooking Royal Tunbridge Wells. The spacious bedrooms are individually decorated and are tastefully furnished and thoughtfully equipped; many rooms overlook the pretty gardens. Public rooms include a comfortable lounge, the Chandelier restaurant and excellent leisure facilities.
ROOMS: 69 en suite (10 fmly) (2 GF) **FACILITIES:** STV ⌧ ℺ Riding Sauna Gym ♫ Steam room Beauty salon Jogging trail ♫ **PARKING:** 120 **NOTES:** ✈ ⊗ in restaurant

Family Rooms | Children's Dishes

★★ 65% Russell
80 London Rd TN1 1DZ
☎ 01892 544833 🖷 01892 515846
e-mail: Sales@russell-hotel.com
web: www.russell-hotel.com
Dir: at junct A26/A264 uphill onto A26, hotel on right

CHILD FACILITIES: Baby listening Ch portions Highchairs Ch discounts Cots Family rms Laundry **NEARBY:** Walks

This detached Victorian property is situated just a short walk from the centre of town. The generously proportioned bedrooms in the main house are pleasantly decorated and well equipped. In addition, there are several smartly appointed self-contained suites in an adjacent building. The public rooms include a lounge, a cosy bar and a restaurant.
ROOMS: 19 en suite 5 annexe en suite (5 fmly) (1 GF) ⊗ in 10 bedrooms s £55-£70; d £68-£85 (incl. bkfst) **LB** **FACILITIES:** **PARKING:** 15 **NOTES:** ✈

Babies Welcome | Children's Dishes

🍺 The Beacon
Tea Garden Ln, Rusthall TN3 9JH
☎ 01892 524252 🖷 01892 534288
e-mail: beaconhotel@btopenworld.com
web: www.the-beacon.co.uk
Dir: From Tunbridge Wells take A264 towards East Grinstead. Pub 1m on L

CHILD FACILITIES: Food/bottle warming Ch licence Ch menu Ch portions Highchairs **NEARBY:** Calverley Park Gardens Leisure centre Cinema Bowling alley

OPEN: 11-11 (Sun 12-10.30) **BAR MEALS:** L served all week 12-2.30 D served all week 6.30-9.30 **RESTAURANT:** L served all week 12-2.30 D served all week 6-9.30 **FACILITIES:** Children's licence Garden: Decking area, 17 acres of garden **ROOMS:** 3 bedrooms 3 en suite s£68.50 d£97 (♦♦♦♦) **PARKING:** 40

LANCASHIRE

Donkeys on Blackpool beach

BLACKPOOL

Blackpool Illuminations
Six mile of illuminations from 400,000 lamps and 75 miles of cabling in this spectacular lightshow, September to November.

Blackpool Zoo Park
FY3 8PP ☎01253 830830
info@blackpoolzoo.freeserve.co.uk
(M55 junct 4, follow brown tourist signs)
Open all year daily, summer 10-6; winter 10-5 or dusk. (Closed 25 Dec).
*£8.50 (ch 6.50). Family (2 ad & 2 ch) £26, (2 ad & 3 ch) £31. Concessions for seniors, disabled people, carers and groups are available.

CHARNOCK RICHARD

Camelot Theme Park
PR7 5LP ☎01257 453044
kingarthur@camelotthemepark.co.uk
(from M6 junct 27/28, or M61 junct 8 follow brown tourist signs)
Open Etr-Oct. Telephone for further details.
*£15 (ch over 1 metre £12, under 1 metre free, pen & disabled £11)

CLITHEROE

Clitheroe Castle Museum BB7 1BA
museum@ribblevalley.gov.uk ☎01200 424635
(follow Clitheroe signs from A59 by-pass. Museum located in castle grounds near town centre).
Open 11-4.30; late Feb-Etr, Sat-Wed; Etr-Oct, daily inc BHs; Nov, Dec & Feb, wknds & school half terms. (Closed Jan)
*£1.70 (ch 25p, pen 85p). Family ticket £3.65

MARTIN MERE

WWT Martin Mere L40 0TA
WWT Martin Mere
info@martinmere.co.uk ☎01704 895181
(signposted from M61, M58 & M6, 6m from Ormskirk, off A59)
Open all year, daily 9.30-5.30 (5 in winter). (Closed 25 Dec).
*£5.75 (ch £3.75, concessions £4.75). Family ticket £15.

PRESTON

Harris Museum & Art Gallery
PR1 2PP ☎01772 258248 🖷01772 258248
harris.museum@preston.gov.uk
(exit M6 at junct 31, follow signs for Preston city centre, park at bus stn car park)
Open all year, Mon-Sat 10-5, Sun 11-4. (Closed BHs).

The National Football Museum
PR1 6RY ☎01772 908442
enquiries@nationalfootballmuseum.com
(2m from M6 juncts 31, 31A or 32. Follow brown tourist signs in Preston)
Open Tue-Sat 10-5, Sun 11-5. (Closed Mon ex BHs). Contact for opening times on match days.

SILVERDALE

RSPB Nature Reserve
LA5 0SW
leighton.moss@rspb.org.uk ☎01524 701601
(M6 junct 35, head west on A501(M) for 0.5m to end. Turn right and head N on A6. Follow brown tourist signs)
Reserve: open daily 9am-Dusk (or sunset if earlier). Visitor Centre daily 9.30-5. Feb-Oct 9.30-4.30 Nov-Jan. Closed 25 Dec.
*£4.50 (ch £1, concessions £3) Family £9. RSPB members Free.

Waterslack Farm, Cafe & Garden Centre
LA5 0UH
welcome@waterslack.com ☎01524 701255
(M6 junct 35, follow A6 towards Milnthorpe. Turn off A6 at Nineteen Acre Lane & follow signs for Leighton Moss Nature Reserve. Pass Reserve, turn right at T-junct & follow signs)
Open Apr-Sep Mon, Wed, Fri & Sat 9.30-6, Tue & Thu 9-5, Sun 10-5; Oct-Mar Mon-Sat 9.30-5, Sun 10.30-5.
Free admission.

WHALLEY

Whalley Abbey
BB7 9SS
office@whalleyabbey.org
☎01524 828400 🖷01524 828401
(just off A59 4m S of Clitheroe)
Open from 5 Jan daily 10-5 (closed around Xmas/New Year).
£2 (ch 50p, pen £1.25) Family (2 ad + children) £4.50

England

ACCRINGTON — Map 07 SD72

Babies Welcome | Family Rooms | Children's Dishes

◆◆◆◆ Maple Lodge Hotel
70 Blackburn Rd, Clayton-Le-Moors BB5 5JH
☎ 01254 301284 ▤ 01254 388152
e-mail: maplelod@aol.com
web: www.maplelodgehotel.co.uk
Dir: Leave M65 at junct 7 follow signs A6185 Clitheroe, after 200yds at T-junct with traffic lights turn right onto A678 hotel 400yds on left

CHILD FACILITIES: Food/bottle warming Ch menu Ch portions Highchairs Ch cutlery Ch discounts under 2s free Cots Family rms D rm with S bed/cot £55-£65 Ch drinks

In the early 18th century this welcoming house formed part of the local country manor; today it enjoys a convenient location close to Junction 7 of the M65. Comfortable, well-equipped bedrooms are provided in the main house and adjoining annexe, while day rooms include a bar and an attractive dining room where creative and carefully cooked dinners (by prior arrangement) and hearty breakfasts are served.
ROOMS: 4 en suite 4 annexe en suite (1 fmly) (4 GF) s £39.50-£44.50; d £54-£59 * ⊗ **FACILITIES:** TVB tea/coffee Direct dial from bedrooms TVL No coaches jacuzzi in 1 room Dinner Last d order 8pm **NOTES:** ✖ ⊗ in restaurant Licensed Cen ht **LB PARKING:** 7

BLACKPOOL — Map 07 SD33

Babies Welcome | Family Rooms | Children's Dishes

★★ 70% Hotel Sheraton
54-62 Queens Promenade FY2 9RP
☎ 01253 352723 ▤ 01253 595499
e-mail: email@hotelsheraton.co.uk
web: www.hotelsheraton.co.uk
Dir: 1m N from Blackpool Tower on promenade towards Fleetwood

CHILD FACILITIES: Baby listening Activities: entertainment in school hols, swimming pool, games room Food/bottle warming Ch menu Ch portions Highchairs Ch discounts under 3s free, 4-9s £15, 10-15s £20 plus seasonal promotions Safe grounds Games consoles Cots Family rms D rm with 1/2 S beds or rm with 2 D beds NEARBY: Seafront location

This family-owned and run hotel is situated at the quieter, northern end of the promenade. Public areas include a choice of spacious lounges with sea views, a large function suite where popular dancing and cabaret evenings are held, and a heated indoor swimming pool. The smartly appointed bedrooms come in a range of sizes and styles.
ROOMS: 104 en suite (45 fmly) s £25-£60; d £50-£120 (incl. bkfst & dinner) **LB FACILITIES:** ⊡ Sauna Table tennis Darts ♫ Xmas **PARKING:** 20 **NOTES:** ✖ ⊗ in restaurant
See advert on opposite page

Babies Welcome | Family Rooms | Children's Dishes

◆◆◆ Craigmore Hotel
8 Willshaw Rd, Gynn Square FY2 9SH
☎ 01253 355098 ▤ 01253 355098
e-mail: blackpoolhotel@fsbdial.co.uk
Dir: N along promenade & golden mile, past the tower. 0.5m to Gynn Rdbt, straight on & Willshaw Rd 1st on right

CHILD FACILITIES: Activities: toys, games Food/bottle warming Ch menu Ch portions Highchairs Ch discounts under 5s 1/3 off, 5-12s 50% Safe grounds Cots Family rms 2 D rms with 2 S beds, D rm with 1 S bed NEARBY: Pleasure beach Blackpool Tower Seafront location

This well-maintained hotel is attractively located overlooking Gynn Square and gardens, with the promenade and tram stops just yards away. Bedrooms are smart and modern, with several suitable for families. There is a comfortable lounge, an additional sun lounge and a patio area. The pretty dining room also contains a small bar.
ROOMS: 9 en suite (3 fmly) s £21-£28; d £42-£46 * ⊗ **FACILITIES:** TVB tea/coffee TVL Dinner Last d order 1pm **NOTES:** ✖ ⊗ in restaurant ⊗ in 1 lounge Licensed Cen ht

◆◆◆ Denely Private Hotel
15 King Edward Av FY2 9TA
☎ 01253 352757
Dir: approximately 1m north of Blackpool Tower

CHILD FACILITIES: Please telephone for details

Just a short stroll from the promenade and Gynn Square Gardens, this welcoming hotel offers comfortable accommodation. A spacious lounge and a bright dining room complement simply furnished bedrooms. Evening meals are available by prior arrangement. The resident owners provide friendly and attentive service.
ROOMS: 9 rms (7 en suite) (3 fmly) d £34-£42 * **FACILITIES:** TVB tea/coffee TVL Dinner Last d order 1pm **NOTES:** ✖ ⊗ in restaurant Cen ht **LB BB PARKING:** 6

Babies Welcome | Family Rooms | Children's Dishes

◆◆◆ Westdean Hotel
59 Dean St FY4 1BP
☎ 01253 342904 ▤ 01253 342926
e-mail: mikeball@westdeanhotel.freeserve.co.uk
web: www.westdeanhotel.com
Dir: along Promenade (from Pleasure Beach towards Blackpool Tower) take 1st right after South Pier into Dean St

CHILD FACILITIES: Food/bottle warming Ch menu Ch portions Highchairs Ch discounts under 12s sharing with parents Videos Cots Family rms D rm with 2 S beds, D with 1 S bed from £50 NEARBY: Near sea

A friendly welcome awaits guests at this well-established private hotel, located within easy reach of the South Promenade and Pleasure Beach. Bedrooms are neatly appointed and well-equipped with modern facilities. Guests have use of a comfortable lounge, a cellar bar and a games room for both adults and children.
ROOMS: 11 rms (10 en suite) (3 fmly) s £22-£30; d £44-£60 * **FACILITIES:** TVB tea/coffee TVL Pool Table **NOTES:** ✖ ⊗ in restaurant Licensed Cen ht **LB PARKING:** 2

How to use this guide & abbreviations are explained on pages 5-7

♦♦♦ Windsor Hotel
53 Dean St FY4 1BP
☎ 01253 400232 📠 01253 346886
e-mail: windsorhotel@btconnect.com
web: www.windsorhotel.co.uk
Dir: M6 junct 32, M55 to lge rdbt, straight on, at mini rdbt right, around supermarket to lights turn left over bridge to next lights, left Dean Street 2nd on right. Turn in front of Texaco garage, hotel on right

CHILD FACILITIES: Please telephone for details

A warm welcome awaits you at this friendly, family-run guest house located close to the South Pier and Pleasure Beach, with other resort attractions just a tram ride away. Cosy bedrooms are neatly decorated and some have stylish four-poster beds. Dinners, by arrangement, are taken in a spacious dining room.
ROOMS: 12 en suite (3 fmly) ⊗ in 9 bedrooms **FACILITIES:** TVB tea/coffee Direct dial from bedrooms TVL **NOTES:** ✖ ⊗ in restaurant Licensed Cen ht **LB PARKING:** 8

Children's
Dishes

🍽 Kwizeen
47-49 Kings St FY1 3EJ
☎ 01253 290045
e-mail: info@kwizeen.co.uk
web: www.kwizeen.co.uk
Dir: From front of Blackpool Winter Gardens, 100yds to King St, and as road forks restaurant 30yds on L

CHILD FACILITIES: Food/bottle warming Ch portions

FOOD: British **STYLE:** Chic **SEATS:** 40 **OPEN:** 12-1.45/6, Closed 21 Feb-10 Mar, last wk Aug, SunL Sat **RESTAURANT:** Fixed L £5.95, main £11-£19.95 **PARKING:** On street

---

CLITHEROE　　　　　　　　　　　　Map 07 SD74

★★ 69% Shireburn Arms
Whalley Rd, Hurst Green BB7 9QJ
☎ 01254 826518 📠 01254 826208
e-mail: sales@shireburnarmshotel.com
web: www.shireburnarmshotel.com
Dir: A59 to Clitheroe, left at lights to Ribchester, follow Hurst Green signs. Hotel on B6243 at entrance to Hurst Green village

CHILD FACILITIES: Please telephone for details

This long established, family-owned hotel dates back to the 17th century and enjoys panoramic views over the Ribble Valley. Rooms are individually designed and thoughtfully equipped. The spacious restaurant, opening onto an attractive patio and garden, offers home-cooked food.
ROOMS: 18 en suite (3 fmly) ⊗ in 3 bedrooms s £48-£70; d £70-£90 (incl. bkfst) **LB FACILITIES:** Xmas **PARKING:** 71 **NOTES:** ⊗ in restaurant

🍸 Assheton Arms
Downham BB7 4BJ
☎ 01200 441227 📠 01200 440581
e-mail: asshetonarms@aol.com
Dir: From A59 take Chatburn turn. In Chatburn follow signs for Downham

CHILD FACILITIES: Please telephone for details

OPEN: 12-3 7-11 (summer Sun open all day) Closed: 1st wk in Jan **BAR MEALS:** L served all week 12-2 D served all week 7-10 Av main course £9 **PARKING:** 12

All AA listed accommodation, restaurants and pubs can be found on the AA's website www.theAA.com

---

THE
OLD ROSINS INN

The Old Rosins is a charming old country inn and restaurant set in the heart of the Lancashire Moors.

Offering a wide selection of dishes appealing to both adults and children, and a number of comfortable en-suite family rooms.

Close to the motorway network, Blackpool, Manchester and The Lake District are all easily accessible, offering fun for all the family!

Treacle Row, Pickup Bank, Hoddlesden, Darwen
Lancashire BB3 3QD
Tel: 01254 771264 Fax: 01254 873894

HOTEL SHERATON
54-62 Queens Promenade, Blackpool FY2 9RP
Tel: 01253 352723
Email: email@hotelsheraton.co.uk

FAMILY OWNED 2 STAR AA HOTEL
Situated on the exclusive Queens Promenade.
104 en-suite bedrooms with colour T.V.,
tea/coffee facilities.

Lifts to all floors • Spacious lounges.
Indoor heated swimming pool • Sauna.
Children's entertainment during children's
holidays (nightly in summer) • Highchairs
• Cots • Children's early dinner menu.
Games room - pool and table tennis.
All family rooms have baby listening.
Family rooms for 5 and 6 available.

DARWEN — Map 07 SD62

🍴 Old Rosins Inn
Treacle Row, Pickup Bank, Hoddlesden BB3 3QD
☎ 01254 771264 📠 01254 873894
Dir: M65 J5, follow signs for Haslingden then R after 2m signed Egworth. 0.5m R & continue for 0.5m

CHILD FACILITIES: Please telephone for details

OPEN: 11-11 (Sun 12-10.30) **BAR MEALS:** L served all week 12-2.30 D served all week 5.30-9 Av main course £5 **RESTAURANT:** L served all week 6.30-9 D served all week Av 3 course à la carte £12 Av 4 course fixed price £15 **FACILITIES:** Garden: Lawns and shrubbery, food served outdoors **ROOMS:** 15 bedrooms 15 en suite s£38.50 d£38.50 (♦♦♦)
PARKING: 200

See advert on page 159

GOOSNARGH — Map 07 SD53

Babies Welcome | Children's Dishes

🍴 Ye Horns Inn
Horns Ln PR3 2FJ
☎ 01772 865230 📠 01772 864299
e-mail: info@yehornsinn.co.uk
web: www.yehornsinn.co.uk
Dir: From M6 J32 take A6 N towards Garstang. At traffic lights turn R onto B5269 towards Goosnargh. In Goosnargh, follow Inn signs

CHILD FACILITIES: Food/bottle warming Ch menu Ch portions Highchairs Safe grounds **NEARBY:** Beacon Fell Country Park
OPEN: 11.30-3 6-11 (Ex Mon) **BAR MEALS:** L served Tue-Sun 12-2 D served all week 7-9.15 Av main course £9 **RESTAURANT:** L served Tue-Sun 12-2 D served all week 7-9.15 Av 3 course à la carte £17 Av 5 course fixed price £18.95 **FACILITIES:** Garden: Large patio area, tables, seating, pond, lawn 🎾 **PARKING:** 70

LANCASTER — Map 07 SD46

Babies Welcome | Family Rooms | Children's Dishes

★★★★ 71% 🏵 Lancaster House
Green Ln, Ellel LA1 4GJ
☎ 01524 844822 📠 01524 844766
e-mail: lancaster@elhmail.co.uk
web: www.elh.co.uk/hotels/lancaster
Dir: M6 junct 33 N towards Lancaster. Through Galgate and into Green Ln. Hotel below university on right

Best Western

CHILD FACILITIES: Baby listening Activities: Sam's Club splash time, welcome pack, toys, board games Food/bottle warming Ch menu Ch portions Highchairs Ch cutlery Ch discounts under 15s free sharing with parents Videos Cots Family rms D rms with S beds Ch drinks Connecting rms Fridge Laundry Changing mats (in family rms) **NEARBY:** Parks Farm Toy workshop Cave Aquarium Castle Waterworld Zoo

continued

This modern hotel enjoys a rural setting south of the city and close to the university. The attractive open-plan, balconied reception and lounge boasts traditional flagstone floors and a roaring log fire in colder months. Bedrooms are spacious and well equipped, and there are excellent leisure facilities. Staff are friendly and keen to please.
ROOMS: 80 en suite (10 fmly) (36 GF) 🚭 in 60 bedrooms s £89-£129; d £89-£129 **LB FACILITIES:** Spa STV 🏊 Sauna Solarium Gym Beauty salon 🎵 Xmas **PARKING:** 100 **NOTES:** 🚭 in restaurant

Babies Welcome | Family Rooms | Children's Dishes

★★★ Thurnham Mill Hotel & Restaurant
Thurnham Mill Ln, Conder Green LA2 0BD
☎ 01524 752852 📠 01524 752477
e-mail: stay@thurnham-mill-hotel.fsnet.co.uk
Dir: M6 junct 33, towards Lancaster. A6 to Galgate, left at lights. 1.75m. At bottom of road left over bridge, then left

CHILD FACILITIES: Activities: colouring, cycle hire Outdoor play area Food/bottle warming Ch menu Ch portions Highchairs Ch cutlery Ch discounts under 5s free, £10 over 5s Safe grounds Cots Family rms 2 D rms with Bbeds, 3 D rms with extra bed/s Laundry **NEARBY:** Walks 12-min drive to sea

This converted cloth mill dates from the 16th century and lies only a few miles from the M6 on the Lancaster Canal. Spacious bedrooms are traditional in style and include a number of family rooms. Dinner can be enjoyed in the Canalside Restaurant, or on sunny days on a popular terrace.
ROOMS: 18 en suite (6 fmly) 🚭 in 1 bedroom **PARKING:** 50
NOTES: 🚭 in restaurant

LONGRIDGE — Map 07 SD63

Babies Welcome | Children's Dishes

🏵 🏵 🏵 The Longridge Restaurant
104-106 Higher Rd PR3 3SY
☎ 01772 784969 📠 01772 785713
e-mail: longridge@heathcotes.co.uk
web: www.heathcotes.co.uk/longridge.htm
Dir: Follow signs for Golf Club & Jeffrey Hill. Higher Rd is beside White Bull Pub in Longridge

CHILD FACILITIES: Activities: colouring Food/bottle warming Ch portions Highchairs **NEARBY:** Cinema
FOOD: Modern British **STYLE:** Classic, Modern **SEATS:** 70
OPEN: 12-2.30/6-10, Closed 1 Jan, MonL Sat **RESTAURANT:** Fixed L £14, Fixed D £25, main £12-£18 **NOTES:** 🚭 area **PARKING:** 10

Don't forget to let proprietors
know when you book that
you're bringing the kids

LYTHAM ST ANNES — Map 07 SD32

★★★★ 67% ◉ Clifton Arms
West Beach, Lytham FY8 5QJ
☎ 01253 739898 ◳ 01253 730657
e-mail: welcome@cliftonarm-lytham.com
web: www.cliftonarm-lytham.com
Dir: on A584 along seafront

CHILD FACILITIES: Baby listening Activities: colouring Food/bottle warming Ch menu Ch portions Highchairs Ch discounts under 3s free Safe grounds Cots Family rms D rm with extra beds £45 per person, 3-8s £9.50, 9-15s £15 Ch drinks Laundry
NEARBY: Swimming pool Cinema Seafront location

This well-established hotel occupies a prime position overlooking Lytham Green and the Ribble Estuary beyond. The bedrooms vary in size and style; front-facing rooms are particularly spacious and some of the side rooms are very stylish and contemporary. There is an elegant restaurant and an open-plan lounge and cocktail bar.
ROOMS: 48 en suite (2 fmly) ⊛ in 25 bedrooms s £68-£98; d £90-£120 (incl. bkfst) LB FACILITIES: STV Xmas PARKING: 50
NOTES: ✖ ⊛ in restaurant

★★★ 67% Chadwick
South Promenade FY8 1NP — THE INDEPENDENTS
☎ 01253 720061 ◳ 01253 714455
e-mail: sales@thechadwickhotel.com
web: www.thechadwickhotel.com
Dir: M6 junct 32 take M55 to Blackpool then A5230 to South Shore. Follow signs for St Annes

CHILD FACILITIES: Baby listening Activities: Indoor play area Food/bottle warming Ch menu Ch portions Highchairs Ch cutlery Ch discounts under 3s free Games consoles Cots Family rms D rm with 1-3 S beds £70-£121 Ch drinks Connecting rms Laundry
NEARBY: Pleasure beach Sealife centre Leisure centre Cinema Parks 100yds to sea

This popular, comfortable and traditional hotel enjoys a seafront location. Bedrooms vary in size and style, but all are very thoughtfully equipped; those at the front boast panoramic sea views. Public rooms are spacious and comfortably furnished. The hotel has a well-equipped, air-conditioned gym and indoor pool.
ROOMS: 75 en suite (28 fmly) (13 GF) s £42-£50; d £62-£72 (incl. bkfst) LB FACILITIES: Spa STV ⊡ Sauna Solarium Gym Jacuzzi Turkish bath Games room Soft play adventure area ♫ Xmas
PARKING: 40 NOTES: ✖ ⊛ in restaurant

See advert on this page

★★ 69% Lindum
63-67 South Promenade FY8 1LZ
☎ 01253 721534 & 722516 ◳ 01253 721364
e-mail: info@lindumhotel.co.uk
web: www.lindumhotel.co.uk
Dir: from M55 follow A5230 & signs for Blackpool Airport. After airport, left at lights to St Annes, right at lights in town centre. 1st left onto seafront. Hotel 250yds on left

CHILD FACILITIES: Baby listening Food/bottle warming Ch menu Ch portions Highchairs Ch discounts Cots Family rms D rm with S beds from £80 Connecting rms Laundry NEARBY: Cinema Mini golf Trampolines Pleasure beach Blackpool Tower Park 100yds to sea

The same family has run this friendly and popular seafront hotel for over 40 years. Well-equipped bedrooms are generally spacious and some enjoy superb coastal views. Extensive public areas include a games room, a choice of lounges and a popular health suite. The open-plan restaurant offers a good choice of well-cooked dishes at breakfast and dinner.
ROOMS: 76 en suite (25 fmly) ⊛ in all bedrooms s £30-£45; d £50-£79 (incl. bkfst) LB FACILITIES: Sauna Solarium Jacuzzi ♫ Xmas
PARKING: 20 NOTES: ⊛ in restaurant

How to use this guide & abbreviations are explained on pages 5-7

MORECAMBE
Map 07 SD46

◆◆◆ Hotel Prospect
363 Marine Rd East LA4 5AQ
☎ 01524 417819 🖷 01524 417819
e-mail: peter@hotel-prospect.fsnet.co.uk
Dir: M6 junct 34/35, follow Morecombe Promenade, premises just before Gala Bingo

CHILD FACILITIES: Please telephone for details

Situated on Morecambe Promenade, this friendly family-run hotel enjoys panoramic views over the bay to the Lakeland Hills beyond. Bedrooms are comfortably proportioned, thoughtfully furnished and carefully decorated. The bright airy dining room extends into a small lounge area, which has its own bar and overlooks the sea. There is an enclosed car park, offering off road parking.

ROOMS: 14 rms (13 en suite) (4 fmly) (2 GF) s £17-£19; d £34-£38 * ⊗ in 2 bedrooms **FACILITIES:** TVB tea/coffee Dinner Last d order 3pm **NOTES:** ⊗ in restaurant Licensed Cen ht **LB BB PARKING:** 14

SLAIDBURN
Map 07 SD75

🍺 Hark to Bounty Inn
Townend BB7 3EP
☎ 01200 446246 🖷 01200 446361
e-mail: manager@hark-to-bounty.co.uk
Dir: From M6 J31 take A59 to Clitheroe then B6478, through Waddington, Newton and onto Slaidburn

CHILD FACILITIES: Please telephone for details

OPEN: 11-11 **BAR MEALS:** L served all week 12-2 D served all week 6-9 Av main course £8.50 **RESTAURANT:** L served Tue-Sun 12-2 D served Tue-Sat 6-9 Av 3 course fixed price £15.95 **FACILITIES:** Children's licence Garden: Large enclosed area **PARKING:** 25

LEICESTERSHIRE

Donington Racetrack Museum

BELVOIR
Belvoir Castle NG32 1PD
info@belvoircastle.com   ☎01476 871002
(between A52 & A607, follow the brown heritage signs from A1, A52, A607 & A46)
Open 16-20 Feb; Apr-Sep, daily (closed Mon & Thu); Mar & Oct Sun only.
*£9 (ch £7 pen £8).

CASTLE DONINGTON
Donington Grand Prix Collection
DE74 2RP   ☎01332 811027
enquiries@doningtoncollection.co.uk
(2m from M1 junct 23a/24 and M42/A42 close to Nottingham Derby and Leicester)
Open daily 10-5 (last admission 4pm). Open later on race days. (Closed over Xmas period - telephone to confirm opening times over this period).

COALVILLE
Snibston Discovery Park LE67 3LN
snibston@leics.gov.uk   ☎01530 278444
(4.5m from M1 junct 22/2m or from A42/M42 junct 13 on A511 on the West side of Coalville)
Open all year, 10-5 (Closed 12-16 Jan & 25-26 Dec).
*£5.70 (ch £3.60, concessions £3.90). Family ticket £17.50.

LEICESTER
National Space Centre LE4 5NS
info@spacecentre.co.uk   ☎0116 261 0261
(off A6, 2m N of city centre)
Tue-Fri 10-5 last entry 3.30pm, Sat-Sun 10-6. School holidays, Mon 12-6 & Tue-Sun 10-6.
*£8.95 (ch 4-16 & concessions £6.95). Family ticket £28.

MOIRA
Conkers DE12 6GA
info@visitconkers.com   ☎01283 216633
(located on B5003 in Moira, signposted from A444 and M42) Open daily, summer 10-6, winter 10-5. (Closed 25 Dec). *£5.95 (ch £3.95, concessions £4.95). Family ticket (2 ad & 2 ch) £17.50.

TWYCROSS
Twycross Zoo Park
CV9 3PX   ☎01827 880250
(On A444 Burton to Nuneaton road, directly off M42 Junct 11)
Open all year, daily 10-6 (4pm in winter). (Closed 25 Dec). Please telephone for prices.

England

BARKESTONE-LE-VALE
Map 08 SK73

Family Rooms | Children's Dishes

◆◆◆◆ 🌱 Woodside Farm
NG13 0HQ
☎ 01476 870336
e-mail: hickling-woodside@supanet.com
web: www.woodsidebandb.co.uk
Dir: from A52 at Bottesford, exit towards Harby & Belvoir Castle. After Redmile crossing, lane leading to Woodside Farm on left approx 0.5m

CHILD FACILITIES: Baby listening Activities: farm animals, board games Outdoor play area Family area Food/bottle warming Ch menu Ch portions Ch cutlery Ch discounts under 3s free in own cot Family rms D rm with S bed & T rm from £40 Ch drinks Laundry **NEARBY:** Adventure park Castle Leisure centre Theme park Walks

A warm welcome awaits guests at this friendly working farm, peacefully located on the Belvoir Castle estate in the Vale of Belvoir within easy reach of Nottingham and Grantham. Bedrooms are smartly appointed and enjoy beautiful views over open countryside. Hearty breakfasts are served in the lounge/dining room, and packed lunches are available on request.
ROOMS: 2 en suite (1 fmly) (1 GF) s £35-£40; d £50-£58 *
FACILITIES: tea/coffee Riding Cycle storage available 340 acres arable dairy **NOTES:** Credit cards not taken ✗ ⊛ Cen ht LB **PARKING:** 4

BOTTESFORD
Map 08 SK83

Babies Welcome | Family Rooms | Children's Dishes

◆◆◆◆ 🛏 The Thatch Hotel & Restaurant
26 High St NG13 0AA
☎ 01949 842330 & 844407 📠 01949 844407
e-mail: thatch.hotelrestaurant@btinternet.com
Dir: turn off A52 signed Bottesford

CHILD FACILITIES: Baby listening Babysitting Activities: colouring Outdoor play area Food/bottle warming Ch portions Highchairs Ch cutlery Safe grounds Cots Family rms D rm with S bed, put up & cot available Laundry

This lovely thatched cottage occupies a prominent location in the centre of the village, just off the A52. There is a comfortable lounge bar and attractive rear gardens, but the hub of the operation is the smartly appointed restaurant, which offers carefully prepared and imaginative dishes. Morning coffee and afternoon teas are readily available. Bedrooms are also smartly appointed and thoughtfully equipped.
ROOMS: 3 en suite (1 fmly) s £40; d £60 * ⊛ **FACILITIES:** TVB tea/coffee Membership cards to leisure centre in Grantham Dinner Last d order 9.30pm **NOTES:** ✗ ⊛ in restaurant Licensed Cen ht
PARKING: 8

CROFT
Map 04 SP59

◆◆◆ Fossebrook
Coventry Rd, Croft LE9 3GP
☎ 01455 283517 📠 01455 283517
Dir: M1 junct 21, outer ring road, B4114 signed Enderby/Narborough, pass police HQ, quarry on right. After turn for Croft, Fossebrook 100yds on left, concealed entrance

CHILD FACILITIES: Please telephone for details

This friendly guest house enjoys a quiet rural location and good access from road networks. Bedrooms are spacious, very comfortable and offer an excellent range of facilities including

continued

videos in all rooms. Breakfast is served in the bright dining room, which overlooks pleasant gardens and grounds.
ROOMS: 5 en suite (1 fmly) (4 GF) s £40; d £40 * ⊛
FACILITIES: TVB tea/coffee No coaches Riding **NOTES:** ✗ Cen ht
PARKING: 16

GADDESBY
Map 08 SK61

◆◆◆◆ 🛏 🍴 The Cheney Arms
Rearsby Ln LE7 4XE
☎ 01664 840260
web: www.cheneyarms.co.uk
Dir: turn off A607 at Rearsby to Gaddesby, 2.5m on left at junct of Main St
CHILD FACILITIES: Please telephone for details

This delightful village inn is peacefully located a short drive from Melton Mowbray. The impressive three-storey, ivy-clad building was originally built for General Cheney. The spacious bedrooms are furnished with well-chosen pine pieces and have many thoughtful touches. Public rooms include a popular public bar and a smart restaurant where an interesting choice of home-made meals are served.
ROOMS: 4 en suite (1 fmly) d £50-£60 * ⊛ **FACILITIES:** TVB tea/coffee Petanque, darts Dinner Last d order 9.30pm **NOTES:** ✗ ⊛ in area of dining room Cen ht **PARKING:** 30

Babies Welcome — This symbol indicates the establishment provides food & bottle warming and highchairs

England

HINCKLEY Map 04 SP49

Babies Welcome	Family Rooms	Children's Dishes

★★★★ 71% 🅱️ 🅱️
Sketchley Grange
Sketchley Ln, Burbage LE10 3HU
☎ 01455 251133 📠 01455 631384
e-mail: reservations@sketchleygrange.co.uk
web: www.sketchleygrange.co.uk
Dir: SE of town, off A5/M69 junct 1, take B4109 to Hinckley. Left at 2nd rdbt. 1st right onto Sketchley Ln

CHILD FACILITIES: Activities: bouncy castle, adventure playground, colouring, activity books Outdoor play area Food/bottle warming Ch menu Ch portions Highchairs Ch discounts under 5s free sharing with parents Safe grounds Cots Family rms D rms with S bed or sofa bed Connecting rms Fridge Laundry NEARBY: National Space Centre Zoo Park Leisure Centre Warwick Castle

Although close to motorway connections the hotel is peacefully set in its own grounds, and enjoys country views. Excellent facilities include the new and stylish Roman's Health and Leisure Spa, complete with a 'Little Romans' crèche, and a choice of bars and dining options. Bedrooms include many extras; many rooms have been recently refurbished.
ROOMS: 52 en suite (9 fmly) (1 GF) 😊 in 15 bedrooms
FACILITIES: Spa STV 🏊 Sauna Solarium Gym Steam room, Hairdressing, Creche, Beauty therapy **PARKING:** 200 **NOTES:** 😊 in restaurant

See advert on page 163

LEICESTER Map 04 SK50

♦♦♦ Stoneycroft Hotel
5-7 Elmfield Av LE2 1RB
☎ 0116 270 7605 📠 0116 270 6067
e-mail: reception@stoneycrofthotel.co.uk
Dir: near city centre on A6 to Market Harborough
CHILD FACILITIES: Please telephone for details
This large hotel provides comfortable accommodation and helpful service. Public rooms include a foyer lounge area, breakfast room and large restaurant/bar area, which serves a good selection of freshly cooked dishes. Bedrooms have modern appointments, including desks and suitable chairs.
ROOMS: 41 en suite (4 fmly) (6 GF) s £44; d £55 * 😊
FACILITIES: TVB tea/coffee Direct dial from bedrooms TVL Pool Table Dinner Last d order 9.30pm **NOTES:** 😊 in restaurant Licensed Cen ht
PARKING: 20

LOUGHBOROUGH Map 08 SK51

♦♦♦ Garendon Park Hotel
92 Leicester Rd LE11 2AQ
☎ 01509 236557 📠 01509 265559
e-mail: info@garendonparkhotel.co.uk
Dir: M1 junct 23/A512 to Loughborough, at 2nd island turn right, at 5th island turn left, at lights turn left. Hotel on right just before next lights
CHILD FACILITIES: Please telephone for details
This late Victorian house is conveniently situated just a short walk from the high street. Bedrooms are individually decorated and feature co-ordinated fabrics and thoughtful touches. Breakfast and dinner are served at individual tables in the smart dining room and guests have the use of a lounge as well as a cosy bar.
ROOMS: 9 en suite (4 fmly) s £37-£45; d £47-£60 * 😊
FACILITIES: STV TVB tea/coffee TVL Dinner Last d order 6pm
NOTES: 😊 in restaurant Licensed Cen ht

MELTON MOWBRAY Map 08 SK71

Babies Welcome	Family Rooms	Children's Dishes

♦♦♦♦ Bryn Barn
38 High St, Waltham-on-the-Wolds LE14 4AH
☎ 01664 464783 & 07791 215614 📠 01664 464138
e-mail: glenarowlands@onetel.com
Dir: off A607 onto High St between Marquis of Granby pub and church, Bryn Barn 200mtrs on right
CHILD FACILITIES: Activities: colouring, puzzles, board games, Lego Food/bottle warming Ch menu Ch portions Highchairs Ch cutlery Ch discounts under 2s free, 2-11s half price Cots Family rms D rm with 1/2 S beds £56 for 2 adults & 1 child Ch drinks (by request) Connecting rms Laundry NEARBY: Family fun park Nature reserve

A warm welcome awaits guests at this attractive, peacefully located cottage within easy reach of Melton Mowbray, Grantham, Rutland Water and Belvoir Castle. Bedrooms are smartly appointed and comfortably furnished, whilst public rooms include an inviting lounge overlooking a wonderful courtyard garden. Dinner can be taken at one of the nearby village pubs.
ROOMS: 4 en suite (2 fmly) (1 GF) s £28-£30; d £45-£48 *
FACILITIES: TV5B tea/coffee TVL No coaches **NOTES:** Credit cards not taken 😊 Cen ht **LB PARKING:** 4

SOMERBY Map 04 SK71

Babies Welcome	Children's Dishes

🍴 Stilton Cheese Inn
High St LE14 2QB
☎ 01664 454394
CHILD FACILITIES: Food/bottle warming Ch menu Ch portions Highchairs Ch cutlery Safe grounds NEARBY: Hill Fort Walks Riding school

OPEN: 12-3 6-11 **BAR MEALS:** L served all week 12-2 D served all week 6-9 Av main course £6.75 **RESTAURANT:** L served all week 12-2 D serve all week 6-9 Av 3 course à la carte £13.50 **FACILITIES:** Garden: Small patio, seats around 20 ✈ **PARKING:** 14

LINCOLNSHIRE

Skegness fair

CLEETHORPES
Pleasure Island Family Theme Park DN35 0PL
pleasureisland@btinternet.com ☎01472 211511
(Follow signs to Pleasure Island from A180)
Open 6 Apr-7 Sep, daily from 10. Wknds during
Sep-Oct & daily during half term (25 Oct-2 Nov).

CONINGSBY
Battle of Britain Memorial Flight Visitor Centre
LN4 4SY ☎01526 344041
bbmf@lincolnshire.gov.uk
(on A153)
Open all year, Mon-Fri, conducted tours 10-3.30.
(Closed 2 wks Xmas). (Phone prior to visiting to
check security situation)
*£3.70 (con £2.20) family £9.60.

GRIMSBY
National Fishing Heritage Centre
DN31 1UZ ☎01472 323345
(follow signs off M180)
Open Apr-Sep, Mon-Thu 10-4, Sat-Sun 11-5
(10.30-5.30 Jul-Sep).

LINCOLN
Museum of Lincolnshire Life
LN1 3LY ☎01522 528448
lincolnshirelife_museum@lincolnshire.gov.uk
(100mtr walk from Lincoln Castle)
Open all year, May-Sep, daily 10-5.30; Oct-Apr,
Mon-Sat 10-5.30, Sun 2-5.30. Closed Sun Oct-
Apr.
*£2.05 (concessions £1.25). Family (2ad+3ch)
£5.35.

SKEGNESS
Skegness Natureland Seal Sanctuary
PE25 1DB ☎01754 764345
natureland@fsbdial.co.uk
(N end of seafront)
Open all year, daily at 10am. Closing times vary
according to season. (Closed 25-26 Dec & 1 Jan).
*£4.95 (ch under 3 free, ch £3.25, pen £3.95).
Family ticket £14.70.

SPALDING
Butterfly & Wildlife Park PE12 9LE
butterflypark@hotmail.com ☎01406 363833
(off A17 at Long Sutton)
Open 20 Mar-end Oct, daily 10-5. (Sep & Oct
10-4).
*£5.50 (ch 3-16 £3.80, pen £4.80). Family ticket
£17-£20. Party rates on application.

♦♦♦♦ Clee House
31-33 Clee Rd DN35 8AD
☎ 01472 200850 📠 01472 200850
e-mail: clee.house@btinternet.com
Dir: on entering town from Grimsby, turn right onto Clee Rd at Isaac's Hill rdbt. 50mtrs house in own grounds on left

CHILD FACILITIES: Please telephone for details

Located close to the town centre, this detached Victorian house retains many original features. Tasty breakfasts and imaginative evening meals are served in the cosy dining room, while a comfortable lounge is also available for residents. Bedrooms are spacious and very well equipped, including several ground floor rooms suitable for less mobile guests.
ROOMS: 10 en suite (6 fmly) (4 GF) ⊗ **FACILITIES:** STV TVB tea/coffee Direct dial from bedrooms TVL Dinner Last d order 9pm
NOTES: ✕ ⊗ in restaurant Licensed Cen ht **PARKING:** 14

♦♦♦ Burlington Guest House
2-4 Albert Rd DN35 8LX
☎ 01472 699071 📠 01472 699071
e-mail: burlington2_4@btopenworld.com
Dir: on the upper Prom. next to library

CHILD FACILITIES: Please telephone for details

This welcoming establishment enjoys a quiet location just off the sea front, with private rear car parking. Bedrooms are neatly presented, and include some ground floor rooms. There is a comfortably appointed residents' bar and breakfast is served in a pleasant dining room.
ROOMS: 12 rms (2 en suite) (3 fmly) (2 GF) **FACILITIES:** TVB tea/coffee TVL No coaches **NOTES:** ⊗ in restaurant Licensed Cen ht
PARKING: 8

Babies Welcome	Family Rooms	Children's Dishes

♦♦♦ The Black Horse Inn
Main Rd LN11 9TJ
☎ 01507 343640 📠 01507 343640
e-mail: barrett@blackhorse1125.freeserve.co.uk
Dir: turn off A157 Lincoln to Louth Road, signed Donington on Bain. In centre of village

CHILD FACILITIES: Outdoor play area Food/bottle warming
Ch menu Ch portions Highchairs Ch discounts Safe grounds Family
rms D rms with S bed **NEARBY:** Walks Working farm

Please note that this establishment has recently changed hands.
An ideal touring base either for The Viking Way, nearby Cadwell Park, Market Rasen or the market town of Louth. A wide range of food and beers is available in this popular inn, and the spacious bedrooms are comfortable and all en-suite.
ROOMS: 8 en suite (4 GF) s fr £26; d fr £44 * ⊗ **FACILITIES:** TVB tea/coffee Pool Table Dinner Last d order 9pm **NOTES:** ⊗ in restaurant ⊗ in 1 lounge Cen ht **LB PARKING:** 60

England

| Babies Welcome | Family Rooms | Children's Dishes |

◆◆◆◆ Elloe Lodge

37 Barrington Gate PE12 7LB
☎ 01406 423207 🖹 01406 423207
e-mail: bandbholbeach@btinternet.com
Dir: in town centre take Church Street from T-lights then 2nd left, 1st house on right

CHILD FACILITIES: Baby listening Outdoor play area Food/bottle warming Ch menu Ch portions Highchairs Ch cutlery Ch discounts Safe grounds Cots Family rms triple rms or D rm with S bed £60 Ch drinks Fridge Laundry Changing mats **NEARBY:** Park Butterfly park Laser Quest Fun farm

This delightful house is peacefully situated in extensive well-tended grounds and gardens, just minutes' walk from the town centre. Bedrooms are well appointed and comfortably furnished. Spacious public areas include an inviting guest lounge and an attractive dining room, where hearty breakfasts are served at individual tables.
ROOMS: 4 en suite (2 fmly) s £28; d £44 * **FACILITIES:** tea/coffee TVL No coaches **NOTES:** ✈ ⊗ Cen ht **LB PARKING:** 10

| Babies Welcome | Family Rooms | Children's Dishes |

★★★ 70% *Washingborough Hall*

Church Hill, Washingborough LN4 1BE
☎ 01522 790340 🖹 01522 792936
e-mail: enquiries@washingboroughhallhotel.com
Dir: on B1190 signed Bardney. Right at mini island, hotel 200yds on left

CHILD FACILITIES: Activities: games, colouring, puzzles Outdoor play area Food/bottle warming Ch menu Ch portions Highchairs Ch discounts Safe grounds Videos Cots Family rms D rm with put up beds from £90, extra bed £15, cot £10 Laundry **NEARBY:** Leisure centre Cinema Walks Park Tenpin bowling

This Georgian manor stands on the edge of the quiet village of Washingborough among attractive gardens, with an outdoor swimming pool in the summer. Public rooms are pleasantly furnished and comfortable, whilst the restaurant offers interesting menus. Bedrooms are individually designed, and most have views out over the grounds and countryside.
ROOMS: 14 en suite (1 fmly) ⊗ in 2 bedrooms **FACILITIES:** ⊰ ▯ **PARKING:** 50 **NOTES:** ⊗ in restaurant

> Please mention AA Family Friendly Places
> to Stay, Eat and Visit when booking

| Babies Welcome | Family Rooms | Children's Dishes |

★★ 73% Hillcrest

15 Lindum Ter LN2 5RT
☎ 01522 510182 🖹 01522 538009
e-mail: reservations@hillcrest-hotel.com
web: www.hillcrest-hotel.com

THE CIRCLE
Selected Individual Hotels
GREAT BRITAIN

Dir: from A15 Wragby Rd and Lindum Rd, turn into Upper Lindum St at sign. Left at bottom for hotel 200mtrs on right

CHILD FACILITIES: Baby listening Food/bottle warming Ch menu Ch portions Highchairs Ch cutlery Ch discounts under 2s free, 2-14s £6 Safe grounds Cots Family rms £85 plus child's price Laundry **NEARBY:** Lincoln Castle Play area Maize Farm

The hospitality offered by Jenny Bennett and her staff is one of the strengths of Hillcrest, which sits in a quiet residential location. Thoughtfully equipped bedrooms come in a variety of sizes and all are well presented and maintained. The cosy dining room and pleasant conservatory offer a good range of freshly prepared food with views out over the adjacent park. A computer room is available for residents.
ROOMS: 14 en suite (5 fmly) (6 GF) ⊗ in 6 bedrooms s £65; d £85-£95 (incl. bkfst) **LB FACILITIES: PARKING:** 8 **NOTES:** ⊗ in restaurant Closed 23 Dec-3 Jan

◆◆◆◆ D'Isney Place Hotel

Eastgate LN2 4AA
☎ 01522 538881 🖹 01522 511321
e-mail: info@disneyplacehotel.co.uk
web: www.disneyplacehotel.co.uk
Dir: 100yds from Lincoln Cathedral. Nearest main roads - A15 & A46
CHILD FACILITIES: Please telephone for details

This charming period town house is located minutes' walk from the cathedral and the historic area of the city. Individually specified bedrooms include rooms with four-poster or half-tester beds, and all come equipped with many extras to guarantee comfort. Breakfasts make use of quality ingredients and are served in bedrooms, or weather permitting, in the delightful private gardens.
ROOMS: 17 en suite (2 fmly) (8 GF) s £59.50-£79.50; d £95-£115 * ⊗ in 10 bedrooms **FACILITIES:** TVB tea/coffee Direct dial from bedrooms **NOTES:** Cen ht **LB PARKING:** 4

| Babies Welcome | Children's Dishes |

◆◆ Jaymar

31 Newland St West LN1 1QQ
☎ 01522 532934 🖹 01522 820182
e-mail: ward.jaymar4@ntlworld.com
Dir: turn off A1 onto A46, proceed to junct with A57 turn right to Lincoln Central. At 1st set of T-lights turn left into Gresham Street then take 2nd right by off licence, Jaymar approx 500mtrs on left

CHILD FACILITIES: Baby listening Babysitting (not registered) Food/bottle warming Ch menu Ch portions Highchairs Ch cutlery Ch discounts under 13s 50% Safe grounds Cots D rm with cot/child's bed £32 Changing mats **NEARBY:** Park Lakes Nature reserve Play zone Cinema

Situated within easy walking distance of the city, this small, friendly guest house offers two well-equipped bedrooms. A full English breakfast, with vegetarian options, is served in the cosy dining room, and an early breakfast, from 5am onwards, is available on request. Children and pets are welcome, and guests can be collected from the bus or railway stations if required.
ROOMS: 2 rms (1 fmly) s £17-£20; d £32-£40 * **FACILITIES:** TVB tea/coffee No coaches **NOTES:** Credit cards not taken ⊗ **LB BB**

England

Babies Welcome | Children's Dishes

🌀 Wig & Mitre
30/32 Steep Hill LN2 1TL
☎ 01522 535190 📠 532402
e-mail: email@wigandmitre.com web: www.wigandmitre.com
Dir: At the top of Steep Hill, adjacent to Lincoln Cathedral and Lincoln Castle car parks

CHILD FACILITIES: Activities: colouring Food/bottle warming Ch portions Highchairs **NEARBY:** Lincoln Cathedral Lincoln Castle Museum of Lincolnshire Life

FOOD: Modern International **STYLE:** Traditional, Bistro **SEATS:** 65 **OPEN:** 8 am-11 pm **RESTAURANT:** main £10.50-£17.50 **NOTES:** ⊗ in restaurant **PARKING:** Public car park adjacent

RAITHBY   Map 08 TF36

🍷 Red Lion Inn
PE23 4DS
☎ 01790 753727
Dir: Take A158 from Horncastle, R at Sausthorpe, keep L into Raithby
CHILD FACILITIES: Please telephone for details

OPEN: 12-3 7-11 **BAR MEALS:** L served Thu-Sun 12-2.30 D served Wed-Mon 7-9.30 Av main course £8 **RESTAURANT:** L served Sat-Sun 12-2.30 D served Wed-Mon 7-10 **FACILITIES:** Food served outside. Terrace patio **NOTES:** Credit cards not taken **PARKING:** 20

SCUNTHORPE   Map 08 SE81

★★★★ 74% 🌀 Forest Pines Hotel
Ermine St, Broughton DN20 0AQ
☎ 01652 650770 📠 01652 650495
e-mail: enquiries@forestpines.co.uk
web: www.forestpines.co.uk
Dir: 200yds from M180 junct 4, on Brigg-Scunthorpe rdbt
CHILD FACILITIES: Please telephone for details
This smart, modern hotel provides a comprehensive range of leisure facilities. A modern health and beauty spa and a championship golf course ensure that it is a popular choice with all guests. A comfortable lounge and extensive public areas
continued

include a choice of dining options, with fine dining available in The Beech Tree Restaurant or more informal eating in the Garden Room or Mulligan's Bar. Bedrooms are modern, spacious and well equipped.
ROOMS: 114 en suite (66 fmly) (41 GF) ⊗ in 77 bedrooms s £79-£99; d £99-£109 (incl. bkfst) **LB FACILITIES: Spa** STV 🏌 Golf 27 Sauna Gym ⚓ Jacuzzi Mountain bikes Jogging track 🎵 Xmas **PARKING:** 300 **NOTES:** ✖ ⊗ in restaurant

SKEGNESS   Map 09 TF56

Babies Welcome | Family Rooms | Children's Dishes

★★★ 67% Vine
Vine Rd, Seacroft PE25 3DB
☎ 01754 763018 & 610611 📠 01754 769845
e-mail: info@thevinehotel.com
Dir: A52 to Skegness, S towards Gibraltar Point, turn right on to Drummond Rd, after 0.5m turn right into Vine Rd

CHILD FACILITIES: Baby listening Activities: colouring Food/bottle warming Ch menu Ch portions Highchairs Safe grounds Cots Family rms 2 rm suites or D rms with S bed Connecting rms **NEARBY:** Leisure park Nature reserve Country park 1m to sea

Reputedly the second oldest building in Skegness, this traditional style hotel offers two character bars. Freshly prepared dishes are served in both the bar and the restaurant; service is both friendly and helpful. The smartly refurbished bedrooms are well equipped and comfortably appointed.
ROOMS: 24 en suite (3 fmly) ⊗ in 6 bedrooms s £60-£70; d £80-£90 (incl. bkfst) **LB FACILITIES:** STV Golf 18 ⚓ Xmas **PARKING:** 50 **NOTES:** ⊗ in restaurant

SLEAFORD   Map 08 TF04

Babies Welcome | Children's Dishes

★★★ 64% The Lincolnshire Oak
East Rd NG34 7EH
☎ 01529 413807 📠 01529 413710
e-mail: reception@lincolnshire-oak.co.uk
web: www.lincolnshire-oak.co.uk
Dir: From A17 (by-pass) exit on A153 into Sleaford. Hotel .75m on left
CHILD FACILITIES: Baby listening Food/bottle warming Ch menu Ch portions Highchairs Ch cutlery Safe grounds Cots Laundry **NEARBY:** Leisure Centre Nature Park Farm Belton House
Located on the edge of the town in well-tended grounds, this hotel has a relaxed and friendly atmosphere. A comfortable open-plan lounge bar is complemented by a cosy restaurant that looks out onto the rear garden. Bedroom styles differ: all rooms are well furnished and suitably equipped, though the 'superior' rooms are more comfortably appointed.
ROOMS: 17 en suite ⊗ in 12 bedrooms s £59-£72; d £72.50-£87.50 (incl. bkfst) **LB FACILITIES:** STV **PARKING:** 80 **NOTES:** ✖ ⊗ in restaurant

England

SOUTH WITHAM   Map 08 SK91

Babies Welcome | Children's Dishes

⬛ Blue Cow Inn & Brewery
High St NG33 5QB
☎ 01572 768432 🖹 01572 768432
e-mail: richard@thirlwell.fslife.co.uk
web: www.thebluecowinn.co.uk
Dir: Between Stamford & Grantham on A1

CHILD FACILITIES: Outdoor play area Food/bottle warming
Ch menu Ch portions Highchairs Ch cutlery NEARBY: Viking Way

OPEN: 12-11 BAR MEALS: L served all week 12-2.30 D served all week
6-9.30 RESTAURANT: L served all week 12-2.30 D served all week 6-9.30
FACILITIES: Garden: Seating for 32 ROOMS: 6 bedrooms 6 en suite
2 family rooms s£40 d£45 (♦♦♦) PARKING: 45

LONDON

Piccadilly Circus

LONDON EC3
Tower of London
EC3N 4AB   ☎0870 756 6060
(Underground - Tower Hill) Open all year, Mar-Oct,
Mon-Sat 9-6, Sun 10-6 last admission 5pm; Nov-
Feb, Tue-Sat 9-5, Sun 10-5 last admission 4pm.
Closed 24-26 Dec & 1 Jan.

LONDON NW1
London Zoo NW1 4RY
marketing@zsl.org   ☎020 7449 6235
(Underground - Camden Town or Regents Park)
Open all year, daily from 10am. Closed 25 Dec.
*£13 ch 3-15 £9.75, concessions £11. Family £41.

Madame Tussaud's & The London Planetarium
NW1 5LR   ☎020 7935 6861
csc@madame-tussauds.com
(Underground - Baker Street) Open all year 10-
5.30 9.30am wknds, 9am summer

LONDON SE1
British Airways London Eye
SE17 PB   ☎0870 500 0600
(Underground - Waterloo/Westminster)
Open May, Mon-Thurs 9.30-8, Fri-Sun 9.30-9, 24-
31 May last flight 10pm; June, Mon-Thu 9.30-9,
Fri-Sun 9.30-10; July-Aug daily 9.30-10; Sep,
Mon-Thurs 9.30-8, Fri-Sun 9.30-9, 1-7 Sep last
flight 10pm; Oct-Dec, daily 9.30-8. Closed 25 Dec
*£11.50 ch under 5 free, ch £5.75, disabled
visitors £9, pen £9. Fast track entry £25.

London Aquarium SE1 7PB
info@londonaquarium.co.uk   ☎020 7967 8000
(Underground-Waterloo & Westminster. On south
bank next to Westminster Bridge, nr Big Ben &
London Eye)
Open all year, daily 10-6. Last admission 1hr
before closing. Closed 25 Dec, late opening over
summer months see website for details.

The London Dungeon
SE1 2SZ   ☎020 7403 7221
londondungeon@merlin-entertainments.com
(Next to London Bridge Station)
Open all year, daily, Apr-Sep 10-5.30; Oct-Mar
10.30-5. Late night opening in the summer.
Telephone for exact times.

LONDON SE10
Cutty Sark Clipper Ship SE10 9HT
info@cuttysark.org.uk   ☎020 8858 2698
(situated in dry dock beside Greenwich Pier)
Open all year, daily 10-4.30 Closed 24-27 Dec.
*£4.25 concessions £3.25. Fam ticket £10.50.
Party 10+ 20% reduction.

LONDON SW7
Natural History Museum SW7 5BD
marketing@nhm.ac.uk   ☎020 7942 5000
(Underground - South Kensington) Mon-Sat 10-
5.50, Sun 11-5.50 last admission 5.30. Closed 24-
26 Dec. Free.

LONDON WC1
British Museum
WC1B 3DG   ☎020 7323 8000
information@thebritishmuseum.ac.uk
(Underground - Russell Sq, Tottenham Court Rd,
Holborn)
Open all year, Gallery: Mon-Sat 10-5.30 & Thu-Fri
10-8.30. Great Court: Sun-Wed 9-6, Thu-Sat 9am-
11pm. (Closed Good Fri, 24-26 Dec & 1 Jan).

E3

The Crown
223 Grove Rd E3 5SN
☎ 020 8981 9998 📠 020 8980 2336
e-mail: crown@singhboulton.co.uk
web: www.singhboulton.co.uk
Dir: Mile End Central Line & District line. Buses 277 to Victoria Park

CHILD FACILITIES: Please telephone for details

OPEN: 12 -11 (Mon 5-11, Wknd phone for details) Closed: 25 Dec **BAR MEALS:** L served Tue-Sun 12.30-3.30 D served Mon-Sun 6.30-10.30 Av main course £10.50 **RESTAURANT:** L served Tue-Sun 12.30-3.30 D served Mon-Sun 6.30-10.30 **FACILITIES:** Children's licence Garden: Paved area at front of pub

E1

Babies Welcome **Children's Dishes**

🌀 Wapping Food
Wapping Hydraulic, Power Station, Wapping Wall E1W 3ST
☎ 020 7680 2080
e-mail: info@wapping-wpt.com
Dir: Turn R from tube, walk E & parallel to the river (approx 4 mins)

CHILD FACILITIES: Outdoor play area Food/bottle warming Ch licence Ch portions Highchairs Safe grounds **NEARBY:** Hackney City Farm River

FOOD: Modern International **STYLE:** Modern Converted Power Station **SEATS:** 100 **OPEN:** 12-3/6.30-11, Closed 24 Dec-3 Jan, D Sun **RESTAURANT:** main £12-£17 **PARKING:** 20

Babies Welcome **Children's Dishes**

🌀 Café Spice Namaste
16 Prescot St E1 8AZ
☎ 020 7488 9242 📠 0171 488 9339
e-mail: pervin@cafespice.co.uk
Dir: Nearest station: Tower Gateway (DLR), Aldgate, Aldgate East, Tower Hill

CHILD FACILITIES: Food/bottle warming Ch portions Highchairs Safe grounds **NEARBY:** Tower of London

FOOD: Indian **STYLE:** Classic **SEATS:** 110 **OPEN:** 12-3/6.15-10.30, Closed BHs, SunL Sat **RESTAURANT:** main £6.75-£15.95 **NOTES:** Smart Dress, Air con **PARKING:** On street; NCP

E14

★★★★★ 🌀
Four Seasons Hotel Canary Wharf
Westferry Circus, Canary Wharf E14 8RS
☎ 020 7510 1999 📠 020 7510 1998
web: www.fourseasons.com/canarywharf
Dir: From A13 follow signs to Canary Wharf, Isle of Dogs and Westferry Circus. Hotel off 3rd exit of Westferry Circus rdbt

CHILD FACILITIES: Please telephone for details

With superb views over the London skyline, this stylish modern hotel enjoys a delightful riverside location. Spacious contemporary bedrooms are particularly thoughtfully equipped. Public areas include the Italian Quadrato Bar and Restaurant and gymnasium. Guests also have complimentary use of the impressive Holmes Place health club and spa. Welcoming staff provide exemplary levels of service and hospitality.

ROOMS: 142 en suite 🚭 in 120 bedrooms s £353-£2115; d £376-£2115 **FACILITIES:** Spa STV 🖰 🛇 Sauna Solarium Gym Jacuzzi 🎵 Xmas **PARKING:** 29

Babies Welcome **Children's Dishes**

🌀 🌀 🌀 Ubon by Nobu
34 Westferry Circus, Canary Wharf E14 8RR
☎ 0207 719 7800 📠 0207 719 7801
e-mail: ubon@noburestaurants.com
web: www.noburestaurants.com
Dir: Restaurant behind Four Seasons Hotel

CHILD FACILITIES: Food/bottle warming Ch portions Highchairs Safe grounds

FOOD: Japanese **STYLE:** Chic, Modern **SEATS:** 120 **OPEN:** 12-2.15/6-10.15, Closed Xmas, all BHs, SunL Sat **RESTAURANT:** main £5-£29.50 **NOTES:** 🚭 area, Air con **PARKING:** Riverside car park

E16

Babies Welcome **Family Rooms** **Children's Dishes**

★★★★ 70% Novotel London ExCel
7 Western Gateway, Royal Victoria Docks E16 1AA
☎ 020 7540 9700 📠 020 7540 9710
e-mail: H3656@accor-hotels.com

CHILD FACILITIES: Babysitting Activities: Lego, welcome pack Food/bottle warming Ch menu Ch portions Highchairs Ch discounts 2 children free sharing with parent Safe grounds Games consoles Cots Family rms Connecting rms Fridge Laundry **NEARBY:** Cutty Sark Greenwich Maritime Museum Tower of London River cruise

This new hotel is situated adjacent to the ExCel exhibition centre and overlooks the Royal Victoria Dock. Design throughout the hotel is contemporary and stylish. Public rooms include a modern coffee station, indoor leisure facilities and a smart bar and restaurant, both with a terrace overlooking the dock. Bedrooms feature modern decor, a bath and separate shower and an extensive range of extras.

ROOMS: 257 en suite (203 fmly) 🚭 in 183 bedrooms s £135-£148; d £155-£161 (incl. bkfst) **LB FACILITIES:** STV Sauna Gym Steam room Xmas **PARKING:** 80

EC1

Babies Welcome **Children's Dishes**

🌀 🌀 Smiths of Smithfield
(Top Floor), 67-77 Charterhouse St EC1M 6HJ
☎ 020 7251 7950 📠 020 7236 5666
e-mail: reservations@smithsofsmithfield.co.uk
Dir: Opposite Smithfield Meat Market

CHILD FACILITIES: Activities: colouring Food/bottle warming Ch menu Ch portions Highchairs Changing facilities **NEARBY:** Cinema

FOOD: Modern British **STYLE:** Modern Minimalist **SEATS:** 80 **OPEN:** 12-3.30/6.30-12, Closed 25-26 Dec, 1 JanL Sat **RESTAURANT:** Fixed L £12.50, main £11-£25 **NOTES:** Air con **PARKING:** NCP: Snowhill

EC1, continued

Babies Welcome

◎ ◎ St John

26 St John St EC1M 4AY
☎ 020 7251 0848 📠 020 7251 4090
e-mail: info@stjohnrestaurant.co.uk
Dir: 100yds from Smithfield Market, northside

CHILD FACILITIES: Food/bottle warming Highchairs Ch cutlery
NEARBY: Globe Theatre HMS Belfast The London Dungeon
Tower of London Children's Museum

FOOD: British **SEATS:** 100 **OPEN:** 12-3/6-11, Closed Xmas, New Year, Easter BH, SunL Sat **NOTES:** Air con **PARKING:** Meters in street

EC3

Babies Welcome | **Family Rooms** | **Children's Dishes**

★★★ 72%
Novotel London Tower Bridge

10 Pepys St EC3N 2NR
☎ 020 7265 6000 📠 020 7265 6060
e-mail: H3107@accor-hotels.com

CHILD FACILITIES: Activities: children's channel TV, goodie bags
Indoor play area Food/bottle warming Ch menu Ch portions
Highchairs Ch cutlery Ch discounts under 5s free, under 16s free
sharing with adults Games consoles Cots Family rms D rms with S
beds Connecting rms Laundry **NEARBY:** Tower of London Tower
Bridge

Located near the Tower of London, this smart hotel is convenient
for Docklands, the City, Heathrow and London City airports.
Bedrooms are spacious, modern, and offer a great range of
facilities, including air conditioning. There is a smart bar and
restaurant and a small gym.
ROOMS: 203 en suite (77 fmly) ⊛ in 145 bedrooms s £160-£270;
d £180-£240 **LB FACILITIES:** STV Sauna Gym Steam Room

N1

◎ ◎ Fifteen

13 Westland Place N1 7LP
☎ 0871 330 1515 📠 020 7251 2749
web: www.fifteenrestaurant.com
Dir: City road, opposite Moorfields Eye Hospital

CHILD FACILITIES: Please telephone for details

FOOD: Modern Italian **STYLE:** Modern **SEATS:** 70
OPEN: 12-2.15/6.30-9.30, Closed BHs, D Sun **RESTAURANT:** main
£24-£29 **NOTES:** ⊛ in restaurant, Air con **PARKING:** On street & NCP

N6

♦♦♦♦ Winchester Pub Hotel

206 Archway Rd, Highgate N6 5BA
☎ 020 8374 1690 📠 020 8374 1690
web: www.winchester-hotel.com
Dir: A1 to London City, pass Highgate Station on left, hotel on left

CHILD FACILITIES: Please telephone for details

This delightful traditional pub is ideally located close to Highgate
tube station and within easy reach of the M1. Spacious bedrooms
are smartly appointed and well equipped. Public areas include a
bar/lounge and an elegant dining area where a good selection of
home-cooked meals and hearty breakfasts are served.
ROOMS: 6 en suite (3 fmly) s £45-£50; d £55-£65 * ⊛ in 3 bedrooms
FACILITIES: STV TVB tea/coffee Dinner Last d order 9.30pm
NOTES: ✱ Licensed Cen ht

N8

♦♦♦ White Lodge Hotel

1 Church Ln, Hornsey N8 7BU
☎ 020 8348 9765 📠 020 8340 7851
Dir: A406 follow sign to Bounds Green, Hornsey High Rd and Church Lane

CHILD FACILITIES: Please telephone for details

This well maintained, friendly guest house enjoys a quiet yet
convenient location close to shops and restaurants. Bedrooms are
traditionally appointed and airy public areas include an attractive
lounge and spacious breakfast room.
ROOMS: 16 rms (8 en suite) (5 fmly) (1 GF) s £34-£36; d £44-£50 *
⊛ in 4 bedrooms **FACILITIES:** TVB tea/coffee TVL No coaches Dinner
Last d order at breakfast **NOTES:** ✱ ⊛ in restaurant ⊛ in 1 lounge
Cen ht

Don't forget our travel accommodation
section at the front of the guide

N19

Children's Dishes

⊚ The Parsee
34 Highgate Hill N19 5NL
☎ 020 7272 9091 📠 020 7687 1139
e-mail: dining@theparsee.co.uk
Dir: Opposite Whittington Hospital

CHILD FACILITIES: Food/bottle warming Ch menu Ch portions
NEARBY: Leisure centre

FOOD: Indian, Parsee **STYLE:** Minimalist **SEATS:** 50 **OPEN:** 6-10.45,
Closed Xmas, 1 Jan, BHs, Sun **RESTAURANT:** main £9.95-£11.95
NOTES: ⊗ area, Air con **PARKING:** On street

NW1

Babies Welcome | Family Rooms | Children's Dishes

★★★★★ ⊚ The Landmark London
222 Marylebone Rd NW1 6JQ
☎ 020 7631 8000 📠 020 7631 8080
e-mail: reservations@thelandmark.co.uk
web: www.landmarklondon.co.uk
Dir: adjacent to Marylebone Station and near Paddington Station

CHILD FACILITIES: Baby listening Nanny Babysitting Activities:
toys Food/bottle warming Ch menu Ch portions Highchairs
Ch cutlery Ch discounts under 14s free Games consoles Videos
Cots Family rms £269-£317 Ch drinks Connecting rms Fridge
Laundry **NEARBY:** Regents Park Zoo Madame Tussaud's Cinema
Museums

Said to be one of the last truly grand railway hotels, The Landmark
boasts a number of stunning features, the most spectacular being
the naturally lit central atrium that forms the focal point of the
hotel. When it comes to eating and drinking there are plenty of
options, including the Cellars for upmarket bar meals. The Winter
Gardens make a beautiful venue for all-day dining, set in the
central atrium. Air-conditioned bedrooms are spacious and have
stunning marble bathrooms.
ROOMS: 299 en suite (60 fmly) ⊗ in 179 bedrooms s £229.12-£388;
d £258.50-£411 **LB** **FACILITIES: Spa** STV ⌨ Sauna Gym Jacuzzi
Beauty treatments and massages ♫ Xmas **PARKING:** 80 **NOTES:** ✖

Babies Welcome | Family Rooms | Children's Dishes

★★★★ 67% ⊚
Novotel London Euston
100-110 Euston Rd NW1 2AJ
☎ 020 7666 9000 📠 020 7766 9100
e-mail: H5309@accor-hotels.com
Dir: between St Pancras & Euston stations

continued

CHILD FACILITIES: Activities: games, activity book Food/bottle
warming Ch menu Ch portions Highchairs Ch cutlery Ch discounts
under 16s free sharing with parents Safe grounds Cots Family rms
Connecting rms Fridge Laundry **NEARBY:** London Planetarium
Zoo Madame Tussaud's Regents Park

This hotel enjoys a central location adjacent to the British Library
and close to some of London's main transport hubs. The style is
modern and contemporary throughout. Bedrooms are spacious
and very well equipped and many have views over the city. Open
plan public areas include a leisure suite.
ROOMS: 312 en suite (21 fmly) ⊗ in 246 bedrooms s fr £160; d fr £160
FACILITIES: STV Sauna Gym Steam room Xmas **NOTES:** ✖

NW3

◆◆◆◆◆ The House Hotel
2 Rosslyn Hill, Hampstead NW3 1PH
☎ 020 7431 8000 📠 020 7433 1775
e-mail: reception@thehousehotel.co.uk
web: www.thehousehotel.co.uk
*Dir: On A502, from Hampstead tube station, down Rosslyn Hill towards
junct with Pond St B518, on corner*

CHILD FACILITIES: Please telephone for details

This elegant house enjoys a prime location close to both
Hampstead and Belsize Park tube stations. Bedrooms are superbly
appointed and particularly well-equipped with mini-bars, CD
players, modem points and safes. Public areas include a
contemporary stylish bar and restaurant. 24-hour room service
from a wide range of local eateries is also offered.
ROOMS: 23 en suite (2 fmly) (8 GF) s £90-£165; d £90-£220 * ⊗ in
18 bedrooms **FACILITIES:** STV TVB tea/coffee Direct dial from
bedrooms No coaches **NOTES:** ⊗ in area of dining room ⊗ in lounges
Licensed Cen ht **PARKING:** 8

◆◆◆◆ Langorf Hotel
20 Frognal, Hampstead NW3 6AG
☎ 020 7794 4483 📠 020 7435 9055
e-mail: langorf@aol.com
web: www.langorfhotel.com
Dir: approx 3m N of Oxford St and 3m S of M1, just off A41 Finchley Rd

CHILD FACILITIES: Please telephone for details

Located on a leafy and mainly residential avenue within easy
walking distance of shops and restaurants, this elegant Edwardian
hotel has been sympathetically renovated to provide high
standards of comfort and facilities. Bedrooms are furnished with
style and flair and a warm welcome is assured.
ROOMS: 31 en suite (4 fmly) (3 GF) s £70-£90; d £85-£110 *
FACILITIES: STV TVB tea/coffee Direct dial from bedrooms Lift TVL No
coaches **NOTES:** ✖ ⊗ in restaurant Licensed Cen ht **PARKING:**

Babies Welcome | Family Rooms | Children's Dishes

◆◆◆ Best Western Swiss Cottage Hotel
4 Adamson Rd, Swiss Cottage NW3 3HP
☎ 020 7722 2281 📠 020 7483 4588
e-mail: reservations@swisscottagehotel.co.uk
web: www.swisscottagehotel.co.uk
*Dir: on A41 go around Swiss cottage pub to Avenue Road, at lights left,
next lights left to Winchester Road, hotel at end of road right*

CHILD FACILITIES: Food/bottle warming Ch portions Highchairs
Ch discounts up to 12s free sharing with parents Safe grounds Cots
Family rms D rms with S beds from £79.50 Connecting rms Laundry
NEARBY: Cinema Regents Park London Zoo

This smart Victorian property enjoys a peaceful residential
location, yet is only minutes' walk from Swiss Cottage tube station.
Bedrooms are comfortable, smartly appointed and well-equipped.

continued on p172

NW3, continued

There is a spacious lounge/bar and room service refreshments and snacks are available. English breakfast is served in the basement dining room.
ROOMS: 59 en suite (8 fmly) (7 GF) s £59.50-£105; d £65-£125 * ⊗ in 23 bedrooms **FACILITIES:** STV TVB tea/coffee Direct dial from bedrooms Lift Dinner Last d order 9.45pm **NOTES:** ✠ ⊗ in restaurant Licensed Cen ht **PARKING:** 4

NW11

| Babies | Family |
| Welcome | Rooms |

♦♦♦ Anchor Hotel
10 West Heath Dr, Golders Green NW11 7QH
☎ 020 8458 8764 ▤ 020 8455 3204
e-mail: reservations@anchor-hotel.co.uk
Dir: North Circular A406 onto A598 Finchley Rd. At tube, left then 1st right

CHILD FACILITIES: Outdoor play area Food/bottle warming Highchairs Ch cutlery Ch discounts under 6s free sharing with parents Safe grounds Cots Family rms from £70 Ch drinks Laundry **NEARBY:** Park Kenwood House

A friendly atmosphere prevails at this privately owned guest house, close to Golders Green tube station and shopping area. Bedrooms are comfortably appointed and well equipped.
ROOMS: 11 rms (8 en suite) (3 fmly) (3 GF) s £30-£57; d £48-£77 * ⊗ in 3 bedrooms **FACILITIES:** TVB tea/coffee Direct dial from bedrooms TVL No coaches **NOTES:** ✠ ⊗ in restaurant ⊗ in lounges Cen ht **PARKING:** 5

SE1

| Babies | Family | Children's |
| Welcome | Rooms | Dishes |

★★★★ 68%
Novotel London City South
Southwark Bridge Rd SE1 9HH
☎ 020 7089 0400 ▤ 020 7089 0410
e-mail: H3269@accor-hotels.com
Dir: junct at Thrale St

CHILD FACILITIES: Activities: colouring, board game Indoor play area Family area Food/bottle warming Ch menu Ch portions Highchairs Ch discounts under 16s free sharing with parents Games consoles Cots Family rms from £79 Connecting rms Fridge Laundry **NEARBY:** Tate Modern London Dungeon Museums

The first of a new generation of Novotels, this newly-built hotel is contemporary in design with smart, modern bedrooms and spacious public rooms. There are a number of options for guests wanting to unwind, including treatments such as reflexology and immersion therapy, while a gymnasium is available for the more energetic.
ROOMS: 182 en suite (139 fmly) ⊗ in 158 bedrooms s £150; d £170 **FACILITIES:** STV Gym **PARKING:** 80

| Babies | Children's |
| Welcome | Dishes |

★★★ 71%
Mercure London City Bankside
71-79 Southwark St SE1 0JA
☎ 020 7902 0800 ▤ 020 7902 0810
e-mail: H2814@accor-hotels.com
Dir: A200 to London Bridge. Left into Southwark St. Hotel 2 mins by car from station

continued

CHILD FACILITIES: Baby listening Nanny Babysitting Family area Food/bottle warming Ch menu Ch portions Highchairs Ch cutlery Ch discounts under 16s free sharing with parents Safe grounds Games consoles Cots Connecting rms Fridge Laundry **NEARBY:** Parks

This smart, contemporary hotel forms part of the rejuvenation of the South Bank. With the City of London just over the river and a number of tourist attractions within easy reach, the hotel is well situated. Facilities include spacious air-cooled bedrooms, a modern bar and the stylish Loft Restaurant.
ROOMS: 144 en suite (24 fmly) (5 GF) ⊗ in 88 bedrooms **FACILITIES:** STV Gym **PARKING:** 3

| Babies | Family | Children's |
| Welcome | Rooms | Dishes |

★★★ 68%
Novotel London Waterloo
113 Lambeth Rd SE1 7LS
☎ 020 7793 1010 ▤ 020 7793 0202
e-mail: h1785@accor-hotels.com
Dir: opposite Houses of Parliament on S bank of River Thames, off Lambeth Bridge, opposite Lambeth Palace

CHILD FACILITIES: Activities: Lego Indoor play area Food/bottle warming Ch menu Ch portions Highchairs Ch discounts under 16s free sharing with parents Games consoles Cots Family rms with sofa bed from £99 Connecting rms Fridge **NEARBY:** Theatres London Eye London Aquarium

This hotel has an excellent location with Lambeth Palace, the Houses of Parliament and Waterloo Station all within a short walk. Bedrooms are spacious and air conditioned, a number of rooms have been designed for less able guests. The open-plan public areas include the Garden Brasserie, the Flag and Whistle Pub and children's play area.
ROOMS: 187 en suite (80 fmly) ⊗ in 158 bedrooms s £140-£155; d £160-£175 **LB FACILITIES:** Sauna Gym Steam room Fitness room **PARKING:** 40

| Babies | Children's |
| Welcome | Dishes |

⊚ ⊚ Cantina Vinopolis
1 Bankside SE1 9BU
☎ 020 7940 8333 ▤ 020 7940 8334
e-mail: cantina@vinopolis.co.uk
Dir: Telephone for directions

CHILD FACILITIES: Food/bottle warming Ch licence Ch portions Highchairs Ch cutlery Safe grounds Changing facilities **NEARBY:** London Eye The London Dungeon Shakespeare's Globe Exhibition and Theatre Aquarium

FOOD: Mediterranean, French **STYLE:** Rustic Country-House **SEATS:** 160 **OPEN:** 12-3/6-10.30, Closed Xmas, New Year, D Sun **RESTAURANT:** Fixed L £15.95, Fixed D £26.95, main £9.50-£15.95 **NOTES:** Smart Dress, ⊗ area, Air con **PARKING:** Street parking (free after 6.30pm)

England

◎ ◎ The Anchor & Hope
36 The Cut SE1 8LP
☎ 020 7928 9898
e-mail: anchorandhope@btconnect.com
CHILD FACILITIES: Ch licence Highchairs Changing facilities
NEARBY: Southbank
FOOD: Traditional European **STYLE:** Bistro **SEATS:** 58
OPEN: 12-2.30/6-10.30, Closed BHs, 25 Dec-1 Jan, SunL Mon
RESTAURANT: main £9.80-£16

Babies Welcome | **Children's Dishes**

◪ The Fire Station ◎
150 Waterloo Rd SE1 8SB
☎ 020 7620 2226 ▤ 020 7633 9161
e-mail: firestation@wizardinns.co.uk
CHILD FACILITIES: Activities: colouring Family area Food/bottle warming Ch menu Ch portions Highchairs Changing facilities
NEARBY: London Eye Aquarium Imax cinema
OPEN: 11-11 (Sun 12-10.30) Closed: 25/26 Dec **BAR MEALS:** L served all week 12-5.30 D served all week 5.30-10.30 Av main course £5.95
RESTAURANT: L served all week 12-2.45 D served all week 5-11 Av 3 course à la carte £20 Av 3 course fixed price £13.50 **FACILITIES:** ✗

SE5

◪ The Sun and Doves
61-63 Coldharbour Ln, Camberwell SE5 9NS
☎ 020 7924 9950 ▤ 020 7924 9330
e-mail: mail@sunanddoves.co.uk
CHILD FACILITIES: Please telephone for details
OPEN: 11-11 Closed: 25/26 Dec **BAR MEALS:** L served all week 12-10.30 D served all week 12-10.30 Av main course £8 **RESTAURANT:** L served all week 11-11 D served all week Av 3 course à la carte £18
FACILITIES: Garden: Secluded, warm, spacious, S facing

SE23

Babies Welcome | **Children's Dishes**

◎ ◎ Babur Brasserie
119 Brockley Rise, Forest Hill SE23 1JP
☎ 020 8291 2400 & 8291 4881 ▤ 020 8291 4881
e-mail: babur_brasserie@compuserve.com
web: www.babur-brasserie.com
Dir: 5 mins walk from Honor Oak Station, where parking is available
CHILD FACILITIES: Family area Food/bottle warming Ch portions Highchairs **NEARBY:** Dulwich Park Blackheath Park

FOOD: Indian **STYLE:** Classic Modern **SEATS:** 56
OPEN: 12.30-2.30/6-11.30, Closed 25-26 DecL Fri **RESTAURANT:** Fixed L £11.95, Fixed D £16.95, main £7.50-£12.95 **NOTES:** ⊗ area, Air con
PARKING: On street

SE24

◎ 3 Monkeys Restaurant
136-140 Herne Hill SE24 9QH
☎ 020 7738 5500 ▤ 020 7738 5505
e-mail: jan@3monkeysrestaurant.com
Dir: Adjacent to Herne Hill Station
CHILD FACILITIES: Please telephone for details
FOOD: Indian **STYLE:** Minimalist **SEATS:** 150 **OPEN:** 6-11, Closed 25 Dec, 1 JanL Mon-Sun **RESTAURANT:** main £9.25-£18.75 **NOTES:** ⊗ area, Air con

SW1

Babies Welcome | **Family Rooms** | **Children's Dishes**

★★★★★ ◎ The Carlton Tower
Cadogan Place SW1X 9PY
☎ 020 7235 1234 ▤ 020 7235 9129
e-mail: contact@carltontower.com
web: www.carltontower.com
Dir: A4 towards Knightsbridge, turn right onto Sloane St. Hotel on left before Cadogan Place
CHILD FACILITIES: Baby listening Nanny Babysitting Food/bottle warming Ch menu Highchairs Safe grounds Videos Cots Family rms £375-£425 Connecting rms Fridge Laundry **NEARBY:** Hyde Park Madame Tussaud's Museums Hamleys toy shop

This impressive hotel enjoys an enviable position in the heart of Knightsbridge, overlooking Cadogan Gardens. Bedrooms vary in size and style and include a number of suites, many with wonderful views of the city. Leisure facilities include a glass-roofed swimming pool, a well-equipped gym and a number of treatment rooms. Dining options Grissini London and the famous Rib Room and Oyster Bar.
ROOMS: 220 en suite (60 fmly) ⊗ in 116 bedrooms s £325; d £325-£3750 **FACILITIES:** Spa STV ▤ ☞ Sauna Gym Jacuzzi Massage and Spa treatments ♫ Xmas **PARKING:** 50 **NOTES:** ✗

Babies Welcome | **Children's Dishes**

★★★★★ ◎ ◎ ◎ ◎ ◎
Mandarin Oriental Hyde Park
66 Knightsbridge SW1X 7LA
☎ 020 7235 2000 ▤ 020 7235 2001
e-mail: molon-reservations@mohg.com
Dir: Harrods on right, hotel 0.5m on left opp Harvey Nichols
CHILD FACILITIES: Babysitting Activities: colouring, toys Food/bottle warming Ch menu Ch portions Highchairs Ch discounts under 12s free sharing with 2 adults Safe grounds Games consoles Videos Cots Ch drinks Connecting rms Fridge Laundry Changing mats **NEARBY:** Hyde Park Tower of London Madame Tussaud's London Zoo London Eye

Situated in fashionable Knightsbridge and overlooking Hyde Park,
continued on p174

SW1, continued

this landmark hotel is a popular venue. Bedrooms, many of which have park views, are appointed to the highest standards with luxurious features such as the finest Irish linen and goose down pillows. Guests have a choice of dining options, from the brasserie style, all day dining Park Restaurant to the chic, award winning Foliage Restaurant. The Mandarin Bar also serves light snacks and cocktails. The stylish spa is a destination in its own right and offers a range of innovative treatments

ROOMS: 200 en suite ⊗ in 106 bedrooms s fr £425; d fr £425 **LB**
FACILITIES: **Spa** STV Sauna Gym Jacuzzi Fitness centre, steam room, relaxation area, sanarium ♫ Xmas **PARKING:** 13 **NOTES:** ✖

Babies Welcome | Family Rooms | Children's Dishes

♦♦♦♦ Windermere Hotel
142/144 Warwick Way, Victoria SW1V 4JE
☎ 020 7834 5163 & 7834 5480 ▤ 020 7630 8831
e-mail: reservations@windermere-hotel.co.uk
web: www.windermere-hotel.co.uk
Dir: from coach stn on Buckingham Palace Rd - opp stn left onto Elizabeth Bridge, then 1st right, take Hugh St to Alderney St, hotel on corner
CHILD FACILITIES: Activities: toys, colouring books Food/bottle warming Ch menu Ch portions Highchairs Ch cutlery Ch discounts Cots Family rms D rm with S beds or extra D beds £129-£149 Connecting rms (laundry nearby) **NEARBY:** Buckingham Palace Parks Museums Zoo London Eye

This relaxed and informal family-run hotel is within easy reach of Victoria Station and many of the capital's attractions. Bedrooms, whilst varying in size, are stylish, comfortable and well equipped. The Pimlico restaurant serves delicious evening meals and hearty cooked breakfasts.
ROOMS: 22 rms (20 en suite) (3 fmly) (4 GF) s £69-£99; d £89-£145 *
⊗ in 8 bedrooms **FACILITIES:** STV TVB tea/coffee Direct dial from bedrooms TVL Dinner Last d order 10.30pm **NOTES:** ✖ ⊗ in restaurant ⊗ in lounges Licensed Cen ht

♦♦♦ Sidney Hotel
68-76 Belgrave Rd SW1V 2BP
☎ 020 7834 2738 ▤ 020 7630 0973
e-mail: reservations@sidneyhotel.com
web: www.sidneyhotel.com
Dir: follow Central London & Victoria signs. Take A23 Vauxhall Bridge road, turn into Charlwood St. Hotel in corner of Charlwood St and Belgrave Rd
CHILD FACILITIES: Please telephone for details
This smart hotel enjoys a convenient location close to Victoria Station and many local attractions. The brightly decorated bedrooms are well equipped and comfortable. The public areas include a bar lounge and an airy breakfast room.

continued

ROOMS: 81 rms (80 en suite) (13 fmly) (9 GF) s £60-£78; d £70-£99 *
⊗ in 30 bedrooms **FACILITIES:** STV TVB tea/coffee Direct dial from bedrooms Lift TVL **NOTES:** ✖ ⊗ in restaurant ⊗ in lounges Licensed Cen ht   *See advert on opposite page*

Children's Dishes
⊛ Al Duca
4-5 Duke of York St SW1Y 6LA
☎ 020 7839 3090 ▤ 020 7839 4050
e-mail: info@alduca-restaurant.co.uk
Dir: 5 mins walk from station towards Piccadilly. R into St James, L into Jermyn St. Duke of York St, halfway along on R
CHILD FACILITIES: Food/bottle warming Ch licence Ch portions **NEARBY:** Trocadero

FOOD: Italian **STYLE:** Modern Italian **SEATS:** 56 **OPEN:** 12-2.30/6-11, Closed Christmas, New Year, BHs, Sun **RESTAURANT:** Fixed L £17.50, Fixed D £24 **NOTES:** Smart Dress, Air con

Children's Dishes
⊛⊛ Drones of Pont Street
1 Pont St SW1X 9EJ
☎ 020 7235 9555 ▤ 020 7235 9566
e-mail: sales@whitestarline.org.uk
CHILD FACILITIES: Food/bottle warming Ch portions **NEARBY:** Hyde Park

FOOD: British, French **STYLE:** Chic **SEATS:** 96 **OPEN:** 12-2.30/6-11, Closed 26 Dec-1 JanL Sat, D Sun **RESTAURANT:** main £9.50-£22
NOTES: Air con **PARKING:** On street

⊛ Just St James
12 St James St SW1A 1ER
☎ 020 7976 2222 ▤ 020 7976 2020
e-mail: bookings@juststjames.com
Dir: Turn R on Piccadilly towards Piccadilly Circus, then R into St James St.
CHILD FACILITIES: Please telephone for details

FOOD: British **STYLE:** Classic Chic **SEATS:** 120 **OPEN:** 12-3.30/6-11.30, Closed 25-26 Dec, 01 Jan, D Sun **RESTAURANT:** Fixed L £16.50, main £13-£18 **NOTES:** Air con **PARKING:** St James Square - meters

Babies Welcome | **Children's Dishes**

Box Wood Café
The Berkeley Hotel, Wilton Place, Knightsbridge SW1X 7RL
☎ 020 7235 1010 ▤ 7235 1011
e-mail: boxwoodcafe@gordonramsay.com

CHILD FACILITIES: Activities: colouring Food/bottle warming Ch menu Ch portions Highchairs Changing facilities
NEARBY: Hyde Park

FOOD: British, American **STYLE:** Modern, Chic **SEATS:** 140
OPEN: 12-3/5.45-11 **RESTAURANT:** main £12.50-£22.50 **NOTES:** Air con **PARKING:** Street parking available

Children's Dishes

Quirinale
North Court, 1 Great Peter St SW1P 3LL
☎ 020 7222 7080
e-mail: info@quirinale.co.uk

CHILD FACILITIES: Food/bottle warming Ch portions Safe grounds
NEARBY: Houses of Parliament Westminster Abbey River Thames St James' Park

FOOD: Italian **STYLE:** Chic **SEATS:** 50 **OPEN:** 12-3/6-12, Closed Xmas & New Year, 2 wks Aug, Sat & Sun **RESTAURANT:** main £12.50-£16 **NOTES:** Air con **PARKING:** Street parking available, NCP

> Many proprietors are happy to provide extra facilities for children, but let them know in advance what you need so they can be prepared

SW3

◆◆◆◆ The Claverley Hotel
13-14 Beaufort Gardens, Knightsbridge SW3 1PS
☎ 020 7589 8541 ▤ 020 7584 3410
e-mail: reservations@claverleyhotel.co.uk
web: www.claverleyhotel.co.uk
Dir: take M4/A4 into London. East on Brompton Rd, Beaufort Gdns is 6th on right after Victoria & Albert Museum

CHILD FACILITIES: Please telephone for details

This privately owned hotel is hidden away in a quiet Knightsbridge leafy cul-de-sac, only minutes' walk from Harrods. Stylish bedrooms are individually designed and some have four-poster beds. Public areas include a delightful reading room where guests can enjoy tea and coffee. Impressive breakfasts are served in the recently refurbished dining room.

ROOMS: 30 rms (27 en suite) (7 fmly) (2 GF) s £60-£120; d £120-£195 * ⊗ in 20 bedrooms **FACILITIES:** STV TVB Direct dial from bedrooms Lift **NOTES:** ✖ ⊗ in restaurant Cen ht **LB**

SW5

Family Rooms

◆◆◆◆ The Mayflower Hotel
26-28 Trebovir Rd SW5 9NJ
☎ 020 7370 0991 ▤ 020 7370 0994
e-mail: info@mayflower-group.co.uk
web: www.mayflowerhotel.co.uk
Dir: From Earls Court Underground; take Earls Court exit, turn first left into Trebovir Rd, hotel on left

continued on p176

SW5, continued

| CHILD FACILITIES: | Babysitting Family area Food/bottle warming Ch discounts under 2s sharing free Safe grounds Cots Family rms D rm with 2 B beds Ch drinks Laundry NEARBY: Parks Adventure play area Cinema |

This smart hotel is located within minutes' walk of Earls Court, close to Olympia and west London's museums and attractions. Stylish, individually designed bedrooms vary in size but all are extremely well equipped and benefit from smart, modern en suites. There is a comfortable, stylish lounge and an airy dining room where breakfast is served.
ROOMS: 46 en suite (4 fmly) (5 GF) s £62-£89; d £79-£140 *
FACILITIES: STV TVB tea/coffee Direct dial from bedrooms Lift
NOTES: ⊗ in restaurant ⊗ in lounges Cen ht **LB PARKING:** 4

| Babies Welcome | Family Rooms | Children's Dishes |

◆◆◆ Rushmore Hotel
11 Trebovir Rd, Earls Court SW5 9LS
☎ 020 7370 3839 & 020 7370 6505 ▤ 020 7370 0274
e-mail: rushmore-reservations@london.com
Dir: turn off A4 onto A3220 (Earls Court Rd) and take 4th street on right, Trebovir Rd. The hotel is 50mtrs on right

| CHILD FACILITIES: | Activities: books, toys Food/bottle warming Ch portions Highchairs Ch cutlery Ch discounts under 12s free sharing with parents Cots Family rms 3/4 bed rms, D rms with S bed from £75 Laundry NEARBY: Parks Kensington Gardens Museums Hamleys toy shop |

This smart private hotel is conveniently located close to the exhibition halls and a short stroll from the tube station. Stylish bedrooms are individually themed and include some rooms suitable for families; most benefit from brand new, modern en-suite shower rooms. A continental buffet breakfast is served in the modern conservatory.
ROOMS: 22 en suite (4 fmly) (4 GF) s £55-£65; d £65-£79 * ⊗ in 4 bedrooms **FACILITIES:** STV TVB tea/coffee Direct dial from bedrooms TVL **NOTES:** ✘ ⊗ in restaurant Cen ht

| Babies Welcome | Family Rooms |

◆◆◆ Swiss House Hotel
171 Old Brompton Rd, South Kensington SW5 0AN
☎ 020 7373 2769 & 7373 9383 ▤ 020 7373 4983
e-mail: recep@swiss-hh.demon.co.uk
web: www.swiss-hh.demon.co.uk
Dir: from A4 turn right down Earls Court Rd, at Old Brompton Rd turn left, pass lights, hotel on right

| CHILD FACILITIES: | Nanny Outdoor play area Food/bottle warming Highchairs Ch discounts under 4s free Safe grounds Cots Family rms D rms with 3 S beds £132-£147 Ch drinks NEARBY: Parks Cinemas Leisure centre Museum |

This delightful private hotel enjoys a prime location in the heart of
continued

South Kensington, within easy reach of London's main attractions, shops and exhibition centres. Smart bedrooms are furnished in pine and are particularly thoughtfully equipped. A continental buffet and freshly-cooked breakfast are served in the cosy dining room.
ROOMS: 16 rms (15 en suite) (7 fmly) (2 GF) ⊗ in 4 bedrooms
FACILITIES: STV TVB Direct dial from bedrooms TVL No coaches
NOTES: ⊗ in restaurant ⊗ in lounges Cen ht

SW7

| Babies Welcome | Family Rooms | Children's Dishes |

◆◆◆◆ Five Sumner Place Hotel
5 Sumner Place, South Kensington SW7 3EE
☎ 020 7584 7586 ▤ 020 7823 9962
e-mail: reservations@sumnerplace.com
web: www.sumnerplace.com
Dir: 300yds from South Kensington tube station, 2nd left off Old Brompton Rd from tube station

| CHILD FACILITIES: | Babysitting Food/bottle warming Ch menu Ch portions Highchairs Ch cutlery Ch discounts under 5s free Cots Family rms adjoining D/T rms £99 Connecting rms Fridge Laundry NEARBY: Hyde Park Museums Cinema Walks |

Situated in a residential area between Old Brompton Road and Fulham Road, this smartly maintained terraced house is a short walk from South Kensington tube station. Individually styled bedrooms are comfortably furnished and tastefully decorated. Breakfast is served in a bright airy conservatory that overlooks the small rear garden.
ROOMS: 13 en suite (4 fmly) (2 GF) s £85-£100; d £130-£152 * ⊗ in 10 bedrooms **FACILITIES:** TVB Direct dial from bedrooms Lift TVL No coaches **NOTES:** ✘ ⊗ in restaurant ⊗ in lounges Cen ht

All AA listed accommodation, restaurants and pubs can be found on the AA's website www.theAA.com

◆◆◆◆ The Gainsborough
7-11 Queensberry Place, South Kensington SW7 2DL
☎ 020 7957 0000 ▤ 020 7957 0001
e-mail: reservations@eeh.co.uk
web: www.eeh.co.uk
Dir: off Cromwell Rd, opposite Natural History Museum in South Kensington

| CHILD FACILITIES: | Please telephone for details |

This smart mid-Georgian townhouse is located in a quiet street near the Natural History Museum in South Kensington. Bedrooms are individually designed and decorated in fine fabrics, with quality furnishings and carefully co-ordinated colours. Guests are
continued

offered a choice of breakfast, served in the attractive dining room. There is a small lounge and 24-hour room service is available.

ROOMS: 49 en suite (5 fmly) s £94-£112; d £152.75-£188 *
FACILITIES: STV TVB tea/coffee Direct dial from bedrooms Lift No coaches **NOTES:** 🛏 😊 in restaurant Licensed Cen ht

SW10

😊 Sophie's Steak House & Bar

311-313 Fulham Rd SW10 9QH
☎ 020 7352 0088 🖹 020 349 9776
e-mail: enquiries@sophiessteakhouse.com
Dir: No 14 bus or from station turn left, at x-roads turn R and along Fulham Rd (10 min walk). Restaurant opposite cinema.

CHILD FACILITIES: Please telephone for details

FOOD: Modern British **STYLE:** Rustic **SEATS:** 92 **OPEN:** 12-12, Closed 25-26 Dec **RESTAURANT:** Fixed L £9.95, main £7.95-£21.95
NOTES: Air con

SW11

😊 Osteria Antica Bologna

23 Northcote Rd SW11 1NG
☎ 020 7978 4771 🖹 020 7978 4771
e-mail: osteria@osteria.co.uk
web: www.osteria.co.uk
Dir: Off Battersea Rise, between Wandsworth & Clapham Commons.

CHILD FACILITIES: Please telephone for details

FOOD: Italian **STYLE:** Rustic **SEATS:** 75 **OPEN:** 12-3/6-11, Closed 24-26 Dec, 31 Dec, 1 Jan **RESTAURANT:** Fixed L £9.50, main £9.50-£17
NOTES: Air con **PARKING:** On street

| Babies Welcome | Children's Dishes |

😊 😊 Ransome's Dock

Battersea SW11 4NP
☎ 020 7223 1611 & 7924 2462 🖹 020 7924 2614
e-mail: chef@ransomesdock.co.uk
Dir: Between Albert Bridge & Battersea Bridge

continued

CHILD FACILITIES: Activities: colouring Food/bottle warming Ch portions Highchairs Ch cutlery Safe grounds
NEARBY: Battersea Park Zoo

FOOD: Modern British **STYLE:** Modern **SEATS:** 55 **OPEN:** from 11/6, Closed Xmas, D Sun **RESTAURANT:** Fixed L £14.75, main £9.50-£20
NOTES: 😊 area, Air con **PARKING:** 20

SW14

| Babies Welcome | Children's Dishes |

◆◆◆◆ 😊 😊 🍽 The Victoria

10 West Temple Sheen SW14 7RT
☎ 020 8876 4238 🖹 020 8878 3464
e-mail: bookings@thevictoria.net
web: www.thevictoria.net
Dir: turn off Upper Richmond Rd onto Temple Sheen Rd, at top of hill road narrows and left into West Temple Sheen

CHILD FACILITIES: Baby listening Activities: colouring Outdoor play area Food/bottle warming Ch menu Ch portions Highchairs Ch discounts under 5s free Safe grounds Cots
NEARBY: Richmond Park

The Victoria is located in a quiet residential area close to Sheen high street. Bedrooms are refreshingly simple, stylish and thoughtfully equipped with a host of extras, including PCs with free broadband Internet access. Public areas consist of a small contemporary seating area, a modern bar and a gastro-pub, which serves highly regarded imaginative European food.
ROOMS: 7 en suite (2 fmly) (3 GF) s £99.50; d £99.50 * 😊
FACILITIES: TVB tea/coffee Direct dial from bedrooms No coaches Dinner Last d order 9.45pm **NOTES:** 🛏 Licensed Cen ht **PARKING:** 14

| Babies Welcome | Children's Dishes |

😊 The Depot Waterfront Brasserie

Tideway Yard, Mortlake High St SW14 8SN
☎ 020 8878 9462 🖹 020 8392 1361
e-mail: speaktous@the-depot.biz.co.uk
Dir: Between Barnes Bridge & Mortlake stations

CHILD FACILITIES: Activities: books, colouring Food/bottle warming Ch menu Ch portions Highchairs Ch cutlery Safe grounds Changing facilities **NEARBY:** River Thames Richmond Park

FOOD: Modern **STYLE:** Modern Bistro **SEATS:** 120 **OPEN:** 12-3/6-10, Closed 24-26 Dec **RESTAURANT:** main £7.85-£14 **NOTES:** 😊 area, Air con

SW15

◆◆◆◆ The Lodge Hotel

52-54 Upper Richmond Rd, Putney SW15 2RN
☎ 020 8874 1598 🖹 020 8874 0910
e-mail: res@thelodgehotellondon.com
Dir: A3, A219 down Putney Hill, right at lights onto upper Richmond Rd, 0.5mile on left, under railway bridge with East Putney Station on right

CHILD FACILITIES: Please telephone for details

This friendly hotel is conveniently located close to east Putney tube station. Attractive public areas include a choice of lounges, a smart bar with satellite TV. An impressive buffet breakfast is served in the garden conservatory. Thoughtfully equipped, comfortable bedrooms include a selection of executive rooms and suites.
ROOMS: 62 en suite (10 fmly) (21 GF) s £69-£109; d £75-£146 * 😊 in 35 bedrooms **FACILITIES:** STV TVB tea/coffee Direct dial from bedrooms TVL **NOTES:** Licensed Cen ht **LB** **PARKING:** 30

SW19

♦♦♦ Worcester House Hotel

38 Alwyne Rd, Wimbledon SW19 7AE
☎ 020 8946 1300 📠 020 8946 9120
e-mail: janet@worcesterhouse.demon.co.uk
web: www.worcesterhousehotel.co.uk
Dir: turn off A3, to Worple Rd & follow to end, turn left & 2nd right to Alwyne Rd

CHILD FACILITIES: Please telephone for details

Guests are assured of a warm welcome at this friendly hotel, which is located in a quiet suburb near Wimbledon town centre. A homely atmosphere prevails throughout, thanks in part to the attractive décor and furnishings; all bedrooms are equipped to a high standard. Breakfast is taken family-style in the cosy dining room.
ROOMS: 9 en suite (2 fmly) (2 GF) s £49.50-£55; d £75 *
FACILITIES: TVB tea/coffee Direct dial from bedrooms No coaches
NOTES: ✗ 🚭 in restaurant Cen ht **PARKING:** 1

♦♦ Wimbledon Hotel

78 Worple Rd, Wimbledon SW19 4HZ
☎ 020 8946 9265 & 8946 1581 📠 020 8946 9265
Dir: M25, A3, Merton exit

CHILD FACILITIES: Please telephone for details

Situated within walking distance of the town centre and transport links, this double-fronted Victorian house provides simple but well-equipped accommodation. English breakfasts are served in the bright, modern dining room and a small television lounge is available.
ROOMS: 14 rms (11 en suite) (6 fmly) **FACILITIES:** TVB tea/coffee Direct dial from bedrooms TVL **NOTES:** ✗ 🚭 in restaurant Cen ht
PARKING: 10

W1

| Babies Welcome | Family Rooms | Children's Dishes |

★★★★★ 🅶 🏨 Athenaeum

116 Piccadilly W1J 7BJ
☎ 020 7499 3464 📠 020 7493 1860
e-mail: info@athenaeumhotel.com
web: www.athenaeumhotel.com
Dir: on Piccadilly, overlooking Green Park

CHILD FACILITIES: Babysitting Activities: free gift and fun pack Food/bottle warming Ch menu Ch portions Highchairs Ch cutlery Safe grounds Games consoles Videos Cots Family rms apartments £415 Ch drinks Connecting rms Fridge Laundry **NEARBY:** Hyde Park Museums Madame Tussaud's

With a discreet address in the heart of Mayfair, this well-loved hotel has become a favourite with many guests over the years for its efficient service and excellent hospitality. Bedrooms are decorated to the highest standard and some have views over Green Park. A row of Edwardian town houses immediately adjacent to the hotel offer a range of spacious and well-appointed apartments. Public rooms include the Bullochs Restaurant, the Windsor Lounge and a cosy cocktail bar.
ROOMS: 157 en suite 🚭 in 58 bedrooms s £265; d £285 **LB**
FACILITIES: Spa STV Sauna Gym Jacuzzi Steam rooms, spa treatments Xmas **NOTES:** ✗

| Children's Dishes | This symbol indicates a children's menu or smaller portions are available |

★★★★★ 🅶 🅶 🅶 The Dorchester

Park Ln W1A 2HJ
☎ 020 7629 8888 📠 020 7409 0114
e-mail: reservations@dorchesterhotel.com
Dir: halfway along Park Ln between Hyde Park Corner & Marble Arch

CHILD FACILITIES: Nanny Babysitting Food/bottle warming Ch menu Ch portions Highchairs Ch cutlery Safe grounds Videos Cots Family rms adjoining rooms Connecting rms Fridge Laundry Changing mats (by request) **NEARBY:** Hyde Park Theatres Cinema

One of London's finest hotels, The Dorchester is sumptuously decorated. The bedrooms, which have been refurbished, are beautifully appointed and feature huge, luxurious baths in marble bathrooms. Leading off from the foyer, The Promenade is the perfect setting for afternoon tea or drinks. In the evenings guests can relax to the sound of live jazz in the bar, and enjoy a cocktail or an Italian meal. Other dining options include the traditional Grill Restaurant and the award-winning Oriental, offering Cantonese cuisine.
ROOMS: 250 en suite 🚭 in 34 bedrooms s £323-£358.37; d £417.13-£546.38 **LB FACILITIES:** Spa STV Sauna Solarium Gym Jacuzzi The Dorchester Spa Health club 🎵 Xmas **PARKING:** 21
NOTES: ✗

| Babies Welcome | Children's Dishes |

★★★★★ 🅶 🅶 Ritz Hotel

150 Piccadilly W1J 9BR
☎ 020 7493 8181 📠 020 7493 2687
e-mail: enquire@theritzlondon.com
web: www.theritzlondon.com
Dir: from Hyde Park Corner E on Piccadilly. Hotel on right after Green Park

CHILD FACILITIES: Nanny (by arrangement) Babysitting (by arrangement) Food/bottle warming Ch menu Ch portions Highchairs Ch discounts under 12s free sharing with parents Videos Cots Connecting rms Laundry **NEARBY:** Museums London Eye

Synonymous with style, sophistication and attention to detail, The Ritz continues its stately progress into the third millennium, having recaptured much of its former glory. All bedrooms are comfortably furnished in Louis XVI style, with fine marble bathrooms and every imaginable comfort. Elegant reception rooms include the Palm Court with its legendary afternoon teas, the beautifully refurbished Rivoli Bar and the sumptuous Ritz Restaurant, complete with gold chandeliers and extraordinary trompe-l'oeil decoration.
ROOMS: 133 en suite 🚭 in 36 bedrooms s fr £353; d fr £429 **LB**
FACILITIES: STV Gym 🎵 Xmas **NOTES:** ✗

| Babies Welcome | Children's Dishes |

★★★★ 70%
Radisson SAS Portman

22 Portman Square W1H 7BG
☎ 020 7208 6000 📠 020 7208 6001
e-mail: sales.london@radissonsas.com
Dir: 100mtrs N of Oxford St and 500mtrs E of Edgware Rd

CHILD FACILITIES: Nanny Babysitting Food/bottle warming Ch menu Ch portions Highchairs Ch discounts free sharing with parents Safe grounds Cots Ch drinks Connecting rms Fridge Laundry **NEARBY:** Park London Eye Cinema

This smart, popular hotel enjoys a prime location a short stroll from Oxford Street and close to all the city's major attractions. The spacious, well-equipped bedrooms are themed ranging from

continued

Oriental through to classical and contemporary Italian decor.
Public areas include a bar and a smart restaurant.
ROOMS: 272 en suite (93 fmly) ⊛ in 129 bedrooms s £186.82;
d £222.07 **LB FACILITIES:** STV ℞ Sauna Solarium Gym ♫ Xmas
PARKING: 400 **NOTES:** ✖

Babies Welcome | Family Rooms | Children's Dishes

♦♦♦♦ Hart House Hotel
51 Gloucester Place, Portman Sq W1U 8JF
☎ 020 7935 2288 🖷 020 7935 8516
e-mail: reservations@harthouse.co.uk
web: www.harthouse.co.uk
Dir: just off Oxford St behind Selfridges, nearest underground is Baker St or Marble Arch

CHILD FACILITIES: Baby listening Babysitting Food/bottle warming Ch portions Highchairs Ch cutlery Ch discounts Cots Family rms D rm with S beds or cot NEARBY: Parks Zoo Madame Tussaud's

This elegant Georgian house enjoys a prime location minutes' walk from both Oxford Street and Madame Tussaud's. Bedrooms and public areas are smartly furnished, stylishly decorated and have been carefully restored to retain much of the house's original character. English breakfast is served in the cottage-style dining room.
ROOMS: 16 en suite (4 fmly) (4 GF) s £65-£75; d £89-£105 * ⊛
FACILITIES: TVB tea/coffee Direct dial from bedrooms TVL No coaches
NOTES: ✖ ⊛ in restaurant ⊛ in lounges Cen ht

Family Rooms | Children's Dishes

♦♦♦♦ Mermaid Suite Hotel
3-4 Blenheim St W1S 1LA
☎ 020 7629 1875 🖷 020 7499 9475
e-mail: info@mermaidsuite.com
Dir: From Bond St underground into Oxford St turn right into New Bond St, then 1st right into Blenheim St

CHILD FACILITIES: Baby listening Nanny Babysitting Food/bottle warming Ch menu Cots Family rms Ch drinks NEARBY: Hyde Park Museums Madame Tussaud's

Enviably located just off Oxford Street, this privately owned hotel
continued

provides excellent accommodation in one of London's best known shopping areas. Bedrooms, on several floors, are all smartly presented and well equipped. There is also a popular Italian restaurant that is open all day.
ROOMS: 30 rms (29 en suite) (4 fmly) ⊛ in 3 bedrooms
FACILITIES: STV TVB tea/coffee Direct dial from bedrooms Dinner Last d order 10pm **NOTES:** ✖ Licensed Cen ht

Babies Welcome | Family Rooms | Children's Dishes

♦♦♦♦ St George Hotel
49 Gloucester Place W1U 8JE
☎ 020 7486 8586 & 020 7486 6567 🖷 020 7486 6567
e-mail: reservations@stgeorge-hotel.net
web: www.stgeorge-hotel.net
Dir: From Marble Arch turn left, to lights, left into Portman St, continue into Gloucester Place, hotel on left

CHILD FACILITIES: Food/bottle warming Ch portions Highchairs Ch discounts under 5s free Safe grounds Cots Family rms D rm with 2 S beds, suite D rm with 3 S beds & S rm Ch drinks Connecting rms Fridge Laundry NEARBY: Madame Tussaud's Parks Cinema

This attractive, Grade II listed house is in the heart of the West End, close to Baker Street tube station. Bedrooms are furnished to a high standard and feature an excellent range of facilities, including modem points, safes, hairdryers and mini fridges. Breakfasts are served in the smart breakfast room and the friendly staff offer a very warm welcome.
ROOMS: 19 en suite (3 fmly) (3 GF) ⊛ in 6 bedrooms
FACILITIES: STV TVB tea/coffee Direct dial from bedrooms No coaches
NOTES: ✖ ⊛ in restaurant ⊛ in 1 lounge Cen ht **LB**

♦♦♦ Bryanston Court
50-60 Great Cumberland Place W1H 8DD
☎ 020 7262 3141 🖷 020 7262 7248
e-mail: info@bryanstonhotel.com
Dir: central London 2mins from Marble Arch and Oxford St
CHILD FACILITIES: Please telephone for details
This terrace of Georgian town houses has been converted to provide accommodation ideally placed for access to central London. The public areas consist of a bar with spacious seating and an elegant breakfast room. Bedrooms vary in size, some being compact, but all are en suite with good facilities.
ROOMS: 54 en suite (4 fmly) s £49-£95; d £69-£120 * **FACILITIES:** STV TVB tea/coffee Direct dial from bedrooms Lift No coaches **NOTES:** ✖ ⊛ in restaurant Licensed Cen ht

---

Please mention AA Family Friendly Places to Stay, Eat and Visit when booking

---

Babies Welcome | Family Rooms | Children's Dishes

♦♦ Lincoln House Hotel
33 Gloucester Place W1U 8HY
☎ 020 7486 7630 🖷 020 7486 0166
e-mail: reservations@lincoln-house-hotel.co.uk
web: www.lincoln-house-hotel.co.uk
Dir: From Marble Arch Station turn left into Oxford St, then left into Portman St which continues into Gloucester Place

CHILD FACILITIES: Food/bottle warming Ch portions Highchairs Safe grounds Cots Family rms D rm with S beds from £85 Fridge NEARBY: Zoo Madame Tussaud's Planetarium Parks

This impressive Georgian townhouse, located close to Oxford Street, is a friendly, family-run establishment. Comfortable bedrooms vary in size and are well equipped. Public areas are
continued on p180

W1, continued

decorated to a high standard with a cottage-style breakfast room on the lower ground floor where breakfast is served.

Lincoln House Hotel, W1

ROOMS: 23 en suite (5 fmly) (6 GF) s £59-£75; d £69-£85 *
FACILITIES: STV TVB tea/coffee Direct dial from bedrooms **NOTES:** ✖ ⊗ in restaurant **PARKING:** 6

Babies Welcome | Children's Dishes

⊗ ⊗ L'Escargot - The Ground Floor Restaurant
48 Greek St W1D 4EF
☎ 020 7439 7474 🖷 020 7437 0790
e-mail: sales@whitestarline.org.uk
web: www.whitestarline.org.uk/LEscargot_Restaurant.htm
Dir: Telephone for directions

CHILD FACILITIES: Food/bottle warming Ch portions Highchairs

FOOD: Modern French **STYLE:** Chic French **SEATS:** 70
OPEN: 12.15-2.15/6-11.30, Closed 25-26 Dec, 1 Jan, SunL Sat
RESTAURANT: Fixed L £14.95, Fixed D £17.95, main £12.95 **NOTES:** Air con **PARKING:** NCP Chinatown, on street parking

⊗ Veeraswamy Restaurant
Mezzanine Floor, Victory House, 99 Regent St W1B 4RS
☎ 020 7734 1401 🖷 020 7439 8434
e-mail: info@realindianfood.com
web: www.realindianfood.com
Dir: Entrance near jnctn of Swallow St and Regent St, in Victory House.

CHILD FACILITIES: Please telephone for details

FOOD: Indian **STYLE:** Modern **SEATS:** 130 **OPEN:** 12-2.30/5.30-11.30, Closed D Xmas **RESTAURANT:** main £14-£21.50 **NOTES:** Air con

Children's Dishes

⊗ ⊗ YMing
35-36 Greek St W1D 5DL
☎ 020 7734 2721 🖷 020 7437 0292
e-mail: cyming2000@blueyonder.co.uk
Dir: Opposite Palace Theatre.

continued

CHILD FACILITIES: Food/bottle warming Ch portions Ch cutlery

FOOD: Chinese **STYLE:** Chic **SEATS:** 60 **OPEN:** 12, Closed 25-26 Dec, 1 Jan, Sun (ex Chinese New Year) **RESTAURANT:** Fixed L £10, Fixed D £15 **NOTES:** ⊗ area, Air con

Babies Welcome | Children's Dishes

⊗ The Wolseley
160 Piccadilly W1J 9EB
☎ 020 7499 6996 🖷 020 7499 6888
Dir: 500mtrs from Underground station

CHILD FACILITIES: Activities: colouring Food/bottle warming Ch portions Highchairs Changing facilities

FOOD: European **STYLE:** Classic **SEATS:** 125 **OPEN:** 7.30-midnight, Closed 24 & 25 Dec, 1Jan, 9am-midnight Sat, 9am-11pm Sun
RESTAURANT: main £5.50-£26 **NOTES:** ⊗ area, Air con

W2

★★★★ 🏠 Pembridge Court
34 Pembridge Gardens W2 4DX
☎ 020 7229 9977 🖷 020 7727 4982
e-mail: reservations@pemct.co.uk
web: www.pemct.co.uk
Dir: off Bayswater Rd at Notting Hill Gate by underground station

CHILD FACILITIES: Please telephone for details

This attractive Victorian town house is in a residential street near the Portobello Market and Notting Hill Gate tube. Individually styled bedrooms are generally spacious and most are air-conditioned. Public areas include two spacious lounges, a small conference room and an airy breakfast room. The hotel features a collection of antique clothing and fans.
ROOMS: 20 en suite (4 fmly) (5 GF) s £125-£165; d £160-£195 (incl. bkfst) **FACILITIES:** STV Membership of local Health Club **PARKING:** 2
NOTES: ⊗ in restaurant RS 24 Dec-1 Jan

Family Rooms

◆◆◆◆ Byron Hotel
36-38 Queensborough Ter W2 3SH
☎ 020 7243 0987 🖷 020 7792 1957
e-mail: byron@capricornhotels.co.uk
web: www.byronhotel.co.uk
Dir: off Bayswater Rd close to Queensway. From Marble Arch follow signs to Notting Hill

CHILD FACILITIES: Babysitting Indoor play area Family area Food/bottle warming Ch cutlery Ch discounts when sharing with parents Cots Family rms D rm with 2/3 S beds £95-120 Connecting rms Laundry Changing mats NEARBY: Hyde Park Kensington Gardens

This charming terraced house has been thoughtfully restored, retaining many original features. Bedrooms are tastefully decorated and thoughtfully equipped with air conditioning, trouser

continued

press and safes. Breakfast is served in the attractive dining room and there is an elegant guest lounge and smart conservatory.
ROOMS: 45 en suite (5 fmly) s £50-£75; d £65-£120 * **FACILITIES:** STV TVB tea/coffee Direct dial from bedrooms Lift TVL **NOTES:** ✝ ⊛ in restaurant Licensed Cen ht **L**

♦♦♦♦ The Duke of Leinster
20 Leinster Gardens W2 3AN
☎ 020 7298 3850 📠 020 7298 3855
e-mail: dukeofleinsterhotel@crystalhotels.co.uk
Dir: in Bayswater/Queensway area

| CHILD FACILITIES: | Baby listening Nanny (on request) Babysitting Food/bottle warming Highchairs Ch cutlery Ch discounts Safe grounds Cots Family rms D rm with 2 S beds, rm with 4 S beds £160 Fridge Laundry | NEARBY: Kensington Gardens |

This smart, well-appointed property is centrally located close to Kensington Gardens and within easy reach of Paddington station. Décor is stylish throughout and bedrooms are tastefully appointed and equipped with a host of thoughtful extras that include mini-bars and safes. Breakfast is served in the modern, airy basement dining room.
ROOMS: 36 en suite (7 fmly) (5 GF) ⊛ in 6 bedrooms
FACILITIES: TVB tea/coffee Direct dial from bedrooms Lift No coaches
NOTES: ✝ ⊛ in restaurant ⊛ in lounges Cen ht

♦♦♦♦ Norfolk Plaza Hotel
29/33 Norfolk Square, Paddington W2 1RX
☎ 020 7723 0792 📠 020 7224 8770
e-mail: teri@norfolkplazahotel.co.uk
web: www.norfolkplazahotel.co.uk
Dir: 300mtrs from Paddington Station. Inside Norfolk Sq, off London St

| CHILD FACILITIES: | Baby listening Food/bottle warming Ch portions Highchairs Ch cutlery Ch discounts Cots Family rms D rms with S beds Fridge Laundry | NEARBY: London attractions |

This popular hotel in the heart of Paddington is located in a quiet residential square, with easy access to the West End. Bedrooms are thoughtfully furnished, particularly well equipped and include a number of split-level suites. Public areas include a smart well appointed bar and lounge, plus an attractive restaurant where breakfast is served.
ROOMS: 87 en suite (6 fmly) (8 GF) s £95-£105; d £120-£130; (room only) * ⊛ in 10 bedrooms **FACILITIES:** STV TVB tea/coffee Direct dial from bedrooms Lift TVL **NOTES:** ✝ ⊛ in restaurant ⊛ in 1 lounge Licensed Cen ht

♦♦♦ Averard Hotel
10 Lancaster Gate W2 3LH
☎ 020 7723 8877 📠 020 7706 0860
e-mail: sales@averard.com
Dir: opposite Hyde Park & Kensington Gdns, 2 mins walk from Lancaster Gate tube stn/10 mins walk from Paddington main line stn

| CHILD FACILITIES: | Food/bottle warming Ch portions Ch discounts Safe grounds Family rms Laundry | NEARBY: Museums Theatres |

Quietly located close to Hyde Park and Kensington Gardens, minutes' walk from Lancaster Gate tube station, this Edwardian property retains much of its original charm. Individually designed bedrooms are well equipped; many are spacious and suitable for families. There is a comfortable lounge, a bar and a stylish breakfast room.
ROOMS: 52 en suite (5 fmly) (2 GF) s £50-£70; d £70-£100 *
FACILITIES: TVB Direct dial from bedrooms Lift **NOTES:** Licensed Cen ht **LB**

♦♦♦ Barry House Hotel
12 Sussex Place, Hyde Park W2 2TP
☎ 020 7723 7340 & 0845 126 7856 📠 020 7723 9775
e-mail: hotel@barryhouse.co.uk
web: www.barryhouse.co.uk
Dir: follow Paddington signs into Sussex Gardens, then turn into Sussex Place

| CHILD FACILITIES: | Food/bottle warming Ch menu Ch portions Ch discounts under 5s free sharing with parents Cots Family rms rms for 3,4 & 5 people £92-£120 | NEARBY: Hyde Park |

Family-run, the Barry House offers friendly accommodation that is conveniently located close to rail and tube links as well as being near Hyde Park. Bedrooms are well-equipped and most rooms are en suite.
ROOMS: 18 rms (15 en suite) (5 fmly) (2 GF) ⊛ in 3 bedrooms
FACILITIES: TVB tea/coffee Direct dial from bedrooms **NOTES:** ✝ ⊛ in restaurant ⊛ in lounges Cen ht

♦♦♦ Kingsway Park Hotel
139 Sussex Gardens W2 2RX
☎ 020 7723 5677 & 7724 9346 📠 020 7402 4352
e-mail: info@kingswaypark-hotel.com
web: www.kingswaypark-hotel.com

| CHILD FACILITIES: | Nanny Family area Food/bottle warming Ch portions Highchairs Ch cutlery Ch discounts Safe grounds Videos Cots Family rms D rm with S beds Ch drinks Connecting rms Fridge Changing mats | NEARBY: London Zoo |

This Victorian property enjoys a central location within walking distance of Marble Arch, Hyde Park and Paddington. Bedrooms offer well-equipped value accommodation. Public areas include a reception lounge and a basement breakfast room adorned with interesting artwork.
ROOMS: 22 en suite (5 fmly) (2 GF) s £40-£65; d £65-£85 * ⊛ in 8 bedrooms **FACILITIES:** STV TVB tea/coffee Direct dial from bedrooms TVL Dinner Last d order 7pm **NOTES:** ✝ ⊛ in restaurant ⊛ in 1 lounge Licensed Cen ht **LB** **PARKING:** 3

W6

Babies Welcome	Family Rooms	Children's Dishes

★★★ 72% *Novotel London West*

1 Shortlands W6 8DR
☎ 020 8741 1555 ▤ 020 8741 2120
e-mail: H0737@accor-hotels.com

Dir: M4 (A4) & A316 junct at Hogarth rdbt. Along Great West Rd, left for Hammersmith before flyover. On Hammersmith Bridge Rd to rdbt, take 5th exit. 1st left into Shortlands, 1st left to hotel main entrance

CHILD FACILITIES: Babysitting Food/bottle warming Ch menu Ch portions Highchairs Ch discounts under 16s free sharing with parents Safe grounds Games consoles Cots Family rms D rms with S beds from £145 Connecting rms Fridge Laundry **NEARBY:** Cinema Park

Situated between Heathrow Airport and the West End, this substantial, purpose-built hotel is a popular base for both business and leisure travellers. Spacious, air-conditioned bedrooms boast a good range of extras and many have additional beds, making them suitable for families. The hotel also has its own paying car park.

ROOMS: 629 en suite (148 fmly) ✆ in 473 bedrooms **FACILITIES:** STV Snooker Gym **PARKING:** 240

Snows-on-the-Green

166 Shepherd's Bush Rd, Brook Green, Hammersmith W6 7PB
☎ 020 7603 2142 ▤ 020 7602 7553
e-mail: sebastian@snowsonthegreenfreeserve.co.uk

Dir: 300yds from station

CHILD FACILITIES: Please telephone for details

FOOD: Modern **STYLE:** Modern **SEATS:** 80 **OPEN:** 12-3/6-11, Closed 24-29 Dec, BHs L Sat, D Sun **RESTAURANT:** Fixed L £12.50, Fixed D £16.50, main £13-£16 **NOTES:** ✆ area, Air con **PARKING:** On street

---

Children's Dishes This symbol indicates a children's menu or smaller portions are available

---

W14

♦♦♦ *Aston Court Hotel*

25/27 Matheson Rd, West Kensington W14 8SN
☎ 020 7602 9954 ▤ 020 7371 1338

CHILD FACILITIES: Please telephone for details

This large corner property is located in a quiet residential area just a few minutes' walk from West Kensington tube station and Olympia. Bedrooms are comfortable and practically furnished. Public areas include a small comfortable lounge bar and an attractive conservatory where English breakfasts are served.

ROOMS: 29 en suite (3 fmly) ✆ in 14 bedrooms **FACILITIES:** STV TVB tea/coffee Direct dial from bedrooms Lift TVL **NOTES:** ✖ Licensed Cen h

W8

Babies Welcome	Children's Dishes

◉ ◉ ◉ Belvedere

Abbotsbury Rd, Holland House, Holland Park W8 6LU
☎ 020 7602 1238 ▤ 020 7610 4382
e-mail: sales@whitestarline.org.uk

Dir: On the Kensington High Street side of Holland Park.

CHILD FACILITIES: Outdoor play area Food/bottle warming Ch portions Highchairs Safe grounds **NEARBY:** Play area

FOOD: Classical French **STYLE:** Chic Traditional **SEATS:** 90 **OPEN:** 12-2.30/6-10.30, Closed D Sun **RESTAURANT:** Fixed L £14.95, Fixed D £24.50, main £14 **NOTES:** Air con **PARKING:** 50

WC1

Babies Welcome	Family Rooms	Children's Dishes

★★★★★ 74% ◉ ◉

Renaissance Chancery Court London

252 High Holborn WC1V 7EN
☎ 020 7829 9888 ▤ 020 7829 9889
e-mail: sales.chancerycourt@renaissancehotels.com

RENAISSANCE HOTELS

Dir: A4 along Piccadilly onto Shaftesbury Av. Into High Holborn, hotel on right

CHILD FACILITIES: Babysitting Activities: activity pack Food/bottle warming Ch portions Highchairs Ch discounts under 12s sharing free Safe grounds Games consoles Cots Family rms from £295 Ch drinks Connecting rms Fridge Laundry **NEARBY:** Park Covent Garden

This is a grand place with splendid public areas, decorated from top to bottom in rare marble. Craftsmen have meticulously restored the sweeping staircases, archways and stately public rooms of the 1914 building. The result is a spacious, relaxed hotel offering everything from stylish, luxuriously appointed bedrooms to a health club and state-of-the-art meeting rooms. The new Pearl restaurant has offers sophisticated cuisine and a memorable ambience.

ROOMS: 356 en suite ✆ in 280 bedrooms s £282-£352.50; d £282-£352.50 **LB FACILITIES:** Spa STV Sauna Gym Jacuzzi Spa treatments by ESPA Xmas **PARKING:** 4 **NOTES:** ✖

Babies Welcome	Family Rooms	Children's Dishes

★★★★ 72% ◎
The Montague on the Gardens
15 Montague St, Bloomsbury WC1B 5BJ
☎ 020 7637 1001 📠 020 7637 2516
e-mail: bookmt@rchmail.com
Dir: just off Russell Square

Red Carnation HOTELS

CHILD FACILITIES: Baby listening Babysitting Activities: colouring, books, games, puzzles, play mats Food/bottle warming Ch menu Ch portions Highchairs Ch cutlery Ch discounts under 5s free Videos Cots Family rms D rm with S bed **£135-225** Laundry Changing mats **NEARBY:** Gardens Cinemas Hamleys toy shop

This stylish hotel is situated right next to the British Museum. A special feature is the alfresco terrace overlooking a delightful garden. Other public rooms include the Blue Door Bistro and Chef's Table, a bar, a lounge and a conservatory where traditional afternoon teas are served. The bedrooms are beautifully appointed and range from split-level suites to more compact rooms.
ROOMS: 104 en suite (18 GF) ◎ in 47 bedrooms s £165-£220; d £195-£265 **LB FACILITIES:** STV Sauna Gym Jacuzzi ♫ Xmas
NOTES: ◎ in restaurant

Babies Welcome	Family Rooms	Children's Dishes

♦♦♦ Euro Hotel
51-53 Cartwright Gardens, Russell Square WC1H 9EL
☎ 020 7387 4321 📠 020 7383 5044
e-mail: reception@eurohotel.co.uk
web: www.eurohotel.co.uk
Dir: M1 junct 1 to Edgware Rd/Marylebone Rd/Euston Rd, right into Judd St, right into Leigh St, over Marchmont St into Cartright Gdns

CHILD FACILITIES: Outdoor play area Food/bottle warming Ch menu Ch portions Highchairs Ch discounts 2s and under free, 16s and under £10 sharing with an adult Safe grounds Videos Cots Family rms D rm with 2-3 S beds **NEARBY:** Parks Museums Zoo

This friendly bed and breakfast enjoys an ideal location in a leafy Georgian crescent. Russell Square tube station with its direct link to Heathrow is only a few minutes' walk away. Bedrooms are well equipped and many have en suite bathrooms. Breakfast is served at individual tables in the attractive dining room.
ROOMS: 34 rms (10 en suite) (9 fmly) (4 GF) s £49-£70; d £69-£89 *
FACILITIES: STV TVB tea/coffee Direct dial from bedrooms ⌕
NOTES: ✖ ◎ in restaurant Cen ht

WC2

◎ Bank Aldwych Restaurant
1 Kingsway WC2B 6XF
☎ 020 7379 9797 📠 020 7379 5070
e-mail: aldres@bankrestaurants.com
web: www.bankrestaurants.com
Dir: 2 mins from The Strand

CHILD FACILITIES: Please telephone for details

FOOD: Modern British **STYLE:** Modern Minimalist **SEATS:** 220
OPEN: 12-2.45/5.30-11, Closed 25-26 Dec, 1-2 Jan, BH's
RESTAURANT: main £11.95-£24 **NOTES:** Air con **PARKING:** NCP Drury Lane

Babies Welcome

◎ Imperial China
White Bear Yard, 25a Lilse St WC2H 7BA
☎ 020 7734 3388 📠 0207 343 833
e-mail: mail@imperial-china.co.uk
Dir: Nearest tube: Leicester Square. From station into Little Newport St, straight ahead into Lilse St and R into White Bear Yard

CHILD FACILITIES: Food/bottle warming Highchairs Changing facilities **NEARBY:** Cinema Parks

FOOD: Cantonese **STYLE:** Traditional **SEATS:** 400 **OPEN:** 12, Closed Xmas **RESTAURANT: NOTES:** ◎ area, Air con

Children's Dishes

◎ ◎ Maggiore's
33 King St, Covent Garden WC2E 8JD
☎ 020 7379 9696 📠 020 7379 6767
e-mail: enquiries@maggiores.uk.com

CHILD FACILITIES: Ch portions **NEARBY:** Covent Garden Theatres Museums

FOOD: Traditional French **STYLE:** Chic, Rustic **SEATS:** 60
OPEN: noon-2.30/5-11, Closed 24-26 Dec & 1 Jan **RESTAURANT:** Fixed L £14.50, main £14.50-£17.50 **NOTES:** ◎ area, Air con **PARKING:** NCP, on street

> How to use this guide & abbreviations are explained on pages 5-7

MERSEYSIDE

HOYLAKE
Map 07 SJ28

★★★ 66% *Kings Gap Court*
CH47 1HE
☎ 0151 632 2073 📠 0151 632 0247
e-mail: kingsgapcourt@aol.com
web: www.kingsgapcourt.co.uk

CHILD FACILITIES: Please telephone for details

In the reign of William III 'Hoyle Lake' was an army staging post from where the invasion of Ireland was launched in 1690, and the 'Kings Gap' area commemorates this slice of history. The lake no longer exists but the hotel that has adopted the name enjoys a peaceful residential location just a short walk from sandy beaches. Modern bedrooms are stylish and comfortable whilst the bright and spacious day rooms include a conservatory restaurant.

ROOMS: 30 en suite (4 fmly) (7 GF) ⊗ in 15 bedrooms **PARKING:** 60
NOTES: ⊗ in restaurant

LIVERPOOL
Map 07 SJ39

★★★★ 69%
Liverpool Marriott Hotel City Centre
1 Queen Square L1 1RH
☎ 0151 476 8000 📠 0151 474 5000
e-mail: liverpool.city@marriotthotels.co.uk
Dir: from city centre follow signs for Queen Sq Parking. Hotel adjacent

Marriott
HOTELS·RESORTS·SUITES

CHILD FACILITIES: Please telephone for details

An impressive modern hotel located in the heart of the city. The
continued

elegant public rooms include a café bar, cocktail bar and the stylish Oliver's Restaurant. The hotel also boasts a well-equipped, indoor leisure health club with pool. Bedrooms are stylishly appointed and benefit from a host of extra facilities.

ROOMS: 146 en suite (29 fmly) ⊗ in 120 bedrooms s £98-£150; d £98-£150 **LB FACILITIES:** STV 🏊 Sauna Solarium Gym Jacuzzi Xmas **PARKING:** 158 **NOTES:** ⊗ in restaurant

★★★★ 68%
Liverpool Marriott Hotel South
Speke Aerodrome L24 8QD
☎ 0151 494 5000 📠 0151 494 5053
e-mail: liverpool.south@marriotthotels.co.uk
Dir: M62 junct 6, take Knowsley Expressway towards Speke. At end of Expressway right onto A561 towards Liverpool. Continue for approx 4 miles, hotel on left just after Estuary Commerce Park

Marriott
HOTELS·RESORTS·SUITES

CHILD FACILITIES: Please telephone for details

Previously Liverpool airport, this hotel has a distinctive look, reflected by its art deco architecture and interior design. The spacious bedrooms are fully air-conditioned and feature a comprehensive range of facilities. Feature rooms include the presidential suite in the base of the old control tower.

ROOMS: 164 en suite (50 fmly) (46 GF) ⊗ in 100 bedrooms s £115-£125; d £115-£125 **FACILITIES:** STV 🏊 ⚘ ✎ Squash Sauna Solarium Gym Jacuzzi Selected use of David Lloyd Leisure Centre adjacent to hotel **PARKING:** 200 **NOTES:** ✈

ST HELENS
Map 07 SJ59

◀ The Red Cat
8 Red Cat Ln WA11 8RU
☎ 01744 882422 📠 01744 886693
e-mail: redcat@amserve.net
Dir: From A580/A570 Junct follow signs for Crank

CHILD FACILITIES: Please telephone for details

OPEN: 12-11 (Sun 12-10.30) **BAR MEALS:** L served Wed-Sun 12-2 D served Wed-Sun 6-9.30 Av main course £8.95 **RESTAURANT:** L served Wed-Sun 12-2 D served Wed-Sun 6-9.30 **FACILITIES:** ✈ **PARKING:** 60

All information was correct at the time of going to press; we recommend you confirm details on booking

NORFOLK

Wells-Next-The-Sea

BANHAM
Banham Zoo NR16 2HE
info@banhamzoo.co.uk ☎01953 887771
(On B1113, signposted off A11 and A140. Follow
brown tourist signs)
Open all year, daily from 10am Closed 25-26 Dec.
Last admission 1 hour before closing.

BRESSINGHAM
Bressingham Steam Museum & Gardens
IP22 2AB
info@bressingham.co.uk ☎01379 686900
(On A1066 2.5m W of Diss. Between Thetford &
Diss) Open: Steam Museum, Dad's Army
collection, Foggy Bottom & Dell Garden Apr-Sep,
daily 10.30-5.30 10.30-4.30 Mar & Oct. Last
admission 1 hour before closing time.
*£7-£10 ch 3-16 £5-£8, pen £6-£8. Family £21-
£30. Season tickets available.

FAKENHAM
Pensthorpe Waterfowl Park & Nature Reserve
NR21 0LN ☎01328 851465
info@pensthorpe.com
(Just outside Fakenham on the A1067 to Norwich)
Open Jan-Mar; daily 10-4, Apr-Dec; 10-5.
*£6 ch £3, pen £5

FILBY
Thrigby Hall Wildlife Gardens NR29 3DR
mail@thrigbyhall.co.uk ☎01493 369477
(On unclass road off A1064, between Acle &
Caister-on-Sea.)
Open all year, daily from 10.
*£6.90 ch 4-14 £4.90, pen £5.90.

GREAT YARMOUTH
Merrivale Model Village
NR30 3JG ☎01493 842097
(Marine parade seafront. Next to Wellington Pier)
Open 3 Apr-28 May, 10-5. 29 May-12 Sep 10-9, 13
Sep-Oct 10-5.
*£3 ch 3-16 £2.50, pen £2.50.

HUNSTANTON
Sea Life Aquarium & Marine Sanctuary
PE36 5BH ☎01485 533576
Open all year, daily from 10. Closed 25 Dec

LENWADE
Dinosaur Adventure Park NR9 5JW
info@dinosaurpark.co.uk ☎01603 876310
(9m from Norwich. Follow Weston Park signs from
A47 or A1067)
Open Etr-8 Sep & Oct half term, daily; 9 Sep-20
Oct, Fri, Sat & Sun.

NORWICH
Norwich Castle Museum NR13 JU
museums@norfolk.gov.uk ☎01603 493625
(City centre)
Open all year, Mon-Fri 10-4.30, Sat 10-5, Sun 1-5;
School holidays Mon-Sat 10-6, Sun 1-5. Closed
24-27 Dec & 1 Jan.
*All zones £5.25 ch 4-16 £3.70, concessions £4.50.

REEDHAM
Pettitts Animal Adventure Park
NR13 3UA ☎01493 700094
(Off A47 at Acle)
Open daily 27 Mar-0ct, 10-5/5.30.
*£7.75 ch 3-15 £7.25, pen/disabled £5.85. Under
3's free.

SHERINGHAM
North Norfolk Railway
NR26 8RA ☎01263 820800
enquiries@nnrailway.com
(from A148 take A1082. Next to large car park by
rdbt in town centre). Open mid Feb-Oct; daily
steam trains; Dec & Jan, Santa specials.
Telephone for details. *£8 (ch under 4 free, ch 4-15
£4.50, pen £7). Family ticket £23.

THURSFORD GREEN
Thursford Collection NR21 0AS
admin@thursfordcollection.co.uk ☎01328 878477
(1m off A148. Halfway between Fakenham and
Holt). Open Good Fri-last Sun in Sep, daily, 12-5.
Closed Sat. *£5.50 (ch under 4 free, ch 4-14 £3,
students £4.75 pen £5.20). Party 15+ £4.75 each.

WEST RUNTON
Norfolk Shire Horse Centre
NR27 9QH ☎01263 837339
bakewell@norfolkshirehorse.fsnet.co.uk
(Off A149)
Open Etr-last Fri in Oct, Sun-Fri; also Sats BHs.
Last admission 3.45pm
*£5.50 ch £3.50, pen £4.50.

BARNEY
Map 09 TF93

◆◆◆◆ The Old Brick Kilns
Little Barney Ln, Barney NR21 0NL
☎ 01328 878305 📠 01328 878948
e-mail: oldbrickkilns@aol.com
Dir: turn off A148 Cromer road onto B1354. Turn 1st right to Barney in approx 300yds turn left down Little Barney Lane, house at end of the lane.

CHILD FACILITIES: Please telephone for details

A delightful country house, originally three separate cottages, which have been carefully converted to provide tastefully decorated accommodation in its own peaceful grounds. Breakfasts and dinner, by prior arrangement, are served at a communal table in the dining room/lounge.

ROOMS: 3 en suite (1 fmly) (1 GF) s £25; d £50 * **FACILITIES:** TVB tea/coffee Direct dial from bedrooms TVL No coaches Fishing Pool Table **NOTES:** ✖ ⊗ Licensed Cen ht **PARKING:** 6

BAWBURGH
Map 05 TG10

Babies Welcome | Children's Dishes

🍺 Kings Head
Harts Ln NR9 3LS
☎ 01603 744977 📠 01603 744990
e-mail: anton@kingshead-bawburgh.co.uk
Dir: From A47 W of Norwich take B1108 W

CHILD FACILITIES: Food/bottle warming Ch licence Ch menu Ch portions Highchairs Ch cutlery Safe grounds Changing facilities NEARBY: Walks

OPEN: 11.30-11 (Sun 12-10.30) Closed: 25-27 Dec(eve) 1 Jan(eve) **BAR MEALS:** L served all week 12-2 D served all week 6.30-9.30 Av main course £12 **RESTAURANT:** L served all week 12-2 D served all week 6.30-9.30 Av 3 course à la carte £22.50 **FACILITIES:** Children's licence Garden: Secluded, landscaped garden with flower beds ✖ **PARKING:** 100

BLAKENEY
Map 09 TG04

🍺 The Kings Arms
Westgate St NR25 7NQ
☎ 01263 740341 📠 01263 740391
e-mail: kingsarms.blakeney@btopenworld.com

CHILD FACILITIES: Please telephone for details

OPEN: 11-11 **BAR MEALS:** L served all week 12-9.30 D served all week 12-9.30 Av main course £7 **FACILITIES:** Garden: Very safe large patio and grass area **PARKING:** 10

BRANCASTER STAITHE
Map 09 TF74

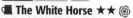
Babies Welcome | Children's Dishes

🍺 The White Horse ★★ ⊛
Main Rd PE31 8BY
☎ 01485 210262 📠 01485 210930
e-mail: reception@whitehorsebrancaster.co.uk
web: www.whitehorsebrancaster.co.uk
Dir: mid-way between King's Lynn & Wells-Next-The-Sea on the A149 coastal road

CHILD FACILITIES: Activities: puzzles, colouring Food/bottle warming Ch menu Highchairs Ch cutlery Safe grounds Changing facilities NEARBY: Sealife Centre Sailing school Near sea

OPEN: 11 -11 (Sun 12-10.30) **BAR MEALS:** L served all week 11.30-3 Av main course £8.50 **RESTAURANT:** L served all week 12-3 D served all week 6-10 Av 3 course à la carte £27 **FACILITIES:** Garden: Sun deck terrace overlooking tidal marshes **ROOMS:** 15 bedrooms 15 en suite 3 family rooms s£72 d£104 **PARKING:** 80

BURNHAM MARKET
Map 09 TF84

◆◆◆◆ Staffordshire House
Station Rd, Docking PE31 8LS
☎ 01485 518709
e-mail: enquiries@staffordshirehouse.com
Dir: located on B1153 (Station Rd) next door but one to duck pond, approx 300yds from church and diagonally opposite Post Office

CHILD FACILITIES: Please telephone for details

This charming, detached property is situated in the centre of the quiet rural village of Docking, and is ideally placed for exploring Burnham Market and the North Norfolk coastline. The individually decorated bedrooms are tastefully furnished and thoughtfully equipped with many useful extras. The house is due to become the hub of an Internet Art Gallery, replacing the former 'antique and interiors' shop.

ROOMS: 3 rms s £32; d £52-£58 * ⊗ **FACILITIES:** TVB tea/coffee No coaches **NOTES:** ✖ ⊗ in restaurant Cen ht **LB** **PARKING:** 4

◆◆◆◆ 🌱 Whitehall Farm
Burnham Thorpe PE31 8HN
☎ 01328 738416 & 07050 247390 📠 01328 730937
e-mail: barrysoutherland@aol.com
web: www.whitehallfarm-accommodation.com
Dir: from Lord Nelson pub in Burnham, head towards Holkam/Wells. Farmhouse last building on right on leaving village

CHILD FACILITIES: Please telephone for details

On an arable farm, this house has large landscaped gardens and a menagerie of animals and offers a relaxing and informal atmosphere. Bedrooms are spacious, comfortable and equipped with DVD, TV and many extras. Communal hearty breakfasts are served in the cosy dining room.

ROOMS: 3 rms (2 en suite) (1 fmly) s £40-£65; d £60-£70 * ⊗ **FACILITIES:** TVB tea/coffee TVL Riding Countryside stewardship access route 560 acres arable **NOTES:** ✖ ⊗ in restaurant Cen ht **PARKING:** 7

BURNHAM THORPE
Map 09 TF84

Babies Welcome | Children's Dishes

🍺 The Lord Nelson
Walsingham Rd PE31 8HL
☎ 01328 738241 📠 01328 738241
e-mail: david@nelsonslocal.co.uk
web: www.nelsonslocal.co.uk

CHILD FACILITIES: Activities: colouring, toys Outdoor play area Food/bottle warming Ch menu Ch portions Highchairs Safe grounds Changing facilities NEARBY: Park Sea life Sanctuary Langham Glass North Norfolk Steam Railway 2-3m to sea

OPEN: 11-3 6-11 (Sun 12-3 6.30-10.30) **BAR MEALS:** L served all week 12-2 D served Mon-Sat 7-9 **RESTAURANT:** L served all week 12-2 D served Mon-Sat 7-9 Av 3 course à la carte £20 **FACILITIES:** Garden: Very large; seating; childrens play area **PARKING:** 30

England

Babies Welcome | Children's Dishes

🍴 The George Hotel ◆◆◆◆
High St NR25 7RN
☎ 01263 740652 ⧉ 01263 741275
e-mail: thegeorge@cleynextthesea.com
Dir: On coast road (A149). Centre of village

CHILD FACILITIES: Outdoor play area Food/bottle warming
Ch licence Ch menu Ch portions Highchairs Changing facilities
NEARBY: Walks Cinema Leisure centre Near sea

Delightful inn situated in the centre of this pretty Norfolk village close to the seal colonies and the famous marshes with its abundance of bird life. Bedrooms are pleasantly decorated and furnished with pine pieces and have many useful extras. Public rooms include a smart lounge area, a restaurant and a choice of bars which feature artwork for sale by a local artist.
OPEN: 11-3 6-11 (all day Apr-Oct & Bank Hols) **BAR MEALS:** L served all week 12-2.30 D served all week 6.30-9.30 Av main course £6.95
RESTAURANT: L served all week 12-2.30 D served all week 6.30-9 Av 3 course à la carte £19 **FACILITIES:** Garden: Mature garden **ROOMS:** 12 bedrooms 12 en suite s£35 d£40 **PARKING:** 15

Babies Welcome | Family Rooms | Children's Dishes

◆◆◆ ♥ Abbott Farm
Walsingham Rd, Binham NR21 0AW
☎ 01328 830519 & 07986 041715 ⧉ 01328 830519
e-mail: abbot.farm@btinternet.com
Dir: leave A148 at Thursford (Crawfish Thai Restaurant) towards Hindringham, then 4m to Binham, in village L on B1388 to Walsingham, Farm 1m on L

CHILD FACILITIES: Activities: toys, books, games Outdoor play area Food/bottle warming Ch menu Ch portions Highchairs Ch cutlery Ch discounts under 5s free, under 12s half price Safe grounds Videos Cots Family rms rm with 3 S beds Ch drinks Fridge Laundry Changing mats **NEARBY:** Walks Play area Short drive to sea

A detached red-brick dormer house situated in a peaceful rural location amid 150 acres of arable farmland. The spacious bedrooms are pleasantly decorated and thoughtfully equipped, the ground-floor room features a very spacious en suite shower. Breakfast is taken in the attractive conservatory, which has superb views across the countryside.
ROOMS: 3 en suite (2 GF) s £22-£24; d £44-£48 * **FACILITIES:** TVB tea/coffee 190 acres arable **NOTES:** Credit cards not taken ⊗ Cen ht **PARKING:** 20

Don't forget our travel accommodation section at the front of the guide

Babies Welcome | Children's Dishes

🍴 The White Horse Inn ◆◆◆◆
Fakenham Rd, East Barsham NR21 0LH
☎ 01328 820645 ⧉ 01328 820645
e-mail: rsteele@btinternet.com

CHILD FACILITIES: Activities: colouring, puzzle books, games
Food/bottle warming Ch menu Ch portions Highchairs Ch cutlery
Safe grounds **NEARBY:** Dinosaur Park Farms

OPEN: 11-3 6-11 **BAR MEALS:** L served all week 12-2 D served all week 7-9.30 **RESTAURANT:** L served all week 12-2 D served all week 7-9.30 **FACILITIES:** Garden: Patio area & enclosed courtyard 🐾 **ROOMS:** 3 bedrooms 3 en suite 2 family rooms s£35 d£50 **PARKING:** 50

🍴 The Boar Inn
NR21 0DX
☎ 01328 829212 ⧉ 01328 829421
Dir: Off A1067 4m S of Fakenham
CHILD FACILITIES: Please telephone for details
OPEN: 11-2.30 6.30-11 (All day 1 May-30 Sep) **BAR MEALS:** L served all week 12-2 D served all week 7-9.30 **RESTAURANT:** L served all week 12-2 D served all week 7-9.30 Av 3 course à la carte £15 **FACILITIES:** Garden: Food served outside. 🐾 **ROOMS:** 5 bedrooms 5 en suite 2 family rooms s£30 d£50 (◆◆◆) **PARKING:** 30

Babies Welcome | Family Rooms | Children's Dishes

◆◆◆◆ The Elmfield Hotel
38 Wellesley Rd NR30 1EU
☎ 01493 859827
e-mail: elmfieldhotel@hotmail.com
Dir: From A47 follow signs for seafront turn left into Wellesley Rd, which is the last turning before the seafront

CHILD FACILITIES: Baby listening Activities: colouring, games, toys Food/bottle warming Ch menu Ch portions Highchairs Ch cutlery Ch discounts under 2s free, 2-11s half price Safe grounds Games consoles Cots Family rms D rm with S beds Ch drinks Fridge Changing mats **NEARBY:** 400 metres to sea

A delightful privately-owned hotel situated just a couple of minutes' walk from the seafront and town centre. Breakfast is served in the spacious dining room and there is a cosy lounge bar. Bedrooms are pleasantly decorated and equipped with many useful extras; some rooms have sea views.
ROOMS: 9 en suite (3 fmly) s £15-£22; d £30-£44 * ⊗ in 1 bedrooms
FACILITIES: TVB tea/coffee No coaches Dinner Last d order am
NOTES: Credit cards not taken 🐾 ⊗ in restaurant ⊗ in 1 lounge Licensed Cen ht **LB BB** **PARKING:** 7

◆◆◆◆ Hamilton Hotel
23-24 North Dr NR30 4EW
☎ 01493 844662
e-mail: enquiries@hamilton-hotel.co.uk
Dir: A47 follow signs for the seafront, turn left at Britannia Pier. Hotel 800yds along the seafront
CHILD FACILITIES: Please telephone for details
Friendly, family-run hotel situated at the quieter end of town overlooking the Venetian Waterways and beach. Breakfast and dinner are taken in the smart dining room, and guests have the use of a cosy bar and residents' lounge. Bedrooms are pleasantly decorated and thoughtfully equipped; some rooms have sea views.
ROOMS: 24 en suite 1 annexe en suite (3 fmly) (2 GF) s £30-£34.50; d £60-£69 * ⊗ **FACILITIES:** TVB tea/coffee Dinner Last d order 6pm **NOTES:** ⊗ in restaurant ⊗ in 1 lounge Licensed Cen ht **LB** **PARKING:** 24

England

GREAT YARMOUTH, continued

◆◆◆ Spindrift Private Hotel
36 Wellesley Rd NR30 1EU
☎ 01493 843772
e-mail: bradleyshouse@btinternet.com
Dir: follow signs for seafront, continue along St Nicholas Rd & Euston Rd then 1st left into Wellesley Rd

CHILD FACILITIES: Please telephone for details

Expect a friendly welcome at this privately owned hotel, which is situated in a tree-lined avenue, just a short walk from the seafront and town centre. Bedrooms are smartly decorated with co-ordinated fabrics and have many thoughtful touches; family rooms are available. Breakfast is served at individual tables in the cosy ground floor breakfast room.
ROOMS: 7 en suite (2 fmly) d £30-£50 * **FACILITIES:** TVB tea/coffee No coaches **NOTES:** Credit cards not taken ✖ ⊗ in restaurant Cen ht LB BB **PARKING:** 1

◆◆◆ Amber Guest House
25 St Georges Rd NR30 2JT
☎ 01493 850676

CHILD FACILITIES: Please telephone for details

Ideally placed for the beach and town centre, this guest house is just a short walk from both Britannia and Wellington Piers. Bedrooms vary in size and style; each one is brightly decorated and soundly appointed. Breakfast is served at individual tables in the open plan lounge/dining room.
ROOMS: 9 rms (3 en suite) (2 fmly) s £18-£25 ; d £40-£55 * **FACILITIES:** TVB tea/coffee TVL No coaches Dinner **NOTES:** Credit cards not taken ✖ ⊗ Cen ht LB BB

Babies Welcome | Family Rooms | Children's Dishes

◆◆◆ Harbour Hotel
20 Pavilion Rd, Gorleston on Sea NR31 6BY
☎ 01493 661031 ▤ 01493 661031
e-mail: jeffchambers@harbourhotel.freeserve.co.uk
Dir: A12 to Gorleston on Sea town centre, follow signs to beach. Hotel 20yds from lighthouse

CHILD FACILITIES: Baby listening Activities: toys, games Indoor play area Food/bottle warming Ch menu Ch portions Highchairs Ch cutlery Ch discounts half price Safe grounds Videos Cots Family rms D rm with S bed, 2 D rms with S and extra D bed Connecting rms Changing mats NEARBY: Theme park Leisure centre 2 mins to sea

Expect a warm welcome at this small, privately-owned hotel, situated near the harbour overlooking the sea. The pleasantly decorated, well-equipped bedrooms vary in size and style; some rooms have lovely sea views. Breakfast is served in the spacious dining room and snacks are offered in the lounge bar during the evening.
ROOMS: 8 rms (4 en suite) (6 fmly) s £35-£46; d £44-£46 * **FACILITIES:** tea/coffee TVL No coaches **NOTES:** Credit cards not taken ✖ ⊗ in restaurant Licensed Cen ht LB **PARKING:** 2

HAPPISBURGH   Map 09 TG13

🍺 The Hill House
NR12 0PW
☎ 01692 650004 ▤ 01692 650004
Dir: 5m from Stalham, 8m from North Walsham

CHILD FACILITIES: Please telephone for details

continued

OPEN: 12-3 (Thu-Sun all day) 7-11 (Summer all day) Rest: 25 Dec Closed eve **BAR MEALS:** L served all week 12-2.30 D served all week 7-9.30 Av main course £6 **RESTAURANT:** L served all week 12-2.30 D served all week 7-9.30 Av 3 course à la carte £14 **FACILITIES:** Garden: Large, by the sea **PARKING:** 20

LARLING   Map 05 TL98

Babies Welcome | Children's Dishes

🍺 Angel Inn
NR16 2QU
☎ 01953 717963 ▤ 01953 718561

CHILD FACILITIES: Outdoor play area Food/bottle warming Ch menu Ch portions Highchairs Ch cutlery Safe grounds NEARBY: Thetford Forest Banham Zoo Snetterton Race Circuit

OPEN: 10-11 **BAR MEALS:** L served Sun-Sat 12-2 D served Sun-Sat 6.30-9.30 Av main course £7.50 **RESTAURANT:** L served all week 12-2 D served all week 6.30-9.30 Av 3 course à la carte £15 **FACILITIES:** Garden: Large, garden tables ✖ **PARKING:** 100

LITTLE FRANSHAM   Map 09 TF9

Babies Welcome | Children's Dishes

🍺 The Canary and Linnet
Main Rd NR19 2JW
☎ 01362 687027 ▤ 01362 687021
e-mail: ben@canaryandlinnet.co.uk
Dir: Situated on A47 between Dereham and Swaffham

CHILD FACILITIES: Food/bottle warming Ch menu Ch portions Highchairs Safe grounds

OPEN: 12-3 6-11 (Sun 12-3 7-10) **BAR MEALS:** L served Mon-Sun 12-2 D served all week 6-9.30 **RESTAURANT:** L served all week 12-2 D served Mon-Sun 6-9.30 **FACILITIES:** Garden **PARKING:** 70

LITTLE WALSINGHAM   Map 09 TF9:

Babies Welcome | Children's Dishes

🍺 Black Lion ◆◆◆◆
Friday Market Place NR22 6DB
☎ 01328 820235 ▤ 01328 821407
e-mail: blacklionwalsingham@btinternet.com
web: www.blacklionwalsingham.com
Dir: From Kings Lynn take A148 and B1105 or from Norwich take A1067 and B1105.

CHILD FACILITIES: Food/bottle warming Ch portions Highchairs NEARBY: Pensthorpe Waterfowl Park & Nature Reserve 4m to sea

OPEN: 11.30-3 (Easter-Oct 11.30-11) 6-11 (Sat 11.30-11, Sun 12-10.30) **BAR MEALS:** L served all week 12-2 D served all week 7-9.30 Av main course £8.50 **RESTAURANT:** L served all week D served all week 7-9.30 Av 3 course à la carte £18 **FACILITIES:** Garden: Courtyard garden, Picnic tables, Well **ROOMS:** 8 bedrooms 8 en suite 1 family rooms s£48.50 d£7(

NORWICH   Map 05 TG20

Babies Welcome | Family Rooms | Children's Dishes

★★★★ 75%
Marriott Sprowston Manor Hotel & Country Club

Marriott HOTELS · RESORTS · SUITES

Sprowston Park, Wroxham Rd, Sprowston NR7 8RP
☎ 01603 410871 ▤ 01603 423911
e-mail: sprowston.manor@marriotthotels.co.uk
Dir: From A11/A47, 2m NE on A115 (Wroxham Rd). Follow signs to Sprowston Park

CHILD FACILITIES: Babysitting Activities: colouring Food/bottle warming Ch menu Ch portions Highchairs Ch discounts under 5s free sharing with parents Safe grounds Videos Cots Family rms D rm with D sofa bed £150 Connecting rms Fridge Laundry Changing mats (on request) **NEARBY:** Cinemas Thrigby Hall 20-min drive to sea

Surrounded by open parkland, this imposing property is set in attractively landscaped grounds and is just a short drive from the city centre. Bedrooms are spacious and feature a variety of decorative styles. The hotel also has extensive banqueting and leisure facilities. Other public rooms include a variety of seating areas and the elegant Manor Restaurant.
ROOMS: 94 en suite (3 fmly) (5 GF) ⊗ in 61 bedrooms s fr £109; d £170 **LB FACILITIES:** Spa STV ⊠ Golf 18 Sauna Solarium Gym ⚓ Xmas **PARKING:** 150 **NOTES:** ✖ ⊗ in restaurant

★★★ 70% The Georgian House THE INDEPENDENTS HOTEL ASSOCIATION
32-34 Unthank Rd NR2 2RB
☎ 01603 615655 ▤ 01603 765689
e-mail: reception@georgian-hotel.co.uk
web: www.georgian-hotel.co.uk
Dir: follow Roman Catholic Cathedral signs from city centre, hotel off inner ring road

CHILD FACILITIES: Please telephone for details

Please note that this establishment has recently changed hands. This pair of Victorian houses has been carefully converted to create a comfortable hotel, which is situated just a short walk from the city centre. Public areas include a cosy bar, a TV lounge and an elegant restaurant. The smartly refurbished bedrooms are well maintained and thoughtfully equipped.
ROOMS: 28 en suite (2 fmly) (10 GF) ⊗ in 20 bedrooms s £64-£81.50; d £90-£120 (incl. bkfst) **LB FACILITIES:** STV **PARKING:** 40 **NOTES:** ⊗ in restaurant Closed 24 Dec-2 Jan

★★★ 67% Wensum Valley Hotel Golf & Country Club
Beech Av, Taverham NR8 6HP
☎ 01603 261012 ▤ 01603 261664
e-mail: enqs@wensumvalley.co.uk
Dir: Turn left off A1067 Norwich to Fakenham road at Taverham into Beech Avenue. Hotel entrance on right next to High School

continued

CHILD FACILITIES: Please telephone for details

Family run hotel set amid 240 acres of Norfolk countryside just a short distance from the city centre. The modern purpose built bedrooms are generally spacious and thoughtfully equipped. Public rooms include a choice of bars, a lounge and a large restaurant overlooking the green. The hotel has superb golf and leisure facilities.
ROOMS: 84 en suite (12 fmly) (32 GF) ⊗ in all bedrooms
FACILITIES: ⊠ Golf 36 Fishing Snooker Sauna Solarium Gym ⚓ Jacuzzi Beauty therapy Golf driving range Hairdressing salon ♫ Xmas **PARKING:** 250 **NOTES:** ✖ ⊗ in restaurant

★★ 70% The Old Rectory
North Walsham Rd, Crostwick NR12 7BG
☎ 01603 738513 ▤ 01603 738712
e-mail: info@therectoryhotel.fsnet.co.uk
web: www.oldrectorycrostwick.com
Dir: left off Norwich ring road onto B1150. Hotel 4m on left opposite St Peters church

CHILD FACILITIES: Please telephone for details

Attractive family-run hotel situated on the outskirts of Norwich city centre. Public rooms feature a superb hexagonal conservatory style dining room, which overlooks the pretty gardens, and guests have the use of a smart lounge as well as a cosy bar and private dining room. Bedrooms are attractively decorated and well equipped.
ROOMS: 13 en suite (8 fmly) (13 GF) ⊗ in 5 bedrooms s £46-£48; d £62.50-£65 (incl. bkfst) **FACILITIES:** ⚓ **PARKING:** 100 **NOTES:** ⊗ in restaurant

Babies Welcome | Family Rooms | Children's Dishes

★★ 64% Cumberland
212-216 Thorpe Rd NR1 1TJ
☎ 01603 434550 ▤ 01603 433355
e-mail: cumberland@paston.co.uk
web: www.cumberlandhotel.co.uk
Dir: Cumberland Hotel is located on the left hand side of Thorpe Road

CHILD FACILITIES: Baby listening Food/bottle warming Ch portions Highchairs Ch cutlery Cots Family rms D rm with D or S bed, Suite from £75 Connecting rms Laundry **NEARBY:** Cinema Ten-pin bowling

Please note that this establishment has recently changed ownership. The hotel is situated just a short drive from the railway station and city centre. Bedrooms are pleasantly decorated and thoughtfully equipped. An interesting choice of freshly prepared dishes is served in the Cape Dutch restaurant and guests also have the use of a smart lounge bar and cosy sitting room.
ROOMS: 22 en suite 4 annexe en suite (3 fmly) (6 GF) ⊗ in 10 bedrooms s £45-£59; d £59-£89 (incl. bkfst) **LB PARKING:** 50 **NOTES:** ✖ ⊗ in restaurant Closed 26-31 Dec

Babies Welcome | Family Rooms | Children's Dishes

◆◆◆◆ Church Farm
Church St, Horsford NR10 3DB
☎ 01603 898020 ▤ 01603 891649
e-mail: churchfarmguesthouse@btopenworld.co.uk
Dir: from A11 take signs for airport, turn left onto B1149, then at 1st x-rds (Woodlands PH on corner) turn into Church St

CHILD FACILITIES: Food/bottle warming Ch menu Ch portions Highchairs Ch cutlery Safe grounds Cots Family rms D rm with adjoining rm with B beds £65 Fridge Changing mats

Ideally situated in a peaceful rural location just a short drive from Norwich airport and the city centre. The spacious bedrooms are smartly decorated, tastefully furnished and have many thoughtful

continued on p190

England

NORWICH, continued

touches. Breakfast is served at individual tables in the open plan conservatory-style lounge/dining room, which overlooks the garden and sun terrace.

Church Farm, Norwich

ROOMS: 10 en suite (1 fmly) (3 GF) s £30-£35; d £45-£50 * ⊗ in 3 bedrooms **FACILITIES:** TVB tea/coffee TVL No coaches **NOTES:** ✖ ⊗ in restaurant Cen ht **PARKING:** 20

| Babies Welcome | Family Rooms | Children's Dishes |

◆◆◆ The Larches
345 Aylsham Rd NR3 2RU
☎ 01603 415420 🖷 01603 465340
web: www.thelarches.com
Dir: on A140 500yds past ring road, on left adjacent to Lloyds Bank

CHILD FACILITIES: Activities: toys Indoor play area Outdoor play area Food/bottle warming Ch menu Ch portions Highchairs Ch cutlery Ch discounts under 5s free, 5-12s half price Safe grounds Cots Family rms D rm with S bed, D with 2 S beds
NEARBY: Parks Leisure centre Swimming pool Cinema River walks

Modern, detached property situated only a short drive from the city centre and airport. The spacious, well-equipped bedrooms are brightly decorated, pleasantly furnished and have co-ordinated soft fabrics. Breakfast is served at individual tables in the smart open plan lounge/dining room. Dinner is available by prior arrangement.
ROOMS: 7 en suite (2 fmly) (1 GF) s fr £30; d fr £40 *
FACILITIES: STV TVB tea/coffee TVL No coaches Dinner Last d order 3pm **NOTES:** ⊗ in area of dining room ⊗ in 1 lounge Cen ht **PARKING:** 10

| Babies Welcome | Family Rooms | Children's Dishes |

◆◆◆ Marlborough House Hotel
22 Stracey Rd, Thorpe Rd NR1 1EZ
☎ 01603 628005 🖷 01603 628005
Dir: adjacent to Norwich railway station on A47, Thorpe to Yarmouth rd

CHILD FACILITIES: Food/bottle warming Ch menu Ch portions Highchairs Ch cutlery Ch discounts 5-12s half price Safe grounds Family rms D rm with S beds Ch drinks

Privately-owned and personally-run small hotel conveniently situated for both the railway station, football ground and just a short walk from the city centre. Bedrooms are pleasantly decorated, soundly maintained and equipped with modern facilities. Public rooms include a cosy lounge bar and a traditionally furnished breakfast room, where separate tables are provided.
ROOMS: 12 rms (7 en suite) (2 fmly) (1 GF) s £30-£40; d £55-£60 * ⊗ in 3 bedrooms **FACILITIES:** TVB tea/coffee TVL Dinner Last d order 4.30pm **NOTES:** Credit cards not taken ✖ ⊗ in restaurant ⊗ in 1 lounge Licensed Cen ht **LB PARKING:** 5

| Babies Welcome | Children's Dishes |

⊛ ⊛ Adlard's Restaurant
79 Upper St Giles St NR2 1AB
☎ 01603 633522 🖷 01603 617733
e-mail: info@adlards.co.uk
web: www.adlards.co.uk
Dir: City centre, 200yds behind the City Hall

CHILD FACILITIES: Food/bottle warming Ch portions Highchairs
NEARBY: Cinema

FOOD: French, European **STYLE:** Modern **SEATS:** 40
OPEN: 12.30-1.45/7.30-10.30, Closed 1 wk after Xmas, SunL Mon
RESTAURANT: Fixed L £17, main £16-£23.50 **NOTES:** Air con

| Babies Welcome | Children's Dishes |

⊛ ⊛ Brummells Seafood Restaurant
7 Magdalen St NR3 1LE
☎ 01603 625555 🖷 01603 766260
e-mail: brummell@brummells.co.uk
web: www.brummells.co.uk
Dir: In city centre, 40yds from Colegate

CHILD FACILITIES: Food/bottle warming Ch portions Highchairs

FOOD: International, Seafood **STYLE:** Chic, Rustic **SEATS:** 30
OPEN: 12/6 **RESTAURANT:** main £16-£32 **NOTES:** Smart Dress, ⊗ area, Air con

| Babies Welcome | Children's Dishes |

⊛ St Benedicts Restaurant
9 St Benedicts St NR2 4PE
☎ 01603 765377 🖷 01603 765377
e-mail: stbens@ukonline.co.uk
Dir: At city end of St Benedicts

CHILD FACILITIES: Activities: Food/bottle warming Ch portions Highchairs **NEARBY:** Museum Farm

FOOD: Modern British **STYLE:** Modern **SEATS:** 42 **OPEN:** 12-2/7-10, Closed 25-31 Dec, Sun-Mon **RESTAURANT:** main £9.50-£11.95
NOTES: ⊗ area **PARKING:** On street, West Wick Pay & Display

---

◆◆◆◆ Fairlawns
26 Hooks Hill Rd NR26 8NL
☎ 01263 824717 🖷 01263 824115
Dir: from A149 turn into Holt Road opp Police Station, then 2nd left and at T-junct turn right

CHILD FACILITIES: Please telephone for details

Lovely Victorian guest house situated a few minutes' walk from the town centre and beach. The smartly decorated bedrooms are pleasantly furnished and equipped with thoughtful extras. Public areas include a comfortable lounge with a small corner bar and a lovely garden with croquet pitch. Guests are assured of a healthy cooked breakfast and dinner is available by prior arrangement.
ROOMS: 5 en suite (1 fmly) s £37-£42; d £50-£55 * ⊗
FACILITIES: TVB tea/coffee TVL No coaches ⬭ ⅃ Dinner Last d order noon **NOTES:** Credit cards not taken ✖ ⊗ in restaurant Licensed Cen ht **LB PARKING:** 6

> Many proprietors are happy to provide extra facilities for children, but let them know in advance what you need so they can be prepared

SNETTISHAM
Map 09 TF63

Babies Welcome | **Family Rooms** | **Children's Dishes**

★★ 70% 🏵 **Rose & Crown**
Old Church Rd PE31 7LX
☎ 01485 541382 📠 01485 543172
e-mail: info@roseandcrownsnettisham.co.uk
web: www.roseandcrownsnettisham.co.uk
Dir: A149 N from Kings Lynn towards Hunstanton. Turn into Snettisham after approx. 10M, then turn into Old Church Rd. Hotel 100yds on L.

CHILD FACILITIES: Activities: crayons and paper, large outside play area Outdoor play area Family area Food/bottle warming Ch menu Ch portions Highchairs Ch cutlery Safe grounds Cots Family rms £15 per child sharing with parents Ch drinks **NEARBY:** Walks Farm Park Near sea

This lovely village centre pub provides comfortable, well equipped bedrooms. A range of quality meals is served in the many dining areas. Service is friendly and a delightful atmosphere prevails. A walled garden is available on sunny days, as is a children's play area.
ROOMS: 11 en suite (3 fmly) 🚭 in all bedrooms s £50-£65; d £70-£100 (incl. bkfst) **LB** ✆ **PARKING:** 70 **NOTES:** 🚭 in restaurant

SWANTON MORLEY
Map 09 TG01

Babies Welcome | **Children's Dishes**

🍺 **Darbys Freehouse**
1&2 Elsing Rd NR20 4NY
☎ 01362 637647 📠 01362 637987
Dir: From A47 (Norwich to King's Lynn) take B1147 to Dereham

CHILD FACILITIES: Activities: toys, games Indoor play area Outdoor play area Family area Food/bottle warming Ch menu Ch portions Highchairs Ch cutlery Safe grounds Changing facilities **NEARBY:** Dinosaur Park Gressenhall Farm & Rural Life Museum Swimming pool Walks

OPEN: 11.30-3 6-11 (Sat 11.30-11, Sun 12-10.30) Rest: Dec 25 Closed Eve
BAR MEALS: L served all week 12-2.15 D served all week 6.30-9.45 Av main course £7.50 **RESTAURANT:** L served all week 12-2.15 D served all week 6.30-9.45 Av 3 course à la carte £18.50 **FACILITIES:** Garden: beer garden, outdoor eating **PARKING:** 75

THORNHAM
Map 09 TF74

Babies Welcome | **Family Rooms** | **Children's Dishes**

★★ 69% 🏵 **Lifeboat Inn**
Ship Ln PE36 6LT
☎ 01485 512236 📠 01485 512323
e-mail: reception@lifeboatinn.co.uk
web: www.lifeboatinn.co.uk
Dir: follow coast road from Hunstanton A149 for approx 6m and take 1st left after Thornham sign

CHILD FACILITIES: Outdoor play area Family area Food/bottle warming Ch menu Ch portions Highchairs Ch discounts £15 per child sharing with 2 adults Cots Family rms D rms with S and B beds Changing mats **NEARBY:** Walks Near sea

This 16th-century smugglers' alehouse enjoys superb views across open meadows to Thornham Harbour. The attractive bedrooms are furnished with pine pieces and have many thoughtful touches. The public rooms have a wealth of character and feature open fireplaces and oak beams. A range of bar meals is available or guests can choose from the à la carte menu in the smart restaurant.
ROOMS: 13 en suite (3 fmly) (1 GF) 🚭 in all bedrooms s £59-£75; d £78-£110 (incl. bkfst) **LB FACILITIES:** Xmas **PARKING:** 120 **NOTES:** 🚭 in restaurant

TITCHWELL
Map 09 TF74

★★ 78% 🏵 🏵 **Titchwell Manor**
PE31 8BB
☎ 01485 210221 📠 01485 210104
e-mail: margaret@titchwellmanor.com
web: www.titchwellmanor.com
Dir: on A149 coast road between Brancaster and Thornham

CHILD FACILITIES: Please telephone for details

A popular venue for golfers, bird watchers and walkers, this family-run hotel is ideally placed for touring the north Norfolk coastline. Bedrooms are comfortable; some in the adjacent annexe offer ground floor access. Smart public rooms include a lounge area, relaxed informal bar and a delightful conservatory restaurant, overlooking the walled garden. Imaginative menus feature quality local produce and fresh fish.
ROOMS: 8 en suite 7 annexe en suite (2 fmly) (3 GF) 🚭 in 9 bedrooms s £55-£100; d £84-£130 (incl. bkfst) **LB FACILITIES:** Xmas **PARKING:** 50 **NOTES:** 🚭 in restaurant

NORTHAMPTONSHIRE

England

BULWICK
Map 04 SP99

Babies Welcome **Children's Dishes**

🍴 The Queen's Head
Main St NN17 3DY
☎ 01780 450272
Dir: Just off the A43 nr Corby, 12m from Peterborough, 2m from Dene Park

CHILD FACILITIES: Family area Food/bottle warming Ch menu Ch portions Highchairs Ch cutlery Safe grounds **NEARBY:** Walks

OPEN: 12-2.30 6-11 **BAR MEALS:** L served Tue-Sun 12-2 D served Tue-Sat 6-9 Av main course £9.95 **RESTAURANT:** L served Tue-Sun 12-2 D served Tue-Sat 6-9 Av 3 course fixed price £20 **FACILITIES:** Garden: Food served outside. Patio area **PARKING:** 40

CORBY
Map 04 SP88

◆◆ 🍴 Raven Hotel
Rockingham Rd NN17 1AG
☎ 01536 202313 🖷 01536 203159
e-mail: ravenhotel@hotmail.com
Dir: A6003 towards Rockingham right into Rockingham Rd, Hotel on right after shopping parade

CHILD FACILITIES: Please telephone for details

Public areas at this hotel are a haven for music lovers, consisting of Peppers bar, filled with a wealth of Beatles memorabilia, and the spacious and comfortable Piano bar where a wide range of popular drinks and bar meals are served. Bedrooms are modern in style.
ROOMS: 17 rms (5 en suite) (3 fmly) (room only) ⊗ in 2 bedrooms
FACILITIES: TVB tea/coffee TVL Pool Table Dinner Last d order 8.45pm **NOTES:** ✖ ⊗ in area of dining room Cen ht **PARKING:** 40

FOTHERINGHAY
Map 04 TL09

Babies Welcome **Children's Dishes**

⚜ The Falcon Inn
PE8 5HZ
☎ 01832 226254 🖷 01832 226046
web: www.huntsbridge.com
Dir: Off A605 follow signpost Fotheringhay

CHILD FACILITIES: Food/bottle warming Ch menu Ch portions Highchairs Ch cutlery Safe grounds **NEARBY:** Walks

FOOD: Modern International **STYLE:** Chic **SEATS:** 45
OPEN: 12-2.15/7-9.30 **RESTAURANT:** Fixed L £12.50, main £9.95-£18.95 **NOTES:** ⊗ in restaurant **PARKING:** 40

NORTHAMPTON
Map 04 SP76

★★★ 71%
Courtyard by Marriott Northampton

Bedford Rd NN4 7YF
☎ 0870 400 7214 🖷 0870 400 7314
e-mail: reservations.northamptoncourtyard@whitbread.com
Dir: M1 junct 15 onto A508 towards Northampton. Follow A45 towards Wellingborough for 2m then A428 towards Bedford, hotel on left

CHILD FACILITIES: Please telephone for details

With its convenient location on the eastern edge of town and easy
continued

access to transport links, this modern hotel is particularly popular with business travellers. Accommodation is spacious, practical, and includes a good range of extras. Open-plan public areas help to create an informal atmosphere and the staff are genuinely friendly.

ROOMS: 104 en suite (50 fmly) (27 GF) ⊗ in 91 bedrooms s £50-£89; d £50-£89 **LB FACILITIES:** STV Gym Xmas **PARKING:** 156
NOTES: ✖ ⊗ in restaurant

◆◆◆◆ Poplars Hotel
33 Cross St, Moulton NN3 7RZ
☎ 01604 643983 🖷 01604 790233
e-mail: info@thepoplarshotel.com
web: www.thepoplarshotel.com
Dir: off A43 into Moulton & follow signs for Moulton College

CHILD FACILITIES: Please telephone for details

Located north of the city in the pretty village of Moulton, this ivy clad period house provides traditional standards of service and warm hospitality. Bedrooms, some of which are located in a quality chalet extension, are filled with a good range of practical extras. Characterful public areas include a cottage-style dining room where imaginative evening meals are served from Monday to Thursday.
ROOMS: 16 rms (12 en suite) (7 fmly) (5 GF) ⊗ in 11 bedrooms
FACILITIES: TVB tea/coffee Direct dial from bedrooms TVL No coaches Dinner Last d order 7.45pm **NOTES:** ⊗ in restaurant ⊗ in 1 lounge Licensed Cen ht **PARKING:** 16

STOKE BRUERNE
Map 04 SP74

Babies Welcome **Children's Dishes**

🍴 The Boat Inn
NN12 7SB
☎ 01604 862428 🖷 01604 864314
e-mail: info@boatinn.co.uk
web: www.boatinn.co.uk
Dir: Just off A508

CHILD FACILITIES: Food/bottle warming Ch licence Ch menu Ch portions Highchairs Changing facilities **NEARBY:** Farm visits Boat trips Walks Canal Museum

OPEN: 9-11 (3-6 closed Mon-Thu in winter) **BAR MEALS:** L served all week 9.30-9 D served all week **RESTAURANT:** L served Tue-Sun 12-2 D served all week 7-9 Av 3 course fixed price £16 **FACILITIES:** Children's licence Garden: Table and grass area by canal **PARKING:** 50

All AA listed accommodation, restaurants and pubs can be found on the AA's website www.theAA.com

NORTHUMBERLAND

The Angel of the North

ALNWICK
Alnwick Castle NE66 1NQ
enquiries@alnwickcastle.com ☎01665 510777
(off A1 on outskirts of town, follow signs for The Alnwick Garden & Castle)
Open 28 Mar-25 Oct, daily 11-5 (last ad 4.15).

BAMBURGH
Bamburgh Castle NE69 7DF
bamburghcastle@aol.com ☎01668 214515
(A1 Belford by-pass, E on B1342 to Bamburgh)
Open 15 Mar-Oct, daily 11-5 (last admission 4.30pm). Other times by prior arrangement.
Grace Darling Museum
NE69 7AE ☎01668 214465
(follow A1, turn off at Bamburgh & follow signposts to Northumbria Coastal route, museum on right)
Open Etr-Oct, daily 10-5 (Sun 12-5).

BARDON MILL
Vindolanda (Chesterholm) NE47 7JN
info@vindolanda.com ☎01434 344277
(signposted from A69 or B6318)
Open Feb-Mar daily 10-5, Apr-Sep 10-6, Oct & Nov 10-5.
*£4.10 (ch £2.90, student & pen £3.80, free admission for disabled). Saver ticket for joint admission to sister site - The Roman Army Museum £6.50 (ch £4.30, pen £5.50)

HOLY ISLAND (LINDISFARNE)
Lindisfarne Priory
TD15 2RX ☎01289 389200
(Can only be reached at low tide across a causeway. Tide tables posted at each end of the causeway) Open all year, Apr-Sep, daily 10-6; Oct, daily 10-4; Nov-Jan, Sat & Sun 10-4. Feb-Mar daily, 10-4 (Closed 24-26 Dec & 1 Jan).
*£3.50 (ch £1.80, concessions £2.60).

HOUSESTEADS
Housesteads Roman Fort
NE47 6NN ☎01434 344363
(2.5m NE of Bardon Mill on B6318)
Open all year, Apr-Sep, daily 10-6; Oct-Mar daily 10-4. (Closed 24-26 Dec & 1 Jan).
*£3.50 (ch £1.80, concessions £2.60). Family £8.80.

BELLINGHAM Map 12 NY88

★★ 69% **Riverdale Hall** THE INDEPENDENTS
NE48 2JT
☎ 01434 220254 ▧ 01434 220457
e-mail: iben@riverdalehall.demon.co.uk
web: www.riverdalehall.demon.co.uk
Dir: turn off B6320, after bridge, hotel on left
CHILD FACILITIES: Please telephone for details

This hotel dates from 1866 and is located outside the village. It boasts its own cricket square and football pitch, and fishing on the Tyne. The well-equipped bedrooms are spacious and some have balconies. Meals are available in the bar or stylish restaurant, where local produce and Thai specialities feature on the menus.
ROOMS: 20 en suite (11 fmly) (3 GF) s £48-£54; d £88-£108 (incl. bkfst) **LB** **FACILITIES:** ▧ Fishing Sauna ♨ ♨ Cricket field Xmas
PARKING: 60 **NOTES:** ⊗ in restaurant

BERWICK-UPON-TWEED Map 12 NT95

| Babies Welcome | Family Rooms | Children's Dishes | |

◆◆◆◆ **Dervaig Guest House**
1 North Rd TD15 1PW
☎ 01289 307378
e-mail: dervaig@talk21.com
Dir: turn off A1 at A1167 (North Road) to town, last house on right before railway bridge
CHILD FACILITIES: Outdoor play area Food/bottle warming Ch menu Ch portions Highchairs Ch discounts under 5s free, 5-12s £7.50 sharing with parents Safe grounds Videos Cots Family rms **NEARBY:** Park Leisure centre Swimming pool Cinema 10-min walk to sea

Lying north of the town centre, this detached Victorian house sits in lovely sheltered gardens, which guests can use. The house has a restful atmosphere and comfortable bedrooms. Breakfast is served in a bright front-facing room decorated with an interesting collection of plates. This is a no-smoking establishment.
ROOMS: 5 en suite (3 fmly) s £25-£45; d £50-£60 * ⊗
FACILITIES: TVB tea/coffee No coaches **NOTES:** ⊗ in restaurant ⊗ in lounges Cen ht **LB** **PARKING:** 8

FALSTONE Map 12 NY78

| Babies Welcome | Family Rooms | Children's Dishes |

◆◆◆◆ 🍴 **Pheasant**
Stannersburn NE48 1DD
☎ 01434 240382 ▧ 01434 240382
e-mail: enquiries@thepheasantinn.com
web: www.thepheasantinn.com
Dir: A68 onto B6320, follow signs for Kielder Water. From A69, B6079, B6320, follow signs to Kielder Water

continued on p194

FALSTONE, continued

> **CHILD FACILITIES:** Baby listening Outdoor play area Family area Food/bottle warming Ch menu Ch portions Highchairs Ch discounts under 3s free, 3-6s discounted Safe grounds Cots Family rms T rm with B beds £80-85 Laundry **NEARBY:** Walks Cycling Sailing Windsurfing

This charming establishment epitomises the traditional country inn; it has character, good food and warm hospitality. Bright modern bedrooms, some with their own entrances, are all contained in stone-built buildings adjoining the inn. Delicious home-cooked meals are served in the bar with its low beamed ceilings and exposed stone walls, or in the attractive dining room. **ROOMS:** 8 annexe en suite (1 fmly) (5 GF) s £35-£45; d £65-£75 * ⊗ **FACILITIES:** TVB tea/coffee No coaches Dinner Last d order 8.50pm **NOTES:** ⊗ in restaurant Cen ht **LB PARKING:** 40

◆◆◆ 🍴 Blackcock

NE48 1AA
☎ 01434 240200
e-mail: blackcock@falstone.fsbusiness.co.uk
web: www.theblackcockinn.com
Dir: off C200 road from Bellingham which can be accessed off A68 or B6320

> **CHILD FACILITIES:** Please telephone for details

This traditional family-run village inn lies close to Kielder Water. A cosy pub, it boasts a homely atmosphere, with a welcoming fire in the bar in the colder weather. Evening meals are served here and in the small restaurant, which is reminiscent of a Victorian parlour. The inn is closed during the day.
ROOMS: 4 en suite (1 fmly) s £35; d £55 * ⊗ **FACILITIES:** TVB tea/coffee Fishing Pool Table Dinner Last d order 8.30pm **NOTES:** ⊗ in restaurant Cen ht **LB PARKING:** 20

GREENHEAD   Map 12 NY66

Babies Welcome | Family Rooms | Children's Dishes

◆◆◆◆ Holmhead

Thirlwall Castle Farm, Hadrians Wall CA8 7HY
☎ 016977 47402 📠 016977 47402
e-mail: holmhead@hadrianswall.freeserve.co.uk
web: www.bandbhadrianswall.com
Dir: from B6318 turn between Ye Olde Forge Tea Rooms & Greenhead Youth Hostel, over bridge, premises 0.25m along Farm Rd

> **CHILD FACILITIES:** Baby listening Activities: games, colouring, puzzles, work sheets Outdoor play area Food/bottle warming Ch portions Highchairs Ch cutlery Ch discounts under 3s free in own cot, under 10s eat for half price, 1/3 off sharing parents' rm Safe grounds Cots Family rms D rm with B bed or small child's bed £86 Ch drinks **NEARBY:** Roman museum Farms

Built upon the course of Hadrian's Wall, this old farmhouse offers comfortable, good value accommodation with the cosy bedrooms being attractively decorated and traditionally furnished. The lounge contains an abundance of books, board games and toys, and Pauline Staff's knowledge of local history and archaeology will be useful for all. A set dinner menu is available, and breakfast can be chosen from "the longest breakfast menu in the world".
ROOMS: 4 en suite 1 annexe en suite (1 fmly) (1 GF) s £38-£41; d £58-£62 * **FACILITIES:** tea/coffee TVL Table tennis Badminton Dinner Last d order 3pm **NOTES:** 🐾 ⊗ Licensed Cen ht **LB PARKING:** 6

>
> **Family Rooms** This symbol indicates family rooms are available, with type of room and prices included if provided

HEDLEY ON THE HILL   Map 12 NZ05

Children's Dishes

🍴 The Feathers Inn

NE43 7SW
☎ 01661 843607 📠 01661 843607

> **CHILD FACILITIES:** Family area Food/bottle warming Ch licence Ch portions **NEARBY:** Leisure pool Beamish Museum

OPEN: 12-3 6-11 (Sun 12-3, 7-10.30) Closed: Dec 25 **BAR MEALS:** L served Sat-Sun 12-2.30 D served Tue-Sun 7-9 Av main course £8.10 **FACILITIES:** Children's licence Tables outside at the front 🐾 **PARKING:** 12

HEXHAM   Map 12 NY96

Babies Welcome | Family Rooms | Children's Dishes

◆◆◆◆ 🐑 Rye Hill

Slaley NE47 0AH
☎ 01434 673259 📠 01434 673259
e-mail: info@ryehillfarm.co.uk
Dir: 5m S of Hexham, off B6306, 1st right after Travellers Rest pub then 1st farm road right

> **CHILD FACILITIES:** Indoor play area Outdoor play area Family area Food/bottle warming Ch menu Ch portions Highchairs Ch cutlery Ch discounts under 2s free Safe grounds Cots Family rms D rm with S bed, S rm with S bed & chair bed from £67 Laundry

Enjoying delightful panoramic views, Rye Hill offers a real farm-stay experience. Accommodation is contained in two converted barns in the main courtyard. Meals are served house-party style at two rustic pine tables overlooking the gardens. A games room and skittles alley are also available. **ROOMS:** 6 en suite (2 fmly) s £30; d £50 * ⊗ **FACILITIES:** TVB tea/coffee TVL Pool Table Games room, Skittle alley 30 acres sheep Dinner Last d order 4pm **NOTES:** ⊗ in restaurant Licensed Cen ht **PARKING:** 6

Babies Welcome | Children's Dishes

🍴 Miners Arms Inn

Main St, Acomb NE46 4PW
☎ 01434 603909
Dir: 17m W of Newcastle on A69, 2m W of Hexham.

> **CHILD FACILITIES:** Activities: books, dominoes Family area Food/bottle warming Ch menu Ch portions (if possible) Highchairs Ch cutlery Safe grounds **NEARBY:** Cinema Park Leisure centre Walks

OPEN: 5-11 Sat 12-11, Sun 12-10.30 Easter, Summer, Xmas Hols 12-11 all wk **BAR MEALS:** L served all week 12-9 D served all week 5-9 Av main course £5.35 **RESTAURANT:** L served all week 12-9 D served all week 5-9 **FACILITIES:** Garden: Secluded sun trap beer garden, seating, BBQ **NOTES:** Credit cards not taken

England

OTTERBURN
Map 12 NY89

Babies Welcome | **Family Rooms** | **Children's Dishes**

★★★ 64% The Otterburn Tower Hotel
NE19 1NS
☎ 01830 520620 📠 01830 521504
e-mail: sales@otterburntower.com
web: www.otterburntower.com
Dir: situated in the village of Otterburn, on A696 Newcastle to Edinburgh road

CHILD FACILITIES: Nanny Babysitting Activities: toys, books Food/bottle warming Ch menu Ch portions Highchairs Ch discounts Safe grounds Cots Family rms D rm with adjoining T rm Laundry

Built by the cousin of William the Conqueror, this mansion is set in its own grounds. The hotel is steeped in history - Sir Walter Scott stayed here in 1812. Bedrooms come in a variety of sizes and some have huge ornamental fireplaces. Though furnished in period style, they are equipped with all modern amenities. The restaurant features 16th-century oak panelling.
ROOMS: 18 en suite (2 fmly) (2 GF) ⊛ in all bedrooms s £75-£90; d £120-£180 (incl. bkfst) **LB FACILITIES:** STV Fishing ♫ Xmas **PARKING:** 70 **NOTES:** ⊛ in restaurant

★★ 68% Percy Arms
NE19 1NR
☎ 01830 520261 📠 01830 520567
e-mail: percyarmshotel@yahoo.co.uk
Dir: centre of Otterburn on A696

CHILD FACILITIES: Please telephone for details

This former coaching inn lies in the centre of the village, with good access to the Northumberland countryside. Real fires warm welcoming public areas in season and guests have a choice of mouth-watering dishes in either the restaurant or cosy bar/bistro. Bedrooms are cheerfully decorated and thoughtfully equipped.
ROOMS: 28 en suite (2 fmly) ⊛ in 2 bedrooms s £45-£68; d £80-£96 (incl. bkfst) **LB FACILITIES:** Fishing Xmas **PARKING:** 74 **NOTES:** ⊛ in restaurant

SEAHOUSES
Map 12 NU23

Babies Welcome | **Family Rooms** | **Children's Dishes**

★★★ 67% Bamburgh Castle
NE68 7SQ
☎ 01665 720283 📠 01665 720848
e-mail: bamburghcastlehotel@btinternet.com
web: www.bamburghcastlehotel.co.uk
Dir: from A1 follow signs for Seahouses, car park entrance on rbt opposite Barclays Bank, automatic barrier will rise

CHILD FACILITIES: Baby listening Activities: games, colouring Outdoor play area Food/bottle warming Ch menu Ch portions Highchairs Ch discounts under 8s sharing free Videos Cots Family rms from £93.50 Fridge Laundry **NEARBY:** Putting green Seafront location

This family run hotel enjoys a seafront location overlooking the harbour. There is a relaxed and friendly atmosphere with professional, friendly staff providing attentive service. Bedrooms vary in size and style with superior rooms being more spacious, all are attractively appointed. Front-facing rooms, plus the main lounge and restaurant all take advantage of the panoramic views out to sea.
ROOMS: 20 en suite (3 fmly) (3 GF) ⊛ in 10 bedrooms s £44.95-£56.95; d £89.90-£99.90 (incl. bkfst) **LB FACILITIES:** ♨ **PARKING:** 30 **NOTES:** ⊛ in restaurant Closed 24-26 Dec & 2wks mid Jan

WARENFORD
Map 12 NU12

Children's Dishes

🍴 Warenford Lodge
NE70 7HY
☎ 01668 213453 📠 01668 213453
e-mail: warenfordlodge@aol.com
Dir: 100yds E of A1,10m N of Alnwick

CHILD FACILITIES: Food/bottle warming Ch portions Safe grounds **NEARBY:** Woodland walks 4m to sea

OPEN: 12-2 Closed Sun Eve, Mon-Tue(Nov-Easter) 7-11 Closed: 25/26 Dec, 1 Jan-31 Jan **BAR MEALS:** L served Sat-Sun 12-1.30 D served Tues-Sun 7-9.30 Av main course £7.20 **RESTAURANT:** L served Sat-Sun 12-1.30 D served Tues-Sun 7-9.30 Av 3 course à la carte £15.20 **FACILITIES:** Garden: More a field than a garden ✈ **PARKING:** 60

NOTTINGHAMSHIRE

CAUNTON
Map 08 SK76

Babies Welcome | **Children's Dishes**

🍴 Caunton Beck
NG23 6AB
☎ 01636 636793 📠 01636 636828
e-mail: cautonbeck@aol.com
Dir: 5m NW of Newark on A616

CHILD FACILITIES: Activities: colouring Food/bottle warming Ch licence Ch portions Highchairs **NEARBY:** Millgate Museum Newark Castle

OPEN: 8am-midnight **BAR MEALS:** L served all week 8am-11pm D served all week 8am-11pm Av main course £13.50 **RESTAURANT:** L served all week 8am-11pm D served all week 8am-11pm Av 3 course à la carte £24 Av 3 course fixed price £13.95 **FACILITIES:** Children's licence Garden: Terrace & lawns **PARKING:** 30

LAXTON
Map 08 SK76

🍴 The Dovecote Inn
Moorhouse Rd NG22 0NU
☎ 01777 871586 📠 01777 871586
e-mail: dovecoteinn@yahoo.co.uk
Dir: Telephone for directions

CHILD FACILITIES: Please telephone for details

OPEN: 11.30-3 6.30-11.30 (Fri-Sat 6-11.30) **BAR MEALS:** L served all week 12-2 D served all week 6.30-9.30 Av main course £9 **RESTAURANT:** L served all week 12-2 D served all week 6.30-9.30 **FACILITIES:** Garden: Table&chairs in front garden **ROOMS:** 2 bedrooms 2 en suite s£35 d£50 (♦♦♦♦) **PARKING:** 45

England

NOTTINGHAM Map 08 SK54

Babies Welcome | Family Rooms | Children's Dishes

⌂ Citilodge

Wollaton St NG1 5FW
☎ 0115 912 8000 📠 0115 912 8080
e-mail: mail@citilodge.co.uk
web: www.citilodge.co.uk
Dir: From M1 junct 26, follow A610 into city centre. Hotel opposite Royal Centre on Wollaton St

CHILD FACILITIES: Food/bottle warming Ch portions Highchairs Cots Family rms D rm with 2 S beds £80 **NEARBY:** Castle Caves Ice skating Bowling Cinema

This city centre lodge offers superior accommodation along with a good range of bar and food options. Bedrooms are spacious and light with warm colour schemes, offering an excellent range of facilities; each bedroom has air-conditioning.
ROOMS: 90 en suite s £58; d £58

Babies Welcome | Family Rooms

♦♦♦ Andrews Private Hotel

310 Queens Rd, Beeston NG9 1JA
☎ 0115 925 4902 📠 0115 9178839
e-mail: andrews.hotel@ntlworld.com
Dir: from A52 take B6006 to Beeston, turn right at 4th lights into Queens Rd, hotel 200mtrs on right

CHILD FACILITIES: Baby listening Food/bottle warming Highchairs Cots Family rms D rm with S bed £55 Laundry **NEARBY:** Nature reserve River walks Leisure centre Theme parks

This pleasant establishment sits close to the shops and park, and is popular with business people and tourists alike. Guests have the use of a comfortable lounge and a separate dining room. Bedrooms, which vary in size, are well presented and suitably equipped.
ROOMS: 10 rms (3 en suite) (1 fmly) (1 GF) s £25-£35; d £45-£50 *
⊗ in 5 bedrooms **FACILITIES:** TVB tea/coffee TVL No coaches
NOTES: Credit cards not taken 🗶 ⊗ in restaurant Cen ht **PARKING:** 6

Family Rooms | Children's Dishes

♦♦♦ Tudor Lodge Hotel

400 Nuthall Rd NG8 5DS
☎ 0115 924 9244 📠 0115 924 9243
e-mail: tudorlodge@commodoreinternational.co.uk
web: www.commodoreinternational.co.uk/tudorlodge
Dir: A610 3miles from junction 26 M1 towards Nottingham

CHILD FACILITIES: Outdoor play area Family area Food/bottle warming Ch menu Ch portions Ch discounts under 5s free Safe grounds Family rms rms with 3 S beds & camp bed Ch drinks **NEARBY:** Park Leisure centre Adventure park Castle

Tudor Lodge is conveniently located for the M1 and the city centre. Accommodation comes in a variety of sizes and styles; the ground floor en suite room is well suited for use by guests with limited mobility. Breakfast is served in the comfortably furnished dining room.
ROOMS: 7 rms (4 en suite) (2 fmly) (3 GF) ⊗ in 3 bedrooms
FACILITIES: TVB tea/coffee Dinner Last d order 8.30pm **NOTES:** 🗶 ⊗ in restaurant ⊗ in lounges Licensed Cen ht **PARKING:** 10

THURGARTON Map 08 SK64

Babies Welcome | Children's Dishes

🍴 The Red Lion

Southwell Rd NG14 7GP
☎ 01636 830351
Dir: On A612 between Nottingham & Southwell

CHILD FACILITIES: Food/bottle warming Ch menu Ch portions Highchairs Ch cutlery Safe grounds **NEARBY:** Bleasby Farm Thurgarton Priory River Trent

OPEN: 11.30-2.30 6.30-11 (Open all day Sat-Sun & BHs) **BAR MEALS:** L served all week 12-2 D served all week 7-10 Av main course £6.95
RESTAURANT: L served all week 12-2 D served all week 7-10
FACILITIES: Garden: Large spacious, well kept 🗶 **PARKING:** 40

OXFORDSHIRE

Children's Corner at Cotswold Wildlife Park

BANBURY
Banbury Museum
OX16 2PQ ☎01295 259855
banburymuseum@cherwell-dc.gov.uk
(M40 junct 11 straight across at first rdbt into
Hennef Way, left at next rdbt into Concord
Avenue, right at next rdbt & left at next rdbt,
Castle Quay Shopping Centre & Museum on right)
Open all year, Mon-Sat, 10-5, Sun 10.30-4.30.

BURFORD
Cotswold Wildlife Park
OX18 4JW ☎01993 823006
(2m S of Burford on the A361)
Open all year, daily (ex 25 Dec) from 10am, last
admission 4.30pm Mar-Sep, 3pm Oct Feb.
*£8 (ch & pen £5.50). Party rate £6.50 (ch £4 pen
£5).

DIDCOT
Didcot Railway Centre OX11 7NJ
didrlyc@globalnet.co.uk ☎01235 817200
(on A4130 at Didcot Parkway Station)
Open all year, Sat & Sun. 25 Mar-17 Apr, 30 Apr-
25 Sep Steamdays Sat & Sun, 23 Apr-2 Oct Wed
13 Jul-31 Aug, 10-4 Steamdays & wkends Mar-
Oct 10-5. *£4-£8 depending on event (ch £3-
£7.50, over 60's £3.50-£6.50).

OXFORD
Oxford University Museum of Natural History
OX1 3PW ☎01865 272950
info@oum.ox.ac.uk
(opposite Keble College)
Open daily 12-5. Times vary at Xmas & Etr.
Pitt Rivers Museum OX1 3PP
prm@prm.ox.ac.uk ☎01865 270927
(10 min walk from Oxford city centre)
Open Mon-Sat 12-4.30 & Sun 2-4.30. (Closed
Xmas & Etr, open BH's)
The Oxford Story OX1 3AJ
info@oxfordstory.co.uk ☎01865 728822
(Follow signs)
Open Jan-Jun & Sep-Dec, Mon-Sat 10-4.30 &
Sun 11-4.30. Jul & Aug daily 9.30-5. Closed 25
Dec.
*£6.95 (ch £5.25, pen £5.75, students £5.95),
Family ticket (2 ad & 2 ch) £22.50.

BANBURY Map 04 SP44

| Family Rooms | Children's Dishes |

♦♦♦ Fairlawns
60 Oxford Rd OX16 9AN
☎ 01295 262461 ▤ 01295 261296
e-mail: fairlawnsgh@aol.com
*Dir: M40 junct 11 towards Banbury, left at 2nd island signposted 'town
centre'. T-junct after 2m, house opposite*

CHILD FACILITIES: Ch portions Highchairs Cots Family rms D rm
with S bed & fold up £59 **NEARBY:** Park Leisure centre Cinema

This extended Edwardian house retains many original features and
enjoys a convenient location. Bedrooms are mixed in size, and all
are neatly furnished, some with direct access to the car park. A
comprehensive breakfast is served in the traditional dining room
and a selection of soft drinks and snacks is also available.
ROOMS: 12 rms (11 en suite) 6 annexe en suite (5 fmly) s £30-£42;
d £40-£52 * ⊗ in 6 bedrooms **FACILITIES:** TVB tea/coffee Direct dial
from bedrooms **NOTES:** ⊗ in restaurant ⊗ in lounges Cen ht
PARKING: 18

BLOXHAM Map 04 SP43

▥ The Elephant & Castle
OX15 4LZ
☎ 01295 720383
e-mail: elephant.bloxham@btinternet.com
Dir: Just off A361

CHILD FACILITIES: Please telephone for details

OPEN: 10-3 5-11 (Sat, Sun-open all day) **BAR MEALS:** L served Mon-Sat
12-2 Av main course £5.50 **RESTAURANT:** L served Mon-Sat 12-2
FACILITIES: Garden: Raised lawn in flower filled garden, patio
PARKING: 20

BRITWELL SALOME Map 04 SU69

| Babies Welcome | Children's Dishes |

⊛ ⊛ The Goose
OX49 5LG
☎ 01491 612304 ▤ 01491 613945
*Dir: M40 J6 take B4009 to Watlington and on towards Benson. Pub on R,
1.5m.*

CHILD FACILITIES: Activities: colouring Food/bottle warming
Ch menu Ch portions Highchairs Safe grounds **NEARBY:** Walks
Well Place Petting zoo Park

FOOD: Modern British **STYLE:** Chic, Rustic **SEATS:** 40 **OPEN:** 12-3/7-11,
Closed 25 Dec, D Sun **RESTAURANT:** main £12-£17 **NOTES:** ⊗ area
PARKING: 35

HENLEY-ON-THAMES Map 04 SU78

♦♦♦♦ ▤ The Knoll
Crowsley Rd. Shiplake RG9 3JT
☎ 0118 940 2705 ▤ 0118 940 2705
e-mail: theknollhenley@aol.com
web: www.theknollhenley.co.uk
*Dir: from Henley take A4155 towards Reading, after 2m left at war
memorial, then 1st right into Crowsley Rd, 3rd house on right*

CHILD FACILITIES: Please telephone for details

The Knoll is set in a quiet residential area in beautiful gardens, just
two miles from Henley-on-Thames. One of the two bedrooms has
a second room attached for children, and both are traditionally
furnished and comfortably equipped. Breakfast includes a
continued on p198

HENLEY-ON-THAMES, continued

delicious array of fresh fruit, muffins, home-made preserves and fresh juices.
ROOMS: 2 en suite (1 fmly) (3 GF) s £49; d £60 *
FACILITIES: TV3B tea/coffee TVL No coaches Free internet access
NOTES: Credit cards not taken ✈ ⊗ in restaurant ⊗ in 1 lounge Cen ht
PARKING: 5

◑ The Five Horseshoes
Maidensgrove RG9 6EX
☎ 01491 641282 ▤ 01491 641086
Dir: A4130 from Henley, onto B480

> **CHILD FACILITIES:** Please telephone for details

OPEN: 11-3 6-11 Rest: Closed evenings Oct-Jun **BAR MEALS:** L served all week 12-2 D served all week 6.30-9.30 Av main course £8
RESTAURANT: L served all week 12-2 D served all week 6.30-9.00 Av 3 course à la carte £18 Av 3 course fixed price £14.95 **FACILITIES:** Garden: 2 gardens lovely views, 1 with a BBQ **PARKING:** 85

◑ The Golden Ball
Lower Assendon RG9 6AH
☎ 01491 574157 ▤ 01491 576653
e-mail: Golden.Ball@theseed.net
Dir: A4130, R onto B480, pub 300yds on L

> **CHILD FACILITIES:** Activities: colouring, toys Family area
> Food/bottle warming Ch menu Ch portions Highchairs Safe grounds
> Changing facilities NEARBY: Walks Parks River Cinema

OPEN: 11-3 6-11 **BAR MEALS:** L served all week 12-2.00 D served all week 7-9.00 Av main course £8.95 **FACILITIES:** Garden: Large south facing garden **PARKING:** 50

HOOK NORTON   Map 04 SP33

> Babies Welcome | Children's Dishes

◑ The Gate Hangs High ◆◆◆◆
Whichford Rd OX15 5DF
☎ 01608 737387 ▤ 01608 737870
e-mail: gatehangshigh@aol
Dir: Off A361 SW of Banbury

> **CHILD FACILITIES:** Family area Food/bottle warming Ch menu
> Ch portions Highchairs Ch cutlery Safe grounds Changing facilities
> NEARBY: Waterfowl Sanctuary

OPEN: 12-3 6-11 (Sun, 12-4, 7-10.30) **BAR MEALS:** L served all week 12-2.30 D served all week 6-10 Av main course £7.95 **RESTAURANT:** L served all week 12-2.30 D served all week 6-10 Av 3 course à la carte £18 Av 3 course fixed price £12.95 **FACILITIES:** Garden: Wonderful views overlooking fields; courtyard **ROOMS:** 4 bedrooms 4 en suite 1 family rooms s£40 d£60 **PARKING:** 30

KELMSCOT   Map 04 SU29

◑ The Plough Inn
GL7 3HG
☎ 01367 253543 ▤ 01367 252514
e-mail: plough@kelmscottgl7.fsnet.co.uk
Dir: From M4 onto A419 then A361 to Lechlade & A416 to Faringdon, pick up signs to Kelmscot

> **CHILD FACILITIES:** Food/bottle warming Ch licence Ch menu
> Ch portions Highchairs Safe grounds NEARBY: River Thames

continued

OPEN: 11-3 (Sun 12-3, 7-10.30) 7-11 **BAR MEALS:** L served all week 12-2.30 D served Mon-Sat 7-9 Av main course £11.50 **RESTAURANT:** L served Tue-Sun 12-2.30 D served Tue-Sat 7-9 Av 3 course à la carte £20 **FACILITIES:** Garden: Grassed area with patio **PARKING:** 4

KINGHAM   Map 04 SP22

◉ The Tollgate Hotel & Restaurant
Church St OX7 6YA
☎ 01608 658389 ▤ 01608 659467
e-mail: info@the-tollgate.com
web: www.the-tollgate.com
Dir: From Chipping Norton, follow signs to Kingham Station, then for Kingham. Restaurant in village centre

> **CHILD FACILITIES:** Please telephone for details

FOOD: European, Oriental **STYLE:** Traditional **SEATS:** 40
OPEN: 12.30-2.30/7-9.30, Closed L Mon, D Mon **RESTAURANT:** Fixed L £10, Fixed D £15.50, main £7.95-£16.95 **NOTES:** ⊗ in restaurant
PARKING: 15

OXFORD   Map 04 SP50

> Babies Welcome | Family Rooms | Children's Dishes

★★★ 70% ◉ Fallowfields
Country House Hotel
Faringdon Rd, Kingston Bagpuize, Southmoor OX13 5BH
☎ 01865 820416 ▤ 01865 821275
e-mail: stay@fallowfields.com
web: www.fallowfields.com
Dir: from A420, take A415 towards Abingdon for 100yds. Right at mini rdbt, through Kingston Bagpuize, Southmoor and Longworth, follow signs

> **CHILD FACILITIES:** Nanny Babysitting Activities: colouring, books,
> toys, board games Food/bottle warming Ch menu Ch portions
> Highchairs Ch discounts £30 when sharing with parents Safe
> grounds Videos Cots Family rms D/T rm with S beds £170-£250
> Ch drinks (by request) Laundry NEARBY: Railway centre Leisure
> centre Swimming pool Horseriding

With a history stretching back over 300 years, this spacious, comfortable hotel provides friendly, old-fashioned service. The thoughtfully equipped bedrooms are very much of this century and are decorated with skill. Public areas include an elegant drawing room and a charming conservatory restaurant in which the hotel's own seasonal produce is served.
ROOMS: 10 en suite (2 fmly) ⊗ in all bedrooms s £95-£115; d £145-£170 (incl. bkfst) **LB FACILITIES:** STV ℚ ♬ Falconry
PARKING: 21 **NOTES:** ⊗ in restaurant

> Babies Welcome | Children's Dishes

◉ Gee's Restaurant
61 Banbury Rd OX2 6PE
☎ 01865 553540 ▤ 01865 310308
e-mail: info@gees-restaurant.co.uk
Dir: M40 J8. From northern ring road, follow signs to city centre through Summertown. Gee's opp Parktown on Banbury Rd

> **CHILD FACILITIES:** Food/bottle warming Ch portions Highchairs
> NEARBY: University Parks Port Meadow Cinema Canal walks
> Punting Cycling

FOOD: British **STYLE:** Classic, Chic **SEATS:** 85 **OPEN:** 12-2.30/6-10.30, Closed 25-26 Dec **RESTAURANT:** Fixed L £12.50, Fixed D £24.95, main £8.95-£19.50 **NOTES:** ⊗ in restaurant, Air con **PARKING:** Street parking

England

SOUTH MORETON
Map 04 SU58

🍴 The Crown Inn
High St OX11 9AG
☎ 01235 812262
Dir: From Didcot take A4130 towards Wallingford. Village on R
CHILD FACILITIES: Please telephone for details
OPEN: 11-3 5.30-11 (Sun 12-3, 7-10.30) Closed: Dec 25-26 **BAR MEALS:** L served all week 12-2 D served all week 7-9.30 Av main course £8.50 **RESTAURANT:** L served all week 12-2 D served all week 7-9.30 **FACILITIES:** Garden: 2 areas with bench style seating **PARKING:** 30

WALLINGFORD
Map 04 SU68

Babies Welcome	Family Rooms	Children's Dishes

★★★ 75% 🍴 Springs Hotel & Golf Club
Wallingford Rd, North Stoke OX10 6BE
☎ 01491 836687 📠 01491 836877
e-mail: info@thespringshotel.com web: www.thespringshotel.com
Dir: off A4074 Oxford-Reading Rd to B4009 - Goring. Club 1m on right
CHILD FACILITIES: Baby listening Food/bottle warming Ch menu Ch portions Highchairs Ch cutlery Ch discounts under 5s free Safe grounds Cots Family rms Laundry **NEARBY:** Zoo
Set on its own golf course, this Victorian mansion has a timeless and peaceful atmosphere. Bedrooms vary in size; many are spacious, and all are generously equipped. The elegant restaurant enjoys splendid views over the spring-fed lake. There is also a comfortable lounge with original features in which to relax.
ROOMS: 31 en suite (3 fmly) (8 GF) ⊗ in 6 bedrooms s £95-£120; d £110-£135 (incl. bkfst) **LB FACILITIES:** STV ⚲ Golf 18 Fishing Sauna ♨ ⚘ Clay pigeon shooting ♫ Xmas **PARKING:** 150 **NOTES:** ⊗ in restaurant

WANTAGE
Map 04 SU38

Children's Dishes

🍴 The Star Inn
Watery Ln, Sparsholt OX12 9PL
☎ 01235 751539 & 751001 📠 01235 751539
e-mail: lee-carina@btconnect.com
Dir: Sparsholt is 4m west of Wantage, take the B4507 Wantage to Ashbury road and turn off R to the village, the Star Inn is signposted
CHILD FACILITIES: Food/bottle warming Ch menu Ch portions Safe grounds **NEARBY:** White Horse Hill Cinema
OPEN: 12-3 6-11 (Sat 12-11,Sun 12-10.30) **BAR MEALS:** L served all week 12-3 D served all week 7-9 Av main course £8 **RESTAURANT:** L served all week 12-2 D served Mon-Sat 7-9 **FACILITIES:** Garden: Food served outside **PARKING:** 20

RUTLAND

EXTON
Map 08 SK91

Babies Welcome	Children's Dishes

🍴 Fox & Hounds
LE15 8AP
☎ 01572 812403 📠 01572 812403
CHILD FACILITIES: Outdoor play area Food/bottle warming Ch menu Ch portions Highchairs Safe grounds **NEARBY:** Rutland Water Falconry Centre

continued

OPEN: 11-3 6-11 **BAR MEALS:** L served all week 12-2 D served all week 6.30-9 Av main course £9 **RESTAURANT:** L served all week 12-2 D served all week 6.30-9 Av 3 course à la carte £18 **FACILITIES:** Garden: Large walled garden & patio area **PARKING:** 20

OAKHAM
Map 04 SK80

🍴 Barnsdale Lodge Hotel ★★★ 🌸
The Avenue, Rutland Water, North Shore LE15 8AH
☎ 01572 724678 📠 01572 724961
e-mail: enquiries@barnsdalelodge.co.uk
web: www.barnsdalelodge.co.uk
CHILD FACILITIES: Please telephone for details

A popular and interesting hotel converted from a farmstead and overlooking Rutland Water. The public areas are dominated by a very successful food operation with informal meals served in the brasserie, and a good range of appealing meals on offer in the more formal restaurant. Real ales including local brews are available. Bedrooms are comfortably appointed with excellent beds and period furnishings, enhanced by contemporary soft furnishings and thoughtful extras.
OPEN: 7-11 **BAR MEALS:** L served all week 12.15-2.15 D served all week 7-9.45 Av main course £10 **RESTAURANT:** L served all week 12.15-2.15 D served all week 7-9.45 Av 3 course à la carte £35 **FACILITIES:** Garden: Courtyard, established garden with lawns **ROOMS:** 46 bedrooms 46 en suite 4 family rooms s£75 d£99.50 **PARKING:** 280
See advert on page 200

Many proprietors are happy to provide extra facilities for children, but let them know in advance what you need so they can be prepared

---

UPPINGHAM
Map 04 SP89

Babies Welcome	Family Rooms	Children's Dishes

★★★ 64% Falcon
The Market Place LE15 9PY
☎ 01572 823535 📠 01572 821620
e-mail: sales@thefalconhotel.com
web: www.thefalconhotel.com
Dir: turn off A47 onto A6003, left at lights, hotel on right
CHILD FACILITIES: Nanny (on request - charged) Babysitting (on request - charged) Activities: board games Food/bottle warming Ch menu Ch portions Highchairs Ch cutlery Ch discounts Safe grounds Cots Family rms D rm with sofa bed £105 Laundry **NEARBY:** Water activity centre

An attractive, 16th-century coaching inn situated in the heart of
continued on p200

England

UPPINGHAM, continued

this bustling market town. Public areas feature an open-plan lounge bar, with a relaxing atmosphere and comfortable sofas. The brasserie area offers a cosmopolitan-style snack menu, while more formal meals are provided in the Garden Terrace Restaurant.
ROOMS: 25 en suite (4 fmly) (3 GF) s £60; d £90-£125 (incl. bkfst) **LB**
FACILITIES: STV Snooker ♫ Xmas **PARKING:** 33 **NOTES:** ⊛ in restaurant

WING   Map 04 SK80

◆◆◆◆ 🚘 🍴 **Kings Arms**
13 Top St LE15 8SE
☎ 01572 737634 📠 01572 737255
e-mail: enquiries@thekingsarms-wing.co.uk
web: www.thekingsarms-wing.co.uk
Dir: 1.5m off A6003 between Uppingham & Oakham. B&B is 100yds on right from village sign
CHILD FACILITIES: Please telephone for details
This traditional village inn with its open fires, flagstone floors and low ceiling beams, dates back to the 17th century. In contrast, the refurbished restaurant has a more contemporary feel and offers a wide range of interesting freshly produced dishes; service is both attentive and friendly. The spacious and well-equipped bedrooms are situated in The Old Bake House and Granny's Cottage, which are nearby in the courtyard.
ROOMS: 8 en suite (4 fmly) (4 GF) s £55-£65; d £65-£75 * ⊛
FACILITIES: TVB tea/coffee Direct dial from bedrooms Dinner Last d order 9pm **NOTES:** ✗ ⊛ in restaurant Cen ht **PARKING:** 15

SHROPSHIRE

Ironbridge Gorge

ATCHAM
Attingham Park SY4 4TP
attingham@nationaltrust.org.uk   ☎01743 708123
(4m SE of Shrewsbury on B4380)
House open mid Mar-Oct, Fri-Tue 12-5, BH Mon 11-5. Deer park & grounds daily Mar-Oct 9am-8pm, Nov-Feb 9am-5pm.
*£5.50 ch £2.75 Family ticket £12.75. Park & Grounds £2.75 ch £1.35. Family £6.75.

COSFORD
The Royal Air Force Museum
TF11 8UP   ☎01902 376200
cosford@rafmuseum.org
(On A41, 1m S of M54 junct 3)
Open all year daily, 10-6 last admission 4.
Closed 24-26 Dec & 1 Jan
Charges made for special events.

CRAVEN ARMS
Secret Hills, The Shropshire Hills Discovery Centre
SY7 9RS   ☎01588 676000
jill.jarrett@shropshire-cc.gov.uk
(On A49, on southern edge of Craven Arms)
Open all year, daily from 10am. Last admission 3.30 Nov-Mar, 4.30 Apr-Oct.
*£4.25 ch £2.75 & pen £3.75, ch under 5 free. Family ticket £12.20. Groups 20+ £3.75 each, ch £2.50 each.

IRONBRIDGE
Ironbridge Gorge Museums TF8 7DQ
info@ironbridge.org.uk   ☎01952 433522
(M54 junct 4, signposted)
Open all year, 10-5. Some small sites closed Nov-Mar. Telephone or write for exact winter details.
£12.95, ch £8.25, pen £11.25. Family £40.

TELFORD
Hoo Farm Animal Kingdom TF6 6DJ
info@hoofarm.com   ☎01952 677917
(M54 junct 6, follow brown tourist signs)
Open 23 Mar-8 Sep, daily 10-6 last admission 5; 10 Sep-22 Nov, Tue-Sun 10-5 last admission 4. Closed Mon ex Halloween. 23 Nov-24 Dec daily 10-5 closes at 1pm 24 Dec. Closed 25 Dec-mid Mar.
*£4.25 ch £3.50, pen £3.75. Family ticket 2 ad & 3 ch £16.

BISHOP'S CASTLE
Map 07 SO38

Babies Welcome | Family Rooms | Children's Dishes

♦♦♦ The Boar's Head
Church St SY9 5AE
☎ 01588 638521 🗋 01588 630126
e-mail: sales@boarsheadhotel.co.uk
Dir: from A488 follow signs to livestock market, continue past market. Inn on L at x-roads

CHILD FACILITIES: Activities: activity packs Food/bottle warming Ch menu Ch portions Highchairs Ch cutlery Ch discounts children only charged for breakfast Cots Family rms D rm with 2 S beds Laundry NEARBY: Farm Maze

Located in the heart of this ancient borough, the inn retains many original features including stone-flagged floors, exposed beams and open fireplaces. A wide range of imaginative food is available in the non-smoking restaurant. The well-equipped bedrooms are situated on the ground floor of a sympathetically converted outbuilding.
ROOMS: 4 en suite (1 fmly) (4 GF) d £60-£70 * FACILITIES: STV TVB tea/coffee Direct dial from bedrooms TVL Pool Table Dinner Last d order 9.30pm NOTES: ⊗ in restaurant ⊗ in 1 lounge Cen ht LB PARKING: 20

CHURCH STRETTON
Map 07 SO49

Babies Welcome | Family Rooms | Children's Dishes

★★★ 68% ⊚ ⊚
Stretton Hall Hotel
THE INDEPENDENTS
All Stretton SY6 6HG
☎ 01694 723224 🗋 01694 724365
e-mail: aa@strettonhall.co.uk
Dir: from Shrewsbury, on A49, right onto B4370 signed All Stretton. Hotel 1m on left opposite The Yew Tree pub

CHILD FACILITIES: Baby listening Babysitting (with notice) Outdoor play area Food/bottle warming Ch menu Ch portions Highchairs Ch cutlery Ch discounts free cots Games consoles Videos Cots Family rms from £130 Ch drinks Laundry Changing mats NEARBY: Working farm

This fine 18th-century country house stands in spacious gardens. Original oak panelling features throughout the lounge bar, lounge and halls. Bedrooms are traditionally furnished and have modern facilities. Family and four-poster rooms are available and the restaurant has been tastefully refurbished.
ROOMS: 12 en suite (1 fmly) s £50-£115; d £80-£130 (incl. bkfst) LB FACILITIES: Xmas PARKING: 70 NOTES: ⊗ in restaurant

Children's Dishes
⊚ The Studio
59 High St SY6 6BY
☎ 01694 722672
Dir: Off A49 to town, L at crossroads onto High Street, 150 yds on L
CHILD FACILITIES: Food/bottle warming Ch portions NEARBY: Walks River
FOOD: Modern British STYLE: Traditional, Rustic SEATS: 30
OPEN: 12-3/7-10, Closed Xmas, 3 wks Jan, MonL Mon-Sat, D Sun
RESTAURANT: main £13.95-£15.95 NOTES: ⊗ in restaurant
PARKING: Street parking

CRAVEN ARMS
Map 07 SO48

📶 The Sun Inn
Corfton SY7 9DF
☎ 01584 861239 & 861503
e-mail: normanspride@aol.com
Dir: on the B4368 7m N of Ludlow
CHILD FACILITIES: Please telephone for details
OPEN: 12-2.30 6-11 BAR MEALS: L served all week 12-2 D served all week 6-9.30 Av main course £7.25 RESTAURANT: L served all week 12-2 D served all week 6-9.30 FACILITIES: Children's licence Garden: 4 benches with tables, pretty views PARKING: 30

IRONBRIDGE
Map 07 SJ60

📶 The Malthouse ♦♦♦♦
The Wharfage TF8 7NH
☎ 01952 433712 🗋 01952 433298
e-mail: enquiries@malthousepubs.co.uk
Dir: Telephone for directions
CHILD FACILITIES: Please telephone for details
OPEN: 11-11 (Sun 12-3 6-10.30) Closed: 25-26 Dec BAR MEALS: L served all week 12-2.30 D served all week 6-9.30 Av main course £8 RESTAURANT: L served all week 12-2 D served all week 6.30-9.45 Av 3 course à la carte £21.20 FACILITIES: Garden: ✹ ROOMS: 6 bedrooms 6 en suite 2 family rooms s£55 d£60 PARKING: 15

LUDLOW
Map 07 SO57

Babies Welcome | Family Rooms | Children's Dishes

♦♦♦♦   The Clive Restaurant with Rooms
Bromfield SY8 2JR
☎ 01584 856565 🗋 01584 856661
e-mail: info@theclive.co.uk
web: www.theclive.co.uk
Dir: 2m N of Ludlow on A39 in village of Bromfield.
CHILD FACILITIES: Activities: colouring Family area Food/bottle warming Ch menu Ch portions Highchairs Ch cutlery Ch discounts £10-£15 Cots Family rms D rm with sofa bed Connecting rms Changing mats NEARBY: Discovery Centre Ludlow Castle

The Clive is just two miles from the busy town of Ludlow and is a convenient base for visiting the local attractions. The bedrooms are spacious and very well equipped, and some are suitable for families and guests with disabilities. Meals are available in the well-known Clive restaurant or the Cookhouse cafe bar. (See entry on page 202).
ROOMS: 15 annexe en suite (9 fmly) (11 GF) s £50-£60; d £70-£85 * FACILITIES: TVB tea/coffee Direct dial from bedrooms Dinner NOTES: ✹ ⊗ Licensed LB PARKING: 100

♦♦♦♦ The Hoopits
Greete SY8 3BS
☎ 01584 879187 🗋 01584 875530
e-mail: thehoopits@talk21.com
web: www.ludlow-thehoopits.co.uk
Dir: On A49 turn towards Ashford, Caynham & Clee Hill. In Caynham village turn right for Greete & Tenbury Wells, Hoopits is 1m on left
CHILD FACILITIES: Please telephone for details
Set in immaculately maintained gardens, The Hoopits occupies a peaceful location within easy distance of Ludlow and the surrounding attractions. Quality period or handcrafted furniture highlights the many original features and breakfast is taken at a
continued on p202

LUDLOW, continued

superb pine table in an elegant dining room. A guest lounge with wood burner is also available.

ROOMS: 3 rms (2 en suite) (1 fmly) (1 GF) s £25; d £50 *
FACILITIES: TVB tea/coffee TVL No coaches Dinner Last d order 10am
NOTES: Credit cards not taken ✻ ☻ Cen ht **LB PARKING:** 10

Babies Welcome | Family Rooms | Children's Dishes

◆◆◆ ⌑ Church Inn
The Buttercross SY8 1AW
☎ 01584 872174 📠 01584 877146
e-mail: Reception@thechurchinn.com
web: www.thechurchinn.com
Dir: in Ludlow town centre at top of Broad St

CHILD FACILITIES: Nanny (by request) Babysitting Family area Food/bottle warming Ch menu Ch portions Highchairs Ch cutlery Safe grounds Cots Family rms D rm with B beds £90 **NEARBY:** Cinema Parks Leisure centre

At the heart of historic Ludlow, this Grade II listed inn has been sympathetically renovated to provide quality accommodation with smart modern bathrooms, some with spa baths. Other areas include a small guest lounge and cosy bar areas, the setting for imaginative food.
ROOMS: 9 en suite (3 fmly) s £40-£50; d £70-£80 * **FACILITIES:** TVB tea/coffee Direct dial from bedrooms No coaches Dinner Last d order 9pm **NOTES:** ☻ in area of dining room ☻ in 1 lounge Cen ht

Family Rooms | Children's Dishes

◆◆◆ Timberstone Bed & Breakfast
Cleestanton SY8 3EL
☎ 01584 823519
e-mail: timberstone1@hotmail.com
Dir: A4117 Ludlow to Kidderminster, left to Bridgnorth on the B4364, follow for 1.5m, right to Cleestanton, take left fork, follow for 1.5m, 1st left, cottage on left

CHILD FACILITIES: Activities: games, books, puzzles Food/bottle warming Ch portions Ch discounts Videos Family rms D rm with extra bed Ch drinks (on request) Laundry **NEARBY:** Educational activity centre

This ancient timber-framed, stone house is quietly located in a rural setting, north-east of Ludlow. It has been painstakingly restored without losing any of its considerable charm. The accommodation comprises one twin and one double-bedded room with their own private bath or shower room. There is a choice of lounge areas, one with log fires and television. Guests all share one table at breakfast.
ROOMS: 2 rms (1 fmly) s £25-£35; d £50-£60 * **FACILITIES:** tea/coffee No coaches reflexology offered **NOTES:** Credit cards not taken ☻ Cen ht **PARKING:** 4

Children's Dishes

⌑ The Cookhouse Cafe Bar
Bromfield SY8 2JR
☎ 01584 856565 & 856665 📠 01584 856661
e-mail: info@thecookhouse.org.uk
web: www.thecookhouse.org.uk
Dir: Telephone for directions

CHILD FACILITIES: Activities: colouring Family area Ch licence Ch menu Ch portions Highchairs Ch cutlery Changing facilities **NEARBY:** Stokesay Castle Secret Hills Discovery Centre Craven Arms Walks

continued

OPEN: 11-11 (Sunday 12-10.30) Closed: 25-26 Dec **BAR MEALS:** L served all week 12-3 D served all week 6-10 Av main course £9 **RESTAURANT:** L served all week 12-3 D served all week 6-10 Av 3 course à la carte £24
FACILITIES: Garden: Courtyard and beer lawn ✻ **PARKING:** 100

MUCH WENLOCK   Map 07 SO69

⌑ The George & Dragon
2 High St TF13 6AA
☎ 01952 727312
Dir: On A458 halfway between Shrewsbury & Bridgnorth

CHILD FACILITIES: Please telephone for details

OPEN: 12-3 (Wknds & summer June-Sep all day) 6-11 (Fri-Sun 12-11, 12-10.30) **BAR MEALS:** L served Mon-Sun 12-2.00 D served Mon-Tue, Thur-Sat 6-9.00 Av main course £7.95 **RESTAURANT:** L served Mon-Sun 12-2.00 D served Mon-Tue, Thur-Sat 6.30-9.00 Av 3 course à la carte £16.95
FACILITIES: ✻

⌑ Longville Arms
Longville in the Dale TF13 6DT
☎ 01694 771206 📠 01694 771742
Dir: From Shrewsbury take A49 to Church Stretton, then B4371 to Longville

CHILD FACILITIES: Please telephone for details

OPEN: 12-3 7-11 Sat & Sun all day **BAR MEALS:** L served all week 12-2.30 D served all week 7-9.30 **RESTAURANT:** L served all week 12-2.30 D served all week 7-9.30 **FACILITIES:** Garden: Patio area
PARKING: 40

MUNSLOW   Map 07 SO58

Family Rooms | Children's Dishes

◆◆◆◆ ⊜ ⌑ Crown Country Inn
SY7 9ET
☎ 01584 841205 📠 01584 841255
e-mail: info@crowncountryinn.co.uk
Dir: A49, turn on to B4368 at Craven Arms, 7m on left, car park opp

CHILD FACILITIES: Baby listening Activities: toys Outdoor play area Family area Food/bottle warming Ch menu Ch portions Ch cutlery Safe grounds Family rms from £70 Ch drinks **NEARBY:** Railway centre Farm Ironbridge Gorge museum

Located between Much Wenlock and Craven Arms, this impressive pastel coloured and half-timbered Tudor inn is full of character and charm with stone floors, exposed beams and blazing log fires during winter. Smart pine furnished bedrooms are located in a sympathetic conversion of the former stable block and spacious public areas include two dining rooms.
ROOMS: 3 en suite (1 fmly) (1 GF) s fr £40; d £60-£65 * ☻
FACILITIES: TVB tea/coffee Dinner Last d order 8.45pm **NOTES:** ☻ in restaurant Cen ht **LB PARKING:** 20

> How to use this guide & abbreviations
> are explained on pages 5-7

NORTON
Map 07 SJ70

Babies Welcome | Children's Dishes

🏨 The Hundred House Hotel ★★ 🏵 🏵
Bridgnorth Rd TF11 9EE
☎ 01952 730353 0845 6446 100 📠 01952 730355
e-mail: reservations@hundredhouse.co.uk
web: www.hundredhouse.co.uk
Dir: On A442 6m N of Bridgnorth, 5 mile south of Telford Centre

CHILD FACILITIES: Outdoor play area Food/bottle warming
Ch menu Ch portions Highchairs Ch cutlery Changing facilities
NEARBY: Enginuity at Ironbridge Museum Severn Valley Steam
Railway Walks Bowling alley

Primarily Georgian, but with parts dating back to the 14th century, this friendly family owned and run hotel offers individually styled, well-equipped bedrooms which have period furniture and attractive soft furnishings. Public areas include cosy bars and intimate dining areas where memorable meals are served.
OPEN: 11am-3 (Sun 11-10.30) 6-11 Closed: 25/26 Dec eve BAR
MEALS: L served all week 12-2.30 D served all week 6-10 Av main course £9.95 RESTAURANT: L served all week 12-2.30 D served Mon-Sat 6-10 Av 3 course à la carte £25 FACILITIES: Garden: Large water garden, herb and rose garden 🎯 ROOMS: 10 bedrooms 10 en suite 3 family rooms s£85 d£125 PARKING: 40

SHREWSBURY
Map 07 SJ41

Babies Welcome | Family Rooms | Children's Dishes

★★★ 77% 🏵 🛎 Albright Hussey
Ellesmere Rd SY4 3AF
☎ 01939 290571 & 290523 📠 01939 291143
e-mail: abhhotel@aol.com
web: www.albrighthussey.co.uk
Dir: 2.5m N of Shrewsbury on A528, follow signs for Ellesmere

CHILD FACILITIES: Baby listening Nanny (by prior arrangement)
Babysitting Food/bottle warming Ch menu Ch portions Highchairs
Ch cutlery Cots Family rms D rm with adjoining room Connecting
rms Laundry

First mentioned in the Domesday Book, this enchanting medieval manor house is complete with a moat. Bedrooms are situated in either the sumptuously appointed main house or in the more modern ambience of the new wing. The intimate restaurant displays an abundance of original features and there is also a comfortable cocktail bar and lounge.
ROOMS: 26 en suite (4 fmly) (8 GF) 🕎 in 16 bedrooms s £79-£105; d £110-£180 (incl. bkfst) LB FACILITIES: 🎵 Jacuzzi Xmas
PARKING: 85 NOTES: 🕎 in restaurant

Babies Welcome | Family Rooms | Children's Dishes

★★★ 67% 🏵 Mytton & Mermaid
Atcham SY5 6QG
☎ 01743 761220 📠 01743 761292
e-mail: admin@myttonandmermaid.co.uk
web: www.myttonandmermaid.co.uk
Dir: from Shrewsbury cross old bridge in Atcham. Hotel beside River Severn opposite main entrance to Attingham Park

CHILD FACILITIES: Baby listening Babysitting Food/bottle
warming Ch menu Ch portions Highchairs Ch discounts under 3s
free Cots Family rms D rm with B beds £80 NEARBY: Park
Farm Walks Cinema Swimming pool Tenpin bowling Ironbridge

Convenient for Shrewsbury, this ivy-clad former coaching inn enjoys a pleasant location beside the River Severn. Some bedrooms, including family suites, are in a converted stable block
continued

adjacent to the hotel. The large lounge bar has been recently refurbished, and there is also a comfortable lounge and brasserie gaining a well-deserved local reputation for the quality of its food.
ROOMS: 11 en suite 7 annexe en suite (1 fmly) 🕎 in 11 bedrooms s £60; d £80-£135 (incl. bkfst) FACILITIES: Fishing 🎵 Xmas
PARKING: 50 NOTES: 🕎 in restaurant

Family Rooms | Children's Dishes

◆◆◆ Sydney House Hotel
Coton Crescent, Coton Hill SY1 2LJ
☎ 01743 354681 📠 01743 354681
e-mail: sydneyhouse@btopenworld.com
web: www.sydneyhousehotel.co.uk
Dir: junct A528 towards Ellesmere & B5067 towards Baschurch. 10mins walk from town centre via Gateway Arts centre & rail station

CHILD FACILITIES: Food/bottle warming Ch menu Ch portions
Ch cutlery Ch discounts under 12s 50% off Family rms D rm with S
bed from £60 Ch drinks Laundry NEARBY: Riverside walks and
trips

Located a few minutes' walk from the river and historic centre, this elegant Edwardian house provides a range of bedrooms equipped with practical and thoughtful extras. Comprehensive breakfasts are taken in a cosy dining room and a lounge with bar is available.
ROOMS: 6 en suite (1 fmly) 🕎 in 4 bedrooms FACILITIES: TVB tea/coffee TVL No coaches NOTES: 🎯 🕎 in restaurant Licensed
PARKING: 7

TELFORD
Map 07 SJ60

◆◆◆ 🏨 Arleston Inn Hotel
Arleston Ln, Wellington TF1 2LA
☎ 01952 501881 📠 01952 506429
Dir: M54 junct 6 left to island, 4th exit signed Lawley, 0.5m on right

CHILD FACILITIES: Please telephone for details

This friendly, picturesque inn is ideally located close to the modern town centre. It provides compact but attractive bedrooms, equipped with modern facilities. Meals are served in the attractive bar or the newly built sun-lounge which overlooks the garden.
ROOMS: 7 en suite FACILITIES: TVB tea/coffee Dinner Last d order 8.45pm NOTES: Credit cards not taken 🎯 🕎 in area of dining room Cen ht

WESTON HEATH
Map 07 SJ71

🏨 The Countess's Arms
TF11 8RY
☎ 01952 691123 📠 01952 691660

CHILD FACILITIES: Please telephone for details

OPEN: 12-11 (Sun 12-10.30) Closed: 25 Dec BAR MEALS: L served all week 12-2.30 D served all week 6-9.30 Av main course £9
RESTAURANT: L served all week 12-2.30 D served all week 6-9.30 Av 3 course à la carte £20 FACILITIES: Garden: Large grassed area 🎯
PARKING: 100

WORFIELD
Map 07 SO79

🏨 The Dog Inn & Davenport Arms
Main St WV15 5LF
☎ 01746 716020 📠 01746 716050
e-mail: thedog@tinyworld.co.uk
Dir: On the Wolverhampton road turn L opposite the Wheel pub over the bridge and turn R in to the village of Worfield the Dog is on the L. Tourist signs on the A454 & A442

CHILD FACILITIES: Please telephone for details

OPEN: 12-2.30 7-11 BAR MEALS: L served all week 12-2 D served all week 7-9.30 RESTAURANT: L served all week 12-2 D served all week 7-9.30 FACILITIES: Children's licence Garden PARKING: 8

SOMERSET

Weston-Super-Mare

BATH

Bath Postal Museum BA1 5LJ
info@bathpostalmuseum.org   ☎01225 460333
(M4 junct 18. Follow A46 to Bath, on entering city fork left at mini rdbt. After all traffic lights into Walcot St. Podium car park facing)
Open all year, Mon-Sat 11-4.30. Last admission Mar-Oct 4.30pm; Oct-Mar 4pm Closed Sun, 25-26 Dec & 1 Jan.

Museum of Costume
BA1 2QH   ☎01225 477785
costume_bookings@bathnes.gov.uk
(M4 junct 18, follow A46 into Bath. Museum near city centre)
Open all year, daily 10-4.30 Closed 25 & 26 Dec.
*£6 ch £4. Family ticket £16.50. Combined ticket with Roman Baths, £12 ch £7.

Roman Baths & Pump Room
BA1 1LZ   ☎01225 477785
romanbaths_bookings@bathnes.gov.uk
(M4 junct 18, A46 into city centre)
Open all year, Mar-Jun & Sep-Oct, daily 9-5; Jul & Aug daily 9am-10; Jan-Feb & Nov-Dec, daily 9.30-4.30. Closed 25 & 26 Dec. Last exit 1hr after closing.
*£9 ch £5. Family ticket £24. Combined ticket with Museum of Costume £12 ch £7. Disabled visitors free admission to ground floor areas.

CRICKET ST THOMAS

The Wildlife Park at Cricket St Thomas
TA20 4DB   ☎01460 30111
teresa.white2@bourne-leisure.co.uk
(3m E of Chard on A30, follow brown heritage signs. Clearly signposted from M5 junct 25)
Open all year, daily 10-dusk, last admission 4pm in summer. Closed 25 Dec.

GLASTONBURY

Glastonbury Abbey BA6 9EL
info@glastonburyabbey.com   ☎01458 832267
(Located on A361 between Frome & Taunton. M5 junct 23, then take A39 to Glastonbury)
Open all year, daily, Jun-Aug 9-6; Sep-May 9.30-6 or dusk, whichever is the earliest. Dec-Feb open at 10am. Closed 25 Dec. *£4 ch 5-15 £1.50, pen & students £3.50. Family ticket £10 2ad+2ch

SPARKFORD

Haynes Motor Museum BA22 7LH
info@haynesmotormuseum.co.uk☎01963 440804
(From A303 follow A359 road towards Castle Cary, the museum is clearly signposted)
Open all year, Mar-Oct, daily 9.30-5.30; Nov-Feb, 10-4.30. Closed 24 & 26 Dec & 1 Jan.* Adult £6.50 ch £3.50, concessions £5. Family £8.50 1 ad & 1 ch, £19 2 ad & 3 ch.

STOKE ST GREGORY

Willow & Wetlands Visitor Centre TA3 6HY
phcoate@globalnet.co.uk   ☎01823 490249
(between North Curry & Stoke St Gregory, signed from A361 & A378)
Open all year, Mon-Fri 9-5 guided tours 10-4, Sat no tours 9-5. Closed Sun.
*Admission free, tour charge: £3.50 ch £1.75, pen £3. Family ticket £8. Credit cards accepted if total admission price exceeds £10.

STREET

The Shoe Museum
BA16 0YA   ☎01458 842169
(M5 Junct 23, take A39 to Street, follow signs for Clarks Village) Open all year. Mon-Fri 10-4.45, Sat 10-1.30 & 2-5, Sun 11-1.30 & 2-5. Closed 10 days over Xmas

WASHFORD

Tropiquaria Animal and Adventure Park
TA23 0QB   ☎01984 640688
office@tropiquaria.co.uk
(On A39, between Williton and Minehead)
Open Apr-Sep, daily 10-6 last entry 4.30; Oct daily 11-5 last entry 4; Nov-Mar wknds 11-4.
Last entry 3.

WESTON-SUPER-MARE

The Helicopter Museum BS24 8PP
BS24 8PP   ☎01934 635227
office@helimuseum.fsnet.co.uk
(outskirts of town on A371, nr M5 junct 21)
Open all year, Nov-Mar Wed-Sun 10-4.30, Apr-Oct 10-5.30 (closed 24-26 Dec & 1 Jan) Open daily during Etr & Summer school hols 10-6.30. *£4.95 (ch under 5 free, ch 5-16 £2.95, pen £3.95). Family ticket (2ad+2ch) £13. Party 12+.

WOOKEY HOLE

Wookey Hole Caves & Papermill BA5 1BB
witch@wookey.co.uk   ☎01749 672243
(M5 junct 22, follow signs via A38 & A371, from Bristol & Bath A39 to Wells then 2m to Wookey Hole)
Open all year, Apr-Oct 10-7; Nov-Mar 10.30-5.30.
*£8.80 ch £5.50, under 4's free.

YEOVILTON

Fleet Air Arm Museum BA22 8HT
info@fleetairarm.com   ☎01935 840565
(On B3151, just off A303)
Open all year, daily ex 24-26 Dec 10-5.30, 4.30 Nov-Mar.

APPLEY · Map 03 ST02

🍴 The Globe Inn
TA21 0HJ
☎ 01823 672327
Dir: From M5 J26 take A38 towards Exeter. Village signposted in 5m

CHILD FACILITIES: Outdoor play area Food/bottle warming Ch menu Ch portions (some) Highchairs Ch cutlery Changing facilities **NEARBY:** Walks

OPEN: 11-3 6.30-11 (closed Mon) **BAR MEALS:** L served Tue-Sun 12-2 D served Tue-Sun 7-10 Av main course £9 **RESTAURANT:** L served Tue-Sun D served Tue-Sun 7-10 **FACILITIES:** Garden: Large garden overlooking countryside ✖ **PARKING:** 30

ASHCOTT · Map 03 ST43

🍴 Ring O'Bells
High St TA7 9PZ
☎ 01458 210232 📠 01458 210880
e-mail: info@ringobells.com
web: www.ringobells.com
Dir: From M5 follow signs A39 & Glastonbury. N off A39 at post office follow signs to church and village hall

CHILD FACILITIES: Activities: board games Outdoor play area Family area Food/bottle warming Ch menu Ch portions Highchairs Ch cutlery Safe grounds **NEARBY:** Nature reserves Walks Peat Moors Visitors Centre Glastonbury

OPEN: 12-3 7-11 (Sun 7-10.30) Closed: 25 Dec **BAR MEALS:** L served all week 12-2 D served all week 7-10 Av main course £6.50 **RESTAURANT:** L served all week 12-2 D served all week 7-10 Av 3 course à la carte £13 **FACILITIES:** Garden: Large, enclosed garden, grass, patio ✖ **PARKING:** 25

BATH · Map 03 ST76

★★★ 72% Cliffe
Cliffe Dr, Crowe Hill, Limpley Stoke BA2 7FY
☎ 01225 723226 📠 01225 723871

Best Western

e-mail: cliffe@bestwestern.co.uk
Dir: A36 S from Bath, at A36/B3108 lights left toward Bradford on Avon, 0.5m. Turn right before bridge through village, hotel on right

CHILD FACILITIES: Baby listening Activities: swimming pool, board games, chess set, colouring Food/bottle warming Ch menu Ch portions Highchairs Ch discounts under 5s free Safe grounds Cots Family rms D rm with S beds from £157 Ch drinks Laundry **NEARBY:** Walks Canal trips Longleat

With stunning countryside views this attractive country house is just a short drive from the city centre of Bath. Bedrooms vary in size and style and are well-equipped; several are particularly spacious and a number of rooms are on the ground floor. The restaurant overlooks the well-tended garden and offers a tempting selection of carefully prepared dishes.

ROOMS: 8 en suite 3 annexe en suite (2 fmly) (4 GF) ⊗ in 4 bedrooms s £90-£100; d £110-£130 (incl. bkfst) **LB** **FACILITIES:** STV 🎣 peaceful gardens Xmas **PARKING:** 20 **NOTES:** ⊗ in restaurant

◆◆◆◆◆ 🏛 Haydon House
9 Bloomfield Park BA2 2BY
☎ 01225 444919 & 427351 📠 01225 444919
e-mail: stay@haydonhouse.co.uk
web: www.haydonhouse.co.uk
Dir: follow signs for A367 Exeter. At large rdbt turn left. After 0.75m right at shopping centre, fork right then 2nd right for 200yds

CHILD FACILITIES: Please telephone for details

This charming house offers excellent standards of comfort and hospitality. The delightful rooms include four-poster and canopied beds and are tastefully decorated with Laura Ashley fabrics, as well as being very well equipped and provided with many thoughtful extras. Special rates are available between November and March. Breakfast is excellent - an interesting feature is the Scotch whisky or rum porridge.

ROOMS: 5 en suite (1 fmly) s £45-£75; d £75-£115 * **FACILITIES:** TVB tea/coffee Direct dial from bedrooms No coaches Sun Terrace **NOTES:** ✖ ⊗ Cen ht **LB** **PARKING:** 1

◆◆◆◆◆ Paradise House Hotel
Holloway BA2 4PX
☎ 01225 317723 📠 01225 482005
e-mail: info@paradise-house.co.uk
web: www.paradise-house.co.uk
Dir: from A36 (Bristol/Warminster road) at Churchill Bridge rdbt take A367, then 3rd left, down hill into cul-de-sac, house 200yds on left

CHILD FACILITIES: Please telephone for details

Set in half an acre of lovely walled gardens, this Georgian house, built in 1720 from mellow Bath stone, is within walking distance of the city centre. Many bedrooms have fine views over the city, and all are decorated in opulent style. Furnishings are elegant and facilities modern. The lounge is comfortable and relaxing and breakfast is served in the smart dining room. Hospitality and service here are friendly and professional.

ROOMS: 11 en suite (2 fmly) (4 GF) s £55-£95; d £65-£165 * **FACILITIES:** TVB tea/coffee Direct dial from bedrooms No coaches Boules pitch **NOTES:** ✖ ⊗ Licensed Cen ht **LB** **PARKING:** 6

◆◆◆◆ Aquae Sulis
174/176 Newbridge Rd BA1 3LE
☎ 01225 420061 & 339064 📠 01225 446077
e-mail: enquiries@aquaesulishotel.com
web: www.aquaesulishotel.com
Dir: take Upper Bristol Rd (A4) from Queens Square towards Bristol. At second lights after Victoria Park fork left. Hotel on right.

CHILD FACILITIES: Baby listening Food/bottle warming Ch portions Ch cutlery Ch discounts under 3s free sharing with parents Safe grounds Cots Family rms D rms with S beds from £69 **NEARBY:** Parks

Located within easy reach of the city centre, this attractive Edwardian house offers a warm and genuine welcome. Bedrooms are of a good size and well equipped with many modern facilities such as Internet/e-mail access. There are two inviting lounges, one with a small bar. Breakfast is taken in the comfortable dining room and a good selection of meals is available in the evening.

ROOMS: 13 en suite (5 fmly) (2 GF) s £49-£65; d £59-£95 * ⊗ **FACILITIES:** STV TVB tea/coffee Direct dial from bedrooms TVL Free use of golf course (clubs/trolley provided) Dinner Last d order 6pm **NOTES:** ⊗ in restaurant ⊗ in 1 lounge Licensed Cen ht **LB** **PARKING:** 12

BATH, continued

◆◆◆◆ Bailbrook Lodge
35/37 London Rd West BA1 7HZ
☎ 01225 859090 🖷 01225 852299
e-mail: hotel@bailbrooklodge.co.uk
web: www.bailbrooklodge.co.uk
Dir: M4 junct 18, take A46 Bath exit at rdbt. Left signed Batheaston, hotel on left. From Bath, A4. At A46 rdbt to Batheaston

CHILD FACILITIES: Please telephone for details

Set in extensive gardens on the eastern edge of the city, this imposing Georgian building offers comfortable accommodation. The well-equipped bedrooms include some with four-poster beds and period furniture. The comfortable lounge includes an honesty bar and is the ideal place to relax at the end of a busy day.
ROOMS: 12 en suite (4 fmly) s £42-£55 * ⊛ in 4 bedrooms
FACILITIES: TVB tea/coffee **NOTES:** ✾ ⊛ in restaurant Licensed Cen ht **LB PARKING:** 12

◆◆◆ Ashgrove
39 Bathwick St BA2 6PA
☎ 01225 421911
Dir: from M4 junct 18, to city centre on London Rd, follow rd to left into Bathwick St. Fire & ambulance station on left, house on right after garage

CHILD FACILITIES: Please telephone for details

Attractive Georgian terraced property ideally situated just a six-minute walk from the city centre. The neatly appointed, brightly decorated bedrooms combine traditional furnishings with modern facilities and a useful range of extras. Breakfast is served at individual tables in the smartly decorated dining room.
ROOMS: 9 rms (6 en suite) ⊛ in 5 bedrooms **FACILITIES:** TVB tea/coffee **NOTES:** ✾ ⊛ in restaurant ⊛ in lounges **PARKING:** 6

Babies Welcome	Family Rooms	Children's Dishes

◆◆◆ Pulteney Hotel
14 Pulteney Rd BA2 4HA
☎ 01225 460991 🖷 01225 460991
e-mail: pulteney@tinyworld.co.uk
web: www.pulteneyhotel.co.uk
Dir: on A36 0.25m from city centre, 100yds from major set traffic lights

CHILD FACILITIES: Outdoor play area Food/bottle warming Ch portions Highchairs Safe grounds Cots Family rms D rms with S beds **NEARBY:** Parks Canal walks Leisure centres Cinema

A warm welcome is assured at this large detached property, situated in a colourful, award-winning garden within walking distance of the city centre. Bedrooms vary in size and are well equipped with useful extra facilities. Full English breakfasts are served in the dining room at individual tables.
ROOMS: 12 rms (11 en suite) 5 annexe en suite (6 fmly) (2 GF) s £40-£50; d £70-£100 * ⊛ in 5 bedrooms **FACILITIES:** TVB tea/coffee TVL **NOTES:** ⊛ in restaurant Cen ht **PARKING:** 18

Babies Welcome	Children's Dishes

◉ The Eastern Eye
8A Quiet St BA1 2JS
☎ 01225 422323 466401 🖷 01225 444484
e-mail: info@easterneye.co.uk
Dir: Town centre

CHILD FACILITIES: Food/bottle warming Ch portions Highchairs

This restaurant has an exceptional interior even by Bath's amazing architectural standards. Always busy the Eastern Eye is rated as one of the top curry houses in the UK. Expertly handled fresh spices make this a must for those who enjoy South Asian cuisine.
continued

The extensive menu is packed with authentic Bengali, North Western and vegetarian dishes that you don't often see.

FOOD: Indian **STYLE: SEATS:** 130 **OPEN:** 12.30-2.15/6-11.30, Closed 25 Dec **RESTAURANT:** Fixed D £18, main £5.50-£11.90 **NOTES:** ⊛ area, Air con
See advert on opposite page

BUCKLAND ST MARY
Map 03 ST21

Babies Welcome	Family Rooms	Children's Dishes

◆◆◆◆ Hillside
TA20 3TQ
☎ 01460 234599 & 07703 633770 🖷 01460 234599
e-mail: royandmarge@hillsidebsm.freeserve.co.uk
Dir: A303, approx 4m S of Ilminster turning, right at the Eagle Tavern, next left (water tower on corner), Hillside approx 500yds on left

CHILD FACILITIES: Activities: books, toys, games Outdoor play area Food/bottle warming Ch portions Highchairs Ch cutlery Ch discounts under 12s Safe grounds Cots Family rms D/T rm with S bed/cot from £60 Ch drinks **NEARBY:** Wildlife park

A warm welcome is assured at this peaceful family home, set in large, attractive gardens and enjoying splendid far-reaching views across open countryside. Bedrooms are spacious and decorated to a high standard with many thoughtful extras. Hearty breakfasts are served hot from the Aga in the bright dining room or the conservatory, which overlooks the garden.
ROOMS: 4 rms (2 en suite) 1 annexe rms (1 fmly) (1 GF) s £27-£35; d £47-£60 * **FACILITIES:** TV4B tea/coffee TVL No coaches **NOTES:** Credit cards not taken ✾ ⊛ Cen ht **LB PARKING:** 4

CHARD
Map 03 ST30

Babies Welcome	Family Rooms	Children's Dishes

◆◆◆ Watermead
83 High St TA20 1QT
☎ 01460 62834 🖷 01460 67448
e-mail: trudy@watermeadguesthouse.co.uk
web: www.watermeadguesthouse.co.uk
Dir: on A30 through the High St continue up the hill from shopping centre

CHILD FACILITIES: Indoor play area Outdoor play area Food/bottle warming Ch menu Ch portions Highchairs Ch discounts Safe grounds Cots Family rms self contained annexe with D & 3 S beds, rm for extra bed, lounge area £60-£80 Fridge **NEARBY:** Wildlife park

This family-run house provides smart and comfortable accommodation. Conveniently located, it is an ideal base from which to explore the area and guests are made to feel at home. Hearty breakfasts are served in the spacious dining room which overlooks the attractive garden. Bedrooms are neatly presented and a very spacious, self-contained suite proves popular with families.
ROOMS: 9 rms (6 en suite) 1 annexe en suite (1 fmly) s £25-£37; d £49-£53 * **FACILITIES:** TVB tea/coffee TVL No coaches **NOTES:** ⊛ Cen ht **LB PARKING:** 10

CLUTTON
Map 03 ST65

🍴 The Hunters Rest ♦♦♦♦
King Ln, Clutton Hill BS39 5QL
☎ 01761 452303 ⊟ 01761 453308
e-mail: info@huntersrest.co.uk
web: www.huntersrest.co.uk
Dir: Follow signs for Wells A37 through village of Pensford, at large rdbt turn L towards Bath, after 100 meters R into country lane, pub 1m up hill

CHILD FACILITIES: Please telephone for details

This inn was originally built around 1750 as a hunting lodge for the Earl of Warwick. Set in delightful countryside, it is conveniently located midway between the varied attractions of Bath, Bristol and Wells. Bedrooms and bathrooms are furnished and equipped to excellent standards, and the ground floor combines the character of a real country inn with an excellent range of home-cooked meals.

OPEN: 11.30-3 6-11 (All day Sun in summer) **BAR MEALS:** L served all week 12-2 D served all week 6.30-9.45 Av main course £8
RESTAURANT: L served all week 12-2 D served all week 6.30-9.45 Av 3 course à la carte £17.50 **FACILITIES:** Garden: Large landscaped areas with country views **ROOMS:** 5 bedrooms 5 en suite 2 family rooms s£57.50 d£80 **PARKING:** 80

CREWKERNE
Map 03 ST40

♦♦♦♦ 🍴 Manor Farm
Wayford TA18 8QL
☎ 01460 78865 & 0776 7620031 ⊟ 01460 78865
web: www.manorfarm.biz
Dir: from Crewkerne take B3165 to Lyme Regis, after 3m in Clapton turn right into Dunsham Lane, 0.5m up hill Manor Farm on right

CHILD FACILITIES: Activities: games, netball, skittles Outdoor play area Food/bottle warming Ch menu Ch portions Highchairs Ch discounts under 12s half price Safe grounds Family rms D rm with 2 S beds £62.50-£75 Laundry NEARBY: Wildlife park

Located off the beaten track, this fine Victorian country house has extensive views over Clapton towards the Axe Valley. The comfortably furnished bedrooms are well equipped; front-facing rooms enjoy splendid views. Breakfast is served at separate tables in the dining room, and a spacious lounge is also provided.

ROOMS: 3 en suite 1 annexe en suite s £30-£35; d £50 *
FACILITIES: STV TVB tea/coffee TVL Fishing Riding 20 acres breeding beef **NOTES:** Credit cards not taken 🐾 ⊗ Cen ht **PARKING:** 14

DINNINGTON
Map 04 ST41

🍴 Dinnington Docks
TA17 8SX
☎ 01460 52397 ⊟ 01460 52397
e-mail: hilary@dinningtondocks.co.uk
Dir: On A303 between South Petherton And Ilminster

CHILD FACILITIES: Outdoor play area Food/bottle warming Ch menu Ch portions Highchairs Ch cutlery Safe grounds Changing facilities NEARBY: Walks Rural, transport & military museums Wildlife Park

OPEN: 11.30-3.30 6-11 **BAR MEALS:** L served all week 12-2.30 D served all week 6-9.30 Av main course £4.50 **RESTAURANT:** L served all week 12-2.30 D served all week 6-9.30 Av 3 course à la carte £11
FACILITIES: Garden: Large garden with children's play area
PARKING: 30

Welcome to Bath's premier unique Indian restaurant. The Mahal of exquisite Indian cuisine with the city's most impressive Georgian interior. Voted by "The Good Curry Guide" as one of the top 100 restaurants. AA Rosette Awards, Les Routiers & le Guide Du Routard. The dining room is a whole floor of a Georgian building with spectacular vaulted ceiling. Designer Curryhouse. Food is well prepared and staff friendly and efficient. **The Observer.** 12 noon to 2.30pm. 6 to 11pm daily. Last orders 6 to 11.30pm daily.

8a Quiet Street, Bath
Tel: 01225 422323/466401 Fax: 01225 444484/466401
www.easterneye.com
email: manager@easterneye.co.uk

DULVERTON
Map 03 SS92

♦♦♦♦ Threadneedle
EX16 9JH
☎ 01398 341598
e-mail: info@threadneedlecottage.co.uk
web: www.threadneedlecottage.co.uk
Dir: on Devon/Somerset border just off B3227 between Oldways End & East Anstey

CHILD FACILITIES: Please telephone for details

Situated on the edge of Exmoor near Dulverton, Threadneedle is built in the style of a Devon longhouse. The spacious, well-appointed family home offers guests comfortable, en suite accommodation. Traditional West Country dishes are served, by prior arrangement, in the light airy dining room, which overlooks the garden and surrounding countryside.

ROOMS: 2 en suite (1 fmly) s £27-£30; d £54-£60 * ⊗
FACILITIES: TVB tea/coffee No coaches Dinner Last d order 10am
NOTES: Credit cards not taken Cen ht **LB PARKING:** 12

FROME
Map 03 ST74

Children's Dishes

🍴 The Horse & Groom
East Woodlands BA11 5LY
☎ 01373 462802 ⊟ 01373 462802
e-mail: horse.and.groom@care4free.net
Dir: Just off Frome by-pass (A361 Shepton Mallet/Devizes rd)

CHILD FACILITIES: Food/bottle warming Ch menu Ch portions NEARBY: Longleat

continued on p208

England

FROME, continued

OPEN: 11.30-2.30 6.30-11 (Sun 12-3, 7-10) **BAR MEALS:** L served
Tue-Sun 12-2 D served Tue-Sat 6.30-9 Av main course £7.50
RESTAURANT: L served Tue-Sun 12-2 D served Tue-Sat 6.30-9 Av 3 course
à la carte £17.80 **FACILITIES:** Garden: Large garden with fruit trees and 7
tables **PARKING:** 20

HOLFORD — Map 03 ST14

♦♦♦♦ Winsors Farm B & B

TA5 1RY
☎ 01278 741435 & 741666 ▤ 01278 741666
e-mail: enq@winsors-farm.co.uk
*Dir: 10m W of Bridgwater on A39. On entering Holford take 1st left at
Plough Inn and Winsors Farm is on the left, 200mtrs from the A39*

CHILD FACILITIES: Please telephone for details

Reputed to be the oldest property in the village, Winsors Farm
dates back to the 16th century and is located on the edge of The
Quantocks. Guests are assured of a warm and friendly welcome
here. The bedrooms are comfortable and well equipped and have
numerous thoughtful extras. Breakfast is served around a large
table in the entrance hall/dining room. Dinner is available by prior
arrangement.
ROOMS: 2 en suite 1 annexe en suite (1 GF) s £30; d £45-£50 *
FACILITIES: TVB tea/coffee TVL No coaches walking, bird and deer
watching **NOTES:** Credit cards not taken Ⓢ Cen ht **PARKING:** 5

ILCHESTER — Map 03 ST52

Babies Welcome | Family Rooms | Children's Dishes

♦♦♦♦ 🍴 Ilchester Arms

Church St BA22 8LN
☎ 01935 840220 ▤ 01935 841353
*Dir: Ilchester exit from A303, turn left at rdbt to Ilchester. Hotel situated on
village square*

CHILD FACILITIES: Activities: playhouse, colouring, toys, jigsaws
Outdoor play area Food/bottle warming Ch menu Ch portions
Highchairs Ch cutlery Ch discounts under 15s free sharing with
parents Safe grounds Cots Family rms D rms with B beds £75
Ch drinks **NEARBY:** Cinema Bowling

Ideally located in the centre of Ilchester, the accommodation here
combines very well equipped, spacious bedrooms with a friendly
and relaxed style of hospitality. Downstairs, guests can choose
from a lively bar or a more relaxed, pleasant bistro area where
delicious home-cooked meals are freshly prepared.
ROOMS: 7 en suite (3 fmly) s £60; d £70 * Ⓢ in 5 bedrooms
FACILITIES: TVB tea/coffee Direct dial from bedrooms Dinner Last d
order 2.30pm **NOTES:** ✹ Ⓢ in restaurant Ⓢ in 1 lounge Cen ht **LB**
PARKING: 22

KILVE — Map 03 ST14

♦♦♦♦ 🍴 Hood Arms Hotel

TA5 1EA
☎ 01278 741210 ▤ 01278 741477
e-mail: bheason1942@aol.com
*Dir: 12m W of Bridgwater on A39, midway between Bridgwater &
Minehead*

CHILD FACILITIES: Please telephone for details

Comfortable, well-equipped bedrooms, with a good range of
facilities, are offered at this 17th-century former coaching inn,
continued

---

centrally located in the village of Kilve. In the beamed bars,
blackboard menus offer a wide range of popular dishes.

ROOMS: 6 en suite (1 fmly) Ⓢ **FACILITIES:** TVB tea/coffee Direct dial
from bedrooms Pool Table Dinner Last d order 9.30pm **NOTES:** Ⓢ in
restaurant Cen ht **PARKING:** 12

LEIGH UPON MENDIP — Map 03 ST64

Babies Welcome | Children's Dishes

🍴 The Bell Inn

BA3 5QQ
☎ 01373 812316
*Dir: head for Bath, then twrds Radstock following the Frome Rd, turn twrds
Mells and then Leigh-upon-Mendip*

CHILD FACILITIES: Activities: colouring Outdoor play area Family
area Food/bottle warming Ch menu Ch portions Highchairs
Ch cutlery Safe grounds **NEARBY:** Cheddar Caves Longleat Bath
Wookey Hole Stourhead

OPEN: 12-3 6-11 **BAR MEALS:** L served all week 12-2 D served all week
6.30-9.30 Av main course £8 **RESTAURANT:** L served all week 12-2 D
served all week 6.30-9 Av 3 course à la carte £15 **FACILITIES:** Garden:
Patio area, grassed area with flower borders ✹ **PARKING:** 24

LITTON — Map 03 ST55

Babies Welcome | Children's Dishes

🍴 The Kings Arms

BA3 4PW
☎ 01761 241301

CHILD FACILITIES: Outdoor play area Food/bottle warming
Ch menu Ch portions Highchairs Safe grounds Changing facilities
NEARBY: Walks Lakes

OPEN: 11-2.30 6-11 (Sun 12-3 7-10.30) **BAR MEALS:** L served all week
12-2.30 D served all week 6.30-10 Av main course £8 **FACILITIES:** Garden
PARKING: 50

England

MINEHEAD
Map 03 SS94

Babies Welcome | Family Rooms | Children's Dishes

◆◆◆ The Old Ship Aground
Quay St TA24 5UL
☎ 01643 702087 ◫ 01643 709066
e-mail: enquiries@oldshipaground.co.uk
Dir: turn right towards Butlins at 1st rdbt after Dunster lights, turn left at rdbt on seafront, proceed to harbour with sea on right, on front

CHILD FACILITIES: Baby listening Outdoor play area Family area Food/bottle warming Ch menu Ch portions Highchairs Safe grounds Cots Family rms D rm with 2 S beds from £50 Laundry NEARBY: Harbourside location Parks Leisure centre Cinema Railway centre Near sea

Located at the edge of the harbour and enjoying views of the bay, the Old Ship Aground offers traditional hospitality within a laid-back atmosphere. Bedrooms are spacious and thoughtfully equipped. Bar food is available and breakfast is served in the large dining/ function room.
ROOMS: 13 en suite (3 fmly) s £25-£30; d £45-£55 * ⊗ in 5 bedrooms FACILITIES: TVB tea/coffee Pool Table Dinner Last d order 9.30pm NOTES: ⊗ in area of dining room Cen ht PARKING: 10

NETHER STOWEY
Map 03 ST13

Babies Welcome | Family Rooms | Children's Dishes

★★ 71% Apple Tree
Keenthorne TA5 1HZ
☎ 01278 733238 ◫ 01278 732693
e-mail: reservations@appletreehotel.com
web: www.appletreehotel.com
Dir: from Bridgwater follow A39 towards Minehead, Hotel on left 2m past Cannington

CHILD FACILITIES: Baby listening Activities: games, cards, books Food/bottle warming Ch menu Ch portions Highchairs Ch cutlery Cots Family rms D bed with S beds £78-83 NEARBY: Animal adventure park Farm Castle Walks Railway centre

Parts of this cottage-style property, convenient for the coast and the M5, date back some 340 years. Bedrooms vary in character and style; some are in an adjoining wing, overlooking the garden. The friendly resident owners and their small team of staff make every effort to ensure an enjoyable stay. Public areas include an attractive conservatory restaurant, a bar and a library lounge.
ROOMS: 14 en suite (2 fmly) (5 GF) ⊗ in 5 bedrooms s £54.50; d £68 (incl. bkfst) LB PARKING: 40 NOTES: ✷ ⊗ in restaurant

◆◆◆◆◆ Castle of Comfort
TA5 1LE
☎ 01278 741264 ◫ 01278 741144
e-mail: reception@castle-of-comfort.co.uk
web: www.castle-of-comfort.co.uk
Dir: on A39, approx 1.3m W of Nether Stowey on left
CHILD FACILITIES: Please telephone for details
Dating in part from the 16th century, this former inn is situated on the northern slopes of the Quantock Hills in an Area of Outstanding Natural Beauty. Bedrooms and bathrooms are well equipped while the public rooms are smart and comfortable. The delightful gardens and a heated swimming pool are available for guests' use in the summer months and cuisine involves imaginative dinners.
ROOMS: 5 en suite 1 annexe en suite (1 fmly) (1 GF) s £41-£91; d £103-£139 * FACILITIES: TVB tea/coffee Direct dial from bedrooms No coaches ✶ Stabling with access to bridle paths and hunting Dinner Last d order noon NOTES: ⊗ Licensed Cen ht LB PARKING: 10

RODE
Map 03 ST85

Babies Welcome | Children's Dishes

The Mill at Rode
BA11 6AG
☎ 01373 831100 ◫ 01373 831144
e-mail: info@themillatrode.co.uk

CHILD FACILITIES: Activities: colouring, books, toys, game consoles Indoor play area Outdoor play area Family area Food/bottle warming Ch licence Ch menu Ch portions Highchairs Ch cutlery Safe grounds Changing facilities NEARBY: Walks Longleat

OPEN: 12 -11 BAR MEALS: L served all week 12 D served all week 10 Av main course £9.50 FACILITIES: Garden: Riverside garden with adult only island ✷ NOTES: Credit cards not taken PARKING: 72

SOMERTON
Map 03 ST42

◆◆◆◆ Somerton Court Country House
TA11 7AH
☎ 01458 274694 ◫ 01458 274693
e-mail: owen@newopaul.freeserve.co.uk
web: www.somertoncourt.co.uk
Dir: turn off A303 at Podimore rdbt onto A372. 2m turn right A3165 to Somerton rd in 3m at bad right bend turn left & follow B&B signs
CHILD FACILITIES: Please telephone for details
Dating back to the 17th century and set in 55 acres of gardens and grounds, Somerton Court Country House offers a tranquil haven for guests wishing to escape the pressures of modern life. The comfortable bedrooms offer lovely views. Breakfast is served in the delightful dining room that overlooks the gardens.
ROOMS: 6 en suite (2 fmly) FACILITIES: TVB tea/coffee Riding NOTES: ✷ ⊗ Licensed Cen ht PARKING: 30

TAUNTON
Map 03 ST22

Babies Welcome | Family Rooms | Children's Dishes

◆◆◆◆ Blorenge House
57 Staple Grove Rd TA1 1DG
☎ 01823 283005 ◫ 01823 283005
e-mail: enquiries@blorengehouse.co.uk
Dir: M5 junct 25 towards cricket ground and Safeways on left. At traffic lights turn left, at 2nd lights turn right, Blorenge House is 150yds up on the left hand side

CHILD FACILITIES: Babysitting Food/bottle warming Ch portions Highchairs Safe grounds Cots Family rms 4 D rms with 1 S bed, 2 D rms with 2 S beds £65-£90 NEARBY: Tenpin bowling Cinema Activity centre

Conveniently situated within walking distance of the town centre, this fine old Victorian property offers spacious accommodation. The individually furnished bedrooms are well-equipped and some feature impressive four-poster beds. A bar-lounge, garden and outdoor swimming pool are available for guests, and evening meals are provided by prior arrangement.
ROOMS: 25 rms (20 en suite) (4 fmly) (3 GF) s fr £29; d fr £49 * ⊗ in 23 bedrooms FACILITIES: TVB tea/coffee TVL ✶ NOTES: ⊗ in restaurant Licensed Cen ht LB PARKING: 25

Babies Welcome | Children's Dishes

◉ Brazz
Castle Bow TA1 1NF
☎ 01823 252000 ◫ 01823 336066
e-mail: taunton@brazz.co.uk
web: www.brazz.co.uk
Dir: From M5 follow signs for Town Centre/Castle Hotel.

continued on p210

TAUNTON, continued

CHILD FACILITIES: Activities: colouring, puzzles Food/bottle warming Ch licence Ch portions Highchairs Safe grounds Changing facilities NEARBY: Vivary Park Cinema Swimming pools Museums

FOOD: Modern European **STYLE:** Modern **SEATS:** 100 **OPEN:** 12-11 **RESTAURANT:** main £7-£15.95 **NOTES:** ⊗ in restaurant, Air con **PARKING:** 35

WELLS   Map 03 ST54

Babies Welcome | **Family Rooms** | **Children's Dishes**

★★ 67% Crown at Wells
Market Place BA5 2RP
☎ 01749 673457 ▤ 01749 679792
e-mail: reception@crownatwells.co.uk
web: www.crownatwells.co.uk
Dir: in Market Place, follow signs for Hotels/Deliveries

CHILD FACILITIES: Activities: Easter egg hunt, colouring, bubbles, quiz Food/bottle warming Ch menu Ch portions Highchairs Ch discounts under 5s free Cots Family rms D rms with S beds from £100 Laundry NEARBY: Palace Park Cinema Walks Cathedral

Retaining its original features and period charm, this historic old inn is situated in the heart of Wells, just a short stroll from the cathedral. Bedrooms vary in size and style and have modern facilities. Public areas focus around Anton's, the popular bistro, with its bold paintings and relaxed atmosphere, and the Penn Bar, an alternative eating option.
ROOMS: 15 en suite (1 fmly) ⊗ in all bedrooms s £50-£80; d £80-£95 (incl. bkfst) **LB PARKING:** 15 **NOTES:** ⊗ in restaurant RS 25 Dec food not available in the evening

Babies Welcome | **Family Rooms** | **Children's Dishes**

◆◆◆◆ ❦ Double-Gate Farm
Godney BA5 1RX
☎ 01458 832217 ▤ 01458 835612
e-mail: doublegatefarm@aol.com
web: www.doublegatefarm.com
Dir: from Wells A39 towards Glastonbury, at Polsham turn right signed Godney/Polsham, approx 2m to x-roads, continue to farmhouse on left after Inn

CHILD FACILITIES: Activities: books, games Food/bottle warming Ch portions Highchairs Ch cutlery Ch discounts free in own cot, babies £5, 1-4s £10, 5-12s £17.50 Cots Family rms large D rm with B beds Ch drinks Fridge Laundry NEARBY: Play park Caves

Surrounded by the Somerset Levels and enjoying splendid views to the Mendips, this farm provides a warm and friendly welcome. Bedrooms are very attractively decorated and are most comfortable, with one room particularly well suited for the less

continued

mobile. Breakfast is served at two refectory style tables where guests can choose from an interesting and extensive menu.
ROOMS: 3 en suite 3 annexe en suite (1 fmly) (1 GF) s £35-£40; d £55-£60 * **FACILITIES:** TVB tea/coffee TVL Snooker Table tennis, darts 100 acres mixed **NOTES:** ✽ ⊗ Cen ht **PARKING:** 9

◆◆◆ Birdwood House
Birdwood, Bath Rd BA5 3EW
☎ 01749 679250
e-mail: s_crane_birdwood@hotmail.com
Dir: from town centre follow signs on one-way system to the Horringtons. Take B3139 for 1.5m, last house on left near double bend sign

CHILD FACILITIES: Please telephone for details

Set in extensive grounds and gardens just a short drive from the town centre, this imposing detached house dates back to the 1850s. The comfortable bedrooms are simply furnished with a number of extra facilities. A conservatory and lounge are also available to guests, while breakfast is taken in the pleasant dining room.
ROOMS: 4 rms (1 en suite) (1 fmly) **FACILITIES:** TVB tea/coffee TVL No coaches ⌂ **NOTES:** Credit cards not taken ✽ ⊗ Cen ht **PARKING:** 12

Babies Welcome | **Children's Dishes**

⌥ The Fountain Inn & Boxer's Restaurant
1 Saint Thomas St BA5 2UU
☎ 01749 672317 ▤ 01749 670825
e-mail: eat@fountaininn.co.uk
Dir: City centre, at junc of A371 & B3139. Follow signs for The Harringtons, The fountain Inn is is on junction of Tor Street & St Thomas Street

CHILD FACILITIES: Activities: kids packs Food/bottle warming Ch menu Ch portions Highchairs Changing facilities NEARBY: Wookey Hole Mendip Way walks Leisure centre Cinema Wells Cathedral

OPEN: 10.30-2.30 6-11 (Sun 12-3,7-10.30) Closed: 25-26 Dec **BAR MEALS:** L served all week 12-2.30 D served all week 6-10 Av main course £6.95 **RESTAURANT:** L served all week 12-2.30 D served all week 6-10 Av 3 course à la carte £16 Av 2 course fixed price £7.50 **FACILITIES:** ✽ **PARKING:** 24

WESTON-SUPER-MARE   Map 03 ST36

Babies Welcome | **Family Rooms** | **Children's Dishes**

★★★ 65% Beachlands
17 Uphill Rd North BS23 4NG
☎ 01934 621401 ▤ 01934 621966
e-mail: info@beachlandshotel.com
web: www.beachlandshotel.com
Dir: M5 junct 21, follow signs for Hospital. At Hospital rdbt follow signs for beach, hotel 300yds before beach

CHILD FACILITIES: Baby listening Activities: colouring Outdoor play area Food/bottle warming Ch menu Ch portions Highchairs Ch discounts £15 sharing with parents, 2nd child £5, babies free Safe grounds Videos Cots Family rms D rms with S beds Ch drinks Connecting rms Laundry NEARBY: Parks Sealife centre Longleat Caves Near sea

This popular hotel has the bonus of a 10-metre indoor pool and sauna. It is very close to the 18-hole links course and a short walk from the seafront. Elegant public areas include a bar, a choice of lounges and a bright dining room. Bedrooms vary slightly in size, but all are well-equipped.
ROOMS: 23 en suite (6 fmly) (11 GF) ⊗ in all bedrooms s £49.75-£72.50; d £79.50-£102.50 (incl. bkfst) **LB FACILITIES:** ⊠ Sauna **PARKING:** 28 **NOTES:** ✽ ⊗ in restaurant Closed 23 Dec-2 Jan

Babies Welcome | Family Rooms | Children's Dishes

★★★ 61% **Royal Hotel**
1 South Pde BS23 1JP
☎ 01934 423100 📠 01934 415135
e-mail: royalwsm@btopenworld.com

CHILD FACILITIES: Outdoor play area Family area Food/bottle warming Ch menu Ch portions Highchairs Ch discounts under 5s free, under 16s £6.95 sharing with parents Safe grounds Cots Family rms D rm with S bed & Z bed Fridge Laundry **NEARBY:** Cinema Leisure centre Park Seafront location

The Royal, which opened in 1810, was the first hotel in Weston and occupies a prime seafront position. Bedrooms are soundly appointed and include both four-poster and family rooms, many having sea views. Public areas include a choice of bars and the refurbished restaurant, offering a range of dishes to meet all tastes. Entertainment is provided during the season with a regular jazz slot on Sundays.

ROOMS: 37 en suite (5 fmly) ⊗ in 9 bedrooms s £56-£62; d £79-£83 (incl. bkfst) **FACILITIES:** STV ♫ **PARKING:** 152 **NOTES:** ⚞

Babies Welcome | Family Rooms | Children's Dishes

♦♦♦ **The Weston Bay Hotel**
2-4 Clevedon Rd BS23 1DG
☎ 01934 628903 📠 01934 417661
e-mail: westonbayhotel@btinternet.com
web: www.westonbayhotel.co.uk
Dir: exit M5 junct 21, 15 min to Weston Bay Hotel follow signs for seafront. Hotel opp the Sea life centre on the seafront.

CHILD FACILITIES: Baby listening Food/bottle warming Ch menu Ch portions Highchairs Ch cutlery Ch discounts Safe grounds Cots Family rms D rm with S beds Ch drinks **NEARBY:** Sea life centre Cave Seafront location

Located on the seafront, this family run hotel provides generally spacious well-equipped bedrooms, all of which have modern en suite facilities. The comfortable guest lounge and attractive breakfast room enjoy sea views. Packed lunches are available on request and guests have use of a small private car park.

ROOMS: 9 en suite (5 fmly) (1 GF) s £39-£49; d £54-£60 * ⊗ in 4 bedrooms **FACILITIES:** TVB tea/coffee TVL No coaches 🍽 Dinner Last d order 7.30pm **NOTES:** ⚞ ⊗ in restaurant Cen ht **LB** **PARKING:** 11

♦♦♦ **Goodrington**
23 Charlton Rd BS23 4HB
☎ 01934 623229
e-mail: vera.bishop@talk21.com
web: www.goodrington.info
Dir: from A370 follow signs to seafront. Left at end of beach lawns, then 3rd left and establishment 50yds on left

CHILD FACILITIES: Please telephone for details

Quietly tucked away in a residential area, the owners of this

continued

charming Victorian house make every effort to ensure guests enjoy their stay. Bedrooms are spacious and comfortably furnished, and there is also an attractive lounge. Families are especially welcome and this is an ideal base for holidays.
ROOMS: 3 rms (2 en suite) (1 fmly) s £20-£24; d £40-£48 *
FACILITIES: TVB tea/coffee TVL No coaches Dinner Last d order 24hr notice **NOTES:** Credit cards not taken ⚞ ⊗ Cen ht

♦♦♦ *Sarnia Hotel*
28 Upper Church Rd BS23 2DX
☎ 01934 629696 📠 01934 629696
e-mail: suefraser@bms-finance.co.uk
Dir: facing Grand Pier, turn right along seafront. Upper Church Rd 0.5m on right after Pavilion Bar. Hotel on right

CHILD FACILITIES: Please telephone for details

This friendly guesthouse is located close to the seafront and within easy walking distance of the town centre. The compact bedrooms are generally well furnished and equipped. A generous breakfast is served in the dining room and guests are welcome to use the lounge bar.

ROOMS: 8 rms (4 en suite) (2 GF) ⊗ **FACILITIES:** TVB tea/coffee **NOTES:** Credit cards not taken ⚞ ⊗ in restaurant Licensed Cen ht

---

WINCANTON   Map 03 ST72

▥ **Bull Inn**
Hardway, nr Bruton BA10 0LN
☎ 01749 812200

CHILD FACILITIES: Please telephone for details

OPEN: 11.30-2.30 6-11 **BAR MEALS:** L served all week 12-2 D served Mon-Sat 6-10 **RESTAURANT:** L served all week 12-2 D served Mon-Sat 7-9.30 **FACILITIES:** Garden: Beer garden with tables&chairs **PARKING:** 30

YEOVIL   Map 03 ST51

♦♦♦♦ ⊛ ⊜ ▥ *Helyar Arms*
Moor Ln, East Coker BA22 9JR
☎ 01935 862332 📠 01935 864129
e-mail: info@helyar-arms.co.uk
web: www.helyar-arms.co.uk
Dir: from A30 or A37 follow signs to East Coker, Pub 100mtrs from St Michaels Church

CHILD FACILITIES: Please telephone for details

Located in a picture book Somerset village close to Yeovil, this 15th-century inn has a first-rate reputation throughout the area. A wealth of beams and an inglenook fireplace add charm to the bar and restaurant. The menu features local beef and fish. Bedrooms are comfortably furnished, a couple are family rooms.

ROOMS: 6 en suite (3 fmly) ⊗ **FACILITIES:** TVB tea/coffee Direct dial from bedrooms Dinner Last d order 9.30pm **NOTES:** ⊗ in area of dining room Cen ht **PARKING:** 40

England

STAFFORDSHIRE

Ride at Alton Towers

ALTON
Alton Towers ST10 4DB
info@alton-towers.com ☎08705 204060
(signposted from M1 junct 23A, M6 junct 15, M1
junct 28 or M6 junct 16)
Open 12 Mar-30 Oct. *From £20 (ch fr £17).
Please telephone for price confirmation.

LICHFIELD
Lichfield Heritage Centre WS13 6LG
info@lichfieldheritage.org.uk ☎01543 256611
(situated on Market Sq in centre of city, easily
accessible from A38, A5 and A51)
Open all year, daily 10-5, Sun 10.30-5. Last
admission 4pm. (Closed Xmas & New Year)

STOKE-ON-TRENT
Ceramica ST6 3DS
info@ceramicauk.com ☎01782 832001
(exit M6 junct 15/16 take A500 leave at A4527
signposted Tunstall. After 0.5 mile turn right onto
B5051 for Burslem. Ceramica is in Old Town Hall.)
Open Mon, Wed-Sat 9.30-5, Sun 10.30-4.30.
*£3.75, (concessions £2.50, under 4's free). Family
ticket (2ad+2ch) £10.
Gladstone Working Pottery Museum ST3 1PQ
gladstone@stoke.gov.uk ☎01782 319232
(M6 junct 15, follow A500 to A50 then follow brown
heritage signs. From M1 follow A50 westbound
then follow brown signs)
Open all year, daily 10-5 (last admission
4pm).Limited opening Xmas & New Year.
*£4.95 (ch £3.50, students & pen £3.95). Family
ticket £14 (2 ad & 3 ch 4-16yrs).

TAMWORTH
Drayton Manor Theme Park & Zoo B78 3TW
info@draytonmanor.co.uk ☎01827 287979
(M42, junct 9, follow brown tourist signs on A409)
Park open end Mar-Oct. Rides from 10.30-5 or 6.
Zoo open all year. Telephone for details.
Tamworth Castle B79 7NA
heritage@tamworth.gov.uk ☎01827 709629
(from M42 junct 10 & M6 junct 12, access via A5)
Open mid Feb-Oct, Tue-Sun 12-5.15. Last
admission 4.30. Nov-mid Feb; Thu-Sun 12-5.15
last admission 4. Telephone to confirm opening
times before visiting. *£4.30 (ch £2.75). Family £13.
Prices subject to change.

CANNOCK Map 07 SJ91

★★★ 67% The Whitehouse Hotel & Restaurant
Marquis Dr, Penkridge Bank Rd WS12 4PR
☎ 01543 422712 ▤ 01543 422639
e-mail: info@thewhitehouse-hotel.co.uk
*Dir: Turn off A34 at rdbt with wooden wigwam, towards Rugeley through
Forest. Hotel approx 2m on right*
CHILD FACILITIES: Please telephone for details
This privately owned and personally run hotel is quietly situated in
the heart of Cannock Chase, only a short drive from Stafford and
the motorway network. Bedrooms are modern and well-equipped.
There is an attractive lounge bar and a pleasant restaurant where
a good selection of grill dishes is available.
ROOMS: 6 en suite ⊛ in 1 bedroom d £65-£125 (incl. bkfst) **LB**
PARKING: 80 **NOTES:** ✕ Closed 26-2 Jan

CAULDON Map 07 SK04

🍴 Yew Tree Inn
ST10 3EJ
☎ 01538 308348 ▤ 01782 212064
CHILD FACILITIES: Family area Food/bottle warming
NEARBY: Alton Towers Dove Dale Manifold Valley
OPEN: 10-2.30 6-11 (Sun 12-3, 7-10.30) **BAR MEALS:** L served Snacks
available during opening hours **FACILITIES: NOTES:** Credit cards not
taken **PARKING:** 50

CHEADLE Map 07 SJ88

Babies Welcome | Children's Dishes

⊛ Thornbury Hall
Lockwood Rd ST10 2DH
☎ 0158 750831 ▤ 750539
e-mail: info@thornburyhall.com
Dir: 7 miles from Stoke-on-Trent
CHILD FACILITIES: Outdoor play area Food/bottle warming
Ch menu Ch portions Highchairs Ch cutlery Safe grounds
NEARBY: Alton Towers Churnet Valley Railway Peak District
FOOD: British, Indian **STYLE:** Classic, Traditional **SEATS:** 60
OPEN: 12-2/6-10 **RESTAURANT:** Fixed L £9, Fixed D £10, main
£5.90-£12.99 **NOTES:** Smart Dress, ⊛ in restaurant, ⊛ area
PARKING: 80

FROGHALL Map 07 SK04

Babies Welcome | Family Rooms | Children's Dishes

♦♦♦ 🌱 Hermitage Working Farm
ST10 2HQ
☎ 01538 266515 ▤ 01538 266155
e-mail: wilma@hermitagefarm.co.uk
Dir: turn off A52 in Froghall onto B5053, farm 0.5m on left at top of hill
CHILD FACILITIES: Baby listening Activities: working farm, toys
Outdoor play area Family area Food/bottle warming Ch menu
Ch portions Highchairs Ch cutlery Ch discounts under 2s free
sharing with parents Safe grounds Cots Family rms D rm with S or
B beds £59-£84 Ch drinks Laundry Changing mats
NEARBY: Leisure centre Alton Towers Gullivers Kingdom Zoo

Parts of this charming old sandstone-built house date back to the
16th century. It is quietly located in an elevated position with
impressive panoramic views. There is traditionally furnished
accommodation in the main house as well as a recently converted

continued

barn, which offers rooms suitable for families. Handy for visiting Alton Towers.
ROOMS: 3 en suite 6 annexe en suite (3 fmly) (3 GF) d £43-£58 * ⊗
FACILITIES: TVB tea/coffee TVL Riding shooting 75 acres beef, sheep, poultry **NOTES:** ✦ ⊗ in restaurant ⊗ in 1 lounge Cen ht **LB**
PARKING: 12

STAFFORD
Map 07 SJ92

◆◆◆ *Bailey Hotel*
63 Lichfield Rd ST17 4LL
☎ 01785 214133 🖷 01785 227920
CHILD FACILITIES: Please telephone for details

Guests can be sure of a warm welcome at this friendly guest house, situated south of the town centre. Bedrooms are traditionally furnished and include a ground floor room for less mobile visitors. Dinner is served most evenings in the cosy dining room and residents have use of a TV lounge.
ROOMS: 10 en suite (1 fmly) (1 GF) ⊗ in 4 bedrooms
FACILITIES: TVB tea/coffee Direct dial from bedrooms TVL No coaches Dinner Last d order 4pm **NOTES:** Credit cards not taken ⊗ in restaurant Licensed Cen ht **PARKING:** 10

STOKE-ON-TRENT
Map 07 SJ84

Babies Welcome **Children's Dishes**

The Elms, Passion of India
Snowhill, Shelton ST1 4LY
☎ 01782 266360 🖷 265172
Dir: Telephone for directions
CHILD FACILITIES: Family area Food/bottle warming Ch licence Ch menu Highchairs Ch cutlery Safe grounds Changing facilities **NEARBY:** Alton Towers

FOOD: Indian **STYLE:** Traditional, Indian **SEATS:** 120 **OPEN:** 6-11.30, Closed 25 Dec, SunL Mon-Sat, D Sun **RESTAURANT:** Fixed D £15, main £6.75-£12.99 **NOTES:** Smart Dress, ⊗ in restaurant **PARKING:** 80

TAMWORTH
Map 07 SK20

◆◆◆◆ *Harlaston Post Office*
Main Rd, Harlaston B79 9JU
☎ 01827 383324 🖷 01827 383746
Dir: turn off M42/A42 at junct 11 onto B5453 to No Man's Heath, turn right for Clifton Campville & straight on for Haunton & Harlaston
CHILD FACILITIES: Please telephone for details

Part of the village stores and post office, this constantly improving, well-maintained guest house is located opposite the ancient church in this idyllic hamlet. The individually styled bedrooms provide a range of modern facilities in addition to thoughtful extras. Hearty cooked breakfasts can be enjoyed in the bright and comfortable dining room.
ROOMS: 4 en suite (1 fmly) (1 GF) **FACILITIES:** STV TVB tea/coffee Direct dial from bedrooms TVL No coaches **NOTES:** Credit cards not taken ✦ ⊗ Cen ht **PARKING:** 5

UTTOXETER
Map 07 SK03

◆◆◆ *Hillcrest*
3 Leighton Rd ST14 8BL
☎ 01889 564627 🖷 01889 564627
e-mail: mridge@hillcrest.fsnet.co.uk
Dir: follow Racecourse signs along A518 to B5017, right at mini-rdbt on B5017 400m, right Wood Leighton, right again Leighton Rd, end on right
CHILD FACILITIES: Please telephone for details
This long-established, friendly, family-run guesthouse is within easy reach of Alton Towers. Bedrooms are equipped with modern facilities and extras such as hairdryers and radios. Two rooms are available in the converted stables and one of these boasts disabled facilities. There is a spacious, comfortable lounge and an attractive dining room.
ROOMS: 7 en suite (5 fmly) **FACILITIES:** TVB tea/coffee TVL No coaches Dinner Last d order 2pm **NOTES:** ✦ ⊗ Licensed Cen ht **PARKING:** 12

SUFFOLK

Beach huts at Southwold

BUNGAY
Otter Trust
NR35 2AF ☎01986 893470 ▤01986 892461
(off A143, 1m W of Bungay)
Open Apr (or Good Fri if earlier) – Oct, daily 10.30-6.

EASTON
Easton Farm Park IP13 0EQ
easton@eastonfarmpark.co.uk ☎01728 746475
(signed from A12 at Wickam Market, and from A1120)
Open Mar-end Sep, daily 10.30-6. Also open Feb &
Oct half term hols.

FLIXTON
Norfolk & Suffolk Aviation Museum NR35 1NZ
nsam.flixton@virgin.net ☎01986 896644
(off A143, take B1062, 2m W of Bungay)
Open Apr-Oct, Sun-Thu 10-5 (last admission 4); Nov-
Mar Tue, Wed & Sun 10-4 (last admission 3) (Closed
late Dec-early Jan).

FRAMLINGHAM
Framlingham Castle
IP8 9BT ☎01728 724189
(on B1116)
Open all year, Apr-Sep, daily 10-6; Oct, daily 10-5;
Nov-Mar, daily 10-4. (Closed 24-26 Dec & 1 Jan).
*£4.20 (ch £2.10, concessions £3.20). Prices &
opening times relate to 2004, for further details phone
or log onto www.english-heritage.org.uk/visits

HORRINGER
Ickworth House, Park & Gardens
IP29 5QF ☎01284 735270 ▤01284 735175
ickworth@ntrust.org.uk
(2.5m S of Bury St Edmunds in the village of
Horringer on the A143)
Open: House 19 Mar-Oct, Mon, Tue, Fri, wknds & BH
Mons 1-5 (4.30 in Oct) last admission 4.30; Garden
open daily 19 Mar-Oct 10-5. Last admission 4.30.
Nov-22 Dec wkdays 10-4; Park daily 7-7.
*House, Garden & Park £6.40 (National Trust
members & ch under 5 free, ch £2.90) Garden & park
£2.95 (ch 85p). Discount for pre-booked parties.

LEISTON
Leiston Abbey
IP16 4TB ☎01728 831354 ▤01728 832500
mo@leistonabbey.fsnet.co.uk
(N of Leiston, off B1069)
Open any reasonable time

Long Shop Steam Museum
IP16 4ES ☎01728 832189 ▤01728 832189
longshop@care4free.net
(Turn off A12, follow B1119 from Saxmundham to
Leiston. Museum is in the middle of town)
Open Apr-Oct, Mon-Sat 10-5, Sun 11-5.

LONG MELFORD
Kentwell Hall CO10 9BA
info@kentwell.co.uk ☎01787 310207
(signposted off A134, between Bury St Edmunds &
Sudbury) Open: Gardens & Farm Sun during Mar,
Apr-Jun. House, Gardens & Farm 14 Jul-early Sep
daily; Oct, Sun only. Also open BHs wknds & school
hols. Historical recreations on selected wknds
throughout year.

LOWESTOFT
East Anglia Transport Museum NR33 8BL
enquiries@eatm.org.uk ☎01502 518459
(3m SW of Lowestoft, follow brown signs from A12,
A146 & B1384)
Open Good Fri & Etr Sat 2-4, Etr Sun-Etr Mon 11-5.
May-Sep, Sun & BHs 11-5; Wed & Sat 2-5 (last entry
1 hour before closing).
*£5 (ch 5-15 & pen £3.50). Price includes rides.

New Pleasurewood Hills
NR32 5DZ ☎01502 586000
info@pleasurewoodhills.co.uk
(Off A12 at Lowestoft)
Open Apr-Oct & Xmas. Telephone for details

STOWMARKET
Museum of East Anglian Life
IP14 1DL ☎01449 612229 ▤01449 672307
meal@meal.fsnet.co.uk
(located in centre of Stowmarket opposite ASDA
Supermarket & is signposted from A14 & B1115).
Open Apr-Oct.

SUFFOLK
Wildlife Park
NR33 7TF ☎01502 740291
(25min S of Gt. Yarmouth, just S of Lowestoft off the
A12) Open all year, daily from 10am. (Closed 25-26
Dec).

WESTLETON
RSPB Nature Reserve Minsmere
IP17 3BY ☎01728 648281 ▤01728 648770
minsmere@rspb.org.uk
(signposted from A12 at Yoxford & Blythburgh and
from Westleton Village.
Open daily (ex closed Tue) 9-9 (or dusk if earlier).
Visitor centre open 9-5 (Nov-Jan 9-4). (Closed 25-26
Dec).
*£5 (ch £1.50, concessions £3). Family ticket £10.
RSPB members free.

WEST STOW
West Stow Anglo Saxon Village IP28 6HG
weststow@stedsbc.gov.uk ☎01284 728718
(off A1101, follow brown heritage signs located 7m
North West of Bury St Edmunds)
Open all year, daily 10-5. Last entry 4pm (3.30 in
Winter) *£5 (ch £4). Family ticket £15. (prices subject
to changes for special events)

ALDEBURGH Map 05 TM45

🏮 Regatta Restaurant
171 High St IP15 5AN
☎ 01728 452011 ◈ 01728 453324
e-mail: regatta.restaurant@aldeburgh.sagegost.co.uk
Dir: Middle of High Street, town centre.

| CHILD FACILITIES: | Please telephone for details |

FOOD: Eclectic **STYLE:** Bistro **SEATS:** 90 **OPEN:** 12-2.30/6-10, Closed Restricted opening in winter, Mon,Tue,Sun evening (Nov-Mar), D Sun **RESTAURANT:** Fixed L £9, Fixed D £12, main £7.50-£18 **NOTES:** ⊗ area, Air con

BURY ST EDMUNDS Map 05 TL86

Babies Welcome | Family Rooms | Children's Dishes

★★★ 75% 🏮 ♨ Ravenwood Hall
Rougham IP30 9JA
☎ 01359 270345 ◈ 01359 270788
e-mail: enquiries@ravenwoodhall.co.uk
Dir: 3m E off A14

CHILD FACILITIES: Baby listening **Activities:** Easter egg hunt, animal feeding, colouring, books, toys, puzzles Outdoor play area Food/bottle warming Ch menu Ch portions Highchairs Ch discounts babies in own cot free Safe grounds Cots Family rms rm with extra S beds £20 per bed Laundry **NEARBY:** Gardens Cinema Leisure centre Museum Saxon village Theatre

Delightful 15th-century property set in seven acres of woodland and landscaped gardens. The building has many original features including carved timbers and inglenook fireplaces. The spacious bedrooms are attractively decorated, tastefully furnished with well-chosen pieces and equipped with many thoughtful touches. Public rooms include an elegant restaurant and a smart lounge bar with an open fire.

ROOMS: 7 en suite 7 annexe en suite (5 GF) ⊗ in all bedrooms s £81-£109; d £106-£149 (incl. bkfst) **LB FACILITIES:** ↳ Riding ⌂ Shooting & fishing Xmas **PARKING:** 150 **NOTES:** ⊗ in restaurant

◆◆◆ Hamilton House
4 Nelson Rd IP33 3AG
☎ 01284 703022 07787 146553 ◈ 01284 703022
Dir: exit A14 onto A1302. follow road for 1m, across rdbt, right after Lloyds Bank. establishment on left

| CHILD FACILITIES: | Please telephone for details |

Expect a warm welcome at this relaxing Edwardian villa, which is situated in a quiet side road just a short walk from the town centre. The spacious bedrooms are brightly decorated and have a good range of facilities. Breakfast is taken at a communal table in the dining room.

ROOMS: 4 rms (2 en suite) (1 fmly) s £22-£25; d £48 *
FACILITIES: TVB tea/coffee No coaches **NOTES:** Credit cards not taken ⊗ Cen ht

DUNWICH Map 05 TM47

Babies Welcome | Children's Dishes

🍺 The Ship Inn
St James St IP17 3DT
☎ 01728 648219 ◈ 01728 648675
e-mail: shipinn@tiscali.co.uk
Dir: N on A12 from Ipswich thru Yoxford, R signed Dunwich

CHILD FACILITIES: Outdoor play area Family area Food/bottle warming Ch menu Ch portions Highchairs **NEARBY:** Parks Walks Leisure centre Cinema

continued

OPEN: 11-11 Sun 12-10.30 **BAR MEALS:** L served all week 12-3 D served all week 6-9.00 Av main course £6.85 **RESTAURANT:** L served all week 12-3 D served all week 7-9.00 **FACILITIES:** Garden: Large terraced area **PARKING:** 10

ELMSWELL Map 05 TL96

Babies Welcome | Family Rooms | Children's Dishes

◆◆◆ Kiln Farm
Kiln Ln IP30 9QR
☎ 01359 240442 & 242604
e-mail: paul-jacky@kilnfarm.fsnet..co.uk
Dir: 1m from junct 47 (Ixworth turnoff) of the A14

CHILD FACILITIES: Baby listening **Activities:** puzzles, toys, bike hire Outdoor play area Food/bottle warming Ch menu Ch portions Highchairs Ch cutlery Ch discounts under 3s free Safe grounds Cots (charge) Family rms D rms with sofa & S beds £55-£65 Ch drinks Laundry **NEARBY:** Walks

Delightful Victorian farmhouse set in a peaceful rural location amid three acres of landscaped grounds with lovely views. Bedrooms are housed in a converted barn; each is pleasantly decorated and furnished in country style. Breakfast is served in the open plan dining room/bar and guests have the use of a cosy lounge.

ROOMS: 3 en suite 4 annexe en suite (1 fmly) (4 GF) s £25-£30; d £48-£55 * ⊗ **FACILITIES:** TV4B tea/coffee No coaches Dinner Last d order 9pm **NOTES:** ⊗ in area of dining room ⊗ in 1 lounge Licensed Cen ht **PARKING:** 10

EYE Map 05 TM17

Babies Welcome | Children's Dishes

🍺 The White Horse Inn ◆◆◆◆
Stoke Ash IP23 7ET
☎ 01379 678222 ◈ 01379 678557
e-mail: mail@whitehorse-suffolk.co.uk
web: www.whitehorse-suffolk.co.uk
Dir: On the main A140 between Ipswich & Norwich

CHILD FACILITIES: **Activities:** colouring, toys Food/bottle warming Ch licence Ch menu Ch portions Highchairs Ch cutlery **NEARBY:** Park Swimming pool Walks

OPEN: 11-11 (Sun 11-10.30) **BAR MEALS:** L served all week 11-9.30 D served all week 11-9.30 Av main course £8 **RESTAURANT:** L served all week 11-9.30 D served all week 11-9.30 Av 3 course à la carte £14.50 **FACILITIES:** Children's licence Garden: Patio & grass area 🎯 **ROOMS:** 7 bedrooms 7 en suite 1 family rooms s£42.50 d£57.50 **PARKING:** 60

HORRINGER Map 05 TL86

Children's Dishes

🍺 Beehive
The Street IP29 5SN
☎ 01284 735260 ◈ 01638 730416
Dir: From A14, 1st turning for Bury St Edmunds, sign for Westley & Ickworth Park

CHILD FACILITIES: Outdoor play area Food/bottle warming Ch menu Ch portions Safe grounds **NEARBY:** Ickworth House, Park and Gardens

OPEN: 11.30-2.30 7-11 Closed: Dec 25-26 **BAR MEALS:** L served all week 12-2 D served Mon-Sat 7-9.45 **RESTAURANT:** L served all week 12-2 D served all week 7-9.45 Av 3 course à la carte £18 **FACILITIES:** Garden: Patio, picnic benches, walled garden 🎯 **PARKING:** 30

England

HOXNE
Map 05 TM17

Babies Welcome | Children's Dishes

🍺 The Swan
Low St IP21 5AS
☎ 01379 668275
e-mail: hoxneswan@supanet.com

CHILD FACILITIES: Food/bottle warming Ch portions Highchairs Safe grounds **NEARBY:** Walks Bressingham Steam Museum & Gardens

OPEN: 11.30-3 (Sun 12-10.30) 6-11 **BAR MEALS:** L served all week 12-2.30 D served all week 7-9.30 Av main course £9 **RESTAURANT:** L served all week 12-2.30 D served all week 7-9.30 Av 3 course à la carte £17.50 **FACILITIES:** Garden: Riverside at rear of Pub; 25 acre lawn & trees **PARKING:** 40

IPSWICH
Map 05 TM14

Babies Welcome | Family Rooms | Children's Dishes

★★★ 71%
Courtyard by Marriott Ipswich

COURTYARD

The Havens, Ransomes Europark IP3 9SJ
☎ 01473 272244 ▤ 01473 272484
e-mail: reservations.ipswich@whitbread.com
Dir: off A14 Ipswich Bypass at 1st junct after Orwell Bridge signed Ransomes Europark. Hotel faces slip road

CHILD FACILITIES: Food/bottle warming Ch menu Ch portions Highchairs Ch discounts Safe grounds Cots Family rms D rms with extra beds from £72 Laundry **NEARBY:** Extensive leisure facilities

Conveniently situated within easy striking distance of the town centre and major road networks, this modern and well-maintained hotel offers stylish accommodation with attractive, spacious bedrooms. The open plan public rooms include a restaurant and bar. Guests also have the use of a small fitness studio.
ROOMS: 60 en suite (28 fmly) (30 GF) ⊗ in 44 bedrooms s £52-£96; d £72-£105 (incl. bkfst) **LB FACILITIES:** STV Gym Guests may use nearby leisure club at special rate **PARKING:** 150 **NOTES:** ✈

LAVENHAM
Map 05 TL94

Babies Welcome | Family Rooms | Children's Dishes

Lavenham Great House Hotel
Market Place CO10 9QZ
☎ 01787 247431 ▤ 01787 248007
e-mail: greathouse@clara.co.uk
web: www.greathouse.co.uk
Dir: from A1141 into Market Ln, hotel just behind cross

continued

CHILD FACILITIES: Baby listening Babysitting Outdoor play area Food/bottle warming Ch portions Highchairs Ch cutlery Ch discounts under 2s free, 3-12s £15, 13+ £20 Cots Family rms rm with 2 D beds, D rm with D bed & sofa bed from £96 Connecting rms Laundry

Essentially, this establishment is a restaurant with rooms housed in an 18th-century Tudor building overlooking the market place. The restaurant is like a little pocket of France and offers high-quality rural cuisine served by French staff. The spacious bedrooms are individually decorated and thoughtfully equipped with many useful extras; some rooms have a separate lounge area.
ROOMS: 5 en suite (2 fmly) s £65-£98; d £76-£150 * ⊗
FACILITIES: TVB tea/coffee Direct dial from bedrooms No coaches Dinner Last d order 9.30pm **NOTES:** ⊗ in restaurant Licensed Cen ht **LB**

LONG MELFORD
Map 05 TL84

Babies Welcome | Family Rooms | Children's Dishes

★★★ 75% 🍴 The Black Lion
Church Walk, The Green CO10 9DN
☎ 01787 312356 ▤ 01787 374557
e-mail: enquiries@blacklionhotel.net
Dir: at junct of A134/A1092, overlooking the green

CHILD FACILITIES: Baby listening Activities: rocking horse, toys, books, puzzles, colouring Food/bottle warming Ch menu Ch portions Highchairs Ch cutlery babies free in own cots Safe grounds Cots Family rms suite - adjoining rooms from £120 Laundry **NEARBY:** Tudor re-enactment Rare breeds farm Gardens

This charming 15th-century hotel is situated on the edge of this bustling town overlooking the green. Bedrooms are generally spacious and each is attractively decorated, tastefully furnished and equipped with useful extras. An interesting range of dishes is served in the lounge bar or guests may choose to dine in the more formal restaurant.
ROOMS: 10 en suite (3 fmly) ⊗ in all bedrooms s £85-£109; d £106-£146 (incl. bkfst) **LB FACILITIES:** Board games Xmas
PARKING: 10 **NOTES:** ⊗ in restaurant

LOWESTOFT
Map 05 TM59

Babies Welcome | Family Rooms | Children's Dishes

◆◆◆◆ Albany Hotel
400 London Rd South NR33 0BQ
☎ 01502 574394 ▤ 01502 581198
e-mail: geoffrey.ward@btclick.com
web: www.albanyhotel-lowesoft.co.uk
Dir: on A12 to Lowestoft from S. Hotel on right just after entering one-way system from Pakefield

CHILD FACILITIES: Baby listening Activities: colouring, jigsaws, board games, toys Food/bottle warming Ch menu Ch portions Highchairs Ch cutlery Ch discounts under 3s free sharing with parents Safe grounds Videos Cots Family rms D rm with 2 S beds £60-£80 Laundry **NEARBY:** Theme park Cinema Wildlife park Mini golf 3-min walk to sea

Expect a warm welcome at this delightful privately owned hotel, which is situated just a short walk from the beach and town centre. The attractively decorated bedrooms are tastefully furnished and have a good range of useful extras. Public rooms feature a smartly appointed lounge with a corner bar and a smart dining room.
ROOMS: 8 rms (6 en suite) (3 fmly) s £22.50-£29.50; d £48-£60 * ⊗
FACILITIES: TVB tea/coffee TVL No coaches Dinner Last d order 2pm
NOTES: ⊗ in restaurant Licensed Cen ht **LB PARKING:** 1

♦♦♦ Coventry House
8 Kirkley Cliff NR33 0BY
☎ 01502 573865 📠 01502 573865
Dir: 0.25m from harbour bridge on southbound A12 (seafront). On right opp Claremont pier

CHILD FACILITIES: Food/bottle warming Ch menu Ch portions Highchairs Ch discounts under 12s half price Safe grounds Cots Family rms D rm with 2 S beds **NEARBY:** Adventure park Seafront location

Expect a warm welcome at this impressive Victorian terrace house, which is situated opposite the pier and seafront. The pleasantly decorated bedrooms are comfortably furnished and thoughtfully equipped; many rooms have lovely sea views. Breakfast and dinner are served in the tastefully appointed dining room and guests also have the use of a comfortable lounge.
ROOMS: 7 rms (5 en suite) (3 fmly) (1 GF) s £20-£27; d £45-£50 * ⊗ in 3 bedrooms **FACILITIES:** TVB tea/coffee TVL No coaches Dinner Last d order breakfast **NOTES:** Credit cards not taken ⊗ in restaurant Cen ht **LB** **PARKING:** 4

SNAPE   Map 05 TM35

⚓ Plough & Sail
Snape Maltings IP17 1SR
☎ 01728 688413 📠 01728 688930
e-mail: enquiries@snapemaltings.co.uk
web: www.snapemaltings.co.uk

CHILD FACILITIES: Activities: word searches, colouring Food/bottle warming Ch licence Ch menu Ch portions Highchairs Ch cutlery Safe grounds Changing facilities **NEARBY:** Easton Farm Park Near sea

OPEN: 11-3 (summer 11-11) 5.30-11 **BAR MEALS:** L served all week 12-2.30 D served all week 7-9 Av main course £6 **RESTAURANT:** L served all week 12-2.30 D served all week 7-9 Av 3 course à la carte £21
FACILITIES: Garden: Enclosed courtyard, paved garden area
PARKING: 100

SUDBURY   Map 05 TL85

♦♦♦ Old Bull Hotel & Restaurant
Church St CO10 2BL
☎ 01787 374120 📠 01787 379044
web: www.theoldbullhotel.co.uk
Dir: on A131 Halstead Rd. 0.25m from town centre
CHILD FACILITIES: Please telephone for details
This 16th-century coaching inn is situated within easy walking distance of the town centre. Bedrooms are pleasantly decorated and equipped with many thoughtful extras. Public rooms include a
continued

---

residents' lounge with plush furnishings and a cosy bar, as well as a smart restaurant.

ROOMS: 7 en suite 3 annexe en suite (4 fmly) ⊗ in 3 bedrooms **FACILITIES:** TVB tea/coffee Direct dial from bedrooms TVL No coaches Dinner Last d order 8.45pm **NOTES:** ⊗ in restaurant ⊗ in 1 lounge Licensed Cen ht **PARKING:** 15

WHEPSTEAD   Map 05 TL85

♦♦♦♦ Folly House Bed & Breakfast
Folly Ln IP29 4TJ
☎ 01284 735207 📠 01284 735207
e-mail: lowerlinda@hotmail.com
Dir: B1066 turn left after post box into Rectory Rd in 1.5m at T junct turn right, turn into Folly Lane

CHILD FACILITIES: Nanny Babysitting Activities: swimming pool, toys, Lego, cards, board games Food/bottle warming Ch menu Ch portions Highchairs Ch cutlery Videos Cots Family rms D rm with 2 S beds from £75 Ch drinks Fridge Laundry Changing mats **NEARBY:** Ickworth House Saxon village Abbey gardens

This former alehouse dates back to the 1830s and is set amid its own landscaped grounds in a peaceful rural location. Breakfast is served in the elegant dining room and guests have the use of a bright conservatory lounge as well as an indoor swimming pool.
ROOMS: 3 rms (1 en suite) (1 fmly) s £30-£35; d £44-£50 *
FACILITIES: TVB tea/coffee TVL No coaches 🚫 ⏰ Dinner Last d order 9am **NOTES:** Credit cards not taken ✖ ⊗ Cen ht **PARKING:** 10

WOODBRIDGE   Map 05 TM24

⊛ ⊛ Captain's Table
3 Quay St IP12 1BX
☎ 01394 383145 📠 01394 388508
Dir: From A12, (Garden centre on left). Quay St is opposite rail station & theatre, restaurant 100 yds on L.

CHILD FACILITIES: Activities: colouring Food/bottle warming Ch menu Ch portions Highchairs Ch cutlery **NEARBY:** Elmhurst Park River walks Cinema Swimming pool Mini boat lake

FOOD: Modern International **STYLE:** Bistro **SEATS:** 50
OPEN: 12-2.30/6.30-10.00, Closed 2 wks Jan, Mon (ex BHs), D Sun (ex BHs) **RESTAURANT:** main £6.95-£15.50 **NOTES:** ⊗ in restaurant
PARKING: 4

This symbol indicates family rooms are available, with type of room and prices included if provided

England

SURREY

Countryside and River Thames at Richmond

CHERTSEY
Thorpe Park
KT16 8PN   ☎0870 444 4466
(M25 junct 11 or 13 and follow signs via A320 to
Thorpe Park)
Open from 5 Apr-2 Nov (ex some off-peak days)
9/10-5/6 (times vary), 7.30pm from 25 Jul-7 Sep,
until 8pm on fireworks night & from noon-11 on Fri
nights.
FARNHAM
Birdworld & Underwaterworld GU10 4LD
bookings@birdworld.co.uk   ☎01420 22140
(3m S of Farnham on A325).
Open daily, 10-6 (summer), 10-4.30 (winter).
GODSTONE
Godstone Farm RH9 8LX
havefun@godstonefarm.co.uk   ☎01883 742546
(M25 junct 6, south of village, signposted).
Open Mar-Oct, 10-6 (last admission 5); Nov-Feb
10-5 (last admission 4). Closed 25 & 26 Dec.
*Contact for admission prices.
GUILDFORD
Dapdune Wharf GU1 4RR
riverwey@nationaltrust.org.uk   ☎01483 561389
(Off Woodbridge Rd to rear of Surrey County
Cricket Ground)
Open Apr-Oct, Thu-Mon 11-5. River trips Thu-Mon
11-5 (conditions permitting). *£2.50 (ch £1.50).
Family ticket £6.50. National Trust Members Free.
TILFORD
Rural Life Centre
GU10 2DL   ☎01252 795571
rural.life@lineone.net
(Off A287, 3m S of Farnham, signposted) Open
late Mar-early Oct, Wed-Sun & BH 10-5; Winter
Wed & Sun only 11-4. *£5 (ch £3 & pen £4).
Family ticket £14 (2ad & 2ch).
WEYBRIDGE
Brooklands Museum
KT13 0QN   ☎01932 857381
info@brooklandsmuseum.com
(M25 junct 10/11, museum off B374).
Open Tue-Sun & BHs 10-5 (4pm in winter).

BAGSHOT   Map 04 SU96

Babies Welcome	Children's Dishes

★★★★★ ◉ ◉ ◉
Pennyhill Park Hotel & The Spa
London Rd GU19 5EU   **ExclusivE**
☎ 01276 471774 📠 01276 473217   HOTELS & GOLF CLUBS
e-mail: enquiries@pennyhillpark.co.uk
web: www.exclusivehotels.co.uk
Dir: on A30 between Bagshot & Camberley opposite Texaco garage

> **CHILD FACILITIES:** Nanny (by prior request) Babysitting
> **Activities:** swimming pool, colouring, puzzles, board games (by prior
> request) Food/bottle warming Ch menu Ch portions Highchairs
> Ch discounts under 5s free Safe grounds Videos interconnecting
> rooms Connecting rms Fridge Laundry **NEARBY:** Legoland
> Windsor Castle

This delightful country house hotel set in 120 acres of grounds
provides every modern comfort. Bedrooms are individually
designed and stylish and have impressive bathrooms. The award
winning Latymer Restaurant is among the range of dining options
and there is a choice of lounges and bars. Leisure facilities include
a jogging trail, a golf course and a new state-of-the-art spa with a
thermal sequencing experience, ozone treated swimming and
hydrotherapy pools along with a comprehensive range of
therapies and treatments.
ROOMS: 26 en suite 97 annexe en suite (6 fmly) (26 GF) ⊛ in 20
bedrooms s £211.50-£646.25; d £229-£646.25 **LB** **FACILITIES:** Spa STV
🖼 ⚲ Golf 9 ⚲ Fishing Snooker Sauna Gym 🎱 Jacuzzi Archery, Clay
pigeon shooting, Plunge pool, Turkish Steam Rm, Volleyball, 🎵 Xmas
PARKING: 500 **NOTES:** ⊛ in restaurant

BRAMLEY   Map 04 TQ04

Babies Welcome	Children's Dishes

Jolly Farmer Inn
High St GU5 0HB
☎ 01483 893355 📠 01483 890484
e-mail: enquiries@jollyfarmer.co.uk
Dir: Onto A3, then A281, Bramley 3m S of Guildford

> **CHILD FACILITIES:** Food/bottle warming Ch menu Ch portions
> Highchairs

OPEN: 11-3 6-11 (Sun 12-3, 7-10.30) **BAR MEALS:** L served all week 12-2
D served all week 6.30-10 Av main course £12 **FACILITIES:** Garden: Large
patio at front and rear **PARKING:** 22

CHIDDINGFOLD   Map 04 SU93

The Swan Inn & Restaurant
Petworth Rd GU8 4TY
☎ 01428 682073 📠 01428 683259
web: www.swaninnandrestaurant.co.uk

> **CHILD FACILITIES:** Please telephone for details

OPEN: 11-3 5.30-11 (Sat 11-11, Sun 12-10.30) **BAR MEALS:** L served all
week 12-2.30 D served all week 6.30-10 Av main course £8
RESTAURANT: L served all week 12-2.30 D served all week 6.30-10 Av 3
course à la carte £20 **FACILITIES:** Garden: Terraced sun trap
PARKING: 25

> Many proprietors are happy to
> provide extra facilities for children,
> but let them know in advance what
> you need so they can be prepared

ELSTEAD   Map 04 SU94

Children's Dishes

🍴 The Woolpack

The Green GU8 6HD
☎ 01252 703106 🗎 01252 703497
Dir: Milford exit off A3. Take the B3001 towards Farnham. Pub on village green in Elstead, about 3 miles from the A3

CHILD FACILITIES: Outdoor play area Family area Food/bottle warming Ch menu Ch portions Safe grounds Changing facilities **NEARBY:** Walks

OPEN: 11-3.00 5.30-11 (Sat 11-11, Sun 12-10.30) **BAR MEALS:** L served all week 12-2 D served all week 7-9.45 Av main course £8.95 **RESTAURANT:** L served all week 12-2 D served all week 7-9.45 **FACILITIES:** Garden: Walled garden at rear **PARKING:** 15

FARNHAM   Map 04 SU84

Children's Dishes

🍴 The Bat & Ball Freehouse

15 Bat & Ball Ln, Boundstone GU10 4SA
☎ 01252 792108 🗎 01252 794564
e-mail: info@thebatandballfarnham.co.uk
Dir: Follow signs to Bird World from Coxbridge Rdbt on A3. Turn Left before Cricketers PH into School Lane. At top cross over staggered Xroad into Sandrock Hill. After 0.25m left into Upper Bourne Lane, follow signs.

CHILD FACILITIES: Activities: games Outdoor play area Family area Food/bottle warming Ch menu Ch portions Safe grounds Changing facilities **NEARBY:** Birdworld Walks Alice Holt Forest Bourne Woods Frensham Ponds

OPEN: 11-3 5.30-11 all day Fri-Sun **BAR MEALS:** L served all week 12-2.15 D served all week 7-9.30 Av main course £7.95 **RESTAURANT:** L served all week 12-2.15 D served all week 7-9.30 **FACILITIES:** Garden: Patio area, seating, suntrap **PARKING:** 40

NEWDIGATE   Map 04 TQ14

Babies Welcome | Children's Dishes

🍴 The Surrey Oaks

Parkgate Rd RH5 5DZ
☎ 01306 631200 🗎 01306 631200
Dir: turn off either A24 or A25 and follow signs to Newdigate, The Surrey Oaks is 1m E of Newdigate Village on the road towards Leigh/Charwood

CHILD FACILITIES: Activities: colouring, swings, slide Outdoor play area Food/bottle warming Ch menu Ch portions Highchairs Safe grounds Changing facilities **NEARBY:** Walks

OPEN: 11.30-2.30 (Sat 11.30-3, 6-11) 5.30-11 (Sun 12-3, 7-10.30) **BAR MEALS:** L served all week 12-2 D served Tue-Sat 7-9 Av main course £8.50 **RESTAURANT:** L served all week 12-2 D served Tue-Sat 7-9 Av 3 course à la carte £15 **FACILITIES:** Garden: Large. Child area, pond, aviary, goat paddock **PARKING:** 75

OCKLEY   Map 04 TQ14

Babies Welcome | Children's Dishes

Bryce's Seafood Restaurant

The Old School House RH5 5TH
☎ 01306 627430 🗎 01306 628274
e-mail: bryces.fish@virgin.net
Dir: From M25 J9 take A24, then A29. 8m S of Dorking on A29

CHILD FACILITIES: Food/bottle warming Ch portions Highchairs Safe grounds **NEARBY:** Walks Pond

continued

FOOD: British, Seafood **STYLE:** Traditional **SEATS:** 50
OPEN: 12-2.30/7-9.30, Closed 25 Dec, 1Jan, D Sun in Nov, Jan & Feb
RESTAURANT: NOTES: ✍ in restaurant **PARKING:** 35

REDHILL   Map 04 TQ25

Children's Dishes

🍴 William IV Country Pub

Little Common Ln, Bletchingly RH1 4QF
☎ 01883 743278
Dir: from M25 J6 take A25 towards Redhill. Turn R at top of Bletchingly High Street

CHILD FACILITIES: Activities: colouring Food/bottle warming Ch menu Ch portions Safe grounds **NEARBY:** Godstone Farm

OPEN: 12-3 6-11 (Sun noon until 10.30) Closed: 25-26 Dec eve **BAR MEALS:** L served all week 12-2.15 D served all week 6.45-9.30 Av main course £7.50 **RESTAURANT:** L served all week 12-2.15 D served all week 6.45-9.30 **FACILITIES:** Garden: Large 2 tier garden, enclosed fence & gates **PARKING:** 10

SOUTH GODSTONE   Map 05 TQ34

Children's Dishes

🍴 Fox & Hounds

Tilbarstow Hill Rd RH9 8LY
☎ 01342 893474 🗎 894503

CHILD FACILITIES: Food/bottle warming Ch portions Safe grounds **NEARBY:** Walks Childrens farm

OPEN: 12-3.30 6-11 (Sun 12-3.30, 7-11) **BAR MEALS:** L served all week 12-2.30 D served all week 7-9.30 Av main course £12 **RESTAURANT:** L served all week 12-2.30 D served all week 7-9.30 Av 3 course à la carte £15 **FACILITIES:** Garden: Large garden **PARKING:** 20

STAINES   Map 04 TQ07

Babies Welcome | Children's Dishes

🍴 The Swan Hotel

The Hythe TW18 3JB
☎ 01784 452494 🗎 01784 461593
e-mail: swan.hotel@fullers.co.uk
Dir: Just off A308, S of Staines Bridge. Minutes from M25, M4 & M3. 5m from Heathrow

CHILD FACILITIES: Food/bottle warming Ch menu Highchairs **NEARBY:** Thorpe Park Cinema Leisure centre Runnymede

OPEN: 11-11 25 Dec 12-3, Sun 12-10.30 **BAR MEALS:** L served all week 12-6 D served all week 6-9.30 Av main course £7.50 **RESTAURANT:** L served all week 12-6 D served all week 6-9.30 **FACILITIES:** Garden: Patio with seating. Overlooks River Thames

WEST CLANDON   Map 04 TQ05

Babies Welcome | Children's Dishes

🍴 Onslow Arms

The Street GU4 7TE
☎ 01483 222447 🗎 01483 211126
e-mail: onslowarms@massivepub.com
Dir: A3 then A247

CHILD FACILITIES: Food/bottle warming Ch portions Highchairs Safe grounds **NEARBY:** Park

OPEN: 11 -11 (Sun 12-10.30) **BAR MEALS:** L served all week 12-2.30 D served all week 7-10 Av main course £7 **RESTAURANT:** L served all week 12.30-2.30 D served all week 7-10 Av 3 course à la carte £30 Av 3 course fixed price £14.50 **FACILITIES:** Garden: Patio, garden, alcove seating **PARKING:** 200

SUSSEX

The Royal Pavilion, Brighton

EAST SUSSEX
ALFRISTON
Drusilla's Park BN26 5QS
info@drusillas.co.uk ☎01323 874100
(Off A27 near Alfriston between Brighton &
Eastbourne)
Open all year, daily 10-6 winter 10-5. Closed 24-26
Dec. *Family super saver tickets: Family of 3
£27.45, family of 4 £36.45, family of 5 £44.95.

BATTLE
Buckleys Yesterday's World TN33 0AQ
info@yesterdaysworld.co.uk ☎01424 775378
(A21 onto A2100 towards Battle, opposite Abbey)
Open all year, winter, daily 10-5; summer, daily 10-
6. Closed 25-26 Dec & 1Jan.
*£4.99 ch £3.75, pen & students £4.75. Family
ticket £16.75. Discount for special needs visitors &
groups of 15+.

BRIGHTON
Museum & Art Gallery
BN1 1EE ☎01273 290900
(A23/M23 from London. Near seafront. New
entrance in the Royal Pavilion Gardens)
Open all year, Tue 10-7, Wed-Sat 10-5 & Sun 2-5.
Closed Mon ex BHs.
Royal Pavilion
BN1 1EE ☎01273 290900
visitor.services@brighton-hove.gov.uk
(M23/A23 from London, situated in centre near
seafront. 15 min walk from train station)
Open all year, Apr-Sep, daily 9.30-5.45, last
admission 5. Oct-May, daily 10-5.15, last
admission 4.30.
*£5.95 ch £3.50, concessions £4.20. Family ticket
£9.20-£15. Groups 20+.£4.95 each.
Sea Life Centre
BN2 1TB ☎01273 604234
slcbrighton@merlinentertainments.biz
(Situated next to Brighton Pier, between Marine
Parade and Madeira Drive).
Open all year, daily ex 25 Dec, 10-6. Last
admission 5. Open later on wknds in summer &
school holidays

EASTBOURNE
***How We Lived Then Museum of Shops & Social
History***
BN21 4NS ☎01323 737143
howwelivedthen@btconnect.com
(Just off seafront, between town centre & theatres)
Open daily all year, 10-5.30 last entry 5pm. Winter
times subject to change, telephone establishment.
*£4 ch 5-15 £3, under 5s free, pen £3.50. Party
10+.
Wish Tower Puppet Museum
BN21 4BU ☎01323 417776
puppet.workshop@virgin.net
(On seafront, W of pier)
Open May-mid Jul & Sep, wknds 11-5;
mid Jul-Aug 11-5.

HASTINGS
Smugglers Adventure
TN34 3HY ☎01424 422964
smugglers@discoverhastings.co.uk
(Follow brown signs along A259 coast road
through Hastings. Use seafront car park and then
take West Cliff railway or follow signed footpath)
Open all year daily, Etr-Sep 10-5.30; Oct-Etr 11-
4.30. Closed 24-26 Dec. *£5.95 ch £3.95,
concessions £4.95. Family ticket £16.50.

NEWHAVEN
Paradise Park & Gardens BN9 0DH
enquiries@paradisepark.co.uk ☎01273 512123
(Signposted off A26 & A259)
Open all year, daily 9-6. Closed 25-26 Dec.
*£5.99, ch £4.99. Family ticket £19.99 2 ad & 3 ch.

WEST SUSSEX
FISHBOURNE
Fishbourne Roman Palace PO19 3QR
adminfish@sussexpast.co.uk ☎01243 785859
(Off A27 onto A259 into Fishbourne. Turn right into
Salthill Rd & right into Roman Way)
Open all year, daily Feb-15 Dec. Feb, Nov-Dec 10-
4; Mar-Jul & Sep-Oct 10-5; Aug 10-6. Winter
wknds 10-4.

LITTLEHAMPTON
Look & Sea! Visitor Centre BN17 5AW
info@lookandsea.co.uk ☎01903 718984
(On harbour front)
Open all year, daily 9-5. *£2.95 ch £2.50, pen &
student £2.50.

SINGLETON
Weald & Downland Open Air Museum
PO18 0EU
office@wealddown.co.uk ☎01243 811348
(6m N of Chichester on A286)
Open all year, Mar-Oct, daily 10.30-6 last
admission 5; Nov-Feb, Sat & Sun 10.30-4, also 26
Dec-1 Jan daily & Feb half term, 10.30-4.
*£7.50 ch & students £4, pen £6.50. Family ticket
2 adults & 3 ch £20. Party.

SUSSEX, EAST

ALFRISTON — Map 05 TQ50

Babies Welcome | Family Rooms | Children's Dishes

★★★ 71% **Deans Place**

Seaford Rd BN26 5TW

 Best Western

☎ 01323 870248 ▤ 01323 870918

e-mail: mail@deansplacehotel.co.uk

Dir: off A27 signed Alfriston & Drusillas Zoo Park. Continue S through village

CHILD FACILITIES: Baby listening Activities: colouring, puzzles, board games Food/bottle warming Ch menu Ch portions Highchairs Ch discounts cots free Safe grounds Cots Family rms 2 D rms with 2 S beds, 2 D rms with 1 S bed standard rate plus £15 per child Ch drinks Laundry **NEARBY:** Walks Zoo Cycle hire 10-min drive to sea

Situated on the southern fringe of the village, this friendly hotel is set in attractive gardens. Bedrooms vary in size and are well appointed with good facilities. A wide range of food is offered including an extensive bar menu and a fine dining option in Harcourt's Restaurant.

ROOMS: 36 en suite (2 fmly) (8 GF) ⊗ in 16 bedrooms s £60-£100; d £100-£138 (incl. bkfst) LB **FACILITIES:** Spa STV ⊰ ♨ ♨ Boules Xmas **PARKING:** 100 **NOTES:** ⊗ in restaurant

◀ **The Sussex Ox**

Milton St BN26 5RL

☎ 01323 870840 ▤ 01323 870715

e-mail: sussexox@aol.com

Dir: Off the A27 between Polegate and Lewes, Signed to Milton Street

CHILD FACILITIES: Please telephone for details

OPEN: 11-3 (Sun 12-3, 6-10.30) 6-11 Rest: 25 Dec Closed eve **BAR MEALS:** L served all week 12-2.30 D served all week 6-9 **RESTAURANT:** L served all week 12-2.30 D served all week 6-9 **FACILITIES:** Garden: **PARKING:** 60

BARCOMBE — Map 05 TQ41

◀ **The Anchor Inn**

Anchor Ln BN8 5BS

☎ 01273 400414 ▤ 01273 401029

Dir: From A26 (Lewes to Uckfield road)

CHILD FACILITIES: Please telephone for details

OPEN: 11-11 (Sun 12-10.30) Closed: 25 & 31 Dec **BAR MEALS:** L served all week 12-3 D served all week 6-9 Av main course £5.95 **RESTAURANT:** L served all week 12-3 D served all week 6-9 **FACILITIES:** Garden: riverside ✈ **PARKING:** 300

BRIGHTON & HOVE — Map 04 TQ30

Babies Welcome | Children's Dishes

⊛ ⊛ **The Gingerman Restaurant**

21A Norfolk Square BN1 2PD

☎ 01273 326688 ▤ 01273 326688

Dir: Telephone for directions

CHILD FACILITIES: Activities: colouring, jigsaws Food/bottle warming Ch portions Highchairs **NEARBY:** 10-min walk to sea

FOOD: Modern European **STYLE:** Modern, Chic **SEATS:** 32 **OPEN:** 12.30-2/7.30-10, Closed 2 wks winter, 2 wks summer, Sun-Mon **RESTAURANT:** **NOTES:** Air con

Babies Welcome | Children's Dishes

⊛ **Sevendials**

1-3 Buckingham Place BN1 3TD

☎ 01273 885555 ▤ 01273 888911

e-mail: sam@sevendialsrestaurant.co.uk

Dir: From Brighton station turn R 0.5m up hill & restaurant situated at Seven Dials rdbt.

CHILD FACILITIES: Activities: colouring Food/bottle warming Ch menu Ch portions Highchairs Safe grounds Changing facilities **NEARBY:** Park 10-min walk to sea

FOOD: European **STYLE:** Modern Chic **SEATS:** 55 **OPEN:** 12-2.30/7-10.30, Closed Xmas & New Year, Mon **RESTAURANT:** Fixed L £10, Fixed D £25, main £15 **NOTES:** ⊗ area **PARKING:** Two mins from restaurant

EASTBOURNE — Map 05 TV69

Babies Welcome | Family Rooms | Children's Dishes

★★★★★ 71% ⊛ ⊛ **Grand**

King Edward's Pde BN21 4EQ

☎ 01323 412345 ▤ 01323 412233

e-mail: reservations@grandeastbourne.com

Dir: on seafront W of Eastbourne, 1m from railway station

CHILD FACILITIES: Baby listening Nanny Babysitting Activities: activity pack playroom open daily Indoor play area Food/bottle warming Ch menu Ch portions Highchairs Ch cutlery Ch discounts under 13s free when sharing, own room 50% discount Safe grounds Games consoles Videos Cots Family rms suites with extra bedrm from £230 Ch drinks Connecting rms Fridge Laundry Changing mats (on request) **NEARBY:** Animal park Fun park 1-min walk to sea

This famous Victorian hotel offers high standards of service and hospitality. The extensive public rooms feature a magnificent Great Hall, with marble columns and high ceilings, where guests can relax and enjoy afternoon tea. The spacious bedrooms provide high levels of comfort and some rooms have balconies with

continued on p222

EASTBOURNE, continued

stunning sea views. There is a choice of restaurants and bars as well as superb leisure facilities.
ROOMS: 152 en suite (20 fmly) s £135-£325; d £165-£385 (incl. bkfst)
LB FACILITIES: Spa 🖪 ⛵ Snooker Sauna Solarium Gym ⛲ Jacuzzi Hairdressing, Beauty therapy 🎵 Xmas **PARKING:** 60 **NOTES:** 🚭 in restaurant

★★★ 66% *York House*
14-22 Royal Pde BN22 7AP
☎ 01323 412918 📠 01323 646238
e-mail: frontdesk@yorkhousehotel.co.uk
web: www.yorkhousehotel.co.uk
Dir: A27 to Eastbourne. On seafront 0.25m E of pier

Best Western

> **CHILD FACILITIES:** Baby listening Ch menu Ch portions Highchairs Ch discounts 1 child under 10 free, 2nd child 50%, 10-14s 50% Cots Family rms Connecting rms Laundry **NEARBY:** Seafront location

With a prime location on the seafront, many rooms enjoy wonderful panoramic views. Bedrooms vary in size but are comfortably and practically fitted. Public areas include a spacious lobby, cosy bar, games room and indoor swimming pool. Parking on the street in front of the hotel only is available.
ROOMS: 87 en suite (15 fmly) (5 GF) 🚭 in 30 bedrooms
FACILITIES: STV 🖪 **NOTES:** 🚭 in restaurant

◆◆◆ Arden Hotel
17 Burlington Place BN21 4AR
☎ 01323 639639 📠 01323 417840
e-mail: mail@ardenhoteleastbourne.freeserve.co.uk
Dir: 50yds from seafront, near bandstand

> **CHILD FACILITIES:** Food/bottle warming Ch portions Highchairs Ch cutlery Ch discounts Cots Connecting rms **NEARBY:** Seafront location

Located close to the seafront and town centre, this friendly hotel provides guests with well appointed rooms. Public areas are tastefully decorated and include a spacious guest lounge and dining room where hearty breakfasts are served.
ROOMS: 12 rms (10 en suite) (1 fmly) (2 GF) s £25-£28; d £50-£56 *
FACILITIES: TVB tea/coffee TVL No coaches **NOTES:** 🚭 Licensed Cen ht **PARKING:** 3

◆◆◆ Camelot Lodge Hotel
35 Lewes Rd BN21 2BU
☎ 01323 725207 📠 01323 722799
e-mail: info@camelotlodgehotel.com
Dir: exit A22 onto A2021, premises approx 0.5m after General Hospital

> **CHILD FACILITIES:** Baby listening Activities: toys, sand pit, trampoline, bikes, balls Outdoor play area Food/bottle warming Ch menu Ch portions Highchairs Ch cutlery Ch discounts under 2s free, under 13s half price if sharing with adults Safe grounds Cots Family rms D rm with S bed/ B beds from £62.50 (on request) **NEARBY:** Zoo Leisure centre Parks Adventure parks 15-min walk to sea

This delightful Edwardian hotel is located within walking distance of the seafront and local amenities. Bedrooms are attractively decorated and feature a range of extra facilities. Guests have the use of a spacious lounge/bar area in which to relax and meals are

continued

served in the bright conservatory dining room. Dinner is available by prior arrangement.
ROOMS: 7 en suite (3 fmly) (1 GF) s £25-£32; d £50-£64 * 🚭
FACILITIES: TVB tea/coffee No coaches Dinner Last d order 24hr notice
NOTES: 🐾 🚭 in restaurant Licensed Cen ht **LB PARKING:** 8

◆◆◆ Sheldon Hotel
9-11 Burlington Place BN21 4AS
☎ 01323 721420 📠 01323 430406
e-mail: sheldonhotel@tiscali.co.uk
Dir: travel W along seafront past the pier. Turn right into Burlington Place

> **CHILD FACILITIES:** Please telephone for details

Just off the hustle-bustle of the main strip, this impressive Victorian house is within a minutes walk from the seafront. Bedrooms vary in size but are comfortably appointed and decorated in a cheerful manner. A smart dining room where traditional home cooked food is served is on offer.
ROOMS: 24 en suite (5 fmly) (2 GF) s £28-£34; d £56-£68 * 🚭
FACILITIES: TVB tea/coffee Direct dial from bedrooms Lift TVL Dinner Last d order 4pm **NOTES:** 🐾 🚭 in restaurant Licensed Cen ht **LB**
PARKING: 18

FIRLE   Map 05 TQ40

🍴 The Ram Inn
BN8 6NS
☎ 01323 858222
e-mail: nikwooller@raminnfirle.net
Dir: R off A27 3m E of Lewes

> **CHILD FACILITIES:** Activities: toys, games, colouring Indoor play area Outdoor play area Family area Food/bottle warming Ch licence Ch menu Ch portions Highchairs Ch cutlery Safe grounds Changing facilities **NEARBY:** Walks

OPEN: 11.30-11 (Sun 12-10.30) Rest: Dec 25 Open 12-2 **BAR MEALS:** L served all week 12-5.30 D served all week Av main course £6.50
FACILITIES: Children's licence Garden: Two gardens 1 with picnic benches, 1 orchard **PARKING:** 10

HARTFIELD   Map 05 TQ43

🍴 Anchor Inn
Church St TN7 4AG
☎ 01892 770424
Dir: On B2110

> **CHILD FACILITIES:** Family area Food/bottle warming Ch menu Ch portions **NEARBY:** Pooh Bridge

OPEN: 11-11 **BAR MEALS:** L served all week 12-2 D served all week 6-10
RESTAURANT: L served all week 12-2.00 D served Tue-Sat 7-9.30
FACILITIES: Garden **PARKING:** 30

HASTINGS & ST LEONARDS   Map 05 TQ80

★★★ 70% ⚐ Beauport Park

Battle Rd TN38 8EA
☎ 01424 851222 📠 01424 852465
e-mail: reservations@beauportprkhotel.co.uk
web: www.beauportparkhotel.co.uk
Dir: 3m N off A2100

CHILD FACILITIES: Please telephone for details

Elegant Georgian manor house set in 40 acres of mature gardens
on the outskirts of Hastings. The individually decorated bedrooms
are tastefully furnished and thoughtfully equipped with modern
facilities. Public rooms convey much of the original character and
feature a large conservatory, a lounge bar, a restaurant and a
further lounge, as well as banqueting rooms.

ROOMS: 25 en suite (2 fmly) ⊗ in 11 bedrooms s £95; d £130 (incl.
bkfst) **LB FACILITIES:** STV ⚲ Golf 18 ⚘ Riding ♬ ⌁ Country walks
round estate ♬ Xmas **PARKING:** 60 **NOTES:** ⊗ in restaurant

★★★ 67% High Beech

Battle Rd TN37 7BS
☎ 01424 851383 📠 01424 854265
e-mail: highbeech@barbox.net
Dir: 400yds from A2100 between Hastings and Battle

CHILD FACILITIES: Please telephone for details

A privately owned hotel situated between the historic towns of
Hastings and Battle in a woodland setting. The generously
proportioned bedrooms are pleasantly decorated and thoughtfully
equipped. Public rooms include St. Patricks Bar, which also
doubles as the lounge area, and the elegant Wedgwood
restaurant where an interesting and varied menu is served.

ROOMS: 17 en suite (4 fmly) ⊗ in all bedrooms s £65-£75; d £95-£125
(incl. bkfst) **LB FACILITIES:** STV **PARKING:** 60 **NOTES:** ✖ ⊗ in
restaurant

LEWES   Map 05 TQ41

Babies | Children's
Welcome | Dishes

🍽 Circa

45 High St BN7 1XT
☎ 01273 471777 📠 488416
e-mail: eat@circacirca.com
web: www.circacirca.com
Dir: At top of High St, just past the Castle Gate

CHILD FACILITIES: Food/bottle warming Ch menu Ch portions
Highchairs Changing facilities **NEARBY:** Lewes Castle Walks

continued

FOOD: International **STYLE:** Modern Chic **SEATS:** 85
OPEN: 12-2.30/6-10, Closed Mon, D Sun **RESTAURANT:** Fixed L £12.95,
Fixed D £27.50, main £12.50 **NOTES:** ⊗ area, Air con **PARKING:** On
street

PEVENSEY   Map 05 TQ60

Babies | Family | Children's
Welcome | Rooms | Dishes

◆◆◆◆ Priory Court Hotel

Castle Rd BN24 5LG
☎ 01323 763150 📠 01323 769030
e-mail: info@priorycourthotel.com
*Dir: at rdbt junct A27/A259 take Pevensey exit and follow main road
through lights hotel on right opposite Pevensey Castle*

CHILD FACILITIES: Outdoor play area Family area Food/bottle
warming Ch menu Ch portions Highchairs Ch cutlery Ch discounts
under 5s free Safe grounds Videos Cots Family rms D rm with S
beds/put up beds from £95 Ch drinks Laundry Changing mats
NEARBY: Castle Science centre Life boat experience 5-min drive
to sea

Retaining many original features, this 15th-century inn is situated
directly opposite the Roman castle. Recently redecorated, the
public rooms are cosy and inviting. Guests can choose from a
wide range of imaginative dishes in the dining room. Bedrooms
are mixed in size; some are suitable for families.

ROOMS: 9 rms (7 en suite) 1 annexe en suite (2 fmly) (2 GF)
s £50-£65; d £80-£95 * **FACILITIES:** TVB tea/coffee Direct dial from
bedrooms Dinner Last d order 9.30pm **NOTES:** ⊗ in restaurant
Licensed Cen ht **LB PARKING:** 40

RUSHLAKE GREEN   Map 05 TQ61

Children's
Dishes

🍽 Horse & Groom

TN21 9QE
☎ 01435 830320 📠 01435 830320
e-mail: chappellhatpeg@aol.com

CHILD FACILITIES: Food/bottle warming Ch portions Safe grounds
NEARBY: Drusillas Park Bluebell Railway Walks

OPEN: 11.30-3 5.30-11 **BAR MEALS:** L served all week 12-2.30 D served
all week 7-9.30 **RESTAURANT:** L served all week 12-2.30 D served all
week 7-9.30 Av 3 course à la carte £20 **FACILITIES:** Garden: Well tended,
views over lake, smart furniture **PARKING:** 20

RYE
Map 05 TQ92

◆◆◆◆ Old Borough Arms Hotel
The Strand TN31 7DB
☎ 01797 222128 ▤ 01797 222128
e-mail: info@oldborougharms.co.uk
web: www.oldborougharms.co.uk
Dir: turn off A259 into the Strand. Hotel is situated at foot of Mermaid Street overlooking Strand Quay

CHILD FACILITIES: Please telephone for details

Expect a warm welcome at this former sailor's inn, which enjoys a peaceful, elevated setting just minutes from town. Bedrooms come in a variety of sizes and styles; each one is pleasantly decorated and thoughtfully equipped. Breakfast is served in the charming dining room and guests have use of the cosy lounge bar.
ROOMS: 9 en suite (2 fmly) (4 GF) s £35-£45; d £60-£95 *
FACILITIES: TVB tea/coffee TVL **NOTES:** ✈ ⊗ Licensed Cen ht
PARKING: 10

◆◆◆ Little Saltcote
22 Military Rd TN31 7NY
☎ 01797 223210 ▤ 01797 224474
e-mail: littlesaltcote.rye@virgin.net
Dir: turn off A268 onto Military Rd, signposted to Appledore. House 300mtrs on left

CHILD FACILITIES: Baby listening Food/bottle warming Ch portions Highchairs Ch cutlery Ch discounts child 50% Safe grounds Videos Cots Family rms D rms with 5 beds, B beds & foldaway from £67.50 Laundry **NEARBY:** Children's farm Rare breed centre Swimming pool 10-min drive to sea

This friendly, family-run guest house sits in quiet surroundings within walking distance of town. Bedrooms are pleasantly decorated and equipped with modern facilities and breakfast is served at individual tables in a smart dining room.
ROOMS: 5 rms (3 en suite) (3 fmly) (1 GF) s £30-£45; d £50-£70 *
FACILITIES: TVB tea/coffee **NOTES:** ⊗ Cen ht **LB** **PARKING:** 3

◆◆◆ Old Vicarage
Rye Harbour TN31 7TT
☎ 01797 222088 ▤ 01797 229620
e-mail: johnathan@oldvicarageryeharbour.fsnet.co.uk
Dir: Just off A259, outside Rye. Well signed to Rye Harbour Nature Reserve, on right

CHILD FACILITIES: Please telephone for details

At the end of Rye Harbour, next to the beach and coastal nature reserve, this house retains a great deal of original charm, which is emphasised by the décor and furniture throughout. Bedrooms are filled with thoughtful extras and the dining room has a Victorian atmosphere, with quality furniture and memorabilia in abundance.
ROOMS: 2 rms ⊗ in 1 bedrooms **FACILITIES:** TVB tea/coffee No coaches **NOTES:** Credit cards not taken ⊗ in restaurant Cen ht
PARKING: 3

SEAFORD
Map 05 TV49

◆◆◆◆ Avondale Hotel
Avondale Rd BN25 1RJ
☎ 01323 890008 ▤ 01323 490598
Dir: from Seaford town centre A259 to Eastbourne. Avondale on left opp town memorial

CHILD FACILITIES: Baby listening Food/bottle warming Ch portions Highchairs Videos Cots Family rms rm with 3 beds and put up bed £60-£80 **NEARBY:** Adventure park Zoo Short walk to sea

A warm welcome is offered by the caring owners at this friendly, family-run hotel which is ideally placed for the Newhaven to Dieppe Seacat ferry service. The bedrooms are attractively decorated, pleasantly furnished and thoughtfully equipped. Breakfast and dinner are served in the attractive dining room and guests also have the use of a cosy lounge.
ROOMS: 16 rms (10 en suite) (4 fmly) (1 GF) s £20-£60; d £40-£65 *
FACILITIES: TVB tea/coffee Lift No coaches Dinner Last d order 10am
NOTES: ✈ ⊗ Licensed Cen ht

UCKFIELD
Map 05 TQ42

★★★★ 74% ◉ ◉
Buxted Park Country House
Buxted TN22 4AY   *Hand*PICKED
☎ 01825 733333 ▤ 01825 732 990
e-mail: buxtedpark@handpicked.co.uk
Dir: From A26 (Uckfield Bypass) take A272 signposted Buxted. Go through traffic lights, hotel is 1 mile on right.

CHILD FACILITIES: Activities: cinema in hotel, games, chess, cycle hire Indoor play area Outdoor play area Family area Food/bottle warming Ch menu Ch portions Highchairs Ch cutlery Ch discounts children £15 when sharing with parents Safe grounds Videos Cots Family rms Connecting rms Fridge Laundry Changing mats **NEARBY:** Gardens Railway centre Castle Llama park Zoo Walks

An attractive Grade II listed Georgian mansion dating back to the 17th century. The property is set amidst 300 acres of beautiful countryside and landscaped gardens. The stylish, thoughtfully equipped bedrooms are split between the main house and the modern Garden Wing. An interesting choice of dishes is served in the original Victorian Orangery.
ROOMS: 44 en suite (6 fmly) (16 GF) ⊗ in 22 bedrooms s £120-£370; d £140-£370 (incl. bkfst) **LB** **FACILITIES:** STV Fishing Snooker Sauna Solarium Gym ⚖ ♨ Beauty salon, clay pigeon shoot, archery, fishing, mountain biking, orienteering Xmas **PARKING:** 150 **NOTES:** ⊗ in restaurant

WINCHELSEA
Map 05 TQ9[?]

◀ The New Inn
German St TN36 4EN
☎ 01797 226252
e-mail: newinnchelsea.co.uk

CHILD FACILITIES: Outdoor play area Family area Food/bottle warming Ch menu Ch portions Highchairs Ch cutlery Safe grounds **NEARBY:** Walks Museums Historic church 1.5m to sea

OPEN: (Open all day every day) **BAR MEALS:** L served all week 12-3 D served all week 6.30-9.30 Av main course £7.95 **RESTAURANT:** L served all week 12-2.30 D served all week 6.30-9.30 Av 3 course à la carte £15
FACILITIES: Garden: Traditional Old English **PARKING:** 20

SUSSEX, WEST

ARUNDEL   Map 04 TQ00

◆◆◆◆ 🌿 Blakehurst Farm

BN18 9QG
☎ 01903 889562 🖷 01903 889562
web: www.blakehurstfarm.co.uk
Dir: 3m E of Arundel, N off A27 dual carriageway, signed Blakehurst

CHILD FACILITIES: Please telephone for details

This fine Georgian property is situated on a working farm and
enjoys good countryside views. Bedrooms are spacious and
cheerfully decorated. Guests have use of the comfortable lounge
and breakfast is taken around a single table. Dinner is available on
request and mountain bikes can be hired.

ROOMS: 3 rms (2 en suite) FACILITIES: TVB tea/coffee TVL 1000 acres
rable NOTES: Credit cards not taken 🏏 ⊗ Cen ht PARKING: 3

BILLINGSHURST   Map 04 TQ02

🍴 Cricketers Arms

Loxwood Rd, Wisborough Green RH14 0DG
☎ 01403 700369
e-mail: sarah@cricketersarms.com
Dir: On the A272, between Billingshurst & Petworth in the middle of
Wisborough Green turn at junction next to the village green, pub is 100 yds
on the right

CHILD FACILITIES: Outdoor play area Food/bottle warming
Ch menu Ch portions   NEARBY: Fishers Farm   Park

OPEN: 11 -11 BAR MEALS: L served Mon-Sun 12-2 D served Mon-Sun
6.30-9.30 RESTAURANT: L served Mon-Sun 12-2 D served Mon-Sun
6.30-9.30 FACILITIES: Garden: Grass area with benches PARKING: 20

BOGNOR REGIS   Map 04 SZ99

◆◆◆ Jubilee

5 Gloucester Rd PO21 1NU
☎ 01243 863016 & 07702 275967 🖷 01243 868017
e-mail: JubileeGuestHouse@breathemail.net
web: www.jubileeguesthouse.com
Dir: from A259 to seafront, house opp Day Entrance to Butlins Family
Entertainment Resort

CHILD FACILITIES: Food/bottle warming Ch portions Highchairs
Ch cutlery Ch discounts half price Cots Family rms D rms with 1 or
2 S beds from £75   NEARBY: Leisure centre   Swimming pool
Cinema   Seafront location

This property is close to Butlin's, the seafront and the town centre.
The brightly decorated and well-equipped bedrooms vary in size,
and all have clock radios and hairdryers. A generous and freshly
continued

cooked breakfast, including provision for vegetarians, is served in
the attractive dining room.

ROOMS: 6 rms (2 en suite) (2 fmly) s fr £25; d fr £50 *
FACILITIES: TVB tea/coffee No coaches NOTES: 🏏 ⊗ in restaurant
Cen ht LB PARKING: 4

CHICHESTER   Map 04 SU80

◆◆◆◆ Old Chapel Forge

Lower Bognor Rd, Lagness PO20 1LR
☎ 01243 264380 🖷 01243 261649
e-mail: cfbarnes@breathemail.net
Dir: from A27 Chichester By-Pass, exit on Bognor rdbt signed
Pagham/Runcton, in S direction. At rdbt turn left onto B2166 Pagham Rd,
continue to Royal Oak PH on right. Left onto Lower Bognor Rd for 0.75m
Old Chapel Forge on right

CHILD FACILITIES: Outdoor play area Food/bottle warming
Ch menu Ch portions Highchairs (booster seat) Ch discounts babies
free, under 14s seasonal discounts Safe grounds Family rms D rm
with 2 S beds, D with S bed £65-£146 Ch drinks Connecting rms
Fridge Laundry   NEARBY: 3-min drive to sea

Old Chapel Forge is located in beautiful rural surroundings and
overlooks sweeping fields. The accommodation takes the form of
a self-contained suite, which includes its own dining area,
comfortable lounge and en suite bedroom. Breakfast is substantial
and of a high quality.
ROOMS: 1 en suite (1 fmly) (1 GF) s £25-£50; d £50-£80 *
FACILITIES: TVB tea/coffee TVL No coaches 🔔 Dinner Last d order
prior to stay NOTES: Credit cards not taken ⊗ Cen ht LB PARKING: 5

🏵 Comme Ça

67 Broyle Rd PO19 6BD
☎ 01243 788724 536307 🖷 01243 530052
e-mail: comme.ca@commeca.co.uk
web: www.commeca.co.uk
Dir: On A286 near Festival Theatre

CHILD FACILITIES: Food/bottle warming Ch menu Ch portions
Highchairs

FOOD: French STYLE: French Rustic SEATS: 100 OPEN: 12-2/6-10.30,
Closed Xmas week & New Year week, BHs, MonL Tue, D Sun
RESTAURANT: Fixed L £16.95, main £12.95-£13.95 NOTES: Smart Dress,
⊗ in restaurant PARKING: 46

England

CLIMPING
Map 04 TQ00

★★★ 78% ⊚ ⊚ Bailiffscourt Hotel & Health Spa
Climping St BN17 5RW
☎ 01903 723511 ▤ 01903 718987
e-mail: bailiffscourt@hshotels.co.uk
web: www.hshotels.co.uk
Dir: turn off A259 at Climping, follow signs for Climping Beach. Hotel 0.5m on right

CHILD FACILITIES: Baby listening Babysitting (unqualified) **Activities:** toys, puzzles Outdoor play area Food/bottle warming Ch menu Ch portions Highchairs Ch cutlery Ch discounts under 3s free, over 3s £25 sharing with parents Videos Cots Family rms D rms with S beds Connecting rms Laundry **NEARBY:** Museum Arundel Wetlands Centre Historic Dockyard Roman palace 200 yds to sea

Dating from just the 1920s, this 'medieval manor' looks like it might have been there for centuries. Bedrooms are spacious and atmospheric in parts, whilst newer rooms provide an impressive contrast of style. There is a choice of cosy lounges, warmed by log fires in the cooler months, and carefully prepared meals are served. A well-equipped spa completes the package.
ROOMS: 9 en suite 30 annexe en suite (25 fmly) (16 GF) s £165-£270; d £185-£450 (incl. bkfst) **LB FACILITIES: Spa** STV ⊡ ↘ ◟ Sauna Gym ♨ Jacuzzi Xmas **PARKING:** 100 **NOTES:** ⊗ in restaurant

GATWICK AIRPORT (LONDON)
Map 04 TQ24

★★★ 75% ⊚ ♨ Stanhill Court
Stanhill Rd, Charlwood RH6 0EP
☎ 01293 862166 ▤ 01293 862773
e-mail: enquiries@stanhillcourthotel.co.uk
web: www.stanhillcourthotel.co.uk
Dir: N of Charlwood towards Newdigate

CHILD FACILITIES: Baby listening Outdoor play area Family area Food/bottle warming Ch menu Ch portions Highchairs Ch cutlery Ch discounts Safe grounds Videos Cots Family rms D rm with S bed or cot £105 Ch drinks Connecting rms Laundry **NEARBY:** Gardens Leisure centre

This hotel dates back to 1881 and enjoys a secluded location in 35 acres of well-tended grounds with views over the Downs. Bedrooms are individually furnished and decorated, and many have four-poster beds. Public areas include a library, a bright bar and a traditional wood-panelled restaurant.
ROOMS: 15 en suite (3 fmly) ⊗ in 3 bedrooms s £75-£95; d £95-£125 (incl. bkfst) **LB FACILITIES:** STV Fishing ♨ ⌁ **PARKING:** 110 **NOTES:** ⊁ ⊗ in restaurant

◆◆◆◆ The Lawn
30 Massetts Rd RH6 7DF
☎ 01293 775751 ▤ 01293 821803
e-mail: info@lawnguesthouse.co.uk
web: www.lawnguesthouse.co.uk
Dir: M23 junct 9, follow signs to A23 (Redhill), at rdbt by Esso garage take 3rd exit, Massetts Rd 300yds on right

CHILD FACILITIES: Please telephone for details

Ideally situated for Gatwick Airport, this fine detached Victorian house offers comfortable bedrooms, equipped with many thoughtful extras. The atmosphere is relaxed, the welcome friendly
continued

and there is even an Internet facility available to guests. A choice of breakfast is served in an attractive dining room.

The Lawn Guest House

ROOMS: 12 en suite (4 fmly) s £40-£45; d £55-£60 * **FACILITIES:** TV tea/coffee Direct dial from bedrooms No coaches **NOTES:** ⊗ Cen ht **PARKING:** 15

HORSHAM
Map 04 TQ13

⊚ Les Deux Garçons
Piries Place RH12 1DF
☎ 01403 271125 ▤ 01403 271022
e-mail: info@lesdeuxgarcons.com
Dir: Follow town centre signs, then sign for Piries Place & car park, situated bottom of car park at entrance to Piries Place

CHILD FACILITIES: **Activities:** competitions, colouring Food/bottle warming Ch menu Ch portions Highchairs Ch cutlery Safe grounds Changing facilities

FOOD: Modern European **STYLE:** Modern Minimalist **SEATS:** 60 **OPEN:** 12-3/7-11, Closed Xmas wk, Sun, Mon **RESTAURANT:** Fixed L £12.90, main £14.90-£23.90 **NOTES:** ⊗ in restaurant, Air con **PARKING:** Parking adjacent to restaurant

HORSTED KEYNES
Map 05 TQ32

◆◆◆◆ The Croft
Lewes Rd RH17 7DP
☎ 01825 790546
e-mail: thecroftbandb@btopenworld.com
Dir: M23 junct 10 turn right at 2nd rdbt (B2028), through Turners Hill/Ardingly, 2nd left Horsted Keynes, right into Lewes Road

CHILD FACILITIES: Please telephone for details

This large, detached, fairly modern house is located in a quiet residential area and provides warm and friendly hospitality. The bedrooms comprise of one double and one twin and are attractively decorated, nicely furnished and well equipped. The freshly cooked breakfast includes several organic options, together with fresh fruit and juices.
ROOMS: 2 rms **FACILITIES:** TVB tea/coffee No coaches Dinner Last d order 24 hours previous **NOTES:** Credit cards not taken ⊗ Cen ht **PARKING:** 4

OVING
Map 04 SU90

⊞ The Gribble Inn
PO20 2BP
☎ 01243 786893 ▤ 01243 788841
e-mail: brianelderfield@hotmail.com
Dir: From A27 take A259. After 1m L at roundabout, 1st R to Oving, 1st L in village

CHILD FACILITIES: Please telephone for details
continued

OPEN: 11-3 5.30-11 (Sun 12-4, 7-10.30) **BAR MEALS:** L served all week 12-2.30 D served all week 6-9.30 Av main course £7.95 **RESTAURANT:** L served all week 12-2.30 D served all week 6-9.30 **FACILITIES:** Garden: Large shaded garden with seating for over 100 **PARKING:** 40

POYNINGS
Map 04 TQ21

Babies Welcome | Children's Dishes

🍺 Royal Oak Inn
The Street BN45 7AQ
☎ 01273 857389 ▤ 01273 857202
e-mail: royaloakpoynings@aol.com
Dir: N on the A23 just outside Brighton, take the A281 (signed for Henfield & Poynings), then follow signs into Poynings village

> **CHILD FACILITIES:** Outdoor play area Family area Food/bottle warming Ch licence Ch menu Ch portions Highchairs **NEARBY:** Walks 10-min drive to sea

OPEN: 11 (Sun 12-10.30) -11 **BAR MEALS:** L served all week 12-2.30 D served all week 6-9.30 Av main course £8 **FACILITIES:** Garden: Large garden with BBQ facilities & nice views **PARKING:** 35

SELSEY
Map 04 SZ89

Babies Welcome | Family Rooms | Children's Dishes

◆◆◆◆ St Andrews Lodge Hotel
Chichester Rd PO20 0LX
☎ 01243 606899 ▤ 01243 607826
e-mail: info@standrewslodge.co.uk
Dir: turn off A27 onto the B2145 for 7 miles. Hotel is on right past Police Station just before the church

> **CHILD FACILITIES:** Food/bottle warming Ch menu Ch portions Highchairs Ch cutlery Ch discounts babies free, 1-4s £5.50, 5-8s £10.50, 9-12s £12.50, 13-16s half price Safe grounds Family rms D rm with 2 S beds (from £65 + children's prices) Ch drinks Connecting rms Fridge **NEARBY:** Walks Cinema Campsite Holiday centre 1m to sea

Located close to the town centre, this hotel provides comfortable accommodation and a warm welcome. Bedrooms are bright and spacious and all have a range of useful extras. There are five rooms in an annexe at the back of the house, and one is adapted for guests with disabilities. Dinner is available by prior arrangement.
ROOMS: 5 en suite 5 annexe en suite (3 fmly) (5 GF) s £30-£50; d £60-£75 * 🚭 **FACILITIES:** TVB tea/coffee Direct dial from bedrooms TVL No coaches **NOTES:** 🚭 in restaurant Licensed Cen ht **LB PARKING:** 12

STEDHAM
Map 04 SU82

Babies Welcome | Children's Dishes

🍺 Hamilton Arms/Nava Thai Restaurant
Hamilton Arms School Ln GU29 0NZ
☎ 01730 812555 ▤ 01730 817459
e-mail: hamiltonarms@hotmail.com
Dir: Off A272 between Midhurst & Petersfield

> **CHILD FACILITIES:** Indoor play area Food/bottle warming Ch menu Ch portions Highchairs Ch cutlery Safe grounds **NEARBY:** Walks Horseracing

OPEN: 11-3 6-11 (Sun 12.00-3.00, 7.00-10.30) Closed: 1 Week Jan **BAR MEALS:** L served Tues-Sun 12-2.30 D served Tues-Sun 6-10.30 Av main course £7.50 **RESTAURANT:** L served Tues-Sun 12-2.30 D served Tues-Sun 6-10.30 Av 3 course à la carte £17 Av 4 course fixed price £19.50 **FACILITIES:** Garden: Lawn with benches and umbrellas **PARKING:** 40

WALDERTON
Map 04 SU71

Babies Welcome | Children's Dishes

🍺 The Barley Mow
PO18 9ED
☎ 023 9263 1321 ▤ 023 9263 1403
e-mail: mowbarley@aol.co.uk
Dir: North Chichester B2146. From Havant B2147. Turn R signed Walderton, the Barley Mow is 100 yds on L

> **CHILD FACILITIES:** Food/bottle warming Ch menu Ch portions Highchairs **NEARBY:** Walks

OPEN: 11-3 6-11.30 (Summer, all day Sun) **BAR MEALS:** L served all week 12-2.15 D served all week 6-9.30 Av main course £4.99 **RESTAURANT:** L served all week 12-2.15 D served all week 6-9.30 **FACILITIES:** Garden: Mature garden, tables, seats, stream **PARKING:** 50

WORTHING
Map 04 TQ10

Babies Welcome | Family Rooms | Children's Dishes

◆◆◆ Manor Guest House
100 Broadwater Rd BN14 8AN
☎ 01903 236028 ▤ 01903 230404
e-mail: stay@manorworthing.com
Dir: At Findon on A24 continue towards Worthing town centre. At lights at St. Marys Church, Manor Guest House is 175yds on left

> **CHILD FACILITIES:** Outdoor play area Family area Food/bottle warming Ch menu Ch portions Highchairs Ch cutlery Ch discounts under 2s free, 2-15s discount Cots Family rms D rm with B bed, D with 2 S beds £100-£120 Laundry Changing mats **NEARBY:** Cinema Theatre Aquarena Arundel Castle Park 0.75m to sea

This attractive guest house is located within walking distance of the centre of Worthing. Bedrooms are smartly presented and include thoughtful extras as a standard. Well-cooked breakfasts and dinner are served in the bright dining room, which has separate tables. Limited parking is also available to guests.
ROOMS: 6 rms (3 en suite) (2 fmly) (1 GF) s £30-£35; d £60-£80 * **FACILITIES:** TVB tea/coffee landscaped gardens Dinner Last d order 7pm **NOTES:** 🚭 Licensed Cen ht **LB PARKING:** 6

TYNE & WEAR

NEWCASTLE UPON TYNE
Map 12 NZ26

Babies Welcome | **Family Rooms**

★★★ 68% Jurys Inn Newcastle

St James Gate, Scotswood Rd NE4 7JH
☎ 0191 201 4400 📠 0191 201 4411
e-mail: jurysinnnewcastle@jurysdoyle.com

CHILD FACILITIES: Food/bottle warming Highchairs Safe grounds Cots Family rms £67 (Sun-Thurs), £75 (Fri-Sat) Connecting rms Laundry **NEARBY:** Life centre Park Leisure centre Metroland

Lying west of the city centre, this modern, stylish hotel is easily accessible from major road networks. Bedrooms provide good guest comfort and are well-equipped. Public areas include a popular bar and restaurant.
ROOMS: 274 en suite 🚭 in 172 bedrooms s £67-£75; d £67-£75
NOTES: ✖

Babies Welcome | **Family Rooms** | **Children's Dishes**

★★★ 67% Novotel Newcastle
Ponteland Rd, Kenton NE3 3HZ
☎ 0191 214 0303 📠 0191 214 0633
e-mail: H1118@accor-hotels.com
Dir: off A1(M) airport junct onto A696, take Kingston Park exit

CHILD FACILITIES: Activities: Lego, games on request, goodie bags Indoor play area Outdoor play area Family area Food/bottle warming Ch menu Ch portions Highchairs Ch cutlery Ch discounts under 5s free, under 16s free sharing with adults Games consoles Videos Cots Family rms D rms with S beds Connecting rms Changing mats (in disabled toilet) **NEARBY:** Cinema Metro Centre Coastline Hadrian's Wall

This modern well proportioned hotel lies just off the bypass and is within easy reach of the airport and city centre. Bedrooms are spacious with a range of extras. The Garden Brasserie offers a flexible dining option and is open until late. There is also a small leisure centre for the more energetic.
ROOMS: 126 en suite (56 fmly) 🚭 in 82 bedrooms **FACILITIES:** STV 🏊 Sauna Gym **PARKING:** 260

◆◆◆ Clifton House Hotel
46 Clifton Rd, Off Grainger Park Rd NE4 6XH
☎ 0191 273 0407 📠 0191 273 0407
e-mail: cliftonhousehotel@hotmail.com
Dir: exit A1, Hexham A69 & City West A1856 junct, take A186 for 2m, right at General Hospital into Grainger Park Rd, left into Clifton Rd

CHILD FACILITIES: Please telephone for details

Situated west of the city in a quiet residential area, this fine period mansion has seen its public areas beautifully restored. They include a cosy residents' bar and elegant dining room. Bedrooms come in a variety of sizes and styles, the en suite rooms providing good levels of comfort.
ROOMS: 11 rms (7 en suite) (3 fmly) 🚭 in 4 bedrooms
FACILITIES: TVB tea/coffee TVL Dinner Last d order 48hrs notice
NOTES: 🚭 in restaurant 🚭 in 1 lounge Licensed Cen ht **PARKING:** 12

TYNEMOUTH
Map 12 NZ36

Babies Welcome | **Children's Dishes**

🏵 Sidney's Restaurant
3-5 Percy Park Rd NE30 4LZ
☎ 0191 257 8500 213 0284 📠 0191 257 9800
e-mail: bookings@sidneys.co.uk
web: www.sidneys.co.uk
Dir: From Newcastle take A1058 to Tynemouth. Restaurant on corner of Percy Park Rd & Front St

CHILD FACILITIES: Activities: colouring, toys Food/bottle warming Ch licence Ch menu Ch portions Highchairs Ch cutlery Safe grounds Changing facilities **NEARBY:** Tynemouth Priory Tynemouth Park Boating lake 2-min walk to sea

FOOD: British, European **STYLE:** Modern, Bistro **SEATS:** 50
OPEN: 12-3/6-12, Closed BHs ex Good Friday, Sun **RESTAURANT:** Fixed L £8.50, Fixed D £12.95, main £10.50-£16.95 **NOTES:** 🚭 in restaurant, Air con **PARKING:** On street

WHICKHAM
Map 12 NZ26

Babies Welcome | **Family Rooms** | **Children's Dishes**

★★★ 69% Gibside Hotel
Front St NE16 4JG
☎ 0191 488 9292 📠 0191 488 8000
e-mail: reception@gibside-hotel.co.uk
web: www.gibside-hotel.co.uk
Dir: off A1(M) towards Whickham on B6317, onto Front Street, 2m on right

CHILD FACILITIES: Baby listening Babysitting (by arrangement) Food/bottle warming Ch licence Ch menu Ch portions Highchairs Ch discounts under 12s free when sharing with parents Safe grounds Cots Family rms £69.50 Connecting rms Fridge Laundry **NEARBY:** Park Metroland Cinema Karting Swimming pool Activity centre

Conveniently located in the village centre, this hotel is close to the Newcastle by-pass and its elevated position affords views over the Tyne Valley. Bedrooms come in two styles, classical and contemporary. Public rooms include the Egyptian-themed Sphinx bar and a more formal restaurant. Secure garage parking is available.
ROOMS: 45 en suite (2 fmly) (13 GF) 🚭 in 10 bedrooms s £45-£59.50; d £60-£71 **LB** **FACILITIES:** STV Golf Academy at The Beamish Park 🎵 Xmas **PARKING:** 28

WARWICKSHIRE

Stratford-upon-Avon Motor Museum

GAYDON
Heritage Motor Centre
CV35 0BJ ☎01926 641188
enquiries@heritage-motor-centre.co.uk
(M40 Junct 12 and take B4100. Heritage motor centre is signposted from this junct)
Open daily 10-5. (Closed 24-26 Dec).
*£8 (ch 5-16 £6, under 5 free, & pen £7). Family ticket £25. Add. charges for outdoor activities

KENILWORTH
Kenilworth Castle
CV8 1NE ☎01926 852078
Open all year, Mar-May daily 10-5; Jun-Aug, daily 10-6; Sep-Oct daily 10-5; Nov-Feb daily 10-4. (Closed 24-26 Dec & 1 Jan). *£4.80 (ch £2.40, concessions £3.60).

MIDDLETON
Ash End House Children's Farm
B78 2BL ☎0121 329 3240
contact@thechildrensfarm.co.uk
(signposted from A4091)
Open daily 10-5 or dusk in winter. (Closed 25 Dec-1 Jan and weekdays in Jan).
*£3.90 (ch £4.90 includes animal feed, pony ride, farm badge & all activities).

RUGBY
The Webb Ellis Rugby Football Museum
CV21 3BY ☎01788 567777
service@webb-ellis.co.uk
(On A428 opposite Rugby School).
Open all year, Mon-Sat 9-5. Phone for holiday opening times.

STRATFORD-UPON-AVON
The Teddy Bear Museum CV37 6LF
info@theteddybearmuseum.com ☎01789 293160
(M40 follow signs to Stratford Town Centre)
Open all year, daily 9.30-5.30 (ex Jan & Feb 10-4.30). Closed 25-26 Dec.
*£2.95 (ch £1.95, concessions £2.45). Family £9.50.

WARWICK
Warwick Castle
CV34 4QU ☎0870 442 2000
customer.information@warwick-castle.com
(2m from M40 exit 15)
Open all year, daily 10-6 (5pm Nov-Mar, 7pm Aug).
*£11.50-£14.50 (ch 4-16 £7.25-£8.75, pen £8.20-£10.50 £33-£39, student £8.75-£10.75). Family ticket (2 ad & 2 ch) £32-£44. Wheelchair bound visitors free. Group discounts are available.

ALDERMINSTER   Map 04 SP24

| Babies Welcome | Family Rooms | Children's Dishes |

◆◆◆◆ 🍴 The Bell
Shipston Rd CV37 8NY
☎ 01789 450414 🖷 01789 450998
e-mail: thebellald@aol.com
web: www.thebellald.co.uk
Dir: on A3400 3m S of Stratford-upon-Avon on Shipston-Oxford road

CHILD FACILITIES: Activities: Food/bottle warming Ch menu Ch portions Highchairs Ch cutlery Ch discounts (by arrangement) Safe grounds Cots Family rms D rms with S beds Ch drinks (on request) Laundry (by arrangement) **NEARBY:** Butterfly farm Warwick Castle Leisure centre Cinema

A focal part of the local community, this former coaching house retains many original features enhanced by quality decor in the public areas. The inn specialises in gastronomic festivals throughout the year and the thoughtfully furnished bedrooms are located in a sympathetically renovated separate house or a quality coach house conversion, accessed via the immaculate gardens.
ROOMS: 6 annexe rms (3 en suite) (2 fmly) (2 GF) s £27-£52; d £48-£70 * ⊗ **FACILITIES:** TVB tea/coffee Dinner Last d order 9.30pm **NOTES:** ⊗ in restaurant ⊗ in lounges Cen ht **LB**
PARKING: 70

HENLEY-IN-ARDEN   Map 04 SP16

◆◆◆◆ Ashleigh House
Whitley Hill B95 5DL
☎ 01564 792315 🖷 01564 794126
e-mail: enquiries@ashleigh-house.fsbusiness.co.uk
Dir: leave A3400 at lights on High St. Along A4189 towards Warwick, Ashleigh House, 1m from lights
CHILD FACILITIES: Please telephone for details

Set in two acres of immaculate grounds, this impressive Edwardian house has been sympathetically upgraded, enhancing the many original features. Spacious bedrooms, some of which are located in former stable blocks, provide both practicality and comfort and ground floor areas include an elegant dining room, conservatory and a lounge.
ROOMS: 6 en suite 5 annexe en suite (2 fmly) (5 GF) s £45-£55; d £55-£69.50 * ⊗ **FACILITIES:** TVB tea/coffee Direct dial from bedrooms TVL No coaches Dinner Last d order before noon **NOTES:** ⊗ in restaurant ⊗ in lounges Licensed Cen ht **LB**
PARKING: 17

KENILWORTH   Map 04 SP27

🍴 Clarendon House
High St CV8 1LZ
☎ 01926 857668 🖷 01926 850669
e-mail: info@clarendonhousehotel.com
web: www.clarendonhousehotel.com
Dir: From A452 pass castle, turn L into Castle Hill and continue into High Street
CHILD FACILITIES: Please telephone for details

OPEN: 11-11 (Sun 12-10.30) Closed: 25-26 Dec, 1 Jan **BAR MEALS:** L served all week 12-10 D served all week 12-10 Av main course £9.50 **RESTAURANT:** L served all week 12-10 D served all week 12-10 Av 3 course à la carte £18 **FACILITIES:** Garden: Patio garden seats about 100. Outdoor heating **ROOMS:** 22 bedrooms 22 en suite 2 family rooms s£57.50 d£79.50 **PARKING:** 35

♦♦♦♦ Bubbenhall House
Paget's Ln CV8 3BJ
☎ 024 7630 2409 🖷 024 7630 2409
e-mail: wharrison@bubbenhallhouse.freeserve.co.uk
Dir: from Leamington on A445, Pagets Lane on right
CHILD FACILITIES: **Please telephone for details**

Located between Leamington Spa and Coventry in extensive mature grounds with an abundance of wildlife, this impressive late Edwardian house, once the home of the Mini's designer, contains many features including a fine Jacobean staircase. Thoughtful extras are provided in the comfortable bedrooms and public areas include an elegant dining room and choice of lounges.
ROOMS: 3 en suite s £40-£45; d £59-£65 * ⊗ **FACILITIES:** TVB tea/coffee TVL No coaches ⚲ ♨ Petanque, spa hot tub **NOTES:** Credit cards not taken ✖ ⊗ in restaurant Cen ht **LB PARKING:** 12

🍴 The Bell Inn
Bell Ln CV23 0QY
☎ 01788 832352 🖷 01788 832352
e-mail: belindagb@aol.com
Dir: Off The Fosseway junction with B4455
CHILD FACILITIES: **Please telephone for details**

OPEN: 12-2.30 7-11 Closed: 26 Dec, 1 Jan **BAR MEALS:** L served Tue-Sun 12-2.30 D served all week 7-11 Av main course £12.50 **RESTAURANT:** L served Tue-Sun 12-2.30 D served all week 7-11 Av 3 course à la carte £30 **FACILITIES:** Garden: overlooks a stream & buttercup meadow ✖

♦♦♦♦ 🍴 The Red Lion Hotel
Main St, Long Compton CV36 5JS
☎ 01608 684221 🖷 01608 684221
e-mail: redlionhot@aol.com
Dir: on A3400 between Chipping Norton & Shipston on Stour
CHILD FACILITIES: **Activities: games, jigsaws, puzzles Outdoor play area Family area Food/bottle warming Ch menu Ch portions Highchairs Ch cutlery Ch discounts Safe grounds Cots Family rms D rm with 3 S beds £80 Laundry NEARBY: Walks Rollingright Stones Wildlife parks**

Located in the pretty rural village of Long Compton, this mid 18th-century posting house retains many original features, highlighted by the rustic furniture throughout the warm and inviting public areas. Bedrooms are furnished with a good range of practical facilities, and menus utilise quality local produce.
ROOMS: 5 en suite (1 fmly) s £40; d £60 * **FACILITIES:** TVB tea/coffee No coaches Pool Table Traditional pub games Dinner Last d order 9pm **NOTES:** ⊗ in area of dining room Cen ht **PARKING:** 60

Babies Welcome	Family Rooms	Children's Dishes

★★★★ 71% Stratford Manor
Warwick Rd CV37 0PY
☎ 01789 731173 🖷 01789 731131
e-mail: stratfordmanor@marstonhotels.com
Dir: M40 junct 15, take A439, hotel 2m on left
CHILD FACILITIES: **Babysitting Activities: activity pack Outdoor play area Food/bottle warming Ch menu Ch portions Highchairs Ch discounts under 15s free sharing with adults Safe grounds Videos Cots Family rms Connecting rms Laundry NEARBY: Warwick Castle Cadbury World Leisure centre**

Just outside Stratford, this hotel is set against a rural backdrop with lovely gardens and ample car parking. Public areas include a lounge bar and a busy split-level restaurant, while the leisure centre boasts a large indoor pool. Service is both professional and helpful. Bedrooms are spacious and well-equipped.
ROOMS: 104 en suite (8 fmly) ⊗ in 52 bedrooms s £124-£134; d £158-£178 (incl. bkfst & dinner) **LB FACILITIES:** Spa STV 🖭 ⚲ Sauna Solarium Gym Beauty treatments Xmas **PARKING:** 250 **NOTES:** ✖ ⊗ in restaurant

♦♦♦♦ 🌿 Clopton Orchard Farm
Lower Clopton, Upper Quinton CV37 8LH
☎ 01386 438669 🖷 01386 438669
e-mail: mail@clopton-orchard.fsnet.co.uk
Dir: from Stratford upon Avon take B4632 signed Broadway. Through Lower Clopton. Farm on right
CHILD FACILITIES: **Please telephone for details**

A warm welcome is assured at this attractive modern farmhouse located between Broadway and Stratford-upon-Avon. Spacious bedrooms are equipped with practical and thoughtful extras and comprehensive breakfasts are taken at one family table.
ROOMS: 2 en suite (1 fmly) s fr £35; d fr £50 * **FACILITIES:** TVB tea/coffee 300 acres arable sheep **NOTES:** Credit cards not taken ✖ ⊗ Cen ht **LB PARKING:** 5

Babies Welcome	Family Rooms	Children's Dishes

♦♦♦♦ Eastnor House Hotel
Shipston Rd CV37 7LN
☎ 01789 268115 🖷 01789 551133
e-mail: enquiries@eastnorhouse.com
Dir: follow A3400 Shipston Rd. Hotel 1st on right, close to Clopton Bridge
CHILD FACILITIES: **Food/bottle warming Ch portions Highchairs Ch cutlery Safe grounds Cots Family rms 2 rms sleeping up to 5 Connecting rms NEARBY: Teddy Bear Museum Warwick Castle**

This late Victorian townhouse is conveniently located for the town centre and many visitor attractions. Run in a warm and friendly manner, it provides very well-equipped accommodation. Separate tables are provided in the traditionally furnished breakfast room.
ROOMS: 10 en suite (3 fmly) (3 GF) s £50-£65; d £66-£85 * **FACILITIES:** TVB tea/coffee Direct dial from bedrooms No coaches **NOTES:** ✖ ⊗ Cen ht **LB PARKING:** 10

♦♦♦ Avon Lodge
Ryon Hill, Warwick Rd CV37 0NZ
☎ 01789 295196
CHILD FACILITIES: **Please telephone for details**

Located in immaculate mature gardens on the outskirts of town, this former Victorian cottage has been tastefully modernised and extended to provide homely and cosy bedrooms. Imaginative breakfasts are taken in an attractive cottage-style dining room.
ROOMS: 6 en suite (1 fmly) **FACILITIES:** TV5B tea/coffee No coaches **NOTES:** Credit cards not taken ⊗ Cen ht **PARKING:** 7

WEST MIDLANDS

Falconry Centre

BIRMINGHAM
Thinktank at Millennium Point B4 7XG
findout@thinktank.ac ☎0121 202 2222
Open daily 10-5 (last entry 4). (Closed 24-26 Dec)

BOURNVILLE
Cadbury World B30 2LD
cadbury.world@csplc.com ☎0121 451 4159
(1m S of A38 Bristol Rd, on A4040 Ring Rd)
Contact information line 0121 451 4180 for
opening times.

DUDLEY
Black Country Living Museum DY1 4SQ
info@bclm.co.uk ☎0121 557 9643
(on A4037, nr Showcase cinema)
Open all year, Mar-Oct daily 10-5; Nov-Feb, Wed-
Sun 10-4. (Telephone for Christmas closing)
*£9.95 (ch 5-18 £5.75, pen £8.75). Family ticket
(2ad+3ch £28) Prices subject to change.

Dudley Zoological Gardens DY1 4QB
marketing@dudleyzoo.org.uk ☎01384 215313
(M5 junct 2 towards Wolverhampton/Dudley.
Signposted)
Open all year, Etr-mid Sep, daily 10-4; mid Sep-
Etr, daily 10-3. (Closed 25 Dec).
*£8.50 (ch 4-15 £5.25, concessions £5.75). Family
ticket £28.50 (2ad+3ch)

SOLIHULL
National Motorcycle Museum
B92 0EJ ☎01675 443311
(near junct 6, of M42, off A45 near NEC)
Open all year, daily 10-6. (Closed 24-26 Dec).
*£5.95 (ch 12 & pen £4.75). Party 20+ £4.95

STOURBRIDGE
The Falconry Centre
DY9 0JB ☎01562 700014
(off A456)
Open all year, daily 10-5 & Sun 11-5. (Closed 25,
26 Dec & Etr Sun).

Babies Welcome | Family Rooms | Children's Dishes

★★★ 67%
Novotel Birmingham Centre
70 Broad St B1 2HT
☎ 0121 643 2000 📠 0121 643 9796
e-mail: h1077@accor-hotels.com

CHILD FACILITIES: Activities: activity pack Indoor play area
Food/bottle warming Ch menu Ch portions Highchairs Ch discounts
under 16s free sharing with parents Games consoles Cots Family
rms D rm with S beds from £70 Ch drinks Connecting rms Fridge
NEARBY: Cadbury World Sealife Centre Cinema Leisure centre

This large, modern, purpose-built hotel benefits from an excellent
city centre location, with the bonus of secure car parking.
Bedrooms are spacious, modern and well equipped. Four rooms
have facilities for less able guests. Public areas include the Garden
Brasserie, function rooms and a fitness room.
ROOMS: 148 en suite (148 fmly) ⊗ in 98 bedrooms s £80-£145;
d £155-£165 (incl. bkfst) **LB FACILITIES:** STV Sauna Gym Jacuzzi
PARKING: 53

Family Rooms | Children's Dishes

♦♦♦ Awentsbury Hotel
21 Serpentine Rd, Selly Park B29 7HU
☎ 0121 472 1258 📠 0121 472 1258
e-mail: ian@awentsbury.com
*Dir: A38 from city centre, at end of dual carriageway & just after fire
station, take 1st left, left again & 1st right*

CHILD FACILITIES: Baby listening Outdoor play area Family area
Food/bottle warming Ch menu Ch portions Ch cutlery Ch discounts
under 5s free Safe grounds Videos Family rms D with foldaway bed
Ch drinks **NEARBY:** Cadbury World Parks

This large Victorian house is quietly located in a residential area,
within easy walking distance of the university and local
restaurants. Bedrooms are simply furnished and many have en
suite showers. Breakfast is taken in a combined lounge and dining
room, overlooking the garden.
ROOMS: 16 rms (7 en suite) (1 fmly) (4 GF) s £40-£50; d £54-£62 *
FACILITIES: TVB tea/coffee Direct dial from bedrooms Dinner Last d
order 7pm **NOTES:** ⊗ Cen ht **PARKING:** 12

♦♦♦ Charde
289 Mackadown Ln, The Cross B33 0NH
☎ 0121 785 2145 📠 0121 785 2149
e-mail: chardeguesthouse@talk21.com
*Dir: M42 to A45 towards Birmingham. Turn right towards Garrets Green,
then at 1st Island turn right. After 0.25 mile turn left into Mackadown Lane*
CHILD FACILITIES: Please telephone for details
This constantly improving guest house, ideally located for both the
city centre and NEC, provides a selection of bedrooms equipped
with a range of thoughtful extras. Breakfast is taken in a cosy
dining room and a bar is also available.
ROOMS: 7 rms (5 en suite) (2 fmly) (3 GF) s £22.50-£27.50; d £45-£50 *
⊗ in 4 bedrooms **FACILITIES:** TVB tea/coffee Dinner Last d order by
arrangement **NOTES:** ✻ Cen ht **LB PARKING:** 7

Many proprietors are happy to
provide extra facilities for children,
but let them know in advance what
you need so they can be prepared

England

Babies Welcome

◉ Chung Ying Garden
17 Thorp St B5 4AT
☎ 0121 666 6622 622 1668 📠 0121 622 5860
e-mail: chungyinggarden@aol.com
Dir: City centre, just off Hurst St, nr Hippodrome Theatre off A38.

CHILD FACILITIES: Food/bottle warming Highchairs Safe grounds Baby changing facilities **NEARBY:** Theatres Bowling alley Cinema

FOOD: Traditional Chinese **STYLE:** Classic Modern **SEATS:** 380
OPEN: noon, Closed Xmas Day **RESTAURANT:** Fixed L £14, Fixed D £16, main £7-£36 **NOTES:** Smart Dress, Air con **PARKING:** 50

◉ Bank Restaurant & Bar
4 Brindley Place B12 JB
☎ 0121 633 7001 0121 633 4466 📠 0121 633 4465
e-mail: birmingham@bankrestaurants.com
Dir: Brindley Place is just off Broad Street (A456), 3mins walk from ICC.
CHILD FACILITIES: Please telephone for details
FOOD: Modern British **STYLE:** Modern Minimalist **SEATS:** 250
OPEN: 12/5.30-10.30, Closed 1-2 Jan, 1 May, BHs **RESTAURANT:** main £9.50-£20 **NOTES:** ✆ area, Air con **PARKING:** 100yds

Babies Welcome | Children's Dishes

◉ Thai Edge Restaurant
Brindley Place B12HS
☎ 0121 643 3993 📠 0121 643 3994
e-mail: vivian@thaiedge.co.uk
Dir: Brindley Place is just off Broad St. (approx 0.5m from B'ham New Street station)
CHILD FACILITIES: Outdoor play area Food/bottle warming Ch licence Ch portions Highchairs **NEARBY:** Sealife Centre Cinema
FOOD: Thai **STYLE:** Modern Minimalist **SEATS:** 100
OPEN: 12-2.30/5.30-11, Closed 25-26 Dec, 1 Jan **RESTAURANT:** Fixed D £17.80, main £7-£28 **NOTES:** Air con

Children's Dishes

◉ ◉ La Toque d'Or
27 Warstone Ln, Hockley B18 6JQ
☎ 0121 233 3655 📠 0121 233 3655
e-mail: didier@latoquedor.co.uk
Dir: 1m N of city centre, 400mtrs from clock tower (in Jewellery Quarter). Telephone for further directions
CHILD FACILITIES: Food/bottle warming Ch portions
FOOD: French **STYLE:** Classic French **SEATS:** 36
OPEN: 12.30-1.30/7-9.30, Closed 1 wk Xmas, 1 wk Etr, 2 wks Aug, Sun-MonL Sat **NOTES:** Air con **PARKING:** NCP - Vyse Street

---

Babies Welcome | Family Rooms | Children's Dishes

★★★ 67%
Novotel Birmingham Airport
B26 3QL
☎ 0121 782 7000 📠 0121 782 0445
e-mail: H1158@accor-hotels.com
Dir: M42 junct 6/A45 to Birmingham, signed to airport. Hotel opposite main terminal

NOVOTEL

CHILD FACILITIES: Activities: colouring, toys, Lego Family area Food/bottle warming Ch menu Ch portions Highchairs Ch discounts under 16s free when sharing with parent Games consoles Cots Family rms D rm with S beds £85-£150 Connecting rms Laundry **NEARBY:** Cadbury's World Drayton Manor Park Sea Life Centre

This large, purpose-built hotel is located opposite the main passenger terminal. Bedrooms are spacious, modern in style and well equipped, including Playstations to keep the children busy. Two rooms have facilities for less able guests. The Garden Brasserie is open from noon until midnight and a full room service is available.
ROOMS: 195 en suite (31 fmly) ✆ in 159 bedrooms s £125-£149; d £135-£159 (incl. bkfst) **FACILITIES:** STV

Babies Welcome | Family Rooms | Children's Dishes

★★★ 64% *Novotel Coventry*
Wilsons Ln CV6 6HL
☎ 024 7636 5000 📠 024 7636 2422
e-mail: h0506@accor-hotels.com
Dir: Follow signs for B4113 towards Longford and Bedworth. 3rd exit on large rdbt

NOVOTEL

CHILD FACILITIES: Activities: Dolfi toys, colouring June-Sept outdoor swimming pool Indoor play area Outdoor play area Food/bottle warming Ch menu Ch portions Highchairs Ch cutlery Ch discounts under 16s free sharing with parents Safe grounds Games consoles Cots Family rms D rms with S beds from £59 Connecting rms Laundry **NEARBY:** Drayton Manor Park Warwick Castle

A modern hotel, convenient for Birmingham, Coventry and the motorway network, offering spacious, well-equipped accommodation. The bright brasserie offers extended dining hours, or alternatively there is an extensive room-service menu. Family rooms and a play area make this a child-friendly hotel.
ROOMS: 98 en suite (15 fmly) ✆ in 70 bedrooms **FACILITIES:** ⚑ Petanque, Pool table **PARKING:** 120

Babies Welcome | Family Rooms | Children's Dishes

♦♦♦ Croft on the Green
23 Stoke Green, off Binley Rd CV3 1FP
☎ 024 7645 7846 🖷 024 7645 7846
e-mail: croftonthegreen@aol.com
web: www.croftonthegreen.co.uk
Dir: from A428 Coventry City Centre towards to Rugby on Binley Rd, turn off onto Stoke Green signed, towards Aldermoor House

CHILD FACILITIES: Activities: books, toys Outdoor play area Food/bottle warming Ch menu Ch portions Highchairs Ch cutlery Ch discounts under 3s free sharing with parents Safe grounds Videos Cots Family rms D rm with 2 S beds £65 Ch drinks Laundry **NEARBY:** Country park

An impresive Victorian villa located within a conservation area close to city centre. A range of practically furnished bedrooms is provided and ground floor areas include a spacious attractive dining room, overlooking the pretty garden and a comfortable lounge bar.
ROOMS: 12 rms (9 en suite) (2 fmly) s £27-£35; d £45-£55 *
FACILITIES: TVB tea/coffee TVL **NOTES:** ✷ ⊗ Licensed Cen ht **PARKING:** 12

ROWLEY REGIS   Map 07 SO98

Babies Welcome | Family Rooms | Children's Dishes

♦♦ Highfield House Hotel
1 Holly Rd, Blackheath B65 0BH
☎ 0121 559 1066 🖷 0121 561 2424
Dir: M5 junct 2, take A4034 (Birchfield Road) towards to Blackheath, joining Oldbury Road, right into Henderson Way, join High St, then Powke Lane, left into Holly Road at 1st traffic lights

CHILD FACILITIES: Food/bottle warming Ch portions Highchairs Ch discounts Safe grounds Cots Family rms D rm with S bed, S & D en-suite rm (price depending on occupancy) Connecting rms **NEARBY:** Parks Leisure centre

Located a few minutes' walk from shops, pubs and restaurants, this extended Victorian house provides good-value accommodation. Comprehensive breakfasts are taken in an attractive, cottage-style dining room and the property benefits from a private car park.
ROOMS: 14 rms (2 en suite) (3 fmly) s £22-£30; d £36-£45 *
FACILITIES: TVB tea/coffee TVL No coaches **NOTES:** ✷ ⊗ in restaurant Licensed Cen ht **BB PARKING:** 10

HAMPTON-IN-ARDEN   Map 04 SP28

Family Rooms | Children's Dishes

♦♦♦ The Cottage
Kenilworth Rd B92 0LW
☎ 01675 442323 🖷 01675 443323
Dir: on A452, 2m from M42, 4m from M6, 3m NEC & B'ham airport

CHILD FACILITIES: Outdoor play area Family area Food/bottle warming Ch menu Ch portions Ch cutlery Ch discounts Videos Cots Family rms D rm with S beds Ch drinks **NEARBY:** Golf Fishing Horseriding Walks Cinema

A fine collection of antique memorabilia adorns the public areas of this delightful cottage, which is an ideal base from which to visit the NEC or to explore the area. A friendly atmosphere and attentive service provide a relaxing environment and many guests return. Freshly cooked traditional breakfasts are served in the cottage dining room and provide a good start to the day.
ROOMS: 9 en suite (2 GF) s £35-£45; d £48-£58 * **FACILITIES:** TVB tea/coffee TVL **NOTES:** Credit cards not taken ⊗ in restaurant Cen ht **PARKING:** 14

WOLVERHAMPTON   Map 07 SO99

Babies Welcome | Family Rooms | Children's Dishes

★★★ 67% Novotel Wolverhampton
Union St WV1 3JN
☎ 01902 871100 🖷 01902 870054
e-mail: H1188@accor-hotels.com
Dir: 6m from M6 junct 10. A454 to Wolverhampton. Hotel on main ring road

 NOVOTEL

CHILD FACILITIES: Activities: games, toys Indoor play area Food/bottle warming Ch menu Ch portions Highchairs Ch discounts under 16s free sharing with parents Safe grounds Games consoles Cots Family rms D rm with S beds Connecting rms **NEARBY:** Zoo Castle Museum Cinema Bowling Leisure Centre

This large, modern, purpose-built hotel stands close to the town centre and ring road. It provides spacious, smartly presented and well-equipped bedrooms, all of which contain convertible bed settees for family occupancy. In addition to the open plan lounge and bar area, there is an attractive brasserie-style restaurant, which overlooks the small outdoor swimming pool.
ROOMS: 132 en suite (10 fmly) ⊗ in 88 bedrooms s £65-£105; d £75-£115 (incl. bkfst) **LB FACILITIES:** STV ✲ **PARKING:** 120

> Many proprietors are happy to provide extra facilities for children, but let them know in advance what you need so they can be prepared

England

ISLE OF WIGHT

Freshwater Bay

BRADING
Isle of Wight Wax Works
PO36 0DQ ☎0870 4584477
waxworks@bradingisleofwight.fsnet.co.uk
(On A3055, in Brading High St)
Open all year, summer 10-5, winter 10.30-4.30
(last admission 1hr before closing)
*£5.50, ch £3.75, under 5 free, pen £4.50. Family
£17 2ad+2ch, Family £20 2ad+3ch. Party 20+.

Lilliput Antique Doll & Toy Museum
PO36 0DJ ☎01983 407231
lilliput.museum@btconnect.com
(A3055 Ryde/Sandown road, in Brading High)
Street Open all year, daily, 10-5. *£1.95, ch & pen
£1.15, ch under 5 free. Party on request.

CARISBROOKE
Carisbrooke Castle
PO30 1XY ☎01983 522107
(1.25m SW of Newport, off B3401)
Open all year, Apr-Sep, daily 10-6 Oct- Mar, daily
10-4. Closed 24-26 Dec & 1 Jan. *£5, ch £2.50,
concessions £3.80.

OSBORNE HOUSE
Osborne House
PO32 6JY ☎01983 200022
(1m SE of East Cowes)
Open House: Apr-Sep, daily 10-6; Oct- Mar, Sun-
Thu guided tours only. Closed 24-26 Dec & 1Jan.
*House & Gardens: £8.50, ch £4.30, concessions
£6.40. Garden only: £5, ch £2.50, concessions
£3.80. Family £21.30 (2ad+3ch).

PORCHFIELD
Colemans Animal Farm PO30 4LX
info@colemansfarm.net ☎01983 522831
(From A3054 Newport-Yarmouth Rd, follow brown
tourist signs.)
Open 20 Mar-7 Nov, Tue-Sun 10-5. Closed Mon,
ex during school and bank holidays.
*£4.95, ch & concessions £3.95

SHANKLIN
Shanklin Chine PO37 6PF
jill@shanklinchine.co.uk ☎01983 866432
(Turn off A3055 into Chine Hollow, Shanklin Old
Village between Crab Inn & Pencil Cottage to
Upper entrance or turn off A3055 at lights left into
Hope Rd & continue on to Esplanade. Lower
entrance Western end)
Open daily Apr-Oct (late May-late Sep illuminated
after dusk. *£3.50, ch under 16 £2, pen & students
£2.50. Family ticket £9. (2 adult & 2 ch £11(2 adult
& 3 ch.) Group rates available.

ALUM BAY
The Needles Old Battery PO30 0JH
jean.pitt@nationaltrust.org.uk ☎01983 754772
(At Needles Headland, W of Freshwater Bay and
Alum Bay, B3322)
Open 28 Mar-Jun & Sep-Oct daily, closed Fri ex
Good Fri 10.30-5; Jul-Aug daily 10.30-5. Property
closes in bad weather. Telephone on day of visit to
check.
*£3.80, ch £1.90. Family ticket £8.50.

The Needles Park PO39 0JD
info@theneedles.co.uk ☎0870 458 0022
(Signposted, on B3322)
Open 23 Mar-30 Oct, daily 10-5. Hours extended
in high season.
*No admission charged for entrance to Park. All
day car park charge £3. Pay-as-you-go attractions
or Supersaver Attraction discount ticket £7.50,
ch £5.50.

ARRETON
Robin Hill Country Park
PO30 2NU ☎01983 527352
(0.5m from Arreton next door to the Hare and
Hounds pub)
Open 25 Mar-3 Nov, daily 10-5 last admission 4.

BLACKGANG
Blackgang Chine Fantasy Park PO38 2HN
info@blackgangchine.com ☎01983 730330
(Follow signs from Ventnor for Whitnell & Niton.
From the village of Niton follow signs for
Blackgang)
Open 22 Mar-Oct daily, 10-5. 18 Jul-4 Sep open
until 10. Combined ticket to chine, sawmill & quay
*£7.50. Saver ticket 4 people £27.

ARRETON   Map 04 SZ58

🍺 The White Lion
PO30 3AA
☎ 01983 528479
e-mail: cthewhitelion@aol.com

CHILD FACILITIES: Please telephone for details

OPEN: 11-12 (Sun 11-10.30) **BAR MEALS:** L served all week 12-9 D served all week 12-9 Av main course £7 **FACILITIES:** Garden: Patio area in pleasant old village location **PARKING:** 6

BEMBRIDGE   Map 04 SZ68

🍺 The Crab & Lobster Inn
32 Foreland Fields Rd PO35 5TR
☎ 01983 872244 ▤ 01983 873495
e-mail: allancrab@aol.com
Dir: Telephone for directions

CHILD FACILITIES: Food/bottle warming Ch licence Ch menu Ch portions Highchairs Ch cutlery Changing facilities
NEARBY: Coastal walks Near sea

OPEN: 11-3 (Wknds & summer all day) 6-11 **BAR MEALS:** L served all week 12-2.30 D served all week 6.00-9.30 Av main course £10
RESTAURANT: L served all week 12-2.30 D served all week 7-9.30 A 3 course à la carte £25 **FACILITIES:** Children's licence Garden: Patio overlooking the beach **PARKING:** 40

BONCHURCH   Map 04 SZ57

🍺 The Bonchurch Inn
Bonchurch Shute PO38 1NU
☎ 01983 852611 ▤ 01983 856657
e-mail: gillian@bonchurch-inn.co.uk
Dir: South coast of the Island

CHILD FACILITIES: Family area Food/bottle warming Ch menu Ch portions Highchairs Safe grounds **NEARBY:** Walks 200yds to sea

OPEN: 11-3.30 6.30-11 Closed: 25 Dec **BAR MEALS:** L served all week 11-2.15 D served all week 6.30-9 **RESTAURANT:** D served all week 6.30-9.30 **FACILITIES:** Garden: Courtyard, patio & fountain **PARKING:** 7

CHALE   Map 04 SZ47

◆◆◆◆◆ Chale Bay Farm
Military Rd PO38 2JF
☎ 01983 730950 ▤ 01983 730395
e-mail: info@chalebayfarm.co.uk
Dir: beside A3055 (Military Rd) in Chale near St Andrews Church

CHILD FACILITIES: Baby listening Activities: toys, jigsaws, books Outdoor play area Food/bottle warming Ch menu Ch portions Highchairs Ch discounts babies free Safe grounds Cots Family rms 2 suites with D & T beds Ch drinks Connecting rms Laundry
NEARBY: Blackgang Chine theme park Dinosaur Farm Fossil hunting trips Near sea

Guests are assured of a warm welcome at Chale Bay Farm, situated on the National Trust Heritage Coastline, with spectacular

continued

coastal and rural views of The Needles and Tennyson Downs. All of the spacious bedrooms, many with their own private patios, are located on the ground floor. In the morning, guests can enjoy hearty, home-cooked breakfasts served at individual tables.

ROOMS: 8 en suite (2 fmly) (8 GF) s £33-£50; d £66-£86 * ⊛ in 2 bedrooms **FACILITIES:** TVB tea/coffee No coaches **NOTES:** ✻ ⊛ in area of dining room ⊛ in lounges Licensed Cen ht **LB PARKING:** 50

FRESHWATER   Map 04 SZ38

★★★ 68% ⊛ Farringford
Bedbury Ln PO40 9TQ
☎ 01983 752500 ▤ 01983 756515
web: www.farringford.co.uk
Dir: A3054, left to Norton Green down Pixlie Hill. Left to Freshwater Bay. At bay turn right into Bedbury Ln, hotel on left

CHILD FACILITIES: Baby listening Nanny Babysitting Activities: disco (Wed school hols) Outdoor play area Food/bottle warming Ch menu Ch portions Highchairs Ch discounts under 5s free, over 5s £10 per day Safe grounds Cots Family rms D, T and triple rms £65-£90 Connecting rms Fridge Laundry Changing mats (on request) **NEARBY:** Tourist Island 2-min drive to sea

Upon seeing Farringford, Alfred Lord Tennyson is said to have remarked "we will go no further, this must be our home" and so it was for some forty years. One hundred and fifty years later, the hotel provides bedrooms ranging in style and size, from large rooms in the main house to adjoining chalet-style rooms. The atmosphere is relaxed and dinner features fresh local produce.
ROOMS: 14 en suite 4 annexe en suite (5 fmly) (4 GF) s £37-£53; d £74-£120 (incl. bkfst) **LB FACILITIES:** ⋏ Golf 9 ⚻ ▨ ⅃ Bowling green ♫ Xmas **PARKING:** 55

ST HELENS   Map 04 SZ68

◆◆◆◆ Sheepstor Cottage
West Green PO33 1XA
☎ 01983 873132
Dir: turn off A3055 onto B3330 coming onto the Green, turn left into Field Lane, Cottage is 3rd house on right

CHILD FACILITIES: Please telephone for details

A friendly welcome awaits you from the proprietor and her family of cats at this cosy cottage-style guest house. The bedrooms are attractively appointed and both offer en suite facilities, while a freshly prepared breakfast can be taken in the pleasant dining room, which enjoys far-reaching views over the surrounding countryside.
ROOMS: 2 en suite (1 fmly) s fr £25; d fr £50 * **FACILITIES:** TVB tea/coffee No coaches **NOTES:** Credit cards not taken ✻ ⊛ Cen ht

SANDOWN   Map 04 SZ58

★★ 68% Riviera
2 Royal St PO36 8LP
☎ 01983 402518 📠 01983 402518
e-mail: enquiries@rivierahotel.org.uk
Dir: pass Heights Leisure Centre and church on left. Turn 2nd right (Melville St), then 2nd right again into Royal St

> **CHILD FACILITIES:** Baby listening Food/bottle warming Ch menu Ch portions Highchairs Ch discounts under 2s free, 3-5s 1/3, 6-10s 1/2, 11-15s 3/4 Safe grounds Cots Family rms D rm with 2 S beds £90 Laundry **NEARBY:** Leisure centres Pier Gardens Tiger Sanctuary 250 yds to sea

Regular guests return year after year to this friendly and welcoming family-run hotel. It is located near to the High Street and just a short stroll from the beach, pier and shops. Bedrooms, including several at ground floor level, are very well furnished and comfortably equipped. Enjoyable home-cooked meals are served in the spacious dining room.
ROOMS: 41 en suite (6 fmly) (10 GF) s £38-£44; d £76-£88 (incl. bkfst & dinner) **LB FACILITIES:** ♫ **PARKING:** 20 **NOTES:** ⊗ in restaurant Closed Nov-Mar

♦♦♦ Carisbrooke House Hotel
11 Beachfield Rd PO36 8NA
☎ 01983 402257 📠 01983 402295
e-mail: carisbrookehotel@aol.com
Dir: follow signs through Sandown town centre and through High Street onto Beachfield Road, hotel 200yds past Post Office on right

> **CHILD FACILITIES:** Activities: colouring, jigsaws, toys Food/bottle warming Ch menu Ch portions Highchairs Ch cutlery Ch discounts under 2s £5, 2-15s 50% Safe grounds Videos Cots Family rms D rms with B beds from £72 **NEARBY:** 2-min walk to sea

Located within walking distance of the town centre and seafront, this delightful family-run hotel provides guests with a warm welcome and comfortable bedrooms. There is a large dining room where full English breakfasts are served at individual tables and guests have access to a bar, which leads through to a cosy television lounge.
ROOMS: 10 rms (8 en suite) (4 fmly) (3 GF) s £20-£25; d £40-£50 *
⊗ **FACILITIES:** TVB tea/coffee TVL **NOTES:** ⊗ in restaurant Licensed Cen ht **LB**

♦♦♦ Culver Lodge Hotel
17 Albert Rd PO36 8AW
☎ 01983 403819 📠 01983 403819
Dir: turn off The Broadway into Station Rd and left into Albert Rd

> **CHILD FACILITIES:** Please telephone for details

This hotel is located in a quiet residential area a short walk from the seafront and town centre. Bedrooms are well equipped and public areas are spacious and include an attractive lounge, bar and games room, while outside, the pool and terrace are ideal areas to enjoy the sun.
ROOMS: 22 en suite (6 fmly) (4 GF) ⊗ **FACILITIES:** TVB tea/coffee TVL ⚲ Pool Table Bike Hire, Table Football, bar billiards Dinner Last d order 7pm **NOTES:** ✖ ⊗ in restaurant ⊗ in 1 lounge Licensed Cen ht **PARKING:** 20

♦♦♦ Fernside Hotel
30 Station Av PO36 9BW
☎ 01983 402356 📠 01983 403647
e-mail: enquiries@fernsidehotel.co.uk
web: www.fernsidehotel.co.uk
Dir: turn off the Broadway opposite Londis shop into Station Avenue, Hotel on left

> **CHILD FACILITIES:** Baby listening Food/bottle warming Ch portions Highchairs Ch cutlery Ch discounts under 3s free, 2-15s reductions Safe grounds Videos Cots Family rms D rms with B beds Ch drinks **NEARBY:** Short walk to sea

Located within walking distance of the town centre and sandy beaches, this family-run hotel provides guests with comfortable bedrooms equipped with useful extra facilities. Some ground floor rooms are available, as are a guest lounge and bar. Full English breakfasts are served at individual tables.
ROOMS: 13 rms (11 en suite) (2 fmly) (3 GF) s £21-£25; d £42-£50 *
FACILITIES: TVB tea/coffee TVL No coaches Dinner Last d order am **NOTES:** ✖ ⊗ Licensed Cen ht **LB PARKING:** 6

SEAVIEW   Map 04 SZ69

★★ 66% *Springvale Hotel & Restaurant*
Springvale PO34 5AN
☎ 01983 612533 📠 01983 812905
e-mail: reception@springvalehotel.com
web: www.springvalehotel.com
Dir: towards Ryde, follow A3055 onto A3330 towards Bembridge. Left at signs to Seaview, follow brown tourist signs for hotel

> **CHILD FACILITIES:** Baby listening Nanny (by arrangement) Activities: fun box with books, toys & games in rm Outdoor play area Food/bottle warming Ch menu Ch portions Highchairs Ch cutlery Ch discounts under 3s free, £2.50 per yr (winter), £3.50 per yr (summer) Cots Family rms D rms with S beds Ch drinks Connecting rms Laundry **NEARBY:** Flamingo Park Puckpool Park Seafront location

A friendly hotel in a quiet beachfront location with views across the Solent. Bedrooms, which differ in shape and size, are attractive and well equipped. Public areas are traditionally furnished and include a cosy bar, dining room and small separate lounge.
ROOMS: 13 en suite (2 fmly) **FACILITIES:** ⚲ Jacuzzi Sailing dinghy hire & tuition, Cruiser Charter ♫ **PARKING:** 1 **NOTES:** ⊗ in restaurant

Babies Welcome	Family Rooms	Children's Dishes

♦♦♦ Northbank Hotel

Circular Rd PO34 5ET
☎ 01983 612227 📠 01983 612227
e-mail: reception@northbankhotel.co.uk
Dir: B3330 from Ryde to Seaview, right into Nettlestone Green, left down the hill into Seaview, hotel on right of High St into Circular Road

CHILD FACILITIES: Baby listening Activities: table tennis, puzzles, games Indoor play area Outdoor play area Family area Food/bottle warming Ch menu Ch portions Highchairs Ch cutlery Ch discounts under 2s £5 per night, 2-12s half price Safe grounds Games consoles Videos Cots Family rms D rms with 2 S beds Ch drinks Connecting rms **NEARBY:** Steam Railway Dinosaur Museum Direct access to sea

The views from Northbank across the Solent to the mainland are stunning, and its delightful gardens run down to a sandy beach. The hotel contains some lovely objets d'art, which add to the ambience of this fine Victorian home. There is a games room, a television room, a library and a bar for guests to enjoy.
ROOMS: 18 rms (6 fmly) s £35-£45; d £70-£90 * **FACILITIES:** TVB tea/coffee TVL No coaches Snooker Day membership to nearby leisure centre Dinner Last d order 8.30pm **NOTES:** ✘ ⊗ in restaurant ⊗ in lounges Licensed **LB PARKING:** 12

SHANKLIN   Map 04 SZ58

Babies Welcome	Family Rooms	Children's Dishes

★★★ 65% Luccombe Hall

8 Luccombe Rd PO37 6RL
☎ 01983 869000 📠 01983 863082
e-mail: enquiries@luccombehall.co.uk
Dir: take A3055 to Shanklin, through old village then 1st left into Priory Rd, left into Popham Rd, 1st right into Luccombe Rd. Hotel on right

CHILD FACILITIES: Baby listening Activities: magician weekly, colouring books, board games, videos, Lego Indoor play area Outdoor play area Food/bottle warming Ch menu Ch portions Highchairs Ch discounts sharing with 2 adults Videos Cots Family rms D rms with S bed & cot/extra bed from £35 per adult; child rates 100%-25% off depending on age Connecting rms Laundry **NEARBY:** Robin Hill Blackgang Chine Seafront location

Appropriately described as 'the view with the hotel', this property was originally built in 1870 as a summer home for the Bishop of Portsmouth. Enjoying an impressive cliff-top location, the hotel benefits from wonderful sea views, delightful gardens and direct access to the beach. Well-equipped bedrooms are comfortably furnished and there is a range of leisure facilities.
ROOMS: 30 en suite (15 GF) (7 GF) s £35-£55; d £70-£110 (incl. bkfst) **FACILITIES:** ⓧ ⓧ Squash Sauna Solarium Gym ⓧ Jacuzzi Games room, Treatment room ♫ Xmas **PARKING:** 20 **NOTES:** ✘ ⊗ in restaurant

Babies Welcome	Family Rooms	Children's Dishes

♦♦♦♦ The Richmond Hotel

23 Palmerston Rd PO37 6AS
☎ 01983 862874 📠 01983 862874
e-mail: richmondhotel.shanklin@virgin.net
web: www.richmondhotel-shanklin.co.uk
Dir: off Shanklin High Stt at Conservative Club & hotel 100mtrs ahead

CHILD FACILITIES: Activities: board games Food/bottle warming Ch menu Ch portions Highchairs Ch cutlery Ch discounts under 2s free, 3-9s half price, 10-12s 3/4 price Safe grounds Videos Cots Family rms 2 D rms with B beds, one with child's bed Ch drinks Connecting rms **NEARBY:** Esplanade with children's activities Gardens 2-min walk to sea

A warm friendly welcome awaits at this delightful hotel located in the centre of town just a few minutes' walk from the beach. Bedrooms are tastefully furnished and have a good range of extra facilities. Public rooms include a cosy lounge and a bar. Dinner is available by prior arrangement.
ROOMS: 9 en suite (2 fmly) s £25; d £50 * ⊗ **FACILITIES:** TVB tea/coffee TVL No coaches Dinner Last d order 1pm **NOTES:** ✘ ⊗ in restaurant Licensed Cen ht **LB PARKING:** 5

Babies Welcome	Family Rooms	Children's Dishes

♦♦♦♦ White House Hotel

Eastcliff Promenade PO37 6AY
☎ 01983 862776 & 867904 📠 01983 865980
e-mail: white_house@netguides.co.uk
Dir: A3055 from Sandown, at 1st lights take B3328, 2nd on left, right at top of hill into Park Rd

CHILD FACILITIES: Baby listening Food/bottle warming Ch menu Ch portions Highchairs Ch cutlery Ch discounts Safe grounds Games consoles Videos Cots Family rms D rms with 1-2 S beds, rm with B beds Ch drinks (on request) Fridge **NEARBY:** Leisure centre Seafront location

A warm welcome is assured at this delightful family-run hotel. From its cliff-top position, many of the comfortable, well-equipped bedrooms enjoy wonderful views of Shanklin Bay. Public areas include a sun lounge, bar, TV lounge and garden. Delicious home-cooked evening meals are available by prior arrangement.
ROOMS: 11 en suite (3 fmly) **FACILITIES:** TVB tea/coffee Direct dial from bedrooms TVL No coaches Dinner Last d order 5pm **NOTES:** ✘ ⊗ in restaurant Licensed Cen ht **PARKING:** 12

This symbol indicates establishments within walking distance or a short drive of the seaside.

England

♦♦♦ Norfolk House Hotel

19 Esplanade PO37 6BN

☎ 01983 863023 📠 01983 863023

e-mail: info@norfolkhousehotel.com

Dir: A3055 Sandown-Shanklin at Arthur's Hill traffic light junct (leaving Lake) turn left onto Hope Road, signed Esplanade, Hotel on right opposite Victorian clock tower

CHILD FACILITIES: Please telephone for details

A warm welcome is assured at this friendly, family-run hotel, located on the sea front with the beach across the road. Bedrooms are comfortable with many extras provided. There is also a bar, lounge and garden for guests' use. A range of drinks and cakes are served during the day.

ROOMS: 9 en suite (2 fmly) (1 GF) s £28-£32; d £56-£64 * ⊗
FACILITIES: TVB tea/coffee TVL Beach nearby Dinner Last d order 5.30pm **NOTES:** ⊗ in restaurant Licensed Cen ht **LB PARKING:** 8

SHORWELL
Map 04 SZ48

🍴 The Crown Inn

Walkers Ln PO30 3JZ

☎ 01983 740293 📠 01983 740293

Dir: From Newport to Carisbrooke High St, then L at rdbt at top of hill, take B3323 to Shorwell

CHILD FACILITIES: Outdoor play area Family area Food/bottle warming Ch menu Ch portions Highchairs Safe grounds Changing facilities **NEARBY:** Blackgang Chine Fantasy Park Carisbrooke Castle Alum Bay Park Dinosaur Museum **5-min drive to sea**

OPEN: 10.30-3 (Sun 12-3) 6-11 (sun eve 6-10:30) **BAR MEALS:** L served all week 12-2.30 D served all week 6-9 Av main course £6.50
RESTAURANT: L served all week 12-2.30 D served all week 6-9 Av 3 course à la carte £12 **FACILITIES:** Garden: Large, sheltered, flower beds, stream, ducks **PARKING:** 70

VENTNOR
Map 04 SZ57

★★★ 66% Eversley

Park Av PO38 1LB

☎ 01983 852244 & 852462 📠 01983 856534

e-mail: eversleyhotel@yahoo.co.uk

web: www.eversleyhotel.com

Dir: on A3055 W of Ventnor, next to Ventnor Park

CHILD FACILITIES: Baby listening Babysitting Outdoor play area Food/bottle warming Ch menu (early tea for under 3s) Ch portions Highchairs Ch discounts sliding scale Safe grounds Cots Family rms D rms with 2 S beds, connecting suites Connecting rms Laundry **NEARBY:** Park 6-min walk to sea

Located west of Ventnor, this hotel enjoys a quiet location with some rooms offering garden and pool views. The spacious restaurant is also used for local functions and there is a bar, television room, lounge area and a card room as well as a new jacuzzi and gym. Bedrooms are generally a good size.

ROOMS: 30 en suite (8 fmly) (2 GF) s £30-£55; d £59-£99 (incl. bkfst)
LB FACILITIES: ⚲ Gym Jacuzzi Childrens play equipment Pool table Xmas **PARKING:** 23 **NOTES:** ⊗ in restaurant Closed 31 Nov-22 Dec & 2 Jan-8 Feb

♦♦♦ Brunswick House

Victoria St PO38 1ET

☎ 01983 852656 📠 01983 855212

e-mail: brunswickhousehotel@btinternet.com

Dir: situated on the A3055 one-way system round the town, immediately before Leslie's Garage on the left-hand side

CHILD FACILITIES: Please telephone for details

Located in the centre of town yet only a short walk from the beach and various local attractions, this property offers comfortable rooms with co-ordinated decor. A small outdoor sitting area is available. Guests can choose from a selection of evening meals, served, as are the hearty English breakfasts, at individual tables.

ROOMS: 5 en suite (3 fmly) s fr £25; d fr £50 * ⊗ **FACILITIES:** TVB tea/coffee TVL Dinner Last d order 9.30pm **NOTES:** ✕ ⊗ in area of dining room Licensed Cen ht **LB**

♦♦ Llynfi Hotel

23 Spring Hill PO38 1PF

☎ 01983 852202 📠 01983 852202

e-mail: info@llynfihotel.co.uk

Dir: A3055 from Shanklin, right before sharp S-bend into St Boniface Rd. Next left into Spring Hill. Hotel 200yds on right

CHILD FACILITIES: Activities: toys on request Food/bottle warming Ch menu Ch portions Highchairs Ch cutlery Ch discounts under 5s free, 5-10s half price, 10-14s ¾ price Safe grounds Videos Cots Family rms 3 D rms with B beds, D rm with 2 B beds **NEARBY:** Gardens Botanic gardens Blackgang Chine **5-min walk to sea**

Guests are assured of a warm welcome to this family-run hotel, located just a short way up the hill from the high street. Bedrooms are bright and comfortably appointed. Extensive public areas include a sunny conservatory with an adjoining terrace, a cosy bar and a dining room, where dinner is served by prior arrangement.

ROOMS: 9 rms (8 en suite) (5 fmly) s £23-£27; d £46-£54 * ⊗ in 2 bedrooms **FACILITIES:** TVB tea/coffee Dinner Last d order 4pm **NOTES:** ✕ ⊗ in restaurant Licensed **LB PARKING:** 7

WILTSHIRE

Longleat House

AVEBURY

Alexander Keiller Museum SN8 1RF
avebury@nationaltrust.org.uk ☎01672 539250
(Turn off A4 on to A4361/B4003)
Open Apr-Oct, daily 10-6 or dusk if earlier; Nov-Mar, 10-4. Closed 24-26 Dec & 1 Jan.*£4.20 ch £2.10.

CALNE

Bowood House & Gardens SN11 0LZ
houseandgardens@bowood.org ☎01249 812102
(Off A4 Chippenham to Calne rd, in Derry Hill village)
Open Apr-Oct, daily 11-6, including BH.
Rhododendron Gardens separate entrance off A342 open 6 weeks during mid Apr-early Jun, 11-6. *House & Gardens £6.60 ch 2-4 £3.25; 5-15 £4.10; pen £5.30. Rhododendrons only £3.60

LACOCK

Lackham Country Park SN15 2NY
daviaj@wiltscoll.ac.uk ☎01249 466800
(3m S of Chippenham, on A350. 6m S of M4 Junct 17)
Open Etr-Aug, Sun & BH Mon, Tue-Thu in Aug 10-5. Last admission 4pm.
*£2 concessions £1.50, up to 2 ch under 16 free.

LONGLEAT

Longleat BA12 7NW
enquiries@longleat.co.uk ☎01985 844400
(Turn off A36 Bath-Salisbury onto A362 Warminster-Frome)
Open 12 Feb-6 Nov *Longleat passport: £16 ch 3-4 yrs & pen £13

SALISBURY

Salisbury Cathedral SP12 EJ
visitors@salcath.co.uk ☎01722 555120
(South of the city centre & Market Sq)
Open all year, daily 7.15-6.15; Jun-Aug, Mon-Sat 7.15-7.15. *Suggested Voluntary Donations: £3.80 ch £2, pen & students £3.30. Family £8.50.
The Medieval Hall (Secrets of Salisbury)
SP1 2EY ☎01722 412472
medieval.hall@ntworld.com
(follow signs within Salisbury Cathedral Close)
Open Apr-Sep, from 11-5. Also open throughout year for pre-booked groups.
*£2.25 ch 7-18 £1, ch under 18 £1.75. Family tickets available

STONEHENGE

Stonehenge
SP4 7DE ☎01980 624715
(2m W of Amesbury on junct A303 and A344/A360)
Open all year, 16 Mar-May, daily 9.30-6; Jun-Aug, daily 9-7; Sep-15 Oct, daily 9.30-6. 16 Oct-15 Mar, daily 9.30-4. Closed 24-26 Dec & 1 Jan.
*£5.20 ch £2.60, concessions £3.90.

STOURHEAD

Stourhead Garden & House BA12 6QD
stourhead@nationaltrust.org.uk ☎01747 841152
(At Stourton off B3092, 3m NW Mere A303, follow brown tourist signs) Garden open all year 9-7 or dusk if earlier. House open 19 Mar-Oct, 11-5 closed on Wed & Thurs; King Alfred tower open 19 Mar-Oct, daily 12-5.
*Garden & House £9.40, Garden or House £5.40; Garden only Nov- end Feb £4.10; King Alfred Tower £2, ch £1

SWINDON

Steam - Museum of The Great Western Railway
SN2 2TA ☎01793 466646
steampostbox@swindon.gov.uk
(From junct 16 of M4 & A420 follow brown signs to 'Outlet Centre' and Museum)
Open daily 10-5 (closed 25-26 Dec & 1Jan).
*£5.95 ch £3.80, pen £3.90 Family ticket £14.70 2ad+2ch

TEFFONT MAGNA

Farmer Giles Farmstead SP3 5QY
tdeane6995@aol.com ☎01722 716338
(11m W of Salisbury, off A303 at Teffont)
Open 18 Mar-5 Nov, daily 10-6, wknds in winter, 10-dusk. Party bookings all year.
*£3.95 ch £2.85, under 2's free & pen £3.50 Family ticket £13.

WESTBURY

Brokerswood Country Park BA13 4EH
woodland.park@virgin.net ☎01373 822238
(Turn off A36 at Bell Inn, Standerwick. Follow brown heritage signs)
Open all year; Park open daily 10-5. Closed Christmas Day, Boxing Day & New Year's Day.
Ring for museum opening hours.
*£3 ch 3-6yrs £2, pen £2.50

WILTON (NEAR SALISBURY)

Wilton House
SP2 0BJ ☎01722 746720
tourism@wiltonhouse.com
(3m W of Salisbury, on the A30, 10m from Stonehenge & A303)
Open 2 Apr-Oct daily 10.30-5.30. Last admission 4.30. House closed Mon, ex BHs.
*£9.75 ch 5-15 £5.50, students & pen £8. Family ticket £24.

BOX · Map 03 ST86

Babies Welcome | **Family Rooms** | **Children's Dishes**

◆◆◆◆◆ White Smocks

Ashley SN13 8AJ
☎ 01225 742154 📠 01225 742212
e-mail: whitesmocksashley@hotmail.com
Dir: on A4 1m W of Box take road opposite Northy Arms, after 200yds at T junct White Smocks is to right of thatched cottage

CHILD FACILITIES: Activities: games, jigsaws, books Outdoor play area Food/bottle warming Ch menu Ch portions Highchairs Ch cutlery Ch discounts babies in cots £5 Safe grounds Videos Cots Family rms D rm with S bed £85 Ch drinks Fridge Laundry Changing mats **NEARBY:** Longleat House Leisure Centre Bowood House

Quietly located in the pleasant village of Ashley, and just a short drive from Bath with its many attractions, White Smocks offers a relaxing escape where guests are encouraged to enjoy the pleasant garden in the summer, real fires in the winter and the jacuzzi all year round. The two bedrooms and bathrooms are immaculately presented and comfortably furnished. Guests are also welcome to use the lounge.
ROOMS: 2 en suite (1 fmly) s £45-£50; d £65-£75 * **FACILITIES:** TVB tea/coffee TVL No coaches **NOTES:** ✖ ⊛ Cen ht **LB PARKING:** 3

Babies Welcome | **Children's Dishes**

🍴 The Quarrymans Arms

Box Hill SN13 8HN
☎ 01225 743569
e-mail: John@quarrymans-arms.co.uk
Dir: Please phone the pub for accurate directions

CHILD FACILITIES: Family area Food/bottle warming Ch menu Ch portions Highchairs Ch cutlery Changing facilities **NEARBY:** Bowood Park

OPEN: 11-3.30 6-11 (all day Fri-Sun) **BAR MEALS:** L served all week 11-3 D served all week 6.30-10.30 Av main course £10 **RESTAURANT:** L served all week 11-3 D served all week 6.30-10.30 Av 3 course à la carte £15 **FACILITIES:** Garden: Small, traditional **PARKING:** 25

BRADFORD-ON-AVON · Map 03 ST86

Babies Welcome | **Family Rooms** | **Children's Dishes**

★★★ 76% ⊛ ⊛ ♨ Woolley Grange

Woolley Green BA15 1TX
☎ 01225 864705 📠 01225 864059
e-mail: info@woolleygrange.com
web: www.luxuryfamilyhotels.com
Dir: Turn off A4 onto B3109. Bradford Leigh, left at crossroads, hotel 0.5m on right at Woolley Green

CHILD FACILITIES: Baby listening Nanny Babysitting Activities: supervised playroom Indoor play area Outdoor play area Family area Food/bottle warming Ch menu Ch portions Highchairs Ch cutlery Ch discounts children free Safe grounds Games consoles Videos Cots Family rms £150-330 Ch drinks Connecting rms Fridge Laundry Changing mats **NEARBY:** Parks Walks Cycling Swimming pool Longleat

This splendid Cotswold manor house is set in beautiful countryside. Children are made especially welcome; there is a trained nanny on duty in the nursery. Bedrooms and public areas are charmingly furnished and decorated in true country-house style, with many thoughtful touches and luxurious extras. The
continued

hotel offers a varied and well-balanced menu selection, including ingredients from the hotel's own garden.
ROOMS: 14 en suite 12 annexe en suite (8 fmly) s £121-£157; d £160-£395 (incl. bkfst & dinner) **LB FACILITIES:** ♨ ⅃♨ ♨ Badminton, Games room, beauty treatments Xmas **PARKING:** 40 **NOTES:** ⊛ in restaurant

Babies Welcome | **Children's Dishes**

🍴 The Dandy Lion

35 Market St BA15 1LL
☎ 01225 863433 📠 01225 869169

CHILD FACILITIES: Food/bottle warming Ch menu Ch portions Highchairs Ch cutlery **NEARBY:** Country Park Swimming pool

OPEN: 10.30-3 6-11 (Sun 11.30-3, 7-10.30) **BAR MEALS:** L served all week 12-2.15 D served all week 7-9.30 Av main course £9.50
RESTAURANT: L served Sun 12-2.15 D served all week 7-9.30
FACILITIES: ✖

BRINKWORTH · Map 03 SU08

Babies Welcome | **Children's Dishes**

🍴 The Three Crowns

SN15 5AF
☎ 01666 510366 📠 01666 510303
Dir: A3102 to Wootton Bassett, then B4042, 5m to Brinkworth

CHILD FACILITIES: Activities: colouring/puzzle booklets Outdoor play area Food/bottle warming Ch menu Ch portions Highchairs Changing facilities

OPEN: 11-3 6-11 Closed: 25-26 Dec **BAR MEALS:** L served all week 12-2 6-9.30 Av main course £15 **RESTAURANT:** L served all week 12-2 D served all week 6.15-9.30 Av 3 course à la carte £20 **FACILITIES:** Garden: Sheltered patio with heaters, well maintained **PARKING:** 40

BURCOMBE · Map 04 SU03

Babies Welcome | **Children's Dishes**

🍴 The Ship Inn

Burcombe Ln SP2 0EJ
☎ 01722 743182 📠 01722 743182
e-mail: neillsev@aol.com
Dir: 2 miles west of Milton on A30

CHILD FACILITIES: Activities: colouring Food/bottle warming Ch menu Ch portions Highchairs Safe grounds **NEARBY:** Wilton House

OPEN: 11-3 6-11 **BAR MEALS:** L served all week 11-2.30 D served all week 6-10 Av main course £6.50 **RESTAURANT:** L served all week 11-2.30 D served all week 6-10 Av 3 course à la carte £16 **FACILITIES:** Children's licence Garden: Garden with river and ducks **PARKING:** 30

CASTLE COMBE · Map 03 ST87

Babies Welcome | **Family Rooms** | **Children's Dishes**

★★★★ ⊛ ⊛ ⊛ ♨ Manor House

SN14 7HR
☎ 01249 782206 📠 01249 782159
e-mail: enquiries@manor-housecc.co.uk
web: www.exclusivehotels.co.uk
Dir: M4 junct 17 follow Chippenham signs onto A420 Bristol, then right onto B4039. Through village, right after crossing bridge

EXCLUSIVE
HOTELS & GOLF CLUB

continued

CHILD FACILITIES: Nanny (prior notice) Babysitting (prior notice) Activities: colouring books, games, jigsaws, books Outdoor play area Food/bottle warming Ch menu Ch portions Highchairs Ch cutlery Ch discounts Safe grounds Cots Family rms D rm connecting triple rm, D rm with S beds Ch drinks (on request) Connecting rms Fridge Laundry Changing mats **NEARBY:** Cotswold Wildlife Park Longleat Safari Park Cinema

This hotel is situated in a secluded valley near the village, where there have been no new buildings for 300 years. There are 365 acres of grounds to enjoy, complete with an Italian garden and 18-hole golf course. Bedrooms, in a row of stone cottages, have been superbly furnished, and public rooms include a number of cosy lounges with roaring fires. Service is a pleasing blend of professionalism and friendliness, while food focuses on top quality local produce.

ROOMS: 22 en suite 26 annexe en suite (8 fmly) (12 GF) d £180-£600 (incl. bkfst) **LB** **FACILITIES:** STV ⚓ Golf 18 ⚓ Fishing Snooker Sauna Gym ⚑ ⚓ Jogging track, croquet lawn Xmas **PARKING:** 100 **NOTES:** ✱ ☺ in restaurant

CHRISTIAN MALFORD
Map 03 ST97

The Rising Sun
Station Rd SN15 4BL
☎ 01249 721571 ▤ 01249 721571
e-mail: risingsun@tesco.net
Dir: From M4 J 17 take B4122 towards Sutton Benger, turn L on to the B4069, pass through after 1m to Christian Malford, turn R into village (station road) pub is the last building on the L

CHILD FACILITIES: Activities: games, colouring Food/bottle warming Ch menu Ch portions Ch cutlery Safe grounds **NEARBY:** Cinema Walks

OPEN: 12-2.30 6.30-11 **BAR MEALS:** L served Tue-Sun 12-2 D served Mon-Sun 6.30-10 Av main course £7 **RESTAURANT:** L served Tue-Sun 12-2 D served Mon-Sun 6.30-10 Av 3 course à la carte £18 **FACILITIES:** Garden: Food served outside, lawn **PARKING:** 15

COLERNE
Map 03 ST87

★★★★   ⚤ Lucknam Park
SN14 8AZ
☎ 01225 742777 ▤ 01225 743536
e-mail: reservations@lucknampark.co.uk
web: www.lucknampark.co.uk
Dir: M4 junct 17, A350 to Chippenham, then A420 to Bristol for 3m. At Ford village, left to Colerne, after 3m right at x-rds. Entrance on right

CHILD FACILITIES: Nanny (prior notice) Babysitting (prior notice) Activities: Lego, board games Outdoor play area Food/bottle warming Ch menu Ch portions Highchairs Ch discounts under 12s £25 or cot £15 Safe grounds Games consoles Videos Cots Family rms suites £490-£640 Ch drinks Connecting rms Fridge Laundry **NEARBY:** Walks Bike rides Equestrian centre 5-side Football pitch Leisure spa

Guests may well feel a theatrical sense of arrival when approaching this Palladian mansion along its magnificent mile-long avenue of beech and lime trees. Surrounded by 500 acres of parkland and beautiful gardens, this fine hotel offers a wealth of choices ranging from enjoying pampering treatments to taking vigorous exercise. Elegant bedrooms and suites are split between the main building and adjacent courtyard. Dining options range from the informal
continued

Pavilion Restaurant, to the formal, and very accomplished, main restaurant.

ROOMS: 23 en suite 18 annexe en suite (16 GF) s fr £225; d £225-£770 **LB** **FACILITIES:** Spa STV ⚓ Riding Snooker Sauna Solarium Gym ⚑ Jacuzzi Whirlpool, Beauty & hair salon, Steam room, Cross country course, Mountain bikes ♫ Xmas **PARKING:** 70 **NOTES:** ✱ ☺ in restaurant

LOWER CHICKSGROVE
Map 03 ST92

◖▌ Compasses Inn ◆◆◆◆
SP3 6NB
☎ 01722 714318 ▤ 01722 714318
e-mail: thecompasses@aol.com
Dir: A30 W from Salisbury, after 10m R signed Chicksgrove

CHILD FACILITIES: Outdoor play area Food/bottle warming Ch menu Ch portions Highchairs Ch cutlery Safe grounds **NEARBY:** Parks Walks Leisure centre Longleat Wilton House Farmer Giles Homestead Rare breeds farm

OPEN: 12-3 6-11 Closed: 25, 26 Dec **BAR MEALS:** L served Tue-Sun 12-2 D served Tue-Sat 7-9 Av main course £12 **RESTAURANT:** L served Tues-Sun 12-2 D served Tues-Sat 7-9 Av 3 course à la carte £20 **FACILITIES:** Garden: Large grass area with nice views, seats 40 **ROOMS:** 4 bedrooms 4 en suite 3 family rooms s£45 d£65 **PARKING:** 30

MALMESBURY
Map 03 ST98

★★★ 75% ☺ ☺ Old Bell
Abbey Row SN16 0AG
☎ 01666 822344 ▤ 01666 825145
e-mail: info@oldbellhotel.com
web: www.oldbellhotel.com
Dir: M4 junct 11, follow A429 north. Left at first rdbt. Left at T-junction. Hotel next to Abbey

CLASSIC BRITISH

CHILD FACILITIES: Please telephone for details

Please note that this establishment has recently changed ownership. Dating back to 1220, the Old Bell is reputed to be the oldest purpose-built hotel in England. Bedrooms vary in size and style; those in the main house are traditionally furnished with antiques, while the newer bedrooms are modelled on a quasi-Japanese theme. Guests have a choice of comfortable sitting areas and dining options. Children are also well-catered for.

ROOMS: 16 en suite 15 annexe en suite (7 GF) ☺ in 12 bedrooms s fr £85; d fr £110 (incl. bkfst) **LB** **FACILITIES:** Spa STV Aromatherapy massages Xmas **PARKING:** 31 **NOTES:** ✱ ☺ in restaurant

MINETY
Map 03 SU09

◖▌ Vale of the White Horse Inn
SN16 9QY
☎ 01666 860175 ▤ 01666 860175
e-mail: jamie@denman.fsbusiness.co.uk
Dir: B4040 6 miles east of Malmesbury.

CHILD FACILITIES: Activities: colouring Food/bottle warming Ch menu Ch portions Highchairs Ch cutlery **NEARBY:** Cotswold Water Park Swindon Railway Museum Bowood House

OPEN: 12-3 6-12 (open all day Sat & Sun) **BAR MEALS:** L served all week 12-2.30 D served all week 6-9.30 Av main course £9.95 **RESTAURANT:** L served all week 2.30-9.30 D served all week 6-9.30 Av 3 course à la carte £17 **FACILITIES:** Garden

England

| Babies Welcome | Family Rooms | Children's Dishes |

◆◆◆◆ 🚲 Fosse Farmhouse Country Hotel

Nettleton Shrub SN14 7NJ
☎ 01249 782286 📠 01249 783066
e-mail: caroncooper@compuserve.com
Dir: off B4039, 1.5m past Castle Combe race circuit take 1st left at Gib Village for farm 1m on right

CHILD FACILITIES: Baby listening Babysitting (prior notice) Activities: Scrabble, crosswords, board games, pedal scooter, skittles Outdoor play area Family area Food/bottle warming Ch menu Ch portions Highchairs Ch cutlery Safe grounds Cots Family rms D rm with S bed £135-£150 **NEARBY:** Bowood House grounds Walks Castle Combe

Set in the quiet Wiltshire countryside close to Castle Combe, this small hotel has well-equipped bedrooms decorated in an individual and interesting style, in keeping with its 18th-century origins. Excellent dinners are served in the farmhouse, and cream teas can be enjoyed in the old stables or the delightful garden.
ROOMS: 3 en suite (1 fmly) s £55-£68; d £85-£135 * ⊗ in 1 bedrooms **FACILITIES:** TVB tea/coffee Golf 18 Dinner Last d order 8.30pm **NOTES:** ⊗ in restaurant Licensed Cen ht **LB PARKING:** 12

| Children's Dishes |

◖ The Silver Plough

White Hill SP5 1DU
☎ 01722 712266 📠 01722 712266
Dir: From Salisbury take A30 towards Andover, Pitton signposted (approx 3m)

CHILD FACILITIES: Indoor play area Outdoor play area Ch menu Ch portions Safe grounds **NEARBY:** Stonehenge Walks Cinema

OPEN: 11-3 6-11 (Sun 12-3, 6-10.30) Rest: 25-26 Dec, 1 Jan Closed eve **BAR MEALS:** L served all week 12-2.30 D served all week 6-9.30 Av main course £8 **RESTAURANT:** L served all week 12-2.30 D served all week 7-9.30 Av 3 course à la carte £18 **FACILITIES:** Garden: Lots of bench tables **PARKING:** 50

| Babies Welcome | Children's Dishes |

◖ Bell Inn

Bell Hill SN12 6SA
☎ 01380 828338
e-mail: Bellseend@aol.com

CHILD FACILITIES: Outdoor play area Food/bottle warming Ch menu Ch portions Highchairs Safe grounds **NEARBY:** Longleat

OPEN: 11-3 5.30-11 **BAR MEALS:** L served all week 11.45-2.15 D served all week 6.15-9.30 Av main course £7 **RESTAURANT:** 11.45-2.15 6.15-9.30 **FACILITIES:** Garden: Lrg, seating for 60 people, beautiful views **PARKING:** 30

| Babies Welcome | Family Rooms | Children's Dishes |

★★★ 70% Stanton Manor Country House Hotel

SN14 6DQ
☎ 01666 837552 📠 01666 837022
e-mail: reception@stantonmanor.co.uk
web: www.stantonmanor.co.uk
Dir: M4 junct 17 onto A429 Malmesbury/Cirencester, within 200yds turn 1st left signed Stanton St Quintin, entrance to hotel on left just after church

CHILD FACILITIES: Baby listening Nanny (on request) Babysitting Activities: books, toys, jigsaws, putting, croquet, pitch & putt Indoor play area Outdoor play area Food/bottle warming Ch menu Ch portions Highchairs Ch cutlery Ch discounts under 5s free sharing with parents Safe grounds Videos Cots Family rms Ch drinks Connecting rms Laundry Changing mats (on request) **NEARBY:** Parks Bowood House GoKart track

Set in seven acres of lovely gardens including a short golf course, this charming Cotswold stone manor house has easy access to the M4. The new owners here are carefully adding further to the quality and comfort of all bedrooms and bathrooms. Public areas are a delight offering both character and comfort. In the restaurant, a short carte of imaginative dishes is supported by a selection of interesting wines.
ROOMS: 23 en suite (2 fmly) (7 GF) ⊗ in 7 bedrooms s fr £88.50; d fr £110 (incl. bkfst) **LB FACILITIES:** STV Golf 9 🎱 ⚓ Xmas **PARKING:** 50 **NOTES:** ⊗ in restaurant

| Babies Welcome | Family Rooms | Children's Dishes |

★★★★ 71% 🌼 Blunsdon House Hotel & Leisure Club

Best Western

Blunsdon SN26 7AS
☎ 01793 721701 📠 01793 721056
e-mail: info@blunsdonhouse.co.uk
web: www.blunsdonhouse.co.uk
Dir: 200 yds off A419 at Swindon, 1m N of Swindon

CHILD FACILITIES: Baby listening Nanny Babysitting Activities: colouring Indoor play area Outdoor play area Family area Food/bottle warming Ch menu Ch portions Highchairs Ch cutlery Ch discounts free sharing with parents Safe grounds Games consoles Videos Cots Family rms D rm with S bed & put up bed Ch drinks Connecting rms Fridge **NEARBY:** Steam Museum Cotswold Wildlife park Water Parks

Located just to the north of Swindon, Blunsdon house is set in 30 acres of well-kept grounds and offers extensive leisure facilities and spacious day rooms. The hotel has a choice of eating and drinking options; there are three bars and two restaurants.

continued

Bedrooms are comfortably furnished, and the contemporary Pavilion rooms are especially spacious.

Blunsdon House Hotel

ROOMS: 118 en suite (14 fmly) (27 GF) ⊗ in 75 bedrooms
FACILITIES: STV ▣ Golf 9 ⚭ Squash Sauna Solarium Gym ♨
Jacuzzi Beauty therapy, Woodland walk, 9 hole par 3 golf course Xmas
PARKING: 300 **NOTES:** ✈ ⊗ in restaurant

Children's Dishes This symbol indicates a children's menu or smaller portions are available

Many proprietors are happy to provide extra facilities for children, but let them know in advance what you need so they can be prepared

| Babies Welcome | Family Rooms | Children's Dishes |

★★★★ 66%
Swindon Marriott Hotel
Pipers Way SN3 1SH
☎ 0870 400 7281 ▤ 0870 400 7381
Dir: M4 junct 15, follow A419, then A4259 to Coate rdbt and B4006 signed 'Old Town'

CHILD FACILITIES: Babysitting Activities: activity packs
Food/bottle warming Ch menu Ch portions Highchairs Ch discounts
up to 16s free when sharing, under 5s free breakfast Safe grounds
Games consoles Cots Family rms T rms with 2 D beds Connecting
rms Laundry

With convenient access to the motorway, this hotel is an ideal base from which to explore Wiltshire and the Cotswolds. The public rooms include a well-equipped leisure centre, Chats café bar and the informal, brasserie-style Mediterrano restaurant.
ROOMS: 156 en suite (42 fmly) ⊗ in 137 bedrooms s £50-£170; d £60-£170 **LB FACILITIES: Spa** STV ▣ ⚭ Sauna Solarium Gym Jacuzzi Steam Room, Health & Beauty, Hair salon, Sports massage therapy
PARKING: 185 **NOTES:** ✈ ⊗ in restaurant

England

SWINDON, continued

Babies Welcome	Family Rooms	Children's Dishes

◆◆◆ Portquin

Broadbush, Broad Blunsdon SN26 7DH
☎ 01793 721261
e-mail: portquin@msn.com
Dir: turn off A419 at Blunsdon onto B4019 signposted Highworth, 0.5m from A419

CHILD FACILITIES: Baby listening Babysitting Activities: games, toys, jigsaws Family area Food/bottle warming Ch portions Highchairs Ch cutlery Ch discounts under 5s free Safe grounds Videos Cots Family rms D rm with 1 or 2 S beds, D rm with 1-3 S beds & sofa Ch drinks Connecting rms Laundry NEARBY: Walks Steam Museum Wildlife Park Water Parks Leisure Centre

Close to Swindon and with views of the Berkshire Downs, this friendly guest house offers a warm welcome. The comfortable rooms vary in shape and size - six are in the main house and three in an adjacent annexe. Full English breakfasts are taken at two large tables in the open-plan kitchen/dining area.
ROOMS: 6 en suite 3 annexe en suite (2 fmly) (4 GF) s £30-£40; d £50-£60 * **FACILITIES:** TVB tea/coffee Direct dial from bedrooms No coaches **NOTES:** ⊗ Cen ht **PARKING:** 12

WHITEPARISH · Map 04 SU22

Babies Welcome	Family Rooms	Children's Dishes

◆◆◆◆◆ 🏅 🍽 Newton Farmhouse

Southampton Rd SP5 2QL
☎ 01794 884416 ▤ 01794 884416
e-mail: reservations@newtonfarmhouse.co.uk
web: www.newtonfarmhouse.co.uk
Dir: Just S of Salisbury- 6 miles, on A36 1m S of junct with A27

CHILD FACILITIES: Baby listening Activities: books, jigsaws, games, toys Food/bottle warming Ch portions Highchairs Ch cutlery Ch discounts babies free, under 12s £10, over 12s £15 Videos Cots Family rms D rms with S beds/cots NEARBY: New Forest Paultons Park

Dating back to the 16th century, this delightful farmhouse was gifted to Lord Nelson's family as part of the Trafalgar estate. The house has been thoughtfully restored and bedrooms, most with four-poster beds, have been adorned with personal touches. Delicious home cooked dinners, which are a speciality, are available by prior arrangement.
ROOMS: 8 en suite (2 GF) s £40-£70 * **FACILITIES:** TVB tea/coffee TVL No coaches ⸙ Dinner Last d order 24hrs notice **NOTES:** Credit cards not taken ✠ ⊗ Cen ht **PARKING:** 10

◆◆◆◆ Brayford

Newton Ln SP5 2QQ
☎ 01794 884216
e-mail: reservations@brayford.org.uk
Dir: turn off A36 at Newton Crossroads, towards Whiteparish, into Newton Lane Brayford is 150yds on right

CHILD FACILITIES: Please telephone for details

A genuine, friendly welcome awaits guests to this comfortable family home. Peacefully located, with rural views over neighbouring farmland, the house is conveniently located just a short drive off the A36. The comfortable bedrooms are well equipped with many thoughtful extras. Guests are invited to relax in the lounge dining room, where a tasty breakfast is served.
ROOMS: 2 rms (1 GF) s £30-£50; d £50-£60 * **FACILITIES:** TVB tea/coffee TVL No coaches **NOTES:** Credit cards not taken ✠ ⊗ Cen ht **PARKING:** 2

WORCESTERSHIRE

EVESHAM · Map 04 SP04

Babies Welcome	Family Rooms	Children's Dishes

★★★ 75% ⊛ 🏅 The Evesham

Coopers Ln, Off Waterside WR11 1DA
☎ 01386 765566 & 0800 716969 (Res) ▤ 01386 765443
e-mail: reception@eveshamhotel.com
web: www.eveshamhotel.com
Dir: Coopers Lane is off road by River Avon

CHILD FACILITIES: Baby listening Activities: games, jigsaws Indoor play area Outdoor play area Food/bottle warming Ch menu Ch portions Highchairs Ch cutlery Ch discounts under 12s £3 for each yr sharing with 2 adults Safe grounds Cots Family rms rms with B beds, extra T beds £175 onwards Connecting rms Fridge Laundry NEARBY: Butterfly Farm Museums Warwick Castle Horse Centre

Dating from 1540 and set in large grounds, this delightful hotel has well-equipped accommodation that includes a selection of quirkily themed rooms - Alice in Wonderland, Egyptian, and Aquarium with a tropical fish tank in the bathroom. A reputation for food is well deserved, with choice particularly strong for vegetarians. Children are especially welcome.
ROOMS: 39 en suite 1 annexe en suite (3 fmly) (11 GF) ⊗ in 20 bedrooms s £74-£87; d £118 (incl. bkfst) **LB FACILITIES:** ⌗ ♫ ♨ **PARKING:** 50 **NOTES:** ⊗ in restaurant Closed 25 & 26 Dec

---

MALVERN · Map 03 SO74

Babies Welcome	Family Rooms	Children's Dishes

★★ 74% Holdfast Cottage

Marlbank Rd, Little Malvern WR13 6NA
☎ 01684 310288 ▤ 01684 311117
e-mail: enquiries@holdfast-cottage.co.uk
web: www.holdfast-cottage.co.uk
Dir: on A4104 midway between Welland and Upper Welland

CHILD FACILITIES: Baby listening Activities: wendy house Outdoor play area Family area Food/bottle warming Ch menu Ch portions Highchairs Ch cutlery Safe grounds Cots (charge) Family rms T rm with 7 bed/cot Ch drinks Laundry Changing mats NEARBY: Malvern Splash Tewkesbury Leisure Centre Cinema

This charming, wisteria-covered hotel lies in attractive grounds at the foot of the Malvern Hills. The public areas offer all the comforts of a country retreat - log fire in the lounge, a cosy bar and an elegant dining room. The bedrooms include many thoughtful touches. The regularly changing menu features fresh local produce, and ice cream and breads are made on the premises.
ROOMS: 8 en suite (1 fmly) ⊗ in all bedrooms s £50-£70; d £84-£94 (incl. bkfst) **LB FACILITIES:** ♫ Walking, bird watching Xmas **PARKING:** 20 **NOTES:** ⊗ in restaurant

Many proprietors are happy to provide extra facilities for children, but let them know in advance what you need so they can be prepared

Babies Welcome | **Children's Dishes**

◄█ **The Red Lion**
4 St Ann's Rd WR14 4RG
☎ 01684 564787

CHILD FACILITIES: **Activities: colouring, books Family area**
Food/bottle warming Ch menu Ch portions Highchairs Ch cutlery
Safe grounds NEARBY: Malvern hills Cinema Theatre Parks
Swimming pool

OPEN: 12-3 5.30-11 Sat-Sun 12-11 **BAR MEALS:** L served all week
12-2.45 D served all week 6-9.30 Av main course £8.99 **RESTAURANT:** L
served all week 12-2.45 D served all week 6-9.30 **FACILITIES:** Garden:
Enclosed courtyard garden ✱

WORCESTER   Map 03 SO85

Babies Welcome | **Children's Dishes**

★★★ 64% **Fownes**
City Walls Rd WR1 2AP
☎ 01905 613151 ▤ 01905 23742
e-mail: reservations@fowneshotel.co.uk
web: www.fownesgroup.co.uk/fownes
*Dir: M5 junct 7 take A44 for Worcester city centre. Turn right at 4th set of
traffic lights into City Walls Rd*

CHILD FACILITIES: **Food/bottle warming Ch menu Ch portions**
Highchairs Cots Connecting rms Laundry NEARBY: Cinema
Museum Cathedral

On the Birmingham Canal and located close to the city centre, this
former Victorian glove factory has been converted into an
interesting-looking, modern hotel with well proportioned
bedrooms. Snacks are available in the lounge bar and the King's
restaurant offers an interesting à la carte menu.
ROOMS: 61 en suite (10 GF) ⊗ in 28 bedrooms s £98.50;
d £79-£104.50 (incl. bkfst) **LB FACILITIES:** Xmas **PARKING:** 82
NOTES: ⊗ in restaurant

Babies Welcome | **Family Rooms** | **Children's Dishes**

◆◆◆◆ **Burgage House**
4 College Precincts WR1 2LG
☎ 01905 25396 ▤ 01905 25396
*Dir: M5 junct 7 towards city centre, at 7th traffic lights (inc. pedestrian
crossings) turn left into Edgar St, College Precinct is pedestrian only street
on the right*

CHILD FACILITIES: **Food/bottle warming Ch portions Highchairs**
Ch cutlery Ch discounts Cots Family rms D rm with S beds
Ch drinks

Located adjacent to the cathedral and many historical attractions,
this impressive Georgian town house retains many original
features, including a fine stone staircase, enhanced by the décor
and furnishing styles throughout. Bedrooms, including the ground
floor Cromwell Room, are spacious and homely. An elegant dining
room is the setting for comprehensive English breakfasts.
ROOMS: 4 en suite (1 fmly) (1 GF) s £30-£35; d £55-£60 *
FACILITIES: TVB tea/coffee **NOTES:** Credit cards not taken ✱ ⊗
Cen ht

Children's Dishes

◄█ **The Salmon's Leap**
42 Severn St WR1 2ND
☎ 01905 726260 ▤ 01905 724151
e-mail: bernardwalker@thesalmonsleap.freeserve.co.uk
*Dir: In City centre, opposite Royal Worcester Porcelain Museum. From M5
J7 follow signs for Museum & Cathedral.*

CHILD FACILITIES: **Activities: bouncy castle (weather permitting),**
play cabin, activity centre Outdoor play area Family area Ch licence
Ch menu Ch portions Highchairs Safe grounds
NEARBY: Worcester Cathedral Civil War Centre Riverside walks
Royal Worcester Porcelain

OPEN: 11.30-11 (Oct-Apr closed Mon lunch - open 5) **BAR MEALS:** L
served all week 12-7.30 D served all week 12-7.30 Av main course £5.50
RESTAURANT: L served all week 12-7.30 D served all week 12-7.30
FACILITIES: Children's licence Garden: Adjacent to pub **PARKING:** 3

YORKSHIRE

Trams at Saltburn's Pier

telephone for up-to-date details.
*£7.20 ch 5-15 £5.10, under 5 free, student & pen
£6.10 Family £21.95. Telephone bookings on
01904 543403 £1 booking fee per person at peak
times.

The York Dungeon
YO1 9RD   ☎01904 632599
yorkdungeons@merlinentertainments.biz
(A64/A19/A59 to city centre)
Open all year, daily 10.30-5 closes 4.30 Oct-Mar.
Closed 25 Dec.

York Castle Museum
☎01904 653611
(City centre, next to Clifford's Tower)
Open all year, Apr-Oct Mon-Sat 9.30-5.30, Sun
10-5.30; Nov-Mar, Mon-Sat 9.30-4, Sun 10-4.
Closed 25-26 Dec & 1 Jan.

EAST RIDING OF YORKSHIRE
KINGSTON-UPON-HULL
The Deep HU1 4DP
info@thedeep.co.uk   ☎01482 381000
(Follow signs from Hull city centre)
Open daily 10-6. Closed 24-25 Dec
*£6.75 ch under 16 £4.75. Family ticket 2 adults
& 2 ch £21

NORTH YORKSHIRE
KIRBY MISPERTON
Flamingo Land Theme Park & Zoo YO17 6UX
info@flamingoland.co.uk   ☎01653 668287
(Turn off A64 onto A169, Pickering to Whitley
road)
Open end Mar-2 Nov from 10. Closing times vary
depending upon season.

NORTH STAINLEY
Lightwater Valley Theme Park HG4 3HT
leisure@lightwatervalley.co.uk ☎0870 458 0060
(3m N of Ripon on the A6108)
Open 23 Mar-7 Apr, weekends only; 13 Apr-26
May inc BH Mon; daily from Jun-2 Sep,
weekends only 7 Sep-13 Oct. daily 19 Oct- 27
Oct.

SALTBURN-BY-THE-SEA
Saltburn Smugglers Heritage Centre
TS12 1HF   ☎01287 625252
(Adjoining Ship Inn, on A174)
Open Apr-Sep, daily 10-6: Winter open by
arrangement only telephone 01642 470836.
*£1.95 ch £1.45. Family ticket £5.80. Party.

YORK
Jorvik YO1 9WT
enquiries@vikingjorvik.com   ☎01904 543403
(Situated in the Coppergate shopping area in city
centre, follow the signs to Jorvik)
Open all year, Apr-Oct daily 10-5; and Viking
festival Nov-Mar daily 10-4 Closed 25 Dec.
Opening times subject to change, please

SOUTH YORKSHIRE
DONCASTER
Earth Centre DN12 4EA
info@earthcentre.org.uk   ☎01709 513933
(Follow brown signs from A1(M) From junct 36
follow brown Earth Centre signs along A630, then
A6023 towards Mexborough. Earth Centre next
right after Coniston Train Stn) Open all year, daily
ex Xmas day 10-5 peak, 10-4 off peak, 10-7
school holidays.

ROTHERHAM
Magna Science Adventure Centre S60 1DX
jeyre@magnatrust.co.uk   ☎01709 720002
(M1 junct 34, follow Templeborough sign off rdbt,
then follow brown heritage signs)

WEST YORKSHIRE
HALIFAX
Eureka! The Museum for Children HX1 2NE
info@eureka.org.uk   ☎01422 330069
(M62 junct 24 follow brown heritage signs to
Halifax centre A629)
Open all year, daily 10-5 except 24-26 Dec
*£5.95. Family Saver ticket £27.50

LEEDS
Royal Armouries Museum LS10 1LT
enquiries@armouries.org.uk   ☎0113 220 1999
(Off A61 close to Leeds centre, follow brown
heritage signs)
Open daily, from 10-5. Closed 24-25 Dec

MIDDLESTOWN
National Coal Mining Museum For England
WF4 4RH
info@ncm.org.uk   ☎01924 848806
(On A642 between Wakefield & Huddersfield)
Open all year, daily 10-5. Closed 24-26 Dec & 1
Jan.

YORKSHIRE, EAST RIDING

BEVERLEY   Map 08 TA03

Children's
Dishes

White Horse Inn
22 Hengate HU17 8BN
☎ 01482 861973 📠 01482 861973
e-mail: anname@talk21.com
Dir: A1079 from York to Beverley

CHILD FACILITIES: **Outdoor play area**   **Food/bottle warming**
Ch menu   **Ch portions**   **NEARBY:**   **The Deep Flamingo Land**

OPEN: 11-11 (Sun 12-10.30)   **BAR MEALS:** L served all week 11-4.45 D
served all week 5-6.45 Av main course £4.50   **FACILITIES:** Garden
NOTES: Credit cards not taken   **PARKING:** 30

BRIDLINGTON   Map 08 TA16

♦♦♦♦ Langdon Hotel
13-16 Pembroke Ter YO15 3BX
☎ 01262 400124 & 673065 📠 01262 605377
Dir: on a terrace facing sea between the harbour and Spa Royal Hall & Theatre

CHILD FACILITIES: **Please telephone for details**

Located opposite the Spa Theatre on the seafront, this family
owned hotel offers comfortable bedrooms. The reception rooms
extend to a small garden porch, cosy bar and lounge where
regular evening entertainment is held. Home cooked meals are
served in the cheerful dining room or the new stylish restaurant.
ROOMS: 31 en suite (10 fmly) s £30-£35; d £60-£70 * **FACILITIES:** TVB
tea/coffee Lift TVL Dinner Last d order 4pm **NOTES:** ✈ ⊗ in
restaurant Licensed Cen ht **LB PARKING:** 5

| Babies | Family | Children's | |
| Welcome | Rooms | Dishes | |

♦♦♦♦ Sunflower Lodge
24 Flamborough Rd YO15 2HX
☎ 01262 400447
e-mail: rosie4infosunlodge@fsmail.net
Dir: follow signs to Leisure World, past church on right. Lodge just past Alexandra Walk

CHILD FACILITIES: **Baby listening Activities: games, colouring,**
toys, dolls house (seasonal), treasure hunts, competitions, parties
Indoor play area Family area Food/bottle warming Ch menu
Ch portions Highchairs Ch cutlery Ch discounts under 2s free, 2-12s
50%, 12-16s 2/3 price when sharing with parents Safe grounds
Games consoles Videos Cots Family rms D rm with B beds from
£69 Ch drinks Fridge Laundry Changing mats NEARBY: Park
Leisure centre Cinema Rock factory Nature trail 2-min walk
to sea

Located just a short stroll from the town centre and sea front,
Sunflower Lodge extends a warm welcome to all guests. The
recently refurbished stylish bedrooms are all very individual,
tastefully decorated and boast many thoughtful extras. A
substantial breakfast is served in the attractive breakfast room.
ROOMS: 3 en suite (2 fmly) s £35-£40; d £52-£70 ⊗ in 2 bedrooms
FACILITIES: TVB tea/coffee No coaches **NOTES:** ✈ ⊗ in restaurant ⊗
in lounges Cen ht **LB**

See advert on this page

SUNFLOWER
LODGE   ♦♦♦♦

ATTENTION ALL CHILDREN - DON'T FORGET YOUR TEDDY!!

Fun-filled family house, nestling
by the sea. Playden with tele-
video/toys/playstation & games
to hire. Dedicated family rooms
from £69.00 B&B open all year
and includes: tele/DVD/radio/CD/
toybox/soft drinks/activity pack/
colouring kit. Resident teddy
awaits. Sammy Sunflower breakfast
menu. Comprehensive baby equipment. Colour brochure
with pleasure. Tel: 01262 400447

24 Flamborough Road, North Bay,
Bridlington, East Yorkshire YO15 2HX
www.smoothhound.co.uk/hotelssunflower
Email: rosie4info@sunlodge.wanadoo.co.uk

♦♦♦ Bay Ridge Hotel
11/13 Summerfield Rd YO15 3LF
☎ 01262 673425 📠 01262 673425/674589
e-mail: bayridgehotel@aol.com
*Dir: towards Bridlington off A614/A165 go to southside seafront. Premises in
Summerfield Rd, off South Marine Drive which is the main south side
seafront*

CHILD FACILITIES: **Please telephone for details**

This friendly guest house, located in a side road just off the
seafront, is family-run and offers value for money
accommodation. Public areas are comfortable and consist of a
spacious bar lounge, separate sitting room and well-appointed
dining room. The modern bedrooms are generously equipped and
comfortable.
ROOMS: 14 rms (12 en suite) (4 fmly) s £23.50-£25; d £47-£50 * ⊗
FACILITIES: TVB tea/coffee TVL Bar billiards, darts, Dominoes Dinner
Last d order 10am **NOTES:** Credit cards not taken ✈ ⊗ in restaurant ⊗
in 1 lounge Licensed Cen ht **LB PARKING:** 6

| Babies | Family | Children's | |
| Welcome | Rooms | Dishes | |

♦♦ Pembroke
6 Pembroke Ter YO15 3BX
☎ 01262 675643 📠 01262 678181
Dir: between the harbour and the Spa Theatre on the seafront.

CHILD FACILITIES: **Activities: toys, colouring books, jigsaws**
Food/bottle warming Ch menu Ch portions Highchairs Ch cutlery
Ch discounts under 5s 1/4 price, over 5s half price Cots Family rms
D rms with 1 or 2 S beds NEARBY: Leisure centre Sewerby Park
& Zoo Bondville miniature village Seafront location

Located in a prime position midway between the spa and the
harbour, this seaside guest house offers traditional

continued on p248

England

BRIDLINGTON, continued

accommodation. A variety of bedrooms are available and spectacular sea views can be enjoyed from many and from the lounge. Meals are served in the basement dining room.
ROOMS: 10 rms (8 en suite) s £22-£23; d £44-£46 * **FACILITIES:** TVB tea/coffee TVL Dinner Last d order noon **NOTES:** ✈ ⊗ in restaurant Licensed **LB**

HUGGATE
Map 08 SE85

Babies Welcome | Children's Dishes

◆◆◆ ⌑ The Wolds Inn
Driffield Rd YO42 1YH
☎ 01377 288217
e-mail: huggate@woldsinn.freeserve.co.uk
Dir: follow signs to Huggate off A166, also brown signs to Wold Inn

CHILD FACILITIES: Food/bottle warming Ch menu Ch portions Highchairs Ch cutlery Safe grounds NEARBY: Walks (Wolds Way) Wharram Percy (medieval village)

Nestling at the end of the highest village in the Yorkshire Wolds, and midway between York and the coastline, this ancient inn offers a rural haven beside the Wolds Way walk. Substantial meals are served in the dining room. Bedrooms, which vary in size, are well equipped and comfortable.
ROOMS: 3 en suite s £27-£33; d £38-£52 * **FACILITIES:** TVB tea/coffee Pool Table Dinner Last d order 9.30pm (9pm Sun)
NOTES: ✈ ⊗ in restaurant Cen ht **BB PARKING:** 50

LOW CATTON
Map 08 SE75

Children's Dishes

⌑ The Gold Cup Inn
YO41 1EA
☎ 01759 371354
Dir: 1m S of A166 or 1m N of A1079, E of York

CHILD FACILITIES: Activities: books Outdoor play area Family area Ch licence Ch menu Ch portions Highchairs Ch cutlery NEARBY: Walks

OPEN: 12-3 6-11 (Sat 12-11, Sun 12-10.30) Rest: Mon closed lunchtime **BAR MEALS:** L served Sun, Tue-Sat 12-2 D served all week 6-9.30 Av main course £6 **RESTAURANT:** L served Sun D served all week 6-9.30 Av 3 course à la carte £16 Av 2 course fixed price £9.75 **FACILITIES:** Garden ✈ **NOTES:** Credit cards not taken **PARKING:** 60

MARKET WEIGHTON
Map 08 SE84

Babies Welcome | Family Rooms | Children's Dishes

◆◆◆ Robeanne House
Driffield Ln, Shiptonthorpe YO43 3PW
☎ 01430 873312 📠 01430 873312
e-mail: robert@robeanne.freeserve.com

CHILD FACILITIES: Activities: toys, feeding animals Family area Food/bottle warming Ch menu Ch portions Highchairs Ch cutlery Ch discounts babies £5, under 10s £12.50 Safe grounds Videos Cots Family rms D rms with S beds Connecting rms Laundry Changing mats NEARBY: Burnby Hall Pocklington York & Beverley

Conveniently located beside the A614, but set far enough back to be a quiet location, this delightful modern family home was built as a farmhouse. Access to York is easy, and the coast and Yorkshire Moors and Dales are also within easy driving distance.
continued

Bedrooms all have countryside views and include a large family room, and a charming wooden chalet is available in the garden.
ROOMS: 2 en suite 2 annexe en suite (2 fmly) (1 GF) s £20-£30; d £45-£55 * ⊗ in 1 bedrooms **FACILITIES:** TVB tea/coffee No coaches outdoor hot tub Dinner Last d order 24hrs prior **NOTES:** ⊗ in restaurant ⊗ in lounges Cen ht **LB PARKING:** 10

SOUTH CAVE
Map 08 SE9?

◆◆◆◆ ⌑ The Fox and Coney Inn
52 Market Place HU15 2AT
☎ 01430 422275 📠 01430 421552
e-mail: foxandconey@aol.com
web: www.foxandconey.com
Dir: At eastern end of M62 follow A63 to 1st junct, left off junct into South Cave, hotel on right after clock tower

CHILD FACILITIES: Please telephone for details

Standing in the centre of the village, this friendly inn provides modern, attractive bedrooms of various sizes which are split between the main building and the adjoining annexe. An extensive range of food is available, either in the bar or in the dining room. The pleasant staff create a relaxed, informal atmosphere.
ROOMS: 12 en suite (2 fmly) (4 GF) s fr £42; d fr £55 * ⊗ in 6 bedrooms **FACILITIES:** STV TVB tea/coffee Direct dial from bedrooms Dinner Last d order 9.30pm **NOTES:** ✈ ⊗ in restaurant ⊗ in 1 lounge Cen ht **LB PARKING:** 21

YORKSHIRE, NORTH

BOLTON ABBEY
Map 07 SE0?

Babies Welcome | Family Rooms | Children's Dishes

★★★ ◎ ◎ ◎
The Devonshire Arms Country House
BD23 6AJ
☎ 01756 710441 📠 01756 710564
e-mail: reservations@thedevonshirearms.co.uk
web: www.devonshirehotels.co.uk
Dir: on B6160, 250yds N of junct with A59

CHILD FACILITIES: Baby listening Nanny (by arrangement) Babysitting (by arrangement) Activities: games Food/bottle warming Ch menu Ch portions Highchairs Ch discounts £25 sharing with parents Videos Cots Family rms D rms with S beds and cots £220-£390 Ch drinks (hot chocolate) Laundry NEARBY: York Dales Bolton Abbey Estate Riverbank Nature trails Lightwater Valley

continued

With stunning views of the Wharfedale countryside, this beautiful hotel, owned by the Duke and Duchess of Devonshire, dates back to the 17th century. Bedrooms are elegantly furnished; those in the old part of the house are particularly spacious, complete with four-posters and fine antiques. The sitting rooms are delightfully cosy with log fires and dedicated staff deliver service with a blend of friendliness and professionalism. The Burlington Restaurant offers highly accomplished dishes, while the brasserie provides a lighter alternative.

ROOMS: 41 en suite (18 GF) ⊗ in 12 bedrooms s £160-£380; d £220-£380 (incl. bkfst) **LB FACILITIES:** ⊠ ९ Fishing Sauna Solarium Gym ⅃♩ ♨ Jacuzzi Laser pigeon shooting, Falconry Xmas **PARKING:** 150 **NOTES:** ⊗ in restaurant

---

BREARTON
Map 08 SE36

Babies Welcome | Children's Dishes

🍴 Malt Shovel Inn

HG3 3BX
☎ 01423 862929
Dir: onto A61 take B6165 towards Knaresborough. Turn at Brearton - 1.5m

CHILD FACILITIES: Food/bottle warming Ch portions Highchairs Ch cutlery **NEARBY:** Lightwater Valley Mother Shiptons Cave Ripley Castle

OPEN: 12-2.30 6.45-11 (Sun 12-2.30, 7-10.30) **BAR MEALS:** L served Tue-Sun 12-2 D served Tue-Sat 7-9 Av main course £6.50 **NOTES:** Credit cards not taken **PARKING:** 20

BROUGHTON
Map 07 SD95

Babies Welcome | Children's Dishes

🍴 The Bull

BD23 3AE
☎ 01756 792065
e-mail: janeneil@thebullatbroughton.co.uk
Dir: On A59 3m from Skipton on A59

CHILD FACILITIES: Activities: colouring Food/bottle warming Ch menu Highchairs Safe grounds Changing facilities **NEARBY:** Skipton Castle Steam railway

OPEN: 12-3 5.30-11 (Sun 12-8) **BAR MEALS:** L served all week 12-2 D served Mon-Sat 6-9 **RESTAURANT:** L all week 12-2 D Mon-Sat 6-9 Av 3 course à la carte £16 **FACILITIES:** Garden **PARKING:** 60

BURNSALL
Map 07 SE06

🍴 The Red Lion ★★ 🏵

By the Bridge BD23 6BU
☎ 01756 720204 📠 01756 720292
e-mail: redlion@dalenet.co.uk
web: www.redlion.co.uk
Dir: A59 E from Skipton. B6160 towards Bolton Abbey, Burnsall 7m

CHILD FACILITIES: Please telephone for details

This delightful 16th-century ferryman's inn stands in a picture postcard village by the River Wharfe, where guests are free to fish in the hotel's own stretch of water. All the well-equipped bedrooms are stylish decorated. The interior is full of old world charm, with a traditional Dales bar, oak floors and panelling, cosy armchairs, sofas and wood-burning stoves. The elegant restaurant makes good use of fresh local ingredients, and breakfasts are memorable.

OPEN: 08.00-11.30 (Sun closes 10.30) **BAR MEALS:** L served all week 12-2.30 D served all week 6-9.30 Av main course £11.50 **RESTAURANT:** L served all week 12-3.00 D served all week 7-9.30 Av 3 course à la carte £27 Av 3 course fixed price £27.95 **FACILITIES:** Garden: Large garden, bordering the river Wharf **ROOMS:** 11 bedrooms 11 en suite 2 family rooms s£57 d£112 **PARKING:** 70

CATTERICK
Map 08 SE29

Babies Welcome | Family Rooms

♦♦♦ Rose Cottage

26 High St DL10 7LJ
☎ 01748 811164
Dir: 5m S of Scotch Corner, take A6136 off A1 into Catterick Village. House opp newsagents

CHILD FACILITIES: Food/bottle warming Highchairs Ch discounts babies free Cots Family rms D rm with S beds & cot/Z bed from £60

Conveniently located for the A1 and for exploring the Dales and Moors, this well maintained guest house lies in the middle of Catterick Village. Bedrooms are nicely presented and comfortable. The cosy public rooms include a cottage style dining room adorned with Mrs Archer's paintings. Dinner is available by arrangement during the summer.

ROOMS: 4 rms (2 en suite) (1 fmly) s £27-£32; d £42-£48 * **FACILITIES:** TVB tea/coffee No coaches Dinner Last d order 9.30am **NOTES:** Credit cards not taken ⊗ in restaurant Cen ht **PARKING:** 4

CRAY
Map 07 SD97

Children's Dishes

🍴 The White Lion Inn

Cray BD23 5JB
☎ 01756 760262 📠 761024
e-mail: admin@whitelioncray.com

CHILD FACILITIES: Activities: games Family area Food/bottle warming Ch menu Ch portions **NEARBY:** The Forbidden Corner Kilnsey Park

OPEN: 11-11 Closed: 25 Dec **BAR MEALS:** L served all week 12-2 D served all week 5.45-8.30 Av main course £8 **FACILITIES:** Garden: Beer garden with 10 trestle tables **ROOMS:** 8 bedrooms 8 en suite 1 family rooms s£40 d£60 (♦♦♦) **PARKING:** 20

EAST WITTON
Map 07 SE18

Babies Welcome | Children's Dishes

🍴 The Blue Lion

DL8 4SN
☎ 01969 624273 📠 01969 624189
e-mail: bluelion@breathemail.net

CHILD FACILITIES: Food/bottle warming Ch portions Highchairs Safe grounds **NEARBY:** Forbidden Corner Cinema Abbey

OPEN: 11-11 **BAR MEALS:** L served all week 12-2.15 D served all week 7-9.30 Av main course £12 **RESTAURANT:** L served Sun 12-2.15 D served all week 7-9.30 Av 3 course à la carte £22.90 **FACILITIES:** Garden: Lrg lawn, beautiful views **PARKING:** 30

ESCRICK
Map 08 SE64

Babies Welcome | Family Rooms | Children's Dishes

★★★ 73% 🏵 Parsonage Country House

York Rd YO19 6LF
☎ 01904 728111 📠 01904 728151
e-mail: reservations@parsonagehotel.co.uk
web: www.parsonagehotel.co.uk
Dir: From A64 take A19 Selby. Follow to Escrick . Hotel on right of St Helens Church.

CHILD FACILITIES: Baby listening Food/bottle warming Ch portions Highchairs Ch discounts under 5s free sharing with parent Safe grounds Cots Family rms Laundry

continued on p250

England

ESCRICK, continued

This 19th-century, former parsonage, has been lovingly restored and extended to provide delightful accommodation, set in well-tended gardens. Bedrooms are smartly appointed and well equipped. Spacious public areas include an elegant restaurant and a choice of attractive lounges.
ROOMS: 12 en suite 34 annexe en suite (4 fmly) (6 GF) ⊗ in 30 bedrooms s £75-£95; d £100-£120 (incl. bkfst) **LB FACILITIES:** STV Able to book tee times at local courses Xmas **PARKING:** 100 **NOTES:** ✈ ⊗ in restaurant

FILEY
Map 08 TA18

◆◆◆◆ Gables
2A Rutland St YO14 9JB
☎ 01723 514750
e-mail: thegablesfiley@aol.com
Dir: leave A165 at Filey, right in town centre into West Ave, 2nd left into Rutland St. The Gables is on corner opp church

> **CHILD FACILITIES:** Activities: books, toys, games, jigsaws Food/bottle warming Ch menu Ch portions Highchairs Ch cutlery Ch discounts under 3s £5, 3-15 half price Safe grounds Cots Family rms D rms with 1 or 2 S beds, B beds Ch drinks Laundry **NEARBY:** Wolds Way Hatherleigh Deep Sea Trawler Filey Brigg

Located in a quiet residential area, just a short stroll from the centre and promenade, this smart Edwardian house extends a warm welcome to all guests. Bedrooms are brightly decorated and well equipped and some are suitable for families. Breakfasts are substantial and a varied evening menu is available.
ROOMS: 5 en suite (3 fmly) **FACILITIES:** TVB tea/coffee No coaches Golf 18 ⚲ Dinner Last d order noon **NOTES:** ⊗ Cen ht **LB PARKING:** 3

HARROGATE
Map 08 SE35

★★ 74% Ascot House
53 Kings Rd HG1 5HJ
☎ 01423 531005 📠 01423 503523
e-mail: admin@ascothouse.com
web: www.ascothouse.com
Dir: follow signs for Town Centre/Conference & Exhibition Centre into Kings Rd, hotel on left after park

> **CHILD FACILITIES:** Baby listening Babysitting (by arrangement) **Activities:** colouring books, jigsaws, toys, board games Food/bottle warming Ch menu Ch portions Highchairs Ch discounts £7.50 sharing with 2 adults Cots Family rms T rm with cot/extra bed £95-£105 Connecting rms Laundry **NEARBY:** Valley Gardens Lightwater Valley Newby Hall & Gardens Harewood House

This late-Victorian house has been tastefully transformed into a friendly and meticulously maintained hotel. Situated a short distance from the International Conference Centre, it provides extremely well-appointed bedrooms, an inviting lounge bar and a dining room offering an interesting choice at dinner.
ROOMS: 19 en suite (2 fmly) (5 GF) ⊗ in all bedrooms s £59-£71; d £87-£112 (incl. bkfst) **LB FACILITIES:** Xmas **PARKING:** 14 **NOTES:** ⊗ in restaurant Closed 29 Dec-4 Jan & 23 Jan-6 Feb

> **Family Rooms** This symbol indicates family rooms are available, with type of room and prices included if provided

HOVINGHAM
Map 08 SE67

★★★ 67% ⚛ Worsley Arms
High St YO62 4LA
☎ 01653 628234 📠 01653 628130
e-mail: worsleyarms@aol.com
Dir: from S take A64, signed York. towards Malton. At dual carriageway left to Hovingham. At Slingsby left, then 2m. Hotel on main street

> **CHILD FACILITIES:** Baby listening Activities: games, videos, piano Outdoor play area Food/bottle warming Ch menu Ch portions Highchairs Ch discounts under 5s free Safe grounds Videos Cots Family rms D rm with S beds from £80 Ch drinks Laundry **NEARBY:** Castle Howard Flamingo Land Helmsley Castle Pickering Steam Railway

Overlooking the village green, this hotel has relaxing and attractive lounges with welcoming open fires. Bedrooms are also comfortable and several are contained in cottages across the green. The restaurant provides interesting quality cooking, with less formal dining in the Cricketers' Bar and Bistro to the rear.
ROOMS: 12 en suite 8 annexe en suite (2 fmly) (4 GF) ⊗ in all bedrooms s £60-£90; d £75-£150 (incl. bkfst) **LB FACILITIES:** ⚲ Squash Shooting Xmas **PARKING:** 25 **NOTES:** ⊗ in restaurant

HUBY
Map 08 SE56

◆◆◆ The New Inn Motel
Main St YO61 1HQ
☎ 01347 810219 📠 01347 810219
e-mail: enquiries@newinnmotel.freeserve.co.uk
Dir: Approach village from A19, left onto Main St. Motel on left

> **CHILD FACILITIES:** Food/bottle warming Ch menu Ch portions Highchairs Ch cutlery Ch discounts under 2s free in own cot Safe grounds Cots Family rms D rm with B beds, D rm with S bed £65-£75 Ch drinks Laundry **NEARBY:** Playing Field Walks Bridle Way

Nestling behind the New Inn, this modern motel style accommodation has a quiet location in the village of Huby, nine miles north of York. Comfortable bedrooms are spacious and neatly furnished, and breakfast is served in the cosy dining room. The reception area hosts an array of tourist information and the resident owners provide a friendly and helpful service.
ROOMS: 8 en suite (3 fmly) (8 GF) s £30-£38; d £44-£52 * ⊗ in 3 bedrooms **FACILITIES:** TVB tea/coffee No coaches **NOTES:** Credit cards not taken ⊗ in restaurant Cen ht **LB PARKING:** 8

KILBURN
Map 08 SE57

◆◆◆ 🍴 Forresters Arms Hotel
YO61 4AH
☎ 01347 868386 & 868550 📠 01347 868386
e-mail: paulcussons@forrestersarms.fsnet.co.uk
web: www.forrestersarms.fsnet.co.uk
Dir: from Thirsk take A170 for 2m then turn right for Kilburn. Follow road for 3m into village

> **CHILD FACILITIES:** Food/bottle warming Ch menu Ch portions Highchairs Ch discounts under 3s free, over 3s £10 Safe grounds Cots Family rms D rm with S bed, D with B beds £72 Connecting rms **NEARBY:** North York Moors Park Monk Park Thirsk Children's Farm

Situated beneath the famous White Horse, and next door to the
continued

enowned 'Mouseman' furniture showroom, this traditional inn
vas built by the Normans in the 12th century. Bedrooms are well
quipped and comfortable and a wide range of popular food is
erved either in the dining room or one of the cosy, characterful
ars.

ROOMS: 10 en suite (1 fmly) (1 GF) s £40; d £52-£62 *
FACILITIES: TVB tea/coffee Direct dial from bedrooms Pool Table
Dinner Last d order 9pm **NOTES:** ⊗ in restaurant Cen ht **LB**
PARKING: 40

KNARESBOROUGH　　　　　　　　　　Map 08 SE35

| Babies Welcome | Family Rooms | Children's Dishes |

♦♦♦♦ 🏠 Newton House

5-7 York Place HG5 0AD
☎ 01423 863539 📠 01423 869748
e-mail: newtonhouse@btinternet.com
web: www.newtonhousehotel.com
Dir: on A59 in Knaresborough, 500yds from town centre

CHILD FACILITIES: Baby listening Babysitting **Activities: toys,
Lego, train sets, dinosaurs, colouring books & pencils, games &
puzzles Family area Food/bottle warming Ch menu Ch portions
Highchairs Ch cutlery Ch discounts under 5s free, 1st child under 16
free, £10 per subsequent child Cots Family rms D rm with S beds
£80-£150 Ch drinks Connecting rms Fridge Changing mats**
**NEARBY: Park Swimming pool Newby Hall Devil's Arrow
Roman Town**

This delightful 18th-century former coaching inn is centrally
ocated and is only two minutes from the river castle and Market
quare. The hotel is entered through its own archway into a
ourtyard. The attractively decorated and very well equipped
edrooms include some four-posters and king-sized doubles.
Guests have use of a comfortable lounge and memorable
maginative breakfasts are served in an attractive dining room.
ROOMS: 9 en suite 2 annexe en suite (3 fmly) (3 GF) s £45; d £75-£90
⊗ **FACILITIES:** TVB tea/coffee Direct dial from bedrooms TVL No
oaches **NOTES:** ⊗ in restaurant Licensed Cen ht **LB PARKING:** 10

MARKINGTON　　　　　　　　　　　Map 08 SE26

★★★ 77% ♨ Hob Green

HG3 3PJ
☎ 01423 770031 📠 01423 771589
e-mail: info@hobgreen.com
web: www.hobgreen.com
*Dir: from A61, 4m N of Harrogate, left at Wormald Green, follow hotel
signs*
CHILD FACILITIES: Please telephone for details

This hospitable country house is set in delightful gardens amidst
olling countryside midway between Harrogate and Ripon. The
nviting lounges boast open fires in season and there is an elegant
continued

SWINTON PARK
LUXURY CASTLE HOTEL

FAMILY FRIENDLY HOTEL
EXCELLENCE IN ENGLAND HOTEL OF THE YEAR 2004
MASHAM, RIPON, NORTH YORKSHIRE HG4 4JH
TEL: (01765) 680900
WWW.SWINTONPARK.COM

restaurant with a small private dining room. The individual
bedrooms come with a host of thoughtful extras.

Hob Green

ROOMS: 12 en suite (1 fmly) ⊗ in all bedrooms s £98.50-£115;
d £115-£125 (incl. bkfst) **LB FACILITIES:** STV ♨ Xmas **PARKING:** 40
NOTES: ⊗ in restaurant

MASHAM　　　　　　　　　　　　　Map 07 SE28

| Babies Welcome | Family Rooms | Children's Dishes |

★★★★ ◎◎ ♨ Swinton Park

HG4 4JH
☎ 01765 680900 📠 01765 680901
e-mail: enquiries@swintonpark.com
web: www.swintonpark.com
*Dir: A1 onto B6267 to Masham. Follow signs through town centre, turn
right onto Swinton Terr. 1m past GC over bridge, up hill. Hotel on right*
continued on p252

England

MASHAM, continued

CHILD FACILITIES: Baby listening Nanny (by arrangement) Babysitting Activities: swings, croquet, kites, mountain bikes, model boats, private cinema, mother & baby massage (by arrangement) Indoor play area Outdoor play area Food/bottle warming Ch menu Ch portions Highchairs Ch cutlery Safe grounds Games consoles Videos Cots Family rms D rms with S & sofa beds Connecting rms Laundry **NEARBY:** 200 acres parklands Lakes Druid's Temple Lightwater Valley

Swinton Park, Masham

Extended during the Victorian and Edwardian eras, the original part of this welcoming castle dates from the 17th century. Bedrooms are luxuriously furnished and come with a host of thoughtful extras. Samuel's restaurant (built by the current owner's great-great-great grandfather) is very elegant and serves imaginative dishes which feature local produce, much being sourced from the Swinton estate.
ROOMS: 30 en suite ✆ in all bedrooms s £100-£350; d £120-£350 (incl. bkfst) **LB FACILITIES: Spa** STV Golf 9 Fishing Riding Snooker Gym ♨ ☂ Jacuzzi Shooting, Falconry, Pony Trekking, cookery school Xmas **PARKING:** 50 **NOTES:** ✆ in restaurant

See advert on page 251

MONK FRYSTON

Map 08 SE52

| Babies Welcome | Family Rooms | Children's Dishes |

★★★ 70% Monk Fryston Hall

LS25 5DU
☎ 01977 682369 📠 01977 683544
e-mail: reception@monkfryston-hotel.co.uk
web: www.monkfrystonhotel.co.uk
Dir: A1/A63 junct towards Selby. Left side in centre of Monk Fryston

CHILD FACILITIES: Baby listening Food/bottle warming Ch menu Ch portions Highchairs Ch discounts 2 children free sharing with parents Cots Family rms D rms with S beds Laundry **NEARBY:** Leisure centre Park Walks

This delightful 16th-century mansion house enjoys a peaceful location in 30 acres of grounds, yet is only minutes' drive from the A1. Many original features have been retained and the public rooms are furnished with antique and period pieces. Bedrooms are individually styled and thoughtfully equipped for both business and leisure guests.
ROOMS: 29 en suite (2 fmly) (5 GF) ✆ in 20 bedrooms s £92-£102; d £116-£171 (incl. bkfst) **LB FACILITIES:** STV ♨ Xmas **PARKING:** 80 **NOTES:** ✆ in restaurant

RICHMOND

Map 07 NZ10

| Babies Welcome | Family Rooms | Children's Dishes |

★★ 67% Frenchgate

59-61 Frenchgate DL10 7AE
☎ 01748 822087 📠 01748 823596
e-mail: info@frenchgatehotel.com
web: www.frenchgatehotel.com
Dir: from Scotch Corner take A6108. Through Richmond to New Queens Rd rdbt, left into Dundas St and left again into Frenchgate

CHILD FACILITIES: Outdoor play area Food/bottle warming Ch menu Ch portions Highchairs Cots Family rms D rms with S beds £95-£120 Laundry **NEARBY:** Yorkshire Dales Walks

Now under new ownership this elegant townhouse dates from the 16th and 17th centuries. Bedrooms are brightly decorated and comfortably equipped. There is an upstairs lounge. At dinner there is a good choice of freshly prepared dishes, and bar meals are also available.
ROOMS: 10 en suite 1 annexe en suite (1 fmly) (3 GF) ✆ in all bedrooms **FACILITIES:** gardens **PARKING:** 9 **NOTES:** ✆ in restaurant

ROSEDALE ABBEY

Map 08 SE79

| Babies Welcome | Children's Dishes |

⬛ The Milburn Arms Hotel ★★ ◉

YO18 8RA
☎ 01751 417312 📠 01751 417541
e-mail: info@millburnarms.co.uk
Dir: A170 W from Pickering 3m, R at sign to Rosedale then 7m N

CHILD FACILITIES: Outdoor play area Food/bottle warming Ch menu Ch portions Highchairs Ch cutlery Safe grounds **NEARBY:** Walks

This attractive inn dates back to the 16th century and enjoys an idyllic and peaceful location. Bedrooms, some in an adjacent stone block, are spacious and smartly appointed. Guests can enjoy carefully prepared food either in the bar or the elegant restaurant.
OPEN: 11.30-3 6-11 Closed: 25 Dec **BAR MEALS:** L served all week 12-2.15 D served all week 6.30-9 Av main course £8 **RESTAURANT:** L served Sun 12-2.30 D served all week 7-9 Av 3 course à la carte £30 **FACILITIES:** Garden: Large lawn area ✱ **ROOMS:** 13 en suite 3 family rooms s£47.50 d£40 **PARKING:** 60

SCARBOROUGH

Map 08 TA08

| Babies Welcome | Family Rooms | Children's Dishes |

◆◆◆◆ 🏠 Croft Hotel

87 Queens Pde YO12 7HT
☎ 01723 373904 📠 01723 350490
e-mail: crofthotel@btinternet.com web: www.crofthotel.co.uk
Dir: follow North Bay Sea Front tourist signs. Head along front towards castle headland. Take only right turn up cliff. Right at top, 1st hotel on left

CHILD FACILITIES: Baby listening Activities: games, Lego Indoor play area Food/bottle warming Ch menu Ch portions Highchairs Ch cutlery Ch discounts under 2s 10% of price, 3-4s 25%, 5-11s 50%, 12-14s 75% Safe grounds Videos Cots Family rms D rm with extra S beds, D rm with B beds **NEARBY:** Peasholm Park Boating Cinema Kinderland 10-min walk to sea

A flexible approach to guests' needs is a key feature of this friendly hotel. It is set in a prime position overlooking the bay, and

continued

guests can enjoy the view from either the comfortable lounge or from the patio in fine weather. A very pleasant bar is provided, and meals are served either here, or in the dining room.
ROOMS: 6 rms (5 en suite) (4 fmly) s £21-£25; d £42-£50 * ⊗
FACILITIES: TVB tea/coffee TVL Golf arranged at local courses Dinner Last d order 6.30pm **NOTES:** ✱ ⊗ in restaurant ⊗ in lounges Licensed Cen ht **LB PARKING:** 4

> Family Rooms Children's Dishes

◆◆◆◆ North End Farm Country
88 Main St, Seamer YO12 4RF
☎ 01723 862965
e-mail: northendfarm@tiscali.co.uk
Dir: A64 onto B1261 through Seamer. Farm on B1261

> **CHILD FACILITIES:** Food/bottle warming Ch menu Ch portions Ch cutlery Ch discounts under 2s free, in own room half price Safe grounds Videos Cots Family rms D rm with cot/extra single £50 Ch drinks (on request) **NEARBY:** Sealife Centre Kinderland Activity Park 10-min drive to sea

Located in Seamer, a village inland from Scarborough, this 18th-century farmhouse contains comfortable, well-equipped bedrooms, all with en suite facilities. Breakfast is served at individual tables in the smart dining room, and the cosy lounge has a large screen colour TV.
ROOMS: 3 en suite s £25-£32; d £40-£48 * **FACILITIES:** TVB tea/coffee TVL No coaches **NOTES:** Credit cards not taken ✱ ⊗ Cen ht
PARKING: 6

> Babies Welcome Family Rooms Children's Dishes

◆◆◆ Jalna House Hotel
168 North Marine Rd YO12 7HZ
☎ 01723 360668 ▤ 01723 360668
e-mail: jalna@btconnect.com
Dir: enter Scarborough on A64, at T-junct (rail station on right). Left, through lights, over 2 rdbts to Peasholm Park. Right, right again

> **CHILD FACILITIES:** Food/bottle warming Ch menu Ch portions Highchairs Ch cutlery Ch discounts Safe grounds Family rms D rms with B beds/cots Ch drinks Fridge **NEARBY:** Scarborough Castle Sea life & Marine sanctuary

A well-furnished guest house close to Peasholme Park and within walking distance of both the North Beach and the town centre. Compact bedrooms are comfortable, there is a cosy lounge and a dining room serving tasty home cooked meals.
ROOMS: 10 rms (6 en suite) (6 fmly) (2 GF) s fr £17; d fr £34 *
FACILITIES: TVB tea/coffee TVL Dinner Last d order noon
NOTES: Credit cards not taken ⊗ in restaurant Licensed Cen ht **LB BB**

SETTLE
Map 07 SD86

> Babies Welcome Family Rooms Children's Dishes

◆◆◆◆ 🍴 Golden Lion
5 Duke St BD24 9DU
☎ 01729 822203 ▤ 01729 824103
e-mail: goldenlion@yorks.net
Dir: in town centre opposite Barclays Bank

> **CHILD FACILITIES:** Food/bottle warming Ch menu Ch portions Highchairs Ch cutlery Safe grounds Cots Family rms D rm with S bed/s £76-£81 **NEARBY:** Walks Three Peaks Railway Falconry Centre Pony trekking

This traditional former coaching inn is centrally located in the town,
continued

---

just a short walk from the railway station. The Golden Lion provides a wide range of freshly prepared meals, served in either the spacious bar or the stylish restaurant. Most of the bedrooms have been refurbished to complement the sparkling new bathrooms.
ROOMS: 12 rms (10 en suite) (2 fmly) **FACILITIES:** TVB tea/coffee Pool Table Dinner Last d order 10pm **NOTES:** ✱ ⊗ in restaurant Cen ht
PARKING: 11

SKIPTON
Map 07 SD95

> Babies Welcome Family Rooms Children's Dishes

★★★ 73% The Coniston
Coniston Cold BD23 4EB
☎ 01756 748080 ▤ 01756 749487
e-mail: info@theconistonhotel.com
Dir: on A65, 6m NW of Skipton

> **CHILD FACILITIES:** Babysitting Activities: colouring, games, outdoor games Food/bottle warming Ch menu Ch portions Highchairs Safe grounds Cots Family rms D rm with S and pull out beds, T rm connecting with D rm £70-£80 Connecting rms Laundry **NEARBY:** Woodland walk Pony trekking Skipton Castle

Privately owned and situated on a 1,200 acre estate centred around a beautiful 24-acre lake this hotel offers guests many exciting outdoor activities. The modern bedrooms are comfortable and most have king-size beds. McLeod's Bar and the main restaurant offer all-day meals and fine dining is available in the evening on both carte and fixed-price menus.
ROOMS: 40 en suite (4 fmly) (20 GF) s £82-£92; d £94-£104 (incl. bkfst) **LB FACILITIES:** STV Fishing Landrover driving, Clay pigeon shooting, Falconry, fishing Xmas **PARKING:** 120 **NOTES:** ⊗ in restaurant

THIRSK
Map 08 SE48

> Babies Welcome Family Rooms Children's Dishes

★★ 75% Golden Fleece
42 Market Place YO7 1LL
☎ 01845 523108 ▤ 01845 523996
e-mail: goldenfleece@bestwestern.co.uk
Dir: off A19 at Thirsk turn off, to the town centre

> **CHILD FACILITIES:** Baby listening Activities: toys Food/bottle warming Ch menu Ch portions Highchairs Ch discounts free Cots Family rms D or T rms with Z beds from £85 Laundry **NEARBY:** Falconry Centre Walks Trekking centre Monk Park Farm Leisure Centre

This delightful hotel began life as a coaching inn, and enjoys a central location in the market square. Bedrooms are comfortably furnished, extremely well equipped and individually styled with beautiful soft furnishings. Guests can eat in the attractive bar, or choose more formal dining in the smart restaurant and are guaranteed friendly, attentive service.
ROOMS: 23 en suite (3 fmly) ⊗ in 4 bedrooms s £65; d £85-£105 (incl. bkfst) **LB FACILITIES:** STV Xmas **PARKING:** 35 **NOTES:** ⊗ in restaurant

THORNTON WATLASS
Map 08 SE28

> Babies Welcome Family Rooms Children's Dishes

★ 69% Buck Inn
HG4 4AH
☎ 01677 422461 ▤ 01677 422447
e-mail: buckwatlass@btconnect.com
Dir: A684 towards Bedale, B6268 towards Masham, after 2m turn right at x-roads to Thornton Watlass, hotel is by Cricket Green

continued on p254

THORNTON WATLASS, continued

CHILD FACILITIES: Babysitting Indoor play area Outdoor play area Family area Food/bottle warming Ch menu Ch portions Highchairs Ch cutlery Safe grounds Cots Family rms D rm with 2 S beds or adjoining rooms with shared bathroom £85-£95 Ch drinks **NEARBY:** Lightwater Valley Theme Park Thorp Perrow Arboretum Wensleydale Railway

Buck Inn, Thornton Watlass

This traditional country inn is situated on the edge of the village green overlooking the cricket pitch. Cricket prints and old photographs are found throughout and an open fire in the bar adds to the warm and intimate atmosphere. Wholesome lunches and dinners are served in the bar or dining room from an extensive menu. Bedrooms are brightly decorated and well equipped. **ROOMS:** 7 rms (5 en suite) (1 fmly) (1 GF) s £45-£50; d £60-£70 (incl. bkfst) **LB FACILITIES:** Fishing Quoits Children's play area ♫ **PARKING:** 10 **NOTES:** ⊗ in restaurant Closed 24 & 25 Dec for accommodation

WESTOW

Map 08 SE76

| Babies Welcome | Family Rooms | Children's Dishes |

♦♦♦♦ ❧ Woodhouse Farm
YO60 7LL
☎ 01653 618378 ▤ 01653 618378
e-mail: stay@wood-house-farm.co.uk
web: www.wood-house-farm.co.uk
Dir: from A64 turn to Kirkham Priory and continue to Westow. Right at T-junct and 0.5m out of village, farm drive on right

CHILD FACILITIES: Baby listening Babysitting Activities: toys, games, books, jigsaws, egg gathering Indoor play area Outdoor play area Family area Food/bottle warming Ch menu Ch portions Highchairs Ch cutlery Ch discounts under 3s free, then dependant on age Safe grounds Games consoles Videos Cots Family rms D rm with B beds & S bed (travel cot available) from £50 Ch drinks Connecting rms Fridge Laundry **NEARBY:** Castle Howard Water World York Castle Yorvick Museum

The owners of this guest house are a young farming family who
continued

open their home and offer caring hospitality. Home made bread, jams and farm produce turn breakfast into a feast, and the views from the house across the open fields are splendid.
ROOMS: 2 en suite (1 fmly) s £20-£30; d £40-£60 * ⊗ **FACILITIES:** TVB tea/coffee 350 acres arable/beef/sheep **NOTES:** Credit cards not taken ✗ ⊗ in restaurant Cen ht **LB PARKING:** 12

WHITBY

Map 08 NZ81

◀ The Magpie Café
14 Pier Rd YO21 3PU
☎ 01947 602058 ▤ 01947 601801
e-mail: ian@magpiecafe.co.uk

CHILD FACILITIES: Please telephone for details

OPEN: 11.30-9 (11.30-6.30 Sun) Closed: 5 Jan-6 Feb Rest: Nov-Mar Closed 6.30 Sun **BAR MEALS:** L served all week 11.30-9 D served all week Av main course £6 **RESTAURANT:** L served all week 11.30-9 D served all week **FACILITIES:** ✗

YORK

Map 08 SE65

| Babies Welcome | Family Rooms | Children's Dishes |

★★★★ 68% York Marriott
Tadcaster Rd YO24 1QQ
☎ 01904 701000 ▤ 01904 702308
e-mail: york@marriotthotels.co.uk
Dir: from A64 at York 'West' onto A1036, follow signs to city centre. Approx 1.5m, hotel on right after church and lights

Marriott
HOTELS · RESORTS · SUITES

CHILD FACILITIES: Babysitting Activities: jigsaws, toys, games, colouring Indoor play area Outdoor play area Food/bottle warming Ch menu Ch portions Highchairs Ch discounts under 5s free sharing with parents Safe grounds Videos Cots Family rms D rm with S beds or sofa beds Ch drinks Connecting rms Fridge Laundry **NEARBY:** Park Museums Maze Flamingo land Cinemas Theatres

Overlooking the racecourse and Knavesmire Parkland, the hotel offers modern accommodation, including family rooms, all with a comfort cooling system. Within the hotel, guests benefit from the use of extensive leisure facilities including indoor pool, putting
continued

green and tennis court. For those guests wishing to explore the historic and cultural attractions of the city there is a daily courtesy mini-bus service to the city centre, less than a mile from the hotel.
ROOMS: 108 en suite (14 fmly) (16 GF) ⊗ in 60 bedrooms
FACILITIES: Spa STV ⊡ ⚲ Sauna Solarium Gym ⚓ Jacuzzi Beauty treatment Xmas **PARKING:** 200 **NOTES:** ✠ ⊗ in restaurant

Babies Welcome	Family Rooms	Children's Dishes

★★★ 77%   Dean Court
Duncombe Place YO1 7EF
☎ 01904 625082 ᐧ 01904 620305
e-mail: info@deancourt-york.co.uk
web: www.deancourt-york.co.uk
Dir: city centre opposite York Minster

Best Western

> **CHILD FACILITIES:** Baby listening Nanny (on request) Babysitting (on request) Activities: games, mementos Food/bottle warming Ch menu Ch portions Highchairs Ch cutlery Ch discounts £20 sharing with adults, cots free Games consoles Videos Cots Family rms Twin, D and T rms with pull out or S beds £165-£185 Ch drinks Connecting rms Laundry NEARBY: Castle Museum Railway Museum Jorvick York Dungeon

This smart hotel enjoys a central location overlooking the Minster. Bedrooms are smartly appointed. Public areas have recently been re-furbished in an elegant, contemporary style and include the popular D.C.H. restaurant which enjoys wonderful views of the cathedral. Service is particularly friendly and efficient and light snacks are served all day in Terry's conservatory café. Valet parking is offered.
ROOMS: 39 en suite (4 fmly) ⊗ in 14 bedrooms s £75-£110; d £110-£190 (incl. bkfst) **LB FACILITIES:** Xmas **PARKING:** 30 **NOTES:** ✠ ⊗ in restaurant

★★ 68% The Groves
8 St Peters Grove, Clifton YO30 6AQ
☎ 01904 559777 ᐧ 01904 627729
e-mail: groves@ecsyork.co.uk
web: www.ecsyork.co.uk
Dir: off A19 at Clifton

> **CHILD FACILITIES:** Please telephone for details

This hotel is peacefully situated on both sides of a quiet side road within easy walking distance of the city and the Minster. Bedrooms offer comfortable, well-equipped accommodation and are available in the main buildings or courtyard. Public areas are split between the two main buildings; dinner is served in the Acorn and Oak restaurant.
ROOMS: 17 en suite 27 annexe en suite (11 fmly) (13 GF) ⊗ in 10 bedrooms s £42; d £84 (incl. bkfst) **LB FACILITIES:** STV **PARKING:** 39 **NOTES:** ⊗ in restaurant RS 19 Dec-3 Jan

> Don't forget our travel accommodation section at the front of the guide

◆◆◆◆ Bronte Guest House
22 Grosvenor Ter, Bootham YO30 7AG
☎ 01904 621066 ᐧ 01904 653434
e-mail: enquiries@bronte-guesthouse.com
web: www.bronte-guesthouse.com
Dir: from A19 north follow signs for city centre, take left turn immediately after Churchill Hotel into Grosvenor Terrace

> **CHILD FACILITIES:** Please telephone for details

Now under new ownership. Beautifully decorated throughout, this family-run guest house offers a friendly atmosphere with comfortable, thoughtfully equipped and individually styled bedrooms. Some rooms have fine period furniture. Hearty breakfasts are served in the tasteful dining room and special diets can also be catered for.
ROOMS: 5 en suite (1 fmly) s £34-£38; d £56-£64 * **FACILITIES:** TVB tea/coffee No coaches **NOTES:** ✠ ⊗ Cen ht **LB PARKING:** 1

Babies Welcome	Family Rooms	Children's Dishes

◆◆◆ Greenside
124 Clifton YO30 6BQ
☎ 01904 623631 ᐧ 01904 623631
e-mail: greenside@amserve.com
web: www.greensideguesthouse.co.uk
Dir: approach city centre on A19 N, at traffic lights straight on for Greenside, on the L opp Clifton Green

> **CHILD FACILITIES:** Baby listening Outdoor play area Family area Food/bottle warming Ch menu Ch portions Highchairs Ch cutlery Ch discounts Safe grounds Cots Family rms D rms with Z beds, adjoining D & T Connecting rms Laundry NEARBY: Rowntree Park Steam Railway Rombalds Moors

Overlooking Clifton Green, this detached house is just within walking distance of the city centre. Accommodation consists of simply furnished bedrooms and there is a cosy lounge and a dining room, where dinners by arrangement and traditional breakfasts are served. It is a family home, and other families are welcome.
ROOMS: 6 rms (3 en suite) (2 fmly) (3 GF) s fr £22; d fr £40 * **FACILITIES:** TVB tea/coffee TVL Children's play area Dinner Last d order 6pm **NOTES:** Credit cards not taken ⊗ in restaurant ⊗ in lounges Licensed Cen ht **LB PARKING:** 6

◆◆◆ Hillcrest
110 Bishopthorpe Rd YO23 1JX
☎ 01904 653160 ᐧ 01904 656168
e-mail: hillcrest@accommodation.gbr.fm
Dir: from A64 take A1036 signed City Centre York West. Take 1st right after Marriott Hotel and at T-junct turn left, Hillcrest 0.33m on right

> **CHILD FACILITIES:** Please telephone for details

A warm welcome awaits you at this conveniently located, central guest house with private parking. The Victorian house has been sympathetically renovated to provide comfortable accommodation. Bedrooms vary in size. The lounge offers a comfortable place in which to relax and breakfasts are served in the small, bright dining room.
ROOMS: 13 rms (7 en suite) (4 fmly) (1 GF) s £24-£29; d £42-£62 * **FACILITIES:** TVB tea/coffee TVL No coaches **NOTES:** ✠ ⊗ Cen ht **LB PARKING:** 8

◆◆◆ Linden Lodge Hotel
Nunthorpe Av, Scarcroft Rd YO23 1PF
☎ 01904 620107 ᐧ 01904 620985
e-mail: bookings@lindenlodge.yorkshire.net
Dir: A64 take York West, follow signs for city centre, past racecourse on right, then 2nd right into Scarcroft Rd, & 2nd right into Nunthorpe Ave

> **CHILD FACILITIES:** Please telephone for details

continued on p256

England

YORK, continued

Friendly service is provided at this well-furnished, comfortable house in a quiet side road a short walk from the city and racecourse. The bedrooms are well-equipped and ground-floor areas include an attractive pine-furnished dining room and comfortable lounge with the benefit of a bar.
ROOMS: 14 rms (10 en suite) (2 fmly) (2 GF) s £26-£29; d £52-£58 * **FACILITIES:** TVB tea/coffee TVL No coaches **NOTES:** ✖ ⊗ Licensed Cen ht **LB**

♦♦♦ St Denys Hotel
St Denys Rd YO1 9QD
☎ 01904 622207 & 646776 ▤ 01904 624800
e-mail: info@stdenyshotel.co.uk
web: www.stdenyshotel.co.uk
Dir: from A64 turn off A1079 York/Hull straight on approx 2.5m, through lights, through Walmgate Bar, left after 500yds. Hotel opp St Denys Church
CHILD FACILITIES: Please telephone for details
Formerly a vicarage, this constantly improving small hotel is located in the heart of the city centre. En suite bedrooms are comfortably furnished and equipped with both practical and homely extras. The neatly appointed dining room leads through to a conservatory lounge with a bar.
ROOMS: 12 en suite (4 fmly) (2 GF) s £40-£50; d £50-£95 * ⊗ **FACILITIES:** TVB tea/coffee Direct dial from bedrooms TVL No coaches **NOTES:** ✖ ⊗ in restaurant Licensed Cen ht **LB PARKING:** 9

YORKSHIRE, SOUTH

SHEFFIELD   Map 08 SK38

★★★★ 70%
Sheffield Marriott Hotel

Kenwood Rd S7 1NQ
☎ 0870 400 7261 ▤ 0870 400 7361
e-mail: eventorganiser.sheffield@marriotthotels.com
Dir: follow A61 past Red Tape Studios on right , right at 2nd lights into St Marys Rd. At rdbt straight across, bear left into London Rd, right at lights, at top of hill straight across 1st and 2nd rdbt
CHILD FACILITIES: Please telephone for details

A smart, modern hotel peacefully located in a residential suburb a few miles from the city centre. Stylishly decorated bedrooms are spacious, quiet and provide very well equipped. The hotel also has an extensive range of leisure facilities. Secure car parking.
ROOMS: 114 en suite (14 fmly) (27 GF) ⊗ in 90 bedrooms s £64-£120; d £78-£140 (incl. bkfst) **LB FACILITIES:** Spa STV ⊠ Fishing Sauna Solarium Gym ♬ Jacuzzi Steam room, Health & beauty treatments **PARKING:** 200 **NOTES:** ⊗ in restaurant

⊛ ⊛ ⊛ Richard Smith at Thyme
32-34 Sandygate Rd S10 5RY
☎ 0114 266 6096 ▤ 0114 266 0279
Dir: From Sheffield centre take A57; at Crosspool turn R onto Sandygate Road. 100yds on R
CHILD FACILITIES: Food/bottle warming Ch portions Highchairs Changing facilities **NEARBY:** Peak District
FOOD: Modern International **STYLE:** Modern, Bistro **SEATS:** 70 **OPEN:** 12-2/6-10, Closed 26 Dec, 1 Jan, D Sun **RESTAURANT:** main £8-£19 **NOTES:** ⊗ in restaurant, Air con

YORKSHIRE, WEST

BRADFORD   Map 07 SE13

Babies Welcome | Family Rooms | Children's Dishes

★★★ 63% Novotel Bradford
6 Roydsdale Way BD4 6SA
☎ 01274 683683 ▤ 01274 651342
e-mail: h0510@accor-hotels.com

Dir: M606 junct 2, exit to Euroway Trading Estate turn right at traffic lights at bottom of slip road, take 2nd right onto Roydsdale Way
CHILD FACILITIES: Babysitting **Activities:** goodie bags, children's channel TV Indoor play area Family area Food/bottle warming Ch menu Ch portions Highchairs Ch cutlery Ch discounts under 16s free sharing with adults Games consoles Cots Family rms D rms with S beds Connecting rms Laundry Changing mats **NEARBY:** X'scape Eureka! Museum National Museum of TV & Photography

This purpose-built hotel stands in an good location for access to the motorway. It provides spacious bedrooms that are comfortably equipped. Open-plan day rooms include a stylish bar, and a lounge that leads into the Garden Brasserie. Several function rooms are also available.
ROOMS: 119 en suite (37 fmly) (9 GF) ⊗ in 69 bedrooms s £60; d £60 **LB FACILITIES:** STV Xmas **PARKING:** 200

HAREWOOD   Map 08 SE34

Babies Welcome | Children's Dishes

⌕ Harewood Arms
Harrogate Rd LS17 9LH
☎ 0113 2886566 ▤ 0113 2886064
e-mail: mail@harewoodarms.co.uk
Dir: On A61 S of Harrogate
CHILD FACILITIES: Food/bottle warming Ch portions Highchairs Safe grounds Changing facilities **NEARBY:** Harewood House
OPEN: 11-11 **BAR MEALS:** L served all week 12-3 D served all week 5-9.30 Av main course £5.50 **RESTAURANT:** L served all week 12-2 D served all week 7-9.30 Av 3 course fixed price £22.95 **FACILITIES:** Garden **PARKING:** 90

All information was correct at the time of going to press; we recommend you confirm details on booking

HAWORTH   Map 07 SE03

♦♦♦♦ 🏛 Aitches
11 West Ln BD22 8DU
☎ 01535 642501
e-mail: aitches@talk21.com
web: www.aitches.co.uk
Dir: enter Haworth, pass steam railway stn, 0.5m, left after Edinburgh Wool shop into Brontë Museum car park, Aitches is to the right of steps to main street

CHILD FACILITIES: Please telephone for details

This pleasant guest house is centrally located on the cobbled main street of this popular village, just one minute's walk from the Brontë Parsonage. Bedrooms are attractively styled, and offer homely and practical extras. Hearty breakfasts and are served in the stylish dining room; pre-booking of dinners is requested.
ROOMS: 4 en suite s £40-£50; d £50-£60 * **FACILITIES:** TVB tea/coffee Dinner Last d order 3pm **NOTES:** ✠ ⊗ Licensed Cen ht **LB**

LEEDS   Map 08 SE23

| Babies Welcome | Family Rooms | Children's Dishes |

★★★ 72% Novotel Leeds Centre
4 Whitehall, Whitehall Quay LS1 4HR
☎ 0113 242 6446 📠 0113 242 6445
e-mail: H3270@accor-hotels.com
Dir: exit M621 junct 3, follow signs to train station. Turn into Aire St and left at lights

NOVOTEL

CHILD FACILITIES: Activities: games, colouring Indoor play area Family area Food/bottle warming Ch menu Ch portions Highchairs Ch cutlery Ch discounts under 16s free sharing with parent Games consoles Videos Cots Family rms £75-£132 Connecting rms Laundry Changing mats NEARBY: Eureka Museum Harewood House Thackray Museum Royal Armouries

With minimalist flair and style, this contemporary hotel provides a quality, value-for-money experience close to the city centre. Spacious, air-conditioned bedrooms are provided, whilst public areas offer deep leather sofas and an eye-catching water feature in reception. Light snacks are provided in the airy bar and the restaurant doubles as a bistro.
ROOMS: 195 en suite (60 fmly) ⊗ in 130 bedrooms s fr £105; d fr £105 * **FACILITIES:** STV Sauna Gym Play station computers in rooms & play area Steam room Xmas **PARKING:** 70

★★★ 68% Bewley's Hotel Leeds
City Walk, Sweet St LS11 9AT
☎ 0113 234 2340 📠 0113 234 2349
e-mail: leeds@BewleysHotels.com
web: www.bewleyshotels.com/leeds_index.htm
Dir: M621 junct 3, at 2nd set of lights turn left, then right and right again. Hotel straight ahead.

CHILD FACILITIES: Please telephone for details

Located on the edge of the city centre, this new hotel has the added advantage of secure underground car parking. Bedrooms are spacious and comfortable. Downstairs, the light and airy bar lounge leads into a brasserie where a wide selection of popular dishes is offered.
ROOMS: 334 en suite (99 fmly) ⊗ in 246 bedrooms s £59; d £59
FACILITIES: STV **PARKING:** 160 **NOTES:** ✠ Closed 24th-26th Dec

CHANNEL ISLANDS

A Golden Tamarind lion monkey in Jersey Zoo

GUERNSEY
FOREST
German Occupation Museum
GY8 0BG   ☎01481 238205
(Behind Forest Church near the airport)
Open Apr-Oct 10-5; Nov-Mar 10-1. Closed Mon.

ROCQUAINE BAY
Fort Grey and Shipwreck Museum
GY7 9BY   ☎01481 265036
admin@museums.gov.gg
(On coast road at Rocquaine Bay)
Open Apr-Sep, 10-5.
*Fort Grey £2.50, pen £1.25; 3 Venue Ticket £9, pen £5.

ST ANDREW
German Military Underground Hospital & Ammunition Store
GY6 8XR   ☎01481 239100
(St Andrews Parish, centre of island)
Open Jul-Aug, daily 10-noon & 2-4.30; May-Jun & Sep, daily 10-noon & 2-4; Apr & Oct, daily 2-4; Mar & Nov, Sun & Thu 2-3.
*£3 ch £1p.

ST PETER PORT
Castle Cornet
GY1 UG   ☎01481 721657
admin@museums.gov.gg
(0.5m from town centre)
Open Apr-Oct, daily 10-5.
*£6 pen £4. 3 venue ticket £9 pen £5

Guernsey Museum & Art Gallery
GY1 1UG   ☎01481 726518
admin@museums.gov.gg
(On the outskirts of St Peter Port set in the Victorian 'Candie gardens')
Open Feb-Dec, daily 10-5.
*£3.50, pen £2.50. 3 venue ticket £9, pen £5.

VALE
Rousse Tower
peter@museum.guernsey.net   ☎01481 726518
(On island's W coast, signposted)
Open Apr-Oct 9-dusk; Nov-Mar Wed, Sat & Sun 9-4.

JERSEY
ST BRELADE
Jersey Lavender Farm JE3 8DS
admin@jerseylavender.co.uk   ☎01534 742933
(On the B25 from St Aubin's Bay to Redhouses)
Open 10 May-18 Sep, Mon-Sat 10-5.
*£3.50, ch under 14 free.

ST CLEMENT'S
Samares Manor
JE2 6QW   ☎01534 870551
barbara@samaresmanor.com
(2m E of St Helier on St Clements Inner Road)
Open 3 Apr-16 Oct.
*£4.95, ch under 16 £1.95, pen £4.50. Sat prices: £3.95, ch under 16 £1.75, pen £3.50.

ST HELIER
Maritime Museum & Occupation Tapestry Gallery
JE2 3ND   ☎01534 811043
marketing@jerseyheritagetrust.org
(Alongside Marina, opposite Liberation Square)
Open all year, daily 10-5. Winter closing at 4pm.
*£5.95, pen/student £5.10. Under 6s free.

ST LAWRENCE
German Underground Hospital
JE3 1FU   ☎01534 860808
info@jerseywartunnels.com
(Bus route 8A from St Helier)
Open 4 Feb-19 Dec, daily 9.30-5.30, last admission 4 *£8 (ch £4, students & serving armed forces £6 & pens £7.)

ST PETER
The Living Legend JE3 7ET
info@jerseyslivinglegend.co.je   ☎01534 485496
(From main town of St Helier, go along main esplanade, turn right to Bel Royal. Turn left and follow road to The Living Legend signposted from the German Underground Hospital)
Open daily, Mar-Nov 9.30-5, Sat & Sun 10-5.
*£7.10, ch 7-13 £4.85, pen £6.80, student £5.50, disabled £5.60.

TRINITY
Durrell Wildlife Conservation Trust
JE3 5BP   ☎01534 860000
info@durrell.org
Open all year, daily 9.30-6, (summer) 9.30-5 (winter). Closed 25 Dec.
*£9.95, ch 4-16 £7.25, pen £8.35.

England

GUERNSEY

ST MARTIN   Map 16

Babies Welcome | **Family Rooms** | **Children's Dishes**

★★★ 75% 🖲 La Barbarie

Saints Rd, Saints Bay GY4 6ES
☎ 01481 235217 📠 01481 235208
e-mail: reservations@labarbariehotel.com
web: www.labarbariehotel.com

CHILD FACILITIES: Baby listening Activities: colouring Food/bottle warming Ch menu Ch portions Highchairs Ch discounts under 2s free Safe grounds Cots Family rms D rm with B beds Connecting rms Laundry **NEARBY:** Park 5-min walk

This former priory dates back to the 17th century and retains much of its charm and style. Staff provide a most friendly and attentive environment, and the modern facilities offer guests a relaxing stay. Excellent choices and fresh local ingredients form the basis of the interesting menus in the attractive restaurant and bar.
ROOMS: 22 en suite (4 fmly) (8 GF) 🚭 in all bedrooms s £43-£59; d £58-£90 (incl. bkfst) **LB FACILITIES:** ₹ **PARKING:** 50 **NOTES:** ✠ 🚭 in restaurant Closed 1 Nov- 25 Feb

HERM

HERM   Map 16

★★★ 70% 🖲 White House

GY1 3HR
☎ 01481 722159 📠 01481 710066
e-mail: hotel@herm-island.com
web: www.herm-island.com
Dir: close to harbour

CHILD FACILITIES: Please telephone for details

Enjoying a unique island setting, this attractive hotel is just a 20 minutes from Guernsey by sea. Set in well-tended gardens, the hotel offers neatly decorated bedrooms, located in either the main house or adjacent cottages; the majority of rooms have sea views. Guests can relax in one of several lounges, enjoy a drink in one of two bars and choose from two dining options.
ROOMS: 17 en suite 23 annexe en suite (23 fmly) (7 GF) s £67-£78; d £134-£198 (incl. bkfst & dinner) **LB FACILITIES:** no TV in bdrms ₹ ✆ ₤♑ Fishing trips, Yacht & Motor boat charters **NOTES:** ✠ 🚭 in restaurant 2 Apr-2 Oct

JERSEY

GOREY   Map 16

Babies Welcome | **Children's Dishes**

🖲 Jersey Pottery Restaurant

Gorey Village JE3 9EP
☎ 01534 850850 📠 01534 856403
e-mail: admin@jerseypottery.com
Dir: In Gorey village, well signposted from main coast road

CHILD FACILITIES: Activities: small cinema Indoor play area Outdoor play area Family area Food/bottle warming Ch menu Ch portions Highchairs Safe grounds Changing facilities **NEARBY:** Jersey Pottery Glaze Craze Near sea

FOOD: Modern British **STYLE:** Rustic **SEATS:** 180 **OPEN:** 12-2.30/7-9, Closed Xmas, Jan, Mid Feb, Mon, Tue, D Sun **RESTAURANT:** Fixed L £15.50, Fixed D £25, main £10.95-£31.50 **NOTES:** 🚭 area **PARKING:** 300

ST BRELADE   Map 16

Babies Welcome | **Family Rooms** | **Children's Dishes**

★★★★ 74% St Brelade's Bay Hotel

JE3 8EF
☎ 01534 746141 📠 01534 747278
e-mail: info@stbreladesbayhotel.com
web: www.stbreladesbayhotel.com
Dir: SW corner of the island

CHILD FACILITIES: Baby listening Babysitting Activities: magician, children's disco, colouring, toys Indoor play area Outdoor play area Food/bottle warming Ch menu Ch portions Highchairs Ch discounts child in cot free, under 5s £25, 5-11s £35, over 12s £45 Safe grounds Videos Cots Family rms D rms with extra beds or B beds from £91 Connecting rms Laundry Changing mats **NEARBY:** Zoo Millbrook Park Cineworld Maritime Museum Living Legend Seafront location

This family hotel overlooking St Brelade's Bay has many loyal guests and members of staff. The attractive tiered gardens and grounds are ablaze with colour during summer. In addition to easy beach access and an extensive range of indoor and outdoor recreational facilities, there is a choice of pools. Most bedrooms have king-size beds, and many have a children's room within the unit. Morning and afternoon tea are included in the tariff.
ROOMS: 72 en suite (50 fmly) s £70-£105; d £100-£170 (incl. bkfst)
FACILITIES: STV ₹ ৎ Snooker Sauna Gym ♑ ₺ Petanque, Mini-gym, Games room, Table tennis ♫ **PARKING:** 60 **NOTES:** ✠ 🚭 in restaurant Closed 3 Oct-21 Apr

How to use this guide & abbreviations are explained on pages 5-7

Babies Welcome | **Family Rooms** | **Children's Dishes**

★★★★ 71% 🖲 🖲 Hotel La Place

Route du Coin, La Haule JE3 8BT
☎ 01534 744261 📠 01534 745164
e-mail: reservations@hotellaplacejersey.com
web: www.hotellaplacejersey.com
Dir: off main St Helier/St Aubin coast road at La Haule Manor (B25). Up hill, 2nd left (to Redhouses), 1st right. Hotel is 100mtrs on right

continued on p260

ST BRELADE, continued

CHILD FACILITIES: Baby listening Babysitting Activities: colouring books Outdoor play area Food/bottle warming Ch menu Ch portions Highchairs Ch cutlery Ch discounts under 4s free, 4-12s 50% Safe grounds Cots Family rms D rm with B beds, Triple rm from £70 Ch drinks (on request) Connecting rms Laundry **NEARBY:** Aqua Park Cinema 10-min walk to sea

Developed around a 17th-century farmhouse, this friendly hotel is well placed for exploration of the island. A range of bedroom types is provided, some rooms have private patios and direct access to the sheltered pool area. The stylish cocktail bar is popular for pre-dinner drinks and a more traditional lounge is available. An interesting menu is offered, making good use of local produce.
ROOMS: 42 en suite (1 fmly) ⊛ in 25 bedrooms s £86-£118; d £130-£232 (incl. bkfst) **LB FACILITIES:** STV ∿ Sauna Discount at Les Ormes Country Club, including golf, gym & indoor tennis Xmas **PARKING:** 100 **NOTES:** ⊛ in restaurant

★★★ 71% Golden Sands
St Brelade's Bay JE3 8EF
☎ 01534 741241 📠 01534 499366
e-mail: goldensands@dolanhotels.com
web: www.dolanhotels.com
Dir: follow signs to St Brelade's Bay. Hotel on coast side of road

CHILD FACILITIES: Babysitting (charge) Activities: playroom, TV with children's channel Indoor play area Food/bottle warming Ch menu Ch portions Highchairs Ch cutlery Ch discounts under 2s free, 2-11s 50%, 12-16s 25% discount Cots Family rms 3 D rms with S beds /B beds approx £186 Laundry **NEARBY:** Seaside location

With direct access to the beach, this popular hotel overlooks the wonderful sandy expanse of St Brelade's Bay. Many of the comfortable bedrooms are seafacing with balconies, guests can relax, breathing in the fresh air and looking out to sea. Public areas include a lounge, bar and restaurant, all of which have bay views.
ROOMS: 62 en suite (5 fmly) s £36-£78; d £72-£104 (incl. bkfst)
FACILITIES: STV Childrens play room ♫ **NOTES:** ✖ ⊛ in restaurant Closed Nov-mid Apr

★★ 72% Beau Rivage
St Brelade's Bay JE3 8EF
☎ 01534 745983 📠 01534 747127
e-mail: beau@jerseyweb.demon.co.uk
web: www.jersey.co.uk/hotels/beau
Dir: seaward side of coast road in centre of St Brelades Bay, 1.5m S of airport

CHILD FACILITIES: Please telephone for details

With direct access to one of Jersey's most popular beaches, residents and non-residents are welcome to this hotel's bar and terrace. Most of the well-equipped bedrooms have wonderful sea views, some the bonus of balconies. Residents have a choice of lounges, plus a sun deck exclusively for their use. Between daily set menus and an extensive carte, a range of dishes featuring English and Continental cuisine is available each evening.
ROOMS: 27 en suite (9 fmly) ⊛ in 1 bedroom s £48-£83; d £64-£134 (incl. bkfst) **LB FACILITIES:** STV Sunbathing terrace ♫ **PARKING:** 16
NOTES: ✖ ⊛ in restaurant RS Nov-Mar

ST HELIER   Map 16

★★★ 67% Apollo
St Saviours Rd JE2 4GJ
☎ 01534 725441 📠 01534 722120
e-mail: reservations@huggler.com
web: www.huggler.com
Dir: on St Saviours Road at its junct with La Motte Street

CHILD FACILITIES: Baby listening Food/bottle warming Ch menu Ch portions Highchairs Ch discounts under 16s free sharing with parents Safe grounds Games consoles Cots Family rms D rm with B beds Ch drinks Laundry **NEARBY:** Cinema Swimming pool 15-min walk to sea

Centrally located, this popular hotel has a relaxed, informal atmosphere. Bedrooms are comfortably furnished and include useful extras. Many guests return regularly to enjoy the variety of leisure facilities including an outdoor pool with water slide and indoor pool with separate jacuzzi. The elegant cocktail bar is an ideal place for a pre-dinner drink.
ROOMS: 85 en suite (5 fmly) s £69-£79; d £92-£112 (incl. bkfst) **LB FACILITIES:** 🏊 ∿ Sauna Solarium Gym Jacuzzi Xmas **PARKING:** 50 **NOTES:** ✖

★★★ 64% Royal
David Place JE2 4TD
☎ 01534 726521 📠 01534 811046
e-mail: royal@bestwestern.co.uk
web: www.royalhoteljersey.com
Dir: follow signs for Ring Rd, pass Queen Victoria rdbt keep left, left at lights, left into Piersons Rd. Follow one-way system to Cheapside, Rouge Bouillon, at A14 turn to Midvale Rd, hotel on left

CHILD FACILITIES: Nanny (by arrangement) Babysitting Activities: (seasonal) face painting Food/bottle warming Ch menu Ch portions Highchairs Ch discounts Cots Family rms Connecting rms Laundry **NEARBY:** Cinema Walks Leisure centre 10-min drive

This long established hotel is located in the centre of town and is within easy walking distance of the business district and shops. It provides individual bedrooms and a range of public areas. Dining choices include the No 27 Bar and Brasserie and the Henry VIII restaurant.
ROOMS: 88 en suite (39 fmly) ⊛ in 16 bedrooms d £85-£138 (incl. bkfst) **LB FACILITIES:** ♫ Xmas **PARKING:** 15 **NOTES:** ✖

TRINITY   Map 16

★★★ 72% Highfield Country

Route d'Ebenezer JE3 5DT
☎ 01534 862194 📠 01534 865342
e-mail: reservations@highfieldjersey.com
web: www.highfieldjersey.com
Dir: on A8 next to Ebenezer Chapel

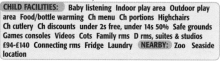

> **CHILD FACILITIES:** Baby listening Indoor play area Outdoor play
> area Food/bottle warming Ch menu Ch portions Highchairs
> Ch cutlery Ch discounts under 2s free, under 14s 50% Safe grounds
> Games consoles Videos Cots Family rms D rms, suites & studios
> £94-£140 Connecting rms Fridge Laundry **NEARBY:** Zoo Seaside
> location

Rurally located, this family-friendly hotel offers spacious,
comfortable bedrooms, some with kitchenette. Public areas are
light and attractively styled, with the conservatory a popular venue
for pre-dinner drinks. Leisure facilities include an indoor pool,
sauna and an outdoor pool. A varied menu is provided at dinner,
and breakfast is a self-service buffet.

ROOMS: 38 en suite (32 fmly) (1 GF) ⊛ in all bedrooms s £62-£71;
d £94-£112 (incl. bkfst) **LB FACILITIES: Spa** 🖼 ↘ Sauna Gym
Petanque **PARKING:** 41 **NOTES:** ✖ ⊛ in restaurant Closed Dec-Mar

ISLE OF MAN

DOUGLAS   Map 06 SC37

★★★ 69% Welbeck

13/15 Mona Dr IM2 4LF
☎ 01624 675663 📠 01624 661545
e-mail: mail@welbeck.com
Dir: at crossroads of Mona & Empress Drive off Central Promenade

> **CHILD FACILITIES:** Baby listening Food/bottle warming Ch menu
> Ch portions Highchairs Ch discounts Safe grounds Videos Cots
> Family rms D & T rms with S beds from £100 Fridge Laundry
> **NEARBY:** Parks Leisure centre Cinema Walks 2-min walk to sea

The Welbeck is a privately owned and personally run hotel
situated within easy reach of the seafront. It offers guests a
friendly welcome and a choice of attractive accommodation,
ranging from well-equipped bedrooms to six newly constructed
luxury apartments, each with its own lounge and small kitchen.
Other facilities include a mini-gym and steam room.
ROOMS: 27 en suite (7 fmly) s £49-£65; d £66-£87 (incl. bkfst)
FACILITIES: STV Gym Steam room **NOTES:** ✖ Closed 19 Dec-5 Jan

> Many proprietors are happy to
> provide extra facilities for children,
> but let them know in advance what
> you need so they can be prepared

Scotland

ABERDEEN CITY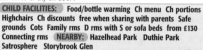

ABERDEENSHIRE

ABERDEEN Map 15 NJ90

| Babies Welcome | Family Rooms | Children's Dishes |

★★★★ 74% 🏵 🏵 **Ardoe House**
South Deeside Rd, Blairs AB12 5YP
☎ 01224 860600 🖷 01224 861283
e-mail: ardoe@macdonald-hotels.co.uk
Dir: 4m W of city off B9077

MACDONALD HOTELS

> **CHILD FACILITIES:** Food/bottle warming Ch menu Ch portions
> Highchairs Ch discounts free when sharing with parents Safe
> grounds Cots Family rms D rms with S or sofa beds from £130
> Connecting rms **NEARBY:** Hazelhead Park Duthie Park
> Satrosphere Storybrook Glen

From its elevated position on the banks of the River Dee, this
baronial-style mansion commands excellent countryside views.
Tastefully decorated bedrooms are located in the main house, or
more modern extension. Public rooms include an impressive
leisure club, cosy lounge and cocktail bar.
ROOMS: 117 en suite (4 fmly) 🚭 in 86 bedrooms s fr £75; d fr £110
(incl. bkfst) **LB FACILITIES:** STV 🖾 ৎ Sauna Solarium Gym Jacuzzi
Petanque Xmas **PARKING:** 250 **NOTES:** 🚭 in restaurant

◆◆◆◆ **Strathisla**
408 Gt Western Rd AB10 6NR
☎ 01224 321026
e-mail: elza@strathisla-guesthouse.co.uk
*Dir: follow A90, over Dee Bridge, straight over rdbt, on dual-carriageway,
over 2nd rdbt to lights, then right into Great Western Rd*

> **CHILD FACILITIES:** Please telephone for details

A comfortable granite-built terraced house on the west side of the
city, Strathisla boasts attractive bedrooms, all individual and
inviting, with added touches such as alarm clocks and a
complimentary slice of cake with the beverage facilities. Vegetarian
options are available at breakfast.
ROOMS: 5 en suite (1 fmly) s £26-£32; d £40-£44 * **FACILITIES:** TVB
tea/coffee No coaches **NOTES:** 🚭 Cen ht **PARKING:** 1

> Many proprietors are happy to
> provide extra facilities for children,
> but let them know in advance what
> you need so they can be prepared

BALLATER Map 15 NO39

| Babies Welcome | Family Rooms | Children's Dishes |

★★ 73% **Loch Kinord**
Ballater Rd, Dinnet AB34 5JY
☎ 01339 885229 🖷 887007
e-mail: ask@kinord.com
Dir: Between Aboyne & Ballater, on A93, in village of Dinnet

THE CIRCLE
Selected Individual Hotels
GREAT BRITAIN

> **CHILD FACILITIES:** Baby listening Babysitting Activities: board
> games, books Outdoor play area Food/bottle warming Ch menu
> Ch portions Highchairs Ch discounts under 10s free
> sharing with parents Safe grounds Videos Cots Family rms D rm
> with S bed £105 Laundry **NEARBY:** Walks

Family-run, this roadside hotel lies between Aboyne and Ballater
and is well located for leisure and sporting pursuits. It has lots of
character and a friendly atmosphere. There are two bars, one
outside and a cosy one inside, plus a dining room in bold, tasteful
colour schemes. Most of the bedrooms have been stylishly
refurbished and boast smart bathrooms.
ROOMS: 21 rms (19 en suite) (3 fmly) (4 GF) 🚭 in 5 bedrooms
s £35-£55; d £50-£85 (incl. bkfst) **LB FACILITIES:** Sauna Jacuzzi Pool
table Xmas **PARKING:** 20 **NOTES:** 🚭 in restaurant

NETHERLEY Map 15 NO89

🍴 **The Lairhillock Inn**
AB39 3QS
☎ 01569 730001 🖷 01569 731175
e-mail: lairhillock@breathemail.net
web: www.lairhillock.com
Dir: From Aberdeen take A90 turn R at Durris turning

> **CHILD FACILITIES:** Please telephone for details

OPEN: 11-2 (Fri 11-2 & 5-12, Sat 11-12, Sun 11-11) 5-11 Closed: 25-26 Dec,
1-2 Jan **BAR MEALS:** L served all week 12-2 D served all week 6-9.30 Av
main course £8 **RESTAURANT:** L served Sun 12-1.30 D served Wed-Mon
7-9.30 Av 3 course à la carte £25 **FACILITIES:** Garden: Small patio in
garden **PARKING:** 100

STONEHAVEN Map 15 NO88

| Babies Welcome | Family Rooms | Children's Dishes |

★★ 66% **County Hotel & Squash Club**
Arduthie Rd AB39 2EH
☎ 01569 764386 🖷 01569 762214
Dir: off A90, opposite railway station

> **CHILD FACILITIES:** Activities: colouring, jigsaws, toys, games
> Indoor play area Food/bottle warming Ch menu Ch portions
> Highchairs Ch cutlery Videos Cots Family rms D rm with S bed, put
> up bed & rm for cot Ch drinks (on request) Laundry (by
> arrangement) Changing mats (on request) **NEARBY:** Seawater
> pool Dunnottar castle Near sea

This small hotel is family-owned and operated. It is situated close
to the railway station. Generally spacious bedrooms are
traditionally decorated. It is popular for its good-value meals
featuring a wide-ranging selection, served in a choice of dining
rooms. The breakfast room displays a fascinating collection of
photographs and posters of a theatrical nature.
ROOMS: 14 en suite (1 fmly) s £40-£46; d £50-£60 (incl. bkfst) **LB**
FACILITIES: Squash Sauna Gym Table tennis **PARKING:** 40
NOTES: ✖

Scotland

STONEHAVEN, continued

| Babies Welcome | Family Rooms | Children's Dishes |

◆◆◆◆ Arduthie House

Ann St AB39 2DA
☎ 01569 762381
e-mail: arduthieguesthouse@btopenworld.com
web: www.arduthieguesthouse.com
Dir: A90 from S, turn into Stonehaven at lights, turn left, then 2nd right (Ann St). House 100yds on left. A90 from N, turn right at lights

> **CHILD FACILITIES:** Baby listening Babysitting Activities: toys, games Family area Food/bottle warming Ch portions Highchairs Ch discounts under 12s Safe grounds Videos Cots Family rms D rm with S bed & cot Laundry **NEARBY:** Storybook Glen Outdoor heated swimming pool Wildlife sanctuary Farm 1-min walk to sea

Arduthie House lies in its terraced garden just off the town centre and provides a welcoming atmosphere. Meticulously maintained throughout, it offers a choice of lounges and a comfortable dining room. Bedrooms feature lots of extras.
ROOMS: 6 rms (5 en suite) (1 fmly) d £54 * **FACILITIES:** TVB tea/coffee TVL No coaches **NOTES:** ✖ ⊗ Cen ht **LB**

ANGUS

ARBROATH   Map 12 NO64

★★ 65% *Hotel Seaforth*

Dundee Rd DD11 1QF
☎ 01241 872232 ⓘ 01241 877473
e-mail: hotelseaforth@ukonline.co.uk
Dir: on southern outskirts, on A92

> **CHILD FACILITIES:** Please telephone for details

This long-established commercial hotel enjoys a seafront location close to many local amenities. Family-run, a welcoming and friendly atmosphere prevails. Spacious, thoughtfully equipped bedrooms all have smart, refurbished bedrooms. Public areas include a popular bar and restaurant that serves a range of good value meals.
ROOMS: 19 en suite (4 fmly) **FACILITIES:** ▨ Snooker Sauna Gym Jacuzzi Steam room **PARKING:** 60 **NOTES:** ⊗ in restaurant

MONTROSE   Map 15 NO75

| Babies Welcome | Family Rooms | Children's Dishes |

◆◆◆ Oaklands

10 Rossie Island Rd DD10 9NN
☎ 01674 672018 ⓘ 01674 672018
e-mail: oaklands1@btopenworld.com
Dir: on A92, S end of town

> **CHILD FACILITIES:** Activities: jigsaws Food/bottle warming Ch portions Highchairs Ch cutlery Ch discounts free when sharing with parents Safe grounds Cots Family rms D rm with S bed Ch drinks Laundry **NEARBY:** Park 5-min drive to sea

A warm welcome and attentive service is assured at this detached house, situated on the south side of the town. Bedrooms come in

continued

a variety of sizes and are well equipped. There is a guest lounge on the ground floor adjacent to the attractive dining room, where hearty breakfasts are served.
ROOMS: 7 en suite (1 fmly) (1 GF) s £25-£30; d £40-£60 * ⊗ in 3 bedrooms **FACILITIES:** TVB tea/coffee TVL No coaches **NOTES:** ⊗ in restaurant Cen ht **PARKING:** 8

ARGYLL & BUTE

ARDUAINE   Map 10 NM71

| Babies Welcome | Family Rooms | Children's Dishes |

★★★ 76% ⊛ ⊛ Loch Melfort

PA34 4XG
☎ 01852 200233 ⓘ 01852 200214
e-mail: reception@lochmelfort.co.uk
web: www.lochmelfort.co.uk
Dir: on A816, midway between Oban and Lochgilphead

> **CHILD FACILITIES:** Baby listening Activities: games Food/bottle warming Ch portions Highchairs Ch cutlery Ch discounts under 5s free, 5-12s £25 sharing with parents Safe grounds Videos Cots Family rms Laundry **NEARBY:** Walks Wildlife park Boat trips Seafront location

Enjoying one of the finest locations on the West Coast, this popular, family-run hotel has outstanding views across Asknish Bay towards the Islands of Jura, Scarba and Shuna. Accommodation is provided in either the balconied rooms of the Cedar wing or the more traditional rooms in the main hotel. Skilfully cooked dinners remain the highlight of any visit.
ROOMS: 7 en suite 20 annexe en suite (2 fmly) ⊗ in 11 bedrooms s £49-£79; d £78-£158 (incl. bkfst) **LB FACILITIES:** Xmas **PARKING:** 65 **NOTES:** ⊗ in restaurant

CONNEL   Map 10 NM93

| Babies Welcome | Family Rooms | Children's Dishes |

★★ 72% Falls of Lora

PA37 1PB
☎ 01631 710483 ⓘ 01631 710694
Dir: hotel set back from A85 from Glasgow, 0.5 mile past Connel sign

> **CHILD FACILITIES:** Baby listening Food/bottle warming Ch menu Ch portions Highchairs Ch discounts Safe grounds Cots Family rms D rms with S beds & B beds Laundry **NEARBY:** Rare breeds park Sealife centre Walks Overlooking loch

Personally run and welcoming, this long-established and thriving holiday hotel enjoys inspiring views over Loch Etive. The spacious ground floor takes in a comfortable, traditional lounge and a bar. Guests can eat in the popular, informal bistro that caters specifically for families from 5pm onwards. Bedrooms come in a variety of styles, ranging from the standard cabin rooms to high quality, luxury rooms.
ROOMS: 30 en suite (4 fmly) (4 GF) s £39-£49; d £43-£119 (incl. bkfst) **LB FACILITIES:** **PARKING:** 40 **NOTES:** Closed mid Dec & Jan

CRINAN   Map 10 NR79

⚓ Crinan Hotel

PA31 8SR
☎ 01546 830261 📠 01546 830292
e-mail: nryan@crinanhotel.com

CHILD FACILITIES: Food/bottle warming Ch licence Ch menu
Ch portions Highchairs Ch cutlery Changing facilities
NEARBY: Kilmartin Museum Walks Near to sea

OPEN: 11 -11 Closed: Xmas & New Year **BAR MEALS:** L served all week
12.30-2.30 D served all week 6.30-8.30 **RESTAURANT:** 12-2.30 D served
all week 7-9 Av 3 course à la carte £22.60 **FACILITIES:** Children's licence
Garden: Patio available **PARKING:** 30

OBAN   Map 10 NM83

◆◆◆◆ Thornloe

Albert Rd PA34 5JD
☎ 01631 562879 📠 01631 562879
e-mail: thornloeoban@aol.com
web: www.thornloeoban.co.uk
*Dir: from A85, turn left at King's Knoll Hotel and pass swimming pool, last
house on right*

CHILD FACILITIES: Please telephone for details

Enjoying stunning views from its elevated position overlooking
Oban Bay, Thornloe is an impressive Victorian house which been
completely refurbished by attentive new owners and is now no
smoking. Bedrooms are comfortable with attractive furnishings
and decoration. The public areas comprise a bright dining room
where hearty breakfasts are served and a conservatory lounge
where guests can relax in comfort.
ROOMS: 8 rms (7 en suite) (2 fmly) s £23.50-£34; d £47-£68 *
FACILITIES: TVB tea/coffee **NOTES:** ✖ ⊗ Cen ht **PARKING:** 5

PORT APPIN   Map 14 NM94

★★★ ⑳ ⑳ ⑳ Airds

PA38 4DF
☎ 01631 730236 📠 01631 730535
e-mail: airds@airds-hotel.com
web: www.airds-hotel.com
Dir: from A828, turn at Appin signed Port Appin. Hotel 2.5m on left.

CHILD FACILITIES: Outdoor play area Food/bottle warming
Ch menu Ch portions Highchairs Ch discounts Safe grounds Videos
Cots Family rms D rm with S beds, suite with sofa bed Ch drinks
Laundry **NEARBY:** Farm Sea Life centre Walks Loch

Stunning views are to be had from this delightful small hotel on
the shores of Loch Linnhe. Finely prepared meals that utilise
first-rate, mostly locally sourced ingredients are served in the
dining room. The bedrooms offer tasteful decor and bathrooms of
a high specification. Lounges are quiet and inviting, with real fires
and attractive artwork. The attentive staff can recommend many
walks.
ROOMS: 12 en suite (2 fmly) (2 GF) ⊗ in all bedrooms s £160-£255;
d £230-£360 (incl. bkfst & dinner) **LB FACILITIES:** Xmas **PARKING:** 21
NOTES: ⊗ in restaurant Closed 5-26 Jan RS Nov - Feb

This symbol indicates establishments
within walking distance or a short
drive of the seaside.

CITY OF EDINBURGH

Edinburgh Castle

EDINBURGH
Camera Obscura & World of Illusions EH1 2ND
info@camera-obscura.co.uk   ☎0131 226 3709
(next to Edinburgh Castle)
Open all year, daily, Apr-Oct 9.30-6; Nov-Mar 10-5.
(Closed 25 Dec). Open later Jul-Aug, phone for
details.

Edinburgh Castle
EH1 2NG   ☎0131 225 9846
Open Apr-Sep, daily 9.30-6. 30Oct-Mar, daily 9.30-
4.30. (Closed 25-26 Dec & 1-2 Jan). *£9.50 (ch
£2, concessions £7).

Edinburgh Dungeon
EH1 1QB   ☎0131 240 1000
edinburghdungeon@merlinentertainments.biz
Open all year (ex 25 Dec).Nov-Feb 11-4, wkends
10.30-4.30, Mar 10.30-4.30, Apr-Jun 10-5, Jul-Aug
10-7, Sep-Oct 10-5.*£9.95 (ch 4-9 £4.95, ch 10-14
£6.95).

Edinburgh Zoo EH12 6TS
marketing@rzss.org.uk   ☎0131 334 9171
(3m W of Edinburgh City Centre on A8 towards
Glasgow)
Open all year, Apr-Sep, daily 9-6; Oct & Mar, daily
9-5; Nov-Feb, daily 9-4.30.
*£8.50 (ch 3-14 & disabled £5.50, student £6.50,
pen £6).

Museum of Childhood
EH1 1TG   ☎0131 529 4142
(On the Royal Mile)
Open all year, Mon-Sat, Jun-Sep 10-6; Oct-May
10-5; (also Sun 12-5 in Jul-Aug).

The People's Story
EH8 8BN   ☎0131 529 4057
(On the Royal Mile)
Open, Mon-Sat 10-5. Also, open Sun during
Edinburgh Festival 2-5.

Royal Museum EH1 1JF
info@nms.ac.uk   ☎0131 247 4219
(5 mins from Edinburgh Castle and the Royal Mile
in city centre)
Open all year, Mon-Sat 10-5, Sun 12-5 (Tue late
opening till 8). (Closed 25 Dec. Phone for times for
26 Dec/1 Jan).

Scotland

EDINBURGH   Map 11 NT27

★★★★ 71% Carlton

North Bridge EH1 1SD

☎ 0131 472 3000 📠 0131 556 2691

PARAMOUNT
GROUP OF HOTELS

e-mail: carlton@paramount-hotels.co.uk

Dir: on North Bridge which links Princes St to the Royal Mile

CHILD FACILITIES: Please telephone for details

The Carlton occupies a city centre location just off the Royal Mile, and has been extensively upgraded to a modern and stylish design. Public areas include an impressive open-plan reception/lobby, modern first floor bar and restaurant and basement leisure club. Bedrooms - many air-conditioned - are generally spacious, with an excellent range of facilities.

ROOMS: 189 en suite (20 fmly) ⊗ in 140 bedrooms s £210-£230; d £225-£245 (incl. bkfst) **LB FACILITIES:** Spa STV ⊠ Squash Sauna Solarium Gym Jacuzzi Table tennis, Dance studio, Creche, Exercise classes ♫ Xmas **PARKING: NOTES:** ✲ ⊗ in restaurant

★★★★ 71%
Novotel Edinburgh Centre

Lauriston Place, Lady Lawson St EH3 9DE

☎ 0131 656 3500 📠 0131 656 3510

NOVOTEL

e-mail: H3271@accor-hotels.com

Dir: from Edinburgh Castle right onto George IV Bridge from Royal Mile. Follow to junct, then right onto Lauriston Pl for hotel 700mtrs on right.

CHILD FACILITIES: Baby listening Babysitting (prior notice) **Activities:** colouring, travel games Indoor play area Family area Food/bottle warming Ch menu Ch portions (on request) Highchairs Ch cutlery (on request) Ch discounts under 16s free sharing with parents Safe grounds Games consoles Videos Cots Family rms D rms with S or sofa beds from £109 Ch drinks (free) Connecting rms Fridge Laundry Changing mats (on request) **NEARBY:** Castle Zoo Gardens Museum 10-min drive to sea

One of the new generation of Novotels, this modern hotel is located in the centre of the city, close to Edinburgh Castle and five minutes from Princes Street. Public areas are contemporary in style and include a smart bar, brasserie style restaurant and indoor leisure facilities. The air-conditioned bedrooms feature a comprehensive range of extras and bathrooms with baths and separate shower cabinets.

ROOMS: 180 en suite (146 fmly) ⊗ in 135 bedrooms s £109-£129; d £109-£129 **LB FACILITIES:** STV ⊠ Sauna Solarium Gym Jacuzzi Xmas **PARKING:** 17

♦♦♦♦ Corstorphine Lodge

186-188 St Johns Rd, Corstorphine EH12 8SG

☎ 0131 539 4237 📠 0131 539 4945

e-mail: corsthouse@aol.com

web: www.corstorphinehotels.co.uk

Dir: from M8 take city bypass N towards city centre for 1m along A8. Hotel on left

CHILD FACILITIES: Activities: bouncy castle, colouring Outdoor play area Family area Food/bottle warming Ch menu Ch portions Highchairs Ch cutlery Ch discounts under 3s free, 3-12s 50% Safe grounds Videos Cots Family rms D rms with S beds from £69 Ch drinks Connecting rms Changing mats (on request) **NEARBY:** Parks Cinema Leisure centres 8-min drive to sea

Occupying two large detached Victorian villas, Corstorphine is conveniently located for both the airport and the city centre. Bedrooms, which vary in size, are tastefully decorated and well equipped. There is a spacious, bright conservatory dining room

continued

---

where traditional, continental or vegetarian breakfasts can be enjoyed at individual tables. Ample off street parking is available.

ROOMS: 12 en suite 5 annexe en suite (8 fmly) (4 GF) s £29-£59; d £49-£109 * **FACILITIES:** STV TVB tea/coffee TVL **NOTES:** ✲ ⊗ Cen ht **LB PARKING:** 14

♦♦♦♦ Sandaig

5 East Hermitage Place, Leith Links EH6 8AA

☎ 0131 554 7357 & 554 7313 📠 0131 467 6389

e-mail: info@sandaigguesthouse.co.uk

web: www.sandaigguesthouse.co.uk

Dir: once in Edinburgh follow signs for Leith. Establishment is located facing Leith Links Park

CHILD FACILITIES: Baby listening Babysitting Food/bottle warming Ch portions Highchairs Ch cutlery Ch discounts under 5s free sharing with parents Videos Cots Family rms D rms with S beds, triple rm from £75 **NEARBY:** Park 10-min drive to sea

Occupying two mid-terrace Victorian houses, Sandaig Guest House overlooks Leith Links north of the city centre. Well-equipped bedrooms come in a variety of sizes and display an imaginative approach to interior design. Bathrooms are particularly impressive.

ROOMS: 9 rms (8 en suite) (2 fmly) s £30-£55; d £48-£95 * **FACILITIES:** TVB tea/coffee Direct dial from bedrooms **NOTES:** ✲ ⊗ Cen ht **LB**

See advert on opposite page

♦♦♦♦ The Walton Hotel

79 Dundas St EH3 6SD

☎ 0131 556 1137 📠 0131 557 8367

e-mail: enquiries@waltonhotel.com

CHILD FACILITIES: Activities: colouring, books, board games, cards Food/bottle warming Ch portions Highchairs Ch discounts under 8s free Safe grounds Cots Family rms 3 D rms with S bed, triple rm with B beds Fridge **NEARBY:** Botanic Gardens Cinema

Set in a Georgian terraced row just north of the city centre, The Walton provides a friendly atmosphere. Smartly decorated and well-furnished in pine, the comfortable bedrooms are well-equipped to include telephones with modem points, radios and hair dryers. Hearty Scottish breakfasts are served at individual tables in the bright cheerful dining room.

ROOMS: 10 en suite (4 fmly) (4 GF) s £45-£69; d £79-£125 * **FACILITIES:** TVB tea/coffee Direct dial from bedrooms **NOTES:** ✲ ⊗ Cen ht **PARKING:** 8

This symbol indicates family rooms are available, with type of room and prices included if provided

Babies Welcome | **Family Rooms** | **Children's Dishes**

♦♦♦ Galloway
22 Dean Park Crescent EH4 1PH
☎ 0131 332 3672 ▤ 0131 332 3672
e-mail: galloway_theclarks@hotmail.com
Dir: 0.5m from Princes St (west end) on A9

CHILD FACILITIES: Activities: games Food/bottle warming
Ch menu Ch portions Highchairs Ch cutlery Ch discounts babies in cots free, 1st child 50%, 2nd child free Cots Family rms D rms with S beds from £50 Ch drinks

Located in a peaceful residential area, conveniently situated for both the shops and bistros north of the city centre, this guest house provides smart, thoughtfully equipped bedrooms. Breakfasts featuring a comprehensive selection of starters and hot dishes are served in the ground floor dining room.
ROOMS: 10 rms (7 en suite) (6 fmly) (1 GF) s £30-£50; d £40-£60 *
FACILITIES: TVB tea/coffee **NOTES:** Cen ht **LB**

Babies Welcome | **Children's Dishes**

◎ ◎ Atrium
10 Cambridge St EH1 2ED
☎ 0131 228 8882 ▤ 0131 228 8808
e-mail: eat@atriumrestaurant.co.uk
Dir: From Princes St, turn into Lothian Rd, 2nd L & 1st R, by the Traverse Theatre.

CHILD FACILITIES: Food/bottle warming Ch licence Ch menu (on request) Ch portions Highchairs Safe grounds **NEARBY:** Princes Street Gardens Edinburgh Castle

FOOD: Modern European **STYLE:** Modern Rustic **SEATS:** 80
OPEN: 12-2/6-10, Closed 25-26 Dec, 1-2 Jan, Sun (apart from Aug)L Sat (apart from Aug) **RESTAURANT:** main £16-£22 **NOTES:** ⊗ in restaurant, Air con **PARKING:** Castle Terrace Car Park

Babies Welcome | **Children's Dishes**

◎ The Vintners Room
The Vaults, 87 Giles St, Leith EH6 6BZ
☎ 0131 554 6767 ▤ 0131 5555653
e-mail: enquiries@thevintersrooms.com
Dir: At the end of Leith Walk; L into Great Junction St, R into Henderson St. Restaurant in old warehouse on R

CHILD FACILITIES: Food/bottle warming Ch portions Highchairs Safe grounds

FOOD: European **STYLE:** Classic **SEATS:** 64 **OPEN:** 12-2/7-10, Closed 15 days from 1st Jan, Mon, D Sun **RESTAURANT:** Fixed L £13, main £15-£19 **NOTES:** ⊗ area **PARKING:** 4

Babies Welcome | **Children's Dishes**

◎ ◎ Off the Wall Restaurant
105 High St, Royal Mile EH1 1SG
☎ 0131 558 1497 ▤ 0131 558 1497
e-mail: otwedinburgh@aol.com
Dir: On Royal Mile near John Knox House - entrance via stairway next to Baillie Fyfes Close (first floor).

CHILD FACILITIES: Food/bottle warming Ch portions Highchairs Ch cutlery Changing facilities **NEARBY:** Museum of Childhood Swimming pool Scottish Museum

FOOD: Modern British **SEATS:** 44 **OPEN:** 12-2.30, Closed 25-26 Dec, 1-2 Jan, Sun **RESTAURANT:** Fixed L £16.50, main £14.95-£19.95 **NOTES:** ⊗ area **PARKING:** NCP

Sandaig Guest House

Situated overlooking Leith Links Park, Sandaig Guest House occupies two mid terraced Victorian villas dating from c1870. All bedrooms are non-smoking, individually designed, en suite and have many extras. Additional facilities include infant high chairs and cots. Sandaig is ideally located for the city centre, just ten minutes away either by car or the regular bus service. Ample free car parking.

◆

5 East Hermitage Place, Leith Links
Edinburgh EH6 8AA
Tel: 0131 554 7357/7313 Fax: 0131 467 6389
Web: www.sandaigguesthouse.co.uk
Email: info@sandaigguesthouse.co.uk

Babies Welcome | **Children's Dishes**

◫ Bennets Bar
8 Leven St EH3 9LG
☎ 0131 229 5143
CHILD FACILITIES: Food/bottle warming Ch menu Highchairs Ch cutlery **NEARBY:** Cinema Park Pitch and putt
OPEN: 11-12.30 (Sun 12.30-11.30) Thu-Sat 11-1 Closed: 25-26 Dec, 1 Jan
BAR MEALS: L served all week 12-2 D served Mon-Sat 5-8.30 Av main course £4.85 **FACILITIES:** ✯

RATHO   Map 11 NT17

Babies Welcome | **Children's Dishes**

◫ The Bridge Inn
27 Baird Rd EH28 8RA
☎ 0131 3331320 ▤ 0131 333 3480
e-mail: info@bridgeinn.com
web: www.bridgeinn.com
Dir: From Newbridge B7030 junction, follow signs for Ratho

CHILD FACILITIES: Activities: colouring, toys, carousel Indoor play area Outdoor play area Family area Food/bottle warming Ch licence Ch menu Ch portions Highchairs Ch cutlery Changing facilities **NEARBY:** Ratho Adventure Centre Walks

OPEN: 12-11 (Sat 11-12, Sun 12.30-11) Closed: 26 Dec, 1 & 2 Jan **BAR MEALS:** L served all week 12-9 Av main course £7 **RESTAURANT:** L served all week 12-2 D served all week 6.30-9 Av 3 course à la carte £22 **FACILITIES:** Children's licence Garden: Landscaped, Patio, enclosed, ducks roaming ✯ **PARKING:** 60

CITY OF GLASGOW

Glasgow Science Centre

GLASGOW

Clydebuilt G51 4BN

clydebuilt@tinyworld.co.uk **☎0141 886 1013**
(M8 junct 25A, 26, follow signs for Braehead shopping centre.)
Open Mon-Thu & Sat 10-5.30; Sun 11-5. (Closed Fri) *£3.50 (ch & concessions £1.75). Family ticket £8

Museum of Transport
G3 8DP **☎0141 287 2720**
(1.5m W of city centre)
Open all year, Mon-Thu & Sat 10-5,
Fri & Sun 11-5.

People's Palace and Winter Gardens
G40 1AT **☎0141 271 2951**
(1m SE of city centre)
Open all year, Mon-Thu & Sat 10-5,
Fri & Sun 11-5.

The Scottish Football Museum
G42 9BA **☎0141 616 6139**
info@scottishfootballmuseum.org.uk
(3m S of city centre, follow brown tourist signs)
Open Mon-Sat 10-5, Sun 11-5. (Closed match days, special events and Xmas/New Year, please telephone in advance for confirmation)
*Museum or stadium tour £5 (concessions & ch under 16 £2.50). Combined ticket £7.50 (concessions & ch under 16 £3.75)

The Tall Ship at Glasgow Harbour G3 8QQ
info@thetallship.com **☎0141 222 2513**
(from M8 junct 19 onto A814 follow signs for 'The Tall Ship')
Open daily Mar-Oct 10-5, Nov-Feb 11-4.
*£4.50 (concessions £3.25, 1 ch free with paying adult/concession, additional ch £2.50).

Tenement House G3 6QN
tenementhouse@nts.org.uk **☎0141 333 0183**
(N of Charing Cross)
Open Mar-Oct, daily 2-5. Weekday morning visits available for pre-booked educational & other groups.
*£3.50 (concession £2.60) Family ticket £9.50. Groups adult £2.80, child/school £1. Admission free to NTS members. For other details please phone 0131 243 9387

Babies Welcome	Family Rooms	Children's Dishes

★★★★ ◉ ◉ 🏠 One Devonshire Gardens
1 Devonshire Gardens G12 0UX
☎ 0141 339 2001 ▤ 0141 337 1663
e-mail: reservations@onedevonshiregardens.com
web: www.onedevonshiregardens.com
Dir: M8 junct 17, follow signs for A82, after 1.5m turn left into Hyndland Rd, 1st right, right at mini rdbt, right at end, continue to end

CHILD FACILITIES: Baby listening Babysitting Activities: colouring Food/bottle warming Ch menu (on request) Ch portions Highchairs Ch discounts children free sharing with parents Safe grounds Games consoles Videos Cots Family rms D rms with S or sofa beds from £225 Ch drinks (on request) Connecting rms Fridge Laundry
NEARBY: Botanic gardens Science Centre Museum Cinema

This renowned townhouse occupies four houses of a Victorian terrace in a residential area. Bedrooms, including a number of suites and four-poster rooms, are stylish, individually designed and thoughtfully equipped to a high standard. Public rooms include a choice of inviting drawing rooms and a smart restaurant offering imaginative cooking. Personal, attentive service is a highlight.
ROOMS: 36 en suite (4 GF) s £145-£485; d £145-£485 **FACILITIES:** STV ✎ Squash Gym Tennis facilities at nearby club **NOTES:** ⊗ in restaurant

Babies Welcome	Family Rooms	Children's Dishes

★★★ 71%
Novotel Glasgow Centre
181 Pitt St G2 4DT
☎ 0141 222 2775 ▤ 0141 204 5438
e-mail: H3136@accor-hotels.com
Dir: next to Strathclyde Police HQ. Close to the SECC, just off Sauchiehall St

CHILD FACILITIES: Indoor play area Food/bottle warming Ch menu Ch portions Highchairs Ch discounts under 16s free sharing with parents Games consoles Cots Family rms D rms with S beds Connecting rms Laundry **NEARBY:** Cinemas Parks Science Centre Museums

Enjoying a convenient city centre location and with limited car-parking spaces, this hotel is ideal for all kinds of guests. Well-equipped bedrooms are brightly decorated and offer functional design. Modern public areas include a brasserie serving a range of meals all day and a small fitness club.
ROOMS: 139 en suite (139 fmly) ⊗ in 90 bedrooms s £65-£99; d £65-£119 **LB FACILITIES:** STV Sauna Gym Pool table, play station Xmas **PARKING:** 19

Don't forget to let proprietors
know when you book that
you're bringing the kids

Babies Welcome	Family Rooms	Children's Dishes

★★★ 63% Bewley's Hotel Glasgow

110 Bath St G2 2EN

☎ 0141 353 0800 📠 0141 353 0900

e-mail: gla@bewleyshotels.com

web: www.bewleyshotels.com

Dir: M8 junct 18, left to Sauchiehall St & right to Birthwood St then left to West Regent St & left into Bath St.

CHILD FACILITIES: Babysitting Food/bottle warming Ch menu Ch portions Highchairs Safe grounds Cots Family rms D rms with S & sofa bed Laundry

In the heart of the city, this modern hotel is ideally suited for leisure breaks. Bedrooms are comfortable and well-equipped, with several enjoying impressive views over the Glasgow skyline. Loop restaurant and bar serves cosmopolitan food all day in a relaxed informal setting.

ROOMS: 103 en suite (47 fmly) ⊗ in 64 bedrooms **FACILITIES:** STV **NOTES:** ✕ Closed 24-26 Dec

◆◆◆◆ Kelvingrove Hotel

944 Sauchiehall St G3 7TH

☎ 0141 339 5011 📠 0141 339 6566

e-mail: kelvingrove.hotel@business.ntl.com

web: www.kelvingrove-hotel.co.uk

Dir: M8 J18 exit 0.5m along road signed Kelvingrove Museum

CHILD FACILITIES: Please telephone for details

This private, well-maintained and friendly hotel lies in a terraced row just west of the city centre and easily spotted in summer with its colourful floral displays. Bedrooms, including several rooms suitable for families, are well equipped and have smart, fully tiled en suite bathrooms. There is a bright breakfast room and a reception lounge that is open 24 hours.

ROOMS: 22 en suite (5 fmly) (3 GF) s £40-£55; d £55-£70; (room only) * **FACILITIES:** TVB tea/coffee Direct dial from bedrooms No coaches **NOTES:** ⊗ Cen ht **LB**

◆◆◆ Clifton Hotel

26-27 Buckingham Ter, Great Western Rd G12 8ED

☎ 0141 334 8080 📠 0141 337 3468

e-mail: kalam@cliftonhotelglasgow.co.uk

Dir: on the Gt Western Road next to the Botanic Gardens

CHILD FACILITIES: Please telephone for details

To the west of the city, this conveniently located hotel forms part of an elegant terraced row. Many of the spacious, attractive bedrooms have recently been refurbished. There is an elegant lounge adjacent to the dining room where hearty breakfasts are served at individual tables.

ROOMS: 23 rms (14 en suite) (6 fmly) (3 GF) s £25-£35; d £55-£75 * **FACILITIES:** STV TVB tea/coffee Direct dial from bedrooms TVL **NOTES:** ⊗ in restaurant Cen ht **PARKING:** 8

◆◆◆ Kelvin Private Hotel

15 Buckingham Ter, Great Western Rd, Hillhead G12 8EB

☎ 0141 339 7143 📠 0141 339 5215

e-mail: enquiries@kelvinhotel.com

web: www.kelvinhotel.com

Dir: M8 J17, A82 Kelvinside/Dumbarton, 1m from motorway on right just before Botanic Gardens

CHILD FACILITIES: Please telephone for details

Two substantial Victorian terraced houses on the west side of the city have been combined to create this friendly private hotel, close to the Botanical Gardens. Bedrooms are comfortably proportioned, attractive and well equipped. The dining room is situated on the first floor and is an appropriate setting for hearty traditional breakfasts, served at individual tables.

ROOMS: 21 rms (9 en suite) (5 fmly) (2 GF) s £24-£42; d £42-£60 * **FACILITIES:** TVB tea/coffee **NOTES:** ⊗ in restaurant Cen ht **PARKING:** 5

How to use this guide & abbreviations are explained on pages 5-7

◆◆◆ Lomond Hotel

6 Buckingham Ter, Great Western Rd, Hillhead G12 8EB

☎ 0141 339 2339 📠 0141 339 0477

e-mail: michael@lomondhotel.freeserve.co.uk

web: www.lomondhotel.co.uk

Dir: M8 J17. Follow A82 Dumbarton for approx 1m, on right before Botanic Gardens

CHILD FACILITIES: Please telephone for details

Situated in the west end of the city in a tree-lined Victorian terrace, the Lomond Hotel offers well maintained, good value accommodation in a friendly environment. Bedrooms are brightly

continued on p270

GLASGOW, continued

appointed and suitably equipped. Hearty breakfasts are served at individual tables in the bright ground floor dining room.

Lomond Hotel, Glasgow

ROOMS: 17 rms (6 en suite) (5 fmly) (3 GF) s £26-£40; d £44-£60 *
FACILITIES: TVB tea/coffee **NOTES:** ⊗ in restaurant ⊗ in lounges Cen ht

♦♦♦ McLays

264/276 Renfrew St, Charing Cross G3 6TT
☎ 0141 332 4796 📠 0141 353 0422
e-mail: info@mclays.com
Dir: exit at junct 18 on the M8 going into Sauchiehall St, turn left into Garnet or Rose St then 3rd left into Buccleuch St this leads into Renfrew St

CHILD FACILITIES: Please telephone for details

This large friendly guest house is conveniently close to the city centre. Bedrooms, several of which have been smartly refurbished, are well equipped. There is a smartly furnished lounge and two dinning rooms where traditional breakfasts are served.
ROOMS: 62 rms (39 en suite) (14 fmly) ⊗ in 20 bedrooms
FACILITIES: STV TVB tea/coffee Direct dial from bedrooms Lift TVL
NOTES: ✹ ⊗ in restaurant ⊗ in 1 lounge Cen ht

Family Rooms | Children's Dishes

♦♦♦ Victorian House

212 Renfrew St G3 6TX
☎ 0141 332 0129 📠 0141 353 3155
e-mail: info@thevictorian.co.uk
Dir: turn left into Garnet St at 1st set of traffic light on Sauchiehall St, E of Charing Cross. Take right into Renfrew St, hotel is 100 yds on left

CHILD FACILITIES: Ch portions Highchairs Ch discounts babies in cots free Cots Family rms D rm with S beds from £66
NEARBY: Parks Leisure centre Cinema

Close to the Art School and Sauchiehall Street, this raised terraced
continued

house has been sympathetically extended to offer a range of well-equipped bedrooms. Some rooms have polished floors and bright modern décor, whilst others are more traditional. There is a comfortable lounge area leading into the breakfast room, which serves buffet style meals.

ROOMS: 58 rms (50 en suite) (13 fmly) (8 GF) s £32-£39; d £46-£56 *
FACILITIES: STV TVB tea/coffee Direct dial from bedrooms **NOTES:** ✹ ⊗ in restaurant Cen ht

♦ Georgian House Hotel

29 Buckingham Ter, Great Western Rd, Kelvinside G12 8ED
☎ 0141 339 0008 & 07973 971563
e-mail: thegeorgianhouse@yahoo.com
web: www.theorgianhousehotel.com
Dir: M8 junct 17 N follow signs to A82 (Dumbarton) Great Western Rd & the hotel is 1.8m on your right just before junction with Queen Margaret Drive & Byres Rd at Royal Botanic Gdns

CHILD FACILITIES: Please telephone for details

Located at the west end of the city and peacefully situated in a tree-lined Victorian terrace near the Botanical Gardens, this friendly private hotel offers good value accommodation. Bedrooms vary in size and are furnished in modern style. Breakfast is served in the first floor combined lounge/dining room.
ROOMS: 11 rms (10 en suite) (4 fmly) (3 GF) s £25-£40; d £48-£100 *
⊗ in 6 bedrooms **FACILITIES:** TVB tea/coffee **NOTES:** ✹ ⊗ in restaurant ⊗ in lounges Cen ht **LB** **PARKING:** 9

Babies Welcome | Children's Dishes

Killermont Polo Club

2002 Maryhill Rd, Maryhill Park G20 0AB
☎ 0141 946 5412 📠 0141 946 0812
Dir: Telephone for directions

CHILD FACILITIES: Activities: colouring books Family area Food/bottle warming Ch licence Ch menu Ch portions Highchairs Safe grounds

continued

Killermont Polo Club

FOOD: Italian **STYLE:** Classic Formal **SEATS:** 80 **OPEN:** 12-2/5-10, Closed New YearL Sun **RESTAURANT:** Fixed L £4.75, main £6.45-£14.50 **NOTES:** Smart Dress, ⊗ area **PARKING:** 40

Babies Welcome | **Children's Dishes**

⊚ ⊚ Rococo
202 West George St G2 2NR
☎ 0141 221 5004 🖷 0141 221 5006
e-mail: res@rococoglasgow.com
web: www.rococoglasgow.com
Dir: City centre

CHILD FACILITIES: Activities: colouring Food/bottle warming Ch menu Ch portions Highchairs Safe grounds **NEARBY:** Cinema

FOOD: French, Scottish **STYLE:** Modern, Chic **SEATS:** 60 **OPEN:** 12-3/5-10, Closed 1 Jan, Sun **RESTAURANT:** main £12.50-£18.95 **NOTES:** ⊗ area, Air con **PARKING:** On street parking or NCP

Babies Welcome | **Children's Dishes**

⊚ ⊚ Stravaigin
30 Gibson St G12 8NX
☎ 0141 334 2665 🖷 0141 334 4099
e-mail: bookings@stravaigin.com
web: www.stravaigin.com
Dir: Next to Glasgow University. 200yds from Kelvinbridge underground

CHILD FACILITIES: Activities: colouring Food/bottle warming Ch licence Ch portions Highchairs **NEARBY:** Parks Walks Leisure centre Cinema

FOOD: Modern **STYLE:** Chic **SEATS:** 76 **OPEN:** 12-2.30/5-11, Closed 25-26 Dec, 1 Jan, MonL Tue-Thu **RESTAURANT:** Fixed L £11.95, Fixed D £13.95, main £10-£22 **NOTES:** ⊗ in restaurant, Air con **PARKING:** On street

Babies Welcome | **Children's Dishes**

⊈ Ubiquitous Chip ⊚ ⊚
12 Ashton Ln G12 8SJ
☎ 0141 334 5007 🖷 0141 337 1302
e-mail: mail@ubiquitouschip.co.uk
web: www.ubiquitouschip.co.uk
Dir: In the west end of Glasgow, off Byres Road

CHILD FACILITIES: Food/bottle warming Ch menu Ch portions Highchairs **NEARBY:** Kelvingrove Park Botanic Gardens

OPEN: 11-12 (12.30-12 Sun) Closed: 25 Dec, 1 Jan **BAR MEALS:** L served all week 12-4 D served all week 4-11 **RESTAURANT:** L served all week 12-2.30 D served all week 5.30-11 **FACILITIES:** ✈

Children's Dishes This symbol indicates a children's menu or smaller portions are available

---

DUMFRIES & GALLOWAY

Museum of Lead Mining

CAERLAVEROCK
WWT Caerlaverock
DG1 4RS ☎01387 770200
(9m SE of Dumfries, signed from A75)
Open daily 10-5 (closed 25 Dec) *£4 (ch £2.50, concessions £3.25) Family £10.50.

CREETOWN
Creetown Gem Rock Museum DG8 7HJ
gem.rock@btinternet.com ☎01671 820357
(follow signs from A75 at Creetown bypass)
Open Etr-Sep, daily 9.30-5.30; Oct-Nov & Mar-Etr, daily 10-4; Dec-Feb, wknds 10-4 or by appointment wkdays. (Closed 23 Dec-Jan). *£3.50 ch £2, concessions £3). Family ticket £9 2ad+3ch).

DUMFRIES
Dumfries Museum & Camera Obscura
DG2 7SW ☎01387 253374
dumfriesmuseum@dumgal.gov.uk
(Take A75 from S Carlisle or SW from Castle) Douglas, museum is situated in Maxwellton area of Dumfries Open all year, Apr-Sep Mon-Sat 10-5, Sun, 2-5; Oct-Mar, Tue-Sat 10-1 & 2-5. *Free except Camera Obscura £1.55 (concessions 80p)

NEW ABBEY
Shambellie House Museum of Costume
DG2 8HQ
info@nms.ac.uk ☎01387 850375
(7m S of Dumfries, on A710)
Open Apr (or Good Fri if earlier)-Oct, 11-5.

THORNHILL
Drumlanrig Castle DG3 4AQ
bre@drumlanrigcastle.org.uk ☎01848 331555
(4m N of Thornhill off A76)
Open early May-late Aug, Castle open seven days a week. Guided tours and restricted route may operate at various times, please verify before visiting. *£6 (ch £2 & pen £4. Grounds only £3. Party 20+ £4 each.

WANLOCKHEAD
Museum of Lead Mining ML12 6UT
ggodfrey@goldpan.co.uk ☎01659 74387
(Signposted from M74 and A76)
Open Apr-2 Nov, daily 10.30-4.30; Jul & Aug 10-5.

CASTLE DOUGLAS — Map 11 NX76

Babies Welcome | Family Rooms | Children's Dishes

★★ 67% Imperial
35 King St DG7 1AA
☎ 01556 502086 🖷 01556 503009
e-mail: david@thegolfhotel.co.uk
web: www.thegolfhotel.co.uk
Dir: off A75 at sign for Castle Douglas, hotel opp town library.

CHILD FACILITIES: Baby listening Outdoor play area Food/bottle warming Ch menu Ch portions Highchairs Ch discounts under 12s 50% Cots Family rms triple rm Laundry **NEARBY:** Park Swimming pool 15 min to sea

Situated in the main street, this former coaching inn, popular with golfers, offers guests well-equipped and cheerfully decorated bedrooms. There is a choice of bars and good-value meals are served either in the foyer bar or the upstairs dining room.
ROOMS: 12 en suite (1 fmly) ⊗ in 6 bedrooms s £40-£50; d £62-£70 (incl. bkfst) LB **FACILITIES:** local pool and sauna/gym 75 yds away **PARKING:** 29 **NOTES:** ⊗ in restaurant Closed 23-26 Dec & 1-3 Jan

CASTLE KENNEDY — Map 10 NX15

Babies Welcome | Children's Dishes

★★ 66% The Plantings Inn
DG9 8SQ
☎ 01581 400633 🖷 01581 400637
e-mail: info@plantings.com

CHILD FACILITIES: Baby listening Activities: colouring, jigsaws Outdoor play area Food/bottle warming Ch menu Ch portions Highchairs Ch cutlery Ch discounts under 5s free, 5-12s £10 Safe grounds Cots Ch drinks Laundry **NEARBY:** Icecream centre Museum Park Swimming pool

Convenient for Stranraer and the Irish ferries, this small hotel focuses on a pleasantly informal eating operation with a wide-ranging menu that offers hearty good-value dishes. Bedrooms are comfortable and smartly furnished; a residents' lounge is also available.
ROOMS: 5 en suite ⊗ in all bedrooms s £35; d £60 (incl. bkfst) LB **FACILITIES:** Xmas **PARKING:** 30

DUMFRIES — Map 11 NX97

Babies Welcome | Family Rooms | Children's Dishes

★★★ 71% ⊛ Cairndale Hotel & Leisure Club
English St DG1 2DF
☎ 01387 254111 🖷 01387 250555
e-mail: sales@cairndale.fsnet.co.uk
web: www.cairndalehotel.co.uk
Dir: from S turn off M6 onto A75 to Dumfries, left at 1st rdbt, cross railway bridge, continue to traffic lights, hotel 1st building on left

CHILD FACILITIES: Baby listening Activities: board games Family area Food/bottle warming Ch menu Ch portions Highchairs Ch cutlery Ch discounts under 12s free sharing with parents Safe grounds Videos Cots Family rms approx £109 Laundry **NEARBY:** Robert Burns house Farm Cream O' Galloway

Within walking distance of the town centre, this hotel provides a wide range of amenities, including leisure facilities and an impressive entertainment centre. Bedrooms range from stylish suites to cosy singles. There's a choice of eating options in the
continued

evening. The Reivers Restaurant is smartly modern with food to match.

ROOMS: 91 en suite (22 fmly) (5 GF) ⊗ in 45 bedrooms s £49-£109; d £69-£149 (incl. bkfst) **LB FACILITIES: Spa** STV ⊠ Sauna Solarium Gym Jacuzzi Steam room, air conditioned gymnasium ♫ Xmas **PARKING:** 120 **NOTES:** ⊗ in restaurant

ISLE OF WHITHORN
Map 11 NX43

🍴 The Steam Packet Inn
Harbour Row DG8 8LL
☎ 01988 500334 ▤ 01988 500627
e-mail: steampacketinn@btconnect.com
web: www.steampacketinn.com
Dir: From Newton Stewart take A714, then A746 to Whithorn, then Isle of Whithorn

CHILD FACILITIES: Activities: colouring, toys Food/bottle warming Ch licence Ch menu Ch portions Highchairs Ch cutlery Changing facilities NEARBY: Gem Rock Museum Park Harbour location

OPEN: 11-11 (Winter open Mon-Thu, 11-3, 6-11) Closed: Dec 25 **BAR MEALS:** L served all week 12-2 D served all week 6.30-9 Av main course £6 **RESTAURANT:** L served all week 12-2 D served all week 6.30-9 **FACILITIES:** Children's licence Garden **PARKING:** 4

KIRKCUDBRIGHT
Map 11 NX65

🍴 Selkirk Arms ★★★
Old High St DG6 4JG
☎ 01557 330402 ▤ 01557 331639
e-mail: reception@selkirkarmshotel.co.uk
web: www.selkirkarmshotel.co.uk

CHILD FACILITIES: Outdoor play area Food/bottle warming Ch licence Ch menu Ch portions Highchairs Safe grounds Changing facilities NEARBY: Kirkcudbright Leisure park Near to sea

The Selkirk Arms is aptly named, as it was originally the hostelry where Robert Burns wrote the *Selkirk Grace*. It is now a smart hotel set in secluded gardens just off the town centre. Public areas include an attractive restaurant, a bistro and lounge bar. **OPEN:** 11 -12 **BAR MEALS:** L served all week 12-2 D served all week 5-9.30 Av main course £6.50 **RESTAURANT:** L served all week 12-2 D served all week 7-9.30 Av 3 course à la carte £25 **FACILITIES:** Children's licence Garden: Beautiful **ROOMS:** 16 bedrooms 16 en suite 3 family rooms s£55 d£80 **PARKING:** 50

LOCKERBIE
Map 11 NY18

Babies Welcome	Family Rooms	Children's Dishes

★★ 65% **Ravenshill House**
12 Dumfries Rd DG11 2EF
☎ 01576 202882 ▤ 01576 202882
e-mail: aaenquiries@ravenshillhotellockerbie.co.uk
web: www.ravenshillhotellockerbie.co.uk
Dir: on A709 which is signed from the A74M Lockerbie junct, W of town centre. Hotel is 0.5m on right

CHILD FACILITIES: Baby listening Outdoor play area Food/bottle warming Ch menu Ch portions Highchairs Ch cutlery Ch discounts under 12s free sharing with parents Safe grounds Cots Family rms 3 D rms with sofa beds Connecting rms NEARBY: Park Quad bikes Castle & Country park Pottery

Set in spacious gardens on the fringe of the town, this friendly, family-run hotel offers cheerful service and good value, home-cooked meals. There are some well-proportioned bedrooms including an ideal two-room family unit.
ROOMS: 8 rms (7 en suite) (2 fmly) ⊗ in 5 bedrooms s £40-£60; d £60-£70 (incl. bkfst) **LB PARKING:** 35 **NOTES:** ⊗ in restaurant

PORTPATRICK
Map 10 NW95

Babies Welcome	Family Rooms	Children's Dishes

★★★ 74% 🌐 **Fernhill**
Heugh Rd DG9 8TD
☎ 01776 810220 ▤ 01776 810596
e-mail: info@fernhillhotel.co.uk
web: www.fernhillhotel.co.uk
Dir: from Stranraer A77 to Portpatrick, 100yds past Portpatrick village sign, turn right before war memorial. Hotel is 1st on left

CHILD FACILITIES: Baby listening Babysitting Activities: colouring, games, croquet Food/bottle warming Ch menu Ch portions Highchairs Ch cutlery Ch discounts children free when sharing with parents Safe grounds Videos Cots Family rms D rm with S bed Ch drinks Connecting rms Laundry NEARBY: Parks Tennis Horse riding Crazy golf Leisure centre Cinema Museums Short walk to sea

Set high above the village, this hotel looks out over the harbour and Irish Sea. A smart conservatory restaurant and some of the bedrooms take advantage of the views. A modern wing offers particularly spacious and well-appointed rooms - some have balconies.
ROOMS: 27 en suite 9 annexe en suite (3 fmly) (8 GF) ⊗ in 10 bedrooms s £50-£87; d £100-£124 (incl. bkfst) **LB FACILITIES:** STV Leisure facilities available at sister hotel in Stranraer Xmas **PARKING:** 45 **NOTES:** ⊗ in restaurant Closed mid-Jan - mid-Feb

Many proprietors are happy to provide extra facilities for children, but let them know in advance what you need so they can be prepared

Scotland

STRANRAER
Map 10 NX06

★★★★ 68% ⊛ North West Castle
DG9 8EH
☎ 01776 704413 ▤ 01776 702646
e-mail: info@northwestcastle.co.uk
web: www.northwestcastle.co.uk
Dir: on seafront, close to Stena ferry terminal

> **CHILD FACILITIES:** Baby listening Babysitting Activities: Indoor play area Food/bottle warming Ch menu Ch portions Highchairs Ch cutlery Ch discounts children free when sharing Videos Cots Family rms D rm with 2 S beds Ch drinks (on request) Connecting rms Fridge Laundry NEARBY: Parks Tennis Horse riding Leisure centre Cinema Museums Short walk to sea

This long-established hotel overlooks the bay and the ferry terminal. The public areas include a classical dining room where a pianist plays during dinner and an adjoining lounge with large leather armchairs and blazing fire in season. There is a shop, leisure centre, and a curling rink that is the focus in winter. Bedrooms are comfortable and spacious.
ROOMS: 70 en suite 2 annexe en suite (22 fmly) ⊛ in 26 bedrooms s £78-£88; d £92-£102 (incl. bkfst & dinner) LB **FACILITIES:** STV ▤ Snooker Sauna Solarium Gym Jacuzzi Curling (Oct-Apr) Games room Xmas **PARKING:** 100 **NOTES:** ⊛ in restaurant

EAST AYRSHIRE

SORN
Map 11 NS52

🏠 🍺 The Sorn Inn ⊛ ⊛
35 Main St KA5 6HU
☎ 01290 551305 ▤ 01290 553470
e-mail: craig@sorninn.com

> **CHILD FACILITIES:** Food/bottle warming Ch licence Ch menu Highchairs Ch cutlery Changing facilities NEARBY: Loudon Castle Theme Park Fishing

Centrally situated in this rural village, which is convenient for many of Ayrshire's attractions, this renovated inn is now a fine dining restaurant with a cosy lounge area. There is also a popular chop house with a more pub-like environment. The freshly decorated bedrooms have comfortable beds and good facilities.
OPEN: 12-2.30 6-11 (Sat-12-12, Sun 12.30-11, Fri 12-2.30, 6-12) **BAR MEALS:** L served Tue-Sun 12-2.30 D served Tue-Sun 6-8 Av main course £8 **RESTAURANT:** L served Wed-Sun 12-2.30 D served Tue-Sun 6-9 Av 3 course fixed price £21 **FACILITIES:** Children's licence ✖ **ROOMS:** 4 bedrooms 4 en suite 1 family rooms s£35 d£70 **PARKING:** 8

EAST LOTHIAN

GIFFORD
Map 12 NT56

★★ 69% Tweeddale Arms
High St EH41 4QU
☎ 01620 810240 ▤ 01620 810488
web: www.tweeddalearmshotel.co.uk
Dir: A1 South from Edinburgh, turn off at Haddington, 4m from Haddington

> **CHILD FACILITIES:** Activities: books,colouring, toys Food/bottle warming Ch menu Ch portions Highchairs Ch cutlery Ch discounts Safe grounds Cots Family rms D rms with S or B beds £80 Laundry NEARBY: Park

In a picturesque setting by the village green, this hotel is enjoying a renaissance under new family ownership. Refurbishment is ongoing, though the original character is being retained. An inviting lounge leads to a small but elegant dining room and the lounge bar is popular for bar meals.
ROOMS: 14 en suite (2 fmly) ⊛ in 10 bedrooms s £49-£65; d £65-£75 (incl. bkfst) LB **FACILITIES:** ♿ Xmas **NOTES:** ✖ ⊛ in restaurant

FALKIRK

BANKNOCK
Map 11 NS77

⊛ ⊛ Glenskirlie House Restaurant
Kilsyth Rd FK4 1UF
☎ 01324 840201 ▤ 01324 841054
e-mail: macaloneys@glenskirliehouse.com
Dir: From Glasgow take A80 towards Stirling. At J4 take A803 signed Kilsyth/Bonnybridge. At T-junct turn R. Hotel 1m on R

> **CHILD FACILITIES:** Food/bottle warming Ch licence Ch menu Ch portions Highchairs Safe grounds Changing facilities NEARBY: Forth and Clyde Canal Falkirk Wheel Stirling Castle Colzium Park

FOOD: British French **STYLE:** Chic, Country-House **SEATS:** 54
OPEN: 12-2/6-9.30, Closed 26-27 Dec, 1-3 Jan, D Mon
RESTAURANT: main £18-£21 **NOTES:** ⊛ in restaurant, ⊛ area, Air con
PARKING: 100

FIFE

St Andrews and the bay

ABERDOUR
Aberdour Castle
KY3 0SL ☎01383 860519
(In Aberdour, 5m E of Forth Bridges on A921)
Open all year, Apr-Sep, daily 9.30-6.30; Oct-Mar,
daily 9.30-4.30. Closed Thu & Fri in winter, 25-26
Dec & 1-2 Jan. *£2.50 (ch 75p, concessions
£1.90) Groups 11+10% discount. Prices valid until
2 Jan 2005. Please telephone for further details.

BURNTISLAND
Burntisland Edwardian Fair Museum
KY3 9AS ☎01592 412860
(in the centre of Burntisland)
Open all year, Mon, Wed, Fri & Sat 10-1 & 2-5;
Tue & Thu 10-1 & 2-7. Closed public holidays)

DUNFERMLINE
Abbot House Heritage Centre KY12 7NE
dht@abbothouse.fsnet.co.uk ☎01383 733266
(city centre)
Open daily 10-5. Last entry to upper exhibitions
4.15. Closed 25 Dec & 1 Jan. *£3 (accompanied
ch under 16 free & concessions £2). Party 20+.

NORTH QUEENSFERRY
Deep Sea World KY11 1JR
info@deepseaworld.co.uk ☎01383 411880
(from N, M90 take exit for Invertkeithing. From S
follow signs to Forth Rd Bridge, 1st exit left.)
Open all year daily from 10, Nov-Mar 10-5, Apr-
Oct 10-6 wkends & school hols 10-6. *£7.50 (ch
3-5 £5.50, concessions £6). Family ticket & group
discounts available.

ST ANDREWS
Castle & Visitor Centre
KY16 9AR ☎01334 477196
Open all year, Apr-Sep, daily 9.30-6.30; Oct-Mar,
daily 9.30-4.30. Closed 25-26 Dec & 1-2 Jan. *£3
(ch £1, concessions £2.30). Joint ticket with St
Andrews Cathedral available £4 (ch £1.25,
concessions £3. Groups 11+ 10% discount. Rates
valid until 2 Jan 2005. Please phone for further
details.

St Andrews Aquarium
KY16 9AS ☎01334 474786
(Signed in town centre)
Open daily from 10.
Please phone for winter opening.

BURNTISLAND
Map 11 NT28

Babies Welcome	Family Rooms	Children's Dishes

★★★ 63% Kingswood
Kinghorn Rd KY3 9LL
☎ 01592 872329 ≣ 01592 873123
e-mail: rankin@kingswoodhotel.co.uk
web: www.kingswoodhotel.co.uk
*Dir: A921 coastal road at Burntisland, right at rdbt, left at T-junct, at bottom
of hill to Kingshorn road, hotel 0.5m on left*

> **CHILD FACILITIES:** Baby listening Activities: toys, books
> Food/bottle warming Ch menu Ch portions Highchairs Ch cutlery
> Ch discounts under 5s free sharing with parents Safe grounds Cots
> Family rms D rm with B beds, family suite Laundry
> **NEARBY:** Parks Swimming pool

Lying in sheltered grounds east of the town, this hotel has views
across the Firth of Forth to Edinburgh. Bedrooms are housed in a
modern extension on the first floor. Public areas include a lounge
bar and extended restaurant where good-value meals are served.
ROOMS: 13 en suite (3 fmly) (1 GF) ◎ in 2 bedrooms s £47-£66;
d £76-£105 (incl. bkfst) **LB FACILITIES: PARKING:** 50 **NOTES:** Closed
26 Dec & 1 Jan

CRAIL
Map 12 NO60

Babies Welcome	Family Rooms	Children's Dishes

★★ 66% Balcomie Links
Balcomie Rd KY10 3TN
☎ 01333 450237 ≣ 01333 450540
e-mail: mikekadir@balcomie.fsnet.co.uk
web: www.balcomie.co.uk
*Dir: follow road to village shops, at junct of High St & Market Gate turn
right. This road becomes Balcomie Rd, hotel on left*

> **CHILD FACILITIES:** Baby listening Food/bottle warming Ch menu
> Ch portions Highchairs Ch cutlery Ch discounts under 14s free
> sharing with parents Safe grounds Cots Family rms £110
> Connecting rms **NEARBY:** 5-min walk to sea

Especially popular with visiting golfers, this family-run hotel on the
east side of the village represents good value for money and has a
relaxing atmosphere. Bedrooms come in a variety of sizes and
styles and offer all the expected amenities. Food is served from
midday in the attractive lounge bar and in the evening also in the
bright cheerful dining room.
ROOMS: 15 rms (13 en suite) (2 fmly) ◎ in 3 bedrooms s £55-£65;
d £85 (incl. bkfst) **LB FACILITIES:** STV Games room ♫ Xmas
PARKING: 25 **NOTES:** ◎ in restaurant

DUNFERMLINE
Map 11 NT08

Babies Welcome	Family Rooms	Children's Dishes

★★★ 74% ◉ Keavil House

Crossford KY12 8QW
☎ 01383 736258 ≣ 01383 621600
e-mail: sales@keavilhouse.co.uk
web: www.keavilhouse.co.uk
Dir: 2m W of Dunfermline on A994

> **CHILD FACILITIES:** Baby listening Nanny (extra cost) Activities:
> colouring, games, books Indoor play area Food/bottle warming
> Ch menu Ch portions Highchairs Ch discounts under 16s free
> sharing with parents Safe grounds Cots Family rms D rms with S
> beds £95-£195 Ch drinks Connecting rms Laundry
> **NEARBY:** Deep sea world Park 4m to sea

continued on p276

DUNFERMLINE, continued

Dating from the 16th century, this former manor house is set in gardens and parkland. Bedrooms come in a variety of sizes and occupy the original house and a modern wing. There is a modern leisure centre and conservatory restaurant which is the focal point of public rooms.

ROOMS: 47 en suite (6 fmly) (17 GF) ⊛ in 28 bedrooms s £55-£115; d £90-£175 (incl. bkfst) **LB FACILITIES: Spa** STV ◪ Sauna Solarium Gym Jacuzzi Aerobics studio, Steam room, Beautician Xmas **PARKING:** 150 **NOTES:** ✈ ⊛ in restaurant

---

ELIE
Map 12 NO40

Babies Welcome | Children's Dishes

⬛ The Ship Inn
The Toft KY9 1DT
☎ 01333 330246 🖷 01333 330864
e-mail: info@ship-elie.com
Dir: Follow A915 & A917 to Elie. Follow signs from High St to Watersport Centre to the Toft.

| CHILD FACILITIES: | Activities: colouring Food/bottle warming Ch licence Ch menu Ch portions Highchairs Ch cutlery Safe grounds NEARBY: Coastal walks Tennis Golf Cinema Seafront location |

OPEN: 11-11 (Sun 12.30-11) Closed: 25 Dec **BAR MEALS:** L served all week 12-2 D served all week 6-9 **RESTAURANT:** L served all week 12-2 D served all week 6-9 **FACILITIES:** Garden: Beer garden, food served outdoors, patio

---

INVERKEITHING
Map 11 NT18

♦♦♦ Forth Craig Private Hotel
90 Hope St KY11 1LL
☎ 01383 418440
e-mail: forthcraighotel@aol.com
Dir: off A90 at 1st exit after Forth Bridge, signed Inverkeithing, for hotel in 0.5m on right next to church

| CHILD FACILITIES: | Please telephone for details |

Neatly maintained throughout, this friendly family-run guest house is set back from the main road at the southern end of the town. It is within easy reach of a park-and-ride facility to Edinburgh. The bright cheery bedrooms are comfortable and well-equipped.
ROOMS: 5 en suite s fr £30; d fr £50 * ⊛ **FACILITIES:** TVB tea/coffee No coaches Dinner Last d order 6pm **NOTES:** ⊛ in restaurant Licensed Cen ht **PARKING:** 8

ST ANDREWS
Map 12 NO51

Babies Welcome | Family Rooms | Children's Dishes

★★★★★ ⊛ ⊛ ⊛ The Old Course Hotel, Golf Resort & Spa
KY16 9SP
☎ 01334 474371 🖷 01334 477668
e-mail: reservations@oldcoursehotel.co.uk
Dir: close to A91 on outskirts of the city

| CHILD FACILITIES: | Baby listening Nanny (on request) Babysitting Activities: children's activity programme Food/bottle warming Ch menu Ch portions Highchairs Ch discounts under 12s free sharing with parents Games consoles Videos Cots Family rms family rms with extra beds Ch drinks Connecting rms Fridge Laundry Changing mats (on request) NEARBY: Castle Museum Country Park Arts centre 5-min walk to sea |

Please note that this establishment has recently changed hands. A haven for golfers, this internationally renowned hotel sits adjacent to the 17th hole of the championship course. Bedrooms vary in size and range from the traditional to the contemporary and stylish fairway rooms, complete with course facing balconies. Day rooms include intimate lounges, a bright conservatory, a well-equipped spa and a range of golf shops. The fine dining 'Road Hole Grill', the seafood bar 'Sands' or the informal Jigger Inn pub prove popular eating venues.

ROOMS: 134 en suite (6 fmly) ⊛ in 118 bedrooms s £230-£580; d £295-£595 (incl. bkfst) **LB FACILITIES: Spa** STV ◪ Golf 18 Sauna Solarium Gym ⚓ Jacuzzi Health spa Steam room Xmas **PARKING:** 150 **NOTES:** ⊛ in restaurant Closed 24-28 Dec

Babies Welcome | Family Rooms | Children's Dishes

★★★ ⊛ ⊛ St Andrews Golf
40 The Scores KY16 9AS
☎ 01334 472611 🖷 01334 472188
e-mail: reception@standrews-golf.co.uk
web: www.standrews-golf.co.uk
Dir: follow signs 'Golf Course' into Golf Place and in 200yds turn right into The Scores

| CHILD FACILITIES: | Baby listening Activities: colouring, board games Outdoor play area Food/bottle warming Ch menu Ch portions Highchairs Ch cutlery Ch discounts under 5s free, 5-14s only pay for meals Safe grounds Videos Cots Family rms D rm with S beds Laundry NEARBY: Sealife centre Castle Park Putting Near sea |

A genuinely warm approach to guest care is found at this delightful, family-run hotel. In a stunning location the views of the beach, golf links and coastline can be enjoyed from the inviting day rooms. There is a choice of bars and an informal atmosphere in Ma Bell's. Bedrooms come in two distinct styles with those on the higher floors offering stylish, modern design and comfort.
ROOMS: 21 en suite (9 fmly) s £115-£170; d £170-£215 (incl. bkfst) **LB FACILITIES:** STV Xmas **PARKING:** 6 **NOTES:** ⊛ in restaurant

Babies Welcome | Family Rooms | Children's Dishes

⬛ ⊛ ⊛ The Inn at Lathones
THE INDEPENDENT
Largoward KY9 1JE
☎ 01334 840494 🖷 01334 840694
e-mail: lathones@theinn.co.uk
web: www.theinn.co.uk
Dir: 5m S of St Andrews on A915, 0.5m before village of Largoward on left just after hidden dip

| CHILD FACILITIES: | Baby listening Outdoor play area Food/bottle warming Ch menu Ch portions Highchairs Ch cutlery Ch discounts under 12s free sharing with parents Safe grounds Cots Family rms rm with 4 bed, rm with 3 beds Ch drinks (on request) Connecting rms Laundry NEARBY: Sea life centre |

A lovely country inn, full of character and individuality, parts of

continued
continue

which date back 400 years. The friendly staff help to create a relaxed atmosphere. Smart contemporary bedrooms are in two separate wings, both accessed from outside. The colourful, cosy restaurant is the main focus, the menu adding a modern style to Scottish and European dishes.

ROOMS: 13 annexe en suite (2 fmly) (11 GF) s £100-£130; d £140-£200 incl. bkfst) LB **FACILITIES:** STV **PARKING:** 35 **NOTES:** ⊗ in restaurant Closed 25-26 Dec & 3-23 Jan RS 24 Dec

◆◆◆◆ The Larches
River Ter, Guardbridge KY16 0XA
☎ 01334 838008 ▤ 01334 838008
e-mail: thelarches@aol.com
Dir: on A919 in Guardbridge turn left at Milton Burn Bridge by phone box/bus stop, house 50yds on left

CHILD FACILITIES: Please telephone for details

Situated in a village northwest of St Andrews, this comfortable guest house stands in mature colourful gardens close to the River Eden. It has a welcoming atmosphere and offers well-equipped

continued

pine-furnished bedrooms. A spacious lounge offers lots to interest guests, including videos, books, board games and a self-service beverage facility.

ROOMS: 3 rms (2 en suite) (2 fmly) (2 GF) s £27-£40; d £50-£60 *
FACILITIES: TVB tea/coffee TVL No coaches **NOTES:** Credit cards not taken ✠ ⊗ Cen ht

HIGHLAND

Highland cow

AVIEMORE
Strathspey Steam Railway
PH22 1PY   ☎01479 810725
information@strathspeyrailway.co.uk
(Off B970)
Open daily Etr. 23-29 Mar, 29 May-30 Sep, Apr, Wed & Sun; May & Oct, Wed, Thu, Sat, Sun & BH Mon, 9.30-4.30 *£9 basic round trip,(ch £4.50) £21 Family roundtrip.

BOAT OF GARTEN
Loch Garten Osprey Centre
PH25 3EF   ☎01479 831476
(Signposted from B970 & A9 at Aviemore, follow 'RSPB Ospreys' signs)
Reserve open at all times. Osprey Centre daily, Apr-Aug 10-6.
*£2.50 ch 50p, concessions £1.50.

CARRBRIDGE
Landmark Forest Theme Park PH23 3AJ
landmarkcentre@btconnect.com ☎01479 841613
(Off A9 between Aviemore & Inverness)
Open all year, daily, Apr-mid Jul 10-6; mid Jul-mid Aug 10-7; Sep-Oct 10-5.30; Nov-Mar 10-5.

CAWDOR
Cawdor Castle IV12 5RD
info@cawdorcastle.com   ☎01667 404401
(On B9090, off A96)
Open May-9 Oct, daily 10-5.30. Last admission 5pm. *£6.50 ch 5-15 £3.70, pen £5.50.

Family ticket £19. Party 20+ £5.70 each. Gardens, grounds & nature trails only £3.50.

DRUMNADROCHIT
Official Loch Ness Monster Exhibition Centre
IV3 6TU
brem@loch-ness-scotland.com ☎01456 450573
(On A82, 12m S Inverness)
Open all year; Etr-May 9.30-5.30; Jun-Sep 9.30-6 9-8.30 Jul & Aug; winter 10-4. Last admission 30mins before closing.

ELPHIN
Highland & Rare Breeds Farm
IV27 4HH   ☎01854 666204
(On A835 in Elphin)
Open Jul & Aug only.
*£3.95 ch £2.95, students & pen £3.50

GAIRLOCH
Gairloch Heritage Museum
IV21 2BP   ☎01445 712287
info@gairlochheritagemuseum.org.uk
(On junct of A382 & B8021. Nr police station & public car park)
Open Apr-Sep, Mon-Sat 10-5; Oct, Mon-Fri 10-1.30 last admission 4.30. Winter months by arrangement.

GLENCOE
Glencoe Visitor Centre
PA39 4HX   ☎01855 811307
(On A82, 17m S of Fort William)
Open - Site all year, daily. Visitor Centre Apr-Aug, daily 9.30-5.30; Mar-Apr & Sep-Oct, daily 10-5; Nov-Feb, Fri-Mon 10-4.
*50p ch & pen 30p. Includes parking.

KINCRAIG
Highland Wildlife Park PH21 1NL
info@highlandwildlifepark.org ☎01540 651270
(On B9152, 7m S of Aviemore)
Open throughout the year, weather permitting. Apr-Oct, 10-6; Jun-Aug 10-7; Nov-Mar 10-4. last entry 2 hours before closing.
*£8 child £5.50, pen £7.

Scotland

AVIEMORE

Map 14 NH81

Babies Welcome | **Family Rooms** | **Children's Dishes**

◆◆◆◆ Ravenscraig
Grampian Rd PH22 1RP
☎ 01479 810278 🖷 01479 810210
e-mail: info@aviemoreonline.com
web: www.aviemoreonline.com
Dir: at north end of Main St on left. 250mtrs N of Police Station

CHILD FACILITIES: Activities: toys, games Food/bottle warming Ch portions Highchairs Ch cutlery Ch discounts 50% sharing with parents Cots Family rms D rms with S beds Laundry

This friendly, family-run guest house is located on the north side of the village, a short walk from local amenities. Bedrooms vary between the traditionally styled rooms in the main house and modern spacious rooms in a brand new chalet style annexe. There is a relaxing lounge and separate dining room, where freshly prepared breakfasts are served at individual tables.
ROOMS: 6 en suite 6 annexe en suite (6 fmly) (6 GF) s £20-£30; d £40-£60 * ⊗ **FACILITIES:** TVB tea/coffee TVL **NOTES:** ✈ ⊗ in restaurant Cen ht **PARKING:** 15

Babies Welcome | **Children's Dishes**

The Old Bridge Inn
Dalfaber Rd PH22 1PU
☎ 01479 811137 🖷 01479 810270
e-mail: highlandcatering@aol.com
web: www.oldbridgeinn.co.uk
Dir: Exit A9 to Aviemore, 1st L to 'Ski road', then 1st L again - 200mtrs

CHILD FACILITIES: Activities: colouring, books, toys Outdoor play area Family area Food/bottle warming Ch licence Ch menu Ch portions Highchairs NEARBY: Highland Wildlife Park Landmark Forest Theme Park

OPEN: 11-11 **BAR MEALS:** L served all week 12-2 D served all week 6-9 Av main course £7 **RESTAURANT:** L served all week 12-2 D served all week 6-9 Av 3 course à la carte £14 **FACILITIES:** Children's licence Garden ✈ **PARKING:** 24

BALLACHULISH

Map 14 NN05

Babies Welcome | **Family Rooms** | **Children's Dishes**

★★★ 71% Ballachulish Hotel
PH49 4JY
☎ 0871 222 3415 🖷 0871 222 3416
e-mail: reservations@freedomglen.co.uk
web: www.freedomglen.co.uk
Dir: on A828, Fort William-Oban road, 3m N of Glencoe

CHILD FACILITIES: Baby listening Food/bottle warming Ch menu Ch portions Highchairs Ch cutlery Ch discounts under 3s free, 3-5s £7.50, 6-10s £17.50, 11-15s £27.50 Cots Family rms D rms with S beds from £160 Ch drinks Laundry NEARBY: Walks Lochside

A relaxed atmosphere prevails at this long-established hotel, which boasts stunning views over Loch Linnhe. Bedrooms vary in size and style and all are comfortably appointed; many have superb views. Inviting public areas include a spacious and comfortable lounge, the informal Ferry Bar and a cocktail bar adjacent to the bold and attractive restaurant.
ROOMS: 54 en suite (4 fmly) s £52.50-£150; d £110-£280 (incl. bkfst & dinner) **LB FACILITIES:** Complimentary Membership of Leisure Club at nearby sister hotel ♫ Xmas **PARKING:** 50 **NOTES:** ⊗ in restaurant Closed 9-23 Dec & 5-27 Jan

◆◆◆◆ Lyn-Leven
West Laroch PH49 4JP
☎ 01855 811392 🖷 01855 811600
Dir: off A82 signed on left West Lorroch

CHILD FACILITIES: Please telephone for details

Genuine Highland hospitality and high standards are part of the appeal of this comfortable guest house. The attractive bedrooms vary in size, are well equipped, offering many thoughtful extra touches. There is a spacious lounge and a smart dining room where delicious home-cooked evening meals and breakfasts are served at individual tables.
ROOMS: 8 en suite 4 annexe en suite (1 fmly) (12 GF) s £24-£30; d £48-£54 * ⊗ in 1 bedrooms **FACILITIES:** TVB tea/coffee TVL Dinne Last d order 7pm **NOTES:** Licensed Cen ht **LB PARKING:** 12

BEAULY

Map 14 NH5

Babies Welcome | **Family Rooms** | **Children's Dishes**

★★★ 72% Priory
The Square IV4 7BX
☎ 01463 782309 🖷 01463 782531
e-mail: reservations@priory-hotel.com
web: www.priory-hotel.com
Dir: signed from A832, into Beauly, hotel in square on left

CHILD FACILITIES: Food/bottle warming Ch menu Ch portions Highchairs Ch cutlery Ch discounts children sharing free Cots Family rms Ch drinks NEARBY: Walks Parks

This popular hotel occupies an enviable location in the town square. There are two standards of accommodation offered, with the executive rooms providing very high standards of comfort an● facilities. A wide range of meals are served throughout the day in the open plan public areas.
ROOMS: 34 en suite (3 fmly) ⊗ in 9 bedrooms s £42.50-£52.50; d £65-£85 (incl. bkfst) **LB FACILITIES:** STV Snooker Xmas **PARKING:** 20 **NOTES:** ✈ ⊗ in restaurant

CARRBRIDGE

Map 14 NH5

Babies Welcome | **Family Rooms** | **Children's Dishes**

◆◆◆◆ Carrmoor
Carr Rd PH23 3AD
☎ 01479 841244 🖷 01479 841244
e-mail: christine@carrmoorguesthouse.co.uk
web: www.carrmoorguesthouse.co.uk
Dir: drive to centre of village & turn into Carr rd opp church & village hall. Carrmoor on left in Carr Rd

CHILD FACILITIES: Baby listening Food/bottle warming Ch menu Ch portions Highchairs Cots Family rms D rm with B beds £66-£70

A welcoming atmosphere prevails at this immaculately maintaine● guest house. Bedrooms feature attractive colour schemes and are well equipped and comfortably modern in appointment. There is

continue●

osy lounge for peaceful relaxation and an inviting dining room where delicious cuisine using quality fresh ingredients is served. egetarian and children's options are available.

OOMS: 6 en suite (1 fmly) (1 GF) s £25.50-£28; d £46-£50 * ☺
ACILITIES: TV1B tea/coffee TVL No coaches Dinner Last d order 8pm
OTES: ☺ in restaurant Licensed Cen ht **PARKING:** 6

Babies Welcome	Family Rooms	Children's Dishes

◆◆◆ Pines Country House
Duthil PH23 3ND
☎ 01479 841220 ▤ 01479 841220 *51
e-mail: Lynn@thepines-duthil.fsnet.co.uk
Dir: A9 to Carrbridge, turn onto A938 Grantown-on-Spey road, 2m to Duthil. 5th house on left

CHILD FACILITIES: Baby listening Activities: soft toys, board games Outdoor play area Food/bottle warming Ch menu Ch portions Highchairs Ch cutlery Ch discounts under 4s free, 4-12s 50% Safe grounds Videos Cots Family rms D rm with adj B bed rm £67 Connecting rms Laundry Changing mats NEARBY: Adventure park Fun house

warm and friendly welcome is assured at this comfortable home which enjoys a delightful rural setting. The bright bedrooms are comfortable, traditionally furnished and offer the expected amenities. Enjoyable home cooked fare is served around a communal table. There is a bright conservatory lounge where guests can watch squirrels feed in the nearby wood.
OOMS: 4 en suite (1 fmly) (1 GF) s £30; d £45 * **FACILITIES:** STV TVB tea/coffee No coaches Dinner Last d order 4pm **NOTES:** ☺ Cen ht **LB PARKING:** 5

CAWDOR   Map 14 NH85

Babies Welcome	Children's Dishes

■ Cawdor Tavern
The Lane IV12 5XP
☎ 01667 404777 ▤ 01667 404777
e-mail: cawdortavern@btopenworld.com
Dir: From A96 (Inverness-Aberdeen) take B9006 & follow signs for Cawdor Castle. Tavern in village centre.

CHILD FACILITIES: Activities: model making, colouring Family area Food/bottle warming Ch licence Ch menu Ch portions Highchairs Ch cutlery Safe grounds Changing facilities NEARBY: Cawdor woods Walks Near sea

OPEN: 11-3 5-11 (May-Oct 11-11) Closed: 25 Dec, 1 Jan **BAR MEALS:** L served all week 12-2 D served all week 5.30-9 Av main course £8.95 **RESTAURANT:** L served all week 12-2 D served all week 6.30-9 Av 3 course à la carte £19.95 **FACILITIES:** Children's licence Garden: Patio area at front of Tavern **PARKING:** 60

DRUMNADROCHIT   Map 14 NH52

Babies Welcome	Family Rooms	Children's Dishes

★★★ 68% ⚕ Polmaily House Hotel
IV63 6XT
☎ 01456 450343 ▤ 01456 450813
e-mail: polmaily@btinternet.com
web: www.polmaily.co.uk
Dir: in Drumnadrochit, next to the monster exhibition, turn onto A831(signed Cannich), hotel 2m on right. 1.5m from Loch Ness

CHILD FACILITIES: Baby listening Nanny (by arrangement) Babysitting Activities: activities 2hrs per day, Monster Club in eve, books, games, indoor & outdoor toys Indoor play area Outdoor play area Family area Food/bottle warming Ch menu Ch portions Highchairs Ch cutlery Ch discounts 2nd child free in low season Safe grounds Games consoles Videos Cots Family rms Suites with D & B beds Connecting rms Fridge Laundry NEARBY: Theme park Castle Cinema Seal watching Quad bikes

Run by a family, this relaxing country house is geared for children, with a pets corner and well-stocked play areas. The 18 acres of lawns and woods also include good leisure facilities, such as a swimming pool, horse riding and tennis. Good home-cooked dinners are also on offer.
ROOMS: 10 en suite (6 fmly) (1 GF) ☺ in all bedrooms s £40-£72; d £80-£144 (incl. bkfst) LB **FACILITIES:** 🏊 ❊ Fishing Riding Solarium ⚕ Indoor/outdoor child's play area, Boating, Pony rides, Beauty massage, bicycles Xmas **PARKING:** 20 **NOTES:** ☺ in restaurant

---

FORT WILLIAM   Map 14 NN17

Babies Welcome	Family Rooms	Children's Dishes

◆◆◆◆ ⚐ Distillery House
Nevis Bridge, North Rd PH33 6LR
☎ 01397 700103 ▤ 01397 702980
e-mail: disthouse@aol.com
Dir: from S, A82 thru Fort William in direction of Inverness. On left after Glen Nevis rdbt (3rd coming thru Fort William). From N, A82 towards Fort William, right at sign after 2nd lights

CHILD FACILITIES: Outdoor play area Food/bottle warming Ch menu Ch portions Highchairs Safe grounds Videos Cots Family rms D rms with 2 or 3 S beds £45-£85 NEARBY: Cinema Leisure park Play area Walks Bike routes

Situated in the grounds of the former Glenlochy Distillery, this friendly guest house was once the distillery manager's home. Bedrooms are attractively decorated, comfortably furnished and very well equipped. There is a relaxing lounge, which features a superb range of games, and a bright airy dining room where traditional Scottish breakfasts are served at individual tables.
ROOMS: 8 en suite (1 fmly) (1 GF) **FACILITIES:** TVB tea/coffee No coaches Fishing **NOTES:** ☺ Cen ht **LB PARKING:** 20

Scotland

◆◆◆◆ Seangan Croft
Seangan Bridge, Banavie PH33 7PB
☎ 01397 773114 & 01397 772228
e-mail: seangan-chalets@fortwilliam59.freeserve.co.uk
Dir: take A82 2m N of Fort William at traffic lights and turn left onto A830. After 1m turn right onto B8004 (Gairlochy), House 2m further than Moorings Hotel opposite An Crann Restaurant.

CHILD FACILITIES: Please telephone for details

This modern bungalow situated on the north side of the Caledonian Canal offers stunning views of Ben Nevis and the ski slopes of Aonach Mor. The bedrooms are contemporary in style and guests have use of a spacious and comfortable lounge. Full breakfasts are served in the neat dining room and if dinner is required guests can eat at the An Crann (The Plough) restaurant across the road, also run by Sinè Ross.
ROOMS: 3 en suite s £25-£35; d £40-£46 * **FACILITIES:** TVB tea/coffee TVL No coaches Last d order 9pm **NOTES:** ✼ ⊗ Licensed Cen ht **LB** **PARKING:** 6

◆◆◆ Glenlochy
Nevis Bridge PH33 6LP
☎ 01397 702909
e-mail: glenlochy1@aol.com
Dir: from Inverness on A82, the guest house is located on left after 2nd set of traffic lights. From South on A82, after 3rd rdbt, located 50m on right.
CHILD FACILITIES: Please telephone for details
The garden of this friendly, family-run guest house marks the end of the famous West Highland Way. Bedrooms are pleasantly decorated and well equipped. There is a comfortable first floor lounge and a bright, airy ground floor dining room, where hearty breakfasts are served at individual tables.
ROOMS: 10 rms (9 en suite) 2 annexe en suite (2 fmly) (7 GF)
s £22-£45; d £45-£70 * **FACILITIES:** TVB tea/coffee TVL No coaches
NOTES: ✼ ⊗ Cen ht **LB** **PARKING:** 13

Map 14 NG81

🍴 Glenelg Inn
IV40 8JR
☎ 01599 522273 ▤ 01599 522283
e-mail: christophermain7@glenelg-inn.com
web: www.glenelg-inn.com
Dir: From Shiel Bridge (A87) take unclassified road to Glenelg
CHILD FACILITIES: Indoor play area Outdoor play area Food/bottle warming Ch menu Ch portions Highchairs Ch cutlery Safe grounds Changing facilities **NEARBY:** 30yds to sea
OPEN: 12-11 (Bar closed lunchtimes during winter) **BAR MEALS:** L served all week 12.30-2 D served all week 6-9.30 **RESTAURANT:** 12.30-2 7.30-9 **FACILITIES:** Garden: Large garden going down to the sea

★★★★ 71% *Inverness Marriott Hotel*
Culcabock Rd IV2 3LP
☎ 01463 237166 ▤ 01463 225208
e-mail: events@marriotthotels.co.uk
Dir: from A9 S, exit Culduthel/Kingsmills 5th exit at rdbt, follow road 0.5m, over mini-rdbt past golf club, hotel on left after lights
CHILD FACILITIES: Please telephone for details
Located on the south side of the city, this smart hotel is popular with both business and leisure guests. Accommodation is provide in spacious, thoughtfully equipped rooms, with those in the newe wing particularly impressive. Well-proportioned public areas include a choice of restaurants and lounges.
ROOMS: 76 en suite 6 annexe en suite (11 fmly) (26 GF) ⊗ in 29 bedrooms **FACILITIES:** Spa STV ⊡ Sauna Solarium Gym ⊥ Hair & beauty salon Steam room **PARKING:** 120 **NOTES:** ⊗ in restaurant

Babies Welcome	Family Rooms	Children's Dishes

★★ 67% The Maple Court
12 Ness Walk IV3 5SQ
☎ 01463 230330 ▤ 01463 237700
e-mail: maplecourt@macleodhotels.co.uk
Dir: off A9 into City Centre, follow one-way system. Over Tomnachurich St Bridge, 1st right onto Ness Walk
CHILD FACILITIES: Activities: colouring, toys Outdoor play area Food/bottle warming Ch menu Ch portions Highchairs Ch cutlery Ch discounts Safe grounds Cots Family rms from £115 **NEARBY:** Park Walks Cinema Pony trekking 3-min walk to sea
Set in gardens on the banks of the River Ness and close to the Eden Court Theatre, this hotel is within a short stroll of the city centre. It has been substantially upgraded and provides smart ground-floor bedrooms and a restaurant serving good-value meals. The friendliness of staff leaves a lasting impression.
ROOMS: 9 en suite (2 fmly) (9 GF) ⊗ in 5 bedrooms s £60-£65; d £80-£90 (incl. bkfst) **LB** **FACILITIES:** ♫ Xmas **PARKING:** 32 **NOTES:** ⊗ in restaurant

Babies Welcome	Family Rooms	Children's Dishes

◆◆◆◆◆ Moyness House
6 Bruce Gardens IV3 5EN
☎ 01463 233836 ▤ 01463 233836
e-mail: stay@moyness.co.uk
web: www.moyness.co.uk
Dir: off A82 Fort William road, almost opposite Highland Regional Council headquarters
CHILD FACILITIES: Activities: toys Outdoor play area Food/bottle warming Ch portions Highchairs Ch cutlery Ch discounts for children sharing with parents Safe grounds Cots Family rms D rm with S bed £80-£86 **NEARBY:** Aquadome Sports centre Ice rink Park Cinema
Situated in a quiet residential area just a short distance from the city centre, this elegant Victorian villa dates back to 1880 and offers beautifully decorated, comfortable bedrooms and well-appointed bathrooms. There is an attractive sitting room and an inviting dining room, where traditional Scottish breakfasts are served. Guests are welcome to use the secluded and well-maintained back garden.
ROOMS: 7 en suite (1 fmly) (2 GF) s £35-£38; d £70-£76 *
FACILITIES: TVB tea/coffee No coaches **NOTES:** ⊗ Cen ht **LB** **PARKING:** 10

♦♦♦ Westbourne

0 Huntly St IV3 5HS
☎ 01463 220700 🖶 01463 220700
-mail: richard@westbourne.org.uk
ir: off A9 to A82 at football stadium, straight across 3 rdbts & Friars
ridge, 1st left from bridge into Wells St, & right into Huntly St

CHILD FACILITIES: Please telephone for details

his house lies on the banks of the River Ness, looking across to
he city centre. Immaculately maintained, this friendly family-run
guest house offers bright modern bedrooms of varying size, all
ttractively furnished in pine and very well equipped. There is also
a ground-floor bedroom, which has been specially furnished for
guests with limited mobility.
ROOMS: 10 en suite (6 fmly) (1 GF) **FACILITIES:** TVB tea/coffee No
coaches **NOTES:** ⊗ Cen ht **PARKING:** 6

Babies Welcome	Family Rooms	Children's Dishes

♦♦♦ Park

51 Glenurquhart Rd IV3 5PB
☎ 01463 231858
e-mail: hendry.robertson@connectfree.co.uk
ir: on A82 leaving town centre, on W side of river

CHILD FACILITIES: Activities: Food/bottle warming Ch menu
Ch portions Highchairs Ch cutlery Ch discounts under 5s free, 5-10s
50% Safe grounds Cots Family rms D rms with S bed
NEARBY: Parks Swimming pool Aquadome

Park Guest House is a substantial, welcoming Victorian villa with
distinctive ivy-clad frontage and a neat front garden. The
bedrooms are comfortable, attractively decorated and well
equipped. There is a peaceful ground-floor lounge and a cheerful
breakfast room where traditional breakfasts are served at
individual tables.
ROOMS: 6 rms (3 en suite) (3 fmly) s £20-£30; d £40-£60 *
FACILITIES: TVB tea/coffee TVL No coaches **NOTES:** ⊗ Cen ht **LB**
PARKING: 6

Babies Welcome	Family Rooms	Children's Dishes

♦♦♦ 🚌 The Old Schoolhouse

Tigh Fasgaidh, Erbusaig IV40 8BB
☎ 01599 534369 🖶 01599 534369
e-mail: cuminecandj@lineone.net
web: www.highland.plus.com/schoolhouse
Dir: turn right in Kyle of Lochalsh towards Plockton. Follow road for 2m to
arrive at Erbusaig. Do not enter village on left but continue for 0.25m, 3rd
house on right

CHILD FACILITIES: Food/bottle warming Ch menu Ch portions
Highchairs Ch cutlery Ch discounts under 2s free, over 2s £5 + £1 for
each year Safe grounds Cots Family rms D/T rm with extra bed
£63-£75 Ch drinks Laundry Changing mats **NEARBY:** Castles
Walks Leisure centre 0.5m to sea

Situated in the quiet hamlet of Erbusaig, just north of the Skye
Bridge, this former school has been skilfully converted to a family
home and guest house. Bedrooms are homely and well equipped
and the lounge is very cosy, with a real fire and small bar. The
intimate dining room provides a pleasant environment to enjoy
chef/patron Calum Cumine's carefully prepared and tasty dinners.
ROOMS: 3 en suite (1 GF) s £35-£45; d £50-£60 * **FACILITIES:** TVB
tea/coffee No coaches Dinner Last d order 5pm **NOTES:** ⊗ in restaurant
Licensed Cen ht **PARKING:** 15

Babies Welcome	Children's Dishes

🍴 Kylesku Hotel

IV27 4HW
☎ 01971 502231 🖶 01971 502313
e-mail: kyleskuhotel@lycos.co.uk
Dir: 35m N of Ullapool on A835, turn into Kylesku, hotel at end of road at
old ferry pier

CHILD FACILITIES: Food/bottle warming Ch licence Ch portions
Highchairs **NEARBY:** Boat trips Walks

OPEN: 11-11.30 (Mon-Thu, Sat 10-11.30 Fri 10-12, Sun 12.30-11) Closed: 1
Nov-28 Feb **BAR MEALS:** L served all week 12-2.30 D served all week 6-9
Av main course £9.50 **RESTAURANT:** D served all week 7-8.30 Av 2
course fixed price £21.95 **FACILITIES:** Garden: overlooking the sea loch
ROOMS: 8 bedrooms 6 en suite 1 family rooms s£40 d£70

Babies Welcome	Children's Dishes	

🍴 The Portland Arms Hotel

KW3 6BS
☎ 01593 721721 🖶 01593 721722
e-mail: info@portlandarms.co.uk
Dir: Beside A99. From Inverness to Wick, hotel on left, 200yds from sign for
Lybster

CHILD FACILITIES: Activities: toys, colouring Food/bottle warming
Ch licence Ch menu Ch portions Highchairs Ch cutlery Changing
facilities **NEARBY:** Swimming pool Bowling alley Cinema Park
0.5m to sea

OPEN: 7.30-11 Closed: Dec 31-Jan 3 **BAR MEALS:** L served all week 12-3
D served all week 5-9 Av main course £8.50 **RESTAURANT:** L served all
week 11.30-3 D served all week 5-9 Av 3 course à la carte £18.50
FACILITIES: Children's licence Food served outside 🎄 **ROOMS:** 22
bedrooms 22 en suite 4 family rooms s£50 d£80 **PARKING:** 20

MUIR OF ORD
Map 14 NH55

★★ 68%  🏨 Ord House
IV6 7UH

THE CIRCLE
Selected Individual Hotels
GREAT BRITAIN

☎ 01463 870492 📄 01463 870492
e-mail: admin@ord-house.co.uk
Dir: off A9 at Tore rdbt onto A832. Follow for 5m into Muir of Ord. Turn left outside Muir of Ord, to Ullapool still on A832. Hotel 0.5m on left

CHILD FACILITIES: Activities: toys Outdoor play area Family area Food/bottle warming Ch menu Ch portions Highchairs Ch cutlery Ch discounts under 5s free, 5-10s 50% when sharing with parents Safe grounds Videos Cots Family rms D rm with S bed or cot from £100 Laundry Changing mats NEARBY: Cinema Waterdome Walks 10-min to sea

Dating back to 1637, this country-house hotel is situated peacefully in wooded grounds and offers brightly furnished and well-proportioned accommodation. Comfortable day rooms reflect the character and charm of the house, with inviting lounges, a cosy snug bar and an elegant dining room where wide-ranging, creative menus are offered.
ROOMS: 11 en suite (2 GF) s fr £50; d fr £100 (incl. bkfst)
FACILITIES: no TV in bdrms 🏐 ⚓ Clay pigeon shooting **PARKING:** 30
NOTES: ⊗ in restaurant Closed Nov-Apr

★ 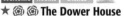 The Dower House
Highfield IV6 7XN
☎ 01463 870090 📄 01463 870090
e-mail: aa@thedowerhouse.co.uk
web: www.thedowerhouse.co.uk
Dir: on Dingwall road A862, 1m from Muir of Ord, on left

CHILD FACILITIES: Baby listening Activities: books, jigsaws, games, cards Outdoor play area Food/bottle warming Ch menu Ch portions Highchairs Ch cutlery Ch discounts children £18 when sharing with parents Safe grounds Cots Family rms Suite with divan bed £165 Connecting rms Laundry NEARBY: Walks Lochs Fishing 10-min drive to sea

This enchanting house enjoys a secluded location on the northern edge of the village. The relaxed, friendly atmosphere and attentive service are key features of the hotel and guests are made to feel that this is a real home from home. The cosy sitting room is full of books, whilst the dining room has quiet elegance and antique furniture. The charming bedrooms come in various sizes; one has its own sitting room.
ROOMS: 5 en suite 2 annexe en suite (1 fmly) (5 GF) ⊗ in all bedrooms s £65-£105; d £110-£150 (incl. bkfst) LB **FACILITIES:** 🏐 Bird watching **PARKING:** 20 **NOTES:** ⊗ in restaurant Closed 25 Dec & 2wks Nov

NAIRN
Map 14 NH85

★★★★ 73% Golf View
The Seafront IV12 4HD

SCOTLAND'S HOTELS OF DISTINCTION

☎ 01667 452301 📄 01667 455267
e-mail: golfview@morton-hotels.com
web: www.morton-hotels.com
Dir: off A96 into Seabank Rd, follow road to end, hotel on right

continued

CHILD FACILITIES: Babysitting Outdoor play area Family area Food/bottle warming Ch menu Ch portions Highchairs Ch discounts from £1.50-£2.50 per year of age Safe grounds Games consoles Videos Cots Family rms D rm with integral B bed room, sleeping 3-8 Laundry NEARBY: Adventure playground Seafront location

Ideally situated adjacent to both the beach and Nairn Golf Club, this hotel has benefited from significant investment. Stylish and well-equipped bedrooms are spacious and include a number of family suites. Public areas include an attractive leisure club. Freshly prepared meals can be enjoyed in both the informal conservatory and restaurant.
ROOMS: 42 en suite (7 fmly) ⊗ in 7 bedrooms s £92-£113; d £139-£236 (incl. bkfst) LB **FACILITIES:** STV ❖ ❖ Sauna Solarium Gym ⚓ Jacuzzi Cycle hire, Swimming pool supervised Xmas **PARKING:** 65 **NOTES:** ⊗ in restaurant

★★★★ 70% Newton
Inverness Rd IV12 4RX
☎ 01667 453144 📄 01667 454026
e-mail: info@morton-hotels.com
web: www.morton-hotels.com
Dir: 15m from Inverness on A96, turn left into tree lined driveway

CHILD FACILITIES: Baby listening Babysitting Outdoor play area Food/bottle warming Ch menu Ch portions Highchairs Safe grounds Cots Family rms Connecting rms Laundry NEARBY: Adventure play park Near sea

The original part of this hotel dates from 1650, while a stylish, modern extension houses a large conference centre and some super bedrooms. Public rooms include spacious lounges, a well-stocked, recently refurbished bar and an elegant restaurant, where much use is made of the abundant local produce.
ROOMS: 56 en suite (2 fmly) ⊗ in 15 bedrooms s £92-£113; d £114-£196 (incl. bkfst) LB **FACILITIES:** STV ❖ Fishing Use of leisure club at sister hotel Xmas **PARKING:** 200 **NOTES:** ⊗ in restaurant Closed 23-27 Dec

PORTNANCON
Map 14 NC46

◆◆◆◆ 🍴 🛏 Port-Na-Con House
Loch Eriboll IV27 4UN
☎ 01971 511367 📄 01971 511367
e-mail: portnacon70@hotmail.com
web: www.port-na-con.info
Dir: 0.25m off A838, on shore of loch, 6m SE of Durness

CHILD FACILITIES: Activities: games, Lego Food/bottle warming Ch portions Highchairs Ch cutlery Ch discounts under 2s free, 2-6s 1/3 reduction, 7-10s 50%, 11-13s 2/3 reduction Cots Family rms D rm with S bed Ch drinks (on request) NEARBY: Walks Seafront location

continued

...lthough it might take nearly a day to reach this secluded guest ...ouse on the shores of Loch Eriboll, few journeys can be better ...ewarded - the tranquillity and picture-book loch and mountain ...cenery will provide an unforgettable memory. Genuine hospitality ...nd attentive service are offered. Bedrooms are comfortable, ...reakfasts are substantial and at dinner wide-ranging menus are ...erved.

ROOMS: 3 rms (1 en suite) (1 fmly) d £40-£42 *
FACILITIES: tea/coffee No coaches local golf & fishing Dinner Last d ...rder 5pm **NOTES:** ☺ Licensed Cen ht **PARKING:** 6

...HIELDAIG   Map 14 NG85

Babies Welcome	Family Rooms	Children's Dishes

★ ◉ ◉ Tigh an Eilean
V54 8XN
☎ 01520 755251 ▤ 01520 755321
...-mail: tighaneileanhotel@shieldaig.fsnet.co.uk
...ir: off A896 onto village road signped Shieldaig, hotel in centre of village ...n loch front

CHILD FACILITIES: Baby listening Activities: toys, jigsaws, shrimping Food/bottle warming Ch menu Ch portions Highchairs Ch cutlery Ch discounts under 8s free, 8-13s 50% Safe grounds Cots Family rms D rm with S bed £120 Laundry **NEARBY:** Seafront location

A superb location on the seafront with views over the bay the ...cing on the cake for this delightful small hotel. Most guests ...nvariably endure a long drive to reach Sheildaig but the ...verriding consensus is that the journey is more than worth the ...ffort. Genuine hospitality and well-developed customer-care skills ...as produced a loyal following that appreciate the superb ...ccommodation, outstanding cooking at dinner and the polished ...et intimate service. The brightly decorated bedrooms vary in size ...ut are furnished to a high standard, though don't expect ...elevisions.

ROOMS: 11 en suite (1 fmly) s fr £55; s fr £120 (incl. bkfst) **LB**
FACILITIES: no TV in bdrms Bird watching, Boat available, Kayaks, ...stronomy **PARKING:** 15 **NOTES:** ☺ in restaurant Closed late Oct-end ...Mar

---

All AA listed accommodation, restaurants and pubs can be found on the AA's website www.theAA.com

---

AA The Hotel Guide 2005
Britain's best-selling hotel guide for all your leisure needs.

Just **AA** sk.

www.theAA.com

SKEABOST BRIDGE   Map 13 NG44

Babies Welcome	Family Rooms	Children's Dishes

★★★ 69% ◉ Skeabost Country House
IV51 9NP
☎ 01470 532202 01470 532215 ▤ 01470 532454
e-mail: reception@skeabostcountryhouse.com
Dir: on A87 north of Portree, left onto A850. Hotel 1.5 miles on right, just beyond Snizort River bridge

CHILD FACILITIES: Baby listening Nanny Babysitting Activities: entertainers, colouring, party packs Indoor play area Outdoor play area Family area Food/bottle warming Ch menu Ch portions Highchairs Ch cutlery Ch discounts Safe grounds Videos Cots Family rms from £110 Ch drinks Fridge Laundry (some) **NEARBY:** Boat trips Walks Pony riding Lochside

This 19th-century house is set amid 12 acres of secluded woodland and gardens, beside the picturesque shore of Loch Snizort. Comfortable public areas include a choice of inviting lounges warmed by roaring log fires. Dinner provides a sense of occasion; the daily-changing, fixed-price menu features tempting, carefully prepared dishes, mostly locally sourced. Bedrooms are provided in a variety of styles.

ROOMS: 17 en suite 4 annexe en suite (1 fmly) (9 GF) ☺ in all bedrooms s £80-£90; d £100-£110 (incl. bkfst) **LB FACILITIES:** STV Golf 9 Fishing Snooker ♫ Xmas **PARKING:** 100 **NOTES:** ✗ ☺ in restaurant

---

SPEAN BRIDGE   Map 14 NN28

◆◆◆◆ Distant Hills
PH34 4EU
☎ 01397 712452 ▤ 01397 712452
e-mail: enquiry@distanthills.com
web: www.distanthills.com
Dir: turn off A82 from Fort William to Inverness onto A86 at junct in village of Spean Bridge. Establishment 0.5m on right

CHILD FACILITIES: Please telephone for details

A warm and friendly welcome is assured at this family-run guest house set in its own well-tended garden. Bedrooms are maintained to a high standard with tasteful modern appointments. There is a spacious split-level lounge, with access to the large garden. Enjoyable home cooked evening meals (by prior arrangement) and hearty Scottish breakfasts are served on individual tables in the peaceful dining room.

ROOMS: 7 en suite s £30-£50; d £42-£50 * ☺ **FACILITIES:** TVB tea/coffee TVL No coaches Dinner Last d order 2pm **NOTES:** ☺ in restaurant Cen ht **PARKING:** 10

STEIN   Map 13 NG25

Babies Welcome	Children's Dishes

◉ Loch Bay Seafood Restaurant
IV55 8GA
☎ 01470 592235 ▤ 592235
e-mail: david@lochbay-seafood-restaurant.co.uk

CHILD FACILITIES: Activities: colouring Food/bottle warming Ch portions Highchairs **NEARBY:** Galleries Tannery Seafront location

FOOD: British, Seafood **STYLE:** Minimalist Bistro **SEATS:** 26
OPEN: 12-2.30/6-9, Closed Nov-Easter (excl. 1wk over Hogmanay), SunL Sat **RESTAURANT:** main £8.50-£30 **NOTES:** ☺ in restaurant **PARKING:** 6

Scotland

STRATHPEFFER Map 14 NH45

 Babies Welcome | Family Rooms | Children's Dishes

◆◆◆ Inver Lodge

IV14 9DL

☎ 01997 421392

e-mail: derbyshire@inverlg.fsnet.co.uk

Dir: from A834 through Strathpeffer centre, turn beside Spa Pavilion signed Bowling Green. Inver Lodge on right

CHILD FACILITIES: Activities: books, toys, games, jigsaws, colouring Food/bottle warming Ch menu Ch portions Highchairs Ch cutlery Ch discounts under 3s free, 4-14s 50% sharing with adults Safe grounds Cots Family rms triple rm with chair bed & cot from £34 Ch drinks Laundry **NEARBY:** Museum Swimming pool Tennis courts Play park Cycle hire

Guests are assured of a warm welcome at this Victorian lodge, situated within easy walking distance of the town centre. Bedrooms are comfortable and well equipped. Imaginative breakfasts, and by prior arrangement, enjoyable home-cooked evening meals, are served at a communal table.

ROOMS: 2 rms (1 fmly) s £25-£28; d £34 * **FACILITIES:** TVB tea/coffee No coaches Fishing and riding can be arranged Dinner Last d order 4pm **NOTES:** ✠ ⊛ Cen ht **LB BB PARKING:** 2

TOMATIN Map 14 NH82

 Babies Welcome | Family Rooms | Children's Dishes

◆◆◆ Glenan Lodge

IV13 7YT

☎ 01808 511217 ▤ 01808 511356

e-mail: enquiries@glenlodge.co.uk

web: www.glenanlodge.co.uk

Dir: turn off A9 to Tomatin, at Little Chef. Sign to Lodge ahead

CHILD FACILITIES: Activities: jigsaws, games Food/bottle warming Ch menu Ch portions Highchairs Ch discounts under 5s free, 5-15s £15 Cots Family rms D rms with 5 beds Ch drinks (chocolate) **NEARBY:** Theme park Loch Ness Visitor Centre

Enjoying a peaceful rural location on the edge of the village, this relaxed and homely guest house offers a warm welcome. The comfortable bedrooms are traditionally furnished and delicious home-cooked evening meals and breakfasts are served in the dining room. A two-mile stretch of the River Findhorn is available for fly fishing, and golfers, walkers and bird watchers are also well provided for locally.

ROOMS: 7 en suite (2 fmly) s £25; d £45 * **FACILITIES:** TVB tea/coffee TVL No coaches Fishing Dinner Last d order 6pm **NOTES:** ⊛ Licensed Cen ht **LB**

TONGUE Map 14 NC5

 Babies Welcome | Children's Dishes

ⓤ Borgie Lodge Hotel

Skerray KW14 7TH

☎ 01641 521332 ▤ 01641 521332

e-mail: info@borgielodgehotel.co.uk

web: www.borgielodgehotel.co.uk

CHILD FACILITIES: Baby listening Babysitting Activities: croquet Outdoor play area Food/bottle warming Ch portions Highchairs Ch cutlery Ch discounts under 3s free, children sharing with parents £10, own room £30 Safe grounds Videos Cots Ch drinks Connecting rms Laundry **NEARBY:** Walks Pony trekking Cycling Leisure pool 1.5m to sea

At the time of going to press, the star classification for this hotel was not confirmed. Please refer to the AA internet site www.theAA.com for current information.

ROOMS: 8 rms (7 en suite) (1 GF) ⊛ in all bedrooms **FACILITIES:** Fishing ⌥ Mountain bikes, Shooting, Stalking, Boating **PARKING:** 20 **NOTES:** ⊛ in restaurant Closed Nov - Feb

TORRIDON Map 14 NG9

Babies Welcome | Children's Dishes

★★★ ⊛ ⊛ ⌥

Loch Torridon Country House

By Achnasheen, Wester Ross IV22 2EY

☎ 01445 791242 ▤ 01445 791296

e-mail: stay@lochtorridonhotel.com

web: www.lochtorridonhotel.com

Dir: from A832 at Kinlochewe, take the A896 towards Torridon, do not turn into village carry on for 1m, hotel on right

CHILD FACILITIES: Baby listening Babysitting Activities: outdoor activities, junior archery Food/bottle warming Ch portions Highchairs Ch cutlery Ch discounts under 10s £20 sharing with parents Safe grounds Videos Cots Laundry **NEARBY:** Walks

Delightfully set amidst inspiring loch and mountain scenery, this elegant Victorian shooting lodge has been beautifully restored to make the most of its many original features. The attractive bedrooms are all individually furnished and most enjoy stunning Highland views. Comfortable day rooms feature fine wood panelling and roaring fires in cooler months. Outdoor activities include shooting, cycling and walking.

ROOMS: 19 en suite (2 GF) ⊛ in all bedrooms s £64-£110; d £101-£33? (incl. bkfst) **LB FACILITIES:** STV Fishing ⌥ Pony trekking, Mountain biking, Archery, Clay pigeon shooting, Falconry Xmas **PARKING:** 20 **NOTES:** ⊛ in restaurant Closed 3-27 Jan

PERTH & KINROSS

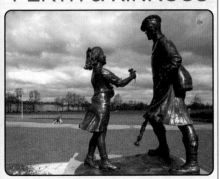

South Inch Gardens, Perth

BLAIR ATHOLL
Blair Castle PH18 5TL
office@blair-castle.co.uk ☎01796 481207
(7m NW of Pitlochry, off A9)
Open, 2 Nov-15 Mar, Tue-Sat 9.30-12.30,
19 Mar-28 Oct, 9.30-4.30.

KINROSS
Loch Leven Castle
KY137AR ☎01786 450000
(on an island in Loch Leven accessible by boat)
from Kinross Open Apr-Sep, daily 9.30-6.30.
*£3.50 (ch £1.20, concessions £2.50). Charge
includes ferry trip.
RSPB Nature Reserve Vane Farm KY13 9LX
vane.farm@rspb.org.uk ☎01577 862355
(on S shore of Loch Leven, via B9097 to
Glenrothes, 2m E M90 junct 5)
Open daily, 10-5. Closed 25-26 Dec, 1-2 Jan.
£3 (ch 50p, concessions £2). Family £6.

PERTH
Branklyn Garden OH2 7BB
aclipson@nts.scot.demon.co.uk ☎01738 625535
(On A85)
Open Apr & Jul-Sep, Fri-Tue 10-5; May-Jun, daily,
10-5. £5 (concessions £3.75) Group adult £4
(child/school £1), groups please book in advance.
Family ticket £13.50. Admission free to NTS
members.

PITLOCHRY
*Scottish & Southern Energy Visitor Centre
Dam & Fish Pass*
PH16 5ND ☎01796 473152
(Turn off A9, 24m N of Perth)
Open Apr-Sep, Mon-Fri 10-5.30. (Weekend
opening Jul, Aug & BHs).

SCONE
Scone Palace PH2 6BD
visits@scone-palace.co.uk ☎01738 552300
(2m NE of Perth on A93)
Open Apr-Oct.

Babies Welcome | Family Rooms | Children's Dishes

★★★★★ ◎◎◎◎ **The Gleneagles Hotel**
PH3 1NF
☎ 01764 662231 📠 01764 662134
e-mail: resort.sales@gleneagles.com
Dir: off A9 at exit for A823 follow signs for Gleneagles Hotel

CHILD FACILITIES: Babysitting Activities: playroom, junior golf
lessons, junior off road driving, riding lessons, kiddies kitchen Indoor
play area Outdoor play area Food/bottle warming Ch menu
Ch portions Highchairs Ch cutlery Ch discounts under 5s free, 6-14s
sharing adults' room £45 Safe grounds Games consoles Videos Cots
Family rms D rm with cot or extra bed £305-£390 Ch drinks
Connecting rms Fridge Laundry

With its international reputation for high standards, this grand
hotel provides something for everyone. Set in a delightful location,
Gleneagles offers a peaceful retreat, as well as many sporting
activities, including the famous championship golf courses.
Afternoon tea is a feature, and cocktails are prepared with flair
and skill at the bar. Amongst the dining options is Strathearn, with
two AA rosettes, as well as some inspired cooking at Andrew
Fairlie at Gleneagles, a restaurant with four rosettes. Service is
always professional, staff are friendly and nothing is too much
trouble.
ROOMS: 270 en suite (115 fmly) (11 GF) ◎ in 149 bedrooms
d £330-£465 (incl. bkfst) **LB FACILITIES: Spa** STV 🖭 ⚹ Golf 18 ☏
Fishing Squash Riding Snooker Sauna Solarium Gym 🎱 ⚷ Jacuzzi
Falconry, Equestrian, Off roading, Golf range, Archery, Clay target shooting
🎵 Xmas **PARKING:** 200

◆◆◆◆ **Merlindale**
Perth Rd PH7 3EQ
☎ 01764 655205 📠 01764 655205
e-mail: merlin.dale@virgin.net
web: www.merlindale.co.uk
*Dir: Leave A9 take A822 through Greenloaning/Braco/Muthill to Crieff.
Follows signs for town centre on A85, 500yds on right Tower Hotel straight
past Houseproud on right Merlindale 4th house on left*

CHILD FACILITIES: Please telephone for details

Situated in a quiet residential area, within walking distance of the
town centre, this delightful detached house stands in well-tended
grounds and offers a warm welcome. The pretty bedrooms are
comfortably furnished and well equipped. There is a spacious
lounge, an impressive library and an elegant dining room, which is
the setting for delicious evening meals and traditional breakfasts.
ROOMS: 3 en suite (1 fmly) **FACILITIES:** TVB tea/coffee No coaches
Dinner Last d order 24 hrs in advance **NOTES:** Credit cards not taken ✈
◎ Cen ht **PARKING:** 3

Scotland

KILLIECRANKIE　　　　　　　　　　　Map 14 NN96

Babies Welcome	Family Rooms	Children's Dishes

★★ 77% ◉ ◉ Killiecrankie House
PH16 5LG
☎ 01796 473220 ▤ 01796 472451
e-mail: enquiries@killiecrankiehotel.co.uk
web: www.killiecrankiehotel.co.uk
Dir: off A9 at Killiecrankie, hotel 3m along B8079 on right

CHILD FACILITIES:　Baby listening　Activities: games　Food/bottle warming　Ch menu　Ch portions　Highchairs　Ch discounts　under 2s free, 2-16s £20　Safe grounds　Cots　Family rms　D rms with sofa beds £79　Ch drinks　Connecting rms　NEARBY:　Walks　Parks　Blair Castle

A long-established hotel set in mature grounds close to the historic Pass of Killiecrankie. Red squirrels are found in the grounds. The owners Tim and Maillie Waters and their charming staff provide friendly and attentive service. Accomplished cooking can be enjoyed in the atmospheric restaurant, and a healthy and tasty selection of dishes can be found in the bar.

ROOMS: 10 en suite (2 fmly) (2 GF) ⊗ in all bedrooms s £79-£99; d £158-£198 (incl. bkfst & dinner) **LB　FACILITIES:** ⚒ ⚓ Xmas **PARKING:** 20 **NOTES:** ⊗ in restaurant Closed 3 Jan - 14 Feb RS Nov, Dec, Feb & Mar

KINROSS　　　　　　　　　　　　　Map 11 NO10

★★★ 75% Green
2 The Muirs KY13 8AS
☎ 01577 863467 ▤ 01577 863180
e-mail: reservations@green-hotel.com
web: www.green-hotel.com
Dir: M90 junct 6 follow signs for Kinross, turn onto A922, hotel situated on this road

CHILD FACILITIES:　Please telephone for details

A long-established hotel offering a wide range of indoor and outdoor activities. Public areas include a classical restaurant and a well-stocked gift shop. The comfortable, well-equipped bedrooms, most of which are generously proportioned, boast attractive colour schemes and smart modern furnishings.

ROOMS: 46 en suite (4 fmly) (14 GF) ⊗ in 12 bedrooms s £85-£105; d £150-£170 (incl. bkfst) **LB　FACILITIES:** STV ⚓ Golf 36 ✑ Fishing Squash Sauna Solarium Gym ⚒ ⚓ Curling in season, Petanque (French boules) Xmas **PARKING:** 60 **NOTES:** ⊗ in restaurant Closed 23-28 Dec excluding Xmas day RS 25 Dec

Babies Welcome	Family Rooms	Children's Dishes

◆◆◆◆ ⦿ Muirs Inn Kinross
49 Muirs KY13 8AU
☎ 01577 862270 ▤ 01577 862270
e-mail: themuirsinn@aol.com
Dir: off M90 junct 6 and follow signs for A922 at T-junct. Inn diagonally opposite on right

CHILD FACILITIES:　Activities: colouring　Food/bottle warming Ch menu　Ch portions　Highchairs　Ch cutlery　Ch discounts　under 5s free　Family rms　adjoining rms　NEARBY:　Leisure centre

A friendly atmosphere prevails at this inn whose buildings date from the 1800s. The main bar boasts exposed stone walls and wood and flagstone floors. Home cooked fare is served in the attractive restaurant. The cosy cottage style bedrooms are well equipped.

ROOMS: 4 en suite (1 fmly) s fr £35; d fr £60 * ⊗ **FACILITIES:** STV TVB tea/coffee Dinner Last o order 9pm **NOTES:** ✖ ⊗ in area of dining room Cen ht **PARKING:** 10

PITLOCHRY　　　　　　　　　　　Map 14 NN95

⦿ Moulin Hotel ★★
11-13 Kirkmichael Rd, Moulin PH16 5EW
☎ 01796 472196 ▤ 01796 474098
e-mail: enquiries@moulinhotel.co.uk
web: www.moulinhotel.co.uk
Dir: From A924 at Pitlochry take A923. Moulin 0.75m

CHILD FACILITIES:　Please telephone for details

Steeped in history, original parts of this friendly hotel date back to 1695. The Moulin bar, serves an excellent choice of bar meals as well as real ales from the hotel's own microbrewery. Alternatively, guests can eat in the comfortable restaurant which overlooks the Moulin Burn. Bedrooms are well equipped, with many having been refurbished.

OPEN: 12-11 (Fri-Sat 12-11.45) **BAR MEALS:** L served all week 12-9.30 D served all week Av main course £7.50 **RESTAURANT:** D served all week 6-9 Av 4 course fixed price £19.95 **FACILITIES:** Garden: Behind hotel, next to stream ✖ **ROOMS:** 15 bedrooms 15 en suite 3 family rooms s£40 d£50 **PARKING:** 40

ST FILLANS　　　　　　　　　　　Map 11 NN62

Babies Welcome	Family Rooms	Children's Dishes

★★★ 68% ◉ ◉ The Four Seasons Hotel
Loch Earn PH6 2NF
☎ 01764 685333 ▤ 01764 685444
e-mail: info@thefourseasonshotel.co.uk
web: www.thefourseasonshotel.co.uk
Dir: on A85, towards W of village facing Loch

CHILD FACILITIES:　Baby listening　Activities: toys　Food/bottle warming　Ch menu　Ch portions　Highchairs　Ch discounts　under 3s free, 3-11s 50%　Safe grounds　Videos　Cots　Family rms　D rm with S & B beds　Laundry　NEARBY:　Wildlife farm　Walks　Loch

Set on the edge of Loch Earn, this welcoming hotel and many of its bedrooms benefit from fine views. There is a choice of lounges, including a library, warmed by log fires during winter. Local produce is used to good effect in both the Meall Reamhar restaurant and the more informal Tarken Room.

ROOMS: 12 en suite 6 annexe en suite (7 fmly) ⊗ in 3 bedrooms s £40-£78; d £80-£106 (incl. bkfst) **LB　FACILITIES:** Xmas **PARKING:** 40 **NOTES:** ⊗ in restaurant Closed 5 Jan-end of Feb RS Nov, Dec, Mar

RENFREWSHIRE

HOUSTON　　　　　　　　　　　　Map 10 NS46

⦿ Fox & Hounds
South St PA6 7EN
☎ 01505 612448 612991 ▤ 01505 614133
e-mail: jonathan@foxandhoundshouston.co.uk
Dir: M8 - Glasgow Airport. A737 - Houston

CHILD FACILITIES:　Please telephone for details

OPEN: 11-12 (11-1am Fri-Sat, 12.30-12 Sun) **BAR MEALS:** L served all week 12-2.30 D served all week 5.30-10 Av main course £7.50 **RESTAURANT:** L served all week 12-2.30 D served all week 5.30-10 Av 3 course à la carte £25 **FACILITIES:** Children's licence **PARKING:** 40

LOCHWINNOCH   Map 10 NS35

Babies Welcome	Family Rooms	Children's Dishes

◆◆◆◆◆ 🏚 🚲 East Lochhead

Largs Rd PA12 4DX
☎ 01505 842610 📠 01505 842610
e-mail: admin@eastlochhead.co.uk
web: www.eastlochhead.co.uk
Dir: from Glasgow take M8 junct 28a for A737 Irvine. At Roadhead rdbt turn right on A760. Premises 2m on left, look for brown tourist sign

> **CHILD FACILITIES:** Baby listening Family area Food/bottle warming Ch menu Ch portions Highchairs Ch cutlery Ch discounts under 5s £10, 5-12s £20 Safe grounds Cots Family rms D rm with 1 S bed Ch drinks Laundry **NEARBY:** Water sports centre Cycle route Kelburn Countryside Centre

A relaxed country-house atmosphere prevails at this former farmhouse, which dates back to the 1800s. Sitting in colourful and immaculately maintained grounds, the house boasts magnificent views over Barr Loch. The stylishly furnished bedrooms are attractive and superbly equipped. There is a combined lounge/dining room where delicious breakfasts are served. A barn has been tastefully converted into five self-contained units with their own private entrances, and a separate barn hosts a function room.
ROOMS: 3 en suite (1 fmly) (1 GF) s £45-£55; d £70-£80 *
FACILITIES: TVB tea/coffee TVL No coaches Cycle hire Dinner Last d order 10am **NOTES:** ⊗ Licensed Cen ht **LB PARKING:** 24

SCOTTISH BORDERS

GALASHIELS   Map 12 NT43

Babies Welcome	Children's Dishes

🍴 Kingsknowles ★★★

1 Selkirk Rd TD1 3HY
☎ 01896 758375 📠 01896 750377
e-mail: enquiries@kingsknowles.co.uk
web: www.kingsknowles.co.uk
Dir: Off A7 at Galashiels/Selkirk rdbt

> **CHILD FACILITIES:** Outdoor play area Food/bottle warming Ch licence Ch menu Ch portions Highchairs Ch cutlery

An imposing turreted mansion, this hotel lies in attractive gardens on the outskirts of town close to the River Tweed. It boasts elegant public areas and many spacious bedrooms, some with excellent views. There is a choice of bars, one with a popular menu to supplement the restaurant.
OPEN: 12-12 **BAR MEALS:** L served all week 11.45-2 D served all week 5.45-9.30 Av main course £6.75 **RESTAURANT:** L served all week 11.45-2 D served all week 5.45-9.30 Av 3 course à la carte £17 Av 5 course fixed price £16.95 **FACILITIES:** Garden: 3.5 acres, lawn, rockery **ROOMS:** 12 bedrooms 12 en suite 3 family rooms s£54 d£89 **PARKING:** 60

Family Rooms	This symbol indicates family rooms are available, with type of room and prices included if provided

LAUDER   Map 12 NT54

Babies Welcome	Family Rooms	Children's Dishes

★★ 67% Lauderdale

1 Edinburgh Rd TD2 6TW
☎ 01578 722231 📠 01578 718642
e-mail: enquiries@lauderdale-hotel.co.uk
web: www.lauderdale-hotel.co.uk
Dir: on A68 from S, drive through centre of Lauder, hotel on right. From Edinburgh, hotel is on left at 1st bend after passing sign for Lauder

> **CHILD FACILITIES:** Baby listening Activities: toys Food/bottle warming Ch menu Ch portions Highchairs Ch discounts Safe grounds Cots Family rms D rm with 2 S beds £110 based on 2 adults & 2 under 12s Laundry **NEARBY:** Stately homes Thirlestone Castle

Lying on the north side of the village with spacious gardens to the side and rear, this friendly hotel is ideally placed for those wishing to stay outside of Edinburgh itself. A good range of meals is served in both the bar and the restaurant. The well-equipped bedrooms come in a variety of sizes.
ROOMS: 10 en suite (1 fmly) ⊗ in all bedrooms s £42; d £70-£80 (incl. bkfst) **FACILITIES:** STV Xmas **PARKING:** 200 **NOTES:** ✕ ⊗ in restaurant

PEEBLES   Map 11 NT24

Babies Welcome	Family Rooms	Children's Dishes

★★★★ 70% Peebles Hotel Hydro

EH45 8LX
☎ 01721 720602 📠 01721 722999
e-mail: info@peebleshydro.com
web: www.peebleshydro.com
Dir: on A702, one third mile out of town

> **CHILD FACILITIES:** Baby listening Activities: summer activities, playroom, colouring, painting, puzzles Indoor play area Outdoor play area Food/bottle warming Ch menu Ch portions Highchairs Ch cutlery Ch discounts (incl high tea & breakfast) Safe grounds Games consoles Videos Cots Family rms D & T rms with B beds in adj rm Connecting rms Laundry **NEARBY:** Leisure centre Walks Parks Neidpath Castle Edinburgh

This privately owned resort hotel benefits from an elevated location with striking views across the valley. Its range of indoor and outdoor leisure activities is second to none and makes the hotel a favourite with families. Accommodation comes in a range of styles and includes a number of family rooms.
ROOMS: 128 en suite (25 fmly) (15 GF) s £114-£125; d £182-£298 (incl. bkfst & dinner) **LB FACILITIES:** Spa STV ⊡ 🏌 Riding Snooker Sauna Solarium Gym ♨ ♨ Badminton, Beautician, Hairdressing, Giant Chess & Draughts, Pitch & Putt 🎵 Xmas **PARKING:** 200 **NOTES:** ✕ ⊗ in restaurant

ST BOSWELLS   Map 12 NT53

Babies Welcome | Children's Dishes

⚓ Buccleuch Arms Hotel ★★
The Green TD6 0EW
☎ 01835 822243 ▤ 01835 823965
e-mail: info@buccleucharmshotel.co.uk
web: www.buccleucharmshotel.co.uk
Dir: On A68, 8m N of Jedburgh

CHILD FACILITIES: Outdoor play area Food/bottle warming
Ch licence Ch menu Ch portions Highchairs Safe
grounds Changing facilities **NEARBY:** Harestanes Visitor Centre
Bowhill Country Park Floors Castle

Formerly a coaching inn, this long-established hotel stands
opposite the village green. The lounge bar is a popular eating
venue and complements the restaurant, and morning coffee and
afternoon tea are served in the attractive lounge with its open fire.
The well-equipped bedrooms come in a variety of sizes.
OPEN: 7.30-11 Closed: 25 Dec **BAR MEALS:** L served all week 12-2 D
served all week 6-9 Av main course £7.50 **RESTAURANT:** L served all
week 12-2 D served all week 6-9 Av 3 course fixed price £21.95
FACILITIES: Garden: Quiet, spacious & peaceful garden **ROOMS:** 19
bedrooms 19 en suite 1 family rooms s£46 d£38.50 **PARKING:** 80

SOUTH AYRSHIRE

AYR   Map 10 NS32

★★★ 72% Savoy Park   THE INDEPENDENTS
16 Racecourse Rd KA7 2UT
☎ 01292 266112 ▤ 01292 611488
e-mail: mail@savoypark.com
*Dir: from A77 follow Holmston Road(A70) for 2m, through Parkhouse
Street, turn left into Beresford Terrace, 1st right into Bellevue Rd*

CHILD FACILITIES: Please telephone for details

This well-established hotel retains many of its traditional values.
Public rooms feature impressive panelled walls, ornate ceilings
and open fires. The restaurant is reminiscent of a Highland
shooting lodge and offers a good value menu to suit all tastes. The
large superior bedrooms retain a classical elegance while others
are smart and modern; all have lovely bathrooms.
ROOMS: 15 en suite (3 fmly) ⊗ in all bedrooms s £75-£85; d £95-£115
(incl. bkfst) **LB FACILITIES:** STV Xmas **PARKING:** 60 **NOTES:** ⊗ in
restaurant

Babies Welcome | Family Rooms | Children's Dishes

◆◆◆ Belmont
15 Park Circus KA7 2DJ
☎ 01292 265588 ▤ 01292 290303
e-mail: belmontguesthouse@btinternet.com
web: www.belmontguesthouse.co.uk
*Dir: off A77 onto A70. At double rdbt follow Town Centre signs. Over
railway bridge and left at traffic lights. After next lights turn right into
Bellevue St. At end of street right into park circus establishment on right*

CHILD FACILITIES: Activities: games, books Food/bottle warming
Ch portions Highchairs Ch cutlery Ch discounts under 10s free,
10-15s half price Cots Family rms rm with 2 D beds, D rm with 1 S
bed, D with 2 S beds from £46 **NEARBY:** Leisure centre Cinema
Bowling Park 5-min walk to sea

continued

Run along traditional lines, Belmont is a terraced house in a quiet
tree-lined area, close to the town centre. Spacious bedrooms
come with thoughtful extras. Public areas include a lounge with a
vast array of books and a comfortable dining room. The hosts
demonstrate a genuine concern for conservation and
environmental issues.
ROOMS: 5 en suite (3 fmly) (2 GF) s £26; d £46 * **FACILITIES:** TVB
tea/coffee TVL No coaches **NOTES:** Cen ht **PARKING:** 5

◆◆◆ Windsor Hotel
6 Alloway Place KA7 2AA
☎ 01292 264689
e-mail: windsorhotel.ayr@ukonline.co.uk
Dir: from centre of Ayr, take A19 through Wellington Sq. Hotel 1st on right.
CHILD FACILITIES: Please telephone for details
This friendly private hotel is situated between the seafront and
town centre. Bedrooms are well presented, with several on the
ground floor and some suitable for families. The upstairs lounge
looks towards the sea, whilst tasty breakfasts are served in the
ground floor dining room.
ROOMS: 10 rms (7 en suite) (4 fmly) (3 GF) s fr £25; d fr £50 * ⊗ in
1 bedrooms **FACILITIES:** TVB tea/coffee TVL No coaches **NOTES:** ⊗
in restaurant Cen ht **LB**

◉ ◉ Fouters
2A Academy St KA7 1HS
☎ 01292 261391 ▤ 01292 619323
e-mail: qualityfood@fouters.co.uk
web: www.fouters.co.uk
Dir: Town centre, opposite Town Hall, down Cobblestone Lane.
CHILD FACILITIES: Please telephone for details
FOOD: International **STYLE:** Traditional, Minimalist **SEATS:** 38
OPEN: 12-2.30/5-10, Closed 4-11 Jan, Sun-Mon **RESTAURANT:** main
£11.95-£19.95 **NOTES:** ⊗ in restaurant, Air con **PARKING:** On street

SOUTH LANARKSHIRE

KIRKMUIRHILL   Map 11 NS74

Children's Dishes

◆◆◆ ♥ Dykecroft
ML11 0JQ
☎ 01555 892226 ▤ 01555 892226
*Dir: from S M74 junct 10 (from N junct 9), take B7078 for 2m, then B7086
to Strathaven for 1.5m, past Boghead, 1st bungalow on left*
CHILD FACILITIES: Outdoor play area Food/bottle warming
Ch menu Ch portions Ch discounts under 2s free sharing with
parents Videos Ch drinks Laundry **NEARBY:** Parks Leisure
centres Swimming pool Loch Quad Bikes
A warm and friendly welcome is assured at this modern
bungalow, situated in an open rural location on the road to
Strathaven. The bedrooms are traditionally furnished and
comfortable. There is a bright airy lounge/dining room that enjoys
lovely countryside views.
ROOMS: 3 rms (3 GF) s £23; d £42 * **FACILITIES:** tea/coffee TVL 60
acres sheep **NOTES:** Credit cards not taken ⊗ Cen ht **PARKING:** 4

How to use this guide & abbreviations
are explained on pages 5-7

STIRLING

WEST DUNBARTONSHIRE

CALLANDER
Map 11 NN60

| Babies Welcome | Family Rooms | Children's Dishes |

◆◆◆◆ 🏛 The Priory Country Guest House
Bracklinn Rd FK17 8EH
☎ 01877 330001 📠 01877 339200
e-mail: judith@bracklinnroad.fsnet.co.uk
Dir: M9 to Stirling, take A84 signed to Crianlarich/Callander. After 7m through Doune, then 6m to Callander. Turn right into Bracklinn Rd, house on R

> **CHILD FACILITIES:** Family area Food/bottle warming Ch portions Highchairs Ch discounts Safe grounds Cots Family rms D rm with 2 S beds **NEARBY:** Walks Park River

Warm, genuine hospitality can be found at this delightful house, set in a peaceful location yet within easy walking distance of the town centre. The stylish bedrooms are tastefully decorated and thoughtfully equipped; one has a four-poster. There is an elegant lounge adjacent to the conservatory dining room, where delicious breakfasts, using local produce, are served.

ROOMS: 9 rms (8 en suite) (1 fmly) (1 GF) s fr £45; d fr £80 *
FACILITIES: TV8B tea/coffee TVL No coaches Golf 18 Golf discount available at local golf club **NOTES:** ⊗ Cen ht **PARKING:** 9

DUNBLANE
Map 11 NN70

| Babies Welcome | Family Rooms | Children's Dishes |

★★★ ◉◉ ⚘ Cromlix House
Kinbuck FK15 9JT
☎ 01786 822125 📠 01786 825450
e-mail: reservations@cromlixhouse.com
web: www.cromlixhouse.com
Dir: off A9 N of Dunblane. Exit B8033 to Kinbuck Village then after village cross narrow bridge drive 200yds on left

> **CHILD FACILITIES:** Baby listening Food/bottle warming Ch portions Highchairs Ch discounts cots free Cots Family rms suites & apartments Connecting rms Fridge **NEARBY:** Ceramic Experience Wildlife Park Cinema Leisure Centre

Nestling in sweeping gardens and surrounded by a 2000-acre estate, Cromlix House is an imposing Victorian mansion, boasting gracious and inviting public areas. Well-appointed bedrooms, the majority of which are suites, are spacious and elegant. The two dining rooms offer contrasting décor but both ideal in which to enjoy the skilfully prepared food.

ROOMS: 14 en suite s £140-£210; d £235-£385 (incl. bkfst) **LB**
FACILITIES: ⚘ Fishing ⚑ Clay pigeon shooting, Falconry, Archery Xmas
PARKING: 51 **NOTES:** ⊗ in restaurant Closed 2-29 Jan RS Oct-Apr

KIPPEN
Map 11 NS69

🍷 Cross Keys Hotel
Main St FK8 3DN
☎ 01786 870293 📠 01786 870293
e-mail: crosskeys@kippen70.fsnet.co.uk
> **CHILD FACILITIES:** Please telephone for details

OPEN: 12-2.30 5.30-11 (Fri-Sat 5.30-12 Sun 12.30-11) Closed: 25 Dec, 1 Jan
BAR MEALS: L served all week 12-2 D served all week 5.30-9 Av main course £6.95 **RESTAURANT:** L served all week 12-2 D served all week 5.30-9 **FACILITIES:** Garden: Small garden with water feature, good views
PARKING: 5

BALLOCH
Map 10 NS38

| Babies Welcome | Family Rooms | Children's Dishes |

★★★★★ 69% ◉ ◉ ◉
De Vere Cameron House
DE VERE ● HOTELS
G83 8QZ
☎ 01389 755565 📠 01389 759522
e-mail: reservations@cameronhouse.co.uk
web: www.devereonline.co.uk/cameronhouse
Dir: M8 (W) junct 30 for Erskine Bridge. Then A82 for Crainlarich. After 14m, at rdbt signed Luss straight on towards Luss, hotel on right

> **CHILD FACILITIES:** Babysitting Activities: Kid's club, creche Indoor play area Outdoor play area Family area Food/bottle warming Ch menu Ch portions Highchairs Ch cutlery Ch discounts Safe grounds Games consoles Videos Cots Family rms D rm with B beds Ch drinks Connecting rms Fridge Laundry **NEARBY:** Blair Drummond Safari Park Stirling Castle Near Loch Lomond

Enjoying an idyllic location on the banks of Loch Lomond, this leisure-orientated hotel offers spacious, well-equipped accommodation. Bedrooms vary in size and style and many boast wonderful views of the loch. A choice of restaurants, bars and lounges, a host of indoor and outdoor sporting activities and a smart spa are just some of the facilities available. Dinner in the Georgian room is a highlight of any stay.

ROOMS: 96 en suite (9 fmly) ⊗ in all bedrooms s £150-£200; d £200-£495 (incl. bkfst) **LB FACILITIES: Spa** STV 🎱 Golf 9 ⚘ Fishing Squash Snooker Sauna Solarium Gym ⚑ Jacuzzi Whole range of outdoor sports, Motor boat on Loch Lomond, Hairdressers Xmas
PARKING: 200 **NOTES:** ✈

Scotland

SCOTTISH ISLANDS

ARRAN, ISLE OF

BLACKWATERFOOT   Map 10 NR92

★★★ 68% **Kinloch**
KA27 8ET
☎ 01770 860444 📠 01770 860447

Best Western

e-mail: reservations@kinlochhotel.eclipse.co.uk
Dir: Ferry from Ardrossan to Brodick, follow signs for Blackwaterfoot, hotel in centre of village

CHILD FACILITIES: Please telephone for details

This family-run hotel overlooks the Mull of Kintyre. Spacious public areas include a choice of lounges, bars and good leisure facilities. Bedrooms offer mixed modern appointments and are gradually being upgraded. The main dining room offers a well-prepared and innovative four course dinner menu, in addition to meals served in the bars.
ROOMS: 43 en suite (7 fmly) (7 GF) ⊗ in 24 bedrooms s £35-£51.50; d £70-£103 (incl. bkfst) **LB FACILITIES:** STV ⊞ Squash Snooker Sauna Gym Beauty therapy ♫ Xmas **PARKING:** 2 **NOTES:** ⊗ in restaurant

See advert on opposite page

BRODICK   Map 10 NS03

Babies Welcome	Family Rooms	Children's Dishes

★★★ 76% ⚙️🏵️ *Auchrannie Country House*
KA27 8BZ
☎ 01770 302234 📠 01770 302812
e-mail: info@auchrannie.co.uk
Dir: turn right from Brodick Ferry terminal, through Brodick village, 2nd left after Brodick Golf Course clubhouse, 300yds to hotel

CHILD FACILITIES: Baby listening Activities: bouncy castle, on-site pools, face painting, colouring, games Indoor play area Food/bottle warming Ch menu Ch portions Highchairs Ch discounts under 16s £20 sharing with parents Safe grounds Cots Family rms D rm with 2 S beds £45-£99 Ch drinks Connecting rms Fridge Laundry **NEARBY:** Brodick Castle Quad & cycle tracks 10-min walk to sea

This Victorian mansion lies in landscaped grounds and provides well-equipped bedrooms. Dine in the 'Garden Restaurant' or the bistro, while a brasserie is also available in the extensive spa centre, which itself offers excellent family accommodation. Residents have their own leisure facilities but will be attracted to the superb spa set in the grounds.
ROOMS: 28 en suite (3 fmly) (4 GF) **FACILITIES: Spa** STV ⊞ ⚲ Snooker Sauna Solarium Gym Hair salon Aromatherapy Shiatsu Hockey Badminton **PARKING:** 50 **NOTES:** 🛪 ⊗ in restaurant

BARRA, ISLE OF

TANGASDALE   Map 13 NF60

★★ 69% **Isle of Barra**
Tangasdale Beach HS9 5XW
☎ 01871 810383 📠 01871 810385
e-mail: barrahotel@aol.com
Dir: left after leaving ferry terminal onto A888, hotel 2m on left

CHILD FACILITIES: Please telephone for details

It may well take you the better part of a day to reach the most westerly hotel in Britain, but few journeys could be better rewarded. First impressions of the hotel promote a real sense of 'wow!' - overlooking the white sands of Halaman Bay and the crystal clear shallows of the Atlantic. The hotel is comfortably furnished and most of the bedrooms enjoy stunning beach and ocean views. Try the scallops at dinner and experience the finest shellfish in British waters. Local staff provide warm hospitality and a wealth of useful knowledge of the island.
ROOMS: 30 en suite (2 fmly) (7 GF) s £42-£49; d £68-£84 (incl. bkfst) **LB FACILITIES:** STV Beach **PARKING:** 50 **NOTES:** ⊗ in restaurant Closed mid Oct-Mar

MULL, ISLE OF

TOBERMORY   Map 13 NM55

Babies Welcome	Family Rooms	Children's Dishes

★★★ 73% **Western Isles**
PA75 6PR
☎ 01688 302012 📠 01688 302297
e-mail: wihotel@aol.com
web: www.mullhotel.com
Dir: from ferry follow signs to Tobermory. Over 1st mini-rdbt in Tobermory then over small bridge and immediate right & follow road to T-junct. Right again then keep left and take 1st left for hotel at top of hill on right

CHILD FACILITIES: Baby listening Activities: games, books, puzzles, colouring Food/bottle warming Ch menu Ch portions Highchairs Ch discounts under 15s free sharing with parents Videos Cots Family rms D rm with Z beds or bed settees Connecting rms Laundry **NEARBY:** Balamory Tour Sea Life Centre Castles Farm Steam Railway

Built in 1883 and standing high above the village, this hotel enjoys spectacular views over Tobermory harbour and the Sound of Mull. Public rooms range from the classical drawing room and restaurant to the bright modern conservatory bar/bistro. Bedrooms come in a variety of styles; the impressive superior rooms include a suite complete with its own piano.
ROOMS: 28 en suite s £45-£114; d £99-£124 (incl. bkfst) **LB FACILITIES:** Xmas **PARKING:** 28 **NOTES:** ⊗ in restaurant Closed 17-27 Dec

Babies Welcome	Family Rooms	Children's Dishes

★★ 69% ⚙️ **Tobermory**
53 Main St PA75 6NT
☎ 01688 302091 📠 01688 302254
e-mail: tobhotel@tinyworld.co.uk
web: www.thetobermoryhotel.com
Dir: on waterfront, overlooking Tobermory Bay

CHILD FACILITIES: Baby listening Activities: books, games, jigsaws, building blocks Indoor play area Food/bottle warming Ch menu Ch portions Highchairs Ch cutlery Ch discounts under 1s free, 1-5s £5, 6-16s 50% when sharing with parents Videos Cots Family rms D rm with S beds & rm for cot Connecting rms Laundry **NEARBY:** Walks Near sea

continued

This friendly hotel, with its pretty pink frontage, sits on the seafront amid other brightly coloured buildings. There is a comfortable lounge where drinks are served (there is no bar) prior to dining in the cosy restaurant. Bedrooms come in a variety of sizes; all are bright and vibrant with the superiors having video TVs.

ROOMS: 16 rms (15 en suite) (3 fmly) (2 GF) ⊗ in all bedrooms s £41-£102; d £82-£102 (incl. bkfst) **LB** **FACILITIES:** Xmas **NOTES:** ⊗ in restaurant Closed Xmas

---

SKYE, ISLE OF

ARDVASAR   Map 13 NG60

★★ 70% *Ardvasar Hotel*
Sleat IV45 8RS
☎ 01471 844223 📠 01471 844495
e-mail: richard@ardvasar-hotel.demon.co.uk
web: www.ardvasarhotel.com
Dir: leave ferry, drive 500mtrs & turn left

CHILD FACILITIES: Please telephone for details

The Isle of Skye is dotted with cosy, welcoming hotels that make touring the island easy and convenient. This hotel ranks highly amongst its peers thanks to great hospitality and a unique preservation of community island spirit that has been carefully preserved for the traveller. The hotel sits less than five minutes' drive from the Mallaig ferry and provides comfortable bedrooms and a cosy bar lounge for residents. Seafood is prominent on menus, and meals can be enjoyed in either the popular bar or the attractive dining room.

ROOMS: 10 en suite (4 fmly) ⊗ in 6 bedrooms
FACILITIES: **PARKING:** 30 **NOTES:** ⊗ in restaurant

EDINBANE   Map 13 NG35

♦♦♦♦ **Shorefield House**
Edinbane IV51 9PW
☎ 01470 582444 📠 01470 582414
e-mail: shorefieldhouse@aol.com
web: www.shorefield.com
Dir: approx 12m from Portree and 8m from Dunvegan, turn off A850 into Edinbane, house 1st on right.

CHILD FACILITIES: Please telephone for details

Shorefield is a modern house lying in its own child-friendly garden just off the road. The comfortable bedrooms include ground floor rooms specially adapted for disabled guests and those with limited mobility. Others are suitable for families and all are thoughtfully equipped to include CD players. Breakfast offers an impressive choice.

ROOMS: 5 en suite (2 fmly) (4 GF) s £30-£40; d £60-£80 *
FACILITIES: tea/coffee TVL No coaches Children's Play Area **NOTES:** ✠ ⊗ Cen ht **PARKING:** 10

UIG   Map 13 NG36

♦♦♦ **Woodbine House**
IV51 9XP
☎ 01470 542243 📠 01470 542243
e-mail: shona_mcclure@hotmail.com
Dir: on entering Uig Bay from Portree, pass Ferry Inn and turn next right onto A855-Staffing Rd, Woodbine Houe is 300yds on right

CHILD FACILITIES: Please telephone for details

Built in the late 1800s, Woodbine House occupies an elevated location overlooking Uig bay and the surrounding countryside and is ideally situated for walking and bird watching. Bedrooms are attractive, well equipped and comfortable. The ground floor lounge and dining room both enjoy lovely views and make a delightful setting for relaxation or delicious evening meals and hearty breakfasts.

ROOMS: 4 en suite (1 fmly) s £20-£35; d £30-£50 * **FACILITIES:** TVB tea/coffee TVL No coaches Dinner Last d order 2pm **NOTES:** ⊗ Cen ht **BB** **PARKING:** 4

Wales

ANGLESEY, ISLE OF

AMLWCH Map 06 SH49

★★ 70% Lastra Farm
Penrhyd LL68 9TF
☎ 01407 830906 🖷 01407 832522
e-mail: booking@lastra-hotel.com
web: www.lastra-hotel.com
Dir: after 'Welcome to Amlwch' sign turn left. Straight across main road, left at T-junct on to Rhosgoch Rd

CHILD FACILITIES: **Please telephone for details**

This 17th-century farmhouse offers pine-furnished, colourfully decorated bedrooms. There is also a comfortable lounge and a cosy bar. A wide range of good-value food is available either in the restaurant or Granary's Bistro. The hotel can cater for functions in a separate purpose built suite.

ROOMS: 5 en suite 3 annexe en suite (1 fmly) s £39.50-£44.50; d £60-£68 (incl. bkfst) **LB** **PARKING:** 40 **NOTES:** ⊗ in restaurant

BRIDGEND

BRIDGEND Map 03 SS97

Babies Welcome | Family Rooms | Children's Dishes

★★★ 69% Heronston
Best Western
Ewenny Rd CF35 5AW
☎ 01656 668811 🖷 01656 767391
e-mail: reservations@heronston-hotel.demon.co.uk
Dir: M4 junct 35, follow signs for Porthcawl, at 4th rdbt turn left towards Ogmore-by-Sea (B4265) hotel 200yds on left

CHILD FACILITIES: **Baby listening Outdoor play area Family area Food/bottle warming Ch menu Ch portions Highchairs Ch discounts under 5s free Safe grounds Cots Family rms D rm with adj room D rm with 2 S beds £75 Connecting rms Laundry** **NEARBY:** **Parks Walks**

Situated within easy reach of the town centre and the M4, this large modern hotel offers spacious well-equipped accommodation, including no-smoking bedrooms and ground floor rooms. Public areas include an open plan lounge/bar, attractive restaurant and a smart leisure & fitness club.

ROOMS: 69 en suite 6 annexe en suite (4 fmly) (37 GF) ⊗ in 21 bedrooms s fr £39.50; d fr £59 (incl. bkfst) **LB** **FACILITIES:** STV Sauna Solarium Gym Jacuzzi Steamroom Xmas **PARKING:** 250 **NOTES:** ⊗ in restaurant

Many proprietors are happy to provide extra facilities for children, but let them know in advance what you need so they can be prepared

CARDIFF

Welsh Industrial Maritime Museum, Cardiff

CARDIFF

Cardiff Castle CF10 3RB
cardiffcastle@cardiff.gov.uk ☎029 2087 8100
(Follow signs to city centre From M4, A48 & A470)
cardiffcastle@cardiff.gov.uk
Open all year, daily (ex 25-26 Dec & 1 Jan) including guided tours, Mar-Oct, 9.30-6 (last tour 5pm); Nov-Feb, 9.30-5.30 (last tour 4pm). Royal Regiment of Wales Museum closed Tue. Queen's Dragoon Guards Museum closed Fri.
*Full conducted tour, military museums, green, Roman Wall & Norman Keep £6 (ch & pen £3.70). Roman Wall, Norman Keep, & military museum £2.90 (ch & pen £1.80).

Millennium Stadium Tours
CF10 1JA ☎029 2082 2228
(M4 Junct 32, take A470 to Cardiff City Centre) Westgate street is opposite Cardiff Castle far end.
Open Mon - Sat, 10-5; Sun 10-4.
£5 (ch up to 16 £2.50, ch under 5 free, concessions £3). Party 20+.

National Museum & Gallery Cardiff CF10 3NP
post@nmgw.ac.uk ☎029 2039 7951
(Civic Centre, 5 mins walk from the city centre, 20 mins walk from bus and train station. M4 junct 32)
Open all year, Tue-Sun 10-5. Closed Mon (ex BHs) & 24-26 Dec.

Techniquest CF10 5BW
info@techniquest.org ☎029 2047 5475
(M4 junct 33, follow A4232 to Cardiff Bay)
Open all year (ex Xmas), Mon-Fri 9.30-4.30; Sat-Sun & BH's 10.30-5, school holidays 9.30-5.
£6.75 (ch 5-16 & con £4.65). Family ticket £18.50 (2ad+3ch). Friend season ticket £48. Groups 10+

ST FAGANS

Museum of Welsh Life CF5 6XB
post@nmgw.ac.uk ☎029 2057 3500
(4m W of Cardiff, 3m from M4 junct 33, along A4232) Open all year 10-5. Closed 24-26 Dec.

TONGWYNLAIS

Castell Coch
CF4 7YS ☎029 2081 0101
(A470 to Tongwynlais junction, then B4262 to castle on top of hill)
Open Apr-May & Oct, daily 9.30-5; Jun-Sep, daily 9.30-6; Nov-Mar, Mon-Sat 9.30-4, Sun 11-4.
Phone for Xmas opening times. £3 (ch 5-15, pen & students £2.50, wheelchair users and assisting companion free. Family ticket (2 ad & 3 ch) £8.50.

Wales

| Babies Welcome | Family Rooms | Children's Dishes |

★★★★ 68% Cardiff Marriott Hotel

Mill Ln CF10 1EZ

☎ 029 2039 9944 📠 029 2039 5578

e-mail: sara.nurse@marriotthotels.co.uk

Dir: M4 junct 29 follow signs City Centre. Turn left into High Street opposite Castle, then 2nd left, at bottom of High St into Mill Lane

CHILD FACILITIES: Food/bottle warming Ch menu Ch portions Highchairs Ch discounts under 5s free Cots Family rms rms with 2 D beds D rm with sofa bed Laundry NEARBY: Cardiff Bay Barry Island resort Cinema

A centrally located modern hotel, with spacious public areas and a good range of services, is ideal for leisure. Eating options include the informal Chats café bar and the contemporary Mediterrano restaurant. Well-equipped bedrooms are comfortable and air-conditioned. The leisure suite includes a gym and good sized pool.
ROOMS: 182 en suite (58 fmly) ⊗ in 127 bedrooms s fr £131; d fr £143 (incl. bkfst) LB **FACILITIES:** STV ⬚ Sauna Solarium Gym Jacuzzi Steam room Xmas **PARKING:** 110 **NOTES:** ✱ ⊗ in restaurant

★★★★ 64% Jurys Cardiff

Mary Ann St CF10 2JH

☎ 029 2034 1441 📠 029 2022 3742

e-mail: info@jurysdoyle.com

Dir: next to Ice Rink, opposite Cardiff International Arena

CHILD FACILITIES: Please telephone for details

This modern hotel is situated opposite the Cardiff International Arena. Bedrooms are largely set around an impressive atrium which houses the reception and offers access to Dylan's restaurant and Kavanagh's Irish bar, whilst those rooms on the executive floor are particularly well appointed.
ROOMS: 146 en suite (6 fmly) ⊗ in 48 bedrooms s £68-£240; d £78-£260 (incl. bkfst) LB **FACILITIES:** STV **PARKING:** 55 **NOTES:** ✱

| Babies Welcome | Family Rooms | Children's Dishes |

★★★ 65%
Quality Hotel & Suites Cardiff

Merthyr Rd, Tongwynlais CF15 7LD

☎ 029 2052 9988 📠 029 2052 9977

e-mail: enquiries@quality-hotels-cardiff.com

web: www.choicehotelseurope.com

Dir: M4 junct 32, take exit for Tongwynlais A4054 off large rdbt, hotel situated on right

continued

CHILD FACILITIES: Babysitting (prearranged) Activities: colouring, games, leisure club Food/bottle warming Ch menu Ch portions Highchairs Ch discounts under 12s free sharing with parents Safe grounds Cots Family rms D rm and suites with S beds from £60 inc breakfast Fridge Laundry NEARBY: Big Pit Cardiff Castle Techniquest Brecon mountain railway

This modern hotel is conveniently located off the M4 with easy access to Cardiff. Guests can enjoy the spacious open plan public areas and impressive leisure facilities and relax in the well-proportioned and equipped bedrooms, which include some suites.
ROOMS: 95 en suite (12 fmly) (19 GF) ⊗ in 38 bedrooms s £57-£96; d £75-£135 LB **FACILITIES:** STV ⬚ Sauna Solarium Gym Jacuzzi Xmas **PARKING:** 130 **NOTES:** ✱ ⊗ in restaurant

| Babies Welcome | Family Rooms |

◆◆◆◆ Big Sleep Hotel

Bute Ter CF10 2FE

☎ 029 2063 6363 📠 029 2063 6364

e-mail: bookings.cardiff@thebigsleephotel.com

Dir: opposite Cardiff International Arena

CHILD FACILITIES: Food/bottle warming Highchairs Ch discounts under 12s free sharing with parents Cots (subject to availability) Family rms D rms with Z beds/B beds £45 - £104 Ch drinks Laundry NEARBY: Techniquest Millennium Stadium

Part of Cardiff's skyline, this city centre hotel offers well-equipped bedrooms ranging from standard to penthouse, with spectacular views over the city towards the bay. There is a bar on the ground floor and secure parking. Continental breakfast is served or 'Breakfast to go' is an alternative for anyone wishing to make an early start.
ROOMS: 81 en suite (6 fmly) d £45-£135 * ⊗ in 40 bedrooms
FACILITIES: STV TVB tea/coffee Direct dial from bedrooms Lift **NOTES:** ⊗ in area of dining room Licensed Cen ht LB **PARKING:** 30

◆◆◆◆ Tanglewood

4 Tygwyn Rd, Penylan CF23 5JE

☎ 029 2047 3447 & 07971546812 📠 0870 7061808

e-mail: reservations@tanglewoodguesthouse.com

web: www.tanglewoodguesthouse.com

Dir: towards Cardiff E & Docks. 3rd exit at rdbt. Next rdbt 1st exit. Left at lights. Turn right just past next lights. Establishment 120yds on right

CHILD FACILITIES: Please telephone for details

An elegant, well-kept former Edwardian residence, Tanglewood is situated in a quiet residential district in its own attractive gardens. The bedrooms are pleasantly decorated and thoughtfully equipped and there is a comfortable lounge overlooking the gardens to relax in.
ROOMS: 4 rms (1 en suite) **FACILITIES:** TVB tea/coffee TVL No coaches **NOTES:** Credit cards not taken ✱ ⊗ Cen ht **PARKING:** 8

⑤ Cutting Edge

Discovery House, Scott Harbour, Cardiff Bay CF10 4PJ
☎ 02920 470780 📠 02920 440876
Dir: Telephone for directions

CHILD FACILITIES: Please telephone for details

FOOD: Modern British **STYLE:** Chic, Minimalist **SEATS:** 45
OPEN: 12-2.30/7-9.30, Closed 25-26 Dec, 31 Dec, BHs, SunL Sat
RESTAURANT: Fixed L £11.95, main £8.50-£16.95 **NOTES:** ⊗ area, Air
con **PARKING:** street parking - vouchers required

⑤ ⑤ da Venditto

7-8 Park Place CF10 3DP
☎ 029 20230781 📠 029 20399949
e-mail: sherry@vendittogroup.co.uk
Dir: In the city centre, opposite the new theatre

CHILD FACILITIES: Food/bottle warming Ch licence Ch portions
Highchairs Ch cutlery **NEARBY:** Cinema Theatre Parks Castle

FOOD: Modern Italian **STYLE:** Modern Italian **SEATS:** 55
OPEN: 12-2.30/6-10.45, Closed Xmas, New Yr, BHs, Sun
RESTAURANT: Fixed L £14.50, Fixed D £32.50 **NOTES:** Air con

CARMARTHENSHIRE

CWMDUAD — Map 02 SN33

◆◆◆◆ Neuadd-Wen

SA33 6XJ
☎ 01267 281438 📠 01267 281438
e-mail: goodbourn@neuaddwen.plus.com
Dir: on A484, 9m N of Carmarthen

CHILD FACILITIES: Baby listening Activities: books, board games,
puzzles Outdoor play area Food/bottle warming Ch menu
Ch portions Highchairs Ch discounts under 3s free, 3-7s 1/4 price,
7-14s half price Games consoles Videos Cots Family rms D rm with
adjoining B bed rm Laundry **NEARBY:** Walks Cinema Leisure
centre

Excellent customer care is assured at this combined post office
and house situated in pretty gardens in an unspoilt village.
Bedrooms are filled with thoughtful extras and there is a choice of
continued

---

guest lounges. One bedroom is contained in a tastefully
renovated, early-Victorian toll cottage across the road. There is an
attractive dining room that serves imaginative dinners utilising
fresh local produce.
ROOMS: 8 rms (6 en suite) (2 fmly) (2 GF) s £19.50-£23.50; d £39-£47
* **FACILITIES:** TVB tea/coffee Direct dial from bedrooms TVL No
coaches Dinner Last d order 6pm **NOTES:** ⊗ in restaurant ⊗ in 1
lounge Licensed Cen ht **LB PARKING:** 12

LLANDEILO — Map 03 SN62

◆◆◆◆ Brynteilo

Manordeilo SA19 7BG
☎ 01550 777040 📠 01550 777884
e-mail: enquiries@brynteilo.com
web: www.brynteilo.com
Dir: on A40, 4m NE of Llandeilo & 8m SW of Llandovery

CHILD FACILITIES: Food/bottle warming Ch portions Highchairs
Ch discounts Cots Family rms D rm with sofa bed & cot

This personally run, no smoking, friendly guest house is situated
just north-east of Llandeilo. In the heart of the Towy Valley and
surrounded by lovely countryside, this establishment offers smart,
modern and well equipped accommodation, that includes a family
room and ground-floor bedrooms. A self-catering flat is also
available. Separate tables are provided in the attractive dining
room.
ROOMS: 11 en suite (1 fmly) (6 GF) s £40-£45; d £50-£55 *
FACILITIES: TVB tea/coffee Direct dial from bedrooms No coaches
Dinner Last d order noon **NOTES:** ✈ ⊗ Licensed Cen ht
PARKING: 15

LLANDOVERY — Map 03 SN73

Babies Welcome | Family Rooms | Children's Dishes

◆◆◆◆◆ Cwn Rhuddan Mansion

SA20 0DX
☎ 01550 721414 📠 01550 721414
e-mail: cwmrhuddan@hotmail.com
*Dir: Travelling from Brecon turn left off A40, in Llandovery, on to A4069.
After 1m turn left and immediately left into drive to house*

CHILD FACILITIES: Baby listening Activities: toys, jigsaws, table
tennis, snooker, collecting eggs in grounds Indoor play area
Food/bottle warming Ch portions Highchairs Ch cutlery
Ch discounts under 3s free, 3-13s half price Safe grounds Videos
Cots Family rms 2 D rms with S bed Ch drinks Laundry Changing
mats **NEARBY:** Dolaucothi Gold Mines Dan-Yr-Ogof caves

This French chateau-style mansion was built in 1871 and stands in
extensive grounds and gardens. In recent years, it has been
extensively and painstakingly restored to provide spacious,
comfortable and tastefully appointed accommodation, including a
four-poster room. There is a choice of lounges, where welcoming
log fires are lit during cold weather. Separate tables are provided
in the elegant breakfast room. The owner has an impressive
collection of motoring memorabilia including vintage vehicles,
which guests are welcome to view.
ROOMS: 3 en suite (2 fmly) ⊗ **FACILITIES:** TVB tea/coffee TVL No
coaches Games lounge, table tennis **NOTES:** Credit cards not taken ⊗ in
restaurant ⊗ in 1 lounge Cen ht **LB PARKING:** 14

CEREDIGION

Seafront at Aberystwyth

ABERAERON

Llanerchaeron
SA48 8DG   ☎01545 570200
llanerchaeron@nationaltrust.org.uk
(2.5m E of Aberaeron off A482)
Open early Apr-late Oct, Wed-Sun & BH Mons 11-5. Last admission 1hr before closing. Park open all year dawn to dusk.
*£5 (ch £2.50). Family ticket £12.

ABERYSTWYTH

National Library of Wales SY23 3BU
holi@llgc.org.uk   ☎01970 632800
(off Penglais Hill, A487 in north area of Aberystwyth)
Open all year, exhibitions, library & reading rooms Mon-Fri 9.30-6, Sat until 5.(Closed BHs & first wk Oct). *Free. Admission to reading rooms available by ticket, proof of identity required. Free admission to permanent exhibition and between 2-3 temporary exhibitions.

CAPEL BANGOR

Rheidol Hydro Electric Power Station & Visitor Centre
SY23 3NF   ☎01970 880667
(off A44 at Capel Bangor)
Open Apr-Oct, daily 10-4 for free tours of the Power Station, fish farm & visitor centre.

CENARTH

The National Coracle Centre
SA38 9JL   ☎01239 710980
martinfowler.coraclecentre@virgin.net
(on A484 between Carmarthen and Cardigan, centre of Cenarth village, beside bridge and river)
Open Etr-Oct, Sun-Fri 10.30-5.30. All other times by appointment.
*£3 (ch £1, concessions £2.50). Party rates 12+.

EGLWYSFACH

RSPB Nature Reserve
SY20 8TA   ☎01654 700222
(6m S of Machynlleth on A487 in Eglwys-Fach)
Open daily, 9am-9pm (or sunset if earlier). Visitor Centre: Apr-Oct 9-5 daily; Nov-Mar 10-4 Wed-Sun. *£3.50 (ch £1, concessions £2.50) Family £7 RSPB members free.

FELINWYNT

Felinwynt Rainforest & Butterfly Centre
SA43 1RT   ☎01239 810882
dandjdevereux@btinternet.com
(from A487 Blaenannerch Airfield turning, turn onto B4333. Signposted 6m N of Cardigan)
Open daily from Etr-Oct.
*£3.95 (ch 4-14 £1.50, pen £3.50)

ABERYSTWYTH   Map 06 SN58

Babies Welcome	Family Rooms	Children's Dishes

★★★ 66% ⊛ Belle Vue Royal
Marine Ter SY23 2BA
☎ 01970 617558   📠 01970 612190
e-mail: reception@bellevueroyalhotel.fsnet.co.uk
Dir: on sea front, 200yds from the pier

> **CHILD FACILITIES:** Baby listening Babysitting (by prior arrangement) **Activities:** colouring books Food/bottle warming Ch menu Ch portions Highchairs Ch discounts under 9s free sharing with parents Cots Family rms D rm with rm for cot 2 S rms with rm for cot £98 - £103 Ch drinks (on request) Laundry **NEARBY:** Cinema Leisure Centre Pier Playground Seafront location

This large hotel dates back more than 170 years and stands on the promenade, a short walk from the shops. Family and sea-view rooms are available and all are well equipped. For dining there are bar meals or a more formal restaurant with a well deserved reputation for its cuisine.
ROOMS: 37 rms (34 en suite) (6 fmly) (1 GF) ⊛ in 10 bedrooms s fr £63; d £93-£106 (incl. bkfst) **LB FACILITIES:** STV Xmas **PARKING:** 14 **NOTES:** ✈ ⊛ in restaurant

Babies Welcome	Family Rooms	Children's Dishes

★★ 66% Four Seasons
50-54 Portland St SY23 2DX
☎ 01970 612120   📠 01970 627458
e-mail: reservations@fourseasonshotel.demon.co.uk
web: www.fourseasonshotel.uk.com
Dir: From railway station, turn left onto Terrace Rd by traffic lights, into North Pde & left onto Queens Rd, then 2nd left into Portland St. Hotel on right

> **CHILD FACILITIES:** Family area Food/bottle warming Ch menu Ch portions Highchairs Ch cutlery Ch discounts under 9s Safe grounds Cots Family rms D rm with D futon, 3 S beds with B beds £70 Connecting rms Laundry **NEARBY:** Leisure centre Cinema Castle 2-min walk to sea

This privately owned hotel is well-maintained and friendly. Bedrooms are well equipped. A cosy lounge is provided, plus a separate bar. A wide choice of food is available.
ROOMS: 16 rms (15 en suite) (2 fmly) ⊛ in 14 bedrooms s £50-£55; d £65-£75 (incl. bkfst) **LB PARKING:** 8 **NOTES:** ✈ ⊛ in restaurant Closed 23 Dec-6 Jan

Babies Welcome	Family Rooms	Children's Dishes

★★ 65% Marine Hotel
The Promenade SY23 2BX
☎ 01970 612444   📠 01970 617435
e-mail: marinehotel1@btconnect.com
web: www.marinehotelaberystwyth.co.uk
Dir: from W on A44. From N or S Wales on A487. On seafront west of pier

> **CHILD FACILITIES:** Outdoor play area Food/bottle warming Ch menu Ch portions Highchairs Ch discounts Safe grounds Cots Family rms most family rms with adjoining bathroom £80 - £125 Connecting rms Changing mats **NEARBY:** Parks Walks Leisure centre Cinema Seafront location

The Marine is a privately owned hotel situated on the promenade overlooking Cardigan Bay. Bedrooms have been tastefully decorated, some have four-poster beds and many have sea views.
continued

The refurbished reception rooms are comfortable and relaxing, and meals are served in the elegant dining room or the bar.
ROOMS: 44 rms (43 en suite) (7 fmly) ⊗ in 1 bedroom s £45-£60; d £60-£95 (incl. bkfst) **LB FACILITIES: Spa** Sauna Solarium Gym Jacuzzi Xmas **PARKING:** 15 **NOTES:** ⊗ in restaurant

♦♦♦♦ Llety Ceiro Country House

Peggy Ln, Bow St, Llandre SY24 5AB
☎ 01970 821900 ▤ 01970 820966
e-mail: marinehotel1@btconnect.com
CHILD FACILITIES: Please telephone for details
Located north of Aberystwyth, this tastefully renovated house is immaculately maintained throughout. Bedrooms are equipped with a range of thoughtful extras in addition to smart modern bathrooms. There is a spacious conservatory lounge in addition to an attractive dining room. Bicycle hire is available.
ROOMS: 10 en suite (2 fmly) (3 GF) s £45-£70; d £60-£80 * ⊗ in 1 bedrooms **FACILITIES:** TVB tea/coffee Direct dial from bedrooms Free use of facilities at sister hotel Dinner Last d order 8pm **NOTES:** ⊗ in restaurant Licensed Cen ht **LB PARKING:** 21

♦♦♦ Queensbridge Hotel

Promenade, Victoria Ter SY23 2DH
☎ 01970 612343 ▤ 01970 617452
Dir: N end of promenade, near Constitution Hill
CHILD FACILITIES: Baby listening Nanny Activities: Food/bottle warming Ch portions Highchairs Ch cutlery Ch discounts Safe grounds Cots Family rms D rms with B beds or 3 S beds £75-£95 Connecting rms Laundry

A friendly private hotel on the promenade. The bedrooms, some suitable for families, are well equipped with modern facilities and many have fine sea views. Facilities include a comfortable lounge and bar, where snacks are available and a lift serves all floors.
ROOMS: 15 en suite (2 fmly) ⊗ in 6 bedrooms **FACILITIES:** TVB tea/coffee Direct dial from bedrooms Lift TVL Golf Di **NOTES:** ⊗ in restaurant ⊗ in 1 lounge Licensed Cen ht **LB PARKING:** 6

♦♦♦ Y Gelli

Dolau, Lovesgrove SY23 3HP
☎ 01970 617834
e-mail: pat.twigg@virgin.net
Dir: off A44 2.75m E of town centre
CHILD FACILITIES: Please telephone for details
Located in spacious grounds on the town's outskirts, this modern detached house contains a range of practically furnished bedrooms and three further rooms are available in an adjacent Victorian property. Comprehensive breakfasts are provided in an attractive dining room and a guest lounge is also available.
ROOMS: 6 rms (2 en suite) 3 annexe rms (1 en suite) (3 fmly) (1 GF) **FACILITIES:** TVB tea/coffee TVL No coaches Snooker Pool Table Table tennis Dinner Last d order early morning **NOTES:** Credit cards not taken ✖ ⊗ Cen ht **PARKING:** 20

 Map 02 SN14

♦♦♦ ◧ Webley Hotel

Poppit Sands, St Dogmaels SA43 3LN
☎ 01239 612085
Dir: from St Dogmaels follow signs to Poppit. Hotel by side of Teifi estuary, 0.5m from Poppit Beach
CHILD FACILITIES: Activities: toys, games, books Food/bottle warming Ch menu Ch portions Highchairs Ch cutlery Ch discounts Cots   NEARBY: 0.5m to sea

This friendly riverside inn overlooks the Teifi Estuary near Poppit Sands on the south bank. There are lovely views from many of the bedrooms, which are smart and modern with good facilities. The bar is popular locally and good-value meals are usually on offer. There is a small cosy lounge for residents and separate tables are provided in the traditionally furnished dining room.
ROOMS: 8 rms (5 en suite) s £25-£35; d £40-£60 * ⊗ **FACILITIES:** TV5B tea/coffee TVL Dinner Last d order 9pm **NOTES:** ⊗ in restaurant ⊗ in lounges Cen ht **LB PARKING:** 53

 Map 02 SN54

♦♦♦ ✿ Dremddu Fawr

Creuddyn Bridge SA48 8BL
☎ 01570 470394
Dir: take A482 towards Aberaeron then 2nd right opposite second-hand car forecourt over bridge. Turn sharp left follow road for approx 300yds
CHILD FACILITIES: Babysitting Activities: Outdoor play area Food/bottle warming Ch menu Ch portions Highchairs Ch cutlery Ch discounts Safe grounds Videos Cots Ch drinks Connecting rms Fridge Laundry Changing mats   NEARBY: Fantasy farm Horse riding Walks Parks Conservation Centre

Located four miles north of Lampeter in a secluded rural area, this Edwardian farmhouse offers two cosy, well-equipped and homely bedrooms and a traditional dining room where delicious home-cooked dinners are served by arrangement.
ROOMS: 2 en suite s £25; d £50 * **FACILITIES:** STV TVB tea/coffee 205 acres beef/sheep Dinner Last d order 7pm **NOTES:** ✖ ⊗ Cen ht **LB PARKING:** 2

Many proprietors are happy to provide extra facilities for children, but let them know in advance what you need so they can be prepared

Wales

CONWY

Eiras Park, Colwyn Bay

BETWS-Y-COED
Conwy Valley Railway Museum
LL24 0AL ☎01690 710568
(signed from the A5 into Old Church Rd, adjacent
to train station)
Open daily, 10-5.30 (ex Xmas)
*£1 (ch & pen 50p). Family ticket £2.50. Steam
train ride £1. Tram ride 80p.

CERRIGYDRUDION
Llyn Brenig Visitor Centre LL21 9TT
llyn.brenig@dwrcymru.com ☎01490 420463
(on B4501 between Denbigh & Cerrigydrudion)
Open mid Mar-Oct, daily 9-5.
Charge made for water sports & fishing.

COLWYN BAY
Welsh Mountain Zoo
LL28 5UY ☎01492 532938
welshmountainzoo@enterprise.net
(A55 coast road, junct 20 signposted Rhos-on-
Sea)
Open all year, Mar-Oct, daily 9.30-6; Nov-Feb,
daily 9.30-5. (Closed 25 Dec)

CONWY
Conwy Castle
LL32 8AY ☎01492 592358
(from A55 or B5106)
Open Apr-May & Oct, daily 9.30-5, Jun-Sep, daily
9.30-6 Nov-Mar, Mon-Sat 9.30-4, Sun 11-4. £3.75
(ch 5-15, pen & students £3.25)
*Family ticket £10.75.

Smallest House
LL32 8BB ☎01492 593484
(leave A55 at Conwy signpost, through town, at
bottom of High St for the quay, turn left)
Open Apr-May & Oct 10-5; Jun & Sep, 10-6; Jul &
Aug 10-9.
*75p (ch under 16 50p, under 5yrs free).

DOLWYDDELAN
Dolwyddelan Castle
LL25 0EJ ☎01690 750366
(on A470 Blaenau Ffestiniog to Betws-y-Coed)
Open all year, Apr-Sep, Mon-Sat 9.30-6.30 & Sun
11-4, Oct-Mar, Mon-Sat 9.30-4, Sun 11-4.
Telephone for Xmas opening times.
*£2 (ch 5-15, pen & students £1.50, wheelchair
users & assisting companion free). Family ticket
(2 ad & 3 ch) £5.50. Group rates available.

Babies Welcome | **Children's Dishes**

◀▌ Ty Gwyn Hotel ◆◆◆◆
LL24 0SG
☎ 01690 710383 710787 ▤ 01690 710383
e-mail: mratcl1050@aol.com
Dir: At Junction of A5/A470, 100 yards S of Waterloo Bridge.
CHILD FACILITIES: Food/bottle warming Ch portions
Highchairs **NEARBY:** Snowdon Slate mines Horse riding
OPEN: 12-2 7-9.30 Rest: Mon-Wed closed in Jan **BAR MEALS:** L served
all week 12-2 D served all week 7-9 Av main course £11 **RESTAURANT:** L
served all week 12-2 D served all week 7-9 Av 3 course à la carte £22
FACILITIES: ✖ **ROOMS:** 13 bedrooms 10 en suite 2 family rooms s£20
d£36 (YYY) **PARKING:** 12

◀▌ White Horse Inn ◆◆◆◆
Capel Garmon LL26 0RW
☎ 01690 710271 ▤ 01690 710721
e-mail: whitehorse@supanet.com
web: www.thewhitehorseinn.org
Dir: Telephone for directions
CHILD FACILITIES: Please telephone for details
OPEN: 11-3 6-11 Closed: 2 wks Jan **BAR MEALS:** L served Sat-Sun 12-2 D
served all week 6.30-9.30 Av main course £7.50 **RESTAURANT:** L served
Sat-Sun 12-2 D served all week 6.30-9.30 Av 3 course à la carte £7.50
ROOMS: 6 bedrooms 6 en suite s£35 d£58 no children overnight
PARKING: 30

Babies Welcome | **Family Rooms** | **Children's Dishes**

◆◆◆ Northwood Hotel
47 Rhos Rd, Rhos-on-Sea LL28 4RS
☎ 01492 549931
e-mail: welcome@northwoodhotel.co.uk
web: www.northwoodhotel.co.uk
*Dir: exit A55 at Rhos-on-Sea, follow signs for Promenade. Turn left at
seafront, after 200yds, turn left (opp building with clock), hotel 150yds on
left*
CHILD FACILITIES: Food/bottle warming Ch menu Ch portions
Highchairs Ch cutlery Ch discounts Safe grounds Videos Cots
Family rms D rm with B beds, D with S bed **NEARBY:** Fishing
Sailing Cycle track Walks 150yds to sea
A short walk from the seafront and shops, Northwood Hotel has a
warm and friendly atmosphere prevails and welcomes back many
regular guests. Bedrooms are furnished in modern style and
freshly prepared meals can be enjoyed in the spacious dining
room/bar while light refreshments are offered in the lounge.
ROOMS: 12 rms (10 en suite) (3 fmly) (2 GF) s £25-£28; d £56-£66 ⊗
in 3 bedrooms **FACILITIES:** TVB tea/coffee TVL No coaches Dinner
Last d order 7pm **NOTES:** ⊗ in restaurant ⊗ in lounges Licensed **LB**
PARKING: 12

◆◆◆◆◆ 🍴 Sychnant Pass House
Sychnant Pass Rd LL32 8BJ
☎ 01492 596868 ▤ 01492 596868
e-mail: bresykes@sychnant-pass-house.co.uk
web: www.sychnant-pass-house.co.uk
*Dir: follow signs to Conwy Town Centre. Past visitor centre then 2nd left
into Uppergate St. Continue out of town for 1.75m on right near top of hill*
CHILD FACILITIES: Please telephone for details

continued

Fine views are to be had from this Edwardian house set in its own landscaped grounds. Bedrooms, including suites and four poster rooms, are individually furnished and equipped with a range of thoughtful extras. Lounges, warmed by open fires in the chillier months, are comfortable and inviting, and imaginative dinners and suppers are served in the attractive dining room.

Sychnant Pass House

ROOMS: 10 en suite (6 fmly) (3 GF) s £60-£120; d £80-£140 * 🚭
FACILITIES: TVB tea/coffee TVL No coaches Riding 🎣 All rooms with video,films & CDs available Dinner Last d order 8.30pm **NOTES:** 🚭 in restaurant 🚭 in 1 lounge Licensed Cen ht **LB PARKING:** 30

◆◆◆◆ Gwern Borter Country Manor
Barkers Ln LL32 8YL
☎ 01492 650360 🖷 01492 650360
e-mail: mail@snowdoniaholidays.co.uk
web: www.snowdoniaholidays.co.uk
Dir: from Conwy take B5106 for 2.25m, turn right onto unclass road towards Rowen for 0.5m then right, then stay left as the road forks (Gwern Borter) 0.5m on left

CHILD FACILITIES: Activities: pet's corner, games room, cycles, skateboards, scooters, horse riding Outdoor play area Family area Food/bottle warming Highchairs Ch cutlery Ch discounts Safe grounds Videos Cots Family rms rms and family cottages Fridge Laundry   NEARBY: 3m to sea

This delightful mansion set in several acres of lawns and gardens has walls covered in climbing plants. Children are very welcome and there is a rustic play area, games room and many farmyard pets. Bedrooms are furnished with period or antique pieces and equipped with modern facilities; one has an Edwardian four-poster bed. There is an elegant lounge and Victorian-style dining room, where freshly cooked breakfasts are served.
ROOMS: 3 en suite (1 fmly) **FACILITIES:** TVB tea/coffee TVL No coaches Riding Sauna Gymnasium Cycle hire, Games room, Pets corner,Play area **NOTES:** 🚭 in restaurant Cen ht **PARKING:** 16

LLANDUDNO   Map 06 SH78

★★★ 69% Dunoon
Gloddaeth St LL30 2DW
☎ 01492 860787 🖷 01492 860031
e-mail: reservations@dunoonhotel.co.uk
web: www.dunoonhotel.co.uk
Dir: exit Promenade at War Memorial by pier onto wide avenue. 200yds from Promenade on right

CHILD FACILITIES: Baby listening Activities: jigsaws, books Outdoor play area Food/bottle warming Ch menu Ch portions Highchairs Ch cutlery Ch discounts under 3s free, 3 - 8s £20, over 9s £30 Videos Cots Family rms 1 D rm 2 S rm £60 per adult Connecting rms Laundry   NEARBY: Bodnant Garden Bodafon Farm Great Orme 5-min walk to sea

This hotel is centrally located in the town and is smart and with a choice of attractive well-equipped accommodation. The restaurant offers freshly prepared tasty meals, whilst lighter snacks and afternoon tea may be taken in one of the lounges or bar.
ROOMS: 50 en suite (7 fmly) s £55-£65; d £96-£130 (incl. bkfst & dinner) **LB FACILITIES:** STV ♫ Xmas **PARKING:** 24 **NOTES:** 🚭 in restaurant Closed 28 Dec - mid-Mar

★★◉◉◉ St Tudno Hotel and Restaurant
The Promenade LL30 2LP
☎ 01492 874411 🖷 01492 860407
e-mail: sttudnohotel@btinternet.com
web: www.st-tudno.co.uk
Dir: on reaching Promenade drive towards the pier, hotel opposite pier entrance & gardens

CHILD FACILITIES: Baby listening Activities: toys, colouring Food/bottle warming Ch menu Ch portions Highchairs Ch discounts up to 12s £20, over 12s £25 sharing with parents Videos Cots Family rms Ch drinks (minibar) Connecting rms Fridge Laundry   NEARBY: Great Orme Cable cars Copper mine Museum Seafront location

A high quality family-owned hotel with friendly, attentive staff, and enjoying fine sea views. The stylish bedrooms are well equipped with mini-bars, robes, satellite TVs with videos and many other thoughtful extras. Public rooms include a lounge, a welcoming bar and a small indoor pool. The Terrace Restaurant, where seasonal and daily-changing menus are offered, has a delightful Mediterranean atmosphere. Afternoon tea is a real highlight.
ROOMS: 19 en suite (4 fmly) 🚭 in 3 bedrooms s £72.50-£82.50; d £105-£210 (incl. bkfst) **LB FACILITIES:** STV 🖭 ♫ Xmas **PARKING:** 12 **NOTES:** 🚭 in restaurant

◆◆◆◆ Lynton House Hotel
80 Church Walks LL30 2HD
☎ 01492 875057 & 875009 🖷 01492 875057
e-mail: jfair75440@aol.com
web: www.lyntonhousehotel.co.uk
Dir: along promenade towards pier, turn right at t-junction by cenotaph, turn left at rdbt immediately after pier, hotel on right

CHILD FACILITIES: Food/bottle warming Ch portions Highchairs Ch discounts Under 2s free, 2-16s half price Cots Family rms D rm with 1 or 2 S beds   NEARBY: Playground Crazy Golf Farm Park Museum Cinema Amusement Arcade Near sea

This immaculately maintained private hotel lies under the Great Orme just off the seafront. Bedrooms are smart and modern, with well chosen decor, and two have four-posters. There is a comfortable lounge for residents and hospitality is warm and welcoming.
ROOMS: 14 en suite (4 fmly) (1 GF) s £33; d £56-£66 *
FACILITIES: TVB tea/coffee Direct dial from bedrooms TVL No coaches **NOTES:** 🚭 in restaurant Licensed Cen ht **LB PARKING:** 7

continued

LLANDUDNO, continued

♦♦♦ Tudno Lodge

66 Church Walks LL30 2HG
☎ 01492 876174 & 0800 6525274
e-mail: tudnolodge@supanet.com
Dir: turn off A55 at Llandudno Junction towards Llandudno, 4m. To top of Mostyn Street, with Empire Hotel opposite, turn left and Lodge is on right

CHILD FACILITIES: Please telephone for details

Peacefully located a few minutes' walk from pier, beach and shops, this Victorian villa retains many features and sympathetic improvements have resulted in homely and thoughtfully equipped bedrooms, some with fine sea views. Breakfasts and dinners are served in an attractive front-facing dining room and a first floor lounge with an open fire is also available.

ROOMS: 7 rms (4 en suite) (3 fmly) s £19-£22; d £38-£44 * ⊛
FACILITIES: TVB tea/coffee TVL No coaches Dinner Last d order 4pm
NOTES: ⊛ in restaurant **LB BB**

Babies Welcome	Family Rooms	Children's Dishes

♦♦♦ Vine House

23 Church Walks LL30 2HG
☎ 01492 876493
e-mail: barryharris@bigfoot.com
Dir: by Great Orme tram station

CHILD FACILITIES: Activities: toys, books Food/bottle warming Ch menu Ch portions Highchairs Ch cutlery Ch discounts under 5s free, 5-15s £5 Safe grounds Cots Family rms £50 for 4 Ch drinks
NEARBY: Parks Walks Leisure centre Cinema Short walk to sea

Vine House is a friendly family run house located a short walk from the seafront and pier, opposite the historic tram station. Bedrooms vary in size and style and include some spacious, stylish refurbished rooms with separate sitting areas and modern bathrooms. All rooms have views of the sea or the Orme.
ROOMS: 5 rms (3 en suite) (1 fmly) s £17-£20; d £34-£40 *
FACILITIES: TVB tea/coffee **NOTES:** ⊛ Cen ht **LB BB**

DENBIGHSHIRE

CORWEN

Map 06 SJ04

Babies Welcome	Family Rooms	Children's Dishes

♦♦♦♦♦ 🚌 Bron-y-Graig

LL21 0DR
☎ 01490 413007 📠 01490 413007
e-mail: business@north-wales-hotel.co.uk
web: www.north-wales-hotel.co.uk
Dir: on A5 eastern edge of Corwen

CHILD FACILITIES: Baby listening Nanny Activities: toys, games Outdoor play area Family area Food/bottle warming Ch menu Ch portions Highchairs Ch cutlery Ch discounts under 5s free, 5-14s reductions Safe grounds Games consoles Videos Cots Family rms D rms with S bed £49 Ch drinks Laundry

Located within a few minutes' walk from town centre, this impressive Victorian house retains many original features including fireplaces, stained glass and a tiled floor in the entrance hall. Bedrooms, complemented by luxurious bathrooms, are thoughtfully furnished and two are located in a sympathetically renovated coach house. Ground floor areas include a traditionally
continued

---

furnished dining room and comfortable guest lounge. A warm welcome, attentive service and imaginative food is assured.

ROOMS: 8 en suite 2 annexe en suite (3 fmly) s £35-£45; d £49 * ⊛
FACILITIES: STV TVB tea/coffee Direct dial from bedrooms Fishing Dinner Last d order 9.30pm **NOTES:** ⊛ in restaurant Licensed Cen ht **LB PARKING:** 15

RUTHIN

Map 06 SJ15

♦♦♦♦ Eyarth Station

Llanfair Dyffryn Clwyd LL15 2EE
☎ 01824 703643 📠 01824 707464
e-mail: stay@eyarthstation.com
Dir: off A525, 1 m S Ruthin. Take lane on right - 600metres to Eyarth Station

CHILD FACILITIES: Please telephone for details

Until 1964 and the Beeching cuts, this was a sleepy country station. A comfortable lounge and outdoor swimming pool occupy the space once taken up by the railway and platforms. Bedrooms are tastefully decorated and full of thoughtful extras. Family rooms are available, and two rooms are in the old stationmaster's house adjoining the main building.
ROOMS: 6 en suite 1 annexe en suite (2 fmly) (4 GF) s £37; d £56 * ⊛ **FACILITIES:** TV1B tea/coffee TVL No coaches 🔾 Dinner Last d order 7pm **NOTES:** ⊛ in restaurant ⊛ in 1 lounge Licensed Cen ht **LB PARKING:** 6

ST ASAPH

Map 06 SJ07

♦♦♦♦ 🍸 Bach-Y-Graig

Tremeirchion LL17 0UH
☎ 01745 730627 📠 01745 730971
e-mail: anwen@bachygraig.co.uk
web: www.bachygraig.co.uk
Dir: from A55 take A525 to Trefnant. At lights turn left A541 to x-roads with white railings, turn left down hill, over river bridge, right

CHILD FACILITIES: Please telephone for details

Dating from the 16th century, this listed building was the first brick-built house in Wales and retains many original features including a wealth of exposed beams and inglenook fireplaces. Bedrooms are furnished with fine period pieces and quality soft fabrics. Ground floor areas include a quiet lounge and a combined sitting and dining room, featuring a superb Jacobean oak table.
ROOMS: 3 en suite (1 fmly) s £35-£40; d £56-£60 * **FACILITIES:** TVB tea/coffee TVL Fishing Woodland trail 200 acres dairy **NOTES:** Credit cards not taken 🔾 ⊛ Cen ht **LB PARKING:** 3

All information was correct at the time of going to press; we recommend you confirm details on booking

FLINTSHIRE

FLINT
Map 07 SJ27

★★★ 66% *Mountain Park Hotel*
Northop Rd, Flint Mountain CH6 5QG
☎ 01352 736000 & 730972 📠 01352 736010
Dir: off A55 for Flint onto A5119, hotel 1 mile on left

CHILD FACILITIES: Please telephone for details

This former farmhouse has modern, well-equipped bedrooms, many on ground-floor level, and have direct access to the car park. It is conveniently situated close to the A55. Facilities include the Sevens Brasserie Restaurant serving modern cuisine; a comfortable lounge bar offering a range of bar meals; and an attractively designed function room. There is also a 9-hole golf course.

ROOMS: 21 annexe en suite (1 fmly) ⊗ in 11 bedrooms
FACILITIES: Golf 9 Jacuzzi **PARKING:** 94 **NOTES:** ✈ ⊗ in restaurant

---

NORTHOP
Map 07 SJ26

🍴 Stables Bar Restaurant
CH7 6AB
☎ 01352 840577 📠 01352 840382
e-mail: info@soughtonhall.co.uk
Dir: From A55, take A5119 through Northop village

CHILD FACILITIES: Please telephone for details

OPEN: 11-11 6-11.30 **BAR MEALS:** L served all week 12-9.30 D served all week 7-9.30 Av main course £12 **RESTAURANT:** L served all week 12-3 D served all week 7-10 **FACILITIES:** Garden: Food served outdoors, patio, ✈ **NOTES:** **PARKING:** 150

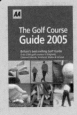

GWYNEDD

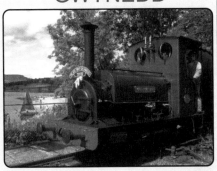

Bala Lake Railway

BANGOR
Penrhyn Castle
LL57 4HN ☎01248 353084
penrhyncastle@nationaltrust.org.uk
(1m E at Bangor, at Llandegai on A5122, just off A55)
Open 23 Mar-Oct, daily (ex Tue) Castle 12-5pm. Grounds and stable block exhibitions 11-5 (Jul & Aug 10-5.30). Last admission 4.30pm. Last audio tour 4pm. *All inclusive ticket: £7 (ch £3.50). Family ticket £17.50. Party 15+ £5.50 p.p. Grounds & stable block only £5 (ch £2.50).

BEDDGELERT
Sygun Copper Mine LL55 4NE
sygunmine@aol.com ☎01766 510100
(1m E of Beddgelert on A498)
Open all year, 10-5.£7.95 (ch £5.95, pen £6.95).

BLAENAU FFESTINIOG
Llechwedd Slate Caverns LL41 3NB
quarrytours@aol.com ☎01766 830306
(Beside A470 1m from Blaenau Ffestiniog)
Open all year, daily from 10am. Last tour 5.15 (Oct-Feb 4.15). (Closed 25-26 Dec & 1 Jan). *Single Tour £8.25 (ch £6.25, pen £7. Reductions for both tours.

CAERNARFON
Segontium Roman Museum LL55 2LN
info@segontium.org.uk ☎01286 675625
(on A4085 towards Beddgelert, approx 1m from Caernarfon)
Open Tue-Sun 12.30-4. Closed Mon except BH

LLANBERIS
Snowdon Mountain Railway LL55 4TY
info@snowdonrailway.co.uk ☎0870 4580033
(on A4086, Caernarfon to Capel Curig road. 7.5m from Caernarfon)
Open 15 Mar-5 Nov, daily from 9am (weather permitting).
*Return £20 (ch £14). Early bird discount on 9am train. (not for July & Aug)
Welsh Slate Museum LL55 4TY
slate@nmgw.ac.uk ☎01286 870630
(0.25m off A4086. The Museum is within Padarn Country Park)
Open Etr-Oct, daily 10-5; Nov-Etr, Sun-Fri 10-4.

ABERDYFI — Map 06 SN69

★★★ 75% Trefeddian
LL35 0SB
☎ 01654 767213 📠 01654 767777
e-mail: info@trefwales.com
web: www.trefwales.com
Dir: 0.5m N of Aberdyfi off A493

CHILD FACILITIES: Please telephone for details

This large privately owned hotel overlooks Cardigan Bay and is surrounded by grounds and gardens. It provides sound modern accommodation with well-equipped bedrooms and bathrooms, plus some luxury rooms with balconies and sea views. Public areas include elegantly furnished lounges, a beauty salon and indoor pool. Children are welcome and recreation areas are provided. The hotel was 100 years old in 2004 and in 2007 the Cave family will celebrate the centenary of their ownership.
ROOMS: 59 en suite (13 fmly) ⊗ in all bedrooms s £73-£93; d £146-£186 (incl. bkfst & dinner) LB **FACILITIES:** ⊠ ℞ Snooker Solarium ⚓ Table tennis, Play area, Beauty salon Xmas **PARKING:** 68 **NOTES:** ⊗ in restaurant

★★ 74% 🏵 Penhelig Arms Hotel & Restaurant
LL35 0LT
☎ 01654 767215 📠 01654 767690
e-mail: info@penheligarms.com
web: www.penheligarms.com
Dir: take A493 coastal road, hotel faces Penhelig harbour

CHILD FACILITIES: Baby listening Nanny (by arrangement) Food/bottle warming Ch portions Highchairs Ch discounts 0-5s £5, over 5s £10 Cots Ch drinks Fridge Laundry **NEARBY:** Talyllyn Railway Pony trekking Walks 5-min walk to sea

Situated opposite the old harbour, this delightful 18th-century hotel overlooks the Dyfi Estuary. The well-maintained bedrooms have good quality furnishings and modern facilities. The public bar retains its original character and is much loved by locals who enjoy the food with its emphasis on seafood.
ROOMS: 10 en suite 5 annexe en suite (4 fmly) ⊗ in all bedrooms s fr £45; d £78-£98 (incl. bkfst) LB **FACILITIES: PARKING:** 14 **NOTES:** ⊗ in restaurant Closed 25 & 26 Dec

★★ 69% *Dovey Inn*
Seaview Ter LL35 0EF
☎ 01654 767332 📠 01654 767996
e-mail: info@doveyinn.com
web: www.doveyinn.com
Dir: In village centre on A493, on R. Dovey, 9m from Machynlleth

CHILD FACILITIES: Please telephone for details

In the heart of Aberdyfi, this inn offers attractive, refurbished rooms which are comfortable and very well equipped; most have

continued

sea views. Downstairs there are four bars where a wide range of dishes, featuring local produce, is available. Breakfast is served in a separate upstairs dining room.
ROOMS: 8 en suite (2 fmly) ⊗ in all bedrooms **FACILITIES:** STV Guest may use facilities at Plas Talgarth Country Club **NOTES:** ✹ ⊗ in restaurant

ABERSOCH — Map 06 SH32

◆◆◆◆ Riverside Hotel
LL53 7HW
☎ 01758 712419 📠 01758 712671
e-mail: info@riversideabersoch.co.uk
web: www.riversideabersoch.co.uk
Dir: on A499 just before entering Abersoch

CHILD FACILITIES: Baby listening Activities: puzzles Food/bottle warming Ch menu Ch portions Highchairs Ch cutlery Ch discounts under 2s free, 2-5s £14, 6-14s £20 Videos Cots Family rms D suites with 2 S beds or B beds, D rms with extra bed Ch drinks Connecting rms **NEARBY:** Walks Leisure Centre Rabbit Farm Go Karting Cinema Near sea

Located close to harbour and town centre with a river bank garden which offers seating for wildfowl observation, this constantly improving hotel provides many thoughtfully equipped bedrooms; some have good family facilities and direct access to the gardens. Other facilities include a Mediterranean-themed restaurant and smart, modern cocktail bar.
ROOMS: 12 en suite (5 fmly) (3 GF) s £55-£62; d £55-£100 * ⊗ **FACILITIES:** TVB tea/coffee Fishing Dinner Last d order 9pm **NOTES:** ✹ ⊗ in restaurant ⊗ in 1 lounge Licensed Cen ht LB **PARKING:** 20

BARMOUTH — Map 06 SH61

★★★ 68% Bae Abermaw
Panorama Hill LL42 1DQ
☎ 01341 280550 📠 01341 280346
e-mail: enquiries@baeabermaw.com
web: www.baeabermaw.com

CHILD FACILITIES: Please telephone for details

This large stone-built Victorian house, now a privately owned and personally run hotel, stands in its own wooded grounds on a hillside with stunning views across the Mawddach estuary. It is decorated and furnished throughout in a striking contemporary style and provides spacious, well-equipped accommodation. Facilities include a room for functions.
ROOMS: 14 en suite (4 fmly) ⊗ in all bedrooms s £86-£103; d £126-£152 (incl. bkfst) LB **FACILITIES:** Xmas **PARKING:** 40 **NOTES:** ✹ ⊗ in restaurant RS Mon

◆◆◆◆ 🍽 Llwyndu Farmhouse
Llanaber LL42 1RR
☎ 01341 280144 📠 01341 281236
e-mail: Intouch@llwyndu-farmhouse.co.uk
web: www.llwyndu-farmhouse.co.uk
Dir: A496 towards Harlech. Where street lights end, on outskirts of Barmouth, take next R

CHILD FACILITIES: Baby listening Activities: books, toys Outdoor play area Food/bottle warming Ch menu Ch portions Highchairs Ch cutlery Ch discounts under 3s £5, 3-12s £15, 12-15s £20 Safe grounds Cots Family rms Four poster rm with put-up bed, 2 D rms with B beds Ch drinks Laundry **NEARBY:** Walks Farms Leisure centre Railways 10-min walk & 5-min drive to sea

continued

This converted 16th-century farmhouse retains many original features including inglenook fireplaces, exposed beams and timbers. There is a cosy lounge for residents and meals can be enjoyed at individual tables in the character dining room. Bedrooms are modern and well equipped; some have four-poster beds. Four rooms are situated in nearby buildings.

Llwyndu Farmhouse

ROOMS: 3 en suite 4 annexe en suite (2 fmly) **FACILITIES:** TVB tea/coffee TVL 4 acres non-working Dinner Last d order 6.30pm **NOTES:** ⊗ Licensed Cen ht **PARKING:** 10

BETWS GARMON   Map 06 SH55

♦♦♦♦ ≋ ⟺ Betws Inn
LL54 7YY
☎ 01286 650324
e-mail: jan@btwsinn.freeserve.co.uk
Dir: on A4085 from Caernarfon to Beddgelert, opp Bryn Gloch Caravan Park
CHILD FACILITIES: Please telephone for details

A former 17th-century village inn on the foothills of the Snowdonia range, this establishment has been lovingly restored and has immense charm and character. Bedrooms are equipped with a wealth of homely extras and a warm welcome and caring services are assured. Imaginative dinners feature both classical and local dishes and the breakfast selection includes home-made bread and preserves.

ROOMS: 3 rms (1 en suite) s £20-£25; d £40-£50 *
FACILITIES: tea/coffee TVL No coaches Dinner Last d order 2pm **NOTES:** Credit cards not taken ✕ ⊗ **PARKING:** 3

CRICCIETH   Map 06 SH43

♦♦♦♦ Glyn-Y-Coed Hotel
Porthmadog Rd LL52 0HP
☎ 01766 522870 01766 523341
e-mail: julie@glyn-y-coed.co.uk
web: www.glynycoedhotel.co.uk
Dir: on main street through Criccieth towards Porthmadoc, 1st hotel on left just past shops
CHILD FACILITIES: Please telephone for details

A warm welcome is assured at this impressive house which overlooks the sea and surrounding mountains. Bedrooms are equipped with lots of thoughtful extras and a comfortable sitting room, garden patio and car park is available in addition to a spacious dining room, the setting for wholesome breakfasts.

ROOMS: 9 en suite 1 annexe en suite (1 fmly) (1 GF) s £45-£60; d £59-£69 * **FACILITIES:** TVB tea/coffee Direct dial from bedrooms **NOTES:** ✕ ⊗ Licensed Cen ht LB **PARKING:** 14

> **Children's Dishes** This symbol indicates a children's menu or smaller portions are available

LLANBEDR   Map 06 SH52

♦♦♦♦ ⌑ Victoria
LL45 2LD
☎ 01341 241213 01341 241644
e-mail: junevicinn@aol.com
Dir: Village centre
CHILD FACILITIES: Please telephone for details

This fine old coaching inn lies on the banks of the River Artro in a very pretty village. Many original features remain, including the Settle bar with its flagged floor, black polished fireplace and unusual circular wooden settle. The menu is extensive and is supplemented by blackboard specials. Bedrooms are spacious and thoughtfully furnished.

ROOMS: 5 en suite s £35-£39; d £56-£65 * ⊗ **FACILITIES:** STV TVB tea/coffee Dinner Last d order 9pm **NOTES:** ✕ ⊗ in restaurant Cen ht LB **PARKING:** 75

LLANBERIS   Map 06 SH56

Babies Welcome | Children's Dishes

⌑ Pen-Y-Gwryd Hotel
LL55 4NT
☎ 01286 870211
Dir: 6m S of Llanberis at head of Gwryd river, close to junction of A4086 & A498. 4 miles from Capel Curig on A4086 on T-Junction with lake in front
CHILD FACILITIES: Indoor play area Outdoor play area Food/bottle warming Ch portions Highchairs **NEARBY:** Snowdonia Lakes River

OPEN: 11-11 Closed: Nov to New Year, mid-week Jan-Feb Rest: wknd opening only **BAR MEALS:** L served all week 12-2 D served all week Av main course £6 **RESTAURANT:** L served all week D served all week 7.30-8 Av 5 course fixed price £20 **FACILITIES:** Garden: Mountain garden with lake and sauna **NOTES:** Credit cards not taken **PARKING:** 25

PORTHMADOG   Map 06 SH53

♦♦♦♦♦ ❧ Tyddyn Du Farm Holidays
Gellilydan, Ffestiniog LL41 4RB
☎ 01766 590281 01766 590281
e-mail: paula@snowdonia-farm.com
web: www.snowdonia-farm-holidays-wales.co.uk
Dir: 1st farmhouse on L after junct of A487/A470 near village of Gellilydan
CHILD FACILITIES: Please telephone for details

Superbly located in an elevated position with stunning views of the surrounding countryside, this constantly improving 400-year-old stone-built property provides a range of spacious, beautifully furnished and equipped bedrooms, sympathetically renovated from former stables and barns. Superb breakfasts are taken in a cosy pine-furnished dining room within the main house, and a guest lounge with log fire is also available. Pets and families are especially welcome.

ROOMS: 4 en suite (4 fmly) (4 GF) **FACILITIES:** TVB tea/coffee TVL ♋ Large garden, duck pond & chickens 150 acres organic/sheep Dinner Last d order 5pm **NOTES:** Credit cards not taken ⊗ Cen ht **PARKING:** 10

PORTMEIRION   Map 06 SH53

★★★ 78% ⊛ Castell Deudraeth
LL48 6EN
☎ 01766 772400 01766 771771
e-mail: castell@portmeirion-village.com
Dir: A4212 for Trawsfynydd/Porthmadog. 1.5m beyond Penrhyndeudraeth, hotel on right
CHILD FACILITIES: Please telephone for details

A refurbished castellated mansion that overlooks Snowdonia and
continued on p304

Wales

PORTMEIRION, continued

the famous Italianate village featured in the 1960's cult series 'The Prisoner'. An original concept, Castell Deudraeth combines traditional materials, such as oak and slate, with state-of-the-art technology and design. Dynamically styled bedrooms boast underfloor heating, real-flame gas fires and wide-screen TVs with DVDs and cinema surround sound. The brasserie-themed dining room provides an informal option at dinner.
ROOMS: 11 en suite (5 fmly) s fr £150; d fr £175 **LB FACILITIES:** Spa STV ♫ Xmas **PARKING:** 30 **NOTES:** ✖

WAUNFAWR   Map 06 SH55

Babies Welcome | Children's Dishes

🍴 Snowdonia Parc Hotel & Brewpub
LL55 4AQ
☎ 01286 650409 & 650218 📠 01286 650409
e-mail: karen@snowdonia-park.co.uk

CHILD FACILITIES: Indoor play area Outdoor play area Family area Food/bottle warming Ch menu Ch portions Highchairs Changing facilities **NEARBY:** Nature parks Horse riding Outdoor water activities 4m to sea

OPEN: 11 -11 **BAR MEALS:** L served all week 11-8.30 D served all week 5-8.30 Av main course £6 **PARKING:** 100

MERTHYR TYDFIL

MERTHYR TYDFIL   Map 03 SQ00

◆◆◆◆ Penrhadw Farm
Pontsticill CF48 2TU
☎ 01685 723481 & 01685 722461 📠 01685 722461
e-mail: info@penrhadwfarm.co.uk
web: www.penrhadwfarm.co.uk
Dir: 5m N of Merthyr Tydfil, map on website
CHILD FACILITIES: Please telephone for details

A warm welcome can be expected at this former Victorian farmhouse in the glorious Brecon Beacons National Park. The house has been totally refurbished to provide quality modern accommodation. The well equipped, spacious, non-smoking bedrooms include two new large suites in cottages adjacent to the main building. There is also a comfortable lounge. Separate tables are provided in the cosy breakfast room.
ROOMS: 5 en suite (2 fmly) (1 GF) s £40-£60 * ◎ **FACILITIES:** STV TVB tea/coffee TVL Dinner Last d order by arrangement **NOTES:** ✖ ◎ in restaurant Cen ht **LB PARKING:** 22

◆◆◆◆ Llwyn Onn
Cwmtaf CF48 2HT
☎ 01685 384384 📠 01685 359310
e-mail: reception@llwynonn.co.uk
Dir: off A470 2m N of Cefn Coed. Directly overlooking Llwyn Onn reservoir
CHILD FACILITIES: Please telephone for details

Fronted by a large and pleasant garden, this delightful house overlooks Llwyn-Onn Reservoir. Bedrooms are spacious, comfortable and tastefully appointed. There is also a comfortable lounge, which opens onto the terrace and garden, as does the bright and pleasant breakfast room.
ROOMS: 9 en suite (3 GF) s £30-£45; d £60-£66 * ◎ **FACILITIES:** STV TVB tea/coffee Direct dial from bedrooms TVL No coaches **NOTES:** ✖ ◎ in restaurant Cen ht **LB PARKING:** 9

MONMOUTHSHIRE

Chepstow Castle

CAERWENT
Caerwent Roman Town
(just off A48)   ☎029 2050 0200
Open-access throughout out the year.

CALDICOT
Caldicot Castle, Museum & Countryside Park
NP26 4HU   ☎01291 420241
caldicotcastle@monmouthshire.gov.uk
(M4 junct 23A onto B4245. From M48 take junct 2 & follow A48 & B4245) Signposted from B4245.
Open Mar-Oct, daily 11-5.

CHEPSTOW
Chepstow Castle
NP6 5EZ   ☎01291 624065
Open Apr-May & Oct, daily 9.30-5; Jun-Sep, daily 9.30-6; Nov-Mar, Mon-Sat 9.30-4, Sun 11-4. Telephone for Xmas opening times. *£3 (ch 5-15, pen & students £2.50, wheelchair users & assisting companion free. Family ticket (2 ad & 3 ch £8.50. Group rates available.

MONMOUTH
Nelson Museum & Local History Centre
NP25 3XA   ☎01600 710630
nelsonmuseum@monmouthshire.gov.uk
(Town centre)
Open all year, Mon-Sat 10-1 & 2-5; Sun 2-5. (Closed Xmas & New Year.)

RAGLAN
Raglan Castle
NP5 2BT   ☎01291 690228
(signposted off A40)
Open Apr-May & Oct, daily 9.30-5; Jun-Sep, daily 9.30-6; Nov-Mar, Mon-Sat 9.30-4, Sun 11-4. Telephone for Xmas opening times. *£2.75 (ch 5-15, pen & students £2.25, wheelchair users and assisting companions free). Family ticket (2 ad & 3 ch) £7.75. Group discounts available.

WHITE CASTLE
White Castle
NP7 8UD   ☎01600 780380
(7m NE of Abergavenny, unclass road N of B4233)
Open Apr-Sep, Wed-Sun & BH Mon 10-5. Monument open and unstaffed on Mon & Tue between Apr-Sep. Telephone for Xmas opening times. *£2 (ch 5-15, pen & students £1.50, wheelchair users & assisting companion free). Family ticket (2 ad & 3 ch) £5.50. Group rates available.

ABERGAVENNY

Map 03 SO21

Babies Welcome | **Children's Dishes**

★★★ 67% ⊛ Angel
15 Cross St NP7 5EN
☎ 01873 857121 ▤ 01873 858059
e-mail: mail@angelhotelabergavenny.com
web: www.angelhotelabergavenny.com
*Dir: follow town centre signs from the rdbt, south of Abergavenny, past
railway and bus stations. Turn left by hotel*

> **CHILD FACILITIES: Babysitting Food/bottle warming Ch menu
> Ch portions Highchairs Safe grounds Cots Connecting rms
> NEARBY: Abergavenny Castle River Usk**

The Angel Hotel has long been a popular venue for both local
people and visitors to the area. Two traditional function rooms and
a ballroom are in regular use. However, those not having called
for a while may be surprised to note the recent changes with a
major refurbishment programme now well underway, resulting in
a comfortable lounge, relaxed bar and award-winning restaurant.
ROOMS: 29 en suite (1 fmly) ⊛ in 14 bedrooms s fr £60; d fr £85
(incl. bkfst) **FACILITIES:** STV ♫ Xmas **PARKING:** 30 **NOTES:** ⊛ in
restaurant Closed 25 Dec RS 24-26 Dec

♦♦♦♦ ❤ Hardwick Farm
NP7 9BT
☎ 01873 853513 & 01873 854238 ▤ 01873 854238
e-mail: carol.hardwickfarm@virgin.net
Dir: 1m from Abergavenny, off A4042, farm sign on R

> **CHILD FACILITIES: Please telephone for details**

Pleasantly and quietly located in Usk Valley with wonderful views,
this large old farmhouse is family run and provides warm and
friendly hospitality. The spacious bedrooms are comfortably
furnished, well equipped and include two that are suitable for
families. Traditional farmhouse breakfasts are served at separate
tables, in the traditionally furnished dining room.
ROOMS: 2 en suite (1 fmly) s £27-£30; d £45-£50 * **FACILITIES:** TVB
tea/coffee 230 acres dairy mixed **NOTES:** Credit cards not taken ⊛ Cen
ht **LB PARKING:** 2

Babies Welcome | **Family Rooms** | **Children's Dishes**

♦♦♦ ❤ Penyclawdd
Llanvihangel Crucorney NP7 7LB
☎ 01873 890591
e-mail: davies@penyclawdd.freeserve.co.uk
web: www.geocities.com/penyclawdd
Dir: take road signed Pantygelli from A465, Hereford/Abergavenny

> **CHILD FACILITIES: Activities: colouring, toys, jigsaws, Lego, ball
> games Food/bottle warming Ch menu Ch portions Highchairs
> Ch cutlery Ch discounts under 4s free, then £1 per yr of age Safe
> grounds Cots Family rms D rm with 2 S beds £50-£75 Ch drinks
> Laundry NEARBY: Park Leisure Centre Falconry Farms**

This attractive modern house is located in immaculate gardens off
the Abergavenny to Hereford road. It offers homely bedrooms
filled with many thoughtful extras. A traditionally furnished dining
room is the setting for imaginative breakfasts, and a comfortable
lounge with wood burner is also available.
ROOMS: 3 rms (1 en suite) (2 fmly) s £25; d £45 * **FACILITIES:** TVB
tea/coffee TVL 160 acres sheep beef, working farm **NOTES:** Credit cards
not taken ✝ ⊛ Cen ht **PARKING:** 6

> Don't forget to let proprietors
> know when you book that
> you're bringing the kids

Children's Dishes

⊛ ⊛ Walnut Tree Inn
Llandewi Skirrid NP7 8AW
☎ 01873 852797 ▤ 01873 859764
e-mail: francesco@thewalnuttreeinn.com
Dir: 3m NE of Abergavenny on B4521

> **CHILD FACILITIES: Food/bottle warming Ch portions Safe grounds
> NEARBY: Walks**

FOOD: Italian **STYLE:** Rustic, Country-House **SEATS:** 70
OPEN: 12-3/700-10.45, Closed 24 Dec-3 Jan, Mon, D BHs, Sun
RESTAURANT: Fixed L £16.50, main £9.75-£25 **NOTES:** ⊛ area
PARKING: 30

LLANTRISANT

Map 03 ST39

◀ The Greyhound Inn
NP15 1LE
☎ 01291 672505 & 673447 ▤ 01291 673255
e-mail: enquiry@greyhound-inn.com
web: www.greyhound-inn.com
*Dir: From M4 take A449 towards Monmouth, 1st jct to Usk, L into Usk Sq.
Take 2nd L signed Llantrisant. 2.5m to inn*

> **CHILD FACILITIES: Please telephone for details**

OPEN: 11-11 (Sun 12-4, 7-11) Closed: 25, 31 Dec, 1 Jan **BAR MEALS:** L
served all week 12-2.15 D served Mon-Sat 6-10 Av main course £7.50
RESTAURANT: L served all week 12-2.15 D served Mon-Sat 6-10.30 Av 3
course à la carte £16.50 **FACILITIES:** Garden: Pond with fountain,
delightful garden ✝ **ROOMS:** 10 bedrooms 10 en suite 2 family rooms
s£50 d£66 **PARKING:** 60

LLANVAIR DISCOED

Map 03 ST49

Babies Welcome | **Children's Dishes**

◀ The Woodland Restaurant & Bar
NP16 6LX
☎ 01633 400313 ▤ 01633 400313
Dir: Telephone for directions

> **CHILD FACILITIES: Outdoor play area Food/bottle warming
> Ch menu Ch portions Highchairs Ch cutlery Safe grounds
> NEARBY: Walks**

OPEN: 11-3 6-11 (Sun 12-3, closed Sun eve) **BAR MEALS:** L served
Tue-Sun 12-2 D served Tue-Sat 6-10 Av main course £13.95
RESTAURANT: L served Tue-Sun 12-2 D served Tue-Sat 6-9.30 Av 3 course
à la carte £25 **FACILITIES:** Garden: Plenty of bench seating, play area
PARKING: 30

MONMOUTH

Map 03 SO51

Babies Welcome | **Family Rooms** | **Children's Dishes**

★★ 65% Riverside
Cinderhill St NP25 5EY
☎ 01600 715577 & 713236 ▤ 01600 712668
e-mail: info@riversidehotelmonmouth.co.uk
*Dir: leave A40 signposted Rockfield & Monmouth hotel on left beyond
garage & before rdbt*

> **CHILD FACILITIES: Baby listening Babysitting (on request)
> Activities: toys, games, jigsaws Family area Food/bottle warming
> Ch menu Ch portions Highchairs Ch cutlery Safe grounds Videos
> Cots Family rms T rms with S beds from £64.95 Connecting rms
> Laundry NEARBY: Farms Leisure centre Cinema Canoeing
> Fishing**

Please note that this establishment has recently changed
ownership. Just a short walk from the famous 13th-century bridge,
continued on p306

MONMOUTH, continued

this hotel offers accommodation in a relaxed and informal atmosphere. Bedrooms are well-equipped and soundly decorated. Public areas include a separate restaurant, a popular bar and a conservatory lounge at the rear of the property.
ROOMS: 17 en suite (2 fmly) ⊛ in 2 bedrooms s £43-£49.95; d £50-£59.95 **LB FACILITIES:** STV Xmas **PARKING:** 30 **NOTES:** ⊛ in restaurant

Babies Welcome	Family Rooms	Children's Dishes

◆◆◆◆ ❦ Penylan Farm

The Hendre NP25 5NL
☎ 01600 716435 ▤ 01600 719391
e-mail: penylan@fsmail.net
Dir: B4233 towards Hendre, prior to Hendre turn for Newcastle, follow road for approx 1.5m, after passing Llangattock Montessori School on left take next left 1st farm on right in approx 0.5m

CHILD FACILITIES: Activities: games, books Outdoor play area Food/bottle warming Ch menu Ch portions Highchairs Ch cutlery Ch discounts under 2s free, under 5s £10, under 15s £15 Safe grounds Videos Cots Family rms connecting D & T rms from £50 Ch drinks Connecting rms **NEARBY:** Farm Cycling Canoeing Walks Leisure centre

This sympathetically renovated converted barn was originally part of the Hendre Estate, and was owned by the Rolls family. Bedrooms are housed in a former granary, and equipped with many thoughtful extras. Breakfasts focus on local produce, and a guest lounge is also available.
ROOMS: 3 rms (2 en suite) d £42-£50 * **FACILITIES:** TVB tea/coffee TVL ♨ 90 acres Beef Dinner Last d order 24hrs prior **NOTES:** Credit cards not taken ✖ ⊛ Cen ht **LB PARKING:** 4

Babies Welcome	Family Rooms	Children's Dishes

◆◆◆ Church Farm

Mitchel Troy NP25 4HZ
☎ 01600 712176
Dir: from A40 S, L onto B4293 for Trelleck before tunnel, 150yds turn L & follow signs to Mitchel Troy. GH on main rd, on L 200 yds beyond campsite

CHILD FACILITIES: Baby listening Activities: cycles, books, toys Outdoor play area Food/bottle warming Ch menu Ch portions Highchairs Ch cutlery Ch discounts children in cots free Safe grounds Games consoles Videos Cots Family rms D rm with 1-2 S beds £50 - £78 Ch drinks Laundry

Located in the village of Mitchel Troy, this 16th-century former farmhouse retains many original features including exposed beams and open fireplaces. A range of bedrooms is provided and a spacious lounge is available in addition to the traditionally furnished dining room where breakfast is served.
ROOMS: 8 rms (6 en suite) (2 fmly) s £22-£30; d £44-£52 * **FACILITIES:** tea/coffee TVL No coaches Dinner Last d order noon **NOTES:** Credit cards not taken ⊛ Cen ht **LB PARKING:** 12

TINTERN PARVA   Map 03 SO50

Babies Welcome	Family Rooms	Children's Dishes

★★★ 68% The Abbey Hotel

THE INDEPENDENTS

NP16 6SF
☎ 01291 689777 ▤ 01291 689727
e-mail: info@theabbeyhoteltintern.com
web: www.theabbeyhoteltintern.com
Dir: M48 junct 2/A466, hotel opposite the abbey ruins

continued

CHILD FACILITIES: Baby listening Babysitting Activities: crayoning Food/bottle warming Ch menu Ch portions Highchairs Ch discounts 5 - 11s sharing with parents £19.50 Safe grounds Cots Family rms family suite £120 Connecting rms Laundry **NEARBY:** Clearwell Caves Forest of Dean Railways

Now refurbished to a high standard and possessing stunning views of nearby Tintern Abbey, this friendly hotel provides modern bedrooms, including a family suite. Diners are spoilt for choice between the brasserie with its daytime carvery, the formal carte service for dinner, and the pleasant hotel bar where lighter meal options are on offer.
ROOMS: 23 en suite ⊛ in 7 bedrooms s £70-£75; d £99-£140 (incl. bkfst) **LB FACILITIES:** Spa STV Fishing Jacuzzi ♫ Xmas **PARKING:** 60 **NOTES:** ⊛ in restaurant

Babies Welcome	Family Rooms	Children's Dishes

★★ 73% ◉ Parva Farmhouse Hotel & Restaurant

THE CIRCLE
Selected Individual Hotels
GREAT BRITAIN

NP16 6SQ
☎ 01291 689411 & 689511 ▤ 01291 689557
e-mail: parva_hoteltintern@hotmail.com
Dir: From S leave M48 junct 2, N edge of village on A466. From N, 10m S of Monmouth town & M50

CHILD FACILITIES: Baby listening Activities: toys, games Food/bottle warming Ch menu Ch portions Highchairs Ch cutlery Videos Cots Family rms Laundry **NEARBY:** Walks Playgrounds Leisure centre

This relaxed and friendly hotel is situated on a sweep of the River Wye with far reaching views of the valley. Originally a farmhouse dating from the 17th century, many of the original features have been retained to provide a lounge full of character, which has a fire in colder months, and an atmospheric restaurant with a popular local following. Bedrooms are tastefully decorated and thoughtfully equipped.
ROOMS: 9 en suite (3 fmly) (1 GF) s £55-£76; d £76-£80 (incl. bkfst) **LB FACILITIES:** Cycle hire **PARKING:** 10 **NOTES:** ⊛ in restaurant

TREDUNNOCK   Map 03 ST89

Babies Welcome	Children's Dishes

🏠 ◉ ◉ 🍴 The Newbridge

NP15 1LY
☎ 01633 451000 ▤ 01633 451001
e-mail: thenewbridge@tinyonline.co.uk
web: www.thenewbridge.co.uk
Dir: Turn off B4236 between Usk & Caerleon at Tredunnock sign

CHILD FACILITIES: Activities: colouring, Lego, books Food/bottle warming Ch portions Highchairs Ch cutlery Safe grounds Changing facilities **NEARBY:** Caerleon Roman Museum

This 200-year-old inn by the River Usk has been renovated and converted into a spacious, traditionally furnished restaurant occupying the ground and first-floor levels. The cuisine is modern British and the dishes on the daily-changing blackboard menu include locally produced meat and fish from Cornwall. Presentation is simple and effective with expertly cooked seafood and pudding dishes. Six smart, modern and well-equipped bedrooms are located in a stone-clad, purpose-built unit adjacent to the restaurant. Winner of the AA Restaurant of the Year for Wales 2004-5.
ROOMS: 6 en suite (2 family) (4GF) ⊛ in all bedrooms s £85-£105; d £95-£125 (inc bkfst) **LB FACILITIES:** STV Fishing Xmas **PARKING:** 6 **NOTES:** ✖

USK   Map 03 SO30

Babies Welcome | **Children's Dishes**

◀ The Nags Head Inn
Twyn Square NP15 1BH
☎ 01291 672820 📠 01291 672720
Dir: On A472

CHILD FACILITIES: Family area Food/bottle warming Ch menu Ch portions Highchairs Safe grounds Changing facilities
NEARBY: Usk Castle River Parks

OPEN: 10-3 5.30-11 Closed: Dec 25 **BAR MEALS:** L served all week 10-2 D served all week 5.30-10.30 Av main course £7.50 **RESTAURANT:** L served all week 11.30-2 D served all week 5.30-10.30
FACILITIES: Garden: ✖

NEATH PORT TALBOT

NEATH   Map 03 SS79

◆◆◆◆◆ Green Lanterns
Hawdref Ganol Farm, Cimla SA12 9SL
☎ 01639 631884 📠 01639 899550
e-mail: caren.jones@btinternet.com
web: www.thegreenlanterns.co.uk
Dir: M4 J43 towards Neath. Take B4287 signposted Cimla & R at x-roads 500yds past comprehensive school, AA signposted

CHILD FACILITIES: Please telephone for details

This 18th-century farmhouse is part of a 46-acre equestrian and pony-trekking centre and has superb views over the surrounding countryside. Bedrooms are spacious, decorated in keeping with the style of the house and equipped with modern facilities. An impressive lounge is provided for residents and features an enormous inglenook fireplace. A separate building is the setting for a comfortable lounge bar, meeting rooms and "T Bones" Restaurant which features a comprehensive menu selection including Welsh black beef steaks.
ROOMS: 4 en suite (2 fmly) ◎ **FACILITIES:** TVB tea/coffee TVL Riding Dinner Last d order 7pm **NOTES:** ◎ in restaurant Licensed Cen ht **PARKING:** 6

PORT TALBOT   Map 03 SS78

Babies Welcome | **Family Rooms** | **Children's Dishes**

★★★ 68% Aberavon Beach
SA12 6QP
☎ 01639 884949 📠 01639 897885
e-mail: sales@aberavonbeach.com
web: www.aberavonbeach.com
Dir: M4 junct 41/A48 & follow signs for Aberavon Beach & Hollywood Park

CHILD FACILITIES: Baby listening Activities: colouring packs Food/bottle warming Ch menu Ch portions Highchairs Ch discounts under 16s sharing with parents free Safe grounds Cots Family rms £89 Connecting rms Laundry **NEARBY:** Leisure Centre/Aquadome Parks Cinema Seafront location

This friendly, purpose-built hotel enjoys a prominent position on the seafront overlooking Swansea Bay. Bedrooms, many of which have sea views, are comfortably appointed and thoughtfully
continued

equipped. Public areas include a leisure suite, open-plan bar and restaurant and a selection of function rooms.
ROOMS: 52 en suite (6 fmly) ◎ in 26 bedrooms s £74-£79; d £84-£89 (incl. bkfst) **LB FACILITIES:** ▣ Sauna Jacuzzi All weather leisure centre ♫ Xmas **PARKING:** 150 **NOTES:** ◎ in restaurant

NEWPORT

NEWPORT   Map 03 ST38

Babies Welcome | **Family Rooms** | **Children's Dishes**

◆◆◆◆ Crescent Guest House
11 Caerau Crescent NP20 4HG
☎ 01633 776677 📠 01633 761279
e-mail: lex4172@aol.com
web: www.crescentguesthouse.com
Dir: M4 junct 27 towards town centre. Through traffic lights with Handpost pub on right. After 50yds left into Caerau Crescent

CHILD FACILITIES: Food/bottle warming Ch menu Ch portions Highchairs Ch cutlery Ch discounts Cots Family rms D rm with 2 S beds, rm with 4 S beds Laundry **NEARBY:** Tredegar House Parks Cinema

Located on a quiet residential avenue within easy walking distance of the centre, this elegant Victorian house retains many original features, including a fine tiled hall and stained glass windows. Bedrooms are comfortable, filled with thoughtful extras and have modern bathrooms. Breakfasts use quality local produce and are taken in an attractive dining room.
ROOMS: 9 en suite (2 fmly) (2 GF) s fr £38; d fr £48 *
FACILITIES: TVB tea/coffee No coaches **NOTES:** ✖ ◎ Cen ht **PARKING:** 5

Babies Welcome | **Children's Dishes**

◎ ◎ The Chandlery
77-78 Lower Dock St NP20 1EH
☎ 01633 256622 📠 01633 256633
Dir: Situated on A48, 0.5 mile from the Royal Gwent Hospital at the foot of George St Bridge

CHILD FACILITIES: Food/bottle warming Ch portions Highchairs Ch cutlery **NEARBY:** Park Cinema Tredegar House Big Pit Museum

FOOD: Modern European **STYLE:** Classic Modern **SEATS:** 70
OPEN: 12-2.30/7-10.30, Closed 1 wk Xmas, Sun-MonL Sat
RESTAURANT: main £9.50-£16.95 **NOTES:** ◎ area, Air con
PARKING: 20

PEMBROKESHIRE

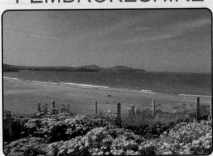

Whitesand, near St David's; Pembrokeshire Coast

AMROTH
Colby Woodland Garden
SA67 8PP ☎01834 811885
(1.5m inland from Amroth beside Carmarthen Bay, follow brown signs from A477)
Open 25 Mar-30 Oct, daily 10-5. *£3.40 (ch £1.70). Family ticket £7.50. Group £2.70 (ch £1.30) NT members free.

FISHGUARD
OceanLab SA64 0DE ☎01348 874737
fishguardharbour-tic@pembrokeshire.gov.uk
(Take A40 to Fishguard, turn at by-pass, follow signs for Stenaline ferry terminal, pass 2 garages, turn right at rdbt & follow signs to Ocean Lab)
Open Apr-Oct 10-6, Nov-Mar 10-4.

PEMBROKE
Pembroke Castle SA71 4LA
☎01646 681510 & 684585
pembroke.castle@talk21.com
(W end of main street)
Open all year, daily, Apr-Sep 9.30-6; Mar & Oct 10-5; Nov-Feb, 10-4; Closed 24-26 Dec & 1 Jan.
*£3 (ch under 16 & pen £2, ch under 5 & wheelchair users free. Family ticket £8.

ST DAVID'S
St David's Bishop's Palace
SA62 6PE ☎01437 720517
(on A487)
Open Apr-May & Oct daily 9.30-5; Jun-Sep, daily 9.30-6; Nov-Mar, Mon-Sat 9.30-4, Sun 11-4. Telephone for Xmas opening times. *£2.50 (ch 5-15, pen & students £2, disabled visitors & assisting companions free). Family ticket (2ad & 3ch) £7. Group discounts available. Prices quoted apply until 31 Mar 2005.

ST FLORENCE
Manor House Wildlife & Leisure Park
SA70 8RJ ☎01646 651201
(on B4318 between Tenby & St Florence)
Open Etr-end Sep, daily 10-6. Please telephone for late opening Jul & Aug.

SCOLTON
Scolton Visitor Centre SA62 5QL
☎01437 731328 (Mus) & 731457 (Park)
(5m N of Haverfordwest, on B4329)
Open; Museum Apr-Oct, Tue-Sun & BHs 10.30-1 & 1.30-5.30; Country Park all year ex 25 & 26 Dec, Etr-Sep 10-7, Oct-Etr 10-6.

Babies Welcome | **Children's Dishes**

⬛ Carew Inn
SA70 8SL
☎ 01646 651267 🖷 01646 650126
e-mail: mandy@carewinn.co.uk
Dir: From A477 take A4075. Inn 400yds opp castle & Celtic cross

CHILD FACILITIES: Activities: colouring Outdoor play area Food/bottle warming Ch menu Ch portions Highchairs Safe grounds Changing facilities **NEARBY:** Carew Castle and Mill Oakwood Leisure Park

OPEN: 11.30-2.30 4.30-11 (Summer & wknd 11-11) Closed: Dec 25 **BAR MEALS:** L served all week 11.30-2 D served all week 6-9 Av main course £6.95 **RESTAURANT:** L served all week 12-2 D served all week 6-9 Av 3 course à la carte £15 Av 2 course fixed price £6.95 **FACILITIES:** Garden: overlooks Carew Castle **PARKING:** 20

Babies Welcome | **Family Rooms** | **Children's Dishes**

◆◆◆◆ College
93 Hill St, St Thomas Green SA61 1QL
☎ 01437 763710
e-mail: colinlarby@aol.com
Dir: towards town centre, follow signs for St Thomas Green car park

CHILD FACILITIES: Baby listening Activities: books, games, puzzles Indoor play area Outdoor play area Food/bottle warming Ch menu Ch portions Highchairs Ch cutlery Ch discounts Videos Cots Family rms D rms with S beds **NEARBY:** Animal parks Theme park Walks 10-min drive to sea

Located in a mainly residential area within easy walking distance of central attractions, this impressive Georgian town house has been upgraded to offer good levels of comfort and facilities. A range of practically equipped bedrooms is provided and public areas include a spacious lounge (where internet access is available) and an attractive pine -furnished dining room, the setting for comprehensive breakfasts.
ROOMS: 8 en suite (3 fmly) s £27-£30; d £45-£50 * 🚭
FACILITIES: TVB tea/coffee TVL Dinner Last d order by prior arrangement **NOTES:** 🚭 in restaurant Cen ht **PARKING:** 2

Babies Welcome | **Children's Dishes**

⬛ Ferry Inn
Pembroke Ferry SA72 6UD
☎ 01646 682947
Dir: A477, off A48, R at garage, signs for Cleddau Bridge, L at roundabout

CHILD FACILITIES: Food/bottle warming Ch menu Ch portions Highchairs Safe grounds Changing facilities **NEARBY:** Oakwood Park Folly Farm

OPEN: 11.30-2.45 7-11 Closed: 25-26 Dec **BAR MEALS:** L served all week 12-2 D served all week 7-10 Av main course £7.50 **RESTAURANT:** L served all week 12-2 D served all week 7-10 Av 3 course à la carte £12 **FACILITIES:** Garden: Beer terrace on edge of river, amazing views ✈ **PARKING:** 12

This symbol indicates the establishment provides food & bottle warming and highchairs

PORTHGAIN   Map 02 SM83

 Babies Welcome | **Children's Dishes**

■ The Sloop Inn
SA62 5BN
☎ 01348 831449 ▤ 01348 831388
-mail: matthew@sloop-inn.freeserve.co.uk

CHILD FACILITIES: Food/bottle warming Ch licence Ch menu
Highchairs Changing facilities   NEARBY: 100yds to sea

OPEN: 11-11 (Sun 12-4, 5.30-10.30) Rest: 25 Dec No food, Limited bar
BAR MEALS: L served all week 12-2.30 D served all week 6-9.30 Av main
ourse £7 RESTAURANT: L served all week 12-2.30 D served all week
-9.30 Av 3 course à la carte £20 FACILITIES: Children's licence Garden:
aised patio area, sun trap, safe ✱ PARKING: 50

ST DAVID'S   Map 02 SM72

Babies Welcome | **Family Rooms** | **Children's Dishes**

★★★ 77% ◉ ◉ Warpool Court
SA62 6BN
☎ 01437 720300 ▤ 01437 720676
-mail: warpool@enterprise.net
web: www.warpoolcourthotel.com
Dir: At Cross Square bear left beside Cartref Restaurant (Goat St). Pass
armers Arms Pub, after 400mtrs take left follow hotel signs, entrance on
ght

CHILD FACILITIES: Baby listening Babysitting (not registered)
Food/bottle warming Ch menu Ch portions Highchairs Ch discounts
babies free, up to 5s £18, 6 -10s £23, 11-14s £29 Safe grounds Cots
Family rms D rms with S beds & B bed from £148 Ch drinks
Laundry   NEARBY: Oakwood Park Folly Farm Coastal walks on
coastal path, 5-min drive to sea

Originally the cathedral choir school, Warpool Court Hotel is set in
landscaped gardens looking out to sea and is within easy walking
distance of the Pembrokeshire coastal path. The lounges are
spacious and comfortable and bedrooms are well furnished and
equipped with modern facilities. The restaurant offers delightful
cuisine.
ROOMS: 25 en suite (3 fmly) s £65-£100; d £130-£200 (incl. bkfst) LB
FACILITIES: ❏ ⚲ Gym ♨ Xmas PARKING: 100 NOTES: ⊛ in
restaurant Closed Jan

Children's Dishes

◉ Morgan's Restaurant
0 Nun St SA62 6NT
☎ 01437 720508 ▤ 01437 720508
-mail: morgans@stdavids.co.uk
web: www.morgans-in-stdavids.co.uk
Dir: 60 yds off Cross Square

CHILD FACILITIES: Food/bottle warming Ch portions
NEARBY: Oceanarium Rare breeds farm Sheepdog displays
Swimming pool Coastal walks 5-min drive to sea

FOOD: European SEATS: 36 OPEN: 6.30-9.30, Closed Jan/Feb (times
may vary out of season), SunL all week RESTAURANT: main £11.50-£18.50
NOTES: Smart Dress, ⊛ in restaurant PARKING: Car park opposite

Don't forget our travel accommodation
section at the front of the guide

TENBY   Map 02 SN10

Family Rooms | **Children's Dishes**

★★★ 71% Heywood Mount
Heywood Ln SA70 8DA
☎ 01834 842087 ▤ 01834 842113
e-mail: reception@heywoodmount.co.uk
web: www.heywoodmount.co.uk
Dir: A478 into Tenby, follow Heywood Mount signs then right into
Serpentine Rd, turn right at T-junct into Heywood Lane, 3rd hotel on left

CHILD FACILITIES: Baby listening Outdoor play area Food/bottle
warming Ch menu Ch portions Ch cutlery Ch discounts when
sharing 4-6s 60%, 7-14s 50% Safe grounds Videos Cots Family rms
D rms with B beds, D rms for 3, D rms for 4 from £130 Fridge
Laundry   NEARBY: Oakwood Park Folly farm Horse riding 0.5m
to sea

This privately owned hotel is situated in a peaceful residential
area, close to Tenby's beaches and town centre. The
well-maintained house is surrounded by extensive gardens, and
public areas include a comfortable lounge, bar, restaurant and
health & fitness spa. Several of the well-appointed and equipped
bedrooms are on the ground floor.
ROOMS: 30 en suite (6 fmly) (10 GF) ⊛ in all bedrooms s £42-£85;
d £84-£170 (incl. bkfst) LB FACILITIES: Spa ⊠ Sauna Solarium No
children 3yrs Gym Jacuzzi ♫ Xmas PARKING: 25 NOTES: ✱ ⊛ in
restaurant

Babies Welcome | **Family Rooms** | **Children's Dishes**

★★★ 69% Fourcroft
North Beach SA70 8AP
☎ 01834 842886 ▤ 01834 842888
e-mail: staying@fourcroft-hotel.co.uk
web: www.fourcroft-hotel.co.uk
Dir: A478, after "Welcome to Tenby" sign left towards North Beach &
walled town. At sea front turn sharp left. Hotel on left

CHILD FACILITIES: Baby listening Activities: games room,
colouring books, board games Indoor play area Outdoor play area
Family area Food/bottle warming Ch menu Ch portions Highchairs
Ch cutlery Ch discounts 5 and under free, 6-14s 50% Safe grounds
Videos Cots Family rms Connecting rms Laundry
NEARBY: Oakwood Theme Park Folly Farm 2-min walk to sea

This friendly, family-run hotel offers a beachfront location,
together with a number of extra facilities that make it particularly
suitable for families with children. Guests have direct access to the
beach through the hotel's clifftop gardens. Bedrooms are of a
good size, with modern facilities.
ROOMS: 40 en suite (12 fmly) ⊛ in 10 bedrooms s £39-£59;
d £78-£118 (incl. bkfst) LB FACILITIES: STV ⊰ Sauna Jacuzzi Table
tennis Giant chess Human Gyroscope Snooker Pool Xmas PARKING: 12
NOTES: ⊛ in restaurant

Wales

WOLF'S CASTLE · Map 02 SM92

◆◆◆◆ 🍺 🍴 The Wolfe Inn
SA62 5LS
☎ 01437 741662 📠 01437 741676
e-mail: eat@the-wolfe.co.uk
web: www.thewolfe.info
Dir: 7m from both Haverfordwest and Fishguard on A40

CHILD FACILITIES: Please telephone for details

This sympathetically renovated period inn retains many original features and is very popular for its imaginative food, featuring good local produce and some regional Italian specialities. Bedrooms, one of which is located in a former hay loft, are equipped with thoughtful extras and the pretty enclosed garden is ablaze with colour during the warmer months.
ROOMS: 2 en suite 1 annexe en suite (2 fmly) ⊗ **FACILITIES:** TVB tea/coffee Dinner Last d order 9pm **NOTES:** ⊗ in restaurant ⊗ in 1 lounge Cen ht **PARKING:** 30

POWYS

BERRIEW · Map 07 SJ10

🍴 The Lion Hotel
SY21 8PQ
☎ 01686 640452 📠 01686 640604
Dir: 5m from Welshpool on A483, R to Berriew. Centre of village next to church.

CHILD FACILITIES: Please telephone for details

OPEN: 12-3 6-11 (Fri 5.30-11, Sat 7-11, Sun 7-10.30) Closed: Dec 25 **BAR MEALS:** L served all week 12-2 D served all week 7-9 Av main course £9.95 **RESTAURANT:** L served all week 12-2 D served Mon-Sat 7-9
FACILITIES: Children's licence Garden: Patio area surrounded by plants
ROOMS: 7 bedrooms 7 en suite 1 family rooms s£55 d£70 **PARKING:** 6

BUILTH WELLS · Map 03 SO05

| Babies Welcome | Family Rooms | Children's Dishes |

★★★ 70% 🌐 ♨ Caer Beris Manor · THE INDEPENDENTS
LD2 3NP
☎ 01982 552601 📠 01982 552586
e-mail: caerberismanor@btinternet.com
web: www.caerberis.co.uk
Dir: from town centre follow signs for A483 Llandovery. Hotel located on left

CHILD FACILITIES: Baby listening Activities: games, jigsaws, books Outdoor play area Family area Food/bottle warming Ch menu Ch portions Highchairs Ch cutlery Ch discounts under 16s free sharing with parents Safe grounds Videos Cots Family rms D rm with 2 S beds £95 Ch drinks Laundry NEARBY: Crazy golf Farms

With extensive landscaped grounds, guests can expect a relaxing stay at this friendly and privately owned hotel. Bedrooms are individually decorated and furnished and retain a feel of a bygone era. A spacious and comfortable lounge and a lounge bar enhance this atmosphere together with the elegant restaurant, complete with 16th-century panelling.
ROOMS: 23 en suite (1 fmly) (3 GF) s £57.50-£67.50; d £95-£105 (incl. bkfst) **LB FACILITIES:** STV Fishing Riding Sauna Gym Clay pigeon shooting Xmas **PARKING:** 32 **NOTES:** ⊗ in restaurant

CRICKHOWELL · Map 03 SO2

| Babies Welcome | Family Rooms | Children's Dishes |

★★★ 68% 🌐 Manor
Brecon Rd NP8 1SE
☎ 01873 810212 📠 01873 811938
e-mail: info@manorhotel.co.uk
web: www.manorhotel.co.uk
Dir: on A40, Crickhowell/Brecon, 0.5m from Crickhowell

CHILD FACILITIES: Baby listening Activities: toys, colouring books, games Family area Food/bottle warming Ch menu Ch portions Highchairs Ch cutlery Safe grounds Cots Family rms D rm with D sofa bed or Z bed £110 Laundry

This impressive manor house set in a stunning location was the birthplace of Sir George Everest. The bedrooms and public areas are elegant, and there are extensive leisure facilities. The restaurant has panoramic views and is the setting for exciting modern cooking. Guests can also dine informally at the nearby Nantyffin Cider Mill, a sister operation of the hotel.
ROOMS: 22 en suite (1 fmly) ⊗ in 8 bedrooms s £45-£65; d £70-£95 (incl. bkfst) **LB FACILITIES:** STV 🏊 Sauna Solarium Gym Jacuzzi Fitness assessment Sunbed Xmas **PARKING:** 200 **NOTES:** ⊗ in restaurant

GARTH · Map 03 SN9

◆◆◆◆ Garth Mill
LD4 4AS
☎ 01591 620572
e-mail: dave@pigsfolly.fsnet.co.uk
Dir: on A483 in village of Garth, 6m SW of Builth Wells

CHILD FACILITIES: Please telephone for details

This former brick works has been sympathetically renovated to provide quality accommodation, with the added benefit of a farm shop and pets' corner complete with llamas, pigs, ducks, chickens and ponies. Spacious bedrooms are both practical and homely, and the dining room is the setting for wholesome food utilising home-reared or local produce. In addition to the residents lounge there is also a large lounge bar where bar meals are available.
ROOMS: 8 rms (4 en suite) (1 fmly) s £30-£50; d £40-£60 * ⊗ **FACILITIES:** TVB tea/coffee Dinner Last d order 9pm **NOTES:** ✖ ⊗ i restaurant ⊗ in lounges Licensed Cen ht **LB PARKING:** 40

Babies Welcome This symbol indicates the establishment provides food & bottle warming and highchairs

LANGAMMARCH WELLS　　　Map 03 SN94

Babies Welcome | Children's Dishes

★★★ ⊛ ⊛ ⚓ **Lake Country House**
D4 4BS
☎ 01591 620202 & 620474 🖷 01591 620457
-mail: info@lakecountryhouse.co.uk
veb: www.lakecountryhouse.co.uk
ir: W from Builth Wells on A483 to Garth (approx 6m). Left for
langammarch Wells, follow hotel signs

CHILD FACILITIES: Baby listening Outdoor play area Food/bottle
warming Ch portions Highchairs Ch discounts free Safe grounds
Cots Ch drinks Connecting rms Laundry　NEARBY: Walks Tennis

xpect good old fashioned values of service and hospitality at this
ictorian country house hotel, which comes complete with a
-hole, par 3 golf course, 50 acres of wooded grounds and a river.
edrooms, including many suites, are individually decorated and
ave many extra comforts as standard. Traditional afternoon teas
re served in the lounge in front of a log fire, and award-winning
uisine is provided in the spacious and elegant restaurant.
OOMS: 19 en suite (2 GF) ⊛ in 6 bedrooms s £105-£170;
£140-£240 (incl. bkfst) LB **FACILITIES:** Golf 9 ⚲ Fishing Snooker ⚓
; Clay pigeon shooting, horse riding, mountain biking, quad biking,
rchery Xmas **PARKING:** 72 **NOTES:** ⊛ in restaurant

LANRHAEADR-YM-MOCHNANT　　　Map 06 SJ12

◆◆◆ **Bron Heulog**
Vaterfall St SY10 0JX
☎ 01691 780521
-mail: kraines@enta.net
ir: Turn off A483 toward Llanrhaeadr (B4396). In village turn right after
SBC bank, Bron Heulog is 1st large house on right
CHILD FACILITIES: Please telephone for details

ocated in the heart of an unspoilt rural village and set on mature
rounds, which are home to two rescued donkeys, this impressive
arly Victorian house has been sympathetically restored to provide
igh standards of comfort and facilities. Bedrooms are equipped
vith thoughtful extras and there is a comfortable lounge.
OOMS: 3 en suite 1 annexe en suite (2 fmly) s £35-£38; d £56-£65 *
ACILITIES: TVB tea/coffee No coaches **NOTES:** ✠ ⊛ Cen ht
ARKING: 8

MONTGOMERY　　　Map 03 SO29

Babies Welcome | Family Rooms | Children's Dishes

★★ 71% ⊛ **Dragon**　　THE INDEPENDENTS
Y15 6PA
☎ 01686 668359 🖷 01686 668287
-mail: reception@dragonhotel.com
veb: www.dragonhotel.com
ir: behind the Town Hall

CHILD FACILITIES: Baby listening Activities: small toy box
Food/bottle warming Ch menu Ch portions Highchairs Ch discounts
€5 per wk when sharing with parents Videos Cots Family rms
Connecting rms Laundry

his fine 17th-century coaching inn stands in the centre of
Montgomery. Beams and timbers from the nearby castle, which
vas destroyed by Cromwell, are visible in the lounge and bar. A
vide choice of soundly prepared, wholesome food is available in
oth the restaurant and bar. Bedrooms are well equipped and
mily rooms are available.
OOMS: 20 en suite (6 fmly) ⊛ in 16 bedrooms s £47-£57; d £79.50
ncl. bkfst) LB **FACILITIES:** ⊡ Sauna ♬ Xmas **PARKING:** 21
OTES: ⊛ in restaurant

RHONDDA CYNON TAFF

Wales

PONTYPRIDD　　　Map 03 ST08

Babies Welcome | Family Rooms | Children's Dishes

★★★ 70% **Llechwen Hall**
Llanfabon CF37 4HP
☎ 01443 742050 & 743020 🖷 01443 742189
e-mail: llechwen@aol.com
web: www.llechwen.com
Dir: A470 N towards Merthyr Tydfil, then A472, then onto A4054 for
Cilfynydd. After 0.25m, turn left at hotel sign & follow to top of hill

CHILD FACILITIES: Baby listening Outdoor play area Food/bottle
warming Ch menu Ch portions Highchairs Ch discounts £15 Safe
grounds Cots Family rms D rm with B beds from £95 Laundry
NEARBY: Rhondda Heritage Park Walks Leisure centre

Set on top of a hill with a stunning approach, this hotel has served
a variety of uses in its 200-year history, including as a private
school and as a magistrates' court. Bedrooms are individually
decorated and well equipped and some are situated in the
comfortable coach house nearby. The Victorian-style public areas
are attractively appointed.
ROOMS: 12 en suite 8 annexe en suite (11 fmly) (4 GF) ⊛ in 8
bedrooms s £54.50-£65.45; d £70-£106.90 (incl. bkfst) LB
FACILITIES: Xmas **PARKING:** 100 **NOTES:** ⊛ in restaurant Closed
25-28 Dec

How to use this guide & abbreviations
are explained on pages 5-7

Wales

SWANSEA

LLANRHIDIAN   Map 02 SS49

★★ 66% *North Gower*

SA3 1EE
☎ 01792 390042 📠 01792 391401
e-mail: enquiries@northgowerhotel.co.uk
web: www.northgowerhotel.co.uk
Dir: on B4295, turn left at Llanrhidian Esso Service Station
CHILD FACILITIES: Please telephone for details

Situated on the Gower Peninsula with delightful views over the sea, this family-owned hotel offers guests a relaxing and comfortable stay. Bedrooms are spacious and airy, whilst public areas consist of a bar full of character and a pleasant restaurant.
ROOMS: 18 en suite (10 fmly) (7 GF) ⊗ in 8 bedrooms
PARKING: 100 **NOTES:** ⊗ in restaurant

See advert on opposite page

PARKMILL (NEAR SWANSEA)   Map 03 SS69

◆◆◆ ❦ *Parc-le-Breos House*

SA3 2HA
☎ 01792 371636 📠 01792 371287
Dir: at village turn right 300yds after Shepherds shop, then next left, signed. Follow private road to end
CHILD FACILITIES: Please telephone for details
This early 19th-century, imposing house is at the end of a forest drive and set in 70 acres of delightful grounds. Many charming original features have been retained in the public rooms, which include a lounge and games room. In the bedrooms, many of which are suitable for family occupancy, comfortable furnishings are provided.
ROOMS: 10 en suite (7 fmly) **FACILITIES:** TVB tea/coffee TVL Riding Games room 65 acres arable horses pigs chickens Dinner Last d order 3pm **NOTES:** Credit cards not taken ✖ Cen ht **PARKING:** 12

SWANSEA   Map 03 SS69

★★★★ ❦ ⊛ ⊛ **Morgans**

Somerset Place SA1 1RR
☎ 01792 484848 📠 01792 484849
e-mail: info@morganshotel.co.uk

continued

This new and stunning hotel has been imaginatively developed from the Port's Authority building near the harbour side. The bedrooms are modern in design with much attention given to guest comfort. Features include big beds, best linen, large screen TV, high ceilings, and DVDs. Public areas enjoy wonderful period elements and guests have a choice of eating and drinking options.
ROOMS: 20 en suite (4 fmly) ⊗ in all bedrooms **FACILITIES:** STV
PARKING: 27 **NOTES:** ✖ ⊗ in restaurant

★★★★ 68%
Swansea Marriott Hotel

The Maritime Quarter SA1 3SS
☎ 0870 400 7282 📠 0870 400 7382
Dir: M4 junct 42, A483 to city centre past Leisure Centre, then follow signs to Maritime Quarter
CHILD FACILITIES: Please telephone for details

Marriott
HOTELS · RESORTS · SUITES

Just opposite City Hall, this busy hotel enjoys fantastic views over the bay and marina. Bedrooms are spacious and equipped with a range of extras. Public rooms include a popular leisure club and Abernethy's restaurant, which overlooks the marina. It is worth noting, however, that lounge seating is limited.
ROOMS: 122 en suite (50 fmly) (11 GF) ⊗ in 90 bedrooms s £75-£12? d £100-£155 (incl. bkfst) **LB FACILITIES:** STV ⊠ Sauna Gym Jacuzzi
PARKING: 122 **NOTES:** ✖ ⊗ in restaurant

◆◆◆◆ **The White House Hotel**

4 Nyanza Ter SA1 4QQ
☎ 01792 473856 📠 01792 455300
e-mail: reception@thewhitehousehotel.co.uk
Dir: on A4118, 1m W of city centre, before Uplands shops
CHILD FACILITIES: Please telephone for details
Part of the shortest early Victorian terrace within fashionable Uplands, this house retains many original features and sympathetic restoration has resulted in a thoughtfully furnished and equipped home of quality. Bedrooms are filled with many extras and the memorable Welsh breakfasts include cockles and laverbread.
ROOMS: 9 en suite (4 fmly) s £38-£48; d £66 * **FACILITIES:** STV TVB tea/coffee Direct dial from bedrooms TVL No coaches Dinner Last d order 8.15pm **NOTES:** ✖ ⊗ in restaurant Cen ht **LB PARKING:** 4

VALE OF GLAMORGAN

BARRY   Map 03 ST16

| Babies Welcome | Family Rooms | Children's Dishes |

★★★ 73% ◎ ⚲ Egerton Grey Country House

Porthkerry CF62 3BZ
☎ 01446 711666 ▤ 01446 711690
e-mail: info@egertongrey.co.uk
web: www.egertongrey.co.uk
Dir: M4 junct 33 follow signs for airport, left at rdbt for Porthkerry, after 500yds turn left down lane between thatched cottages

CHILD FACILITIES: Baby listening **Activities:** books, teddies, games **Food/bottle warming Ch menu Ch portions Highchairs Ch cutlery Ch discounts £10 per child Videos Cots Family rms D rm with 2 S beds £140 Laundry (NEARBY:** Country Park Leisure Club Walks

This former rectory enjoys a peaceful setting and views over delightful countryside with distant glimpses of the sea. The non-smoking bedrooms are spacious and individually furnished. Public areas offer charm and elegance, and include an airy lounge and restaurant, which has been sympathetically converted from the billiards room.

ROOMS: 10 en suite (4 fmly) s £89.50-£95; d £100-£130 (incl. bkfst) LB **FACILITIES:** STV ⚑ 丄 9 hole golf course 200 yds away. Xmas **PARKING:** 41 **NOTES:** ⊗ in restaurant

---

EAST ABERTHAW   Map 03 ST06

| Babies Welcome | Children's Dishes | 🛝 |

⬛ Blue Anchor Inn

CF62 3DD
☎ 01446 750329 ▤ 01446 750077
Dir: Telephone for directions

CHILD FACILITIES: Food/bottle warming Ch menu Highchairs **Ch cutlery Safe grounds (NEARBY:** 10-min walk to sea

OPEN: 11-11 (Sun 12-10.30) **BAR MEALS:** L served Mon-Sat 12-2 D served Mon-Fri 6-8 Av main course £6.95 **RESTAURANT:** L served Sun 12-2.30 D served Mon-Sat 7-9.30 Av 3 course à la carte £20 Av 3 course fixed price £13.95 **FACILITIES:** Garden: Patio style ✹ **PARKING:** 70

Many proprietors are happy to provide extra facilities for children, but let them know in advance what you need so they can be prepared

---

The
North Gower Hotel

The North Gower Hotel is the ideal choice for those who enjoy the tranquillity of the countryside and the easy access to the city.

Guests can relax in our large public bar and restaurant overlooking the Loughor Estuary. Enjoy a meal from our extensive bar menu or special boards. Families are welcome with various room classifications available.

Visit our web site:
www.northgowerhotel.co.uk

Llanrhidian, North Gower, Swansea SA3 1EE
Tel: 01792 390042 Fax: 01792 391401
Email: enquiries@northgowerhotel.co.uk

HENSOL   Map 03 ST07

★★★★ 71% Vale Hotel Golf & Spa Resort

Hensol Park CF72 8JY
☎ 01443 667800 ▤ 01443 665850
e-mail: reservations@vale-hotel.com
web: www.vale-hotel.com
Dir: M4 junct 34, towards Pendoylan, hotel is signposted, approx 3 mins drive from junct.

CHILD FACILITIES: Please telephone for details

A wealth of leisure facilities are offered at this large and modern, purpose-built complex, including two golf courses and a driving range, extensive health spa, gym, swimming pool, squash courts and an orthopaedic clinic. Public areas are spacious and attractive, whilst bedrooms, many of which have balconies, are well appointed.

ROOMS: 29 en suite 114 annexe en suite (17 fmly) (36 GF) ⊗ in 71 bedrooms s £80-£160; d £90-£180 **LB FACILITIES:** Spa STV ⚑ Golf 36 ⚑ Fishing Squash Riding Sauna Solarium Gym 丄 Jacuzzi Beauty & Hydrotherapy treatments, Children's club, Indoor training arena **PARKING:** 300 **NOTES:** ✹ ⊗ in restaurant

Ireland

NORTHERN IRELAND

Botanic Gardens, Belfast

BELFAST

Belfast Zoological Gardens BT36 7PN
blackrhonda@belfastcity.gov.uk ☎028 9077 6277
(from M2 junct 4 signed to Glengormley. Follow
signs off rdbt to Belfast zoo)
Open all year (ex 25 Dec), daily Apr-Sep 10-5;
Oct-Mar 10-2.30.
*Summer: £6.70 (ch £3.40), Winter: £5.40 (£2.70).
Under 4's, pen and disabled free of charge.

CO ARMAGH - AMARGH

Armagh Planetarium BT61 9DB
kate@armaghplanet.com ☎028 3752 3689
(on main Armagh-Belfast road close to mall) City
centre Open, Mon-Fri 2-4.45. Presentations Mon-
Fri 3pm. Closed Sat, Sun & BHs.

Saint Patrick's Trian Visitor Complex BT61 7BA
info@saintpatrickstrian.com ☎028 37 521801
(City centre) Open all year, Mon-Sat 10-5, Sun 2-
5; Jul-Aug, Mon-Sat 10-5.30, Sun 2-5. Last tour
1hr before closing. *£4 (ch £2.25, pen & student
£2.75). Family ticket £10

CO DOWN - DOWNPATRICK

The St Patrick Centre
BT30 6LZ ☎028 4461 9000
director@saintpatrickcentre.com
(follow A7 from Belfast, follow brown signs.
Situated in Downpatrick, off Market Street)
Open all year Oct-Mar, Mon-Sat, 10-5 & St
Patricks Day 9.30-7; Apr-May & Sep, Mon-Sat
9.30-5.30, Sun 1-5.30 (morning opening on
request), Jun-Aug Mon-Sat 9.30-6, Sun 10-6.
(Last admission 1.5 hrs before closing).
*£4.75 (ch £2.35, concessions £3.15) family ticket
(2ad+2ch) £11.55 groups 25+

PORTAFERRY

Exploris Aquarium BT22 1NZ
info@ards-council.gov.uk ☎028 4272 8062
(A20 or A2 or A25 to Strangford Ferry Service)
Open all year, Mon-Fri 10-6, Sat 11-6, Sun 1-6.
(Sep-Feb closing 1 hr earlier).

CO TYRONE - OMAGH

Ulster American Folk Park BT78 5QY
info@uafp.co.uk ☎028 8224 3292
(5m NW Omagh on A5)
Open Etr-Sep, daily 10.30-6, Sun & BH 11-6.30;
Oct-Etr Mon-Fri 10.30-5. Last admission 1hr
30mins before closing. *£4 (ch & pen £2.50).
Family ticket £10. Children under 5yrs free.

CO ANTRIM

LARNE Map 01 D5

◆◆◆ GH **Derrin**

2 Prince's Gardens BT40 1RQ
☎ 028 2827 3269 & 2827 3762 ▯ 028 2827 3269
e-mail: info@derrinhouse.co.uk
*Dir: off A8 (Harbour Highway) for A2 coastal route, after lights at Main St,
take 1st road on left*

CHILD FACILITIES: **Please telephone for details**

Just a short walk from the town centre, and a minute's drive from
the harbour, this comfortable Victorian house offers smartly
decorated modern bedrooms with a wide range of amenities. The
spacious lounge invites peaceful relaxation, whilst hearty
breakfasts are offered in the stylish dining room.
ROOMS: 6 rms (4 en suite) (2 fmly) s £22-£27; d £40-£48 * ⊗
FACILITIES: TVB tea/coffee TVL No coaches **NOTES:** ⊗ in restaurant
Cen ht **PARKING:** 5

BELFAST

BELFAST Map 01 D5

Babies Welcome | **Children's Dishes**

⊚ **Cayenne**

7 Ascot House, Shaftesbury Square BT2 7DB
☎ 028 90331532 ▯ 028 90261575
e-mail: reservations@cayennerestaurant.com
Dir: Shaftesbury Square

CHILD FACILITIES: **Food/bottle warming Ch licence Ch portions**
Highchairs Safe grounds NEARBY: Odyssey

FOOD: Modern International **STYLE:** Modern Chic **SEATS:** 130
OPEN: 12-2.15/6-11.15, Closed 25-26 Dec, 12 Jull. Sat & Sun
RESTAURANT: main £11.50-£22.50 **NOTES:** ⊗ area, Air con
PARKING: Dublin Rd

Babies Welcome | **Children's Dishes**

⊚ **Beatrice Kennedy**

44 University Rd BT7 1NJ
☎ 028 90202290 ▯ 028 90 202291
e-mail: reservations@beatrice-kennedy.co.uk
web: www.beatrice-kennedy.co.uk
Dir: Adjacent to Queens University on the main University Road

CHILD FACILITIES: **Food/bottle warming Ch menu Ch portions**
Highchairs Ch cutlery

FOOD: International **STYLE:** Traditional, Country-House **SEATS:** 75
OPEN: 12.30-3/5-10.30, Closed 24-26 Dec, 1 Jan, Easter, MonL Mon-Sat, D
Mon **RESTAURANT:** Fixed D £17.50, main £9-£16 **PARKING:** On street

All AA listed accommodation, restaurants
and pubs can be found on the AA's
website www.theAA.com

Ireland

CO DOWN

CO FERMANAGH

DOWNPATRICK   Map 01 D5

ENNISKILLEN   Map 01 C

◆◆◆◆◆ **Pheasants Hill Country House**

37 Killyleagh Rd BT30 9BL
☎ 028 4483 8707 & 4461 7246 ▨ 028 4461 7246
e-mail: info@pheasantshill.com
web: www.pheasantshill.com
Dir: on A22, 3m N of Downpatrick

> **CHILD FACILITIES:** Please telephone for details

This modern farmhouse enjoys a rural setting on the border of The Quoile Pondage, just north of the town. Surrounded by fields, this working farm has pigs and horses and grows organic crops. The stylish bedrooms feature country-style furniture and there is a comfortable lounge. The farm shop sells a wide range of organic goods.
ROOMS: 5 en suite (1 fmly) (1 GF) d £62-£65 * **FACILITIES:** STV TVB tea/coffee TVL 12 acres rare breeds **NOTES:** ✻ ⊛ Cen ht **LB**
PARKING: 10

NEWTOWNARDS   Map 01 D5

Babies Welcome	Family Rooms	Children's Dishes

◆◆◆◆◆ GH **Edenvale House**

130 Portaferry Rd BT22 2AH
☎ 028 9181 4881 ▨ 028 9182 6192
e-mail: edenvalehouse@hotmail.com
web: www.edenvalehouse.com
Dir: between Newtownards and Greyabbey, 2m from Newtownards on A20

> **CHILD FACILITIES:** Baby listening Babysitting Activities: pony rides, hen feeding, egg collection, climbing frame, swing, books, toys Outdoor play area Food/bottle warming Ch menu Ch portions Highchairs Ch cutlery Ch discounts under 8s free, then £10 per extra bed Safe grounds Games consoles Videos Cots Family rms D rm with S bed or cot Ch drinks Connecting rms Laundry
> **NEARBY:** Fun Park By lough

A genuine warm welcome is provided at this beautifully restored Georgian house, set in its own grounds and furnished with antiques. Bedrooms are delightfully decorated in period style and feature many thoughtful extras, and one of the elegant lounges enjoys views across Strangford Lough towards the Mountains of Mourne. Breakfast is served at a communal table and a particularly good selection of home-made and local produce is offered.
ROOMS: 3 en suite (2 fmly) s £45; d £65 * **FACILITIES:** TVB tea/coffee No coaches Riding ♫ **NOTES:** ⊛ Cen ht **PARKING:** 15

Babies Welcome	Family Rooms	Children's Dishes

★★★★ 72% **Killyhevlin**

BT74 6RW
☎ 028 6632 3481 ▨ 028 6632 4726
e-mail: info@killyhevlin.com
web: www.killyhevlin.com
Dir: 2m S, off A4

> **CHILD FACILITIES:** Baby listening Nanny (on request) Babysitting (on request) Outdoor play area Food/bottle warming Ch menu Ch portions Highchairs Ch discounts under 4s free sharing with parent Cots Family rms D rm with S bed Connecting rms Laundry
> **NEARBY:** Teen Park

A modern, stylish hotel nestling on the shores of Lough Erne, just south of the town. Bedrooms are particularly spacious, well equipped, and many enjoy fine views. An open-plan restaurant and informal bar complement the comfortable lounges. Staff throughout are friendly and helpful.
ROOMS: 43 en suite (32 fmly) (9 GF) ⊛ in 12 bedrooms s £67.50-£80 d £95-£120 (incl. bkfst) **LB FACILITIES:** STV Fishing Leisure club due t open early 2005 ♫ Xmas **PARKING:** 500 **NOTES:** ✻ Closed 25 Dec

Babies Welcome	Family Rooms	Children's Dishes

◆◆◆◆ GH **Arch House Tullyhona Farm**

Marble Arch Rd, Florencecourt BT92 1DE
☎ 028 6634 8452
e-mail: tullyguest60@hotmail.com
Dir: through Enniskillen follow A4, Sligo road for 2.5m then A32 & follow signs for Marble Arch Caves. Turn right at NT sign for Florencecourt

> **CHILD FACILITIES:** Baby listening Nanny Activities: playhouse, slide, climbing frame, quad bike rides, colouring, jigsaws, toys Indoor play area Outdoor play area Family area Food/bottle warming Ch menu Ch portions Highchairs Ch cutlery Ch discounts 50% when sharing Safe grounds Games consoles Videos Cots Family rms D rms with S beds from £70 Laundry Changing mats (on request) **NEARBY:** Playpark Cave tours Leisure centre Cinema Lake

This delightful house nestles in a tranquil country setting very close to the Marble Arch Caves and the National Trust property at Florencecourt. Tullyhona's restaurant is open for all-day breakfasts, as well as a range of traditional evening meals. The stylish, recently refurbished bedrooms offer modern comforts.
ROOMS: 4 en suite (4 fmly) s £25-£30; d £45-£55 * ⊛
FACILITIES: TVB TVL Riding Farm tours, trampoline, swing, table tennis slide Dinner Last d order 5.30pm **NOTES:** ⊛ in restaurant ⊛ in 1 lounge Cen ht **LB PARKING:** 8

Babies	Family
Welcome	Rooms

♦♦♦♦ GH **Dromard House**
Tamlaght BT74 4HR
☎ 028 6638 7250
e-mail: dromardhouse@yahoo.co.uk
web: www.dromardhouse.com
Dir: 2m from Enniskillen, on A4 (Belfast Rd)

CHILD FACILITIES: Activities: **toys Outdoor play area Food/bottle warming Highchairs Ch cutlery Ch discounts under 5s free, 5-12s 50% Safe grounds Cots Family rms D rm with S bed £50 Laundry** **NEARBY:** **Marble Arch Caves Cinema Park Swimming pool**

This popular, smartly presented house enjoys its own woodland trail down to the shores of beautiful Lough Erne. The attractively decorated bedrooms, with separate access, are located in a smartly converted, spacious stable block. Hearty breakfasts are taken in the main house.

ROOMS: 4 annexe en suite s £25; d £40 * **FACILITIES:** TVB tea/coffee No coaches Fishing Woodland trail to lough shore **NOTES:** Credit cards not taken ⊗ Cen ht **PARKING:** 4

CO LONDONDERRY

COLERAINE   Map 01 C6

Babies	Family	Children's
Welcome	Rooms	Dishes

♦♦♦♦ GH **Bellevue Country House**
43 Greenhill Rd, Aghadowey BT51 4EU
☎ 028 7086 8797 ▤ 028 7086 8780
e-mail: info@bellevuecountryhouse.co.uk
web: www.bellevuecountryhouse.co.uk
Dir: 7m S of Coleraine, 3m N of Garvagh. on B66 just off A29

CHILD FACILITIES: **Outdoor play area Food/bottle warming Ch menu Ch portions Highchairs Ch cutlery Ch discounts under 8s free Safe grounds Cots Family rms D rm with 2 S beds Ch drinks Connecting rms Changing mats** **NEARBY:** **Leisure centres Cinemas Walks**

This fine country house, dating back to 1840, is peacefully situated in its own grounds. A variety of bedrooms are offered, including a family room and ground-floor accommodation, and there is also a comfortable drawing room available for guests' use. Generous breakfasts are freshly prepared and served around one large table.

ROOMS: 3 en suite (1 fmly) (1 GF) s £25-£30; d £45-£47 * **FACILITIES:** TVB tea/coffee TVL No coaches Fishing **NOTES:** Credit cards not taken ✈ ⊗ Cen ht **PARKING:** 9

LIMAVADY   Map 01 C6

Babies	Family	Children's
Welcome	Rooms	Dishes

★★★★ 70% ⊚
Radisson SAS Row Park Resort   *Radisson*
BT49 9LB
☎ 028 7772 2222 ▤ 028 7772 2313
e-mail: reservations@radissonroepark.com
Dir: on A2 Londonderry/Limavady road, 16m from Londonderry, 1m from Limavady

CHILD FACILITIES: Babysitting Activities: **(seasonal) Indoor play area Food/bottle warming Ch menu Ch portions Highchairs Ch discounts under 5s free, 5-12s £6.50 when sharing with parents Safe grounds Cots Family rms D rm with 2 S beds & sofa bed Ch drinks Connecting rms Laundry** **NEARBY:** **Country park Leisure centre 20-min drive to sea**

This impressive, popular hotel sits centrally within its own modern golf resort. The spacious, modern bedrooms are well-equipped and many have excellent views of the fairways and surrounding estate. The Greens Restaurant provides a refreshing dining experience and the Coach House brasserie offers a lighter menu. Leisure options are extensive.

ROOMS: 118 en suite (15 fmly) ⊗ in 76 bedrooms **FACILITIES:** STV ☒ Golf 18 Fishing Sauna Solarium Gym ♨ ⅃ Jacuzzi Floodlit driving range, Outside tees, Golf training academy, Bicycle hire ♫ Xmas **PARKING:** 300 **NOTES:** ✈

Babies	Children's
Welcome	Dishes

⊚ **The Lime Tree**
60 Catherine St BT49 9DB
☎ 028 77764300
e-mail: info@limetreerest.com
Dir: Entering Limavady from the Derry side, the restaurant on right on small slip road

CHILD FACILITIES: Activities: **Food/bottle warming Ch menu Ch portions Highchairs Ch cutlery** **NEARBY:** **Roe Valley Country Park**

FOOD: Traditional **STYLE:** Rustic **SEATS:** 30 **OPEN:** 6-9, Closed 1 wk Nov, 1 wk end Feb/Mar, 1 wk Jul, Sun-Mon (ex Dec)L Mon-Sun **RESTAURANT:** Fixed D £12.95, main £12.95-£17.50 **PARKING:** 15

CO TYRONE

DUNGANNON   Map 01 C5

♦♦♦♦ GH **Millbrook Bed & Breakfast**
46 Moy Rd BT71 7DT
☎ 028 8772 3715
Dir: on A29 1m S of Dungannon, 0.25m N of M1 motorway
CHILD FACILITIES: Please telephone for details

This well-presented bungalow is situated just outside the town, with easy access to main routes. Comfortably furnished ground floor bedrooms and a new guest lounge are complemented by a substantial freshly prepared breakfast, with the warm and natural hospitality displayed by the owners being a memorable feature.

ROOMS: 3 en suite (3 GF) s £30; d £45 * **FACILITIES:** TVB tea/coffee No coaches **NOTES:** Credit cards not taken ✈ ⊗ Cen ht **PARKING:** 4

REPUBLIC OF IRELAND

Trinity College "Sphere Within a Sphere"

CO CLARE
BALLYVAUGHAN
Aillwee Cave
fiona@aillweecave.ie ☎065 7077036
(3m S of Ballyvaughan. Signposted from Galway and Ennis)
Open all year from 10am mornings only in Dec.
*€9 ch €5, pen €7. Family ticket €22-€26
BUNRATTY
Bunratty Castle & Folk Park
reservations@shannondev.ie ☎061 360788
(8 miles from Limerick city on N18 road to Ennis)
Open all year, daily 9-5.30, 9.30 Apr-May & Sep-Oct last admission 4.15pm. Folk Park also open Jun-Aug 9-6 last admission 5.15pm. Last admission to Castle 4pm all year. Closed Good Fri & 24-26 Dec. *Castle €10.50 ch €5.95, pen €6.95 & student €8.50.
QUIN
Craggaunowen The Living Past Experience
reservations@shannondev.ie ☎061 360788
(signed from N18 Limerick to Galway road, off R462 from Cratloe and R469 from Ennis)
Open daily mid Apr-mid Oct, daily 10-6 (last admission 5pm). *€7 (ch €4.20, pen & students €5.60).

CO CORK
CARRIGTWOHILL (CARRIGTOHILL)
Fota Wildlife Park
info@fotawildlife.ie ☎021 4812 678
(Situated 10km E of Cork City. Take the Cobh road from the N25 Cork - Waterford road)
Open all year 17 Mar-Sep daily, 10-6 Sun 11-6 Oct-17 Mar wknds only. Last admission 5.
CLONAKILITY
West Cork Model Village Railway
modelvillage@eircom.net ☎023 33224
(from Cork N71 West Cork left at junct for Inchydoney island, signed at road junction. Village is on bay side of Clonakilty)
Open Feb-Oct daily 11-5, Jul-Aug, daily, extended hours 10-6. *€6 (concessions €4.50). Family ticket €19, Party 12+.

CO DONEGAL
LETTERKENNY
Glenveagh National Park & Castle
talchorn@duchas.ie ☎074 9137090

(off N56 onto L77)
Open daily 17 Mar-1st Sun in Nov.
Park: free, *Castle €2.75 ch & students €1.25, pen €2. Family ticket €7, group 20+ €2.

CO DUBLIN
DUBLIN
The Chester Beatty Library
info@cbl.ie ☎023 33224
(10 mins walk from Trinity College, up Dame St towards Christ Church Cathedral)
Open all year, May-Sep, Mon-Fri 10-5; Oct-Apr, Tue-Fri 10-5, Sat 11-5, Sun 1-5. Closed BHs.
Dublin Zoo
info@dublinzoo.ie ☎01 474 8900
(10 mins bus ride from City Centre)
Open Mar-Oct, Mon-Sat 9.30-6, Sun 10.30-6; Nov-Feb, daily 10.30-dusk.
National History Museum
education@nmi@indigo.ie ☎01 6777444
(in city centre)
Open all year, Tue-Sat 10-5, Sun 2-5. Closed Mon, Xmas day & Good Fri.
MALAHIDE
Fry Model Railway
fryrailway@dublintourism.ie
☎01 8463779 & 8462184
(in grounds of Malahide Castle, 8m N of Dublin city centre, follow signs for Malahide)
Open Apr-Sep, Mon-Sat 10-5, Sun & PH 2-6; Parties at other times by arrangement. Closed 1-2 on fri. *€6.25 (ch €3.75, concessions €5.25). Family ticket €17.50. Combined ticket for related attractions available.

CO WEXFORD
FERRYCARRIG
Irish National Heritage Park
info@inhp.com ☎053 20733
(3m from Wexford on N11)
Open daily 9.30-6.30. (Last admission 5, times subject to seasonal variations). *€7.50 (pen & students €6). Family (2ad & up to 3ch) €19. Group rates available on request.

CO WICKLOW
ENNISKERRY
Powerscourt Gardens Exhibition
☎01 2046000
(just off N11 S of Bray, next to Enniskerry)
Open daily 9.30-5.30. Winter time may vary.
Waterfall open daily 9.30-7, (Summer) 10.30-dusk, (Winter). *Gardens & House Exhibition €8 (ch under 16 €4.50 ch under 5 free & students €7). Gardens only €6 (ch under 16 €3.50 ch under 5 free & students €5.50). House Exhibition only €2.50 (ch under 16 €1.60 ch under 5 free & students €2.20). Waterfall €4 (ch under 16 €3 ch under 5 free & students €3.50).

Ireland

CO CAVAN

CAVAN
Map 01 C4

★★★ 67% **Kilmore**
Dublin Rd
☎ 049 4332288 🖹 049 4332458
e-mail: kilmore@quinn-hotels.com
Dir: approx 3km from Cavan on N3

CHILD FACILITIES: Please telephone for details

Located on the outskirts of Cavan, easily accessible from the main N3 route, this comfortable hotel features spacious and welcoming public areas. Good food is served in the Annalee Restaurant, which is always appreciated by guests returning from nearby fishing or golf.
ROOMS: 39 en suite (17 fmly) (19 GF) s €75-€85; d €115-€125 (incl. bkfst) **LB FACILITIES:** STV free use of facilities at Slieve Russell Golf & Country Club ♫ Xmas **PARKING:** 450 **NOTES:** ✖ ⊗ in restaurant Closed 25 Dec

CO CLARE

BALLYVAUGHAN
Map 01 B3

Babies Welcome	Family Rooms	Children's Dishes

♦♦♦♦ GH **Cappabhaile House**
Newtown
☎ 065 7077260 🖹 065 7077300
e-mail: cappabhaile@oceanfree.net
Dir: 1km outside Ballyvaughan towards Aillwee Cave

CHILD FACILITIES: Nanny Activities: toys, jigsaws, books, pool table Indoor play area Outdoor play area Family area Food/bottle warming Ch menu Ch portions Highchairs Ch cutlery Ch discounts under 3s free Safe grounds Cots Family rms D rms with S or D beds & cot Ch drinks **NEARBY:** Parks Leisure centres Cinema Aillwee Cave 3m to sea

Cappabhaile House has been recently built using local stone and natural materials, on a 12-acre site on the outskirts of the village in the heart of The Burren. The hosts are happy to assist guests with planning walks and hill climbs, or with archaeological or botanical information. The spacious bedrooms are suitable for families and are very well appointed. Guests can relax in the comfortable lounge or enjoy a game of pool in the games room. An 18-hole pitch and putt course surrounds the house. An extensive breakfast menu is on offer, with home baking a speciality.
ROOMS: 8 en suite (4 fmly) **FACILITIES:** TVB tea/coffee Direct dial from bedrooms No coaches Pool Table 18 hole pitch & putt **NOTES:** ✖ ⊗ Cen ht **PARKING:** 20

BUNRATTY
Map 01 B3

♦♦♦♦ T&C **Park House**
Low Rd
☎ 061 369902 🖹 061 369903
e-mail: parkhouse@eircom.net
Dir: from N18 take Bunratty exit, turn left at castle, pass Folk Park. Park House 4th house on left

CHILD FACILITIES: Please telephone for details

A purpose-built guest house with spacious bedrooms within walking distance of the castle. There is a comfortable guest lounge and a lovely garden; and Mairead Bateman's home baking can be sampled on arrival.
ROOMS: 6 en suite (1 fmly) s €45; d €64-€70 * **FACILITIES:** STV TVB tea/coffee **NOTES:** ✖ ⊗ Cen ht **PARKING:** 6

ENNIS
Map 01 B3

Babies Welcome	Family Rooms	Children's Dishes

♦♦♦♦ GH **Fountain Court**
Lahinch Rd
☎ 065 6829845 🖹 065 6845030
e-mail: kyran@fountain-court.com
Dir: 2m from Ennis on N85 on left

CHILD FACILITIES: Food/bottle warming Ch portions Highchairs Ch discounts under 5s free, 5-14s £20 sharing with parents Cots Family rms D rms with S beds £85 Fridge **NEARBY:** Cinema Leisure centres Sea world National park 20-min drive to sea

Set in four acres of mature gardens on an elevated site, this comfortable guest house is family run. The majority of bedrooms are spacious and tastefully decorated. Guests can relax in the elegant lounge. There is also a games room.
ROOMS: 18 en suite (4 fmly) s €45-€50; d €75-€100 * ⊗ **FACILITIES:** STV TVB tea/coffee Direct dial from bedrooms **NOTES:** ✖ ⊗ in restaurant ⊗ in lounges Licensed Cen ht **LB PARKING:** 25

CO CORK

BALTIMORE
Map 01 B1

★★★ 67% ⊛
Baltimore Harbour Resort Hotel & Leisure Centre
☎ 028 20361 🖹 028 20466
e-mail: info@bhrhotel.ie
Dir: S from Cork city N71 to Skibbereen, continue on R595 13km to Baltimore

CHILD FACILITIES: Please telephone for details

Overlooking the natural harbour of Baltimore, this family orientated leisure hotel is perfect for a relaxing break. Bedrooms are well appointed and most have a sea view. The popular bar and sun room open out onto the patio and gardens.
ROOMS: 64 en suite (30 fmly) **FACILITIES:** ⊡ Sauna Gym ⌂ Jacuzzi Table Tennis, In-house video channel, Indoor bowls ♫ **PARKING:** 80 **NOTES:** ✖ ⊗ in restaurant Closed Jan RS Nov-Dec & Feb-mid Mar

Ireland

BANTRY
Map 01 B2

Babies Welcome | Family Rooms | Children's Dishes

★★★ 64% **Westlodge**
☎ 027 50360 📠 027 50438
e-mail: reservations@westlodgehotel.ie
Dir: N71 to West Cork

CHILD FACILITIES: Baby listening Babysitting Activities: The Mighty Ducks Club, games Indoor play area Outdoor play area Family area Food/bottle warming Ch menu Ch portions Highchairs Ch cutlery Ch discounts Safe grounds Videos Cots Family rms D rm with S beds £170 Ch drinks Connecting rms Laundry
NEARBY: Cinema Walks Near sea

A superb leisure centre and good children's facilities makes this hotel very popular with families. The situation on the outskirts of the town also makes it an ideal base for touring west Cork and south Kerry. All the staff are friendly and hospitable.
ROOMS: 90 en suite (20 fmly) (20 GF) ⊛ in 15 bedrooms
FACILITIES: STV ⊡ ◊ Squash Snooker Sauna Solarium Gym ⌀ Jacuzzi Pitch & Putt, wooded walks ♬ **PARKING:** 400 **NOTES:** ✘ Closed 23-27 Dec

CORK
Map 01 B2

Babies Welcome | Family Rooms | Children's Dishes

★★★★ 69% **Silver Springs Moran**
Tivoli
☎ 021 4507533 📠 021 4507641
e-mail: silverspringsinfo@morangroup.ie
Dir: N8 south Silver Springs exit and right across overpass then right for hotel on left

CHILD FACILITIES: Babysitting Food/bottle warming Ch menu Ch portions Highchairs Ch discounts under 5s free, under 12s £15 Games consoles Videos Cots Family rms 2 D beds per rm from £130 Connecting rms Fridge Laundry Changing mats
NEARBY: Fota Wildlife Park Cinemas Funworld Bowling Cork Opera House

The public areas of this hotel have undergone major development recently, resulting in a smart, contemporary feeling. Bedrooms are comfortable, many offering good views over the river Lee. Guests have use of a nearby leisure centre.
ROOMS: 109 en suite (29 fmly) ⊛ in 17 bedrooms s €98-€140; d €130-€180 (incl. bkfst) LB **FACILITIES:** STV ⊡ ◊ Squash Snooker Sauna Gym Jacuzzi Aerobics classes Xmas **PARKING:** 325 **NOTES:** ✘ ⊛ in restaurant Closed 24-26 Dec

◆◆◆ GH **Abbeypoint House**
Western Rd
☎ 021 4275526 & 4274091 📠 021 4251955
e-mail: info@abbeypoint.com
Dir: from city centre via Washington St, pass Jury's Hotel, Western Rd on left. Through traffic lights at UCC Gates, Abbeypoint on right
CHILD FACILITIES: Please telephone for details
A Victorian red brick house, located opposite the University College Cork and within walking distance of the city centre. Bedrooms vary in size, and all are well equipped. There is a 'set down' arrivals area at front of house and private lock-up parking available at the rear.
ROOMS: 8 en suite (5 fmly) s €40-€60; d €64-€100 *
FACILITIES: TVB tea/coffee Direct dial from bedrooms TVL No coaches
NOTES: ✘ ⊛ Cen ht **PARKING:** 10

KINSALE
Map 01 B2

◆◆◆ GH **The White House**
Pearse St, The Glen
☎ 021 4772125 📠 021 4772045
e-mail: whitehse@indigo.ie
Dir: from Cork on N71 towards Macroom/Killarney, left at Halfway Rdbt onto R607 or take R600 (airport road) into Kinsale. House in town centre, parking at rear
CHILD FACILITIES: Please telephone for details
Centrally located among the narrow, twisting streets of Kinsale, this guest house dates back to 1850. A welcoming hostelry with a comfortable bar, a choice of bistro or restaurant for dining and a convenient car park.
ROOMS: 10 en suite (2 fmly) **FACILITIES:** STV TVB tea/coffee Direct dial from bedrooms Dinner Last d order 10pm **NOTES:** ✘ ⊛ in restaurant Licensed Cen ht

CO DONEGAL

FAHAN
Map 01 C6

◆◆◆◆◆ ⊜ GH
St John's Country House & Restaurant
☎ 074 936 0289 📠 074 936 0612
e-mail: stjohnsrestaurant@eircom.net
CHILD FACILITIES: Please telephone for details
This 18th-century house has panoramic views across Lough Swilly to Inch Island. Food takes pride of place and local lamb and seafood feature on the menus. Bedrooms vary in size, and there is a cosy bar with a turf fire. Just half an hour's drive from the Giant's Causeway, the house is ideally located for exploring this lovely area.
ROOMS: 5 en suite (2 fmly) **FACILITIES:** TVB tea/coffee Direct dial from bedrooms TVL No coaches Dinner Last d order 7pm **NOTES:** ✘ ⊛ Licensed Cen ht **PARKING:** 60

CO DUBLIN

DUBLIN   Map 01 D4

★★★ 67% Bewley's Hotel Ballsbridge
Merrion Rd, Ballsbridge
☎ 01 6681111 ⓕ 01 6681999
e-mail: bb@bewleyshotels.com

CHILD FACILITIES: Please telephone for details

This stylish hotel is conveniently situated near the RDS Showgrounds. It offers comfortable, good value accommodation. Lunch and dinner are available in O'Connell's Restaurant and food is available all day in the spacious lounge café, which is a popular meeting place. Secure underground car parking is available at a nominal fee.

ROOMS: 220 en suite (25 fmly) ☺ in 140 bedrooms s €99; d €99
PARKING: 240 **NOTES:** ✖ ☺ in restaurant Closed 24-26 Dec

★★★ 67% The Carnegie Court
North St, Swords
☎ 01 8404384 ⓕ 01 8404505
e-mail: info@carnegiecourt.com
Dir: from Dublin Airport take N1 towards Belfast. At 5th rdbt take 1st exit for Swords, then sharp left for hotel

CHILD FACILITIES: Please telephone for details

This modern hotel has been tastefully built and is conveniently located close to Dublin Airport just off the N1 in Swords village. The air conditioned bedrooms are well appointed, and many are particularly spacious. Public areas include a select residents' lounge, contemporary Courtyard Restaurant and a dramatically designed Harp Bar. Extensive parking is provided.

ROOMS: 36 en suite (4 fmly) ☺ in 7 bedrooms **FACILITIES:** STV ♫
PARKING: 150 **NOTES:** ✖ ☺ in restaurant Closed 25-26 Dec

How to use this guide & abbreviations are explained on pages 5-7

★★★ 65% Bewleys Hotel Leopardstown
Central Park, Leopardstown Rd
☎ 01 2935 000 ⓕ 021 2935 099
e-mail: leop@bewleyshotel.com

CHILD FACILITIES: Please telephone for details

This newly built hotel is conveniently situated close to the Central Business Park and Leopardstown Race Course, and serviced by the Luas Line. Contemporary in style the open-plan public areas include a spacious lounge bar, Brasserie and a selection of

continued

conference rooms. Bedrooms are well appointed. There is free underground parking.

ROOMS: 306 rms **NOTES:** Credit cards not taken

★★★ 65% Bewley's Hotel Newlands Cross
Newlands Cross, Naas Rd
☎ 01 4640140 ⓕ 01 4640900
e-mail: res@bewleyshotels.com
Dir: M50 junct 9 take N7 Naas road, hotel near N7- Belgard Rd junct at Newlands Cross

CHILD FACILITIES: Please telephone for details

This modern hotel is situated on the outskirts of Dublin off the N7 and close to M50. Bedrooms are well-furnished and prices are competitive. The restaurant is open for casual dining all day and serves more formal meals in the evening. There is a comfortable lounge and bar and ample car parking.

ROOMS: 258 en suite ☺ in 183 bedrooms s €79; d €79
FACILITIES: STV **PARKING:** 200 **NOTES:** ✖ ☺ in restaurant Closed 24-26 Dec

Babies Welcome	Family Rooms	Children's Dishes	

◆◆◆◆ GH Ferryview House
96 Clontarf Rd, Clontarf
☎ 01 8335893 ⓕ 01 8532141
e-mail: ferryview@oceanfree.net
Dir: follow coast road from city centre via Fairview heading N to Clontarf Rd, just beyond Yacht Pub. On left, 2.5m from City Centre

CHILD FACILITIES: Baby listening Food/bottle warming Ch menu Ch portions Highchairs Ch discounts under 2s free Safe grounds Cots Family rms **NEARBY:** 5-min drive to sea

Situated on the coast road 2.5 miles from the city centre on the 130 bus route, this house is conveniently located between Dublin Airport, the Point Theatre and the city centre. Tastefully refurbished to provide relaxing and cheerful accommodation, equipped with all facilities. Free secure parking provided. The Bull Island Bird Sanctuary, Dollymount Beach and three golf course are all nearby.

ROOMS: 8 en suite (3 fmly) (2 GF) s €60-€76; d €80-€90 * ☺
FACILITIES: STV TVB tea/coffee Direct dial from bedrooms TVL
NOTES: ✖ ☺ in restaurant ☺ in 1 lounge Cen ht **PARKING:** 8

Ireland

Babies Welcome | **Family Rooms** | **Children's Dishes**

♦♦♦♦ GH *Glenshandan Lodge*

Dublin Rd, Swords
☎ 01 8408838 📠 01 8408838
e-mail: glenshandan@eircom.net

CHILD FACILITIES: Outdoor play area Family area Food/bottle warming Ch menu Ch portions Highchairs Ch cutlery Games consoles Videos Cots Family rms D rms with S beds £100 NEARBY: Castle Heritage Centres Cinema Zoo 10-min to sea

Family and dog-friendly house, where the hospitable owners are attentive and offer good facilities including e-mail access. Bedrooms are comfortable and one is adapted for wheelchair users. Secure parking available. Close to pubs, restaurants, golf, airport and the Kennel Club.
ROOMS: 9 en suite (5 fmly) **FACILITIES:** TVB tea/coffee TVL **NOTES:** ⊗ in restaurant Cen ht **PARKING:** 10

Babies Welcome | **Family Rooms** | **Children's Dishes**

♦♦♦ GH St Aiden's

32 Brighton Rd, Rathgar
☎ 01 4902011 📠 01 4920234
e-mail: staidens@eircom.net
Dir: turn off M50 junct 11 towards city centre. Premises 3rd left after traffic lights in Terenure village

CHILD FACILITIES: Nanny (by pre-booked arrangement) Babysitting Activities: toys, jigsaws, books Outdoor play area Food/bottle warming Ch menu Ch portions Highchairs Ch cutlery Ch discounts under 6s free, 6-12s 50% Safe grounds Videos Cots Family rms D rms with S beds from €110 Ch drinks (juices only) Fridge Laundry (limited) Changing mats NEARBY: Parks

A fine Victorian house situated in a residential tree-lined road just 15 minutes from the city centre. The well-proportioned reception rooms are comfortable and relaxing, and a hospitality trolley is available for guests. Bedrooms vary in size from spacious family rooms to snug singles, and all offer modern comforts.
ROOMS: 8 en suite (2 fmly) s €40-€65; d €80-€90 *
FACILITIES: STV TVB tea/coffee Direct dial from bedrooms No coaches **NOTES:** ✗ ⊗ Cen ht **LB PARKING:** 4

KILLINEY
Map 01 D4

Babies Welcome | **Family Rooms** | **Children's Dishes**

★★★★ 68% Fitzpatrick Castle

☎ 01 2305400 📠 01 2305430
e-mail: reservations@fitzpatricks.com
Dir: from Dun Laoghaire port turn left, on coast road right at lights, left at next lights. Follow to Dalkey , right at McDonaghs pub, immediate left, up hill, hotel at top

CHILD FACILITIES: Babysitting Activities: colouring (seasonal) kids clubs Food/bottle warming Ch menu Ch portions Highchairs Ch discounts under 12s free sharing with parents Safe grounds Games consoles Videos Cots Family rms 2 K beds with S bed £25 supplement Connecting rms Laundry NEARBY: Leisure centre on site Walks Horseriding Cinema 5-min drive to sea

Situated on Killiney Hill, this converted castle has been extensively refurbished. Bedrooms are comfortable, many with stunning views of Dublin city and bay. Facilities include a large lounge, excellent leisure centre and a choice of restaurants.
ROOMS: 113 en suite (42 fmly) ⊗ in 50 bedrooms s €180-€205; d €220-€245 **LB FACILITIES:** STV 🏊 Sauna Solarium Gym Jacuzzi Beauty/hairdressing salon, Steam room ♫ **PARKING:** 300 **NOTES:** ✗ ⊗ in restaurant

---

CO GALWAY

CLIFDEN
Map 01 A4

Babies Welcome | **Family Rooms** | **Children's Dishes**

♦♦♦♦♦ 🛏 GH Byrne's Mal Dua House

Galway Rd
☎ 095 21171 & 0800 904 7532 📠 095 21739
e-mail: info@maldua.com
Dir: From Galway on N59, establishment on right approx 1km from Clifden. From Westport on N59, left at T-junct in town, then 1km

CHILD FACILITIES: Baby listening Babysitting Activities: donkey feeding, toys, games Indoor play area Outdoor play area Family area Food/bottle warming Ch menu Ch portions Highchairs Ch cutlery Ch discounts under 3s free, 3-12s 25% discount Safe grounds Videos Cots Family rms D rm with 2 S beds Ch drinks Laundry NEARBY: Leisure centre Pony trekking Sailing Surfing Fishing 5-min drive to sea

Set in the outskirts of Clifden, this house offers a relaxed atmosphere of luxury, with a warm welcome from the proprietors. An excellent dinner and breakfast is served in the delightful dining room, which overlooks the lovely garden. Spacious bedrooms are individually decorated with thoughtful extras. Guided tours, bicycles and fishing tackle are available for hire.
ROOMS: 14 en suite (2 fmly) (3 GF) s €50-€75; d €100-€150 *
FACILITIES: STV TVB tea/coffee Direct dial from bedrooms TVL ⏜ Bicycles & fishing rods for rent Dinner Last d order 9pm **NOTES:** ✗ ⊗ Licensed Cen ht **LB PARKING:** 20

GALWAY
Map 01 B3

♦♦♦♦ T&C Atlantic Heights

2 Cashelmara, Knocknacarra Cross, Salthill
☎ 091 529466 & 528830 📠 091 529466
e-mail: atlanticheights@galway.iol.ie
Dir: 1km from Salthill Promenade in upper Salthill on R336. 0.25m on right after Spinnaker House Hotel, before t-junct

CHILD FACILITIES: Please telephone for details

This fine balconied house overlooks Galway Bay, where enthusiastic hosts, Robbie and Madeline Mitchell, take great pride in their home. All bedrooms have TV, tea and coffee making facilities, telephone, hairdryer and many thoughful extras. An extensive breakfast menu, served late if required, features home baking. Laundry service available.
ROOMS: 6 en suite (3 fmly) s €40-€60; d €70-€95 *
FACILITIES: STV TVB tea/coffee Direct dial from bedrooms **NOTES:** ⊗ Cen ht **LB PARKING:** 6

LEENANE
Map 01 A4

♦♦♦♦ GH Killary Lodge

☎ 095 42276 & 42245 📠 095 42314
e-mail: lodge@killary.com
Dir: N59 from Leenane towards Clifden for 3m. As road turns away from Killary Harbour, follow sign for Killary Lodge (in trees on right). Turn right 0.75m to lodge

CHILD FACILITIES: Please telephone for details

In a spectacular setting, overlooking the only fjord in Ireland, Killary Lodge features hand-crafted beech furniture and home cooking in an informal, relaxed atmosphere. A wide range of
continued

outdoor pursuits is available nearby, including archery, tennis, orienteering, hill walking, and sailing.
ROOMS: 12 en suite 9 annexe en suite (8 fmly) (3 GF) s €43-€53; d €86-€106 * **FACILITIES:** Direct dial from bedrooms ⚲ Sauna Various leisure activities Dinner Last d order 8pm **NOTES:** ⊗ Licensed Cen ht
LB PARKING: 30

OUGHTERARD
Map 01 B4

Babies Welcome | **Family Rooms** | **Children's Dishes**

◆◆◆◆◆ T&C **Waterfall Lodge**
☎ 091 552168
e-mail: kdolly@eircom.net
Dir: on N59, 1st house on left after hotel

CHILD FACILITIES: Baby listening Babysitting Family area Food/bottle warming Ch menu Ch portions Highchairs Ch discounts under 4s free, over 4s 50% Games consoles Videos Cots Family rms D rms with S beds **NEARBY:** Park Walks Pony Trekking Leisure centre Boat trips Fishing

An elegant period residence beside a river and waterfall, with private fishing. Set in an idyllic location, yet close to the village, the house has antique furnishings, wooden floors, and log fires. The en suite bedrooms are all well appointed and equipped, and the owner, Mrs Dolly, ensures a warm welcome. Activities available nearby include pony trekking, mountain climbing, golf and fishing, and there are plenty of pubs and restaurants.
ROOMS: 6 en suite (2 fmly) s €50; d €80 * **FACILITIES:** TVB TVL No coaches Fishing **NOTES:** Credit cards not taken ✖ ⊗ Cen ht
PARKING: 8

RENVYLE
Map 01 A4

★★★ 70% 🌐 **Renvyle House Hotel**
☎ 095 43511 📠 095 43515
e-mail: info@renvyle.com
Dir: N59 W of Galway towards Clifden Pass through Oughterard & Maam Cross, at Recess turn right, Kylemore turn left, Letterfrack turn right, hotel 5m
CHILD FACILITIES: Please telephone for details

This comfortable house has been operating as a hotel for over 120 years. Located on the unspoilt coast of Connemara, many leisure pursuits are available. There are spacious lounges, a library, and a range of well equipped bedrooms available, but it is the relaxed friendly staff that make a visit here memorable.
ROOMS: 68 en suite (8 fmly) ⊗ in 5 bedrooms s €30-€130; d €60-€250 (incl. bkfst) **LB FACILITIES:** STV ⚲ Golf 9 ⚲ Fishing Riding Snooker ♪♫ ⚲ Clay pigeon shooting ♫ Xmas **PARKING:** 60
NOTES: ⊗ in restaurant Closed 6 Jan-14 Feb

How to use this guide & abbreviations are explained on pages 5-7

CO KERRY

BALLYHEIGE
Map 01 A2

★★★ 68% *The White Sands*
☎ 066 7133102 📠 066 7133357
e-mail: whitesands@eircom.net
Dir: 18km from Tralee town on coast road in North Kerry, hotel on left on main street.

IRISH COUNTRY HOTELS

CHILD FACILITIES: Please telephone for details

Friendly staff welcome guests to this family run hotel, situated beside the beach and close to golf clubs. Attractively decorated throughout, facilities include a lounge bar, traditional pub, good restaurant and comfortable bedrooms.
ROOMS: 81 en suite **FACILITIES:** STV ♫ **PARKING:** 40
NOTES: Closed Nov-Feb RS Mar-Apr & Oct

CAHERDANIEL
Map 01 A2

★★★ 66% 🌐 **Derrynane**
☎ 066 9475136 📠 066 9475160
e-mail: info@derrynane.com
Dir: just off main road. 2 mins' walk

Best Western

CHILD FACILITIES: Please telephone for details

Super clifftop location overlooking Derrynane Bay with spectacular views adding a stunning dimension to this well run hotel where pleasant, efficient staff contributes to the very relaxed atmosphere. Public areas include spacious lounges, bar and restaurant, an outdoor heated pool in the garden. Bedrooms are well appointed and most enjoy the views.
ROOMS: 73 en suite (30 fmly) ⊗ in 40 bedrooms s €95-€120; d €150-€180 (incl. bkfst) **LB FACILITIES:** STV ⚲ ⚲ Sauna Solarium Gym Steam room, seaweed therapy room ♫ **PARKING:** 60 **NOTES:** ✖ ⊗ in restaurant Closed 4 Oct-15 Apr

---

CASTLEGREGORY
Map 01 A2

◆◆◆ T&C **Griffin's Palm Beach Country House**
Goulane, Conor Pass Rd
☎ 066 7139147 📠 066 7139073
e-mail: griffinspalmbeach@eircom.net
Dir: 1m from Stradbally village
CHILD FACILITIES: Please telephone for details

This farmhouse is ideally location from which to explore the Dingle Peninsula and unspoilt beaches along the coastline. There are fine views over Tralee Bay from the comfortable bedrooms. Guests can enjoy the delightful garden from the dining room and
continued on p324

Ireland

CASTLEGREGORY — Map 01 A2

sitting room. Mrs Griffin believes in a warm welcome and her home baking is a feature on the breakfast menu.

Griffin's Palm Beach Country House, Castlegregory

ROOMS: 8 rms (6 en suite) (3 fmly) (1 GF) s €32-€35; d €64-€70 *
FACILITIES: tea/coffee TVL **NOTES:** ⊗ Cen ht **PARKING:** 10

KENMARE — Map 01 B2

| Babies Welcome | Family Rooms | Children's Dishes |

★★★★ ◎ ◎ ♨ Sheen Falls Lodge

☎ 064 41600 ◻ 064 41386
e-mail: info@sheenfallslodge.ie
Dir: from Kenmare take N71 to Glengarriff over suspension bridge, take 1st left

CHILD FACILITIES: Babysitting Activities: (seasonal) Outdoor play area Food/bottle warming Ch menu Ch portions Highchairs Ch discounts Safe grounds Games consoles Videos Cots Family rms Connecting rms Laundry NEARBY: Pet farm Cinema Muckross House

This former fishing lodge has been developed into a beautiful hotel run by an amenable team of staff. The cascading Sheen Falls are floodlit at night, forming a romantic backdrop to the enjoyment of award-winning cuisine in La Cascade restaurant. Bedrooms are very comfortably appointed, many of the suites are particularly spacious. The leisure centre and beauty therapy facilities offer a number of exclusive treatments.
ROOMS: 66 en suite (14 fmly) (14 GF) ⊗ in 10 bedrooms d €275-€415 LB **FACILITIES:** STV ⊡ ੧ Fishing Riding Snooker Sauna Solarium Gym ♫ Jacuzzi Table tennis,steam room,clay pigeon shooting,cycling,vintage car rides,library ♫ Xmas **PARKING:** 76 **NOTES:** ✈ ⊗ in restaurant Closed 2 Jan-1 Feb RS December

KILLARNEY — Map 01 B2

| Babies Welcome | Family Rooms | Children's Dishes |

★★★ 69% Castlerosse

☎ 064 31144 ◻ 064 31031
e-mail: castler@iol.ie
Dir: from Killarney town take R562 for Killorglin and The Ring of Kerry, hotel 1.5km from town on left

CHILD FACILITIES: Babysitting Activities: children's club Indoor play area Food/bottle warming Ch menu Ch portions Highchairs Ch discounts Safe grounds Videos Cots Family rms Connecting rms Laundry NEARBY: National Park Farm Cinema Leisure centre

A lovely location on 6,000 acres of land overlooking Lough Leane. Bedrooms are well appointed and comfortable. The restaurant
continued

enjoys panoramic views from its elevated position. Golf available on site, together with a leisure centre.
ROOMS: 121 en suite (27 fmly) ⊗ in 4 bedrooms s €60-€110; d €90-€170 (incl. bkfst) LB **FACILITIES:** ⊡ Golf 9 ੧ Sauna Gym Jacuzzi Golfing & riding arranged ♫ **PARKING:** 100 **NOTES:** ✈ ⊗ in restaurant Closed Dec-Feb

| Babies Welcome | Family Rooms | Children's Dishes |

★★★ 61% Darby O'Gills

Lissivigeen, Mallow Rd
☎ 064 34168 & 34919 ◻ 064 36794
e-mail: darbyogill@eircom.net
Dir: turn off N22 (Cork road) to N72(Mallow)

CHILD FACILITIES: Baby listening Activities: toys, colouring Food/bottle warming Ch menu Ch portions Highchairs Ch cutlery Ch discounts under 4s free sharing with parents Safe grounds Videos Cots Family rms Laundry NEARBY: Country park Wildlife park Pet farm Aquarium Cinema

This modern country house hotel is situated just a five minute drive from the town centre it is an ideal location for touring the Ring of Kerry. Accommodation includes well-equipped bedrooms, Cluricaunes restaurant and traditional music is played in Darby's bar during the season.
ROOMS: 25 en suite (7 fmly) **FACILITIES:** STV ♫ Xmas **PARKING:** 150 **NOTES:** ✈

| Babies Welcome | Family Rooms |

◆◆◆◆◆ GH Earls Court House

Woodlawn Junction, Muckross Rd
☎ 064 34009 ◻ 064 34366
e-mail: info@killarney-earlscourt.ie
Dir: on Muckross Road turn left at traffic lights, B&B is 100yds on left

CHILD FACILITIES: Nanny Food/bottle warming Highchairs Ch discounts under 5s free, 5-12s £15 Safe grounds Videos Cots Family rms D rms with S beds from £120 Ch drinks (on request) Connecting rms Laundry NEARBY: Killarney National Park Farms

A distinctive yellow building, contemporary in design and
continued

purpose-built, with the added facility of balconies adjoining most bedrooms. Elegance and luxury can be seen in the decor and the antique furnishings throughout the house. There is a comfortable lounge where rich fabrics have been used to create a setting for relaxation.
ROOMS: 20 en suite (3 fmly) s €70-€120; d €95-€140 *
FACILITIES: STV TVB tea/coffee Direct dial from bedrooms Lift TVL
NOTES: ⊗ Licensed Cen ht **PARKING:** 24

♦♦♦♦ T&C *Applecroft House*
Woodlawn Rd
☎ 064 32782
e-mail: applecroft@eircom.net
Dir: from Killarney take N71 Muckross road for 500mtrs, left at Shell filling station, down Woodlawn Rd for 500mtrs, sign on left
CHILD FACILITIES: Please telephone for details

Applecroft is a family home tucked away in a residential area, with beautiful landscaped gardens. Bedrooms are spacious and there is great attention to detail in the decoration. Guests can relax in the lounge or on the patio. The breakfast room overlooks the garden.
ROOMS: 5 en suite (2 fmly) ⊗ **FACILITIES:** STV TVB TVL **NOTES:** ✖
⊗ in restaurant ⊗ in 1 lounge Cen ht **PARKING:** 5

KILLORGLIN   Map 01 A2

♦♦♦ 🐾 Dromin Farmhouse
Milltown Post Office
☎ 066 9761867
e-mail: drominfarmhouse@yahoo.com
Dir: 3km from Killorglin and Milltown. Turn off N70 approx 1km from Killorglin at sign after factory. House straight on, 2km
CHILD FACILITIES: Please telephone for details

Set on a sheep and cattle farm with fantastic mountain views, this elevated bungalow is conveniently near to local beaches, golf, fishing and horse-riding. A private TV lounge is available for guests, and babysitting can be arranged. Evening meals are served, but reservations are appreciated.
ROOMS: 4 en suite (2 fmly) s €35-€42; d €54-€60 *
FACILITIES: TVB tea/coffee TVL 42 acres dairy sheep Dinner Last d order noon **NOTES:** ✖ ⊗ Cen ht **PARKING:** 10

WATERVILLE   Map 01 A2

♦♦♦♦ GH Brookhaven House
New Line Rd
☎ 066 947 4431 📠 066 947 4724
e-mail: brookhaven@esatclear.ie
Dir: on N70, on Ring of Kerry, 1km N of Waterville
CHILD FACILITIES: Please telephone for details

A new and imposing two storey house in an acre of garden, overlooking the Waterville Golf Course and the Atlantic Ocean. Bedrooms are spacious and individually decorated, with

continued

spectacular views. The lounge has an open turf fire and plenty of books.
ROOMS: 5 en suite (5 fmly) s €60-€80; d €80-€120 *
FACILITIES: STV TVB tea/coffee Direct dial from bedrooms TVL
NOTES: ✖ ⊗ Cen ht **LB PARKING:** 16

CO KILDARE

STRAFFAN   Map 01 D4

★★★★★ 84% 🏵 🏵 🏵 ⚐
The Kildare Hotel & Golf Club
☎ 01 6017200 📠 01 6017298
e-mail: resortsales@kclub.ie
Dir: from Dublin take N4, exit for R406, hotel entrance is on right in Straffan
CHILD FACILITIES: Please telephone for details

The Kildare Hotel and Golf Club, affectionately known as The K Club, will be the home of 2006 Ryder Cup. Two golf courses will be added to with a new spa facility to complement the truly luxurious bedrooms and suites. Public areas are opulently furnished, many of them with views of the formal gardens. Really fine cuisine is served in the elegant Byerly Turk restaurant, with a little less formal dining in Legends, the restaurant in the golf pavillion.
ROOMS: 69 en suite 10 annexe en suite (10 fmly) **FACILITIES: Spa**
STV ▣ Golf 18 Fishing Snooker Sauna Solarium Gym 💆 ♨ Jacuzzi
Beauty salon Driving range Golf tuition Fishing tuition Horse riding nearby
♫ Xmas **PARKING:** 205 **NOTES:** ✖ ⊗ in restaurant

CO KILKENNY

KILKENNY   Map 01 C3

♦♦♦♦ GH Butler House
Patrick St
☎ 056 776 5707 & 772 2828 📠 056 776 5626
e-mail: res@butler.ie
Dir: follow signs for city centre. In centre near Kilkenny Castle
CHILD FACILITIES: Please telephone for details

Once the dower house of Kilkenny Castle, this fine Georgian building fronts onto the main street with secluded gardens at the rear, through which guests stroll to have full breakfast in Kilkenny

continued on p326

Ireland

KILKENNY, continued

Design Centre. Continental breakfast is served in bedrooms, which feature contemporary décor. There is a comfortable foyer lounge.
ROOMS: 13 en suite (4 fmly) s €80-€195; d €125-€210 *
FACILITIES: STV TVB tea/coffee Direct dial from bedrooms No coaches Dinner Last d order 10pm **NOTES:** ✉ ⊗ Licensed Cen ht **LB**
PARKING: 24

CO LIMERICK

ADARE
Map 01 B3

Family Rooms | Children's Dishes

◆◆◆◆ GH Carrigane House
Rienroe
☎ 061 396778
e-mail: carrigane.house@oceanfree.net
Dir: take left turn at rdbt on N21, 0.25m Limerick side of Adare onto Croom road, then 2nd house on right

CHILD FACILITIES: Nanny Babysitting Activities: board games, electronic games, cards Outdoor play area Family area Food/bottle warming Ch portions Ch discounts under 2s free, 2-12s 50% Safe grounds Games consoles Videos Cots Family rms D rms with S beds from £81 NEARBY: Leisure centre Cinema Walks

Set in its own grounds, guests can be assured of a warm welcome at this purpose built house. A relaxing lounge is available for guests' comfort, while breakfast is a particular treat. Ample car parking to the front of the building is provided.
ROOMS: 6 en suite (3 fmly) (1 GF) s €45-€50; d €65 *
FACILITIES: TVB tea/coffee TVL **NOTES:** Credit cards not taken ✉ ⊗ Cen ht **PARKING:** 10

◆◆◆◆ T&C Coatesland House
Tralee/Killarney Rd, Graigue
☎ 061 396372 ◈ 061 396833
e-mail: coatesfd@indigo.ie
Dir: from Adare follow N21 Killarney road for less than 1km. House on left beside W W Doherty's Garage

CHILD FACILITIES: Please telephone for details

Coatesland House, situated on the main Killarney road five minutes from Adare village, is a very well appointed house featuring attractive bedrooms, all with en suite facilities. Proprietors Florence and Donal Hogan are welcoming and friendly and give superb attention to detail. Dinner is available. Nearby

continued

activities include hunting, fishing, golf and there is also an equestrian centre.
ROOMS: 6 en suite (2 fmly) s €45-€50; d €70-€76 * ⊛
FACILITIES: STV TVB tea/coffee Direct dial from bedrooms TVL
NOTES: ⊗ in restaurant Cen ht **PARKING:** 20

Babies Welcome | Family Rooms | Children's Dishes

◆◆◆ T&C Adare Lodge
Kildimo Rd
☎ 061 396629 ◈ 061 395060
e-mail: info@adarelodge.com
Dir: in village turn right at bank, 2nd B&B on right

CHILD FACILITIES: Family area Food/bottle warming Ch portions Highchairs Safe grounds Videos Family rms D rm with S bed NEARBY: Park Go Karting Horseriding

This smartly presented house is located within minutes of the village of Adare.
ROOMS: 6 en suite (2 fmly) (6 GF) s €50-€60; d €70-€80
FACILITIES: TVB tea/coffee TVL **NOTES:** ✉ ⊗ Cen ht **PARKING:** 6

KILMALLOCK
Map 01 B3

◆◆◆◆◆ ✿ Flemingstown House
☎ 063 98093 ◈ 063 98546
e-mail: info@flemingstown.com
Dir: on R512 Kilmallock/Fermoy, establishment 2m from Kilmallock

CHILD FACILITIES: Please telephone for details

A lovely 18th-century farmhouse which has been modernised to provide stylish en suite facilities throughout. Public rooms include a comfortably furnished sitting room with antiques, and a dining room with beautiful stained glass windows. At breakfast much of the produce comes from the owners' own farm. Dinner is available by arrangement. The area is excellent for walkers, riders, anglers and golfers.
ROOMS: 5 en suite (2 fmly) s €55-€60; d €80-€95 *
FACILITIES: TVB tea/coffee Riding 102 acres beef Dinner Last d order 3pm **NOTES:** ✉ ⊗ Cen ht **PARKING:** 12

LIMERICK
Map 01 B3

Babies Welcome | Family Rooms | Children's Dishes

★★★★ 68% ⊛ Radisson SAS
Ennis Rd
☎ 061 326666 ◈ 327418
e-mail: reservations.limerick@radissonsas.com
Dir: on N18 (Ennis Road), 5 mins from city centre, 15 mins from Shannon Airport

continued

CHILD FACILITIES: Baby listening Babysitting Activities: leisure centre club activities, colouring, books Outdoor play area Food/bottle warming Ch menu Ch portions Highchairs Ch cutlery Ch discounts under 17s free sharing with parents Safe grounds Videos Cots Family rms D rms with 2 S beds £130 Connecting rms Fridge Laundry **NEARBY:** Aillwee Caves Castle & Folk Park Woods

Situated between Limerick city and Shannon International Airport this smart new hotel has comfortable lounge areas and a choice of dining options, the contemporary style Porters Restaurant offers fine dining while more casual fair is available in Heron's Irish Pub. Bedrooms are spacious and very well appointed. There is extensive leisure facilities.

ROOMS: 154 en suite (7 fmly) ⊛ in 70 bedrooms s €90-€120; d €110-€130 (incl. bkfst) **FACILITIES: Spa** STV ▣ ❑ Sauna Solarium Gym ♫ Xmas **PARKING:** 300 **NOTES:** ✻ ⊛ in restaurant

CO LONGFORD

LONGFORD   Map 01 C4

♦♦♦♦ ❦ *Longford Country House-Cumiskeys*
Ennybegs
☎ 043 23320 ▤ 043 23516
e-mail: kc@iol.ie
web: www.longfordcountryhouse.com
Dir: 3rd exit off 2nd rdbt on N4 Longford bypass, 3m,left at x-rds after Old Forge Pub, 2nd house on right

CHILD FACILITIES: Please telephone for details

A hospitable, Tudor-style house. The parlour has a wrought iron spiral stairway to the library loft, as well as a cosy sitting room with turf fire and a dining room where dinner is served by prior arrangement. Other facilities include a games room and pitch and putt. Self-catering cottages are also available.

ROOMS: 6 rms (5 en suite) (2 fmly) ⊛ **FACILITIES:** TVB tea/coffee TVL Pitch & putt course Games room Aromatherapy Dinner Last d order noon **NOTES:** ✻ ⊛ in restaurant ⊛ in 1 lounge Cen ht **PARKING:** 20

CO MAYO

WESTPORT   Map 01 B4

| Babies Welcome | Family Rooms | Children's Dishes |

★★★ 76% **Hotel Westport Conference & Leisure Centre**
Newport Rd
☎ 098 25122 ▤ 098 26739
e-mail: reservations@hotelwestport.ie
Dir: N5 to Westport, right at end of Castlebar St turn, 1st right, 1st left, follow to end

continued

CHILD FACILITIES: Baby listening Activities: 0-3s Cubs Corner, 4-10s Panda Club, face painting, movies, children's goody bag Indoor play area Outdoor play area Food/bottle warming Ch menu Ch portions Highchairs Ch discounts under 3s free Safe grounds Videos Cots Family rms D rm with 2 S beds, D rm with S beds Connecting rms Fridge **NEARBY:** Zoo Cineplex 15 -min drive to sea

Located opposite the grounds of Westport House, yet within walking distance of the town, this hotel offers welcoming public areas, a spacious restaurant and comfortable bedrooms. Leisure guests are well catered for by the enthusiastic and friendly team.
ROOMS: 129 en suite (36 fmly) s €120-€150; d €210-€260 (incl. bkfst) **LB FACILITIES:** STV ▣ Sauna Solarium Gym Jacuzzi Children's pool Jet stream Lounger pool Steam room, sauna ♫ Xmas **PARKING:** 220 **NOTES:** ✻ ⊛ in restaurant

| Babies Welcome | Family Rooms | Children's Dishes | |

★★★ 69% ⊛ **The Atlantic Coast Hotel**
The Quay
☎ 098 29000 ▤ 098 29111
e-mail: info@atlanticcoasthotel.com
Dir: N5 follow signs into Westport then Louisburgh on R335 1m from Westport

CHILD FACILITIES: Nanny Babysitting Activities: children's club, discos, pool games, cinema trips, games, toys, books, jigsaws Food/bottle warming Ch menu Ch portions Highchairs Ch discounts under 4s free Safe grounds Videos Cots Family rms D rms with S beds £20 per child Connecting rms Fridge Laundry **NEARBY:** Westport House Cinema 10-min drive to sea

This distinctive hotel is in a former mill and has been renovated to a good contemporary standard with modern facilities. Many of the rooms have sea views, as has the award-winning restaurant on the fourth floor. The ground floor has comfortable lounge areas and a lively bar. Spa and treatment rooms have recently been added to the leisure centre.
ROOMS: 85 en suite (6 fmly) ⊛ in 28 bedrooms s fr €90; d fr €140 (incl. bkfst) **FACILITIES: Spa** STV ▣ Sauna Solarium Gym Treatment rooms/Hydrotherapy ♫ Xmas **PARKING:** 60 **NOTES:** ✻ ⊛ in restaurant Closed 23-27 Dec

Ireland

CO TIPPERARY

CASHEL
Map 01 C3

Babies Welcome	Family Rooms	Children's Dishes

♦♦♦♦ GH **Aulber House**
Deerpark ROI
☎ 062 63713 📠 062 63715
e-mail: beralley@eircom.net
Dir: From Cashel on N74. Last house on left

> **CHILD FACILITIES:** Outdoor play area Food/bottle warming
> **Ch portions Highchairs Ch cutlery Ch discounts under 5s £15 Safe grounds Games consoles Videos Cots Family rms D rm with S beds £120 Ch drinks N Connecting rms Changing mats**
> **NEARBY:** Parks Walks Leisure centre Cinema

A newly-built guest house, set in landscaped gardens just five minutes' walk from the Rock of Cashel and town centre. Spacious bedrooms are thoughtfully furnished and equipped, and include one fitted for the less mobile. Relax by the open fire in the sitting room, or enjoy views from the first floor lounge.
ROOMS: 12 en suite (2 fmly) (3 GF) **FACILITIES:** STV TVB tea/coffee Direct dial from bedrooms TVL **NOTES:** 🟊 ⊗ Cen ht **PARKING:** 20

♦♦♦ T&C **Ashmore House**
John St
☎ 062 61286 📠 062 62789
e-mail: ashmorehouse@eircom.net
Dir: turn off N8 in centre of town onto John St, house 100yds on right
> **CHILD FACILITIES:** Please telephone for details

Ashmore House is set in a pretty walled garden in the town centre with an enclosed car park. Guests have use of a large sitting and dining room, and bedrooms come in a variety of sizes from big family rooms to a more compact double.
ROOMS: 5 en suite (2 fmly) ⊗ **FACILITIES:** STV TVB tea/coffee TVL Dinner Last d order 24hrs notice **NOTES:** 🟊 ⊗ in restaurant Cen ht **PARKING:** 6

NENAGH
Map 01 B3

Babies Welcome	Family Rooms	Children's Dishes

♦♦♦ T&C **Ashley Park House**
☎ 067 38223 & 06738013 📠 067 38013
e-mail: margaret@ashleypark.com
Dir: on N52, 4m N of Nenagh, signed on left then turn left under arch
> **CHILD FACILITIES:** Baby listening Babysitting Activities: games, jigsaws, toys, colouring, painting Indoor play area Outdoor play area Family area Food/bottle warming Ch menu Ch portions Highchairs Ch cutlery Ch discounts under 2s free, 2-8s £10 Safe grounds Cots Family rms D rms with S beds Laundry Changing mats
> **NEARBY:** Burr Castle Leisure centre Tennis Cinema Horseriding

An attractive, colonial style Georgian farmhouse, built in 1770. Set in gardens which run down to Lake Orna, it offers comfortable, spacious bedrooms, with quality antique furnishings. Breakfast is served in the dining room overlooking the lake, and dinner can be taken by prior arrangement.
ROOMS: 5 en suite (3 fmly) s €50-€55; d €90-€100 *
FACILITIES: TV2B tea/coffee TVL Golf 18 Fishing Snooker Dinner Last d order 4pm **NOTES:** Credit cards not taken ⊗ Licensed Cen ht
PARKING: 30

CO WATERFORD

DUNGARVAN
Map 01 C2

Babies Welcome	Family Rooms	Children's Dishes

♦♦♦♦♦ 🍽 **Castle Country House**
Millstreet, Cappagh
☎ 058 68049 📠 058 68099
e-mail: castlefm@iol.ie
Dir: N72, take R671 for 3.5m, right at Millstreet, house 200yds on right
> **CHILD FACILITIES:** Nanny Food/bottle warming Ch menu
> **Ch portions Highchairs Ch discounts under 3s free, 3-12s 50% Safe grounds Cots Family rms D rm with 2 S beds** **NEARBY:** Farm Walks Fun fair Play park

This delightful house is to be found in the west wing of a 15th century castle. Guests are spoilt by host Joan Nugent who loves to cook and hunt out antiques for her visitors to enjoy. She is helped by her husband Emmett who enjoys showing off his high-tech dairy farm and is a fount of local knowledge. Bedrooms are spacious and enjoy lovely views. There is a river walk and a beautiful garden to relax in.
ROOMS: 5 en suite (1 fmly) s €50-€60; d €80-€90 *
FACILITIES: TVB tea/coffee Fishing Farm tour 200 acres dairy & beef Dinner Last d order 5pm **NOTES:** ⊗ Licensed Cen ht **LB** **PARKING:** 11

TRAMORE
Map 01 C2

♦♦♦♦ T&C *Glenorney*
Newtown
☎ 051 381056 📠 051 381103
e-mail: glenoney@iol.ie
Dir: on R675 opposite the Tramore Golf Club
> **CHILD FACILITIES:** Please telephone for details

A beautifully spacious and luxurious home with spectacular views of Tramore Bay, located opposite a championship golf course. Great attention has been paid to detail and there is an extensive breakfast menu. Bedrooms are tastefully decorated and the lounge is comfortably furnished, there is also a sun room, patio and private garden for guests.
ROOMS: 6 en suite (2 fmly) (3 GF) **FACILITIES:** TVB tea/coffee Direct dial from bedrooms TVL **NOTES:** 🟊 ⊗ Cen ht **PARKING:** 6

> Please mention AA Family Friendly Places
> to Stay, Eat and Visit when booking

WATERFORD   Map 01 C2

★★★ 70% **Tower**
The Mall
☎ 051 875801 ▤ 051 870129
e-mail: info@thw.ie
Dir: opp Reginald's Tower in town centre. Hotel at end of quay on N25

CHILD FACILITIES: Please telephone for details

An extensive refurbishment programme has given this long-established hotel a new look that includes two smart restaurants, a riverside bar and upgraded bedrooms. The leisure centre is about to be further developed. Good car parking is provided to the rear of the hotel.

RGOMS: 139 en suite (20 fmly) s €79-€135; d €134-€230 (incl. bkfst) **LB FACILITIES:** ⊠ Sauna Solarium Gym Jacuzzi ♬ Xmas **PARKING:** 90 **NOTES:** ✈ ⊛ in restaurant Closed 24-28 Dec

Babies Welcome | Family Rooms | Children's Dishes

★★★ 64% **Ivory's Hotel**
Tramore Rd
☎ 051 358888 ▤ 051 358899
e-mail: info@ivoryshotel.ie
Dir: from city centre take N25 to Cork. 600yds take exit to Tramore R675. Hotel on right

CHILD FACILITIES: Babysitting Activities: colouring Outdoor play area Food/bottle warming Ch menu Ch portions Highchairs Ch discounts under 5s free, 5-10s 50% Safe grounds Cots Family rms family apartment from £150   **NEARBY:** Kiddies fun zone Leisure centre Cinema Park 7-min drive to sea

This friendly, family-owned, modern hotel is well located just off the Cork Road. Many of the comfortable rooms are suitable for families, and an outdoor play area is also provided. McGinty's, the popular pub carvery, serves food throughout the day, and dinner is served in the Bistro.

ROOMS: 40 en suite (20 fmly) (20 GF) ⊛ in 20 bedrooms s €85-€125; d €120-€180 (incl. bkfst) **LB FACILITIES:** STV **PARKING:** 120 **NOTES:** ⊛ in restaurant Closed 24-28 Dec

CO WESTMEATH

ATHLONE   Map 01 C4

Babies Welcome | Family Rooms | Children's Dishes

★★★ 70% ⊛ **Hodson Bay**
Hodson Bay
☎ 090 6442000 ▤ 090 6442020
e-mail: info@hodsonbayhotel.com
Dir: from N6 take N61 to Roscommon. Turn right. Hotel 1km on Lough Ree

CHILD FACILITIES: Babysitting Activities: Penguin Kids Activity Camp Indoor play area Food/bottle warming Ch menu Ch portions Highchairs Ch discounts under 2s free sharing with parents Safe grounds Games consoles Videos Cots Family rms D rm with S beds £27 per child Connecting rms Laundry (dry cleaning) **NEARBY:** Pet farm Kids' activity centre Boat trips

On the shores of Lough Rea and close to the River Shannon this hotel has its own marina and is surrounded by Athlone Golf course. Public areas include comfortable lounges, carvery bar, an attractive restaurant and excellent banqueting and leisure facilities.
continued

The spacious bedrooms have been designed to capture the magnificent lake views.

ROOMS: 133 en suite (23 fmly) ⊛ in 3 bedrooms s €75-€180; d €55-€240 (incl. bkfst) **LB FACILITIES:** STV ⊠ Golf 18 Fishing Sauna Gym Steam room, play room, beauty salon ♬ Xmas **PARKING:** 300 **NOTES:** ✈ ⊛ in restaurant

CO WEXFORD

ARTHURSTOWN   Map 01 C2

Babies Welcome | Family Rooms | Children's Dishes

◆◆◆◆ T&C **Glendine Country House**
☎ 051 389500 & 389258 ▤ 051 389677
e-mail: glendinehouse@eircom.net
Dir: from Rosslare, N25 for 5m, at 1st & 2nd rdbts left, R733, 32km towards Wellingtonbridge

CHILD FACILITIES: Baby listening Nanny Activities: working farm, games, jigsaws, toys Outdoor play area Family area Food/bottle warming Ch menu Ch portions Highchairs Ch cutlery Ch discounts under 2s free, over 2s 50% Safe grounds Games consoles Videos Cots Family rms D rm with 2 S beds £120 Ch drinks Connecting rms Changing mats **NEARBY:** Arboretum Maze Near sea

A Georgian house in its own grounds overlooking the estuary in Arthurstown, and next to the village of Ballyhack where the local ferry crosses to and from Passage East in Waterford. Glendine is a well-maintained house with attractive gardens, a play area for children, and plenty of car parking space. Inside there is a spacious sitting room with TV, a separate dining room, and comfortable en suite bedrooms, one of which has a second bedroom attached which is useful for family or friends.
ROOMS: 4 en suite (1 fmly) s €60-€80; d €100-€110 *
FACILITIES: TVB tea/coffee TVL Pool Table Small café Cookery courses **NOTES:** ⊛ Licensed Cen ht **LB PARKING:** 20

Many proprietors are happy to provide extra facilities for children, but let them know in advance what you need so they can be prepared

KILMUCKRIDGE · Map 01 D3

◆◆◆◆ T&C *Ballygarran House*
Ballygarran
☎ 053 30164 📠 053 30490
e-mail: ballygarran@iol.ie
Dir: from Wexford, turn off R742 towards Kilmuckridge, right in village, house at top

CHILD FACILITIES: Please telephone for details

A friendly welcome awaits guests to this lovely old parochial house. A new extension contains bedrooms and receptions rooms, and imaginative decor and comfort features throughout. Breakfast is a feast and evening meals are available by reservation. There are restaurants, pubs, an award winning beach and five golf courses nearby.
ROOMS: 6 en suite (1 fmly) **FACILITIES:** TVB TVL Dinner **NOTES:** ✈ ⊗ Cen ht **PARKING:** 12

CO WICKLOW

AVOCA · Map 01 D3

◆◆◆ T&C *Cherrybrook Country Home*
☎ 0402 35179 📠 0402 35765
e-mail: cherrybandb@eircom.net
Dir: from Avoca, at Fitzgeralds Bar turn right, 4th house on right

CHILD FACILITIES: Please telephone for details

Set in the village made famous by TV series 'Ballykissangel' Cherrybrook has fine gardens with a barbeque area. It is a well presented house with a guest lounge and dining room. Bedrooms are attractively decorated. Evening meals are available by prior arrangement.
ROOMS: 5 en suite (2 fmly) **FACILITIES:** TVB tea/coffee TVL Last d order noon **NOTES:** ✈ ⊗ Cen ht **PARKING:** 5

DELGANY · Map 01 D3

★★★★ 62% *Glenview*
Glen O' the Downs
☎ 01 2873399 📠 01 2877511
e-mail: glenview@iol.ie
Dir: from Dublin city centre follow signs for N11, past Bray on southbound N11

CHILD FACILITIES: Please telephone for details

In a lovely hillside location overlooking terraced gardens this hotel boasts an excellent range of leisure facilities. Impressive public areas provide a conservatory bar, lounge and choice of dining options. Bedrooms are spacious and some enjoy excellent views over the valley. Championship golf, horse riding and many tourist amenities are available nearby.
ROOMS: 70 en suite (11 fmly) (16 GF) ⊛ in 11 bedrooms
FACILITIES: Spa STV ⊠ Snooker Sauna Solarium Gym 𝄞 Jacuzzi Aerobics studio, Massage, Beauty treatment room ♫ **PARKING:** 200
NOTES: ✈ ⊗ in restaurant

DUNLAVIN · Map 01 C3

Babies Welcome | Family Rooms | Children's Dishes

◆◆◆◆ ❦ Tynte House
☎ 045 401561 📠 045 401586
e-mail: info@tyntehouse.com
Dir: N81 at Hollywood Cross, right at Dunlavin, follow finger signs for Tynte House, past market house in town centre

CHILD FACILITIES: Baby listening **Activities:** tennis, basketball, pool, soccer nets **Indoor play area Outdoor play area Food/bottle warming Ch menu Ch portions Highchairs Ch cutlery Ch discounts** under 3s free, 4-12s 50-60% discount **Safe grounds Games consoles Videos Cots Family rms D rm with 2 S beds Ch drinks Laundry**
NEARBY: Leisure centre Playbarn

A gracious 19th-century farmhouse standing in the square of this quiet country village. The friendly hosts have carried out a lot of restoration and facilities now include bedrooms, self-catering
continued

apartments in an adjoining courtyard, a laundry, tennis courts, children's play area and indoor games room.
ROOMS: 7 en suite (2 fmly) s fr €44; d fr €70 * ☻ in 2 bedrooms
FACILITIES: TVB tea/coffee Direct dial from bedrooms TVL Golf 18 ♋
Pool Table Playground games room with table tennis 200 acres arable
beef Dinner Last d order Noon **NOTES:** ☻ in restaurant ☻ in lounges
Cen ht **LB PARKING:** 16

NEWTOWNMOUNTKENNEDY
Map 01 D3

ⓤ Marriott Druids Glen Hotel & Country Club
☎ 01 2870800 📠 2870801
e-mail: mhrs.dubgs.reception@marriotthotels.com
Dir: N11 s'bound, off at Newtownmountkennedy. Follow signs for hotel

CHILD FACILITIES: Babysitting (on request) **Activities:** colouring
Indoor play area Outdoor play area Food/bottle warming Ch menu
Ch portions Highchairs Ch discounts Safe grounds Videos Cots
Family rms Ch drinks Connecting rms Fridge Laundry
NEARBY: Wicklow Mountain National Park Sealife Centre 10-min
drive to sea

At the time of going to press, the star classification for this hotel
was not confirmed. Please refer to the AA internet site
www.theAA.com for current information.
ROOMS: 148 en suite ☻ in 106 bedrooms **FACILITIES: Spa** STV 📺
Golf 18 Sauna Gym Jacuzzi 🎵 **PARKING:** 350 **NOTES:** ✈ ☻ in
restaurant

Index

The Automobile Association would like to thank the following agencies for their assistance in the preparation of this book:

Digital Vision 1, 5, 6, 7, 10

The remaining images are held in the Association's own library (AA WORLD TRAVEL LIBRARY) with contributions from the following:

Stuart Abrahams 258; Pat Aithie 301; Adrian Baker 262; Peter Baker 16r, 220, 231; M Birkitt 93, 129, 152, 162; Jamie Blandford 272, 314; Ian Burgum 293, 298, 304; Steve Day 239, 318; Kenya Doran 132; Derek Forss 234; Van Greaves 139, 157, 212; Mike Hayward 200; A J Hopkins 12; Nick Jenkins 16l, 296; Caroline Jones 14, 76, 82, 107, 204; Max Jourdan 4, 121, 168; Andrew Lawson 197; Cameron Lees 193, 246; Tom Mackie 80, 185, 214; Andrew Midgeley 102; John Miller 74; Roger Moss 72; George Munday 315; Rich Newton 229; Ken Paterson 265, 285; Tony Souter 15; James Tims 218; Wyn Voysey 8, 142; Stephen Whitehorne 268, 277; Harry Williams 2, 148, 292.

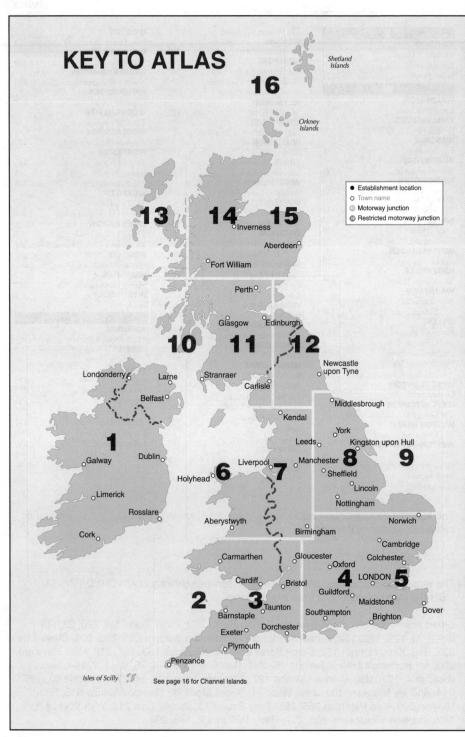

KEY TO ATLAS

Shetland Islands

16

Orkney Islands

- ● Establishment location
- ○ Town name
- Ⓜ Motorway junction
- Ⓡ Restricted motorway junction

13 **14** **15**

Inverness

Aberdeen

Fort William

Perth

Glasgow Edinburgh

10 **11** **12**

Newcastle upon Tyne

Londonderry Larne Stranraer

Belfast Carlisle

Middlesbrough

Kendal

York

Leeds Kingston upon Hull

1 Liverpool **7** Manchester **8** **9**

Galway Dublin Sheffield

Holyhead **6** Lincoln

Limerick Nottingham

Rosslare

Cork Norwich

Aberystwyth

Birmingham

Cambridge

Carmarthen Gloucester Colchester

Cardiff Oxford

Bristol **4** LONDON **5**

2 **3** Guildford

Taunton Southampton Maidstone

Barnstaple Brighton Dover

Exeter Dorchester

Plymouth

Penzance

Isles of Scilly

See page 16 for Channel Islands

© Automobile Association Developments Limited 2004

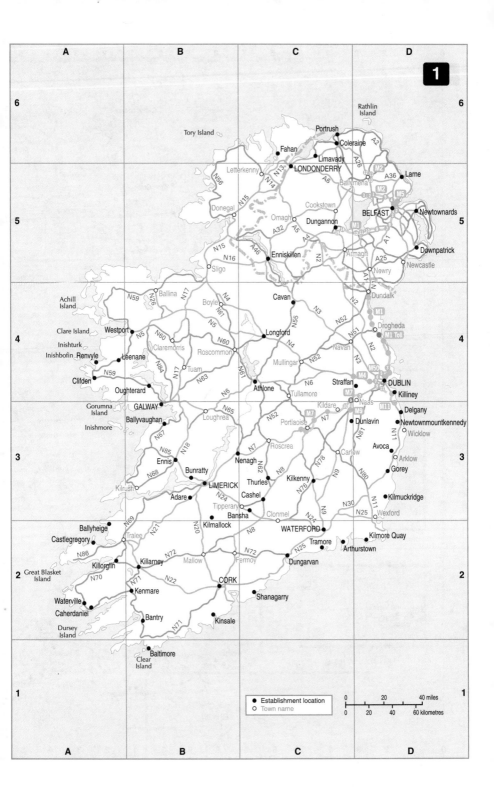

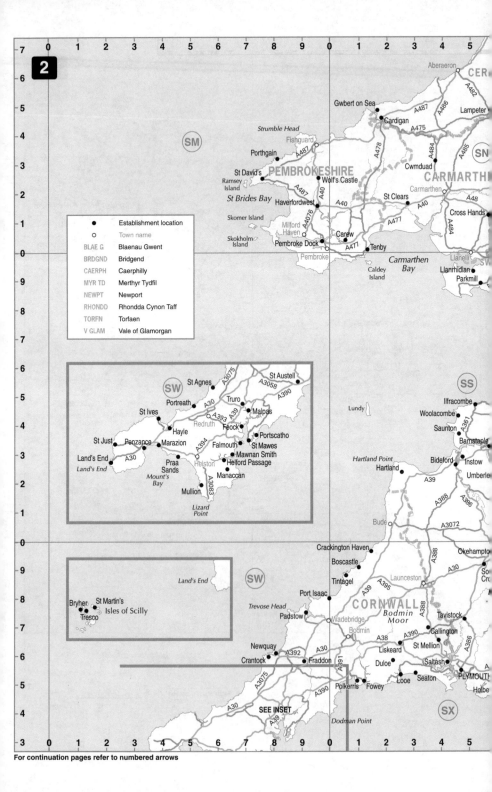

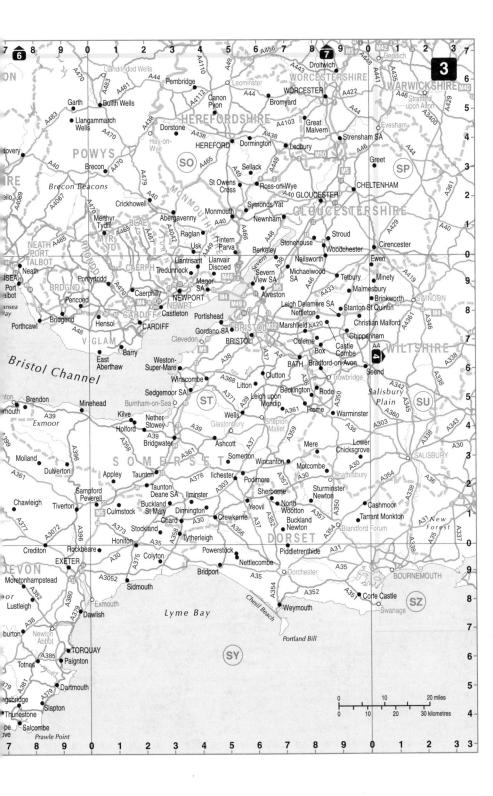

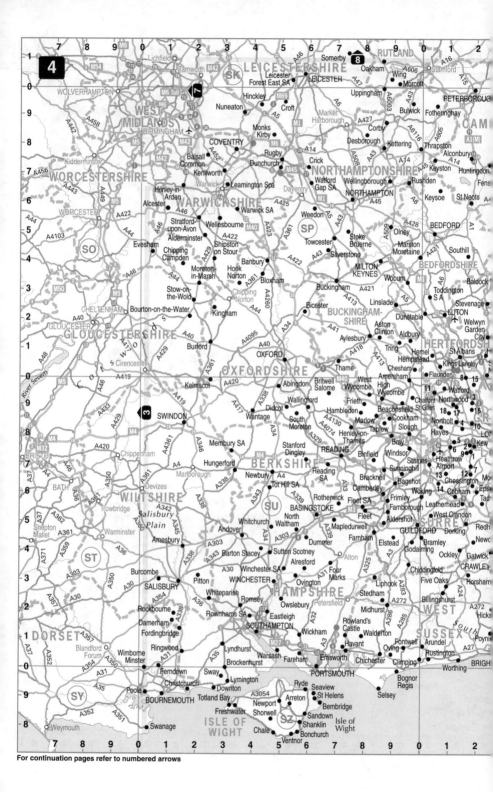

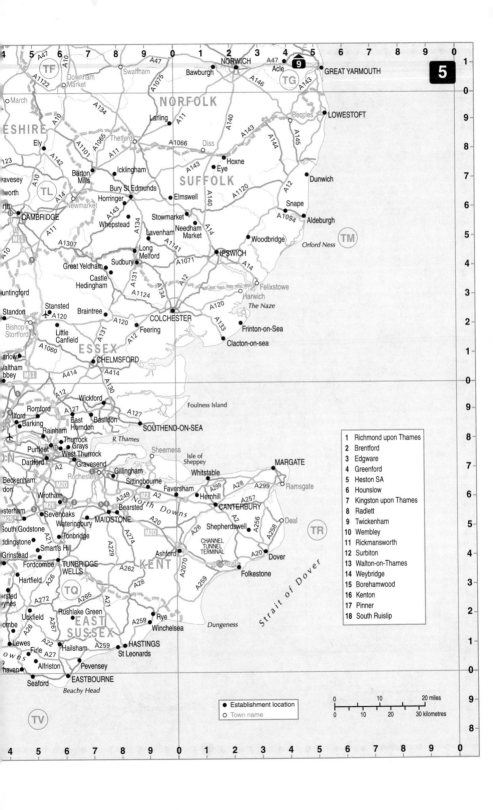

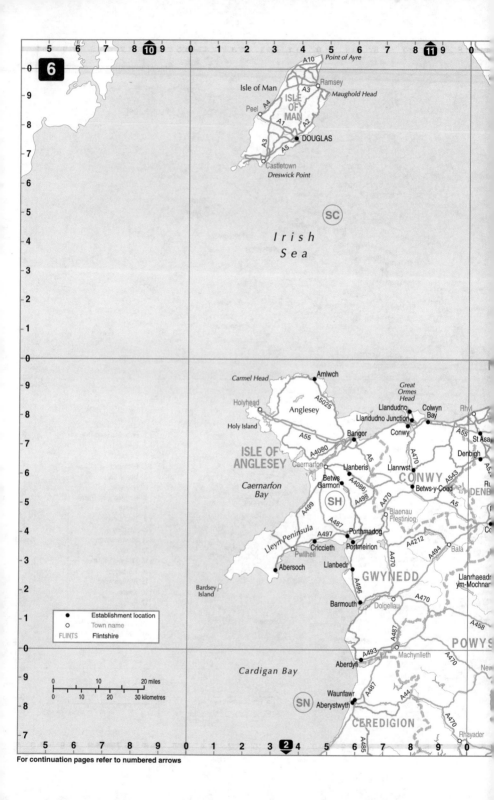

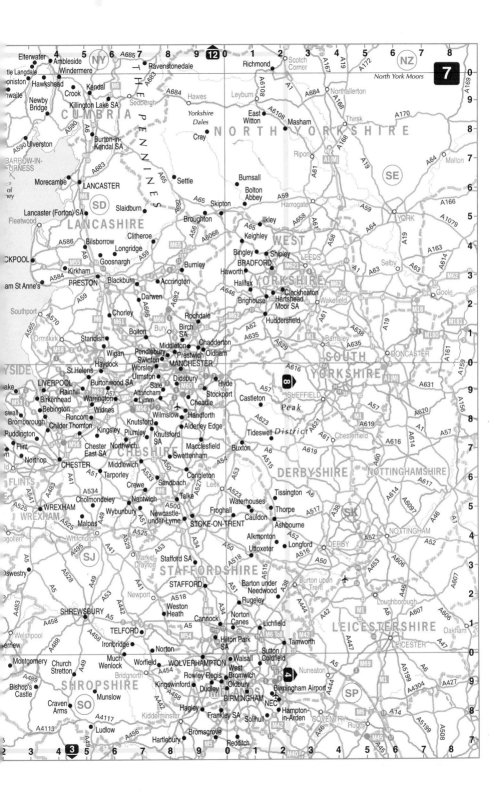

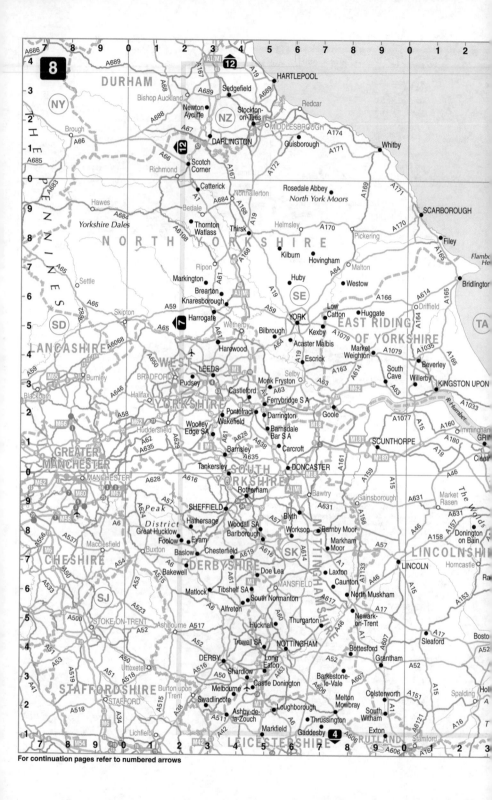

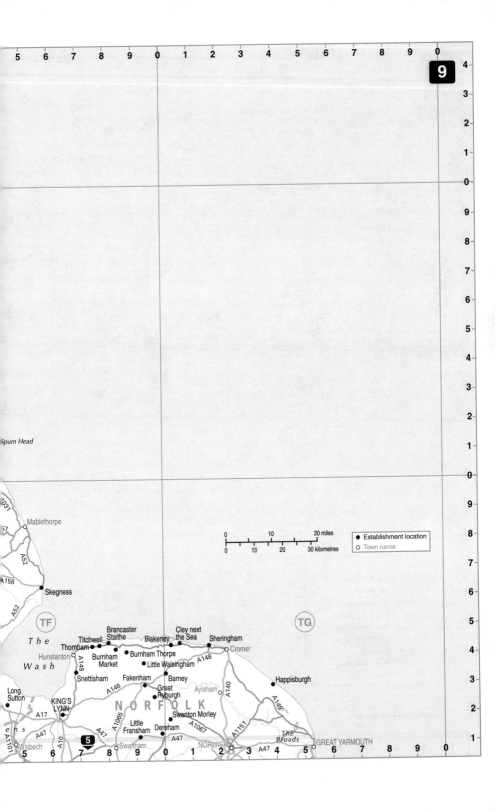

Spurn Head

Mablethorpe

Skegness

TF

The
Wash

Hunstanton

Long
Sutton

KING'S
LYNN

A17

A10

A47

Wisbech

A1101

Swaffham

5

NORFOLK

Thornham
Titchwell
Brancaster
Staithe
Burnham
Market

Burnham Thorpe

Snettisham

Fakenham

Little Walsingham

Barney

Great
Ryburgh

Little
Fransham

Dereham

Swanton Morley

A1067

Blakeney

Cley next
the Sea

Sheringham

Cromer

A148

A140

Aylsham

A1151

Happisburgh

A149

The
Broads

GREAT YARMOUTH

NORWICH

A47

TG

| 0 | | 10 | | 20 miles |
| 0 | 10 | 20 | 30 kilometres | |

● Establishment location
○ Town name

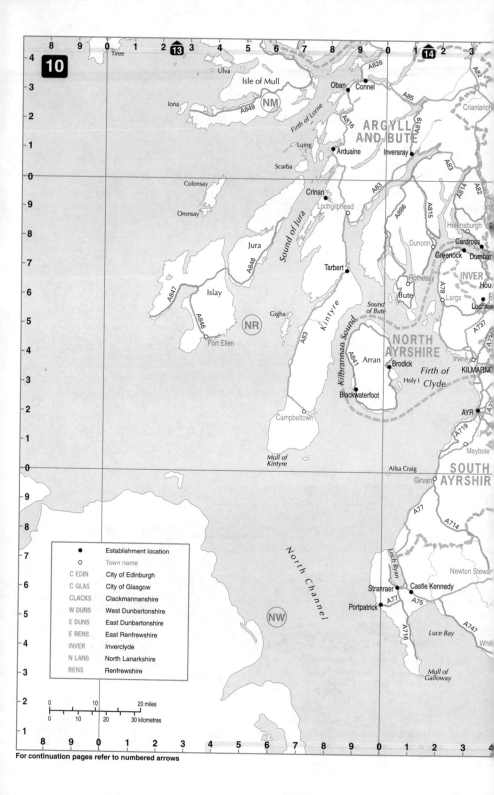

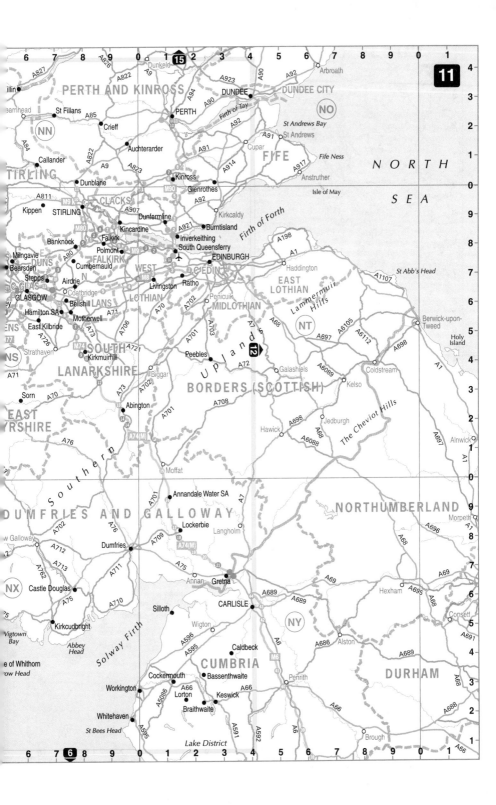

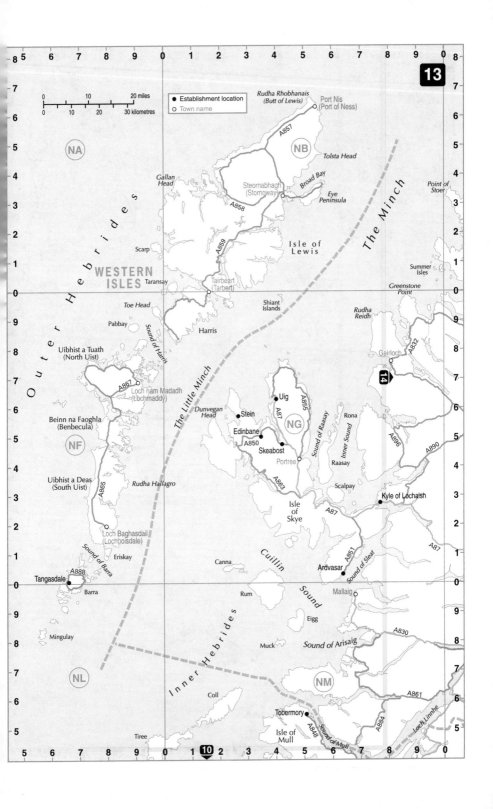

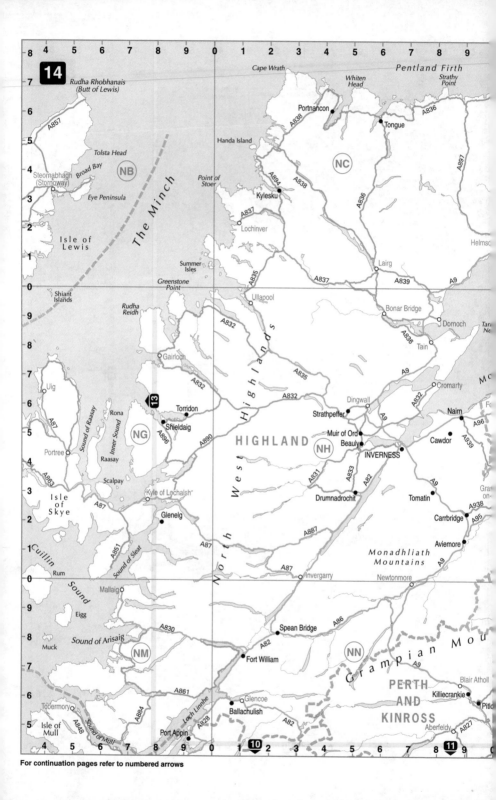

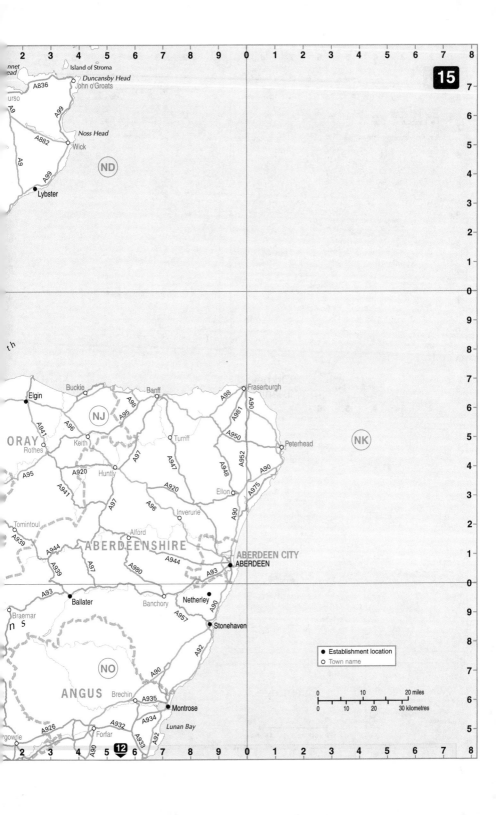

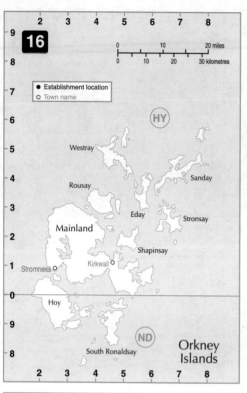

Orkney Islands

- ● Establishment location
- ○ Town name

HY

ND

Westray

Rousay

Sanday

Eday

Stronsay

Mainland

Shapinsay

Stromness ○   Kirkwall ○

Hoy

South Ronaldsay

0   10   20 miles
0   10   20   30 kilometres

Shetland Islands

HP

Unst

Yell   Fetlar

Whalsay

Mainland

Lerwick ●

Bressay

HU

0   10   20 miles
0   10   20   30 kilometres

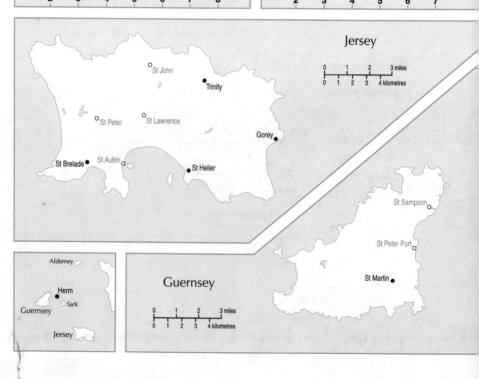

Jersey

St John

Trinity ●

St Peter ○   St Lawrence ○

Gorey ●

St Brelade ●   St Aubin ○   St Helier ●

0   1   2   3 miles
0   1   2   3   4 kilometres

Guernsey

St Sampson ○

St Peter Port ○

St Martin ●

Alderney

Herm

Guernsey   ○ Sark

Jersey

0   1   2   3 miles
0   1   2   3   4 kilometres

Readers' Report form

Please send this form to:
　AA Family Friendly Places to Stay
　AA Lifestyle Guides
　15th Floor
　Fanum House
　Basingstoke RG21 4EA

　or fax: 01256 491647
　or e-mail: lifestyleguides@theAA.com

Please use this form to recommend any establishment you have visited, whether it is included in the guide or not. You can also help us to improve the guide by completing the short questionnaire on the reverse.

The AA does not undertake to arbitrate between you and establishment management, nor to obtain compensation or engage in correspondence.

Date:

Your name (block capitals)

Your address (block capitals)

....

....

....

e-mail address: ....

(Please *only* give us your e-mail address if you wish to hear from us about other products and services from the AA and partners by e-mail)

Name of Establishment

Comments

....

....

....

....

....

....

....essary)

(please attach a separate s

PTO

Readers' Report Form

Have you bought this guide before? ☐ yes   ☐ no

Have you bought any other accommodation, restaurant, pub or food guides recently? If yes, which ones?

....

....

Why did you buy this guide? (circle all that apply)

holiday   short break   overnight stop

other...

How often do you stay in a hotel or B&B (circle one choice)

more than once a month   once a month   once in 2-3 months

once in six months   once a year   less than once a year

Please answer these questions to help us improve the guide:

Which of these factors are most important when choosing a place to stay or eat?

Price   Location   Awards/Ratings   Service

or/Surroundings   Previous experience   Recommendation

for Children   Other...

d the editorial features in the guide? ....

Descr, **location atlas?**...

Information the guide do you find the most useful when
hment? (circle as many as are applicable)

Can you suggest

                        Advertisement   Star/Diamond rating

....ies

nts to this guide?
....